PENGUIN CLASSICS

A TREATISE OF HUMAN NATURE

DAVID HUME (1711–76) devoted himself from early youth to 'philosophy and general learning'. *A Treatise of Human Nature* (1739–40) 'fell dead-born from the Press', by his own account, but is now regarded as his masterwork. He recast it and added to its teaching in essays, inquiries, and dissertations on philosophical, moral, political, economic, and literary topics. His historical interests yielded the *History of England* (1754–62), while *Dialogues concerning Natural Religion*, published posthumously in 1779, completed what he had to say about religion. Foiled in an attempt to become a university professor, he was a tutor, judge advocate, aide-de-camp, librarian, diplomat, and senior civil servant, just before enjoying retirement amidst his friends in Edinburgh from 1769. At one time the object of religious intolerance in Scotland and largely ignored in England, Hume received the adulation of France on arriving there in 1763 as secretary to the British Ambassador. Adam Smith said: 'I have always considered him, both in his lifetime and since his death, as approaching as nearly to the idea of a perfectly wise and virtuous man, as perhaps the nature of human frailty will admit.'

ERNEST CAMPBELL MOSSNER was appointed Professor of English at the University of Texas in 1947, and subsequently Professor of English and Philosophy. He is the author of the following books: *Bishop Butler and the Age of Reason*, *The Forgotten Hume* and *The Life of David Hume*. He edited *New Letters of David Hume* with R. Klibansky, and *David Hume: A Letter from a Gentleman to his Friend in Edinburgh* with J. V. Price. He has been the recipient of Columbia, Guggenheim and Fulbright fellowships.

PENGUIN CLASSICS

A TREATISE OF HUMAN NATURE

DAVID HUME (1711–76) devoted himself from early youth to philosophy and general learning. *A Treatise of Human Nature* (1739–40) 'fell dead-born from the Press' by his own account, but is now regarded as his masterwork. He recast it and added to it, resulting in essays, enquiries, and dissertations on philosophical, moral, political, economic and literary topics. His historical interests yielded the *History of England* (1754–62), while *Dialogues concerning Natural Religion*, published posthumously in 1779, completed what he had to say about religion. Foiled in an attempt to become a university professor, he was a tutor, judge advocate, librarian, secretary, diplomat and senior civil servant just before enjoying retirement amidst his friends in Edinburgh from 1769. A target for the odium of religious intolerance in Scotland and largely ignored in England, Hume received the adulation of France on arriving there in 1763 as secretary to the British Ambassador. Adam Smith said, 'I have always considered him, both in his lifetime and since his death, as approaching as nearly to the idea of a perfectly wise and virtuous man, as perhaps the nature of human frailty will admit.'

ERNEST C. MOSSNER was appointed Instructor of English at the University of Texas in 1937, and subsequently Professor of English and Philosophy. He is the author of the following books: *Bishop Butler and the Age of Reason*, *The Forgotten Hume* and *The Life of David Hume*. He edited *New Letters of David Hume* with R. Klibansky, and *David Hume: 'Letters from a Gentleman to his Friend in Edinburgh'* with J. V. Price. He has been the recipient of Guggenheim and Rockefeller Fellowships.

DAVID HUME

A TREATISE OF HUMAN NATURE

EDITED WITH
AN INTRODUCTION BY
ERNEST C. MOSSNER

PENGUIN BOOKS

PENGUIN BOOKS

Published by the Penguin Group
Penguin Books Ltd, 80 Strand, London WC2R 0RL, England
Penguin Putnam Inc., 375 Hudson Street, New York, New York 10014, USA
Penguin Books Australia Ltd, 250 Camberwell Road, Camberwell, Victoria 3124, Australia
Penguin Books Canada Ltd, 10 Alcorn Avenue, Toronto, Ontario, Canada M4V 3B2
Penguin Books India (P) Ltd, 11 Community Centre, Panchsheel Park, New Delhi – 110 017, India
Penguin Books (NZ) Ltd, Cnr Rosedale and Airborne Roads, Albany, Auckland, New Zealand
Penguin Books (South Africa) (Pty) Ltd, 24 Sturdee Avenue, Rosebank 2196, South Africa

Penguin Books Ltd, Registered Offices: 80 Strand, London WC2R 0RL, England

www.penguin.com

First published 1739 and 1740
Published in Pelican Books 1969
Reprinted in Penguin Classics 1985

042

Set in Georgian Linotype

Printed and bound in Great Britain by Clays Ltd, Elcograf S.p.A.

ISBN-13: 978–0–140–43244–2

www.greenpenguin.co.uk

MIX
Paper from responsible sources
FSC www.fsc.org FSC™ C018179

Penguin Books is committed to a sustainable future for our business, our readers and our planet. This book is made from Forest Stewardship Council™ certified paper.

CONTENTS

INTRODUCTION

DAVID HUME is the greatest of British philosophers, and his greatness, it is now believed, reveals itself most strikingly in the first as well as the most sustained and systematic of his works: *A Treatise of Human Nature.* Berkeley published his *New Theory of Vision* (1709) when he was twenty-four and *A Treatise of the Principles of Human Knowledge* a year later. Also, A. J. Ayer, in our own day, published *Language, Truth and Logic* (1935) when he was twenty-five. Nevertheless, the appearance of the three volumes of Hume's *Treatise* by the time he was twenty-nine still warrants a claim for the author's outstanding philosophical precocity. Not that Hume later in life exulted over his youthful ardour: 'So vast an Undertaking, plan'd before I was one and twenty, & compos'd before twenty five, must necessarily be very defective. I have repented my Haste a hundred, & a hundred times.' Modern readers, however, are likely to be deeply moved and teased into thought by the elements in the *Treatise* which haunted the mature Hume: the nakedness of intellectual self-exposure, the provocative assaults on established systems, and the aggressive presentation of a revolutionary account of man's nature. With justice Sir Isaiah Berlin has written of Hume: 'No man has influenced the history of philosophy to a deeper and more disturbing degree.'

The remarkable achievement of the *Treatise* was the product of a young Scot born in Edinburgh on 26 April 1711, son of Joseph Home of Ninewells in Berwickshire, and Katherine Falconer, daughter of a distinguished advocate who became Lord President of the Court of Session, Scotland's supreme civil court. Joseph Home was also an advocate, educated at the universities of Edinburgh and Utrecht, and according to his son, who never knew him, he 'passed for a man of Parts'. He died in 1713 leaving David 'with an elder Brother and a Sister under the care of [their] Mother, a woman of singular Merit, who, though young and handsome, devoted herself entirely to the rearing and educating of her Children', such being the philosopher's tribute to a much-loved parent. David always remained on excellent terms with his family, though he saw fit to change the spelling of his name at the time of his first visit to England in 1734, when he found that the natives could not be persuaded that the pronunciation was *Hume* however spelled.

After a period of private tutoring, David signed the Matriculation Book at Edinburgh University on 27 February 1723; he was in his twelfth year and, following customary practice, did not bother to take a degree. For two or three years, however, he was exposed to considerable indoctrination in the New Philosophy, particularly that of Sir Isaac Newton. The subjects that he presumably studied included – besides the ancient languages – Logic and Metaphysics, Mathematics, Ethics, History, and Natural Philosophy. Though his family wished him to take up the profession of the law, 'I found', he confesses in his brief autobiography, 'an unsurmountable Aversion to every thing but the pursuits of Philosophy and general Learning: and while they fancyed I was pouring over Voet and Vinnius, Cicero and Virgil were the Authors which I was secretly devouring.'

Early in 1729 he gave up all pretence of the law and threw himself with 'Boldness of Temper' into 'some new Medium, by which Truth might be establisht' which 'open'd up to me a new Scene of Thought, which transported me beyond Measure, & made me, with an Ardor natural to young men, throw up every other Pleasure or Business to apply entirely to it.' 'The Law,' he continues, 'which was the Business I design'd to follow, appear'd nauseous to me, & I cou'd think of no other way of pushing my Fortune in the World but that of a Scholar & Philosopher.' In the course of the eight years of intensive study which followed, he was brought to the verge of a breakdown, and he described fully his case-history in an autobiographical letter, just quoted, to a London physician, very likely Dr John Arbuthnot, the famous satirist and wit. These years of study and frustration were the gestation period of the *Treatise*. The time-scheme involved is suggested by three statements of Hume's, which are not to be taken too rigidly: namely, that the work was *projected* before he left college in 1725 or 1726 aged fourteen or fifteen, was *planned* before he was twenty-one in 1732, and was *composed* before he was twenty-five in 1736.

What this 'new Scene of Thought' was we cannot be sure without new evidence. Yet a survey of the available evidence justifies a reasoned conjecture. The subtitle to the *Treatise* provides an important clue: 'Being An Attempt to introduce the experimental Method of Reasoning into Moral Subjects'. The 'new Medium, by which Truth might be establisht', is thus the experimental method. Newton, at the close of the *Opticks* (1704), had thrown down a challenge which Hume was not alone among philosophers of the Enlightenment in accepting: 'If natural Philosophy in all its parts by pursuing the inductive method, shall at length be perfected, the bounds of moral philosophy will also be enlarged.' Now moral philosophy, as opposed to natural philosophy, comprises what in Hume's terminology are the understanding, the passions, morals, politics, and criticism: in short, the entire science of man discovered empirically and systematically. What he was fomenting was a Copernican revolution in philosophy because 'moral philosophy is in the same condition as natural, with regard to astronomy before the time of Copernicus.' He was convinced of both the fundamental significance of his ideas and the difficulty of getting them accepted: 'My Principles are . . . so remote from all the vulgar Sentiments on this Subject, that were they to take place, they wou'd produce almost a total Alteration in Philosophy: & . . . Revolutions of this kind are not easily brought about.'

Some clues to the development of Hume's thought in the pre-*Treatise* years are to be found among surviving early memoranda (1729–40) organized under three loose headings: 'Natural Philosophy', 'Philosophy', and 'General'. This third section contains many items on ethics and religion that might have been expected to appear under 'Philosophy'. Item 257, for example, is the very essence of Hume's position in ethics: 'The Moderns have not treated Morals so well as the Antients merely from their Reasoning turn which carry'd them away from Sentiment.' Notes 2 and 3 of the second section are from the Abbé Dubos, a great advocate of sentiment in ethics and aesthetics. Of forty notes in the same 'Philosophy' section, sixteen are from the sceptic Pierre Bayle and a note on the reverse of the last sheet is a sentence from Epicharmus, which in translation reads: 'Keep sober and remember to be sceptical.' Five notes are provided by *De Origine Mali* by William King, a rationalistic Archbishop of Dublin. Hume probably used the copiously annotated translation of 1731 by Edmund Law, which was printed with John Gay's introductory essay of philosophical importance as a source for associationism in psychology and utilitarianism in morals.

On the topic of Hume's religious scepticism, we have a tantalizing reference to a document which supplemented the notes in the early memoranda: 'tis not long ago [some time before 1751] that I burn'd an old Manuscript Book, wrote before I was twenty which contain'd, Page after Page, the gradual Progress of my Thoughts on that head.' The nature of this scepticism is elaborated upon: 'It begun with an anxious Search after Arguments, to confirm the common Opinion: Doubts stole in, dissipated, return'd, were again dissipated, return'd again and it was a perpetual Struggle of a restless Imagination against Inclination, perhaps against Reason.'

From the introduction to the *Treatise*, we learn that Hume placed himself in the empirical tradition of Bacon, Newton, Locke, Shaftesbury, Mandeville, Hutcheson, and Butler, 'who have begun to put the science of man on a new footing and have engaged the attention, and excited the curiosity of the public.' The 'new footing' was to base all reasoning concerning human nature entirely upon experience. Hume differed from the others only in seeking to cover all aspects of human nature except the small area that was purely a priori, also in accepting the results of the investigation come what may. The others stopped short, at one point or another. It is a significant but frequently overlooked aspect of the *Treatise* that, at its outset, it was intended as a complete system of the moral sciences.

More names mentioned by Hume in the *Treatise* and its two sequels, the *Abstract* (1740) and *A Letter from a Gentleman* (1745), of which more shortly, are Clarke, Cudworth, Huet, Leibniz, Tillotson, and Wollaston. To cite these is not to give an exhaustive list of Hume's sources: the age was not given to scrupulous documentation.

Outlining to the London physician in 1734 the history of his period of illness and his prospects Hume stated that he was hastening to take up employment with a merchant in Bristol, having formed 'a Resolution to forget myself, & every thing that is past, to engage myself, as far as is possible, in that Course of Life, & to toss about the World, from the one Pole to the other, till I leave this Distemper behind me'. Since he was dismissed within a few months for trying to improve his master's English, this 'very feeble Trial for entering into a more active Scene of Life' was not taken too seriously, but it sufficed to complete his return to good health; thereafter, he was ready to resume his studies. He did so in France, attractive beyond measure to the Scot with a sense of history and to the aspiring man of letters.

Pausing briefly in Paris, Hume met the Chevalier Ramsay, who considered employing him as a translator but decided he was 'too full of himself, to humble his pregnant, active, protuberant Genius to drudge at translation.' He then settled down at Rheims for a year to learn the language and cultivate '*l'Art de Vivre*, the art of society and conversation', which he regarded the French as having in large measure perfected. From Rheims he went in 1735 to La Flèche, in Anjou, and in two years basically completed the composition of the *Treatise*. The attraction of La Flèche, a small country town, came partly from 'the Cheapness of it', and partly from the presence of a 'College of a hundred Jesuits, which is esteem'd the most magnificent both for Buildings & Gardens of any belonging to that Order in France or even in Europe.' The college had a library of 40,000 books, and it was noted as a centre of Cartesianism, understandably, for René Descartes was educated there from 1604 to 1612.

More specific information about Hume's association with the Jesuits comes to light in a letter dated 7 June 1762, which deals with the philosopher's most notorious piece of writing, the essay 'Of Miracles'. Although originally designed for inclusion in the *Treatise*, the piece first appeared in 1748 as part of *Philosophical Essays concerning Human Understanding*, later renamed and subsequently known as the *Enquiry concerning Human Understanding*. Writing to the Reverend George Campbell, who had published a *Dissertation on Miracles* (1762) against his essay, Hume explains its inception:

> It may perhaps amuse you to learn the first hint, which suggested to me that argument which you have so strenuously attacked. I was walking in the cloisters of the Jesuits' College of La Flèche, a town in which I passed two years of my youth, and engaged in a conversation with a Jesuit of some parts and learning, who was relating to me, and urging some nonsensical miracle performed in their convent, when I was tempted to dispute against him; and as my head was full of the topics of my *Treatise of Human Nature*, which I was at that time composing, this argument immediately occurred to me, and I thought it very much gravelled my companion; but at last he observed to me, that it was impossible for that argument to have any solidity, because it operated equally against the Gospel as the Catholic miracles; – which observation I thought proper to admit as a sufficient answer. I believe you will allow [he concludes in a jocular strain] that the freedom at least of this reasoning makes it somewhat extraordinary to have been the produce of a convent of Jesuits, tho perhaps you may think the sophistry of it savours plainly of the place of its birth.

After he had completed the manuscript of the *Treatise* and was on his way to Paris from La Flèche, Hume wrote on 26 August 1737 a letter of some importance for determining the background to his book and the expectations he had formed concerning it: 'I shall submit all my Performances to your Examination,' he advised a friend in England, '& to make you enter into them more easily, I desire of you, if you have Leizure, to read once over le Recherche de la Verité of Pere Malcbranche, the Principles of Human Knowledge by Dr Berkeley, some of the more metaphysical Articles of Bailes Dictionary; such as those [... of] Zeno, & Spinoza. Des-Cartes Meditations wou'd also be useful but [I] don't know if you will find it easily among your Acquaintances. These Books,' he suggests, 'will make you easily comprehend the metaphysical Parts of my Reasoning and as to the Rest, they have so little Dependence on all former systems of Philosophy, that your natural Good Sense will afford you Light enough to judge of their Force & Solidity.' The 'metaphysical Parts' of his reasoning refer to Book I, 'Of the Understanding'; the 'rest', to Books II and III. It can hardly escape notice that the required list of readings divides itself into two quite different groups. The first is the scepticism of Bayle and Berkeley; the second is the rationalism of Descartes and Malebranche. From the *Treatise* itself, it is evident that he approves of the scepticism and disapproves of the rationalism.

If Hume found 'perfect Tranquillity in France' suitable for composition, difficulties of many kinds assailed him in London on his return. 'I have been here near 3 months alwise within a Week of agreeing with Printers,' he admitted in December 1737, '& I ... did not forget the Work itself during that Time, where I began to feel some Passages weaker for the Style & Diction than I cou'd have wisht. The Nearness & Greatness of the Event rouz'd up my Attention, & made me more difficult to please.' In addition to concern over matters of style, his letter revealed, he was having second thoughts about some of the contents of the *Treatise*, 'some Reasonings concerning Miracles, which I once thought of publishing with the rest, but which I am afraid will give too much Offence even as the World is dispos'd at present.' It appears that he wished to submit his manuscript to Dr Joseph Butler, author of a famous series of sermons on human nature (1726) and the *Analogy of Religion* (1736), the one living theologian for whom Hume had intellectual respect:

> I wou'd be glad to be introduc'd to him. I am at present castrating my Work, that is, cutting off its noble Parts, that is, endeavouring it shall give as little Offence as possible; before which I cou'd not pretend to put it into the D[octo]rs hands. This is a Piece of Cowardice, for which I blame myself; tho I believe none of my Friends will blame me. But I was resolv'd not to be an Enthusiast, in Philosophy, while I was blaming other Enthusiasms.

In the event, Hume did not meet Butler, but he did not replace the 'noble Parts' until he published the *Philosophical Essays concerning Human Understanding*, realizing full well that the essay 'Of Miracles' belonged with the one entitled 'Of a Particular Providence and a Future State', as illustrative of the 'experimental Method of Reasoning' in the realm of religion. By 1748, he was sure enough of himself to announce to an intimate friend: 'I won't justify the prudence of this step, any other way than by expressing my indifference about all the consequences that may follow.'

As for the publication of the *Treatise*, three considerations delayed its appearance. Hume desired to be absolutely independent and to seek no help from a patron or a list of personally solicited subscribers. Next, he wished to publish anonymously. Finally, he bargained for rights to a first edition only and would not contract for future additions to the *Treatise*. On 26 September 1738, he signed an agreement with John Noon, at the White Hart, near Mercer's Chapel in Cheapside. Noon was a flourishing publisher, with a respectable number of books on his list, most of them works on religion, general learning, and philosophy. Hume assigned to Noon all rights for a first edition of 1,000 copies of the *Treatise of Human Nature* in two volumes octavo. In return, Hume was to get £50 payable in six months and twelve bound copies. Also, it was agreed that if Hume wished to bring out a second edition, he would buy up the unsold copies or pay a penalty of £50. By 1740 Hume believed he had concluded 'somewhat of a hasty Bargain' with Noon, and he looked elsewhere for a publisher of the third volume of the *Treatise*.

'Nothing excites an Author's Attention so much as the receiving the Proofs from the Press, as the Sheets are gradually thrown off': thus Hume towards the end of his life, and it would also be true of the last months of 1738. In the closing week of January 1739, John Noon published in boards: *A Treatise of Human Nature: Being an Attempt to introduce the experimental Method of Reasoning into Moral Subjects.* 'Book I, Of the Understanding. Book II, Of the Passions. Ten Shillings.' Book III, 'Of Morals', was being revised and did not reach print until November 1740, when it was published by Thomas Longman.

With the first two volumes published, Hume arranged to sail to Berwick but was storm-bound in London during February. The delay afforded him an opportunity to present copies of his book to various people, among them Dr Butler and Pierre Desmaizeaux, London correspondent of the *Bibliothèque britannique* and the *Bibliothèque raisonnée*, French-language periodicals published in the Netherlands. On reaching his home in Scotland in March, Hume distributed more copies, and one of these found its way to Francis Hutcheson, then Professor of Moral Philosophy at Glasgow University and, by reputation, his country's leading philosopher.

There is no known reaction of Butler's to the *Treatise*, but Hutcheson sent an encouraging message: 'I perused the first volume, & a great part, indeed almost all the second. And was everywhere surprised with a great acuteness of thought and reasoning in a mind wholly disengaged from the prejudices of the Learned as well as those of the Vulgar.' Hutcheson signified dissent from Hume's tenets 'as yet', but promised a more careful reading of the book in the coming vacation. He also expressed his willingness to meet the author. Desmaizeaux provided another crumb of comfort in a friendly blurb appearing in the April, May, and June issue for 1739 of the *Bibliothèque raisonnée*: 'A gentleman, named Mr *Hume*, has published a *Treatise of Human Nature*.... Those who demand the new will find satisfaction here. The author reasons on his own grounds; he goes to the bottom of things and traces out new routes. He is very original.' Elsewhere, Hume got a bad press. The *Neuen Zeitungen von gelehrten Sachen* of 28 May 1737, published at Leipzig (and therefore probably unknown to Hume, though the nature and tone of its kind of comment became depressingly familiar), described him as a 'new free-thinker' whose 'evil intentions are sufficiently betrayed in the subtitle of [his] work, taken from Tacitus: *Rara temporum felicitas, ubi sentire, quae velis; & quae sentias, dicere licet*'. The long-awaited review of the *Treatise* in the English periodical, the *History of the Works of the Learned*, which appeared in the November and December issues was, in its first part, a piece of abuse similar to that in the *Neuen Zeitungen*, though grossly extended. Finally, the *Bibliothèque britannique* for the last quarter of 1739 wrote off the *Treatise* as a 'system of logic, or rather of metaphysics, as original as can be, in which the author ... advances the most unheard-of paradoxes.' Thus an eighteenth-century tradition was set of confining comment on the *Treatise* to a wilful misinterpretation, mainly of Book I, 'Of the Understanding', and of abandoning any attempt at reasoned rebuttal in favour of vulgar raillery.

In the long interval before the *History of the Works of the Learned* printed its notice of the *Treatise*, Hume made a third attempt and composed an abstract intending to submit it to that same periodical. In the wake of the 'somewhat abusive' notice, as he called it, he decided to have the abstract published as an anonymous pamphlet. This was announced on 11 March 1740 in the *Daily Advertiser* as *An Abstract of a late Philosophical Performance, entitled A Treatise of Human Nature, &c. Wherein the chief Argument and Design of that Book, which has met with such Opposition, and has been represented in so terrifying a Light, is further illustrated and explain'd.* No copy of a pamphlet with this highly-charged title has been discovered so far, although three copies are extant of one more simply described as *An Abstract of a Book lately Published; Entituled, a Treatise of Human Nature, &c. Wherein the Chief Argument of that Book is farther Illustrated and Explain'd.* Consequently, it is impossible to say whether or not Hume toned down anything more than the title.

According to the *Abstract*, the 'Chief Argument' of Book I of the *Treatise* is that of causation. The movement gained by a billiard ball when struck by another ball provides Hume with his illustration: 'This is as perfect an instance of the relationship of cause and effect as any which we know, either by sensation or reflection. Let us therefore examine it.' The examination concludes that there are but three circumstances determining the relation between the cause and the effect and that these are contiguity, priority, and constant conjunction. Prior to experience, anything may be the cause of anything, and whatever we can imagine is possible. It is experience, custom, and not abstract reason which is the guide of life. The *Abstract* notes that the philosophy contained in the *Treatise* is sceptical in tendency but not to the exclusion of all knowledge: nature is too strong for the stupor attendant on the total suspension of belief. A true understanding of the working of the mind, as revealed by an analysis of causation, is stressed by Hume because it is the key to his teaching that man, a *feeling* rather than primarily a *reasoning* creature, lives in a naturalistic universe open to empirical investigation.

In *My Own Life*, written several months before his death in 1776, Hume was to declare that 'Never literary Attempt was more unfortunate than my Treatise of human Nature. It fell *dead-born from the Press;* without reaching such distinction as even to excite a Murmur among the Zealots.' This piece of self-mockery is not entirely true, as is evinced by the fact that Hume saw fit to compose and publish the *Abstract*. There is also the affair of the second sequel, published in 1745: *A Letter from a Gentleman to His Friend in Edinburgh*: 'Containing Some Observations on A Specimen of the Principles concerning Religion and Morality, *said to be* maintain'd in a Book lately publish'd, intituled, *A Treatise of Human Nature*, &c.'

On his return to Scotland in 1740, Hume had continued his career as a man of letters by turning essayist, a two-volume selection of his writings appearing in the following two years. But the vexing question of a 'settlement' remained unanswered. How was he to be provided for in life? In 1744–5, the Lord Provost of Edinburgh prevailed on Hume to stand candidate for the chair of Moral Philosophy at the University, the town council having certain rights in the election of professors. The Edinburgh clergy, for the most part, and among them the Principal of the University, were opposed to Hume as the author of subversive doctrines propagated in the *Treatise*. They went so far as to write a pamphlet or pamphlets against him. Meantime, Hume took a post as companion to a young nobleman who turned out to be a harmless lunatic. From the mad Marquess of Annandale's country house at Weldehall, near St Albans, without a copy of the *Treatise* to hand, Hume on receiving the accusations wrote a letter to the Provost to vindicate his philosophical standpoint. An eager friend rushed the letter into print, but to no avail in the campaign for the professorship. This was lost, not only because of the attacks by the 'Zealots', but also because, unknown to Hume, a majority of the town council were opposed to the Provost and to any and all of his candidates for office.

If the *Abstract* in the main was a straightforward analysis of causation, the *Letter from a Gentleman* was an impassioned self-defence against six charges:

(1) 'Universal Scepticism',

(2) 'Principles leading to downright Atheism, by denying the Doctrine of Causes and Effects',

(3) 'Errors concerning the very Being and Existence of a God',

(4) 'Errors concerning God's being the first Cause, and prime Mover of the Universe',

(5) 'denying the Immortality of the Soul, and the Consequences flowing from this Denial', and

(6) 'sapping the Foundations of Morality, by denying the natural and essential Differences betwixt Right and Wrong, Good and Evil, Justice and Injustice; making the Differences only artificial, and to arise from human Conventions and Compacts.'

It was this last charge that rankled sorest in Hume's mind. Following the methodological and psychological groundwork of Books I and II, Book III was the crux of the *Treatise*, namely, an attempt to establish a purely naturalistic ethics based on the facts of human nature and divorced from the realm of the a priori. The integrity of his moral character was always of the highest importance to Hume, and he resented the misrepresentation of his arguments as the attempts of an evil man to condone vice.

Nevertheless, there begins in the *Letter from a Gentleman* the public repudiation of the youthful *Treatise* on the score of its manner. 'I am indeed of Opinion', Hume wrote at the close, 'that the Author had better delayed the publishing of that Book; not on account of any dangerous Principles contained in it, but because on more mature Consideration he might have rendered it much less imperfect by further Corrections and Revisals.' In the last months of his life, he struck the same note in the Advertisement that was to appear in the first posthumous edition of *Essays and Treatises* of 1777, and on this occasion completely disowned the *Treatise*:

> Most of the principles and reasonings contained in this volume were published in a work in three volumes, called *A Treatise of Human Nature*, a work which the author had projected before he left College, and which he wrote and published not long after. But not finding it successful, he was sensible of his error in going to press too early, and he cast the whole anew in the following pieces, where some negligences in his former reasoning, and more in the expression are, he hopes, corrected. ... Henceforth, the author desires that the following pieces may alone be regarded as containing his philosophical sentiments and principles.

This Advertisement, he remarked sardonically, is a complete answer to 'that bigotted silly Fellow Beattie', whose

Essay on the Origin and Immutability of Truth; in opposition to Sophistry and Scepticism (1770) stigmatized Hume's *Treatise* as 'the vile effusion of a hard and stupid heart that mistakes its own restlessness for the activity of genius, and its own captiousness for sagacity of understanding.' Immanuel Kant was later to come to Hume's defence and to retort with mordant irony, 'I should think that Hume might fairly have laid as much claim to common sense as Beattie and, in addition, to a critical reason such as Beattie did not possess. ...' The *Treatise*, which had never been acknowledged publicly during his lifetime, was acknowledged posthumously by Hume in both *My Own Life* and the above Advertisement – but acknowledged only to disown.

Unlike most men, who are more prone to believe than to doubt, Hume, a sceptic by temperament, found it more congenial to doubt than to believe. He was also a sceptic by philosophical conviction. Such absolute certainty as exists for man, he argued, is present only in the a priori provinces of pure logic and pure mathematics, where comparisons of ideas give rise to assurance. Here we have knowledge. In the realm of matter of fact, there can be no absolute certainty, because no logical fallacy occurs in denying existence: whatever is, may not be. Here we have proofs and probability. Proofs are 'those arguments, which are deriv'd from the relation of cause and effect, and which are entirely free from doubt and uncertainty'. Probability is 'that evidence, which is still attended with uncertainty'. A test case will settle the question of the difference between a proof and a probability, namely, the rising of the sun tomorrow. No certainty attaches to this, but it would be ridiculous to say that this happening is only probable. The proof lies in our experience of the sun rising today and on previous mornings. In both proofs and probability, the latter the 'very guide of life' according to Dr Butler, the basic concept is cause-and-effect.

Insofar as Hume restricted himself to the Science of Man – and this he did in great part – he was restricting himself to matter of fact, to the practical consequences of his empirical investigation of the nature of man. Confessedly, when dealing with metaphysics proper, he sometimes found himself in a mood of 'philosophical melancholy', such as the one described towards the close of Book I of the *Treatise*. 'When I look abroad, I foresee on every side, dispute, contradiction, anger, calumny and detraction.' (How prescient he was!) 'When I turn my eye inward, I find nothing but doubt and ignorance.' Such a mood, however, is immediately dispelled when nature asserts itself: 'I dine, I play a game of backgammon, I converse, and am merry with my friends; and when after three or four hours' amusement, I wou'd return to these speculations, they appear so cold, and strain'd, and ridiculous, that I cannot find in my heart to enter into them any farther.' Metaphysical or Pyrrhonian or total scepticism is impossible to maintain. It is a matter for the closet only, and when out of the closet nature always asserts itself and the passions take dominion over reason. The Science of Man cannot be detached from the affairs of life; it is a practical matter and demands a practical philosopher, one who wishes to live his philosophy. 'Be a philosopher', cautioned Hume in the *Enquiry concerning Human Understanding*; 'but amidst all your philosophy be still a man.' There is ample reason to believe that Hume was primarily cautioning himself.

Nevertheless, it will not do to describe Hume's philosophy simply as sceptical or agnostic. For while it was partly destructive, it was also largely constructive. However paradoxical it may sound, Hume's scepticism was 'creative scepticism'. The subtitle to the *Treatise* ought to have put this question of creativity beyond argument: the introduction of empirical or scientific method into the study of 'moral subjects'; in modern terminology, those designated as including psychology, ethics, religion, history, political science, economics, aesthetics and criticism. These subjects are treated sceptically in that they are denied the possibility of certainty and are relegated to the realm of probability or, at best, of 'proofs', that is, the very highest probability. They are treated creatively because, freed from the shackles of metaphysical apriority, they are examined in the light of all available evidence. Man emerges, not as the ancient Socratic-Platonic and the modern Cartesian-Leibnizian *thinking animal*, but as a creature dominated by sentiment, emotion, passion, appetite. Hume was no doubt deliberately over-simplifying the issue for polemical purposes when he wrote in Book II that 'We speak not strictly and philosophically when we talk of the combat of passion and reason. Reason is, and ought only to be the slave of the passions, and can never pretend to any other office than to serve and obey them.' But reason is not to be outlawed and is still essential: 'We have ... no choice left but betwixt a false reason and none at all.'

The grand plan of a *Treatise of Human Nature* in five volumes was never completed. 'Of the Understanding', 'Of the Passions', and 'Of Morals' were published, but not 'Of Politics' nor 'Of Criticism'. Why did not Hume carry out his plan and why did he ultimately repudiate the *Treatise* with its systematic approach to the study of human nature, surely to be reckoned, along with the schemes of Bacon, Adam Smith, Bentham, and Spencer, as among the most grandiose ever projected by British philosophers? Simply because, as he came to realize, the *Treatise* was so organized and so presented that few contemporaries had a glimmering of what he taught.

Without too much oversimplification, it may be said that Hume's entire life centred on the *Treatise*: first to compose it, then, in turn, to explain it, to defend it, and to rewrite it. Arguing, fondly, that it was not so much the matter at fault as the manner, he recast it in the two *Enquiries*. Later, he presented the unwritten part in the form of essays, dissertations, and history. Finally, he disowned the *Treatise* in favour of the rewritings. Yet today common opinion has it that the *Treatise* is his philosophical masterpiece, and that his posthumous publication, *Dialogues concerning Natural Religions*, is his greatest literary success. The first and the last, therefore, reveal Hume at his very best. This is not to disparage the two *Enquiries*, which, together with the *Abstract*, form the best simplified introduction to Hume's philosophy.

The year 1745 spent as tutor to the mad Marquess of Annandale must have been one of the most fruitful of Hume's career. With plenty of time on his hands he composed the *Letter from a Gentleman*, experimented with writing the history of England, and worked on the first *Enquiry* of 1748. The following years, 1746–8, were hardly available for sustained philosophical writing. In 1746 he became secretary to General St Clair and acted as Judge Advocate during the descent on the coast of Brittany, an *opéra bouffe* military expedition. And in 1747–8 he was secretary and aide-de-camp to the same general on a military embassy to Vienna and Turin. These years were 'almost the only Interruptions which my Studies have received in the Course of my Life: I passed them agreeably and in good Company: And my Appointments, with my Frugality, had made me reach a Fortune, which I call independant, though most of my Friends were inclined to smile when I said so: In short I was now Master of near a thousand Pound.' These years were also good experience for the future historian.

'In 1751,' wrote Hume in *My Own Life* and with obvious satisfaction, 'I removed from the Countrey to the Town; the true Scene for a man of Letters.' And despite temporary residence in Paris and London, he remained a citizen of Edinburgh for the rest of his life. A feeble effort to secure the chair of Logic at Glasgow University in 1751 came to nothing. Even his friend and admirer Adam Smith, the Professor of Moral Philosophy, was timorous of speaking out for him. The life of letters produced many publications, and beginning in 1753 Hume began to issue, as *Essays and Treatises*, collections of his philosophical works – all but the unfortunate *Treatise* and the associated pamphlets, the *Abstract* and the *Letter from a Gentleman*. And from 1754 to 1762 he brought out six volumes of the *History of England*, a prodigious piece of scholarship which was made possible by his being appointed Keeper of the Advocates' Library in Edinburgh in 1752.

In that same year appeared the *Political Discourses*, a work which was largely to take the place of the unwritten fourth book of the *Treatise*; it supplied the theoretical basis of 'Of Politics', just as the *History* supplied the practical application. Book V of the *Treatise*, also unwritten, was adumbrated in several essays on aesthetics, notably 'Of Tragedy' and 'Of the Standard of Taste'. In short, by 1757, the name of David Hume was known throughout Great Britain and on the Continent as Britain's most famous (and infamous) man of letters. In 1762 Boswell named him 'the greatest writer in BRITTAIN'.

With the Treaty of Paris of 1763 ending the Seven Years War, normal diplomacy was re-established between Britain and France. Named ambassador, the pious Lord Hertford appointed David Hume to be his personal secretary, a choice that was applauded in France as the most felicitous possible. He later became Secretary to the Embassy and briefly chargé d'affaires. For three years Hume received the adulation of France and, returning to England early in 1766, he brought over the famous and much persecuted Jean-Jacques Rousseau to provide him with political sanctuary and a pension from the king. The paranoiac Rousseau shortly turned against his benefactor, however, and Hume had no choice but to defend his own moral integrity in a pamphlet, *A Concise and Genuine Account of the Dispute between Mr Hume and Mr Rousseau*. It is worth noting that no mention is made of this painful episode in his autobiography, and Rousseau's *Confessions* stops just before this point.

After a year in London as Under-Secretary of State, Northern Department under General Conway, Lord Hertford's brother, Hume settled down in 1769 to a philosophical retreat in his native city. His income had been considerably augmented by his public service: 'I was desirous of trying what Superfluity could produce, as I had formerly made an Experiment of Competency.' Accordingly, he had his first and only house built in the fashionable New Town on St Andrew's

Square. In jest, Nancy Ord named the location St David's Street.

'My Company was not unacceptable to the young and careless, as well as to the Studious and literary: And as I took a particular Pleasure in the Company of modest women, I had no Reason to be displeased with the Reception I met with from them.' So wrote the philosopher in his autobiography. The latest of these 'modest women' was the young daughter of Robert Ord, Lord Chief Baron of the Scottish Exchequer. Hume was her devoted admirer, had her choose the wallpaper for his new house, and finally during his last illness declared his attachment to her: 'It is the best placd attachment of my life, and will surely be the last.' It was; as signal proof in a codicil to his will he had written: 'I leave to Mrs Anne Ord, Daughter of the late Chief Baron, ten Guineas to buy a Ring, as a Memorial of my Friendship and Attachment to so amiable and accomplished a Person.'

To chart the dissemination and reception of Hume's teaching in the *Treatise* is to recognize that it is sometimes the fate of genius to anticipate its age by a century or two. Thus, *le bon Thomas Reid*, as the French admirers of the Common Sense philosophy saluted him, acknowledged in 1764 that he 'never thought of calling in question the principles commonly received with regard to human understanding, until the "Treatise of Human Nature" was published.' The same Reid, however, did not hesitate to describe the *Treatise* as a 'monster'! Probably thinking back to the year 1773, Kant asserted that Hume's teaching 'first interrupted my dogmatic slumber', but it is believed that all he knew of the *Treatise* was a passage quoted by Beattie in his *Essay on ... Truth*. In 1776, Bentham mentioned the startling effect on him of reading, some time previously, Book III of the *Treatise*: 'That the foundations of all *virtue* are laid in *utility* is there demonstrated. . . . For my own part, I well remember, no sooner had I read that part of the work which touches on this subject than I felt as if scales had fallen from my eyes. I then, for the first time, learned to call the cause of the People the cause of Virtue.' Yet so much of the full development of doctrinal utilitarianism was foreign to Hume's sceptical point of view.

After Hume died on 25 August 1776, many years indeed went past before the *Treatise* was viewed as a philosophical classic worthy of serious study. There was no second edition until 1817, and no rush to read it then or later in the nineteenth century. John Stuart Mill apparently never thought to open it. If the uncut pages of his copy of the *Philosophical Works* of Hume in Harvard University Library are sufficient evidence, the first book alone of the *Treatise* was read by William James. There was a German translation published in 1790–92, but no French one until 1878, and a partial affair (Book I) at that. In the twentieth century, the story is somewhat different. There have been new German and French translations, in 1906 and 1946 respectively; also, the *Treatise* has appeared in Russian (1906 and 1965–6), Spanish (1923), Italian (1926), Japanese (1933 and 1952), Polish (1951 and 1962), Hebrew (Book I only, 1954).

Despite the cry of a frustrated Hegelian in 1865, 'Hume is our Politics, Hume is our Trade, Hume is our Philosophy, Hume is our Religion – it wants little but Hume were even our Taste', such a millennium was and is still some way off. Unprejudiced Hume scholarship may be said to begin, however, with the publication by Norman Kemp Smith in *Mind*, 1905, of two articles entitled 'The Naturalism of Hume'. These were subsequently expanded to book form in *The Philosophy of David Hume* (1941), which remains the best all-round study of the philosopher and gives priority of attention to the *Treatise*. Kemp Smith's pioneering work was ably seconded by Charles W. Hendel in the U.S.A. and André-Louis Leroy in France.

The climate of philosophical opinion as these interpreters were at work is indicated by Stuart Hampshire: 'When I began the study of philosophy in 1933, Hume's arguments were not taken seriously by most academic philosophers, particularly not in Oxford: they were dismissed as plausible sophistries, which the student was expected quickly to expose; and his conclusions the mere extravagances of scepticism, with implications which no one could seriously accept.' T. H. Green's Introduction to the *Treatise* (1874) was regarded as a complete refutation of this scepticism. 'Suddenly,' according to Hampshire, 'in the late 1930's, all this, at least in England, changed.' The reason given is the interesting one that Hume's sceptical and naturalistic point of view was endorsed by philosophers who, like Hume, had perceived there was 'no hope of a rational insight into the structure of reality'. By way of illustration, Hampshire draws a parallel between Hume and the Wittgenstein of the later works. Both see philosophy as a kind of 'anthropology of knowledge', and both focus attention on the role of belief in understanding the world around us.

As a result of such changes in the key of thought, many philosophers in our time have looked for kinship with Hume: naturalists; positivists; pragmatists; ethical relativists; linguistic analysts; operationalists; even phenomenologists. Husserl in his *Logical Investigations*, according to a modern exponent, provides a good example of someone finding that Hume is on his side: '[Hume] suffers from the delusion that he is an empirical psychologist, when in fact he is engaged in a "pure" phenomenological analysis of the mind, intuiting directly the essence of the various mental acts.' Albert Einstein's biographer states flatly that 'the philosopher whose views Einstein felt helped him most was David Hume.' Bertrand Russell, whose own philosophical progress has been described as a progress from Descartes to Hume, goes so far in the apotheosis of Hume as to allege in a short story, among the collection *Nightmares of Eminent Persons*, that there is a particularly painful chamber in Hell inhabited by philosophers who have refuted Hume. 'These philosophers', concludes Russell drily, 'though in Hell have not yet learned wisdom.'

Nothing too much should be predicated on the *Treatise* as a source of hints for fantasy and philosophical kinship. Its lasting value is that it initiates the reader into the drama of a supreme effort of investigating human nature. In this work will be found the challenging pathos of the reversal of the lofty hopes of human rationality, as well as the cathartic experience of anatomizing human emotions. But here, finally, is the recovery of a balanced and reconciling view of both the intellectual capacity and the generosity of man.

SUGGESTIONS FOR FURTHER READING

HUME

Philosophical Works ed. T. H. Green and T. H. Grose, 4 vols. London 1874–5. Long out of print; reprinted 1964, Scientia Verlag Aalen. Contains all the non-historical works with the exception of the following two:

An Abstract of a Treatise of Human Nature (1740) ed. J. M. Keynes and P. Sraffa. Cambridge 1938.

A Letter from a Gentleman to his friend in Edinburgh (1745) ed. E. C. Mossner and J. V. Price. Edinburgh 1967.

CORRESPONDENCE AND LIFE

Letters of Eminent Persons addressed to David Hume ed. J. H. Burton. Edinburgh 1849.

The Letters of David Hume ed. J. Y. T. Greig, 2 vols. Oxford 1932.

New Letters of David Hume ed. R. Klibansky and E. C. Mossner. Oxford 1954.

Mossner, E. C., *The Life of David Hume*. London and Austin 1954.

CRITICAL STUDIES

Basson, A. H., *David Hume*. London 1958.

Flew, Antony, *Hume's Philosophy of Belief*. London and New York 1961.

Hendel, C. W., *Studies in the Philosophy of David Hume*. New York revised ed. 1963.

Laird, John, *Hume's Philosophy of Human Nature*. London 1932.

Leroy, André-Louis, *David Hume*. Paris 1953.

MacNabb, D. G. C., *David Hume: His Theory of Knowledge and Morality*. London 1951.

Passmore, J. A., *Hume's Intentions*. Cambridge 1952.

Smith, N. Kemp, *The Philosophy of David Hume*. London 1941.

Suggestions for Further Reading

Stewart, J. B., *The Moral and Political Philosophy of David Hume*. New York 1963.

David Hume: A Symposium ed. D. F. Pears. London 1963.

Hume: A Collection of Critical Essays ed. V. C. Chappell. New York 1966.

A NOTE ON THE TEXT

THE 'Hanley' copy in the Humanities Research Center, University of Texas, has been reproduced exactly except that long S's and digraphs have been modernized.

Also the following corrections have been made from:

(1) Hume's own list of errata for Books I and II.

(2) Hume's own 'second thoughts' and errata in the Appendix to Book III, which have been put in their proper places as directed.

(3) The list of corrections in Hume's own hand found in a copy of the *Treatise* bearing the bookplate of Henry Home of Kames. See Walter Nethery, 'Hume's Manuscript Corrections in a Copy of "A Treatise of Human Nature"', in *Papers of the Bibliographical Society of America* 57 (1963), 446–7.

(4) Further errata and inconsistencies of spelling as noted by the present editor.

(5) Hume's page references have been altered to conform to this edition.

No use has been made of the changes listed in the British Museum copy of the *Treatise* once owned by George Chalmers because they are not in Hume's hand, although there is some indication that they are based on the author's own list. See Raymond Klibansky, Appendix to *Hume: Theory of Politics* (ed. Frederick Watkins), Edinburgh 1953.

Facsimile of the title-page of the first edition (1739). The quotation means 'Seldom are men blessed with times in which they may think what they like, and say what they think.'

A

TREATISE

OF

Human Nature:

BEING

An ATTEMPT to introduce the experimental Method of Reasoning

INTO

MORAL SUBJECTS.

by David Hume Esqr.

Rara temporum felicitas, ubi sentire, quæ velis; & quæ sentias, dicere licet. TACIT.

VOL. I.

OF THE

UNDERSTANDING.

LONDON:
Printed for JOHN NOON, at the *White-Hart*, near *Mercer's-Chapel*, in *Cheapside*.

MDCCXXXIX.

ADVERTISEMENT

My design in the present work is sufficiently explain'd in the introduction. *The reader must only observe, that all the subjects I have there plann'd out to my self, are not treated of in these two volumes. The subjects of the* understanding *and* passions *make a compleat chain of reasoning by themselves; and I was willing to take advantage of this natural division, in order to try the taste of the public. If I have the good fortune to meet with success, I shall proceed to the examination of* morals, politics, *and* criticism; *which will compleat this* Treatise of human nature. *The approbation of the public I consider as the greatest reward of my labours; but am determin'd to regard its judgment, whatever it be, as my best instruction.*

THE CONTENTS

PART II

Of love and hatred

PART III

Of the will and direct passions

The Contents

BOOK III: OF MORALS

PART I

Of virtue and vice in general

PART II

Of justice and injustice

PART III

Of the other virtues and vices

INTRODUCTION

Nothing is more usual and more natural for those, who pretend to discover any thing new to the world in philosophy and sciences, than to insinuate the praises of their own systems, by decrying all those, which have been advanced before them. And indeed were they content with lamenting that ignorance, which we still lie under in the most important questions, that can come before the tribunal of human reason, there are few, who have an acquaintance with the sciences, that would not readily agree with them. 'Tis easy for one of judgment and learning, to perceive the weak foundation even of those systems, which have obtained the greatest credit, and have carried their pretensions highest to accurate and profound reasoning. Principles taken upon trust, consequences lamely deduced from them, want of coherence in the parts, and of evidence in the whole, these are every where to be met with in the systems of the most eminent philosophers, and seem to have drawn disgrace upon philosophy itself.

Nor is there requir'd such profound knowledge to discover the present imperfect condition of the sciences, but even the rabble without doors may judge from the noise and clamour, which they hear, that all goes not well within. There is nothing which is not the subject of debate, and in which men of learning are not of contrary opinions. The most trivial question escapes not our controversy, and in the most momentous we are not able to give any certain decision. Disputes are multiplied, as if every thing was uncertain; and these disputes are managed with the greatest warmth, as if every thing was certain. Amidst all this bustle 'tis not reason, which carries the prize, but eloquence; and no man needs ever despair of gaining proselytes to the most extravagant hypothesis, who has art enough to represent it in any favourable colours. The victory is not gained by the men at arms, who manage the pike and the sword;

but by the trumpeters, drummers, and musicians of the army.

From hence in my opinion arises that common prejudice against metaphysical reasonings of all kinds, even amongst those, who profess themselves scholars, and have a just value for every other part of literature. By metaphysical reasonings, they do not understand those on any particular branch of science, but every kind of argument, which is any way abstruse, and requires some attention to be comprehended. We have so often lost our labour in such researches, that we commonly reject them without hesitation, and resolve, if we must for ever be a prey to errors and delusions, that they shall at least be natural and entertaining. And indeed nothing but the most determined scepticism, along with a great degree of indolence, can justify this aversion to metaphysics. For if truth be at all within the reach of human capacity, 'tis certain it must lie very deep and abstruse; and to hope we shall arrive at it without pains, while the greatest geniuses have failed with the utmost pains, must certainly be esteemed sufficiently vain and presumptuous. I pretend to no such advantage in the philosophy I am going to unfold, and would esteem it a strong presumption against it, were it so very easy and obvious.

'Tis evident, that all the sciences have a relation, greater or less, to human nature; and that however wide any of them may seem to run from it, they still return back by one passage or another. Even *Mathematics, Natural Philosophy, and Natural Religion*, are in some measure dependent on the science of MAN; since they lie under the cognizance of men, and are judged of by their powers and faculties. 'Tis impossible to tell what changes and improvements we might make in these sciences were we thoroughly acquainted with the extent and force of human understanding, and cou'd explain the nature of the ideas we employ, and of the operations we perform in our reasonings. And these improvements are the more to be hoped for in natural religion, as it is not content with instructing us in the nature of superior powers, but carries its views farther, to their disposition towards us, and our duties towards them; and consequently we ourselves are not only the beings, that reason, but also one of the objects, concerning which we reason.

If therefore the sciences of Mathematics, Natural Philosophy, and Natural Religion, have such a dependence on the knowledge of man, what may be expected in the other sciences, whose connexion with human nature is more close and intimate? The sole end of logic is to explain the principles and operations of our reasoning faculty, and the nature of our ideas: morals and criticism regard our tastes and sentiments: and politics consider men as united in society, and dependent on each other. In these four sciences of *Logic, Morals, Criticism and Politics,* is comprehended almost every thing, which it can any way import us to be acquainted with, or which can tend either to the improvement or ornament of the human mind.

Here then is the only expedient, from which we can hope for success in our philosophical researches, to leave the tedious lingering method, which we have hitherto followed, and instead of taking now and then a castle or village on the frontier, to march up directly to the capital or center of these sciences, to human nature itself; which being once masters of, we may every where else hope for an easy victory. From this station we may extend our conquests over all those sciences, which more intimately concern human life, and may afterwards proceed at leisure to discover more fully those, which are the objects of pure curiosity. There is no question of importance, whose decision is not compriz'd in the science of man; and there is none, which can be decided with any certainty, before we become acquainted with that science. In pretending therefore to explain the principles of human nature, we in effect propose a compleat system of the sciences built on a foundation almost entirely new, and the only one upon which they can stand with any security.

And as the science of man is the only solid foundation for the other sciences, so the only solid foundation we can give to this science itself must be laid on experience and observation. 'Tis no astonishing reflection to consider, that the application of experimental philosophy to moral subjects should come after that to natural at the distance of above a whole century; since we find in fact, that there was about the same interval betwixt the origins of these sciences; and that reckoning from THALES to SOCRATES, the space of time is nearly equal to that betwixt my Lord BACON* and some late philosophers in *England*, who have begun to put the science of man on a new footing, and have engaged the attention, and excited the curiosity of the public. So true it is, that however other nations may rival us in poetry, and excel us in some other agreeable arts, the improvements in reason and philosophy can only be owing to a land of toleration and of liberty.

Nor ought we to think, that this latter improvement in the science of man will do less honour to our native country than the former in natural philosophy, but ought rather to esteem it a greater glory, upon account of the greater importance of that science, as well as the necessity it lay under of such a reformation. For to me it seems evident, that the essence of the mind being equally unknown to us with that of external bodies, it must be equally impossible to form any notion of its powers and qualities otherwise than from careful and exact experiments, and the observation of those particular effects, which result from its different circumstances and situations. And tho' we must endeavour to render all our principles as universal as possible, by tracing up our experiments to the utmost, and explaining all effects from the simplest and fewest causes, 'tis still certain we cannot go beyond experience; and any hypothesis, that pretends to discover the ultimate original qualities of human nature, ought at first to be rejected as presumptuous and chimerical.

I do not think a philosopher, who would apply himself so earnestly to the explaining the ultimate principles of the soul, would show himself a great master in that very science of human nature, which he pretends to explain, or very knowing in what is naturally satisfactory to the mind of

* Mr *Locke*, my Lord *Shaftsbury*, Dr *Mandeville*, Mr *Hutchinson* [Hutcheson], Dr *Butler*, &c.

man. For nothing is more certain, than that despair has almost the same effect upon us with enjoyment, and that we are no sooner acquainted with the impossibility of satisfying any desire, than the desire itself vanishes. When we see, that we have arrived at the utmost extent of human reason, we sit down contented; tho' we be perfectly satisfied in the main of our ignorance, and perceive that we can give no reason for our most general and most refined principles, beside our experience of their reality; which is the reason of the mere vulgar, and what it required no study at first to have discovered for the most particular and most extraordinary phaenomenon. And as this impossibility of making any farther progress is enough to satisfy the reader, so the writer may derive a more delicate satisfaction from the free confession of his ignorance, and from his prudence in avoiding that error, into which so many have fallen, of imposing their conjectures and hypotheses on the world for the most certain principles. When this mutual contentment and satisfaction can be obtained betwixt the master and scholar, I know not what more we can require of our philosophy.

But if this impossibility of explaining ultimate principles should be esteemed a defect in the science of man, I will venture to affirm, that 'tis a defect common to it with all the sciences, and all the arts, in which we can employ ourselves, whether they be such as are cultivated in the schools of the philosophers, or practised in the shops of the meanest artizans. None of them can go beyond experience, or establish any principles which are not founded on that authority. Moral philosophy has, indeed, this peculiar disadvantage, which is not found in natural, that in collecting its experiments, it cannot make them purposely, with premeditation, and after such a manner as to satisfy itself concerning every particular difficulty which may arise. When I am at a loss to know the effects of one body upon another in any situation, I need only put them in that situation, and observe what results from it. But should I endeavour to clear up after the same manner any doubt in moral philosophy, by placing myself in the same case with that which I consider, 'tis evident this reflection and premeditation would so disturb the operation of my natural principles, as must render it impossible to form any just conclusion from the phaenomenon. We must therefore glean up our experiments in this science from a cautious observation of human life, and take them as they appear in the common course of the world, by men's behaviour in company, in affairs, and in their pleasures. Where experiments of this kind are judiciously collected and compared, we may hope to establish on them a science, which will not be inferior in certainty, and will be much superior in utility to any other of human comprehension.

BOOK I

OF THE UNDERSTANDING

PART I

Of Ideas, their Origin, Composition, Connexion, Abstraction, &c.

SECT. I
Of the Origin of our Ideas

ALL the perceptions of the human mind resolve themselves into two distinct kinds, which I shall call IMPRESSIONS and IDEAS. The difference betwixt these consists in the degrees of force and liveliness, with which they strike upon the mind, and make their way into our thought or consciousness. Those perceptions, which enter with most force and violence, we may name *impressions*; and under this name I comprehend all our sensations, passions and emotions, as they make their first appearance in the soul. By *ideas* I mean the faint images of these in thinking and reasoning; such as, for instance, are all the perceptions excited by the present discourse, excepting only, those which arise from the sight and touch, and excepting the immediate pleasure or uneasiness it may occasion. I believe it will not be very necessary to employ many words in explaining this distinction. Every one of himself will readily perceive the difference betwixt feeling and thinking. The common degrees of these are easily distinguished; tho' it is not impossible but in particular instances they may very nearly approach to each other. Thus in sleep, in a fever, in madness, or in any very violent emotions of soul, our ideas may approach to our impressions: As on the other hand it sometimes happens, that our impressions are so faint and low, that we cannot distinguish them from our ideas. But notwithstanding this near resemblance in a few instances, they are in general so very different, that no-one can make a scruple to rank them under distinct heads, and assign to each a peculiar name to mark the difference*.

There is another division of our perceptions, which it will be convenient to observe, and which extends itself both to our impressions and ideas. This division is into SIMPLE and COMPLEX. Simple perceptions or impressions and ideas are such as admit of no distinction nor separation. The complex are the contrary to these, and may be distinguished into parts. Tho' a particular colour, taste, and smell are qualities all united together in this apple, 'tis easy to perceive they are not the same, but are at least distinguishable from each other.

Having by these divisions given an order and arrangement to our objects, we may now apply ourselves to consider with the more accuracy their qualities and relations. The first circumstance, that strikes my eye, is the great resemblance betwixt our impressions and ideas in every other particular, except their degree of force and vivacity. The one seem to be in a manner the reflexion of the other; so that all the perceptions of the mind are double, and appear both as impressions and ideas. When I shut my eyes and think of my chamber, the ideas I form are exact representations of the impressions I felt; nor is there any circumstance of the one, which is not to be found in the other. In running over my other perceptions, I find still the same resemblance and representation. Ideas and impressions appear always to correspond to each other. This circumstance seems to me remarkable, and engages my attention for a moment.

Upon a more accurate survey I find I have been carried

*I here make use of these terms, *impression and idea*, in a sense different from what is usual, and I hope this liberty will be allowed me. Perhaps I rather restore the word, idea, to its original sense, from which Mr *Locke* had perverted it, in making it stand for all our perceptions. By the terms of impression I would not be understood to express the manner, in which our lively perceptions are produced in the soul, but merely the perceptions themselves; for which there is no particular name either in the *English* or any other language, that I know of.

away too far by the first appearance, and that I must make use of the distinction of perceptions into *simple and complex*, to limit this general decision, *that all our ideas and impressions are resembling*. I observe, that many of our complex ideas never had impressions, that corresponded to them, and that many of our complex impressions never are exactly copied in ideas. I can imagine to myself such a city as the *New Jerusalem*, whose pavement is gold and walls are rubies, tho' I never saw any such. I have seen *Paris*; but shall I affirm I can form such an idea of that city, as will perfectly represent all its streets and houses in their real and just proportions?

I perceive, therefore, that tho' there is in general a great resemblance betwixt our *complex* impressions and ideas, yet the rule is not universally true, that they are exact copies of each other. We may next consider how the case stands with our *simple* perceptions. After the most accurate examination, of which I am capable, I venture to affirm, that the rule here holds without any exception, and that every simple idea has a simple impression, which resembles it; and every simple impression a correspondent idea. That idea of red, which we form in the dark, and that impression, which strikes our eyes in sun-shine, differ only in degree, not in nature. That the case is the same with all our simple impressions and ideas, 'tis impossible to prove by a particular enumeration of them. Every one may satisfy himself in this point by running over as many as he pleases. But if any one should deny this universal resemblance, I know no way of convincing him, but by desiring him to shew a simple impression, that has not a correspondent idea, or a simple idea, that has not a correspondent impression. If he does not answer this challenge, as 'tis certain he cannot, we may from his silence and our own observation establish our conclusion.

Thus we find, that all simple ideas and impressions resemble each other; and as the complex are formed from them, we may affirm in general, that these two species of perception are exactly correspondent. Having discover'd this relation, which requires no farther examination, I am curious to find some other of their qualities. Let us consider how they stand with regard to their existence, and which of the impressions and ideas are causes, and which effects.

The *full* examination of this question is the subject of the present treatise; and therefore we shall here content ourselves with establishing one general proposition, *That all our simple ideas in their first appearance are deriv'd from simple impressions, which are correspondent to them, and which they exactly represent.*

In seeking for phaenomena to prove this proposition, I find only those of two kinds; but in each kind the phaenomena are obvious, numerous, and conclusive. I first make myself certain, by a new review, of what I have already asserted, that every simple impression is attended with a correspondent idea, and every simple idea with a correspondent impression. From this constant conjunction of resembling perceptions I immediately conclude, that there is a great connexion betwixt our correspondent impressions and ideas, and that the existence of the one has a considerable influence upon that of the other. Such a constant conjunction, in such an infinite number of instances, can never arise from chance; but clearly proves a dependence of the impressions on the ideas, or of the ideas on the impressions. That I may know on which side this dependence lies, I consider the order of their *first appearance*; and find by constant experience, that the simple impressions always take the precedence of their correspondent ideas, but never appear in the contrary order. To give a child an idea of scarlet or orange, of sweet or bitter, I present the objects, or in other words, convey to him these impressions; but proceed not so absurdly, as to endeavour to produce the impressions by exciting the ideas. Our ideas upon their appearance produce not their correspondent impressions, nor do we perceive any colour, or feel any sensation merely upon thinking of them. On the other hand we find, that any impressions either of the mind or body is constantly followed by an idea, which resembles it, and is only different in the degrees of force and liveliness. The constant conjunction of our resembling perceptions, is a convincing proof, that the one are the causes of the other; and this priority of the impressions is an equal proof, that our impressions are the causes of our ideas, not our ideas of our impressions.

To confirm this I consider another plain and convincing phaenomenon; which is, that where-ever by any accident the faculties, which give rise to any impressions, are obstructed in their operations, as when one is born blind or deaf; not only the impressions are lost, but also their correspondent ideas; so that there never appear in the mind the least traces of either of them. Nor is this only true, where the organs of sensation are entirely destroy'd, but likewise where they have never been put in action to produce a particular impression. We cannot form to ourselves a just idea of the taste of a pineapple, without having actually tasted it.

There is however one contradictory phaenomenon, which may prove, that 'tis not absolutely impossible for ideas to go before their correspondent impressions. I believe it will readily be allow'd, that the several distinct ideas of colours, which enter by the eyes, or those of sounds, which are convey'd by the hearing, are really different from each other, tho' at the same time resembling. Now if this be true of different colours, it must be no less so of the different shades of the same colour, that each of them produces a distinct idea, independent of the rest. For if this shou'd be deny'd, 'tis possible, by the continual gradation of shades, to run a colour insensibly into what is most remote from it; and if you will not allow any of the means to be different, you cannot without absurdity deny the extremes to be the same. Suppose therefore a person to have enjoyed his sight for thirty years, and to have become perfectly well acquainted with colours of all kinds, excepting one particular shade of blue, for instance, which it never has been his fortune to meet with. Let all the different shades of that colour, except that single one, be plac'd before him, descending gradually from the deepest to the lightest; 'tis plain, that he will perceive a blank, where that shade is wanting, and will be sensible, that there is a greater distance in that place betwixt the contiguous colours, than in any other. Now I ask, whether 'tis possible for him, from his own imagination, to supply this deficiency, and raise up to himself the idea of that particular shade, tho' it had never been conveyed to him by his senses? I believe there are few but will be of opinion that he can; and this may serve as a proof, that the simple ideas are not always derived from the correspondent impressions; tho' the instance is so particular and singular, that 'tis scarce worth our observing, and does not merit that for it alone we should alter our general maxim.

But besides this exception, it may not be amiss to remark on this head, that the principle of the priority of impressions to ideas must be understood with another limitation, *viz.* that as our ideas are images of our impressions, so we can form secondary ideas, which are images of the primary; as appears from this very reasoning concerning them. This is not, properly speaking, an exception to the rule so much as an explanation of it. Ideas produce the images of themselves in new ideas; but as the first ideas are supposed to be derived from impressions, it still remains true, that all our simple ideas proceed either mediately or immediately, from their correspondent impressions.

This then is the first principle I establish in the science of human nature; nor ought we to despise it because of the simplicity of its appearance. For 'tis remarkable, that the present question concerning the precedency of our impressions or ideas, is the same with what has made so much noise in other terms, when it has been disputed whether there be any *innate ideas,* or whether all ideas be derived from sensation and reflexion. We may observe, that in order to prove the ideas of extension and colour not to be innate, philosophers do nothing but shew, that they are conveyed by our senses. To prove the ideas of passion and desire not to be innate, they observe that we have a preceding experience of these emotions in ourselves. Now if we carefully examine these arguments, we shall find that they prove nothing but that ideas are preceded by other more lively perceptions, from which they are derived, and which they represent. I hope this clear stating of the question will remove all disputes concerning it, and will render this principle of more use in our reasonings, than it seems hitherto to have been.

SECT. II

Division of the subject

SINCE it appears, that our simple impressions are prior to their correspondent ideas, and that the exceptions are very rare, method seems to require we should examine our impressions, before we consider our ideas. Impressions may be divided into two kinds, those of SENSATION and those of REFLEXION. The first kind arises in the soul originally, from unknown causes. The second is derived in a great measure from our ideas, and that in the following order. An impression first strikes upon the senses, and makes us perceive heat or cold, thirst or hunger, pleasure or pain of some kind or other. Of this impression there is a copy taken by the mind, which remains after the impression ceases; and this we call an idea. This idea of pleasure or pain, when it returns upon the soul, produces the new impressions of desire and aversion, hope and fear, which may properly be called impressions of reflexion, because derived from it. These again are copied by the memory and imagination, and become ideas; which perhaps in their turn give rise to other impressions and ideas. So that the impressions of reflexion are only antecedent to their correspondent ideas; but posterior to those of sensation, and deriv'd from them. The examination of our sensations belongs more to anatomists and natural philosophers than to moral; and therefore shall not at present be enter'd upon. And as the impressions of reflection, *viz.* passions, desires, and emotions, which principally deserve our attention, arise mostly from ideas, 'twill be necessary to reverse that method, which at first sight seems most natural; and in order to explain the nature and principles of the human mind, give a particular account of ideas, before we proceed to impressions. For this reason I have here chosen to begin with ideas.

SECT. III

Of the ideas of the memory and imagination

WE find by experience, that when any impression has been present with the mind, it again makes its appearance there as an idea; and this it may do after two different ways: either when in its new appearance it retains a considerable degree of its first vivacity, and is somewhat intermediate betwixt an impression and an idea; or when it intirely loses that vivacity, and is a perfect idea. The faculty, by which we repeat our impressions in the first manner, is called the MEMORY, and the other the IMAGINATION. 'Tis evident at first sight, that the ideas of the memory are much more lively and strong than those of the imagination, and that the former faculty paints its objects in more distinct colours, than any which are employ'd by the latter. When we remember any past event, the idea of it flows in upon the mind in a forcible manner; whereas in the imagination the perception is faint and languid, and cannot without difficulty be preserv'd by the mind steddy and uniform for any considerable time. Here then is a sensible difference betwixt one species of ideas and another. But of this more fully hereafter*.

There is another difference betwixt these two kinds of ideas, which is no less evident, namely that tho' neither the ideas of the memory nor imagination, neither the lively nor faint ideas can make their appearance in the mind, unless their correspondent impressions have gone before to prepare the way for them, yet the imagination is not restrain'd to the same order and form with the original impressions; while the memory is in a manner ty'd down in that respect, without any power of variation.

*Part III. Sect. 5.

'Tis evident, that the memory preserves the original form, in which its objects were presented, and that where-ever we depart from it in recollecting any thing, it proceeds from some defect or imperfection in that faculty. An historian may, perhaps, for the more convenient carrying on of his narration, relate an event before another, to which it was in fact posterior; but then he takes notice of this disorder, if he be exact; and by that means replaces the idea in its due position. 'Tis the same case in our recollection of those places and persons, with which we were formerly acquainted. The chief exercise of the memory is not to preserve the simple ideas, but their order and position. In short, this principle is supported by such a number of common and vulgar phaenomena, that we may spare ourselves the trouble of insisting on it any farther.

The same evidence follows us in our second principle, *of the liberty of the imagination to transpose and change its ideas.* The fables we meet with in poems and romances put this entirely out of question. Nature there is totally confounded, and nothing mentioned but winged horses, fiery dragons, and monstrous giants. Nor will this liberty of the fancy appear strange, when we consider, that all our ideas are copy'd from our impressions, and that there are not any two impressions which are perfectly inseparable. Not to mention, that this is an evident consequence of the division of ideas into simple and complex. Where-ever the imagination perceives a difference among ideas, it can easily produce a separation.

SECT. IV

Of the connexion or association of ideas

As all simple ideas may be separated by the imagination, and may be united again in what form it pleases, nothing wou'd be more unaccountable than the operations of that faculty, were it not guided by some universal principles, which render it, in some measure, uniform with itself in all times and places. Were ideas entirely loose and unconnected, chance alone wou'd join them; and 'tis impossible the same simple ideas should fall regularly into complex ones (as they commonly do) without some bond of union among them, some associating quality, by which one idea naturally introduces another. This uniting principle among ideas is not to be consider'd as an inseparable connexion; for that has been already excluded from the imagination: Nor yet are we to conclude, that without it the mind cannot join two ideas; for nothing is more free than that faculty: but we are only to regard it as a gentle force, which commonly prevails, and is the cause why, among other things, languages so nearly correspond to each other; nature in a manner pointing out to every one those simple ideas, which are most proper to be united into a complex one. The qualities, from which this association arises, and by which the mind is after this manner convey'd from one idea to another, are three, *viz.* RESEMBLANCE, CONTIGUITY in time or place, and CAUSE and EFFECT.

I believe it will not be very necessary to prove, that these qualities produce an association among ideas, and upon the appearance of one idea naturally introduce another. 'Tis plain, that in the course of our thinking, and in the constant evolution of our ideas, our imagination runs easily from one idea to any other that *resembles* it, and that this quality alone is to the fancy a sufficient bond and association. 'Tis likewise evident, that as the senses, in changing their objects, are necessitated to change them regularly, and take them as they lie *contiguous* to each other, the imagination must by long custom acquire the same method of thinking, and run along the parts of space and time in conceiving its objects. As to the connexion, that is made by the relation of *cause and effect,* we shall have occasion afterwards to examine it to the bottom, and therefore shall not at present insist upon it. 'Tis sufficient to observe, that there is no relation, which produces a stronger connexion in the fancy, and makes one idea more readily recall another, than the relation of cause and effect betwixt their objects.

That we may understand the full extent of these relations, we must consider, that two objects are connected together in the imagination, not only when the one is immediately resembling, contiguous to, or the cause of the other, but also when there is interposed betwixt them a third object, which bears to both of them any of these relations. This may be carried on to a great length; tho' at the same time we may observe, that each remove considerably weakens the relation. Cousins in the fourth degree are connected by *causation*, if I may be allowed to use that term; but not so closely as brothers, much less as child and parent. In general we may observe, that all the relations of blood depend upon cause and effect, and are esteemed near or remote, according to the number of connecting causes interpos'd betwixt the persons.

Of the three relations above-mentioned this of causation is the most extensive. Two objects may be consider'd as plac'd in this relation, as well when one is the cause of any of the actions or motions of the other, as when the former is the cause of the existence of the latter. For as that action or motion is nothing but the object itself, consider'd in a certain light, and as the object continues the same in all its different situations, 'tis easy to imagine how such an influence of objects upon one another may connect them in the imagination.

We may carry this farther, and remark, not only that two objects are connected by the relation of cause and effect, when the one produces a motion or any action in the other, but also when it has a power of producing it. And this we may observe to be the source of all the relations of interest and duty, by which men influence each other in society, and are plac'd in the ties of government and subordination. A master is such-a-one as by his situation, arising either from force or agreement, has a power of directing in certain particulars the actions of another, whom we call servant. A judge is one, who in all disputed cases can fix by his opinion the possession or property of any thing betwixt any members of the society. When a person is possess'd of any power, there is no more required to convert it into action, but the exertion of the will; and *that* in every case is consider'd as possible, and in many as probable; especially in the case of authority, where the obedience of the subject is a pleasure and advantage to the superior.

These are therefore the principles of union or cohesion among our simple ideas, and in the imagination supply the place of that inseparable connexion, by which they are united in our memory. Here is a kind of ATTRACTION, which in the mental world will be found to have as extraordinary effects as in the natural, and to shew itself in as many and as various forms. Its effects are every where conspicuous; but as to its causes, they are mostly unknown, and must be resolv'd into *original* qualities of human nature, which I pretend not to explain. Nothing is more requisite for a true philosopher, than to restrain the intemperate desire of searching into causes, and having establish'd any doctrine upon a sufficient number of experiments, rest contented with that, when he sees a farther examination would lead him into obscure and uncertain speculations. In that case his enquiry wou'd be much better employ'd in examining the effects than the causes of his principle.

Amongst the effects of this union or association of ideas, there are none more remarkable, than those complex ideas, which are the common subjects of our thoughts and reasoning, and generally arise from some principle of union among our simple ideas. These complex ideas may be divided into *Relations*, *Modes*, and *Substances*. We shall briefly examine each of these in order, and shall subjoin some considerations concerning our *general* and *particular* ideas, before we leave the present subject, which may be consider'd as the elements of this philosophy.

SECT. V

Of relations

THE word RELATION is commonly used in two senses considerably different from each other. Either for that quality, by which two ideas are connected together in the imagination, and the one naturally introduces the other, after the manner above-explained; or for that particular circumstance, in which, even upon the arbitrary union of two ideas in the fancy, we may think proper to compare them. In common language the former is always the sense, in which we use the word, relation; and 'tis only in philosophy, that we extend it to mean any particular subject of comparison, without a connecting principle. Thus distance will be allowed by philosophers to be a true relation, because we acquire an idea of it by the comparing of objects: But in a common way we say, *that nothing can be more distant than such or such things from each other, nothing can have less relation*; as if distance and relation were incompatible.

It may perhaps be esteemed an endless task to enumerate all those qualities, which make objects admit of comparison, and by which the ideas of *philosophical* relation are produced. But if we diligently consider them, we shall find that without difficulty they may be compriz'd under seven general heads, which may be considered as the sources of all *philosophical* relation.

(1) The first is *resemblance*: And this is a relation, without which no philosophical relation can exist; since no objects will admit of comparison, but what have some degree of resemblance. But tho' resemblance be necessary to all philosophical relation, it does not follow, that it always produces a connexion or association of ideas. When a quality becomes very general, and is common to a great many individuals, it leads not the mind directly to any one of them; but by presenting at once too great a choice, does thereby prevent the imagination from fixing on any single object.

(2) *Identity* may be esteem'd a second species of relation. This relation I here consider as apply'd in its strictest sense to constant and unchangeable objects; without examining the nature and foundation of personal identity, which shall find its place afterwards. Of all relations the most universal is that of identity, being common to every being, whose existence has any duration.

(3) After identity the most universal and comprehensive relations are those of *Space* and *Time*, which are the sources of an infinite number of comparisons, such as *distant, contiguous, above, below, before, after*, &c.

(4) All those objects which admit of *quantity*, or *number*, may be compar'd in that particular; which is another very fertile source of relation.

(5) When any two objects possess the same *quality* in common, the *degrees*, in which they possess it, form a fifth species of relation. Thus of two objects, which are both heavy, the one may be either of greater, or less weight than the other. Two colours, that are of the same kind, may yet be of different shades, and in that respect admit of comparison.

(6) The relation of *contrariety* may at first sight be regarded as an exception to the rule, *that no relation of any kind can subsist without some degree of resemblance*. But let us consider, that no two ideas are in themselves contrary, except those of existence and non-existence, which are plainly resembling, as implying both of them an idea of the object; tho' the latter excludes the object from all times and places, in which it is supposed not to exist.

(7) All other objects, such as fire and water, heat and cold, are only found to be contrary from experience, and from the contrariety of their *causes* or *effects*; which relation of cause and effect is a seventh philosophical relation, as well as a natural one. The resemblance implied in this relation, shall be explain'd afterwards.

It might naturally be expected, that I should join *difference* to the other relations. But that I consider rather as a negation of relation, than as any thing real or positive.

Difference is of two kinds as oppos'd either to identity or resemblances. The first is call'd a difference of *number*; the other of *kind*.

SECT. VI

Of modes and substances

I WOU'D fain ask those philosophers, who found so much of their reasonings on the distinction of substance and accident, and imagine we have clear ideas of each, whether the idea of *substance* be deriv'd from the impressions of sensation or reflection? If it be convey'd to us by our senses, I ask, which of them; and after what manner? If it be perceiv'd by the eyes, it must be a colour; if by the ears, a sound; if by the palate, a taste; and so of the other senses. But I believe none will assert, that substance is either a colour, or a sound, or a taste. The idea of substance must therefore be deriv'd from an impression of reflection, if it really exist. But the impressions of reflection resolve themselves into our passions and emotions; none of which can possibly represent a substance. We have therefore no idea of substance, distinct from that of a collection of particular qualities, nor have we any other meaning when we either talk or reason concerning it.

The idea of a substance as well as that of a mode, is nothing but a collection of simple ideas, that are united by the imagination, and have a particular name assigned them, by which we are able to recal, either to ourselves or others, that collection. But the difference betwixt these ideas consists in this, that the particular qualities, which form a substance, are commonly refer'd to an unknown *something*, in which they are supposed to inhere; or granting this fiction should not take place, are at least supposed to be closely and inseparably connected by the relations of contiguity and causation. The effect of this is, that whatever new simple quality we discover to have the same connexion with the rest, we immediately comprehend it among them, even tho' it did not enter into the first conception of the substance. Thus our idea of gold may at first be a yellow colour, weight, malleableness, fusibility; but upon the discovery of its dissolubility in *aqua regia*, we join that to the other qualities, and suppose it to belong to the substance as much as if its idea had from the beginning made a part of the compound one. The principle of union being regarded as the chief part of the complex idea, gives entrance to whatever quality afterwards occurs, and is equally comprehended by it, as are the others, which first presented themselves.

That this cannot take place in modes, is evident from considering their nature. The simple ideas of which modes are formed, either represent qualities, which are not united by contiguity and causation, but are dispers'd in different subjects; or if they be all united together, the uniting principle is not regarded as the foundation of the complex idea. The idea of a dance is an instance of the first kind of modes; that of beauty of the second. The reason is obvious, why such complex ideas cannot receive any new idea, without changing the name, which distinguishes the mode.

SECT. VII

Of abstract ideas

A VERY material question has been started concerning *abstract* or *general* ideas, *whether they be general or particular in the mind's conception of them.* A* great philosopher has disputed the receiv'd opinion in this particular, and has asserted, that all general ideas are nothing but particular ones, annexed to a certain term, which gives them a more extensive signification, and makes them recal upon occasion other individuals, which are similar to them. As I look upon this to be one of the greatest and most valuable discoveries that has been made of late years in the republic of letters,

* Dr *Berkeley*.

I shall here endeavour to confirm it by some arguments, which I hope will put it beyond all doubt and controversy.

'Tis evident, that in forming most of our general ideas, if not all of them, we abstract from every particular degree of quantity and quality, and that an object ceases not to be of any particular species on account of every small alteration in its extension, duration and other properties. It may therefore be thought, that here is a plain dilemma, that decides concerning the nature of those abstract ideas, which have afforded so much speculation to philosophers. The abstract idea of a man represents men of all sizes and all qualities; which 'tis concluded it cannot do, but either by representing at once all possible sizes and all possible quantities, or by representing no particular one at all. Now it having been esteemed absurd to defend the former proposition, as implying an infinite capacity in the mind, it has been commonly infer'd in favour of the latter; and our abstract ideas have been suppos'd to represent no particular degree either of quantity or quality. But that this inference is erroneous, I shall endeavour to make appear, *first*, by proving, that 'tis utterly impossible to conceive any quantity or quality, without forming a precise notion of its degrees: And *secondly* by showing, that tho' the capacity of the mind be not infinite, yet we can at once form a notion of all possible degrees of quantity and quality, in such a manner at least, as, however imperfect, may serve all the purposes of reflection and conversation.

To begin with the first proposition, *that the mind cannot form any notion of quantity or quality without forming a precise notion of the degrees of each*; we may prove this by the three following arguments. First, We have observ'd, that whatever objects are different are distinguishable, and that whatever objects are distinguishable are separable by the thought and imagination. And we may here add, that these propositions are equally true in the *inverse*, and that whatever objects are separable are also distinguishable, and that whatever objects are distinguishable are also different. For how is it possible we can separate what is not distinguishable, or distinguish what is not different? In order therefore to know, whether abstraction implies a separation, we need only consider it in this view, and examine, whether all the circumstances, which we abstract from in our general ideas, be such as are distinguishable and different from those, which we retain as essential parts of them. But 'tis evident at first sight, that the precise length of a line is not different nor distinguishable from the line itself; nor the precise degree of any quality from the quality. These ideas, therefore, admit no more of separation than they do of distinction and difference. They are consequently conjoined with each other in the conception; and the general idea of a line, notwithstanding all our abstractions and refinements, has in its appearance in the mind a precise degree of quantity and quality; however it may be made to represent others, which have different degrees of both.

Secondly, 'tis confest, that no object can appear to the senses; or in other words, that no impression can become present to the mind, without being determin'd in its degrees both of quantity and quality. The confusion, in which impressions are sometimes involv'd, proceeds only from their faintness and unsteadiness, not from any capacity in the mind to receive any impression, which in its real existence has no particular degree nor proportion. That is a contradiction in terms; and even implies the flattest of all contradictions, *viz.* that 'tis possible for the same thing both to be and not to be.

Now since all ideas are deriv'd from impressions, and are nothing but copies and representations of them, whatever is true of the one must be acknowledg'd concerning the other. Impressions and ideas differ only in their strength and vivacity. The foregoing conclusion is not founded on any particular degree of vivacity. It cannot therefore be affected by any variation in that particular. An idea is a weaker impression; and as a strong impression must necessarily have a determinate quantity and quality, the case must be the same with its copy or representative.

Thirdly, 'tis a principle generally receiv'd in philosophy,

that every thing in nature is individual, and that 'tis utterly absurd to suppose a triangle really existent, which has no precise proportion of sides and angles. If this therefore be absurd in *fact and reality*, it must also be absurd *in idea*; since nothing of which we can form a clear and distinct idea is absurd and impossible. But to form the idea of an object, and to form an idea simply is the same thing; the reference of the idea to an object being an extraneous denomination, of which in itself it bears no mark or character. Now as 'tis impossible to form an idea of an object, that is possest of quantity and quality, and yet is possest of no precise degree of either; it follows, that there is an equal impossibility of forming an idea, that is not limited and confin'd in both these particulars. Abstract ideas are therefore in themselves individual, however they may become general in their representation. The image in the mind is only that of a particular object, tho' the application of it in our reasoning be the same, as if it were universal.

This application of ideas beyond their nature proceeds from our collecting all their possible degrees of quantity and quality in such an imperfect manner as may serve the purposes of life, which is the second proposition I propos'd to explain. When we have found a resemblance* among several objects, that often occur to us, we apply the same name to all of them, whatever differences we may observe in the degrees of their quantity and quality, and whatever other differences may appear among them. After we have acquired

*[The following note is inserted from Hume's Appendix to Book III.]

'Tis evident, that even different simple ideas may have a similarity or resemblance to each other; nor is it necessary, that the point or circumstance of resemblance shou'd be distinct or separable from that in which they differ. *Blue* and *green* are different simple ideas, but are more resembling than *blue* and *scarlet*; tho' their perfect simplicity excludes all possibility of separation or distinction. 'Tis the same case with particular sounds, and tastes and smells. These admit of infinite resemblances upon the general appearance and comparison, without having any common circumstance the same. And of this we may be certain, even from the very abstract terms *simple idea*. They comprehend all simple ideas under them. These resemble each other a custom of this kind, the hearing of that name revives the idea of one of these objects, and makes the imagination conceive it with all its particular circumstances and proportions. But as the same word is suppos'd to have been frequently applied to other individuals, that are different in many respects from that idea, which is immediately present to the mind; the word not being able to revive the idea of all these individuals, only touches the soul, if I may be allow'd so to speak, and revives that custom, which we have acquir'd by surveying them. They are not really and in fact present to the mind, but only in power; nor do we draw them all out distinctly in the imagination, but keep ourselves in a readiness to survey any of them, as we may be prompted by a present design or necessity. The word raises up an individual idea, along with a certain custom; and that custom produces any other individual one, for which we may have occasion. But as the production of all the ideas, to which the name may be apply'd, is in most cases impossible, we abridge that work by a more partial consideration, and find but few inconveniences to arise in our reasoning from that abridgment.

For this is one of the most extraordinary circumstances in the present affair, that after the mind has produc'd an individual idea, upon which we reason, the attendant custom, reviv'd by the general or abstract term, readily suggests any other individual, if by chance we form any reasoning, that agrees not with it. Thus shou'd we mention the word, triangle, and form the idea of a particular equilateral one to correspond to it, and shou'd we afterwards assert *that the three angles of a triangle are equal to each other*, the other individuals of a scalenum and isosceles, which we overlook'd at first, immediately crowd in upon us, and make us perceive the falshood of this proposition, tho' it be true with

---

in their simplicity. And yet from their very nature, which excludes all composition, this circumstance, in which they resemble, is not distinguishable nor separable from the rest. 'Tis the same case with all the degrees in any quality. They are all resembling, and yet the quality, in any individual, is not distinct from the degree.

relation to that idea, which we had form'd. If the mind suggests not always these ideas upon occasion, it proceeds from some imperfection in its faculties; and such a one as is often the source of false reasoning and sophistry. But this is principally the case with those ideas which are abstruse and compounded. On other occasions the custom is more entire, and 'tis seldom we run into such errors.

Nay so entire is the custom, that the very same idea may be annext to several different words, and may be employ'd in different reasonings, without any danger of mistake. Thus the idea of an equilateral triangle of an inch perpendicular may serve us in talking of a figure, of a rectilineal figure, of a regular figure, of a triangle, and of an equilateral triangle. All these terms, therefore, are in this case attended with the same idea; but as they are wont to be apply'd in a greater or lesser compass, they excite their particular habits, and thereby keep the mind in a readiness to observe, that no conclusion be form'd contrary to any ideas, which are usually compriz'd under them.

Before those habits have become entirely perfect, perhaps the mind may not be content with forming the idea of only one individual, but may run over several, in order to make itself comprehend its own meaning, and the compass of that collection, which it intends to express by the general term. That we may fix the meaning of the word, figure, we may revolve in our mind the ideas of circles, squares, parallelograms, triangles of different sizes and proportions, and may not rest on one image or idea. However this may be, 'tis certain *that* we form the idea of individuals, whenever we use any general term; *that* we seldom or never can exhaust these individuals; and *that* those, which remain, are only represented by means of that habit, by which we recal them, whenever any present occasion requires it. This then is the nature of our abstract ideas and general terms; and 'tis after this manner we account for the foregoing paradox, *that some ideas are particular in their nature, but general in their representation.* A particular idea becomes general by being annex'd to a general term; that is, to a term, which from a customary conjunction has a relation to many other particular ideas, and readily recals them in the imagination.

The only difficulty, that can remain on this subject, must be with regard to that custom, which so readily recals every particular idea, for which we may have occasion, and is excited by any word or sound, to which we commonly annex it. The most proper method, in my opinion, of giving a satisfactory explication of this act of the mind, is by producing other instances, which are analogous to it, and other principles, which facilitate its operation. To explain the ultimate causes of our mental actions is impossible. 'Tis sufficent, if we give any satisfactory account of them from experience and analogy.

First then I observe, that when we mention any great number, such as a thousand, the mind has generally no adequate idea of it, but only a power of producing such an idea, by its adequate idea of the decimals, under which the number is comprehended. This imperfection, however in our ideas, is never felt in our reasonings; which seems to be an instance parallel to the present one of universal ideas.

Secondly, we have several instances of habits, which may be reviv'd by one single word; as when a person, who has by rote any periods of a discourse, or any number of verses, will be put in remembrance of the whole, which he is at a loss to recollect, by that single word or expression, with which they begin.

Thirdly, I believe every one, who examines the situation of his mind in reasoning, will agree with me, that we do not annex distinct and compleat ideas to every term we make use of, and that in talking of *government, church, negotiation, conquest,* we seldom spread out in our minds all the simple ideas, of which these complex ones are compos'd. 'Tis however observable, that notwithstanding this imperfection we may avoid talking nonsense on these subjects, and may perceive any repugnance among the ideas, as well as if we had a full comprehension of them. Thus if instead of saying, *that in war the weaker have always recourse to negotiation*, we shou'd say, *that they have always recourse to conquest*, the custom, which we have acquir'd of attributing certain relations to ideas, still follows the words, and makes us immediately perceive the absurdity of that proposition; in the same manner as one particular idea may serve us in reasoning concerning other ideas, however different from it in several circumstances.

Fourthly, As the individuals are collected together, and plac'd under a general term with a view to that resemblance, which they bear to each other, this relation must facilitate their entrance in the imagination, and make them be suggested more readily upon occasion. And indeed if we consider the common progress of the thought, either in reflection or conversation, we shall find great reason to be satisfy'd in this particular. Nothing is more admirable, than the readiness, with which the imagination suggests its ideas, and presents them at the very instant, in which they become necessary or useful. The fancy runs from one end of the universe to the other in collecting those ideas, which belong to any subject. One would think the whole intellectual world of ideas was at once subjected to our view, and that we did nothing but pick out such as were most proper for our purpose. There may not, however, be any present, beside those very ideas, that are thus collected by a kind of magical faculty in the soul, which, tho' it be always most perfect in the great geniuses, and is properly what we call a genius, is however inexplicable by the utmost efforts of human understanding.

Perhaps these four reflections may help to remove all difficulties to the hypothesis I have propos'd concerning abstract ideas, so contrary to that, which has hitherto prevail'd in philosophy. But to tell the truth I place my chief confidence in what I have already prov'd concerning the impossibility of general ideas, according to the common method of explaining them. We must certainly seek some new system on this head, and there plainly is none beside what I have propos'd. If ideas be particular in their nature, and at the same time finite in their number, 'tis only by custom they can become general in their representation, and contain an infinite number of other ideas under them.

Before I leave this subject I shall employ the same principles to explain that *distinction of reason,* which is so much talk'd of, and is so little understood, in the schools. Of this kind is the distinction betwixt figure and the body figur'd; motion and the body mov'd. The difficulty of explaining this distinction arises from the principle above explain'd, *that all ideas, which are different, are separable.* For it follows from thence, that if the figure be different from the body, their ideas must be separable as well as distinguishable; if they be not different, their ideas can neither be separable nor distinguishable. What then is meant by a distinction of reason, since it implies neither a difference nor separation?

To remove this difficulty we must have recourse to the foregoing explication of abstract ideas. 'Tis certain that the mind wou'd never have dream'd of distinguishing a figure from the body figur'd, as being in reality neither distinguishable, nor different, nor separable; did it not observe, that even in this simplicity there might be contain'd many different resemblances and relations. Thus when a globe of white marble is presented, we receive only the impression of a white colour dispos'd in a certain form; nor are we able to separate and distinguish the colour from the form. But observing afterwards a globe of black marble and a cube of white, and comparing them with our former object, we find two separate resemblances, in what formerly seem'd, and really is, perfectly inseparable. After a little more practice of this kind, we begin to distinguish the figure from the colour by a *distinction of reason*; that is, we consider the figure and colour together, since they are in effect the same and undistinguishable; but still view them in different aspects, according to the resemblances, of which they are susceptible. When we wou'd consider only the figure of the globe of white marble, we form in reality an idea both of the figure and colour, but tacitly carry our eye to its resemblance with the globe of black marble: And in the same manner, when we wou'd consider its colour only, we turn our view to its resemblance with the cube of white marble. By this means we accompany our ideas with a kind of reflection, of which custom renders us, in a great measure, insensible. A person, who desires us to consider the figure of a globe of white marble without thinking on its colour, desires an impossibility; but his meaning is, that we shou'd consider the colour and figure together, but still keep in our eye the resemblance to the globe of black marble, or that to any other globe of whatever colour or substance.

PART II

Of the ideas of space and time

SECT. I

Of the infinite divisibility of our ideas of space and time

WHATEVER has the air of a paradox, and is contrary to the first and most unprejudic'd notions of mankind is often greedily embrac'd by philosophers, as shewing the superiority of their science, which cou'd discover opinions so remote from vulgar conception. On the other hand, any thing propos'd to us, which causes surprize and admiration, gives such a satisfaction to the mind, that it indulges itself in those agreeable emotions, and will never be persuaded that its pleasure is entirely without foundation. From these dispositions in philosophers and their disciples arises that mutual complaisance betwixt them; while the former furnish such plenty of strange and unaccountable opinions, and the latter so readily believe them. Of this mutual complaisance I cannot give a more evident instance than in the doctrine of infinite divisibility, with the examination of which I shall begin this subject of the ideas of space and time.

'Tis universally allow'd, that the capacity of the mind is limited, and can never attain a full and adequate conception of infinity: And tho' it were not allow'd, 'twou'd be sufficiently evident from the plainest observation and experience. 'Tis also obvious, that whatever is capable of being divided *in infinitum*, must consist of an infinite number of parts, and that 'tis impossible to set any bounds to the number of parts, without setting bounds at the same time to the division. It requires scarce any induction to conclude from hence, that the *idea*, which we form of any finite quality, is not infinitely divisible, but that by proper distinctions and separations we may run up this idea to inferior ones, which will be perfectly simple and indivisible. In rejecting the infinite capacity of the mind, we suppose it may arrive at an end in the division of its ideas; nor are there any possible means of evading the evidence of this conclusion.

'Tis therefore certain, that the imagination reaches a *minimum*, and may raise up to itself an idea, of which it cannot conceive any sub-division, and which cannot be diminished without a total annihilation. When you tell me of the thousandth and ten thousandth part of a grain of sand, I have a distinct idea of these numbers and of their different proportions; but the images, which I form in my mind to represent the things themselves, are nothing different from each other, nor inferior to that image, by which I represent the grain of sand itself, which is suppos'd so vastly to exceed them. What consists of parts is distinguishable into them, and what is distinguishable is separable. But whatever we may imagine of the thing, the idea of a grain of sand is not distinguishable, nor separable into twenty, much less into a thousand, ten thousand, or an infinite number of different ideas.

'Tis the same case with the impressions of the senses as with the ideas of the imagination. Put a spot of ink upon paper, fix your eye upon that spot, and retire to such a distance, that at last you lose sight of it; 'tis plain, that the moment before it vanish'd the image or impression was perfectly indivisible. 'Tis not for want of rays of light striking on our eyes, that the minute parts of distant bodies convey not any sensible impression; but because they are remov'd beyond that distance, at which their impressions were reduc'd to a *minimum*, and were incapable of any farther diminution. A microscope or telescope, which renders them visible, produces not any new rays of light, but only spreads those, which always flow'd from them; and by that means both gives parts to impressions, which to the naked eye appear simple and uncompounded, and advances to a *minimum*, what was formerly imperceptible.

We may hence discover the error of the common opinion, that the capacity of the mind is limited on both sides, and that 'tis impossible for the imagination to form an adequate idea, of what goes beyond a certain degree of minuteness as well as of greatness. Nothing can be more minute, than some ideas, which we form in the fancy; and images, which appear to the senses; since there are ideas and images perfectly simple and indivisible. The only defect of our senses is, that they give us disproportion'd images of things, and represent as minute and uncompounded what is really great and compos'd of a vast number of parts. This mistake we are not sensible of; but taking the impressions of those minute objects, which appear to the senses, to be equal or nearly equal to the objects, and finding by reason, that there are other objects, vastly more minute, we too hastily conclude, that these are inferior to any idea of our imagination or impression of our senses. This however is certain, that we can form ideas, which shall be no greater than the smallest atom of the animal spirits of an insect a thousand times less than a mite: And we ought rather to conclude, that the difficulty lies in enlarging our conceptions so much as to form a just notion of a mite, or even of an insect a thousand times less than a mite. For in order to form a just notion of these animals, we must have a distinct idea representing every part of them; which, according to the system of infinite divisibility, is utterly impossible, and according to that of indivisible parts or atoms, is extremely difficult, by reason of the vast number and multiplicity of these parts.

SECT. II

Of the infinite divisibility of space and time

WHEREVER ideas are adequate representations of objects, the relations, contradictions and agreements of the ideas are all applicable to the objects; and this we may in general observe to be the foundation of all human knowledge. But our ideas are adequate representations of the most minute parts of extension; and thro' whatever divisions and sub-divisions we may suppose these parts to be arriv'd at, they can never become inferior to some ideas, which we form. The plain consequence is, that whatever *appears* impossible and contradictory upon the comparison of these ideas, must be *really* impossible and contradictory, without any farther excuse or evasion.

Every thing capable of being infinitely divided contains an infinite number of parts; otherwise the division would be stopt short by the indivisible parts, which we should immediately arrive at. If therefore any finite extension be infinitely divisible, it can be no contradiction to suppose, that a finite extension contains an infinite number of parts: And *vice versa*, if it be a contradiction to suppose, that a finite extension contains an infinite number of parts, no finite extension can be infinitely divisible. But that this latter supposition is absurd, I easily convince myself by the consideration of my clear ideas. I first take the least idea I can form of a part of extension, and being certain that there is nothing more minute than this idea, I conclude, that whatever I discover by its means must be a real quality of extension. I then repeat this idea once, twice, thrice, &c. and find the compound idea of extension, arising from its repetition, always to augment, and become double, triple, quadruple, &c. till at last it swells up to a considerable bulk, greater or smaller, in proportion as I repeat more or less the same idea. When I stop in the addition of parts, the idea of extension ceases to augment; and were I to carry on the addition *in* *infinitum*, I clearly perceive, that the idea of extension must also become infinite. Upon the whole, I conclude, that the idea of an infinite number of parts is individually the same idea with that of an infinite extension; that no finite extension is capable of containing an infinite number of parts; and consequently that no finite extension is infinitely divisible*.

I may subjoin another argument propos'd by a noted author†, which seems to me very strong and beautiful. 'Tis evident, that existence in itself belongs only to unity, and is never applicable to number, but on account of the unites, of which the number is compos'd. Twenty men may be said to exist; but 'tis only because one, two, three, four, &c. are existent; and if you deny the existence of the latter, that of the former falls of course. 'Tis therefore utterly absurd to suppose any number to exist, and yet deny the existence of unites; and as extension is always a number, according to the common sentiment of metaphysicians, and never resolves itself into any unite or indivisible quantity, it follows, that extension can never at all exist. 'Tis in vain to reply, that any determinate quantity of extension is an unite; but such-a-one as admits of an infinite number of fractions, and is inexhaustible in its sub-divisions. For by the same rule these twenty men *may be consider'd as an unite.* The whole globe of the earth, nay the whole universe *may be consider'd as an unite.* That term of unity is merely a fictitious denomination, which the mind may apply to any quantity of objects it collects together; nor can such an unity any more exist alone than number can, as being in reality a true number. But the unity, which can exist alone, and whose existence is necessary to that of all number, is of

*It has been objected to me, that infinite divisibility supposes only an infinite number of *proportional* not of *aliquot* parts, and that an infinite number of proportional parts does not form an infinite extension. But this distinction is entirely frivolous. Whether these parts be call'd *aliquot* or *proportional*, they cannot be inferior to those minute parts we conceive; and therefore cannot form a less extension by their conjunction.

†Mons. *Malezieu* [Nicholas Malezieu, *Élements de Géometrie de M. le duc de Bourgogne* (Paris 1715)].

another kind, and must be perfectly indivisible, and incapable of being resolved into any lesser unity.

All this reasoning takes place with regard to time; along with an additional argument, which it may be proper to take notice of. 'Tis a property inseparable from time, and which in a manner constitutes its essence, that each of its parts succeeds another, and that none of them, however contiguous, can ever be co-existent. For the same reason, that the year 1737. cannot concur with the present year 1738. every moment must be distinct from, and posterior or antecedent to another. 'Tis certain then, that time, as it exists, must be compos'd of indivisible moments. For if in time we could never arrive at an end of division, and if each moment, as it succeeds another, were not perfectly single and indivisible, there would be an infinite number of co-existent moments, or parts of time; which I believe will be allow'd to be an arrant contradiction.

The infinite divisibility of space implies that of time, as is evident from the nature of motion. If the latter, therefore, be impossible, the former must be equally so.

I doubt not but it will readily be allow'd by the most obstinate defender of the doctrine of infinite divisibility, that these arguments are difficulties, and that 'tis impossible to give any answer to them which will be perfectly clear and satisfactory. But here we may observe, that nothing can be more absurd, than this custom of calling a *difficulty* what pretends to be a *demonstration*, and endeavouring by that means to elude its force and evidence. 'Tis not in demonstrations as in probabilities, that difficulties can take place, and one argument counter-ballance another, and diminish its authority. A demonstration, if just, admits of no opposite difficulty; and if not just, 'tis a mere sophism, and consequently can never be a difficulty. 'Tis either irrefutible, or has no manner of force. To talk therefore of objections and replies, and ballancing of arguments in such a question as this, is to confess, either that human reason is nothing but a play of words, or that the person himself, who talks so, has not a capacity equal to such subjects. Demonstrations may be difficult to be comprehended, because of the abstractedness of the subject; but can never have any such difficulties as will weaken their authority, when once they are comprehended.

'Tis true, mathematicians are wont to say, that there are equally strong arguments on the other side of the question, and that the doctrine of indivisible points is also liable to unanswerable objections. Before I examine these arguments and objections in detail, I will here take them in a body, and endeavour by a short and decisive reason to prove at once, that 'tis utterly impossible they can have any just foundation.

'Tis an establish'd maxim in metaphysics, *That whatever the mind clearly conceives includes the idea of possible existence*, or in other words, *that nothing we imagine is absolutely impossible*. We can form the idea of a golden mountain, and from thence conclude that such a mountain may actually exist. We can form no idea of a mountain without a valley, and therefore regard it as impossible.

Now 'tis certain we have an idea of extension; for otherwise why do we talk and reason concerning it? 'Tis likewise certain, that this idea, as conceiv'd by the imagination, tho' divisible into parts or inferior ideas, is not infinitely divisible, nor consists of an infinite number of parts: For that exceeds the comprehension of our limited capacities. Here then is an idea of extension, which consists of parts or inferior ideas, that are perfectly indivisible: consequently this idea implies no contradiction: consequently 'tis possible for extension really to exist conformable to it: and consequently all the arguments employ'd against the possibility of mathematical points are mere scholastick quibbles, and unworthy of our attention.

These consequences we may carry one step farther, and conclude that all the pretended demonstrations for the infinite divisibility of extension are equally sophistical; since 'tis certain these demonstrations cannot be just without proving the impossibility of mathematical points; which 'tis an evident absurdity to pretend to.

SECT. III

Of the other qualities of our ideas of space and time

No discovery cou'd have been made more happily for deciding all controversies concerning ideas, than that abovemention'd, that impressions always take the precedency of them, and that every idea, with which the imagination is furnish'd, first makes its appearance in a correspondent impression. These latter perceptions are all so clear and evident, that they admit of no controversy; tho' many of our ideas are so obscure, that 'tis almost impossible even for the mind, which forms them, to tell exactly their nature and composition. Let us apply this principle, in order to discover farther the nature of our ideas of space and time.

Upon opening my eyes, and turning them to the surrounding objects, I perceive many visible bodies; and upon shutting them again, and considering the distance betwixt these bodies, I acquire the idea of extension. As every idea is deriv'd from some impression, which is exactly similar to it, the impressions similar to this idea of extension, must either be some sensations deriv'd from the sight, or some internal impressions arising from these sensations.

Our internal impressions are our passions, emotions, desires and aversions; none of which, I believe, will ever be asserted to be the model, from which the idea of space is deriv'd. There remains therefore nothing but the senses, which can convey to us this original impression. Now what impression do our senses here convey to us? This is the principal question, and decides without appeal concerning the nature of the idea.

The table before me is alone sufficient by its view to give me the idea of extension. This idea, then, is borrow'd from, and represents some impression, which this moment appears to the senses. But my senses convey to me only the impressions of colour'd points, dispos'd in a certain manner.

If the eye is sensible of any thing farther, I desire it may be pointed out to me. But if it be impossible to shew any thing farther, we may conclude with certainty, that the idea of extension is nothing but a copy of these colour'd points, and of the manner of their appearance.

Suppose that in the extended object, or composition of colour'd points, from which we first receiv'd the idea of extension, the points were of a purple colour; it follows, that in every repetition of that idea we wou'd not only place the points in the same order with respect to each other, but also bestow on them that precise colour, with which alone we are acquainted. But afterwards having experience of the other colours of violet, green, red, white, black, and of all the different compositions of these, and finding a resemblance in the disposition of colour'd points of which they are compos'd, we omit the peculiarities of colour, as far as possible, and found an abstract idea merely on that disposition of points, or manner of appearance, in which they agree. Nay even when the resemblance is carry'd beyond the objects of one sense, and the impressions of touch are found to be similar to those of sight in the disposition of their parts; this does not hinder the abstract idea from representing both, upon account of their resemblance. All abstract ideas are really nothing but particular ones, considered in a certain light; but being annexed to general terms, they are able to represent a vast variety, and to comprehend objects, which, as they are alike in some particulars, are in others vastly wide of each other.

The idea of time, being deriv'd from the succession of our perceptions of every kind, ideas as well as impressions, and impressions of reflection as well as of sensation, will afford us an instance of an abstract idea, which comprehends a still greater variety than that of space, and yet is represented in the fancy by some particular individual idea of a determinate quantity and quality.

As 'tis from the disposition of visible and tangible objects we receive the idea of space, so from the succession of ideas and impressions we form the idea of time, nor is it possible for time alone ever to make its appearance, or be taken notice of by the mind. A man in a sound sleep, or strongly occupy'd with one thought, is insensible of time; and according as his perceptions succeed each other with greater or less rapidity, the same duration appears longer or shorter to his imagination. It has been remark'd by a* great philosopher, that our perceptions have certain bounds in this particular, which are fix'd by the original nature and constitution of the mind, and beyond which no influence of external objects on the senses is ever able to hasten or retard our thought. If you wheel about a burning coal with rapidity, it will present to the senses an image of a circle of fire; nor will there seem to be any interval of time betwixt its revolutions; meerly because 'tis impossible for our perceptions to succeed each other with the same rapidity, that motion may be communicated to external objects. Wherever we have no successive perceptions, we have no notion of time, even tho' there be a real succession in the objects. From these phaenomena, as well as from many others, we may conclude, that time cannot make its appearance to the mind, either alone, or attended with a steady unchangeable object, but is always discover'd by some *perceivable* succession of changeable objects.

To confirm this we may add the following argument, which to me seems perfectly decisive and convincing. 'Tis evident, that time or duration consists of different parts: For otherwise we cou'd not conceive a longer or shorter duration. 'Tis also evident, that these parts are not co-existent: For that quality of the co-existence of parts belongs to extension, and is what distinguishes it from duration. Now as time is compos'd of parts, that are not co-existent; an unchangeable object, since it produces none but co-existent impressions, produces none that can give us the idea of time; and consequently that idea must be deriv'd from a succession of changeable objects, and time in its first appearance can never be sever'd from such a succession.

Having therefore found, that time in its first appearance to

* Mr *Locke*.

the mind is always conjoin'd with a succession of changeable objects, and that otherwise it can never fall under our notice, we must now examine whether it can be *conceiv'd* without our conceiving any succession of objects, and whether it can alone form a distinct idea in the imagination.

In order to know whither any objects, which are join'd in impression, be separable in idea, we need only consider, if they be different from each other; in which case, 'tis plain they may be conceiv'd apart. Every thing, that is different, is distinguishable; and every thing, that is distinguishable, may be separated, according to the maxims above-explain'd. If on the contrary they be not different, they are not distinguishable; and if they be not distinguishable, they cannot be separated. But this is precisely the case with respect to time, compar'd with our successive perceptions. The idea of time is not deriv'd from a particular impression mix'd up with others, and plainly distinguishable from them; but arises altogether from the manner, in which impressions appear to the mind, without making one of the number. Five notes play'd on a flute give us the impression and idea of time; tho' time be not a sixth impression, which presents itself to the hearing or any other of the senses. Nor is it a sixth impression, which the mind by reflection finds in itself. These five sounds making their appearance in this particular manner, excite no emotion in the mind, nor produce an affection of any kind, which being observ'd by it can give rise to a new idea. For *that* is necessary to produce a new idea of reflection, nor can the mind, by revolving over a thousand times all its ideas of sensation, ever extract from them any new original idea, unless nature has so fram'd its faculties, that it feels some new original impression arise from such a contemplation. But here it only takes notice of the *manner*, in which the different sounds make their appearance; and that it may afterwards consider without considering these particular sounds, but may conjoin it with any other objects. The ideas of some objects it certainly must have, nor is it possible for it without these ideas ever to arrive at any conception of time; which since it appears not as any primary distinct impression, can plainly be nothing but different ideas, or impressions, or objects dispos'd in a certain manner, that is, succeeding each other.

I know there are some who pretend, that the idea of duration is applicable in a proper sense to objects, which are perfectly unchangeable; and this I take to be the common opinion of philosophers as well as of the vulgar. But to be convinc'd of its falsehood we need but reflect on the foregoing conclusion, that the idea of duration is always deriv'd from a succession of changeable objects, and can never be convey'd to the mind by any thing stedfast and unchangeable. For it inevitably follows from thence, that since the idea of duration cannot be deriv'd from such an object, it can never in any propriety or exactness be apply'd to it, nor can any thing unchangeable be ever said to have duration. Ideas always represent the objects or impressions, from which they are deriv'd, and can never without a fiction represent or be apply'd to any other. By what fiction we apply the idea of time, even to what is unchangeable, and suppose, as is common, that duration is a measure of rest as well as of motion, we shall consider* afterwards.

There is another very decisive argument, which establishes the present doctrine concerning our ideas of space and time, and is founded only on the simple principle, *that our ideas of them are compounded of parts, which are indivisible*. This argument may be worth the examining.

Every idea, that is distinguishable, being also separable, let us take one of those simple indivisible ideas, of which the compound one of *extension* is form'd, and separating it from all others, and considering it apart, let us form a judgment of its nature and qualities.

'Tis plain it is not the idea of extension. For the idea of extension consists of parts; and this idea, according to the supposition, is perfectly simple and indivisible. Is it therefore nothing? That is absolutely impossible. For as the compound idea of extension, which is real, is compos'd of such ideas; were these so many non-entities, there wou'd be

*Sect. 5.

a real existence composed of non-entities; which is absurd. Here therefore I must ask, *What is our idea of a simple and indivisible point?* No wonder if my answer appear somewhat new, since the question itself has scarce ever yet been thought of. We are wont to dispute concerning the nature of mathematical points, but seldom concerning the nature of their ideas.

The idea of space is convey'd to the mind by two senses, the sight and touch; nor does any thing ever appear extended, that is not either visible or tangible. That compound impression, which represents extension, consists of several lesser impressions, that are indivisible to the eye or feeling, and may be call'd impressions of atoms or corpuscles endow'd with colour and solidity. But this is not all. 'Tis not only requisite, that these atoms shou'd be colour'd or tangible, in order to discover themselves to our senses; 'tis also necessary we shou'd preserve the idea of their colour or tangibility in order to comprehend them by our imagination. There is nothing but the idea of their colour or tangibility, which can render them conceivable by the mind. Upon the removal of the ideas of these sensible qualities, they are utterly annihilated to the thought or imagination.

Now such as the parts are, such is the whole. If a point be not consider'd as colour'd or tangible, it can convey to us no idea; and consequently the idea of extension, which is compos'd of the ideas of these points, can never possibly exist. But if the idea of extension really can exist, as we are conscious it does, its parts must also exist; and in order to that, must be consider'd as colour'd or tangible. We have therefore no idea of space or extension, but when we regard it as an object either of our sight or feeling.

The same reasoning will prove, that the indivisible moments of time must be fill'd with some real object or existence, whose succession forms the duration, and makes it be conceivable by the mind.

SECT. IV

Objections answer'd

OUR system concerning space and time consists of two parts, which are intimately connected together. The first depends on this chain of reasoning. The capacity of the mind is not infinite; consequently no idea of extension or duration consists of an infinite number of parts or inferior ideas, but of a finite number, and these simple and indivisible: 'Tis therefore possible for space and time to exist conformable to this idea: And if it be possible, 'tis certain they actually do exist conformable to it; since their infinite divisibility is utterly impossible and contradictory.

The other part of our system is a consequence of this. The parts, into which the ideas of space and time resolve themselves, become at last indivisible; and these indivisible parts, being nothing in themselves, are inconceivable when not fill'd with something real and existent. The ideas of space and time are therefore no separate or distinct ideas, but merely those of the manner or order, in which objects exist: Or, in other words, 'tis impossible to conceive either a vacuum and extension without matter, or a time, when there was no succession or change in any real existence. The intimate connexion betwixt these parts of our system is the reason why we shall examine together the objections, which have been urg'd against both of them, beginning with those against the finite divisibility of extension.

I. The first of these objections, which I shall take notice of, is more proper to prove this connexion and dependance of the one part upon the other, than to destroy either of them. It has often been maintain'd in the schools, that extension must be divisible, *in infinitum*, because the system of mathematical points is absurd; and that system is absurd, because a mathematical point is a non-entity, and consequently can never by its conjunction with others form a real existence. This wou'd be perfectly decisive, were there no medium betwixt the infinite divisibility of matter, and the non-entity of mathematical points. But there is evidently a medium, *viz.* the bestowing a colour or solidity on these points; and the absurdity of both the extremes is a demonstration of the truth and reality of this medium. The system of *physical* points, which is another medium, is too absurd to need a refutation. A real extension, such as a physical point is suppos'd to be, can never exist without parts, different from each other; and wherever objects are different, they are distinguishable and separable by the imagination.

II. The second objection is deriv'd from the necessity there wou'd be of *penetration*, if extension consisted of mathematical points. A simple and indivisible atom, that touches another, must necessarily penetrate it; for 'tis impossible it can touch it by its external parts, from the very supposition of its perfect simplicity, which excludes all parts. It must therefore touch it intimately, and in its whole essence, *secundum se, tota, & totaliter*; which is the very definition of penetration. But penetration is impossible: Mathematical points are of consequence equally impossible.

I answer this objection by substituting a juster idea of penetration. Suppose two bodies containing no void within their circumference, to approach each other, and to unite in such a manner that the body, which results from their union, is no more extended than either of them; 'tis this we must mean when we talk of penetration. But 'tis evident this penetration is nothing but the annihilation of one of these bodies, and the preservation of the other, without our being able to distinguish particularly which is preserv'd and which annihilated. Before the approach we have the idea of two bodies. After it we have the idea only of one. 'Tis impossible for the mind to preserve any notion of difference betwixt two bodies of the same nature existing in the same place at the same time.

Taking then penetration in this sense, for the annihilation of one body upon its approach to another, I ask any one, if he sees a necessity, that a colour'd or tangible point should be annihilated upon the approach of another colour'd or tangible point? On the contrary, does he not evidently perceive, that from the union of these points there results an object, which is compounded and divisible, and may be distinguish'd into two parts, of which each preserves its existence distinct and separate, notwithstanding its contiguity to the other? Let him aid his fancy by conceiving these points to be of different colours, the better to prevent their coalition and confusion. A blue and a red point may surely lie contiguous without any penetration or annihilation. For if they cannot, what possibly can become of them? Whether will the red or the blue be annihilated? Or if these colours unite into one, what new colour will they produce by their union?

What chiefly gives rise to these objections, and at the same time renders it so difficult to give a satisfactory answer to them, is the natural infirmity and unsteadiness both of our imagination and senses, when employ'd on such minute objects. Put a spot of ink upon paper, and retire to such a distance, that the spot becomes altogether invisible; you will find, that upon your return and nearer approach the spot first becomes visible by short intervals; and afterwards becomes always visible; and afterwards acquires only a new force in its colouring without augmenting its bulk; and afterwards, when it has encreas'd to such a degree as to be really extended, 'tis still difficult for the imagination to break it into its component parts, because of the uneasiness it finds in the conception of such a minute object as a single point. This infirmity affects most of our reasonings on the present subject, and makes it almost impossible to answer in an intelligible manner, and in proper expressions, many questions which may arise concerning it.

III. There have been many objections drawn from the *mathematics* against the indivisibility of the parts of extension; tho' at first sight that science seems rather favourable to the present doctrine; and if it be contrary in its *demonstrations*, 'tis perfectly conformable in its *definitions*. My present business then must be to defend the definitions, and refute the demonstrations.

A surface is *defin'd* to be length and breadth without depth: A line to be length without breadth or depth: A point to be what has neither length, breadth nor depth. 'Tis evident that all this is perfectly unintelligible upon any other supposition than that of the composition of extension by indivisible points or atoms. How else cou'd any thing exist without length, without breadth, or without depth?

Two different answers, I find, have been made to this argument; neither of which is in my opinion satisfactory. The first is, that the objects of geometry, those surfaces, lines and points, whose proportions and positions it examines, are mere ideas in the mind; and not only never did, but never can exist in nature. They never did exist; for no one will pretend to draw a line or make a surface entirely conformable to the definition: They never can exist; for we may produce demonstrations from these very ideas to prove, that they are impossible.

But can any thing be imagin'd more absurd and contradictory than this reasoning? Whatever can be conceiv'd by a clear and distinct idea necessarily implies the possibility of existence; and he who pretends to prove the impossibility of its existence by any argument deriv'd from the clear idea, in reality asserts, that we have no clear idea of it, because we have a clear idea. 'Tis in vain to search for a contradiction in any thing that is distinctly conceiv'd by the mind. Did it imply any contradiction, 'tis impossible it cou'd ever be conceiv'd.

There is therefore no medium betwixt allowing at least the possibility of indivisible points, and denying their idea; and 'tis on this latter principle, that the second answer to the foregoing argument is founded. It has been * pretended, that tho' it be impossible to conceive a length without any breadth, yet by an abstraction without a separation, we can consider the one without regarding the other; in the same manner as we may think of the length of the way betwixt two towns, and overlook its breadth. The length is insepar-

* *L'Art de penser* [Arnold and Nicole, *La Logique, ou L'Art de Penser* (Paris 1662)].

able from the breadth both in nature and in our minds; but this excludes not a partial consideration, and a *distinction of reason*, after the manner above explain'd.

In refuting this answer I shall not insist on the argument, which I have already sufficiently explain'd, that if it be impossible for the mind to arrive at a *minimum* in its ideas, its capacity must be infinite, in order to comprehend the infinite number of parts, of which its idea of any extension wou'd be compos'd. I shall here endeavour to find some new absurdities in the reasoning.

A surface terminates a solid; a line terminates a surface; a point terminates a line; but I assert, that if the *ideas* of a point, line or surface were not indivisible, 'tis impossible we shou'd ever conceive these terminations. For let these ideas be suppos'd infinitely divisible; and then let the fancy endeavour to fix itself on the idea of the last surface, line or point; it immediately finds this idea to break into parts; and upon its seizing the last of these parts, it loses its hold by a new division, and so on *in infinitum*, without any possibility of its arriving at a concluding idea. The number of fractions bring it no nearer the last division, than the first idea it form'd. Every particle eludes the grasp by a new fraction; like quick-silver, when we endeavour to seize it. But as in fact there must be something, which terminates the idea of every finite quantity; and as this terminating idea cannot itself consist of parts of inferior ideas; otherwise it wou'd be the last of its parts, which finish'd the idea, and so on; this is a clear proof, that the ideas of surfaces, lines and points admit not of any division; those of surfaces in depth; of lines in breadth and depth; and of points in any dimension.

The *schoolmen* were so sensible of the force of this argument, that some of them maintain'd, that nature has mix'd among those particles of matter, which are divisible *in infinitum*, a number of mathematical points, in order to give a termination to bodies; and others eluded the force of this reasoning by a heap of unintelligible cavils and distinctions. Both these adversaries equally yield the victory. A man who hides himself, confesses as evidently the superiority of his enemy, as another, who fairly delivers his arms.

Thus it appears, that the definitions of mathematics destroy the pretended demonstrations; and that if we have the idea of indivisible points, lines and surfaces conformable to the definition, their existence is certainly possible: but if we have no such idea, 'tis impossible we can ever conceive the termination of any figure; without which conception there can be no geometrical demonstration.

But I go farther, and maintain, that none of these demonstrations can have sufficient weight to establish such a principle, as this of infinite divisibility; and that because with regard to such minute objects, they are not properly demonstrations, being built on ideas, which are not exact, and maxims, which are not precisely true. When geometry decides any thing concerning the proportions of quantity, we ought not to look for the utmost *precision* and exactness. None of its proofs extend so far. It takes the dimensions and proportions of figures justly; but roughly, and with some liberty. Its errors are never considerable; nor wou'd it err at all, did it not aspire to such an absolute perfection.

I first ask mathematicians, what they mean when they say one line or surface is EQUAL to, or GREATER, or LESS than another? Let any of them give an answer, to whatever sect he belongs, and whether he maintains the composition of extension by indivisible points, or by quantities divisible *in infinitum*. This question will embarrass both of them.

There are few or no mathematicians, who defend the hypothesis of indivisible points; and yet these have the readiest and justest answer to the present question. They need only reply, that lines or surfaces are equal, when the numbers of points in each are equal; and that as the proportion of the numbers varies, the proportion of the lines and surfaces is also vary'd. But tho' this answer be *just*, as well as obvious; yet I may affirm, that this standard of equality is entirely *useless*, and that it never is from such a comparison we determine objects to be equal or unequal with respect to each other. For as the points, which enter into the composition of any line or surface, whether perceiv'd by the sight or touch, are so minute and so confounded with each other, that 'tis utterly impossible for the mind to compute their number, such a computation will never afford us a standard, by which we may judge of proportions. No one will ever be able to determine by an exact numeration, that an inch has fewer points than a foot, or a foot fewer than an ell or any greater measure; for which reason we seldom or never consider this as the standard of equality or inequality.

As to those, who imagine, that extension is divisible *in infinitum*, 'tis impossible they can make use of this answer, or fix the equality of any line or surface by a numeration of its component parts. For since, according to their hypothesis, the least as well as greatest figures contain an infinite number of parts; and since infinite numbers, properly speaking, can neither be equal nor unequal with respect to each other; the equality or inequality of any portions of space can never depend on any proportion in the number of their parts. 'Tis true, it may be said, that the inequality of an ell and a yard consists in the different numbers of the feet, of which they are compos'd; and that of a foot and a yard in the number of the inches. But as that quantity we call an inch in the one is suppos'd equal to what we call an inch in the other, and as 'tis impossible for the mind to find this equality by proceeding *in infinitum* with these references to inferior quantities; 'tis evident, that at last we must fix some standard of equality different from an enumeration of the parts.

There are some*, who pretend, that equality is best defin'd by *congruity*, and that any two figures are equal, when upon the placing of one upon the other, all their parts correspond to and touch each other. In order to judge of this definition let us consider, that since equality is a relation, it is not, strictly speaking, a property in the figures themselves, but arises merely from the comparison, which the mind makes betwixt them. If it consists, therefore, in this imaginary application and mutual contact of parts, we must at least

*See Dr *Barrow's* mathematical lectures [Isaac Barrow, *Lectiones Mathematicae* (London 1685)].

have a distinct notion of these parts, and must conceive their contact. Now 'tis plain, that in this conception we wou'd run up these parts to the greatest minuteness, which can possibly be conceiv'd; since the contact of large parts wou'd never render the figures equal. But the minutest parts we can conceive are mathematical points; and consequently this standard of equality is the same with that deriv'd from the equality of the number of points; which we have already determin'd to be a just but an useless standard. We must therefore look to some other quarter for a solution of the present difficulty.

[*]There are many philosophers, who refuse to assign any standard of *equality*, but assert, that 'tis sufficient to present two objects, that are equal, in order to give us a just notion of this proportion. All definitions, say they, are fruitless, without the perception of such objects; and where we perceive such objects, we no longer stand in need of any definition. To this reasoning I entirely agree; and assert, that the only useful notion of equality, or inequality, is deriv'd from the whole united appearance and the comparison of particular objects.

'Tis evident, that the eye, or rather the mind is often able at one view to determine the proportions of bodies, and pronounce them equal to, or greater or less than each other, without examining or comparing the number of their minute parts. Such judgments are not only common, but in many cases certain and infallible. When the measure of a yard and that of a foot are presented, the mind can no more question, that the first is longer than the second, than it can doubt of those principles, which are the most clear and self-evident.

There are therefore three proportions, which the mind distinguishes in the general appearance of its objects, and calls by the names of *greater*, *less* and *equal*. But tho' its decisions concerning these proportions be sometimes infallible, they are not always so; nor are our judgments of this

[* The following paragraph is inserted from Hume's Appendix to Book III.]

kind more exempt from doubt and error, than those on any other subject. We frequently correct our first opinion by a review and reflection; and pronounce those objects to be equal, which at first we esteem'd unequal; and regard an object as less, tho' before it appear'd greater than another. Nor is this the only correction, which these judgments of our senses undergo; but we often discover our error by a juxta-position of the objects; or where that is impracticable, by the use of some common and invariable measure, which being successively apply'd to each, informs us of their different proportions. And even this correction is susceptible of a new correction, and of different degrees of exactness, according to the nature of the instrument, by which we measure the bodies, and the care which we employ in the comparison.

When therefore the mind is accustom'd to these judgments and their corrections, and finds that the same proportion which makes two figures have in the eye that appearance, which we call *equality*, makes them also correspond to each other, and to any common measure, with which they are compar'd, we form a mix'd notion of equality deriv'd both from the looser and stricter methods of comparison. But we are not content with this. For as sound reason convinces us that there are bodies *vastly* more minute than those, which appear to the senses; and as a false reason wou'd persuade us, that there are bodies *infinitely* more minute; we clearly perceive, that we are not possess'd of any instrument or art of measuring, which can secure us from all error and uncertainty. We are sensible, that the addition or removal of one of these minute parts, is not discernible either in the appearance or measuring; and as we imagine, that two figures, which were equal before, cannot be equal after this removal or addition, we therefore suppose some imaginary standard of equality, by which the appearances and measuring are exactly corrected, and the figures reduc'd entirely to that proportion. This standard is plainly imaginary. For as the very idea of equality is that of such a particular appearance corrected by juxta-position or a common measure, the notion of any correction beyond what we have instruments and art to make, is a mere fiction of the mind, and useless as well as incomprehensible. But tho' this standard be only imaginary, the fiction however is very natural; nor is any thing more usual, than for the mind to proceed after this manner with any action, even after the reason has ceas'd, which first determin'd it to begin. This appears very conspicuously with regard to time; where tho' 'tis evident we have no exact method of determining the proportions of parts, not even so exact as in extension, yet the various corrections of our measures, and their different degrees of exactness, have given us an obscure and implicit notion of a perfect and entire equality. The case is the same in many other subjects. A musician finding his ear become every day more delicate, and correcting himself by reflection and attention, proceeds with the same act of the mind, even when the subject fails him, and entertains a notion of a compleat *tierce* or *octave*, without being able to tell whence he derives his standard. A painter forms the same fiction with regard to colours. A mechanic with regard to motion. To the one *light* and *shade*; to the other *swift* and *slow* are imagin'd to be capable of an exact comparison and equality beyond the judgments of the senses.

We may apply the same reasoning to CURVE and RIGHT lines. Nothing is more apparent to the senses, than the distinction betwixt a curve and a right line; nor are there any ideas we more easily form than the ideas of these objects. But however easily we may form these ideas, 'tis impossible to produce any definition of them, which will fix the precise boundaries betwixt them. When we draw lines upon paper or any continu'd surface, there is a certain order, by which the lines run along from one point to another, that they may produce the entire impression of a curve or right line; but this order is perfectly unknown, and nothing is observ'd but the united appearance. Thus even upon the system of indivisible points, we can only form a distant notion of some unknown standard to these objects. Upon that of infinite divisibility we cannot go even this length; but are reduc'd meerly to the general appearance, as the rule by which we determine lines to be either curve or right ones. But tho' we can give no perfect definition of these lines, nor produce any very exact method of distinguishing the one from the other; yet this hinders us not from correcting the first appearance by a more accurate consideration, and by a comparison with some rule, of whose rectitude from repeated trials we have a greater assurance. And 'tis from these corrections, and by carrying on the same action of the mind, even when its reason fails us, that we form the loose idea of a perfect standard to these figures, without being able to explain or comprehend it.

'Tis true, mathematicians pretend they give an exact definition of a right line, when they say, *it is the shortest way betwixt two points*. But in the first place I observe, that this is more properly the discovery of one of the properties of a right line, than a just definition of it. For I ask any one, if upon mention of a right line he thinks not immediately on such a particular appearance, and if 'tis not by accident only that he considers this property? A right line can be comprehended alone; but this definition is unintelligible without a comparison with other lines, which we conceive to be more extended. In common life 'tis established as a maxim, that the streightest way is always the shortest; which would be as absurd as to say, the shortest way is always the shortest, if our idea of a right line was not different from that of the shortest way betwixt two points.

Secondly, I repeat what I have already establish'd, that we have no precise idea of equality and inequality, shorter and longer, more than of a right line or a curve; and consequently that the one can never afford us a perfect standard for the other. An exact idea can never be built on such as are loose and undeterminate.

The idea of a *plain surface* is as little susceptible of a precise standard as that of a right line; nor have we any other means of distinguishing such a surface, than its general appearance. 'Tis in vain, that mathematicians represent a plain surface as produc'd by the flowing of a right line. 'Twill immediately be objected, that our idea of a surface is as independent of this method of forming a surface, as our idea of an ellipse is of that of a cone; that the idea of a right line is no more precise than that of a plain surface; that a right line may flow irregularly, and by that means form a figure quite different from a plane; and that therefore we must suppose it to flow along two right lines, parallel to each other, and on the same plane; which is a description, that explains a thing by itself, and returns in a circle.

It appears, then, that the ideas which are most essential to geometry, *viz.* those of equality and inequality, of a right line and a plain surface, are far from being exact and determinate, according to our common method of conceiving them. Not only we are incapable of telling, if the case be in any degree doubtful, when such particular figures are equal; when such a line is a right one, and such a surface a plain one; but we can form no idea of that proportion, or of these figures, which is firm and invariable. Our appeal is still to the weak and fallible judgment, which we make from the appearance of the objects, and correct by a compass or common measure; and if we join the supposition of any farther correction, 'tis of such-a-one as is either useless or imaginary. In vain shou'd we have recourse to the common topic, and employ the supposition of a deity, whose omnipotence may enable him to form a perfect geometrical figure, and describe a right line without any curve or inflexion. As the ultimate standard of these figures is deriv'd from nothing but the senses and imagination, 'tis absurd to talk of any perfection beyond what these faculties can judge of; since the true perfection of any thing consists in its conformity to its standard.

Now since these ideas are so loose and uncertain, I wou'd fain ask any mathematician what infallible assurance he has, not only of the more intricate and obscure propositions of his science, but of the most vulgar and obvious principles? How can he prove to me, for instance, that two right lines cannot have one common segment? Or that 'tis impossible to draw more than one right line betwixt any two points?

Shou'd he tell me, that these opinions are obviously absurd, and repugnant to our clear ideas; I wou'd answer, that I do not deny, where two right lines incline upon each other with a sensible angle, but 'tis absurd to imagine them to have a common segment. But supposing these two lines to approach at the rate of an inch in twenty leagues, I perceive no absurdity in asserting, that upon their contact they become one. For, I beseech you, by what rule or standard do you judge, when you assert, that the line, in which I have suppos'd them to concur, cannot make the same right line with those two, that form so small an angle betwixt them? You must surely have some idea of a right line, to which this line does not agree. Do you therefore mean, that it takes not the points in the same order and by the same rule, as is peculiar and essential to a right line? If so, I must inform you, that besides that in judging after this manner you allow, that extension is compos'd of indivisible points (which, perhaps, is more than you intend) besides this, I say, I must inform you, that neither is this the standard from which we form the idea of a right line; nor, if it were, is there any such firmness in our senses or imagination, as to determine when such an order is violated or preserv'd. The original standard of a right line is in reality nothing but a certain general appearance; and 'tis evident right lines may be made to concur with each other, and yet correspond to this standard, tho' corrected by all the means either practicable or imaginable.

[*]To whatever side mathematicians turn, this dilemma still meets them. If they judge of equality, or any other proportion, by the accurate and exact standard, *viz.* the enumeration of the minute indivisible parts, they both employ a standard, which is useless in practice, and actually establish the indivisibility of extension, which they endeavour to explode. Or if they employ, as is usual, the inaccurate standard, deriv'd from a comparison of objects, upon their general appearance, corrected by measuring and

[* The following paragraph is inserted from Hume's Appendix to Book III.]

juxta position; their first principles, tho' certain and infallible, are too coarse to afford any such subtile inferences as they commonly draw from them. The first principles are founded on the imagination and senses: The conclusion, therefore, can never go beyond, much less contradict these faculties.

This may open our eyes a little, and let us see, that no geometrical demonstration for the infinite divisibility of extension can have so much force as what we naturally attribute to every argument, which is supported by such magnificent pretensions. At the same time we may learn the reason, why geometry fails of evidence in this single point, while all its other reasonings command our fullest assent and approbation. And indeed it seems more requisite to give the reason of this exception, than to shew that we really must make such an exception, and regard all the mathematical arguments for infinite divisibility as utterly sophistical. For 'tis evident, that as no idea of quantity is infinitely divisible, there cannot be imagin'd a more glaring absurdity, than to endeavour to prove, that quantity itself admits of such a division; and to prove this by means of ideas, which are directly opposite in that particular. And as this absurdity is very glaring in itself, so there is no argument founded on it, which is not attended with a new absurdity, and involves not an evident contradiction.

I may give as instances those arguments for infinite divisibility, which are deriv'd from the *point of contact*. I know there is no mathematician, who will not refuse to be judg'd by the diagrams he describes upon paper, these being loose draughts, as he will tell us, and serving only to convey with greater facility certain ideas, which are the true foundation of all our reasoning. This I am satisfy'd with, and am willing to rest the controversy merely upon these ideas. I desire therefore our mathematician to form, as accurately as possible, the ideas of a circle and a right line; and I then ask, if upon the conception of their contact he can conceive them as touching in a mathematical point, or if he must necessarily imagine them to concur for some space. Which-ever side he chuses, he runs himself into equal difficulties. If he affirms, that in tracing these figures in his imagination, he can imagine them to touch only in a point, he allows the possibility of that idea, and consequently of the thing. If he says, that in his conception of the contact of those lines he must make them concur, he thereby acknowledges the fallacy of geometrical demonstrations, when carry'd beyond a certain degree of minuteness; since 'tis certain he has such demonstrations against the concurrence of a circle and a right line; that is, in other words, he can prove an idea, *viz.* that of concurrence, to be *incompatible* with two other ideas, *viz.* those of a circle and right line; tho' at the same time he acknowledges these ideas to be *inseparable.*

SECT. V

The same subject continu'd

IF the second part of my system be true, *that the idea of space or extension is nothing but the idea of visible or tangible points distributed in a certain order*; it follows, that we can form no idea of a vacuum, or space, where there is nothing visible or tangible. This gives rise to three objections, which I shall examine together, because the answer I shall give to one is a consequence of that which I shall make use of for the others.

First, It may be said, that men have disputed for many ages concerning a vacuum and a plenum, without being able to bring the affair to a final decision; and philosophers, even at this day, think themselves at liberty to take party on either side, as their fancy leads them. But whatever foundation there may be for a controversy concerning the things themselves, it may be pretended, that the very dispute is decisive concerning the idea, and that 'tis impossible men cou'd so long reason about a vacuum, and either refute or defend it, without having a notion of what they refuted or defended.

Secondly, If this argument shou'd be contested, the reality

or at least possibility of the *idea* of a vacuum may be prov'd by the following reasoning. Every idea is possible, which is a necessary and infallible consequence of such as are possible. Now tho' we allow the world to be at present a plenum, we may easily conceive it to be depriv'd of motion; and this idea will certainly be allow'd possible. It must also be allow'd possible, to conceive the annihilation of any part of matter by the omnipotence of the deity, while the other parts remain at rest. For as every idea, that is distinguishable, is separable by the imagination; and as every idea, that is separable by the imagination, may be conceiv'd to be separately existent; 'tis evident, that the existence of one particle of matter, no more implies the existence of another, than a square figure in one body implies a square figure in every one. This being granted, I now demand what results from the concurrence of these two possible ideas of *rest* and *annihilation*, and what must we conceive to follow upon the annihilation of all the air and subtile matter in the chamber, supposing the walls to remain the same, without any motion or alteration? There are some metaphysicians, who answer, that since matter and extension are the same, the annihilation of one necessarily implies that of the other; and there being now no distance betwixt the walls of the chamber, they touch each other; in the same manner as my hand touches the paper, which is immediately before me. But tho' this answer be very common, I defy these metaphysicians to conceive the matter according to their hypothesis, or imagine the floor and roof, with all the opposite sides of the chamber, to touch each other, while they continue in rest, and preserve the same position. For how can the two walls, that run from south to north, touch each other, while they touch the opposite ends of two walls, that run from east to west? And how can the floor and roof ever meet, while they are separated by the four walls, that lie in a contrary position? If you change their position, you suppose a motion. If you conceive any thing betwixt them, you suppose a new creation. But keeping strictly to the two ideas of *rest* and *annihilation*, 'tis evident, that the idea, which results from them, is not that of a contact of parts, but something else; which is concluded to be the idea of a vacuum.

The third objection carries the matter still farther, and not only asserts, that the idea of a vacuum is real and possible, but also necessary and unavoidable. This assertion is founded on the motion we observe in bodies, which, 'tis maintain'd, wou'd be impossible and inconceivable without a vacuum, into which one body must move in order to make way for another. I shall not enlarge upon this objection, because it principally belongs to natural philosophy, which lies without our present sphere.

In order to answer these objections, we must take the matter pretty deep, and consider the nature and origin of several ideas, lest we dispute without understanding perfectly the subject of the controversy. 'Tis evident the idea of darkness is no positive idea, but merely the negation of light, or more properly speaking, of colour'd and visible objects. A man, who enjoys his sight, receives no other perception from turning his eyes on every side, when entirely depriv'd of light, than what is common to him with one born blind; and 'tis certain such-a-one has no idea either of light or darkness. The consequence of this is, that 'tis not from the mere removal of visible objects we receive the impression of extension without matter; and that the idea of utter darkness can never be the same with that of vacuum.

Suppose again a man to be supported in the air, and to be softly convey'd along by some invisible power; 'tis evident he is sensible of nothing, and never receives the idea of extension, nor indeed any idea, from this invariable motion. Even supposing he moves his limbs to and fro, this cannot convey to him that idea. He feels in that case a certain sensation or impression, the parts of which are successive to each other, and may give him the idea of time: But certainly are not dispos'd in such a manner, as is necessary to convey the idea of space or extension.

Since then it appears, that darkness and motion, with the utter removal of every thing visible and tangible, can never give us the idea of extension without matter, or of a vacuum;

the next question is, whether they can convey this idea, when mix'd with something visible and tangible?

'Tis commonly allow'd by philosophers, that all bodies, which discover themselves to the eye, appear as if painted on a plain surface, and that their different degrees of remoteness from ourselves are discover'd more by reason than by the senses. When I hold up my hand before me, and spread my fingers, they are separated as perfectly by the blue colour of the firmament, as they cou'd be by any visible object, which I cou'd place betwixt them. In order, therefore, to know whether the sight can convey the impression and idea of a vacuum, we must suppose, that amidst an entire darkness, there are luminous bodies presented to us, whose light discovers only these bodies themselves, without giving us any impression of the surrounding objects.

We must form a parallel supposition concerning the objects of our feeling. 'Tis not proper to suppose a perfect removal of all tangible objects: we must allow something to be perceiv'd by the feeling; and after an interval and motion of the hand or other organ of sensation, another object of the touch to be met with; and upon leaving that, another; and so on, as often as we please. The question is, whether these intervals do not afford us the idea of extension without body?

To begin with the first case; 'tis evident, that when only two luminous bodies appear to the eye, we can perceive, whether they be conjoin'd or separate; whether they be separated by a great or small distance; and if this distance varies, we can perceive its increase or diminution, with the motion of the bodies. But as the distance is not in this case any thing colour'd or visible, it may be thought that there is here a vacuum or pure extension, not only intelligible to the mind, but obvious to the very senses.

This is our natural and most familiar way of thinking; but which we shall learn to correct by a little reflection. We may observe, that when two bodies present themselves, where there was formerly an entire darkness, the only change, that is discoverable, is in the appearance of these two objects, and that all the rest continues to be as before, a perfect negation of light, and of every colour'd or visible object. This is not only true of what may be said to be remote from these bodies, but also of the very distance; which is interpos'd betwixt them; *that* being nothing but darkness, or the negation of light; without parts, without composition, invariable and indivisible. Now since this distance causes no perception different from what a blind man receives from his eyes, or what is convey'd to us in the darkest night, it must partake of the same properties: And as blindness and darkness afford us no ideas of extension, 'tis impossible that the dark and undistinguishable distance betwixt two bodies can ever produce that idea.

The sole difference betwixt an absolute darkness and the appearance of two or more visible luminous objects consists, as I said, in the objects themselves, and in the manner they affect our senses. The angles, which the rays of light flowing from them, form with each other; the motion that is requir'd in the eye, in its passage from one to the other; and the different parts of the organs, which are affected by them; these produce the only perceptions, from which we can judge of the distance.[*] But as these perceptions are each of them simple and indivisible, they can never give us the idea of extension.

We may illustrate this by considering the sense of feeling, and the imaginary distance or interval interpos'd betwixt tangible or solid objects. I suppose two cases, *viz.* that of a man supported in the air, and moving his limbs to and fro, without meeting any thing tangible; and that of a man, who feeling something tangible, leaves it, and after a motion, of which he is sensible, perceives another tangible object; and I then ask, wherein consists the difference betwixt these two cases? No one will make any scruple to affirm, that it consists meerly in the perceiving those objects, and that the sensation, which arises from the motion, is in both cases the same: And as that sensation is not capable of conveying to us an idea of extension, when unaccompany'd with some

[* See Appendix, p. 678, for further comment.]

other perception, it can no more give us that idea, when mix'd with the impressions of tangible objects; since that mixture produces no alteration upon it.

But tho' motion and darkness, either alone, or attended with tangible and visible objects, convey no idea of a vacuum or extension without matter, yet they are the causes why we falsly imagine we can form such an idea. For there is a close relation betwixt that motion and darkness, and a real extension, or composition of visible and tangible objects.

First, We may observe, that two visible objects appearing in the midst of utter darkness, affect the senses in the same manner, and form the same angle by the rays, which flow from them, and meet in the eye, as if the distance betwixt them were fill'd with visible objects, that give us a true idea of extension. The sensation of motion is likewise the same, when there is nothing tangible interpos'd betwixt two bodies, as when we feel a compounded body, whose different parts are plac'd beyond each other.

Secondly, We find by experience, that two bodies, which are so plac'd as to affect the senses in the same manner with two others, that have a certain extent of visible objects interpos'd betwixt them, are capable of receiving the same extent, without any sensible impulse or penetration, and without any change on that angle, under which they appear to the senses. In like manner, where there is one object, which we cannot feel after another without an interval, and the perceiving of that sensation we call motion in our hand or organ of sensation; experience shews us, that 'tis possible the same objects may be felt with the same sensation of motion, along with the interpos'd impression of solid and tangible objects, attending the sensation. That is, in other words, an invisible and intangible distance may be converted into a visible and tangible one, without any change on the distant objects.

Thirdly, We may observe, as another relation betwixt these two kinds of distance, that they have nearly the same effects on every natural phaenomenon. For as all qualities, such as heat, cold, light, attraction, &c. diminish in proportion to the distance; there is but little difference observ'd, whether this distance be mark'd out by compounded and sensible objects, or be known only by the manner, in which the distant objects affect the senses.

Here then are three relations betwixt that distance, which conveys the idea of extension, and that other, which is not fill'd with any colour'd or solid object. The distant objects affect the senses in the same manner, whether separated by the one distance or the other; the second species of distance is found capable of receiving the first; and they both equally diminish the force of every quality.

These relations betwixt the two kinds of distance will afford us an easy reason, why the one has so often been taken for the other, and why we imagine we have an idea of extension without the idea of any object either of the sight or feeling. For we may establish it as a general maxim in this science of human nature, that wherever there is a close relation betwixt two ideas, the mind is very apt to mistake them, and in all its discourses and reasonings to use the one for the other. This phaenomenon occurs on so many occasions, and is of such consequence, that I cannot forbear stopping a moment to examine its causes. I shall only premise, that we must distinguish exactly betwixt the phaenomenon itself, and the causes, which I shall assign for it; and must not imagine from any uncertainty in the latter, that the former is also uncertain. The phaenomenon may be real, tho' my explication be chimerical. The falshood of the one is no consequence of that of the other; tho' at the same time we may observe, that 'tis very natural for us to draw such a consequence; which is an evident instance of that very principle, which I endeavour to explain.

When I receiv'd the relations of *resemblance, contiguity* and *causation*, as principles of union among ideas, without examining into their causes, 'twas more in prosecution of my first maxim, that we must in the end rest contented with experience, than for want of something specious and plausible, which I might have display'd on that subject. 'Twou'd have been easy to have made an imaginary dissection of the brain, and have shewn, why upon our conception of any idea, the animal spirits run into all the contiguous traces, and rouze up the other ideas, that are related to it. But tho' I have neglected any advantage, which I might have drawn from this topic in explaining the relations of ideas, I am afraid I must here have recourse to it, in order to account for the mistakes that arise from these relations. I shall therefore observe, that as the mind is endow'd with a power of exciting any idea it pleases; whenever it dispatches the spirits into that region of the brain, in which the idea is plac'd; these spirits always excite the idea, when they run precisely into the proper traces, and rummage that cell, which belongs to the idea. But as their motion is seldom direct, and naturally turns a little to the one side or the other; for this reason the animal spirits, falling into the contiguous traces, present other related ideas in lieu of that, which the mind desir'd at first to survey. This change we are not always sensible of; but continuing still the same train of thought, make use of the related idea, which is presented to us, and employ it in our reasoning, as if it were the same with what we demanded. This is the cause of many mistakes and sophisms in philosophy; as will naturally be imagin'd, and as it wou'd be easy to show, if there was occasion.

Of the three relations above-mention'd that of resemblance is the most fertile source of error; and indeed there are few mistakes in reasoning, which do not borrow largely from that origin. Resembling ideas are not only related together, but the actions of the mind, which we employ in considering them, are so little different, that we are not able to distinguish them. This last circumstance is of great consequence; and we may in general observe, that wherever the actions of the mind in forming any two ideas are the same or resembling, we are very apt to confound these ideas, and take the one for the other. Of this we shall see many instances in the progress of this treatise. But tho' resemblance be the relation, which most readily produces a mistake in ideas, yet the others of causation and contiguity may also concur in the same influence. We might produce the figures of poets and orators, as sufficient proofs of this, were it as usual, as it is reasonable, in metaphysical subjects to draw our arguments from that quarter. But lest metaphysicians shou'd esteem this below their dignity, I shall borrow a proof from an observation, which may be made on most of their own discourses, *viz.* that 'tis usual for men to use words for ideas, and to talk instead of thinking in their reasonings. We use words for ideas, because they are commonly so closely connected, that the mind easily mistakes them. And this likewise is the reason, why we substitute the idea of a distance, which is not consider'd either as visible or tangible, in the room of extension, which is nothing but a composition of visible or tangible points dispos'd in a certain order. In causing this mistake there concur both the relations of *causation* and *resemblance*. As the first species of distance is found to be convertible into the second, 'tis in this respect a kind of cause; and the similarity of their manner of affecting the senses, and diminishing every quality, forms the relation of resemblance.

After this chain of reasoning and explication of my principles, I am now prepar'd to answer all the objections that have been offer'd, whether deriv'd from *metaphysics* or *mechanics.* The frequent disputes concerning a vacuum, or extension without matter, prove not the reality of the idea, upon which the dispute turns; there being nothing more common, than to see men deceive themselves in this particular; especially when by means of any close relation, there is another idea presented, which may be the occasion of their mistake.

We may make almost the same answer to the second objection, deriv'd from the conjunction of the ideas of rest and annihilation. When every thing is annihilated in the chamber, and the walls continue imoveable, the chamber must be conceiv'd much in the same manner as at present, when the air that fills it, is not an object of the senses. This annihilation leaves to the *eye,* that fictitious distance, which is discover'd by the different parts of the organ, that are affected, and by the degrees of light and shade; and to the *feeling*, that which consists in a sensation of motion in the hand, or other member of the body. In vain shou'd we search any farther. On whichever side we turn this subject, we shall find that these are the only impressions such an object can produce after the suppos'd annihilation; and it has already been remark'd, that impressions can give rise to no ideas, but to such as resemble them.

Since a body interpos'd betwixt two others may be suppos'd to be annihilated, without producing any change upon such as lie on each hand of it, 'tis easily conceiv'd, how it may be created anew, and yet produce as little alteration. Now the motion of a body has much the same effect as its creation. The distant bodies are no more affected in the one case, than in the other. This suffices to satisfy the imagination, and proves there is no repugnance in such a motion. Afterwards experience comes in play to persuade us that two bodies, situated in the manner above-describ'd, have really such a capacity of receiving body betwixt them, and that there is no obstacle to the conversion of the invisible and intangible distance into one that is visible and tangible. However natural that conversion may seem, we cannot be sure it is practicable, before we have had experience of it.

Thus I seem to have answer'd the three objections above-mention'd; tho' at the same time I am sensible, that few will be satisfy'd with these answers, but will immediately propose new objections and difficulties. 'Twill probably be said, that my reasoning makes nothing to the matter in hand, and that I explain only the manner in which objects affect the senses, without endeavouring to account for their real nature and operations. Tho' there be nothing visible or tangible interpos'd betwixt two bodies, yet we find *by experience*, that the bodies may be plac'd in the same manner, with regard to the eye, and require the same motion of the hand in passing from one to the other, as if divided by something visible and tangible. This invisible and intangible distance is also found *by experience* to contain a capacity of receiving body, or of becoming visible and tangible. Here is the whole of my system; and in no part of it have I endeavour'd to explain the cause, which separates bodies after this manner, and gives them a capacity of receiving others betwixt them, without any impulse or penetration.

I answer this objection, by pleading guilty, and by confessing that my intention never was to penetrate into the nature of bodies, or explain the secret causes of their operations. For besides that this belongs not to my present purpose, I am afraid, that such an enterprize is beyond the reach of human understanding, and that we can never pretend to know body otherwise than by those external properties, which discover themselves to the senses. As to those who attempt any thing farther, I cannot approve of their ambition, till I see, in some one instance at least, that they have met with success. But at present I content myself with knowing perfectly the manner in which objects affect my senses, and their connexions with each other, as far as experience informs me of them. This suffices for the conduct of life; and this also suffices for my philosophy, which pretends only to explain the nature and causes of our perceptions, or impressions and ideas.*

I shall conclude this subject of extension with a paradox, which will easily be explain'd from the foregoing reason-

* [The following note is inserted from Hume's Appendix to Book III.]

As long as we confine our speculations to *the appearances* of objects to our senses, without entering into disquisitions concerning their real nature and operations, we are safe from all difficulties, and can never be embarrass'd by any question. Thus, if it be ask'd, if the invisible and intangible distance, interpos'd betwixt two objects, be something or nothing: 'Tis easy to answer, that it is *something*, viz. a property of the objects, which affect the *senses* after such a particular manner. If it be ask'd, whether two objects, having such a distance betwixt them, touch or not: It may be answer'd, that this depends upon the definition of the word, *touch*. If objects be said to touch, when there is nothing *sensible* interpos'd betwixt them, these objects touch: If objects be said to touch, when their *images* strike contiguous parts of the eye, and when the hand *feels* both objects

ing. This paradox is, that if you are pleas'd to give to the invisible and intangible distance, or in other words, to the capacity of becoming a visible and tangible distance, the name of a vacuum, extension and matter are the same, and yet there is a vacuum. If you will not give it that name, motion is possible in a plenum, without any impulse *in infinitum*, without returning in a circle, and without penetration. But however we may express ourselves, we must always confess, that we have no idea of any real extension without filling it with sensible objects, and conceiving its parts as visible or tangible.

As to the doctrine, that time is nothing but the manner, in which some real objects exist; we may observe, that 'tis liable to the same objections as the similar doctrine with regard to extension. If it be a sufficient proof, that we have the idea of a vacuum, because we dispute and reason concerning it; we must for the same reason have the idea of time without any changeable existence; since there is no subject of dispute more frequent and common. But that we really have no such idea, is certain. For whence shou'd it be deriv'd? Does it arise from an impression of sensation or

successively, without any interpos'd motion, these objects do not touch. The appearances of objects to our senses are all consistent; and no difficulties can ever arise, but from the obscurity of the terms we make use of.

If we carry our enquiry beyond the appearances of objects to the senses, I am afraid, that most of our conclusions will be full of scepticism and uncertainty. Thus if it be ask'd, whether or not the invisible and intangible distance be always full of *body*, or of something that by an improvement of our organs might become visible or tangible, I must acknowledge, that I find no very decisive arguments on either side; tho' I am inclin'd to the contrary opinion, as being more suitable to vulgar and popular notions. If *the Newtonian* philosophy be rightly understood, it will be found to mean no more. A vacuum is asserted: That is, bodies are said to be plac'd after such a manner, as to receive bodies betwixt them, without impulsion or penetration. The real nature of this position of bodies is unknown. We are only acquainted with its effects on the senses, and its power of receiving body. Nothing is more suitable to that philosophy, than a modest scepticism to a certain degree, and a fair confession of ignorance in subjects, that exceed all human capacity.

of reflection? Point it out distinctly to us, that we may know its nature and qualities. But if you cannot point out *any such impression*, you may be certain you are mistaken, when you imagine you have *any such idea.*

But tho' it be impossible to shew the impression, from which the idea of time without a changeable existence is deriv'd; yet we can easily point out those appearances, which make us fancy we have that idea. For we may observe, that there is a continual succession of perceptions in our mind; so that the idea of time being ever present with us; when we consider a stedfast object at five-a-clock, and regard the same at six; we are apt to apply to it that idea in the same manner as if every moment were distinguish'd by a different position, or an alteration of the object. The first and second appearances of the object, being compar'd with the succession of our perceptions, seem equally remov'd as if the object had really chang'd. To which we may add, what experience shews us, that the object was susceptible of such a number of changes betwixt these appearances; as also that the unchangeable or rather fictitious duration has the same effect upon every quality, by encreasing or diminishing it, as that succession, which is obvious to the senses. From these three relations we are apt to confound our ideas, and imagine we can form the idea of a time and duration, without any change or succession.

SECT. VI

Of the idea of existence and of external existence

It may not be amiss, before we leave this subject, to explain the ideas of *existence* and of *external existence*; which have their difficulties, as well as the ideas of space and time. By this means we shall be the better prepar'd for the examination of knowledge and probability, when we understand perfectly all those particular ideas, which may enter into our reasoning.

There is no impression nor idea of any kind, of which we have any consciousness or memory, that is not conceiv'd as existent; and 'tis evident, that from this consciousness the most perfect idea and assurance of *being* is deriv'd. From hence we may form a dilemma, the most clear and conclusive that can be imagin'd, *viz.* that since we never remember any idea or impression without attributing existence to it, the idea of existence must either be deriv'd from a distinct impression, conjoin'd with every perception or object of our thought, or must be the very same with the idea of the perception or object.

As this dilemma is an evident consequence of the principle, that every idea arises from a similar impression, so our decision betwixt the propositions of the dilemma is no more doubtful. So far from there being any distinct impression, attending every impression and every idea, that I do not think there are any two distinct impressions, which are inseparably conjoin'd. Tho' certain sensations may at one time be united, we quickly find they admit of a separation, and may be presented apart. And thus, tho' every impression and idea we remember be consider'd as existent, the idea of existence is not deriv'd from any particular impression.

The idea of existence, then, is the very same with the idea of what we conceive to be existent. To reflect on any thing simply, and to reflect on it as existent, are nothing different from each other. That idea, when conjoin'd with the idea of any object, makes no addition to it. Whatever we conceive, we conceive to be existent. Any idea we please to form is the idea of a being; and the idea of a being is any idea we please to form.

Whoever opposes this, must necessarily point out that distinct impression, from which the idea of entity is deriv'd, and must prove, that this impression is inseparable from every perception we believe to be existent. This we may without hesitation conclude to be impossible.

Our foregoing* reasoning concerning the *distinction* of

*Part I. Sect. 7.

ideas without any real *difference* will not here serve us in any stead. That kind of distinction is founded on the different resemblances, which the same simple idea may have to several different ideas. But no object can be presented resembling some object with respect to its existence, and different from others in the same particular; since every object, that is presented, must necessarily be existent.

A like reasoning will account for the idea of *external existence.* We may observe, that 'tis universally allow'd by philosophers, and is besides pretty obvious of itself, that nothing is ever really present with the mind but its perceptions or impressions and ideas, and that external objects become known to us only by those perceptions they occasion. To hate, to love, to think, to feel, to see; all this is nothing but to perceive.

Now since nothing is ever present to the mind but perceptions, and since all ideas are deriv'd from something antecedently present to the mind; it follows, that 'tis impossible for us so much as to conceive or form an idea of any thing specifically different from ideas and impressions. Let us fix our attention out of ourselves as much as possible: Let us chase our imagination to the heavens, or to the utmost limits of the universe; we never really advance a step beyond ourselves, nor can conceive any kind of existence, but those perceptions, which have appear'd in that narrow compass. This is the universe of the imagination, nor have we any idea but what is there produc'd.

The farthest we can go towards a conception of external objects, when suppos'd *specifically* different from our perceptions, is to form a relative idea of them, without pretending to comprehend the related objects. Generally speaking we do not suppose them specifically different; but only attribute to them different relations, connexions and durations. But of this more fully hereafter*.

* Part IV. Sect. 2.

PART III

Of knowledge and probability

SECT. I
Of knowledge

THERE are * seven different kinds of philosophical relation, *viz. resemblance, identity, relations of time and place, proportion in quantity or number, degrees in any quality, contrariety, and causation.* These relations may be divided into two classes; into such as depend entirely on the ideas, which we compare together, and such as may be chang'd without any change in the ideas. 'Tis from the idea of a triangle, that we discover the relation of equality, which its three angles bear to two right ones; and this relation is invariable, as long as our idea remains the same. On the contrary, the relations of *contiguity* and *distance* betwixt two objects may be changed merely by an alteration of their place, without any change on the objects themselves or on their ideas; and the place depends on a hundred different accidents, which cannot be foreseen by the mind. 'Tis the same case with *identity* and *causation.* Two objects, tho' perfectly resembling each other, and even appearing in the same place at different times, may be numerically different: And as the power, by which one object produces another, is never discoverable merely from their idea, 'tis evident *cause* and *effect* are relations, of which we receive information from experience, and not from any abstract reasoning or reflection. There is no single phaenomenon, even the most simple, which can be accounted for from the qualities of the objects,

* Part I. Sect. 5.

as they appear to us; or which we cou'd foresee without the help of our memory and experience.

It appears, therefore, that of these seven philosophical relations, there remain only four, which depending solely upon ideas, can be the objects of knowledge and certainty. These four are *resemblance, contrariety, degrees in quality, and proportions in quantity or number*. Three of these relations are discoverable at first sight, and fall more properly under the province of intuition than demonstration. When any objects *resemble* each other, the resemblance will at first strike the eye, or rather the mind; and seldom requires a second examination. The case is the same with *contrariety*, and with the *degrees* of any *quality*. No one can once doubt but existence and non-existence destroy each other, and are perfectly incompatible and contrary. And tho' it be impossible to judge exactly of the degrees of any quality, such as colour, taste, heat, cold, when the difference betwixt them is very small; yet 'tis easy to decide, that any of them is superior or inferior to another, when their difference is considerable. And this decision we always pronounce at first sight, without any enquiry or reasoning.

We might proceed, after the same manner, in fixing the *proportions* of *quantity* or *number*, and might at one view observe a superiority or inferiority betwixt any numbers, or figures; especially where the difference is very great and remarkable. As to equality or any exact proportion, we can only guess at it from a single consideration; except in very short numbers, or very limited portions of extension; which are comprehended in an instant, and where we perceive an impossibility of falling into any considerable error. In all other cases we must settle the proportions with some liberty; or proceed in a more *artificial* manner.

I have already observ'd, that geometry, or the *art*, by which we fix the proportions of figures; tho' it much excels both in universality and exactness, the loose judgments of the senses and imagination; yet never attains a perfect precision and exactness. Its first principles are still drawn from the general appearance of the objects; and that appearance can never afford us any security, when we examine the prodigious minuteness of which nature is susceptible. Our ideas seem to give a perfect assurance, that no two right lines can have a common segment; but if we consider these ideas, we shall find, that they always suppose a sensible inclination of the two lines, and that where the angle they form is extremely small, we have no standard of a right line so precise as to assure us of the truth of this proposition. 'Tis the same case with most of the primary decisions of the mathematics.

There remain, therefore, algebra and arithmetic as the only sciences, in which we can carry on a chain of reasoning to any degree of intricacy, and yet preserve a perfect exactness and certainty. We are possest of a precise standard, by which we can judge of the equality and proportion of numbers; and according as they correspond or not to that standard, we determine their relations, without any possibility of error. When two numbers are so combin'd, as that the one has always an unite answering to every unite of the other, we pronounce them equal; and 'tis for want of such a standard of equality in extension, that geometry can scarce be esteem'd a perfect and infallible science.

But here it may not be amiss to obviate a difficulty, which may arise from my asserting, that tho' geometry falls short of that perfect precision and certainty, which are peculiar to arithmetic and algebra, yet it exceeds the imperfect judgments of our senses and imagination. The reason why I impute any defect to geometry, is, because its original and fundamental principles are deriv'd merely from appearances; and it may perhaps be imagin'd, that this defect must always attend it, and keep it from ever reaching a greater exactness in the comparison of objects or ideas, than what our eye or imagination alone is able to attain. I own that this defect so far attends it, as to keep it from ever aspiring to a full certainty: But since these fundamental principles depend on the easiest and least deceitful appearances, they bestow on their consequences a degree of exactness, of which these consequences are singly incapable. 'Tis impossible for the eye to determine the angles of a chiliagon to be equal to 1996 right angles, or make any conjecture, that approaches this proportion; but when it determines, that right lines cannot concur; that we cannot draw more than one right line between two given points; its mistakes can never be of any consequence. And this is the nature and use of geometry, to run us up to such appearances, as, by reason of their simplicity, cannot lead us into any considerable error.

I shall here take occasion to propose a second observation concerning our demonstrative reasonings, which is suggested by the same subject of the mathematics. 'Tis usual with mathematicians, to pretend, that those ideas, which are their objects, are of so refin'd and spiritual a nature, that they fall not under the conception of the fancy, but must be comprehended by a pure and intellectual view, of which the superior faculties of the soul are alone capable. The same notion runs thro' most parts of philosophy, and is principally made use of to explain our abstract ideas, and to shew how we can form an idea of a triangle, for instance, which shall neither be an isosceles nor scalenum, nor be confin'd to any particular length and proportion of sides. 'Tis easy to see, why philosophers are so fond of this notion of some spiritual and refin'd perceptions; since by that means they cover many of their absurdities, and may refuse to submit to the decisions of clear ideas, by appealing to such as are obscure and uncertain. But to destroy this artifice, we need but reflect on that principle so oft insisted on, *that all our ideas are copy'd from our impressions.* For from thence we may immediately conclude, that since all impressions are clear and precise, the ideas, which are copy'd from them, must be of the same nature, and can never, but from our fault, contain any thing so dark and intricate. An idea is by its very nature weaker and fainter than an impression; but being in every other respect the same, cannot imply any very great mystery. If its weakness render it obscure, 'tis our business to remedy that defect, as much as possible, by keeping the idea steady and precise; and till we have done so, 'tis in vain to pretend to reasoning and philosophy.

SECT. II

Of probability; and of the idea of cause and effect

THIS is all I think necessary to observe concerning those four relations, which are the foundation of science; but as to the other three, which depend not upon the idea, and may be absent or present even while *that* remains the same, 'twill be proper to explain them more particularly. These three relations are *identity, the situations in time and place, and causation.*

All kinds of reasoning consist in nothing but a *comparison*, and a discovery of those relations, either constant or inconstant, which two or more objects bear to each other. This comparison we may make, either when both the objects are present to the senses, or when neither of them is present, or when only one. When both the objects are present to the senses along with the relation, we call *this* perception rather than reasoning; nor is there in this case any exercise of the thought, or any action, properly speaking, but a mere passive admission of the impressions thro' the organs of sensation. According to this way of thinking, we ought not to receive as reasoning any of the observations we may make concerning *identity*, and the *relations of time* and *place*; since in none of them the mind can go beyond what is immediately present to the senses, either to discover the real existence or the relations of objects. 'Tis only *causation*, which produces such a connexion, as to give us assurance from the existence or action of one object, that 'twas follow'd or preceded by any other existence or action; nor can the other two relations be ever made use of in reasoning, except so far as they either affect or are affected by it. There is nothing in any objects to persuade us, that they are either always *remote* or always *contiguous*; and when from experience and observation we discover, that their relation in this particular is invariable, we always conclude there is some secret *cause*, which separates or unites them. The same reasoning extends to *identity*. We readily suppose an object may continue individually the same, tho' several times absent from and present to the senses; and ascribe to it an identity, notwithstanding the interruption of the perception, whenever we conclude, that if we had kept our eye or hand constantly upon it, it wou'd have convey'd an invariable and uninterrupted perception. But this conclusion beyond the impressions of our senses can be founded only on the connexion of *cause and effect*; nor can we otherwise have any security, that the object is not chang'd upon us, however much the new object may resemble that which was formerly present to the senses. Whenever we discover such a perfect resemblance, we consider, whether it be common in that species of objects; whether possibly or probably any cause cou'd operate in producing the change and resemblance; and according as we determine concerning these causes and effects, we form our judgment concerning the identity of the object.

Here then it appears, that of those three relations, which depend not upon the mere ideas, the only one, that can be trac'd beyond our senses, and informs us of existences and objects, which we do not see or feel, is *causation*. This relation, therefore, we shall endeavour to explain fully before we leave the subject of the understanding.

To begin regularly, we must consider the idea of *causation*, and see from what origin it is deriv'd. 'Tis impossible to reason justly, without understanding perfectly the idea concerning which we reason; and 'tis impossible perfectly to understand any idea, without tracing it up to its origin, and examining that primary impression, from which it arises. The examination of the impression bestows a clearness on the idea; and the examination of the idea bestows a like clearness on all our reasoning.

Let us therefore cast our eye on any two objects, which we call cause and effect, and turn them on all sides, in order to find that impression, which produces an idea of such prodigious consequence. At first sight I perceive, that I must not search for it in any of the particular *qualities* of the objects; since, which-ever of these qualities I pitch on, I find some object, that is not possest of it, and yet falls under the denomination of cause or effect. And indeed there is nothing existent, either externally or internally, which is not to be consider'd either as a cause or an effect; tho' 'tis plain there is no one quality, which universally belongs to all beings, and gives them a title to that denomination.

The idea, then, of causation must be deriv'd from some *relation* among objects; and that relation we must now endeavour to discover. I find in the first place, that whatever objects are consider'd as causes or effects, are *contiguous*; and that nothing can operate in a time or place, which is ever so little remov'd from those of its existence. Tho' distant objects may sometimes seem productive of each other, they are commonly found upon examination to be link'd by a chain of causes, which are contiguous among themselves, and to the distant objects; and when in any particular instance we cannot discover this connexion, we still presume it to exist. We may therefore consider the relation of CONTIGUITY as essential to that of causation; at least may suppose it such, according to the general opinion, till we can find a more * proper occasion to clear up this matter, by examining what objects are or are not susceptible of juxta-position and conjunction.

The second relation I shall observe as essential to causes and effects, is not so universally acknowledg'd, but is liable to some controversy. 'Tis that of PRIORITY of time in the cause before the effect. Some pretend that 'tis not absolutely necessary a cause shou'd precede its effect; but that any object or action, in the very first moment of its existence, may exert its productive quality, and give rise to another object or action, perfectly co-temporary with itself. But beside that experience in most instances seems to contradict this opinion, we may establish the relation of priority

* Part IV. Sect. 5.

by a kind of inference or reasoning. 'Tis an establish'd maxim both in natural and moral philosophy, that an object, which exists for any time in its full perfection without producing another, is not its sole cause; but is assisted by some other principle, which pushes it from its state of inactivity, and makes it exert that energy, of which it was secretly possest. Now if any cause may be perfectly co-temporary with its effect, 'tis certain, according to this maxim, that they must all of them be so; since any one of them, which retards its operation for a single moment, exerts not itself at that very individual time, in which it might have operated; and therefore is no proper cause. The consequence of this wou'd be no less than the destruction of that succession of causes, which we observe in the world; and indeed, the utter annihilation of time. For if one cause were co-temporary with its effect, and this effect with *its* effect, and so on, 'tis plain there wou'd be no such thing as succession, and all objects must be co-existent.

If this argument appear satisfactory, 'tis well. If not, I beg the reader to allow me the same liberty, which I have us'd in the preceding case, of supposing it such. For he shall find, that the affair is of no great importance.

Having thus discover'd or suppos'd the two relations of *contiguity* and *succession* to be essential to causes and effects, I find I am stopt short, and can proceed no farther in considering any single instance of cause and effect. Motion in one body is regarded upon impulse as the cause of motion in another. When we consider these objects with the utmost attention, we find only that the one body approaches the other; and that the motion of it precedes that of the other, but without any sensible interval. 'Tis in vain to rack ourselves with *farther* thought and reflection upon this subject. We can go no *farther* in considering this particular instance.

Shou'd any one leave this instance, and pretend to define a cause, by saying it is something productive of another, 'tis evident he wou'd say nothing. For what does he mean by *production*? Can he give any definition of it, that will not be the same with that of causation? If he can; I desire it may be produc'd. If he cannot; he here runs in a circle, and gives a synonimous term instead of a definition.

Shall we then rest contented with these two relations of contiguity and succession, as affording a compleat idea of causation? By no means. An object may be contiguous and prior to another, without being consider'd as its cause. There is a NECESSARY CONNEXION to be taken into consideration; and that relation is of much greater importance, than any of the other two above-mention'd.

Here again I turn the object on all sides, in order to discover the nature of this necessary connexion, and find the impression, or impressions, from which its idea may be deriv'd. When I cast my eye on the *known qualities* of objects, I immediately discover that the relation of cause and effect depends not in the least on *them*. When I consider their *relations*, I can find none but those of contiguity and succession; which I have already regarded as imperfect and unsatisfactory. Shall the despair of success make me assert, that I am here possest of an idea, which is not preceded by any similar impression? This wou'd be too strong a proof of levity and inconstancy; since the contrary principle has been already so firmly establish'd, as to admit of no farther doubt; at least, till we have more fully examin'd the present difficulty.

We must, therefore, proceed like those, who being in search of any thing, that lies conceal'd from them, and not finding it in the place they expected, beat about all the neighbouring fields, without any certain view or design, in hopes their good fortune will at last guide them to what they search for. 'Tis necessary for us to leave the direct survey of this question concerning the nature of that *necessary connexion*, which enters into our idea of cause and effect; and endeavour to find some other questions, the examination of which will perhaps afford a hint, that may serve to clear up the present difficulty. Of these questions there occur two, which I shall proceed to examine, *viz.*

First, For what reason we pronounce it *necessary*, that

every thing whose existence has a beginning, shou'd also have a cause?

Secondly, Why we conclude, that such particular causes must *necessarily* have such particular effects; and what is the nature of that *inference* we draw from the one to the other, and of the *belief* we repose in it?

I shall only observe before I proceed any farther, that tho' ideas of cause and effect be deriv'd from the impressions of reflection as well as from those of sensation, yet for brevity's sake, I commonly mention only the latter as the origin of these ideas; tho' I desire that whatever I say of them may also extend to the former. Passions are connected with their objects and with one another; no less than external bodies are connected together. The same relation, then, of cause and effect, which belongs to one, must be common to all of them.

SECT. III

Why a cause is always necessary

To begin with the first question concerning the necessity of a cause: 'Tis a general maxim in philosophy, that *whatever begins to exist, must have a cause of existence*. This is commonly taken for granted in all reasonings, without any proof given or demanded. 'Tis suppos'd to be founded on intuition, and to be one of those maxims, which tho' they may be deny'd with the lips, 'tis impossible for men in their hearts really to doubt of. But if we examine this maxim by the idea of knowledge above-explain'd, we shall discover in it no mark of any such intuitive certainty; but on the contrary shall find, that 'tis of a nature quite foreign to that species of conviction.

All certainty arises from the comparison of ideas, and from the discovery of such relations as are unalterable, so long as the ideas continue the same. These relations are *resemblance, proportions in quantity and number, degrees of any quality, and contrariety*; none of which are imply'd in this proposition, *Whatever has a beginning has also a cause of existence*. That proposition therefore is not intuitively certain. At least any one, who wou'd assert it to be intuitively certain, must deny these to be the only infallible relations, and must find some other relation of that kind to be imply'd in it; which it will then be time enough to examine.

But here is an argument, which proves at once, that the foregoing proposition is neither intuitively nor demonstrably certain. We can never demonstrate the necessity of a cause to every new existence, or new modification of existence, without shewing at the same time the impossibility there is, that any thing can ever begin to exist without some productive principle; and where the latter proposition cannot be prov'd, we must despair of ever being able to prove the former. Now that the latter proposition is utterly incapable of a demonstrative proof, we may satisfy ourselves by considering, that as all distinct ideas are separable from each other, and as the ideas of cause and effect are evidently distinct, 'twill be easy for us to conceive any object to be non-existent this moment, and existent the next, without conjoining to it the distinct idea of a cause or productive principle. The separation, therefore, of the idea of a cause from that of a beginning of existence, is plainly possible for the imagination; and consequently the actual separation of these objects is so far possible, that it implies no contradiction nor absurdity; and is therefore incapable of being refuted by any reasoning from mere ideas; without which 'tis impossible to demonstrate the necessity of a cause.

Accordingly we shall find upon examination, that every demonstration, which has been produc'd for the necessity of a cause, is fallacious and sophistical. All the points of time and place,* say some philosophers, in which we can suppose any object to begin to exist, are in themselves equal; and unless there be some cause, which is peculiar to one time

*Mr *Hobbes*.

and to one place, and which by that means determines and fixes the existence, it must remain in eternal suspence; and the object can never begin to be, for want of something to fix its beginning. But I ask; Is there any more difficulty in supposing the time and place to be fix'd without a cause, than to suppose the existence to be determin'd in that manner? The first question that occurs on this subject is always, *whether* the object shall exist or not: The next, *when* and *where* it shall begin to exist. If the removal of a cause be intuitively absurd in the one case, it must be so in the other: And if that absurdity be not clear without a proof in the one case, it will equally require one in the other. The absurdity, then, of the one supposition can never be a proof of that of the other; since they are both upon the same footing, and must stand or fall by the same reasoning.

The second argument,* which I find us'd on this head, labours under an equal difficulty. Every thing, 'tis said, must have a cause; for if any thing wanted a cause, *it* wou'd produce *itself*; that is, exist before it existed; which is impossible. But this reasoning is plainly unconclusive; because it supposes, that in our denial of a cause we still grant what we expressly deny, *viz.* that there must be a cause; which therefore is taken to be the object itself; and *that*, no doubt, is an evident contradiction. But to say that any thing is produc'd, or to express myself more properly, comes into existence, without a cause, is not to affirm, that 'tis itself its own cause; but on the contrary in excluding all external causes, excludes *a fortiori* the thing itself, which is created. An object, that exists absolutely without any cause, certainly is not its own cause; and when you assert, that the one follows from the other, you suppose the very point in question, and take it for granted, that 'tis utterly impossible any thing can ever begin to exist without a cause, but that upon the exclusion of one productive principle, we must still have recourse to another.

'Tis exactly the same case with the † third argument, which has been employ'd to demonstrate the necessity of a

* Dr *Clarke* and others. † Mr *Locke.*

cause. Whatever is produc'd without any cause, is produc'd by *nothing*; or in other words, has nothing for its cause. But nothing can never be a cause, no more than it can be something, or equal to two right angles. By the same intuition, that we perceive nothing not to be equal to two right angles, or not to be something, we perceive, that it can never be a cause; and consequently must perceive, that every object has a real cause of its existence.

I believe it will not be necessary to employ many words in shewing the weakness of this argument, after what I have said of the foregoing. They are all of them founded on the same fallacy, and are deriv'd from the same turn of thought. 'Tis sufficient only to observe, that when we exclude all causes we really do exclude them, and neither suppose nothing nor the object itself to be the causes of the existence; and consequently can draw no argument from the absurdity of these suppositions to prove the absurdity of that exclusion. If every thing must have a cause, it follows, that upon the exclusion of other causes we must accept of the object itself or of nothing as causes. But 'tis the very point in question, whether every thing must have a cause or not; and therefore, according to all just reasoning, it ought never to be taken for granted.

They are still more frivolous, who say, that every effect must have a cause, because 'tis imply'd in the very idea of effect. Every effect necessarily presupposes a cause; effect being a relative term, of which cause is the correlative. But this does not prove, that every being must be preceded by a cause; no more than it follows, because every husband must have a wife, that therefore every man must be marry'd. The true state of the question is, whether every object, which begins to exist, must owe its existence to a cause; and this I assert neither to be intuitively nor demonstratively certain, and hope to have prov'd it sufficiently by the foregoing arguments.

Since it is not from knowledge or any scientific reasoning, that we derive the opinion of the necessity of a cause to every new production, that opinion must necessarily arise from observation and experience. The next question, then, shou'd naturally be, *how experience gives rise to such a principle*? But as I find it will be more convenient to sink this question in the following, *Why we conclude, that such particular causes must necessarily have such particular effects, and why we form an inference from one to another?* we shall make that the subject of our future enquiry. 'Twill, perhaps, be found in the end, that the same answer will serve for both questions.

SECT. IV

Of the component parts of our reasonings concerning cause and effect

THO' the mind in its reasonings from causes or effects carries its view beyond those objects, which it sees or remembers, it must never lose sight of them entirely, nor reason merely upon its own ideas, without some mixture of impressions, or at least of ideas of the memory, which are equivalent to impressions. When we infer effects from causes, we must establish the existence of these causes; which we have only two ways of doing, either by an immediate perception of our memory or senses, or by an inference from other causes; which causes again we must ascertain in the same manner, either by a present impression, or by an inference from *their* causes, and so on, till we arrive at some object, which we see or remember. 'Tis impossible for us to carry on our inferences *in infinitum*; and the only thing, that can stop them, is an impression of the memory or senses, beyond which there is no room for doubt or enquiry.

To give an instance of this, we may chuse any point of history, and consider for what reason we either believe or reject it. Thus we believe that CAESAR was kill'd in the senate-house on the *ides* of *March*; and that because this fact is establish'd on the unanimous testimony of historians, who agree to assign this precise time and place to that event.

Here are certain characters and letters present either to our memory or senses; which characters we likewise remember to have been us'd as the signs of certain ideas; and these ideas were either in the minds of such as were immediately present at that action, and receiv'd the ideas directly from its existence; or they were deriv'd from the testimony of others, and that again from another testimony, by a visible gradation, 'till we arrive at those who were eye-witnesses and spectators of the event. 'Tis obvious all this chain of argument or connexion of causes and effects, is at first founded on those characters or letters, which are seen or remember'd, and that without the authority either of the memory or senses our whole reasoning wou'd be chimerical and without foundation. Every link of the chain wou'd in that case hang upon another; but there wou'd not be any thing fix'd to one end of it, capable of sustaining the whole; and consequently there wou'd be no belief nor evidence. And this actually is the case with all *hypothetical* arguments, or reasonings upon a supposition; there being in them, neither any present impression, nor belief of a real existence.

I need not observe, that 'tis no just objection to the present doctrine, that we can reason upon our past conclusions or principles, without having recourse to those impressions, from which they first arose. For even supposing these impressions shou'd be entirely effac'd from the memory, the conviction they produc'd may still remain; and 'tis equally true, that all reasonings concerning causes and effects are originally deriv'd from some impression; in the same manner, as the assurance of a demonstration proceeds always from a comparison of ideas, tho' it may continue after the comparison is forgot.

SECT. V

Of the impressions of the senses and memory

IN this kind of reasoning, then, from causation, we employ materials, which are of a mix'd and heterogeneous nature, and which, however connected, are yet essentially different from each other. All our arguments concerning causes and effects consist both of an impression of the memory or senses, and of the idea of that existence, which produces the object of the impression, or is produc'd by it. Here therefore we have three things to explain, *viz. First*, The original impression. *Secondly*, The transition to the idea of the connected cause or effect. *Thirdly*, The nature and qualities of that idea.

As to those *impressions*, which arise from the *senses*, their ultimate cause is, in my opinion, perfectly inexplicable by human reason, and 'twill always be impossible to decide with certainty, whether they arise immediately from the object, or are produc'd by the creative power of the mind, or are deriv'd from the author of our being. Nor is such a question any way material to our present purpose. We may draw inferences from the coherence of our perceptions, whether they be true or false; whether they represent nature justly, or be mere illusions of the senses.

When we search for the characteristic, which distinguishes the *memory* from the imagination, we must immediately perceive, that it cannot lie in the simple ideas it presents to us; since both these faculties borrow their simple ideas from the impressions, and can never go beyond these original perceptions. These faculties are as little distinguish'd from each other by the arrangement of their complex ideas. For tho' it be a peculiar property of the memory to preserve the original order and position of its ideas, while the imagination transposes and changes them, as it pleases; yet this difference is not sufficient to distinguish them in their operation, or make us know the one from the other; it being impossible to recal the past impressions, in order to compare them with our present ideas, and see whether their arrangement be exactly similar. Since therefore the memory is known, neither by the order of its *complex* ideas, nor the nature of its *simple* ones; it follows, that the difference betwixt it and the imagination lies in its superior force and vivacity. A man may indulge his fancy in feigning any past scene of adventures; nor wou'd there be any possibility of distinguishing this from a remembrance of a like kind, were not the ideas of the imagination fainter and more obscure.

[*] It frequently happens, that when two men have been engag'd in any scene of action, the one shall remember it much better than the other, and shall have all the difficulty in the world to make his companion recollect it. He runs over several circumstances in vain; mentions the time, the place, the company, what was said, what was done on all sides; till at last he hits on some lucky circumstance, that revives the whole, and gives his friend a perfect memory of every thing. Here the person that forgets receives at first all the ideas from the discourse of the other, with the same circumstances of time and place; tho' he considers them as mere fictions of the imagination. But as soon as the circumstance is mention'd, that touches the memory, the very same ideas now appear in a new light, and have, in a manner, a different feeling from what they had before. Without any other alteration, beside that of the feeling, they become immediately ideas of the memory, and are assented to.

Since, therefore, the imagination can represent all the same objects that the memory can offer to us, and since those faculties are only distinguish'd by the different *feeling* of the ideas they present, it may be proper to consider what is the nature of that feeling. And here I believe every one will readily agree with me, that the ideas of the memory are more *strong* and *lively* than those of the fancy.

A painter, who intended to represent a passion or emotion

[* The following two paragraphs are inserted from Hume's Appendix to Book III.]

of any kind, wou'd endeavour to get a sight of a person actuated by a like emotion, in order to enliven his ideas, and give them a force and vivacity superior to what is found in those, which are mere fictions of the imagination. The more recent this memory is, the clearer is the idea; and when after a long interval he would return to the contemplation of his object, he always finds its ideas to be much decay'd, if not wholly obliterated. We are frequently in doubt concerning the ideas of the memory, as they become very weak and feeble; and are at a loss to determine whether any image proceeds from the fancy or the memory, when it is not drawn in such lively colours as distinguish that latter faculty. I think, I remember such an event, says one; but am not sure. A long tract of time has almost worn it out of my memory, and leaves me uncertain whether or not it be the pure offspring of my fancy.

And as an idea of the memory, by losing its force and vivacity, may degenerate to such a degree, as to be taken for an idea of the imagination; so on the other hand an idea of the imagination may acquire such a force and vivacity, as to pass for an idea of the memory, and counterfeit its effects on the belief and judgment. This is noted in the case of liars; who by the frequent repetition of their lies, come at last to believe and remember them, as realities; custom and habit having in this case, as in many others, the same influence on the mind as nature, and infixing the idea with equal force and vigour.

Thus it appears, that the *belief* or *assent,* which always attends the memory and senses, is nothing but the vivacity of those perceptions they present; and that this alone distinguishes them from the imagination. To believe is in this case to feel an immediate impression of the senses, or a repetition of that impression in the memory. 'Tis merely the force and liveliness of the perception, which constitutes the first act of the judgment, and lays the foundation of that reasoning, which we build upon it, when we trace the relation of cause and effect.

SECT. VI

Of the inference from the impression to the idea

'Tis easy to observe, that in tracing this relation, the inference we draw from cause to effect, is not deriv'd merely from a survey of these particular objects, and from such a penetration into their essences as may discover the dependance of the one upon the other. There is no object, which implies the existence of any other if we consider these objects in themselves, and never look beyond the ideas which we form of them. Such an inference wou'd amount to knowledge, and wou'd imply the absolute contradiction and impossibility of receiving any thing different. But as all distinct ideas are separable, 'tis evident there can be no impossibility of that kind. When we pass from a present impression to the idea of any object, we might possibly have separated the idea from the impression, and have substituted any other idea in its room.

'Tis therefore by EXPERIENCE only, that we can infer the existence of one object from that of another. The nature of experience is this. We remember to have had frequent instances of the existence of one species of objects; and also remember, that the individuals of another species of objects have always attended them, and have existed in a regular order of contiguity and succession with regard to them. Thus we remember to have seen that species of object we call *flame*, and to have felt that species of sensation we call *heat*. We likewise call to mind their constant conjunction in all past instances. Without any farther ceremony, we call the one *cause* and the other *effect*, and infer the existence of the one from that of the other. In all those instances, from which we learn the conjunction of particular causes and effects, both the causes and effects have been perceiv'd by the senses, and are remembered: But in all cases, wherein we reason concerning them, there is only one perceiv'd or remember'd, and the other is supply'd in conformity to our past experience.

Thus in advancing we have insensibly discovered a new relation betwixt cause and effect, when we least expected it, and were entirely employ'd upon another subject. This relation is their CONSTANT CONJUNCTION. Contiguity and succession are not sufficient to make us pronounce any two objects to be cause and effect, unless we perceive, that these two relations are preserv'd in several instances. We may now see the advantage of quitting the direct survey of this relation, in order to discover the nature of that *necessary connexion*, which makes so essential a part of it. There are hopes, that by this means we may at last arrive at our propos'd end; tho' to tell the truth, this new-discover'd relation of a constant conjunction seems to advance us but very little in our way. For it implies no more than this, that like objects have always been plac'd in like relations of contiguity and succession; and it seems evident, at least at first sight, that by this means we can never discover any new idea, and can only multiply, but not enlarge the objects of our mind. It may be thought, that when we learn not from one object, we can never learn from a hundred, which are all of the same kind, and are perfectly resembling in every circumstance. As our senses shew us in one instance two bodies, or motions, or qualities in certain relations of succession and contiguity; so our memory presents us only with a multitude of instances, wherein we always find like bodies, motions, or qualities in like relations. From the mere repetition of any past impression, even to infinity, there never will arise any new original idea, such as that of a necessary connexion; and the number of impressions has in this case no more effect than if we confin'd ourselves to one only. But tho' this reasoning seems just and obvious; yet as it would be folly to despair too soon, we shall continue the thread of our discourse; and having found, that after the discovery of the constant conjunction of any objects, we always draw an inference from one object to another, we shall now examine the nature of that inference, and of the transition from the impression to the idea. Perhaps 'twill appear in the end, that the necessary connexion depends on the inference, instead of the inference's depending on the necessary connexion.

Since it appears, that the transition from an impression present to the memory or senses to the idea of an object, which we call cause or effect, is founded on past *experience*, and on our remembrance of their *constant conjunction*, the next question is, Whether experience produces the idea by means of the understanding or imagination; whether we are determin'd by reason to make the transition, or by a certain association and relation of perceptions. If reason determin'd us, it wou'd proceed upon that principle, *that instances, of which we have had no experience, must resemble those, of which we have had experience, and that the course of nature continues always uniformly the same.* In order therefore to clear up this matter, let us consider all the arguments, upon which such a proposition may be suppos'd to be founded; and as these must be deriv'd either from *knowledge* or *probability*, let us cast our eye on each of these degrees of evidence, and see whether they afford any just conclusion of this nature.

Our foregoing method of reasoning will easily convince us, that there can be no *demonstrative* arguments to prove, *that those instances, of which we have had no experience, resemble those, of which we have had experience.* We can at least conceive a change in the course of nature; which sufficiently proves, that such a change is not absolutely impossible. To form a clear idea of any thing, is an undeniable argument for its possibility, and is alone a refutation of any pretended demonstration against it.

Probability, as it discovers not the relations of ideas, consider'd as such, but only those of objects, must in some respects be founded on the impressions of our memory and senses, and in some respects on our ideas. Were there no mixture of any impression in our probable reasonings, the conclusion wou'd be entirely chimerical: And were there no mixture of ideas, the action of the mind, in observing the relation, wou'd, properly speaking, be sensation, not reasoning. 'Tis therefore necessary, that in all probable reasonings there be something present to the mind, either seen or remember'd; and that from this we infer something connected with it, which is not seen nor remember'd.

The only connexion or relation of objects, which can lead us beyond the immediate impressions of our memory and senses, is that of cause and effect; and that because 'tis the only one, on which we can found a just inference from one object to another. The idea of cause and effect is deriv'd from *experience*, which informs us, that such particular objects, in all past instances, have been constantly conjoin'd with each other: And as an object similar to one of these is suppos'd to be immediately present in its impression, we thence presume on the existence of one similar to its usual attendant. According to this account of things, which is, I think, in every point unquestionable, probability is founded on the presumption of a resemblance betwixt those objects, of which we have had experience, and those, of which we have had none; and therefore 'tis impossible this presumption can arise from probability. The same principle cannot be both the cause and effect of another; and this is, perhaps, the only proposition concerning that relation, which is either intuitively or demonstratively certain.

Shou'd any one think to elude this argument; and without determining whether our reasoning on this subject be deriv'd from demonstration or probability, pretend that all conclusions from causes and effects are built on solid reasoning: I can only desire, that this reasoning may be produc'd, in order to be expos'd to our examination. It may, perhaps, be said, that after experience of the constant conjunction of certain objects, we reason in the following manner. Such an object is always found to produce another. 'Tis impossible it cou'd have this effect, if it was not endow'd with a power of production. The power necessarily implies the effect; and therefore there is a just foundation for drawing a conclusion from the existence of one object to that of its usual attendant. The past production implies a power: The power implies a new production: And the new production is what we infer from the power and the past production.

'Twere easy for me to shew the weakness of this reasoning, were I willing to make use of those observations, I have already made, that the idea of *production* is the same with that of *causation*, and that no existence certainly and demonstratively implies a power in any other object; or were it proper to anticipate what I shall have occasion to remark afterwards concerning the idea we form of *power* and *efficacy*. But as such a method of proceeding may seem either to weaken my system, by resting one part of it on another, or to breed a confusion in my reasoning, I shall endeavour to maintain my present assertion without any such assistance.

It shall therefore be allow'd for a moment, that the production of one object by another in any one instance implies a power; and that this power is connected with its effect. But it having been already prov'd, that the power lies not in the sensible qualities of the cause; and there being nothing but the sensible qualities present to us; I ask, why in other instances you presume that the same power still exists, merely upon the appearance of these qualities? Your appeal to past experience decides nothing in the present case; and at the utmost can only prove, that that very object, which produc'd any other, was at that very instant endow'd with such a power; but can never prove, that the same power must continue in the same object or collection of sensible qualities; much less, that a like power is always conjoin'd with like sensible qualities. Shou'd it be said, that we have experience, that the same power continues united with the same object, and that like objects are endow'd with like powers, I wou'd renew my question, *why from this experience we form any conclusion beyond those past instances, of which we have had experience.* If you answer this question in the same manner as the preceding, your answer gives still occasion to a new question of the same kind, even *in infinitum*; which clearly proves, that the foregoing reasoning had no just foundation.

Thus not only our reason fails us in the discovery of the *ultimate connexion* of causes and effects, but even after experience has inform'd us of their *constant conjunction*, 'tis impossible for us to satisfy ourselves by our reason, why we shou'd extend that experience beyond those particular instances, which have fallen under our observation. We suppose, but are never able to prove, that there must be a resemblance betwixt those objects, of which we have had experience, and those which lie beyond the reach of our discovery.

We have already taken notice of certain relations, which make us pass from one object to another, even tho' there be no reason to determine us to that transition; and this we may establish for a general rule, that wherever the mind constantly and uniformly makes a transition without any reason, it is influenc'd by these relations. Now this is exactly the present case. Reason can never shew us the connexion of one object with another, tho' aided by experience, and the observation of their constant conjunction in all past instances. When the mind, therefore, passes from the idea or impression of one object to the idea or belief of another, it is not determin'd by reason, but by certain principles, which associate together the ideas of these objects, and unite them in the imagination. Had ideas no more union in the fancy than objects seem to have to the understanding, we cou'd never draw any inference from causes to effects, nor repose belief in any matter of fact. The inference, therefore, depends solely on the union of ideas.

The principles of union among ideas, I have reduc'd to three general ones, and have asserted, that the idea or impression of any object naturally introduces the idea of any other object, that is resembling, contiguous to, or connected with it. These principles I allow to be neither the *infallible* nor the *sole* causes of an union among ideas. They are not the infallible causes. For one may fix his attention during some time on any one object without looking farther. They are not the sole causes. For the thought has evidently a very irregular motion in running along its objects, and may leap from the heavens to the earth, from one end of the creation to the other, without any certain method or order. But tho' I allow this weakness in these three relations, and this irregularity in the imagination; yet I assert that the only *general* principles, which associate ideas, are resemblance, contiguity and causation.

There is indeed a principle of union among ideas, which at first sight may be esteem'd different from any of these, but will be found at the bottom to depend on the same origin. When ev'ry individual of any species of objects is found by experience to be constantly united with an individual of another species, the appearance of any new individual of either species naturally conveys the thought to its usual attendant. Thus because such a particular idea is commonly annex'd to such a particular word, nothing is requir'd but the hearing of that word to produce the correspondent idea; and 'twill scarce be possible for the mind, by its utmost efforts, to prevent that transition. In this case it is not absolutely necessary, that upon hearing such a particular sound, we shou'd reflect on any past experience, and consider what idea has been usually connected with the sound. The imagination of itself supplies the place of this reflection, and is so accustom'd to pass from the word to the idea, that it interposes not a moment's delay betwixt the hearing of the one, and the conception of the other.

But tho' I acknowledge this to be a true principle of association among ideas, I assert it to be the very same with that betwixt the ideas of cause and effect, and to be an essential part in all our reasonings from that relation. We have no other notion of cause and effect, but that of certain objects, which have been *always conjoin'd* together, and which in all past instances have been found inseparable. We cannot penetrate into the reason of the conjunction. We only observe the thing itself, and always find that from the constant conjunction the objects acquire an union in the imagination. When the impression of one becomes present to us, we immediately form an idea of its usual attendant; and consequently we may establish this as one part of the definition of an opinion or belief, that 'tis *an idea related to or associated with a present impression.*

Thus tho' causation be a *philosophical* relation, as implying contiguity, succession, and constant conjunction, yet 'tis only so far as it is a *natural* relation, and produces an union among our ideas, that we are able to reason upon it, or draw any inference from it.

SECT. VII

Of the nature of the idea or belief

THE idea of an object is an essential part of the belief of it, but not the whole. We conceive many things, which we do not believe. In order then to discover more fully the nature of belief, or the qualities of those ideas we assent to, let us weigh the following considerations.

'Tis evident, that all reasonings from causes or effects terminate in conclusions, concerning matter of fact; that is, concerning the existence of objects or of their qualities. 'Tis also evident, that the idea of existence is nothing different from the idea of any object, and that when after the simple conception of any thing we wou'd conceive it as existent, we in reality make no addition to or alteration on our first idea. Thus when we affirm, that God is existent, we simply form the idea of such a being, as he is represented to us; nor is the existence, which we attribute to him, conceiv'd by a particular idea, which we join to the idea of his other qualities, and can again separate and distinguish from them. But I go farther; and not content with asserting, that the conception of the existence of any object is no addition to the simple conception of it, I likewise maintain, that the belief of the existence joins no new ideas to those, which compose the idea of the object. When I think of God, when I think of him as existent, and when I believe him to be existent, my idea of him neither encreases nor diminishes. But as 'tis certain there is a great difference betwixt the simple conception of the existence of an object, and the belief of it, and as this difference lies not in the parts or composition of the idea, which we conceive; it follows, that it must lie in the *manner*, in which we conceive it.

Suppose a person present with me, who advances propositions, to which I do not assent, *that* Caesar *dy'd in his bed, that silver is more fusible than lead, or mercury heavier than gold*; 'tis evident, that notwithstanding my incredulity, I clearly understand his meaning, and form all the same ideas, which he forms. My imagination is endow'd with the same powers as his; nor is it possible for him to conceive any idea, which I cannot conceive; or conjoin any, which I cannot conjoin. I therefore ask, Wherein consists the difference betwixt believing and disbelieving any proposition? The answer is easy with regard to propositions, that are prov'd by intuition or demonstration. In that case, the person, who assents, not only conceives the ideas according to the proposition, but is necessarily determin'd to conceive them in that particular manner, either immediately or by the interposition of other ideas. Whatever is absurd is unintelligible; nor is it possible for the imagination to conceive any thing contrary to a demonstration. But as in reasonings from causation, and concerning matters of fact, this absolute necessity cannot take place, and the imagination is free to conceive both sides of the question, I still ask, *Wherein consists the difference betwixt incredulity and belief?* since in both cases the conception of the idea is equally possible and requisite.

'Twill not be a satisfactory answer to say, that a person, who does not assent to a proposition you advance; after having conceiv'd the object in the same manner with you; immediately conceives it in a different manner, and has different ideas of it. This answer is unsatisfactory; not because it contains any falsehood, but because it discovers not all the truth. 'Tis confest, that in all cases, wherein we dissent from any person, we conceive both sides of the question; but as we can believe only one, it evidently follows, that the belief must make some difference betwixt that conception to which we assent, and that from which we dissent. We may mingle, and unite, and separate, and confound, and vary our ideas in a hundred different ways; but 'till there appears some principle, which fixes one of these different situations, we have in reality no opinion: And this principle, as it plainly makes no addition to our precedent ideas, can only change the *manner* of our conceiving them.

All the perceptions of the mind are of two kinds, *viz.* impressions and ideas, which differ from each other only in their different degrees of force and vivacity. Our ideas are copy'd from our impressions, and represent them in all their parts. When you wou'd any way vary the idea of a particular object, you can only encrease or diminish its force and vivacity.[*] If you make any other change on it, it represents a different object or impression. The case is the same as in colours. A particular shade of any colour may acquire a new degree of liveliness or brightness without any other variation. But when you produce any other variation, 'tis no longer the same shade or colour. So that as belief does nothing but vary the manner, in which we conceive any object, it can only bestow on our ideas an additional force and vivacity. An opinion, therefore, or belief may be most accurately defin'd, A LIVELY IDEA RELATED TO OR ASSOCIATED WITH A PRESENT IMPRESSION†.

[* See Appendix, p. 678, for further comment.]

† We may here take occasion to observe a very remarkable error, which being frequently inculcated in the schools, has become a kind of establish'd maxim, and is universally received by all logicians. This error consists in the vulgar division of the acts of the understanding, into *conception, judgment* and *reasoning*, and in the definitions we give of them. Conception is defin'd to be the simple survey of one or more ideas: Judgment to be the separating or uniting of different ideas: Reasoning to be the separating or uniting of different ideas by the interposition of others, which show the relation they bear to each other. But these distinctions and definitions are faulty in very considerable articles. For *first*, 'tis far from being true, that in every judgment, which we form, we unite two different ideas; since in that proposition, *God is*, or indeed any other, which regards existence, the idea of existence is no distinct idea, which we unite with that of the object, and which is capable of forming a compound idea by the

Here are the heads of those arguments, which lead us to this conclusion. When we infer the existence of an object from that of others, some object must always be present either to the memory or senses, in order to be the foundation of our reasoning; since the mind cannot run up with its inferences *in infinitum*. Reason can never satisfy us that the existence of any one object does ever imply that of another; so that when we pass from the impression of one to the idea or belief of another, we are not determin'd by reason, but by custom or a principle of association. But belief is somewhat more than a simple idea. 'Tis a particular manner of forming an idea: And as the same idea can only be vary'd by a variation of its degrees of force and vivacity; it follows upon the whole, that belief is a lively idea produc'd by a relation to a present impression, according to the foregoing definition.

[*] This operation of the mind, which forms the belief of any matter of fact, seems hitherto to have been one of the greatest mysteries of philosophy; tho' no one has so much

[* The following paragraph is inserted from Hume's Appendix to Book III.]

---

union. *Secondly,* As we can thus form a proposition, which contains only one idea, so we may exert our reason without employing more than two ideas, and without having recourse to a third to serve as a medium betwixt them. We infer a cause immediately from its effect; and this inference is not only a true species of reasoning, but the strongest of all others, and more convincing than when we interpose another idea to connect the two extremes. What we may in general affirm concerning these three acts of the understanding is, that taking them in a proper light, they all resolve themselves into the first, and are nothing but particular ways of conceiving our objects. Whether we consider a single object, or several; whether we dwell on these objects, or run from them to others; and in whatever form or order we survey them, the act of the mind exceeds not a simple conception; and the only remarkable difference, which occurs on this occasion, is, when we join belief to the conception, and are persuaded of the truth of what we conceive. This act of the mind has never yet been explain'd by any philosopher; and therefore I am at liberty to propose my hypothesis concerning it; which is, that 'tis only a strong and steady conception of any idea, and such as approaches in some measure to an immediate impression.

as suspected, that there was any difficulty in explaining it. For my part I must own, that I find a considerable difficulty in the case; and that even when I think I understand the subject perfectly, I am at a loss for terms to express my meaning. I conclude, by an induction which seems to me very evident, that an opinion or belief is nothing but an idea, that is different from a fiction, not in the nature, or the order of its parts, but in the *manner* of its being conceiv'd. But when I wou'd explain this *manner*, I scarce find any word that fully answers the case, but am oblig'd to have recourse to every one's feeling, in order to give him a perfect notion of this operation of the mind. An idea assented to *feels* different from a fictitious idea, that the fancy alone presents to us: And this different feeling I endeavour to explain by calling it a superior *force*, or *vivacity*, or *solidity*, or *firmness*, or *steadiness*. This variety of terms, which may seem so unphilosophical, is intended only to express that act of the mind which renders realities more present to us than fictions, causes them to weigh more in the thought and gives them a superior influence on the passions and imagination. Provided we agree about the thing, 'tis needless to dispute about the terms. The imagination has the command over all its ideas, and can join, and mix, and vary them in all the ways possible. It may conceive objects with all the circumstances of place and time. It may set them, in a manner, before our eyes in their true colours, just as they might have existed. But as it is impossible, that that faculty can ever, of itself, reach belief, 'tis evident, that belief consists not in the nature and order of our ideas, but in the manner of their conception, and in their feeling to the mind. I confess, that 'tis impossible to explain perfectly this feeling or manner of conception. We may make use of words, that express something near it. But its true and proper name is *belief*, which is a term that every one sufficiently understands in common life. And in philosophy we can go no farther, than assert, that it is something *felt* by the mind, which distinguishes the ideas of the judgment from the fictions of the imagination. It gives them more force and influence; makes them appear of greater importance; infixes them in the mind; and renders them the governing principles of all our actions.

This definition will also be found to be entirely conformable to every one's feeling and experience. Nothing is more evident, than that those ideas, to which we assent, are more strong, firm and vivid, than the loose reveries of a castle-builder. If one person sits down to read a book as a romance, and another as a true history, they plainly receive the same ideas, and in the same order; nor does the incredulity of the one, and the belief of the other hinder them from putting the very same sense upon their author. His words produce the same ideas in both; tho' his testimony has not the same influence on them. The latter has a more lively conception of all the incidents. He enters deeper into the concerns of the persons: represents to himself their actions, and characters, and friendships, and enmities: He even goes so far as to form a notion of their features, and air, and person. While the former, who gives no credit to the testimony of the author, has a more faint and languid conception of all these particulars; and except on account of the style and ingenuity of the composition, can receive little entertainment from it.

SECT. VIII

Of the causes of belief

HAVING thus explain'd the nature of belief, and shewn that it consists in a lively idea related to a present impression; let us now proceed to examine from what principles it is deriv'd, and what bestows the vivacity on the idea.

I wou'd willingly establish it as a general maxim in the science of human nature, *that when any impression becomes present to us, it not only transports the mind to such ideas as are related to it, but likewise communicates to them a share of its force and vivacity*. All the operations of the mind depend in a great measure on its disposition, when it performs them; and according as the spirits are more or less elevated, and the attention more or less fix'd, the action will always have more or less vigour and vivacity. When therefore any object is presented, which elevates and enlivens the thought, every action, to which the mind applies, will be more strong and vivid, as long as that disposition continues. Now 'tis evident the continuance of the disposition depends entirely on the objects, about which the mind is employ'd; and that any new object naturally gives a new direction to the spirits, and changes the disposition; as on the contrary, when the mind fixes constantly on the same object, or passes easily and insensibly along related objects, the disposition has a much longer duration. Hence it happens, that when the mind is once inliven'd by a present impression, it proceeds to form a more lively idea of the related objects, by a natural transition of the disposition from the one to the other. The change of the objects is so easy, that the mind is scarce sensible of it, but applies itself to the conception of the related idea with all the force and vivacity it acquir'd from the present impression.

If in considering the nature of relation, and that facility of transition, which is essential to it, we can satisfy ourselves concerning the reality of this phaenomenon, 'tis well: But I must confess I place my chief confidence in experience to prove so material a principle. We may, therefore, observe, as the first experiment to our present purpose, that upon the appearance of the picture of an absent friend, our idea of him is evidently inliven'd by the *resemblance*, and that every passion, which that idea occasions, whether of joy or sorrow, acquires new force and vigour. In producing this effect there concur both a relation and a present impression. Where the picture bears him no resemblance, or at least was not intended for him, it never so much as conveys our thought to him: And where it is absent, as well as the person; tho' the mind may pass from the thought of the one to that of the other; it feels its idea to be rather weaken'd than inliven'd by that transition. We take a pleasure in viewing the picture of a friend, when 'tis set before us; but when 'tis remov'd rather choose to consider him directly, than by reflexion in an image, which is equally distant and obscure.

The ceremonies of the *Roman Catholic* religion may be consider'd as experiments of the same nature. The devotees of that strange superstition usually plead in excuse of the mummeries, with which they are upbraided, that they feel the good effect of those external motions, and postures, and actions, in inlivening their devotion, and quickening their fervour, which otherwise wou'd decay away, if directed entirely to distant and immaterial objects. We shadow out the objects of our faith, say they, in sensible types and images, and render them more present to us by the immediate presence of these types, than 'tis possible for us to do merely by an intellectual view and contemplation. Sensible objects have always a greater influence on the fancy than any other; and this influence they readily convey to those ideas, to which they are related, and which they resemble. I shall only infer from these practices, and this reasoning, that the effect of resemblance in inlivening the idea is very common; and as in every case a resemblance and a present impression must concur, we are abundantly supply'd with experiments to prove the reality of the foregoing principle.

We may add force to these experiments by others of a different kind in considering the effects of *contiguity*, as well as of *resemblance*. 'Tis certain, that distance diminishes the force of every idea, and that upon our approach to any object; tho' it does not discover itself to our senses; it operates upon the mind with an influence that imitates an immediate impression. The thinking on any object readily transports the mind to what is contiguous; but 'tis only the actual presence of an object, that transports it with a superior vivacity. When I am a few miles from home, whatever relates to it touches me more nearly than when I am two hundred leagues distant; tho' even at that distance the reflecting on any thing in the neighbourhood of my friends and family naturally produces an idea of them. But as in this latter case, both the objects of the mind are ideas; notwithstanding there is an easy transition betwixt them; that transition alone is not able to give a superior vivacity to any of the ideas, for want of some immediate impression.*

No one can doubt but causation has the same influence as the other two relations of resemblance and contiguity. Superstitious people are fond of the relicts of saints and holy men, for the same reason that they seek after types and images, in order to inliven their devotion, and give them a more intimate and strong conception of those exemplary lives, which they desire to imitate. Now 'tis evident, one of the best relicks a devotee cou'd procure, wou'd be the handywork of a saint; and if his cloaths and furniture are ever to

*[The following note is inserted from Hume's Appendix to Book III.]

Naturane nobis, inquit, datum dicam, an errore quodam, ut, cum ea loca videamus, in quibus memoria dignos viros acceperimus multum esse versatos, magis moveamur, quam siquando eorum ipsorum aut facta audiamus, aut scriptum aliquod legamus? velut ego nunc moveor. Venit enim mihi Platonis in mentem: quem accipimus primum hic disputare solitum: Cujus etiam illi hortuli propinqui non memoriam solûm mihi afferunt, sed ipsum videntur in conspectu meo hic ponere. Hic Speusippus, hic Xenocrates, hic ejus auditor Polemo; cujus ipsa illa sessio fuit, quam videamus. Equidem etiam curiam nostram, hostiliam dico, non hanc novam, quae mihi minor esse videtur postquam est major, solebam intuens Scipionem, Catonem, Laelium, nostrum vero in primis avum cogitare. Tanta vis admonitionis inest in locis; ut non sine causa ex his memoriae ducta sit disciplina. Cicero de Finibus, lib. 5.

['Should I,' he said, 'attribute to instinct or to some kind of illusion the fact that when we see those places in which we are told notable men spent much of their time, we are more powerfully affected than when we hear of the exploits of the men themselves or read something written? This is just what is happening to me now; for I am reminded of Plato who, we are told, was the first to make a practice of holding discussions here. Those gardens of his near by do not merely put me in mind of him; they seem to set the man himself before my very eyes. Speusippus was here; so was Xenocrates; so was his pupil, Polemo, and that very seat which we may view was his.

'Then again, when I looked at our Senate-house (I mean the old building of Hostilius, not this new one; when it was enlarged, it diminished in my estimation), I used to think of Scipio, Cato, Laelius and in particular of my own grandfather.

'Such is the power of places to evoke associations; so it is with good reason that they are used as a basis for memory training.']

be consider'd in this light, 'tis because they were once at his disposal, and were mov'd and affected by him; in which respect they are to be consider'd as imperfect effects, and as connected with him by a shorter chain of consequences than any of those, from which we learn the reality of his existence. This phaenomenon clearly proves, that a present impression with a relation of causation may enliven any idea, and consequently produce belief or assent, according to the precedent definition of it.

But why need we seek for other arguments to prove, that a present impression with a relation or transition of the fancy may inliven any idea, when this very instance of our reasonings from cause and effect will alone suffice to that purpose? 'Tis certain we must have an idea of every matter of fact, which we believe. 'Tis certain, that this idea arises only from a relation to a present impression. 'Tis certain, that the belief super-adds nothing to the idea, but only changes our manner of conceiving it, and renders it more strong and lively. The present conclusion concerning the influence of relation is the immediate consequence of all these steps; and every step appears to me sure and infallible. There enters nothing into this operation of the mind but a present impression, a lively idea, and a relation or association in the fancy betwixt the impression and idea; so that there can be no suspicion of mistake.

In order to put this whole affair in a fuller light, let us consider it as a question in natural philosophy, which we must determine by experience and observation. I suppose there is an object presented, from which I draw a certain conclusion, and form to myself ideas, which I am said to believe or assent to. Here 'tis evident, that however that object, which is present to my senses, and that other, whose existence I infer by reasoning, may be thought to influence each other by their particular powers or qualities; yet as the phaenomenon of belief, which we at present examine, is merely internal, these powers and qualities, being entirely unknown, can have no hand in producing it. 'Tis the present impression, which is to be consider'd as the true and real cause of the idea, and of the belief which attends it. We must therefore endeavour to discover by experiments the particular qualities, by which 'tis enabled to produce so extraordinary an effect.

First then I observe, that the present impression has not this effect by its own proper power and efficacy, and when consider'd alone, as a single perception, limited to the present moment. I find, that an impression, from which, on its first appearance, I can draw no conclusion, may afterwards become the foundation of belief, when I have had experience of its usual consequences. We must in every case have observ'd the same impression in past instances, and have found it to be constantly conjoin'd with some other impression. This is confirm'd by such a multitude of experiments, that it admits not of the smallest doubt.

From a second observation I conclude, that the belief, which attends the present impression, and is produc'd by a number of past impressions and conjunctions; that this belief, I say, arises immediately, without any new operation of the reason or imagination. Of this I can be certain, because I never am conscious of any such operation, and find nothing in the subject, on which it can be founded. Now as we call every thing CUSTOM, which proceeds from a past repetition, without any new reasoning or conclusion, we may establish it as a certain truth, that all the belief, which follows upon any present impression, is deriv'd solely from that origin. When we are accustom'd to see two impressions conjoin'd together, the appearance or idea of the one immediately carries us to the idea of the other.

Being fully satisfy'd on this head, I make a third set of experiments, in order to know, whether any thing be requisite, beside the customary transition, towards the production of this phaenomenon of belief. I therefore change the first impression into an idea; and observe, that tho' the customary transition to the correlative idea still remains, yet there is in reality no belief nor persuasion. A present impression, then, is absolutely requisite to this whole operation; and when after this I compare an impression with an idea, and find that their only difference consists in their different degrees of force and vivacity, I conclude upon the whole, that belief is a more vivid and intense conception of an idea, proceeding from its relation to a present impression.

Thus all probable reasoning is nothing but a species of sensation. 'Tis not solely in poetry and music, we must follow our taste and sentiment, but likewise in philosophy. When I am convinc'd of any principle, 'tis only an idea, which strikes more strongly upon me. When I give the preference to one set of arguments above another, I do nothing but decide from my feeling concerning the superiority of their influence. Objects have no discoverable connexion together; nor is it from any other principle but custom operating upon the imagination, that we can draw any inference from the appearance of one to the existence of another.

'Twill here be worth our observation, that the past experience, on which all our judgments concerning cause and effect depend, may operate on our mind in such an insensible manner as never to be taken notice of, and may even in some measure be unknown to us. A person, who stops short in his journey upon meeting a river in his way, foresees the consequences of his proceeding forward; and his knowledge of these consequences is convey'd to him by past experience, which informs him of such certain conjunctions of causes and effects. But can we think, that on this occasion he reflects on any past experience, and called to remembrance instances, that he has seen or heard of, in order to discover the effects of water on animal bodies? No surely; this is not the method, in which he proceeds in his reasoning. The idea of sinking is so closely connected with that of water, and the idea of suffocating with that of sinking, that the mind makes the transition without the assistance of the memory. The custom operates before we have time for reflection. The objects seem so inseparable, that we interpose not a moment's delay in passing from the one to the other. But as this transition proceeds from experience, and not from any primary connexion betwixt the ideas, we must necessarily acknowledge, that experience may produce a belief and a judgment of causes and effects by a secret operation, and without being once thought of. This removes all pretext, if there yet remains any, for asserting that the mind is convinc'd by reasoning of that principle, *that instances of which we have no experience, must necessarily resemble those, of which we have.* For we here find, that the understanding or imagination can draw inferences from past experience, without reflecting on it; much more without forming any principle concerning it, or reasoning upon that principle.

In general we may observe, that in all the most establish'd and uniform conjunctions of causes and effects, such as those of gravity, impulse, solidity, &c. the mind never carries its view expressly to consider any past experience: Tho' in other associations of objects, which are more rare and unusual, it may assist the custom and transition of ideas by this reflection. Nay we find in some cases, that the reflection produces the belief without the custom; or more properly speaking, that the reflection produces the custom in an *oblique* and *artificial* manner. I explain myself. 'Tis certain, that not only in philosophy, but even in common life, we may attain the knowledge of a particular cause merely by one experiment, provided it be made with judgment, and after a careful removal of all foreign and superfluous circumstances. Now as after one experiment of this kind, the mind, upon the appearance either of the cause or the effect, can draw an inference concerning the existence of its correlative; and as a habit can never be acquir'd merely by one instance; it may be thought, that belief cannot in this case be esteem'd the effect of custom. But this difficulty will vanish, if we consider, that tho' we are here suppos'd to have had only one experiment of a particular effect, yet we have many millions to convince us of this principle; *that like objects, plac'd in like circumstances, will always produce like effects*; and as this principle has establish'd itself by a sufficient custom, it bestows an evidence and firmness on any opinion, to which it can be apply'd. The connexion of the ideas is not habitual after one experiment; but this connexion is comprehended under another principle, that is habitual; which brings us back to our hypothesis. In all cases we transfer our experience to instances, of which we have no experience, either *expressly* or *tacitly*, either *directly* or *indirectly*.

I must not conclude this subject without observing, that 'tis very difficult to talk of the operations of the mind with perfect propriety and exactness; because common language has seldom made any very nice distinctions among them, but has generally call'd by the same term all such as nearly resemble each other. And as this is a source almost inevitable of obscurity and confusion in the author; so it may frequently give rise to doubts and objections in the reader, which otherwise he wou'd never have dream'd of. Thus my general position, that an opinion or belief is *nothing but a strong and lively idea deriv'd from a present impression related to it*, may be liable to the following objection, by reason of a little ambiguity in those words *strong and lively*. It may be said, that not only an impression may give rise to reasoning, but that an idea may also have the same influence; especially upon my principle, *that all our ideas are deriv'd from correspondent impressions.* For suppose I form at present an idea, of which I have forgot the correspondent impression, I am able to conclude from this idea, that such an impression did once exist; and as this conclusion is attended with belief, it may be ask'd, from whence are the qualitites of force and vivacity deriv'd, which constitute this belief? And to this I answer very readily, *from the present idea.* For as this idea is not here consider'd, as the representation of any absent object, but as a real perception in the mind, of which we are intimately conscious, it must be able to bestow on whatever is related to it the same quality, call it *firmness, or solidity, or force, or vivacity*, with which the mind reflects upon it, and is assur'd of its present existence. The idea here supplies the place of an impression, and is entirely the same, so far as regards our present purpose.

Upon the same principles we need not be surpriz'd to hear of the remembrance of an idea; that is, of the idea of an idea, and of its force and vivacity superior to the loose conceptions of the imagination. In thinking of our past thoughts we not only delineate out the objects, of which we were thinking, but also conceive the action of the mind in the meditation, that certain *je-ne-sçai-quoi*, of which 'tis impossible to give any definition or description, but which every one sufficiently understands. When the memory offers an idea of this, and represents it as past, 'tis easily conceiv'd how that idea may have more vigour and firmness, than when we think of a past thought, of which we have no remembrance.

After this any one will understand how we may form the idea of an impression and of an idea, and how we may believe the existence of an impression and of an idea.

SECT. IX

Of the effects of other relations and other habits

HOWEVER convincing the foregoing arguments may appear, we must not rest contented with them, but must turn the subject on every side, in order to find some new points of view, from which we may illustrate and confirm such extraordinary, and such fundamental principles. A scrupulous hesitation to receive any new hypothesis is so laudable a disposition in philosophers, and so necessary to the examination of truth, that it deserves to be comply'd with, and requires that every argument be produc'd, which may tend to their satisfaction, and every objection remov'd, which may stop them in their reasoning.

I have often observ'd, that, beside cause and effect, the two relations of resemblance and contiguity, are to be consider'd as associating principles of thought, and as capable of conveying the imagination from one idea to another. I have also observ'd, that when of two objects connected together by any of these relations, one is immediately present to the memory or senses, not only the mind is convey'd to its co-relative by means of the associating principle; but likewise conceives it with an additional force and vigour, by the united operation of that principle, and of the present impression. All this I have observ'd, in order to confirm by analogy, my explication of our judgments concerning cause and effect. But this very argument may, perhaps, be turn'd against me, and instead of a confirmation of my hypothesis, may become an objection to it. For it may be said, that if all the parts of that hypothesis be true, *viz. that* these three species of relation are deriv'd from the same principles; *that* their effects in inforcing and inlivening our ideas are the same; and *that* belief is nothing but a more forcible and vivid conception of an idea; it shou'd follow, that that action of the mind may not only be deriv'd from the relation of cause and effect, but also from those of contiguity and resemblance. But as we find by experience, that belief arises only from causation, and that we can draw no inference from one object to another, except they be connected by this relation, we may conclude, that there is some error in that reasoning, which leads us into such difficulties.

This is the objection; let us now consider its solution. 'Tis evident, that whatever is present to the memory, striking upon the mind with a vivacity, which resembles an immediate impression, must become of considerable moment in all the operations of the mind, and must easily distinguish itself above the mere fictions of the imagination. Of these impressions or ideas of the memory we form a kind of system, comprehending whatever we remember to have been present, either to our internal perception or senses; and every particular of that system, join'd to the present impressions, we are pleas'd to call a *reality*. But the mind stops not here. For finding, that with this system of perceptions, there is another connected by custom, or if you will, by the relation of cause or effect, it proceeds to the consideration of their ideas; and as it feels that 'tis in a manner necessarily determin'd to view these particular ideas, and that the custom or relation, by which it is determin'd, admits not of the least change, it forms them into a new system, which it likewise dignifies with the title of *realities*. The first of these systems is the object of the memory and senses; the second of the judgment.

'Tis this latter principle, which peoples the world, and brings us acquainted with such existences, as by their removal in time and place, lie beyond the reach of the senses and memory. By means of it I paint the universe in my imagination, and fix my attention on any part of it I please. I form an idea of ROME, which I neither see nor remember; but which is connected with such impressions as I remember to have received from the conversation and books of travellers and historians. This idea of *Rome* I place in a certain situation on the idea of an object, which I call the globe. I join to it the conception of a particular government, and religion, and manners. I look backward and consider its first foundation; its several revolutions, successes, and misfortunes. All this, and every thing else, which I believe, are nothing but ideas; tho' by their force and settled order, arising from custom and the relation of cause and effect, they distinguish themselves from the other ideas, which are merely the offspring of the imagination.

As to the influence of contiguity and resemblance, we may observe, that if the contiguous and resembling object be comprehended in this system of realities, there is no doubt but these two relations will assist that of cause and effect, and infix the related idea with more force in the imagination. This I shall enlarge upon presently. Mean while I shall carry my observation a step farther, and assert, that even where the related object is but feign'd, the relation will serve to enliven the idea, and encrease its influence. A poet, no doubt, will be the better able to form a strong description of the *Elysian* fields, that he prompts his imagination by the view of a beautiful meadow or garden; as at another time he may by his fancy place himself in the midst of these fabulous regions, that by the feign'd contiguity he may enliven his imagination.

But tho' I cannot altogether exclude the relations of resemblance and contiguity from operating on the fancy in this manner, 'tis observable that, when single, their influence is very feeble and uncertain. As the relation of cause and effect is requisite to persuade us of any real existence, so is this persuasion requisite to give force to these other relations. For where upon the appearance of an impression we not only feign another object, but likewise arbitrarily, and of our mere good-will and pleasure give it a particular relation to the impression, this can have but a small effect upon the mind; nor is there any reason, why, upon return of the same impression, we shou'd be determin'd to place the same object in the same relation to it. There is no manner of necessity for the mind to feign any resembling and contiguous objects; and if it feigns such, there is as little necessity for it always to confine itself to the same, without any difference or variation. And indeed such a fiction is founded on so little reason, that nothing but pure *caprice* can determine the mind to form it; and that principle being fluctuating and uncertain, 'tis impossible it can ever operate with any considerable degree of force and constancy. The mind forsees and anticipates the change; and even from the very first instant feels the looseness of its actions, and the weak hold it has of its objects. And as this imperfection is very sensible in every single instance, it still encreases by experience and observation, when we compare the several instances we may remember, and form a *general rule* against the reposing any assurance in those momentary glimpses of light, which arise in the imagination from a feign'd resemblance and contiguity.

The relation of cause and effect has all the opposite advantages. The objects it presents are fixt and unalterable. The impressions of the memory never change in any considerable degree; and each impression draws along with it a precise idea, which takes its place in the imagination, as something solid and real, certain and invariable. The thought is always determin'd to pass from the impression to the idea, and from that particular impression to that particular idea, without any choice or hesitation.

But not content with removing this objection, I shall endeavour to extract from it a proof of the present doctrine. Contiguity and resemblance have an effect much inferior to causation; but still have some effect, and augment the conviction of any opinion, and the vivacity of any conception. If this can be prov'd in several new instances, beside what we have already observ'd, 'twill be allow'd no inconsiderable argument, that belief is nothing but a lively idea related to a present impression.

To begin with contiguity; it has been remark'd among the *Mahometans* as well as *Christians*, that those *pilgrims*, who have seen MECCA or the HOLY LAND are ever after more faithful and zealous believers, than those who have not had that advantage. A man, whose memory presents him with a lively image of the *Red-Sea, and the Desert, and Jerusalem, and Galilee*, can never doubt of any miraculous events, which are related either by *Moses or the Evangelists*. The lively idea of the places passes by an easy transition to the facts, which are suppos'd to have been related to them by contiguity, and encreases the belief by encreasing the vivacity of the conception. The remembrance of these fields and rivers has the same influence on the vulgar as a new argument; and from the same causes.

We may form a like observation concerning *resemblance*. We have remark'd, that the conclusion, which we draw from a present object to its absent cause or effect, is never founded on any qualities, which we observe in that object, consider'd in itself; or, in other words, that 'tis impossible to determine, otherwise than by experience, what will result from any phaenomenon, or what has preceeded it. But tho' this be so evident in itself, that it seem'd not to require any proof; yet some philosophers have imagin'd that there is an apparent cause for the communication of motion, and that a reasonable man might immediately infer the motion of one body from the impulse of another, without having recourse to any past observation. That this opinion is false will admit of an easy proof. For if such an inference may be drawn merely from the ideas of body, of motion, and of impulse, it must amount to a demonstration, and must imply the absolute impossibility of any contrary supposition. Every effect, then, beside the communication of motion, implies a formal contradiction; and 'tis impossible, not only that it can exist, but also that it can be conceiv'd. But we may soon satisfy ourselves of the contrary, by forming a clear and consistent idea of one body's moving upon another, and of its rest immediately upon the contact; or of its returning back in the same line, in which it came; or of its annihilation; or circular or elliptical motion: and in short, of an infinite number of other changes, which we may suppose it to undergo. These suppositions are all confident and natural; and the reason, why we imagine the communication of motion to be more consistent and natural not only than those suppositions, but also than any other natural effect, is founded on the relation of *resemblance* betwixt the cause and effect, which is here united to experience, and binds the objects in the closest and most intimate manner to each other, so as to make us imagine them to be absolutely inseparable. Resemblance, then, has the same or a parallel influence with experience; and as the only immediate effect of experience is to associate our ideas together, it follows, that all belief arises from the association of ideas, according to my hypothesis.

'Tis universally allow'd by the writers on optics, that the eye at all times sees an equal number of physical points, and that a man on the top of a mountain has no larger an image presented to his senses, than when he is coop'd up in the narrowest court or chamber. 'Tis only by experience that he infers the greatness of the object from some peculiar qualities of the image; and this inference of the judgment he confounds with sensation, as is common on other occasions. Now 'tis evident, that the inference of the judgment is here much more lively than what is usual in our common reasonings, and that a man has a more vivid conception of the vast extent of the ocean from the image he receives by the eye, when he stands on the top of a high promontory, than merely from hearing the roaring of the waters. He feels a more sensible pleasure from its magnificence; which is a proof of a more lively idea: And he confounds his judgment with sensation; which is another proof of it. But as the inference is equally certain and immediate in both cases, this superior vivacity of our conception in one case can proceed from nothing but this, that in drawing an inference from the sight, beside the customary conjunction, there is also a resemblance betwixt the image and the object we infer; which strengthens the relation, and conveys the vivacity of the impression to the related idea with an easier and more natural movement.

No weakness of human nature is more universal and conspicuous than what we commonly call CREDULITY, or a too easy faith in the testimony of others; and this weakness is also very naturally accounted for from the influence of resemblance. When we receive any matter of fact upon human testimony, our faith arises from the very same origin as our inferences from causes to effects, and from effects to causes; nor is there any thing but our *experience* of the governing principles of human nature, which can give us any assurance of the veracity of men. But tho' experience be the true standard of this, as well as of all other judgments, we seldom regulate ourselves entirely by it; but have a remarkable propensity to believe whatever is reported, even concerning apparitions, enchantments, and prodigies, however contrary to daily experience and observation. The words or discourses of others have an intimate connexion with certain ideas in their mind; and these ideas have also a connexion with the facts or objects, which they represent. This latter connexion is generally much over-rated, and commands our assent beyond what experience will justify; which can proceed from nothing beside the resemblance betwixt the ideas and the facts. Other effects only point out their causes in an oblique manner; but the testimony of men does it directly, and is to be consider'd as an image as well as an effect. No wonder, therefore, we are so rash in drawing our inferences from it, and are less guided by experience in our judgments concerning it, than in those upon any other subject.

As resemblance, when conjoin'd with causation, fortifies our reasonings; so the want of it in any very great degree is able almost entirely to destroy them. Of this there is a remarkable instance in the universal carelessness and stupidity of men with regard to a future state, where they show as obstinate an incredulity, as they do a blind credulity on other occasions. There is not indeed a more ample matter of wonder to the studious, and of regret to the pious man, than to observe the negligence of the bulk of mankind concerning their approaching condition; and 'tis with reason, that many eminent theologians have not scrupled to affirm, that tho' the vulgar have no formal principles of infidelity, yet they are really infidels in their hearts, and have nothing like what we can call a belief of the eternal duration of their souls. For let us consider on the one hand what divines have display'd with such eloquence concerning the importance of eternity; and at the same time reflect, that tho' in matters of rhetoric we ought to lay our account with some exaggeration, we must in this case allow, that the strongest figures are infinitely inferior to the subject: And after this let us view on the other hand the prodigious security of men in this particular: I ask, if these people really believe what is inculcated on them, and what they pretend to affirm; and the answer is obviously in the negative. As belief is an act of the mind arising from custom, 'tis not strange the want of resemblance shou'd overthrow what custom has establish'd, and diminish the force of the idea, as much as that latter principle encreases it. A future state is so far remov'd from our comprehension, and we have so obscure an idea of the manner, in which we shall exist after the dissolution of the body, that all the reasons we can invent, however strong in themselves, and however much assisted by education, are never able with slow imaginations to surmount this difficulty, or bestow a sufficient authority and force on the idea. I rather choose to ascribe this incredulity to the faint idea we form of our future condition, deriv'd from its want of resemblance to the present life, than to that deriv'd from its remoteness. For I observe, that men are every where concern'd about what may happen after their death, provided it regard this world; and that there are few to whom their name, their family, their friends, and their country are in any period of time entirely indifferent.

And indeed the want of resemblance in this case so entirely destroys belief, that except those few, who upon cool reflection on the importance of the subject, have taken care by repeated meditation to imprint in their minds the arguments for a future state, there scarce are any, who believe the immortality of the soul with a true and establish'd judgment; such as is deriv'd from the testimony of travellers and historians. This appears very conspicuously wherever men have occasion to compare the pleasures and pains, the rewards and punishments of this life with those of a future; even tho' the case does not concern themselves, and there is no violent passion to disturb their judgment. The *Roman Catholicks* are certainly the most zealous of any sect in the christian world; and yet you'll find few among the more sensible people of that communion, who do not blame the *Gunpowder-treason*, and the massacre of St *Bartholemew*, as cruel and barbarous, tho' projected or executed against those very people, whom without any scruple they condemn to eternal and infinite punishments. All we can say in excuse for this inconsistency is, that they really do not believe what they affirm concerning a future state; nor is there any better proof of it than the very inconsistency.

We may add to this a remark; that in matters of religion men take a pleasure in being terrify'd, and that no preachers are so popular, as those who excite the most dismal and gloomy passions. In the common affairs of life, where we feel and are penetrated with the solidity of the subject, nothing can be more disagreeable than fear and terror; and 'tis only in dramatic performances and in religious discourses, that they ever give pleasure. In these latter cases the imagination reposes itself indolently on the idea; and the passion, being soften'd by the want of belief in the subject, has no more than the agreeable effect of enlivening the mind, and fixing the attention.

The present hypothesis will receive additional confirmation, if we examine the effects of other kinds of custom, as well as of other relations. To understand this we must consider that custom, to which I attribute all belief and reasoning, may operate upon the mind in invigorating an idea after two several ways. For supposing that in all past experience we have found two objects to have been always conjoin'd together, 'tis evident, that upon the appearance of one of these objects in an impression, we must from custom make an easy transition to the idea of that object, which usually attends it; and by means of the present impression and easy transition must conceive that idea in a stronger and more lively manner, than we do any loose floating image of the fancy. But let us next suppose, that a mere idea alone, without any of this curious and almost artificial preparation, shou'd frequently make its appearance in the mind, this idea must by degrees acquire a facility and force; and both by its firm hold and easy introduction distinguish itself from any new and unusual idea. This is the only particular, in which these two kinds of custom agree; and if it appear, that their effects on the judgment are similar and proportionable, we may certainly conclude, that the foregoing explication of that faculty is satisfactory. But can we doubt of this agreement in their influence on the judgment, when we consider the nature and effects of EDUCATION?

All those opinions and notions of things, to which we have been accustom'd from our infancy, take such deep root, that 'tis impossible for us, by all the powers of reason and experience, to eradicate them; and this habit not only approaches in its influence, but even on many occasions prevails over that which arises from the constant and inseparable union of causes and effects. Here we must not be contented with saying, that the vividness of the idea produces the belief: We must maintain that they are individually the same. The frequent repetion of any idea infixes it in the imagination; but cou'd never possibly of itself produce belief, if that act of the mind was, by the original constitution of our natures, annex'd only to a reasoning and comparison of ideas. Custom may lead us into some false comparison of ideas. This is the utmost effect we can conceive of it. But 'tis certain it cou'd never supply the place of that comparison, nor produce any act of the mind, which naturally belong'd to that principle.

A person, that has lost a leg or an arm by amputation, endeavours for a long time afterwards to serve himself with them. After the death of any one, 'tis a common remark of the whole family, but especially of the servants, that they can scarce believe him to be dead, but still imagine him to be in his chamber or in any other place, where they were accustom'd to find him. I have often heard in conversation, after talking of a person, that is any way celebrated, that one, who has no acquaintance with him, will say, *I have never seen such-a-one, but almost fancy I have; so often have I heard talk of him*. All these are parallel instances.

If we consider this argument from *education* in a proper light, 'twill appear very convincing; and the more so, that 'tis founded on one of the most common phaenomena, that is any where to be met with. I am persuaded, that upon examination we shall find more than one half of those opinions, that prevail among mankind, to be owing to education, and that the principles, which are thus implicitely embrac'd, over-ballance those, which are owing either to abstract reasoning or experience. As liars, by the frequent repetition of their lies, come at last to remember them; so the judgment, or rather the imagination, by the like means, may have ideas so strongly imprinted on it, and conceive them in so full a light, that they may operate upon the mind in the same manner with those, which the senses, memory or reason present to us. But as education is an artificial and not a natural cause, and as its maxims are frequently contrary to reason, and even to themselves in different times and places, it is never upon that account recogniz'd by philosophers; tho' in reality it be built almost on the same foundation of custom and repetition as our reasonings from causes and effects *.

SECT. X

Of the influence of belief

BUT tho' education be disclaim'd by philosophy, as a fallacious ground of assent to any opinion, it prevails nevertheless in the world, and is the cause why all systems are apt to be rejected at first as new and unusual. This perhaps will be the fate of what I have here advanc'd concerning *belief*, and tho' the proofs I have produc'd appear to me perfectly conclusive, I expect not to make many proselytes to my opinion. Men will scarce ever be persuaded, that effects of such consequence can flow from principles, which are seemingly so inconsiderable, and that the far greatest part of our reasonings with all our actions and passions, can be deriv'd from nothing but custom and habit. To obviate this objection, I shall here anticipate a little what wou'd more properly fall under our consideration afterwards, when we come to treat of the passions and the sense of beauty.

There is implanted in the human mind a perception of pain and pleasure, as the chief spring and moving principle of all its actions. But pain and pleasure have two ways of making their appearance in the mind; of which

*In general we may observe, that as our assent to all probable reasonings is founded on the vivacity of ideas, it resembles many of those whimsies and prejudices, which are rejected under the opprobrious character of being the offspring of the imagination. By this expression it appears that the word, imagination, is commonly us'd in two different senses; and tho' nothing be more contrary to true philosophy, than this inaccuracy, yet in the following reasonings I have often been oblig'd to fall into it. When I oppose the imagination to the memory, I mean the faculty, by which we form our fainter ideas. When I oppose it to reason, I mean the same faculty, excluding only our demonstrative and probable reasonings. When I oppose it to neither, 'tis indifferent whether it be taken in the larger or more limited sense, or at least the context will sufficiently explain the meaning.

the one has effects very different from the other. They may either appear in impression to the actual feeling, or only in idea, as at present when I mention them. 'Tis evident the influence of these upon our actions is far from being equal. Impressions always actuate the soul, and that in the highest degree; but 'tis not every idea which has the same effect. Nature has proceeded with caution in this case, and seems to have carefully avoided the inconveniences of two extremes. Did impressions alone influence the will, we should every moment of our lives be subject to the greatest calamities; because, tho' we foresaw their approach, we should not be provided by nature with any principle of action, which might impel us to avoid them. On the other hand, did every idea influence our actions, our condition would not be much mended. For such is the unsteadiness and activity of thought, that the images of every thing, especially of goods and evils, are always wandering in the mind; and were it mov'd by every idle conception of this kind, it would never enjoy a moment's peace and tranquillity.

Nature has, therefore, chosen a medium, and has neither bestow'd on every idea of good and evil the power of actuating the will, nor yet has entirely excluded them from this influence. Tho' an idle fiction has no efficacy, yet we find by experience, that the ideas of those objects, which we believe either are or will be existent, produce in a lesser degree the same effect with those impressions, which are immediately present to the senses and perception. The effect, then, of belief is to raise up a simple idea to an equality with our impressions, and bestow on it a like influence on the passions. This effect it can only have by making an idea approach an impression in force and vivacity. For as the different degrees of force make all the original difference betwixt an impression and an idea, they must of consequence be the source of all the differences in the effects of these perceptions, and their removal, in whole or in part, the cause of every new resemblance they acquire. Wherever we can make an idea approach the impressions in force and vivacity, it will likewise imitate them in its influence on the mind; and *vice versa*, where it imitates them in that influence, as in the present case, this must proceed from its approaching them in force and vivacity. Belief, therefore, since it causes an idea to imitate the effects of the impressions, must make it resemble them in these qualities, and is nothing but *a more vivid and intense conception of any idea*. This, then, may both serve as an additional argument for the present system, and may give us a notion after what manner our reasonings from causation are able to operate on the will and passions.

As belief is almost absolutely requisite to the exciting our passions, so the passions in their turn are very favourable to belief; and not only such facts as convey agreeable emotions, but very often such as give pain, do upon that account become more readily the objects of faith and opinion. A coward, whose fears are easily awaken'd, readily assents to every account of danger he meets with; as a person of a sorrowful and melancholy disposition is very credulous of every thing, that nourishes his prevailing passion. When any affecting object is presented, it gives the alarm, and excites immediately a degree of its proper passion; especially in persons who are naturally inclined to that passion. This emotion passes by an easy transition to the imagination; and diffusing itself over our idea of the affecting object, makes us form that idea with greater force and vivacity, and consequently assent to it, according to the precedent system. Admiration and surprize have the same effect as the other passions; and accordingly we may observe, that among the vulgar, quacks and projectors meet with a more easy faith upon account of their magnificent pretensions, than if they kept themselves within the bounds of moderation. The first astonishment, which naturally attends their miraculous relations, spreads itself over the whole soul, and so vivifies and enlivens the idea, that it resembles the inferences we draw from experience. This is a mystery, with which we may be already a little acquainted, and which we shall have farther occasion to be let into in the progress of this treatise.

After this account of the influence of belief on the passions, we shall find less difficulty in explaining its effects on the imagination, however extraordinary they may appear. 'Tis certain we cannot take pleasure in any discourse, where our judgment gives no assent to those images which are presented to our fancy. The conversation of those, who have acquir'd a habit of lying, tho' in affairs of no moment, never gives any satisfaction; and that because those ideas they present to us, not being attended with belief, make no impression upon the mind. Poets themselves, tho' liars by profession, always endeavour to give an air of truth to their fictions; and where that is totally neglected, their performances, however ingenious, will never be able to afford much pleasure. In short, we may observe, that even when ideas have no manner of influence on the will and passions, truth and reality are still requisite, in order to make them entertaining to the imagination.

But if we compare together all the phaenomena that occur on this head, we shall find, that truth, however necessary it may seem in all works of genius, has no other effect than to procure an easy reception for the ideas, and to make the mind acquiesce in them with satisfaction, or at least without reluctance. But as this is an effect, which may easily be supposed to flow from that solidity and force, which, according to my system, attend those ideas that are establish'd by reasonings from causation; it follows, that all the influence of belief upon the fancy may be explained from that system. Accordingly we may observe, that wherever that influence arises from any other principles beside truth or reality, they supply its place, and give an equal entertainment to the imagination. Poets have form'd what they call a poetical system of things, which tho' it be believ'd neither by themselves nor readers, is commonly esteem'd a sufficient foundation for any fiction. We have been so much accustom'd to the names of MARS, JUPITER, VENUS, that in the same manner as education infixes any opinion, the constant repetition of these ideas makes them enter into the mind with facility, and prevail upon the fancy, without influencing the judgment. In like manner tragedians always borrow their fable, or at least the names of their principal actors, from some known passage in history; and that not in order to deceive the spectators; for they will frankly confess, that truth is not in any circumstance inviolably observed; but in order to procure a more easy reception into the imagination for those extraordinary events, which they represent. But this is a precaution, which is not required of comic poets, whose personages and incidents, being of a more familiar kind, enter easily into the conception, and are received without any such formality, even tho' at first sight they be known to be fictitious, and the pure off-spring of the fancy.

This mixture of truth and falsehood in the fables of tragic poets not only serves our present purpose, by shewing, that the imagination can be satisfy'd without any absolute belief or assurance; but may in another view be regarded as a very strong confirmation of this system. 'Tis evident, that poets make use of this artifice of borrowing the names of their persons, and the chief events of their poems, from history, in order to procure a more easy reception for the whole, and cause it to make a deeper impression on the fancy and affections. The several incidents of the piece acquire a kind of relation by being united into one poem or representation; and if any of these incidents be an object of belief, it bestows a force and vivacity on the others, which are related to it. The vividness of the first conception diffuses itself along the relations, and is convey'd, as by so many pipes or canals, to every idea that has any communication with the primary one. This, indeed, can never amount to a perfect assurance; and that because the union among the ideas is, in a manner, accidental: But still it approaches so near, in its influence, as may convince us, that they are deriv'd from the same origin. Belief must please the imagination by means of the force and vivacity which attends it; since every idea, which has force and vivacity, is found to be agreeable to that faculty.

To confirm this we may observe, that the assistance is

mutual betwixt the judgment and fancy, as well as betwixt the judgment and passion; and that belief not only gives vigour to the imagination, but that a vigorous and strong imagination is of all talents the most proper to procure belief and authority. 'Tis difficult for us to withold our assent from what is painted out to us in all the colours of eloquence; and the vivacity produc'd by the fancy is in many cases greater than that which arises from custom and experience. We are hurried away by the lively imagination of our author or companion; and even he himself is often a victim to his own fire and genius.

Nor will it be amiss to remark, that as a lively imagination very often degenerates into madness or folly, and bears it a great resemblance in its operations; so they influence the judgment after the same manner, and produce belief from the very same principles. When the imagination, from any extraordinary ferment of the blood and spirits, acquires such a vivacity as disorders all its powers and faculties, there is no means of distinguishing betwixt truth and falshood; but every loose fiction or idea, having the same influence as the impressions of the memory, or the conclusions of the judgment, is receiv'd on the same footing, and operates with equal force on the passions. A present impression and a customary transition are now no longer necessary to inliven our ideas. Every chimera of the brain is as vivid and intense as any of those inferences, which we formerly dignify'd with the name of conclusions concerning matters of fact, and sometimes as the present impressions of the senses.

[*] We may observe the same effect of poetry in a lesser degree; and this is common both to poetry and madness, that the vivacity they bestow on the ideas is not deriv'd from the particular situations or connexions of the objects of these ideas, but from the present temper and disposition of the person. But how great soever the pitch may be, to which this vivacity rise, 'tis evident, that in poetry it never has the same *feeling* with that which arises in the mind,

[* The following three paragraphs are inserted from Hume's Appendix to Book III.]

when we reason, tho' even upon the lowest species of probability. The mind can easily distinguish betwixt the one and the other; and whatever emotion the poetical enthusiasm may give to the spirits, 'tis still the mere phantom of belief or persuasion. The case is the same with the idea, as with the passion it occasions. There is no passion of the human mind but what may arise from poetry; tho' at the same time the *feelings* of the passions are very different when excited by poetical fictions, from what they are when they arise from belief and reality. A passion, which is disagreeable in real life, may afford the highest entertainment in a tragedy, or epic poem. In the latter case it lies not with that weight upon us: It feels less firm and solid: And has no other than the agreeable effect of exciting the spirits, and rouzing the attention. The difference in the passions is a clear proof of a like difference in those ideas, from which the passions are deriv'd. Where the vivacity arises from a customary conjunction with a present impression; tho' the imagination may not, in appearance, be so much mov'd; yet there is always something more forcible and real in its actions, than in the fervors of poetry and eloquence. The force of our mental actions in this case, no more than in any other, is not to be measur'd by the apparent agitation of the mind. A poetical description may have a more sensible effect on the fancy, than an historical narration. It may collect more of those circumstances, that form a compleat image or picture. It may seem to set the object before us in more lively colours. But still the ideas it presents are different to the *feeling* from those, which arise from the memory and the judgment. There is something weak and imperfect amidst all that seeming vehemence of thought and sentiment, which attends the fictions of poetry.

We shall afterwards have occasion to remark both the resemblances and differences betwixt a poetical enthusiasm, and a serious conviction. In the mean time I cannot forbear observing, that the great difference in their feeling proceeds in some measure from reflection and *general rules.* We observe, that the vigour of conception, which fictions receive from poetry and eloquence, is a circumstance merely accidental, of which every idea is equally susceptible; and that such fictions are connected with nothing that is real. This observation makes us only lend ourselves, so to speak, to the fiction: But causes the idea to feel very different from the eternal establish'd persuasions founded on memory and custom. They are somewhat of the same kind: But the one is much inferior to the other, both in its causes and effects.

A like reflection on *general rules* keeps us from augmenting our belief upon every encrease of the force and vivacity of our ideas. Where an opinion admits of no doubt, or opposite probability, we attribute to it a full conviction; tho' the want of resemblance, or contiguity, may render its force inferior to that of other opinions. 'Tis thus the understanding corrects the appearances of the senses, and makes us imagine, that an object at twenty foot distance seems even to the eye as large as one of the same dimensions at ten.

We may observe the same effect of poetry in a lesser degree; only with this difference, that the least reflection dissipates the illusions of poetry, and places the objects in their proper light. 'Tis however certain, that in the warmth of a poetical enthusiasm, a poet has a counterfeit belief, and even a kind of vision of his objects: And if there be any shadow of argument to support this belief, nothing contributes more to his full conviction than a blaze of poetical figures and images, which have their effect upon the poet himself, as well as upon his readers.

SECT. XI

Of the probability of chances

But in order to bestow on this system its full force and evidence, we must carry our eye from it a moment to consider its consequences, and explain from the same principles some other species of reasoning, which are deriv'd from the same origin.

Those philosophers, who have divided human reason into *knowledge and probability*, and have defin'd the first to be *that evidence, which arises from the comparison of ideas*, are oblig'd to comprehend all our arguments from causes or effects under the general term of probability. But tho' every one be free to use his terms in what sense he pleases; and accordingly in the precedent part of this discourse, I have follow'd this method of expression; 'tis however certain, that in common discourse we readily affirm, that many arguments from causation exceed probability, and may be receiv'd as a superior kind of evidence. One wou'd appear ridiculous, who wou'd say, that 'tis only probable the sun will rise to-morrow, or that all men must dye; tho' 'tis plain we have no further assurance of these facts, than what experience affords us. For this reason, 'twould perhaps be more convenient, in order at once to preserve the common signification of words, and mark the several degrees of evidence, to distinguish human reason into three kinds, viz. *that from knowledge, from proofs, and from probabilities*. By knowledge, I mean the assurance arising from the comparison of ideas. By proofs, those arguments, which are deriv'd from the relation of cause and effect, and which are entirely free from doubt and uncertainty. By probability, that evidence, which is still attended with uncertainty. 'Tis this last species of reasoning, I proceed to examine.

Probability or reasoning from conjecture may be divided into two kinds, *viz*. that which is founded on *chance*, and that which arises from *causes*. We shall consider each of these in order.

The idea of cause and effect is deriv'd from experience, which presenting us with certain objects constantly conjoin'd with each other, produces such a habit of surveying them in that relation, that we cannot without a sensible violence survey them in any other. On the other hand, as chance is nothing real in itself, and properly speaking, is merely the negation of a cause, its influence on the mind is contrary to that of causation; and 'tis essential to it, to leave the imagination perfectly indifferent, either to consider the existence or non-existence of that object, which is regarded as contingent. A cause traces the way to our thought, and in a manner forces us to survey such certain objects, in such certain relations. Chance can only destroy this determination of the thought, and leave the mind in its native situation of indifference; in which, upon the absence of a cause, 'tis instantly re-instated.

Since therefore an entire indifference is essential to chance, no one chance can possibly be superior to another, otherwise than as it is composed of a superior number of equal chances. For if we affirm that one chance can, after any other manner, be superior to another, we must at the same time affirm, that there is something, which gives it the superiority, and determines the event rather to that side than the other: That is, in other words, we must allow of a cause, and destroy the supposition of chance; which we had before establish'd. A perfect and total indifference is essential to chance, and one total indifference can never in itself be either superior or inferior to another. This truth is not peculiar to my system, but is acknowledg'd by every one, that forms calculations concerning chances.

And here 'tis remarkable, that tho' chance and causation be directly contrary, yet 'tis impossible for us to conceive this combination of chances, which is requisite to render one hazard superior to another, without supposing a mixture of causes among the chances, and a conjunction of necessity in some particulars, with a total indifference in others. Where nothing limits the chances, every notion, that the most extravagant fancy can form, is upon a footing of equality; nor can there be any circumstance to give one the advantage above another. Thus unless we allow, that there are some causes to make the dice fall, and preserve their form in their fall, and lie upon some one of their sides, we can form no calculation concerning the laws of hazard. But supposing these causes to operate, and supposing likewise all the rest to be indifferent and to be determin'd by chance, 'tis easy to arrive at a notion of a superior combination of chances. A dye, that has four sides mark'd with a certain number of spots, and only two with another, affords us an obvious and easy instance of this superiority. The mind is here limited by the causes to such a precise number and quality of the events; and at the same time is undetermin'd in its choice of any particular event.

Proceeding then in that reasoning, wherein we have advanc'd three steps; *that* chance is merely the negation of a cause, and produces a total indifference in the mind; *that* one negation of a cause and one total indifference can never be superior or inferior to another; and *that* there must always be a mixture of causes among the chances, in order to be the foundation of any reasoning: We are next to consider what effect a superior combination of chances can have upon the mind, and after what manner it influences our judgment and opinion. Here we may repeat all the same arguments we employ'd in examining that belief, which arises from causes; and may prove after the same manner, that a superior number of chances produces our assent neither by *demonstration* nor *probability*. 'Tis indeed evident, that we can never by the comparison of mere ideas make any discovery, which can be of consequence in this affair, and that 'tis impossible to prove with certainty, that any event must fall on that side where there is a superior number of chances. To suppose in this case any certainty, were to overthrow what we have establish'd concerning the opposition of chances, and their perfect equality and indifference.

Shou'd it be said, that tho' in an opposition of chances 'tis impossible to determine with *certainty*, on which side the event will fall, yet we can pronounce with certainty, that 'tis more likely and probable, 'twill be on that side where there is a superior number of chances, than where there is an inferior: Shou'd this be said, I wou'd ask, what is here meant by *likelihood and probability*? The likelihood and probability of chances is a superior number of equal chances; and consequently when we say 'tis likely the event will fall on the side, which is superior, rather than on the inferior, we do no more than affirm, that where there is a superior number of chances there is actually a superior, and where there is an inferior there is an inferior; which are identical propositions, and of no consequence. The question is, by what means a superior number of equal chances operates upon the mind, and produces belief or assent; since it appears, that 'tis neither by arguments deriv'd from demonstration, nor from probability.

In order to clear up this difficulty, we shall suppose a person to take a dye, form'd after such a manner as that four of its sides are mark'd with one figure, or one number of spots, and two with another; and to put this dye into the box with an intention of throwing it: 'Tis plain, he must conclude the one figure to be more probable than the other, and give the preference to that which is inscrib'd on the greatest number of sides. He in a manner believes, that this will lie uppermost; tho' still with hesitation and doubt, in proportion to the number of chances, which are contrary. And according as these contrary chances, diminish, and the superiority encreases on the other side, his belief acquires new degrees of stability and assurance. This belief arises from an operation of the mind upon the simple and limited object before us; and therefore its nature will be the more easily discover'd and explain'd. We have nothing but one single dye to contemplate, in order to comprehend one of the most curious operations of the understanding.

This dye form'd as above, contains three circumstances worthy of our attention. *First*, Certain causes, such as gravity, solidity, a cubical figure, *&c.* which determine it to fall, to preserve its form in its fall, and to turn up one of its sides. *Secondly*, A certain number of sides, which are suppos'd indifferent. *Thirdly*, A certain figure, inscrib'd on each side. These three particulars form the whole nature of the dye, so far as relates to our present purpose; and consequently are the only circumstances regarded by the mind in its forming a judgment concerning the result of such a throw. Let us, therefore, consider gradually and carefully what must be the influence of these circumstances on the thought and imagination.

First, We have already observ'd, that the mind is determin'd by custom to pass from any cause to its effect, and that upon the appearance of the one, 'tis almost impossible for it not to form an idea of the other. Their constant conjunction in past instances has produc'd such a habit in the mind, that it always conjoins them in its thought, and infers the existence of the one from that of its usual attendant. When it considers the dye as no longer supported by the box, it cannot without violence regard it as suspended in the air; but naturally places it on the table, and views it as turning up one of its sides. This is the effect of the intermingled causes, which are requisite to our forming any calculation concerning chances.

Secondly, 'Tis suppos'd, that tho' the dye be necessarily determin'd to fall, and turn up one of its sides, yet there is nothing to fix the particular side, but that this is determin'd entirely by chance. The very nature and essence of chance is a negation of causes, and the leaving the mind in a perfect indifference among those events, which are suppos'd contingent. When therefore the thought is determin'd by the causes to consider the dye as falling and turning up one of its sides, the chances present all these sides as equal, and make us consider every one of them, one after another, as alike probable and possible. The imagination passes from the cause, *viz.* the throwing of the dye, to the effect, *viz.* the turning up one of the six sides; and feels a kind of impossibility both of stopping short in the way, and of forming any other idea. But as all these six sides are incompatible, and the dye cannot turn up above one at once, this principle directs us not to consider all of them at once as lying uppermost; which we look upon as impossible: Neither does it direct us with its entire force to any particular side; for in that case this side wou'd be consider'd as certain and inevitable; but it directs us to the whole six sides after such a manner as to divide its force equally among them. We conclude in general, that some one of them must result from the throw: We run all of them over in our minds: The determination of the thought is common to all; but no more of its force falls to the share of any one, than what is suitable to its proposition with the rest. 'Tis after this manner the original impulse, and consequently the vivacity of thought, arising from the causes, is divided and split in pieces by the intermingled chances.

We have already seen the influence of the two first qualities of the dye, *viz.* the *causes*, and the *number* and *indifference* of the sides, and have learn'd how they give an impulse to the thought, and divide that impulse into as many parts as there are unites in the number of sides. We must now consider the effects of the third particular, *viz.* the *figures* inscrib'd on each side. 'Tis evident that where several sides have the same figure inscrib'd on them, they must concur in their influence on the mind, and must unite upon one image or idea of a figure all those divided impulses, that were dispers'd over the several sides, upon which that figure is inscrib'd. Were the question only what side will be turn'd up, these are all perfectly equal, and no one cou'd ever have any advantage above another. But as the question is concerning the figure, and as the same figure is presented by more than one side; 'tis evident, that the impulses belonging to all these sides must re-unite in that one figure, and become stronger and more forcible by the union. Four sides are suppos'd in the present case to have the same figure inscrib'd on them, and two to have another figure. The impulses of the former are, therefore, superior to those of the latter. But as the events are contrary, and 'tis impossible both these figures can be turn'd up; the impulses likewise become contrary, and the inferior destroys the superior, as far as its strength goes. The vivacity of the idea is always proportionable to the degrees of the impulse or tendency to the transition; and belief is the same with the vivacity of the idea, according to the precedent doctrine.

SECT. XII

Of the probability of causes

WHAT I have said concerning the probability of chances can serve to no other purpose, than to assist us in explaining the probability of causes; since 'tis commonly allow'd by philosophers, that what the vulgar call chance is nothing but a secret and conceal'd cause. That species of probability, therefore, is what we must chiefly examine.

The probabilities of causes are of several kinds; but are all deriv'd from the same origin, *viz. the association of ideas to a present impression.* As the habit, which produces the association, arises from the frequent conjunction of objects, it must arrive at its perfection by degrees, and must acquire new force from each instance, that falls under our observation. The first instance has little or no force: The second makes some addition to it: The third becomes still more sensible; and 'tis by these slow steps, that our judgment arrives at a full assurance. But before it attains this pitch of perfection, it passes thro' several inferior degrees, and in all of them is only to be esteem'd a presumption or probability. The gradation, therefore, from probabilities to proofs is in many cases insensible; and the difference betwixt these kinds of evidence is more easily perceiv'd in the remote degrees, than in the near and contiguous.

'Tis worthy of remark on this occasion, that tho' the species of probability here explain'd be the first in order, and naturally takes place before any entire proof can exist, yet no one, who is arriv'd at the age of maturity, can any longer be acquainted with it. 'Tis true, nothing is more common than for people of the most advanc'd knowledge to have attain'd only an imperfect experience of many particular events; which naturally produces only an imperfect habit and transition: But then we must consider, that the mind, having form'd another observation concerning the connexion of causes and effects, gives new force to its reasoning from that observation; and by means of it can build an argument on one single experiment, when duly prepar'd and examin'd. What we have found once to follow from any object, we conclude will for ever follow from it; and if this maxim be not always built upon as certain, 'tis not for want of a sufficient number of experiments, but because we frequently meet with instances to the contrary; which leads us to the second species of probability, where there is a *contrariety* in our experience and observation.

'Twou'd be very happy for men in the conduct of their lives and actions, were the same objects always conjoin'd together, and we had nothing to fear but the mistakes of our own judgment, without having any reason to apprehend the uncertainty of nature. But as 'tis frequently found, that one observation is contrary to another, and that causes and effects follow not in the same order, of which we have had experience, we are oblig'd to vary our reasoning on account of this uncertainty, and take into consideration the contrariety of events. The first question, that occurs on this head, is concerning the nature and causes of the contrariety.

The vulgar, who take things according to their first appearance, attribute the uncertainty of events to such an uncertainty in the causes, as makes them often fail of their usual influence, tho' they meet with no obstacles nor impediment in their operation. But philosophers observing, that almost in every part of nature there is contain'd a vast variety of springs and principles, which are hid, by reason of their minuteness or remoteness, find that 'tis at least possible the contrariety of events may not proceed from any contingency in the cause, but from the secret operation of contrary causes. This possibility is converted into certainty by farther observation, when they remark, that upon an exact scrutiny, a contrariety of effects always betrays a contrariety of causes, and proceeds from their mutual hindrance and opposition. A peasant can give no better reason for the stopping of any clock or watch than to say, that commonly it does not go right: But an artizan easily perceives, that the same force in the spring or pendulum has always the same influence on the wheels; but fails of its usual effect, perhaps by reason of a grain of dust, which puts a stop to the whole movement. From the observation of several parallel instances, philosophers form a maxim, that the connexion betwixt all causes and effects is equally necessary, and that its seeming uncertainty in some instances proceeds from the secret opposition of contrary causes.

But however philosophers and the vulgar may differ in their explication of the contrariety of events, their inferences from it are always of the same kind, and founded on the same principles. A contrariety of events in the past may give us a kind of hesitating belief for the future after two several ways. *First*, By producing an imperfect habit and transition from the present impression to the related idea. When the conjunction of any two objects is frequent, without being entirely constant, the mind is determin'd to pass from one object to the other; but not with so entire a habit, as when the union is uninterrupted, and all the instances we have ever met with are uniform and of a piece. We find from common experience, in our actions as well as reasonings, that a constant perseverance in any course of life produces a strong inclination and tendency to continue for the future; tho' there are habits of inferior degrees of force, proportion'd to the inferior degrees of steadiness and uniformity in our conduct.

There is no doubt but this principle sometimes takes place, and produces those inferences we draw from contrary phaenomena; tho' I am persuaded, that upon examination we shall not find it to be the principle, that most commonly influences the mind in this species of reasoning. When we follow only the habitual determination of the mind, we make the transition without any reflection, and interpose not a moments delay betwixt the view of one object and the belief of that, which is often found to attend it. As the custom depends not upon any deliberation, it operates immediately, without allowing any time for reflection. But this method of proceeding we have but few instances of in our probable reasonings; and even fewer than in those, which are deriv'd from the uninterrupted conjunction of objects. In the former species of reasoning we commonly take knowingly into consideration the contrariety of past events; we compare the different sides of the contrariety, and carefully weigh the experiments, which we have on each side: Whence we may conclude, that our reasonings of this kind arise not *directly* from the habit, but in an *oblique* manner; which we must now endeavour to explain.

'Tis evident, that when an object is attended with contrary effects, we judge of them only by our past experience, and always consider those as possible, which we have observ'd to follow from it. And as past experience regulates our judgment concerning the possibility of these effects, so it does that concerning their probability; and that effect, which has been the most common, we always esteem the most likely. Here then are two things to be consider'd, *viz.* the *reasons* which determine us to make the past a standard for the future, and the *manner* how we extract a single judgment from a contrariety of past events.

First we may observe, that the supposition, *that the future resembles the past*, is not founded on arguments of any kind, but is deriv'd entirely from habit, by which we are determin'd to expect for the future the same train of objects, to which we have been accustom'd. This habit or determination to transfer the past to the future is full and perfect; and consequently the first impulse of the imagination in this species of reasoning is endow'd with the same qualities.

But, secondly, when in considering past experiments we find them of a contrary nature, this determination, tho' full and perfect in itself, presents us with no steady object, but offers us a number of disagreeing images in a certain order and proportion. The first impulse, therefore, is here broke into pieces, and diffuses itself over all those images, of which each partakes an equal share of that force and vivacity, that is deriv'd from the impulse. Any of these past events may again happen; and we judge, that when they do happen, they will be mix'd in the same proportion as in the past.

If our intention, therefore, be to consider the proportions of contrary events in a great number of instances, the images presented by our past experience must remain in their *first form*, and preserve their first proportions. Suppose, for instance, I have found by long observation, that of twenty ships, which go to sea, only nineteen return. Suppose I see at present twenty ships that leave the port: I transfer my past experience to the future, and represent to my self nineteen of these ships as returning in safety, and one as perishing. Concerning this there can be no difficulty. But as we frequently run over those several ideas of past events, in order to form a judgment concerning one single event, which appears uncertain; this consideration must change the *first form* of our ideas, and draw together the divided images presented by experience; since 'tis to *it* we refer the determination of that particular event, upon which we reason. Many of these images are suppos'd to concur, and a superior number to concur on one side. These agreeing images unite together, and render the idea more strong and lively, not only than a mere fiction of the imagination, but also than any idea, which is supported by a lesser number of experiments. Each new experiment is as a new stroke of the pencil, which bestows an additional vivacity on the colours, without either multiplying or enlarging the figure. This operation of the mind has been so fully explain'd in treating of the probability of chance, that I need not here endeavour to render it more intelligible. Every past experiment may be consider'd as a kind of chance; it being uncertain to us, whether the object will exist conformable to one experiment or another: And for this reason every thing that has been said on the one subject is applicable to both.

Thus upon the whole, contrary experiments produce an imperfect belief, either by weakening the habit, or by dividing and afterwards joining in different parts, that *perfect* habit, which makes us conclude in general, that instances, of which we have no experience, must necessarily resemble those of which we have.

To justify still farther this account of the second species of probability, where we reason with knowledge and reflection from a contrariety of past experiments, I shall propose the following considerations, without fearing to give offence by that air of subtilty, which attends them. Just reasoning ought still, perhaps, to retain its force, however subtile; in the same manner as matter preserves its solidity in the air, and fire, and animal spirits, as well as in the grosser and more sensible forms.

First, We may observe, that there is no probability so great as not to allow of a contrary possibility; because otherwise 'twou'd cease to be a probability, and wou'd become a certainty. That probability of causes, which is most extensive, and which we at present examine, depends on a contrariety of experiments; and 'tis evident an experiment in the past proves at least a possibility for the future.

Secondly, The component parts of this possibility and probability are of the same nature, and differ in number only, but not in kind. It has been observ'd, that all single chances are entirely equal, and that the only circumstance, which can give any event, that is contingent, a superiority over another, is a superior number of chances. In like manner, as the uncertainty of causes is discover'd by experience, which presents us with a view of contrary events, 'tis plain, that when we transfer the past to the future, the known to the unknown, every past experiment has the same weight, and that 'tis only a superior number of them, which can throw the ballance on any side. The possibility, therefore, which enters into every reasoning of this kind, is compos'd of parts, which are of the same nature both among themselves, and with those, that compose the opposite probability.

Thirdly, We may establish it as a certain maxim, that in all moral as well as natural phaenomena, wherever any cause consists of a number of parts, and the effect encreases or diminishes, according to the variation of that number, the effect, properly speaking, is a compounded one, and arises from the union of the several effects, that proceed from each part of the cause. Thus because the gravity of a body encreases or diminishes by the encrease or diminution of its parts, we conclude that each part contains this quality and contributes to the gravity of the whole. The absence or presence of a part of the cause is attended with that of a proportionable part of the effect. This connexion or constant conjunction sufficiently proves the one part to be the cause of the other. As the belief, which we have of any event, encreases or diminishes according to the number of chances or past experiments, 'tis to be consider'd as a compounded effect, of which each part arises from a proportionable number of chances or experiments.

Let us now join these three observations, and see what conclusion we can draw from them. To every probability there is an opposite possibility. This possibility is compos'd of parts, that are entirely of the same nature with those of the probability; and consequently have the same influence on the mind and understanding. The belief, which attends the probability, is a compounded effect, and is form'd by the concurrence of the several effects, which proceed from each part of the probability. Since therefore each part of the probability contributes to the production of the belief, each part of the possibility must have the same influence on the opposite side; the nature of these parts being entirely the same. The contrary belief, attending the possibility, implies a view of a certain object, as well as the probability does an opposite view. In this particular both these degrees of belief are alike. The only manner then, in which the superior number of similar component parts in the one can exert its influence, and prevail above the inferior in the other, is by producing a stronger and more lively view of its object. Each part presents a particular view; and all these views uniting together produce one general view, which is fuller and more distinct by the greater number of causes or principles, from which it is deriv'd.

The component parts of the probability and possibility, being alike in their nature, must produce like effects; and the likeness of their effects consists in this, that each of them presents a view of a particular object. But tho' these parts be alike in their nature, they are very different in their quantity and number; and this difference must appear in the effect as well as the similarity. Now as the view they present is in both cases full and entire, and comprehends the object in all its parts, 'tis impossible that in this particular there can be any difference; nor is there any thing but a superior vivacity in the probability, arising from the concurrence of a superior number of views, which can distinguish these effects.

Here is almost the same argument in a different light. All our reasonings concerning the probability of causes are founded on the transferring of past to future. The transferring of any past experiment to the future is sufficient to give us a view of the object; whether that experiment be single, or combin'd with others of the same kind; whether it be entire, or oppos'd by others of a contrary kind. Suppose, then, it acquires both these qualities of combination and opposition, it loses not upon that account its former power of presenting a view of the object, but only concurs with and opposes other experiments, that have a like influence. A question, therefore, may arise concerning the manner both of the concurrence and opposition. As to the *concurrence*, there is only the choice left betwixt these two hypotheses. *First*, That the view of the object, occasion'd by the transference of each past experiment, preserves itself entire, and only multiplies the number of views. Or, *secondly*, That it runs into the other similar and correspondent views, and gives them a superior degree of force and vivacity. But that the first hypothesis is erroneous, is evident from experience, which informs us, that the belief, attending any reasoning, consists in one conclusion, not in a multitude of similar ones, which wou'd only distract the mind, and in many cases wou'd be too numerous to be comprehended distinctly by any finite capacity. It remains, therefore, as the only reasonable opinion, that these similar views run into each other, and unite their forces; so as to produce a stronger and clearer view, than what arises from any one alone. This is the manner, in which past experiments concur, when they are transfer'd to any future event. As to the manner of their *opposition;* 'tis evident, that as the contrary views are incompatible with each other and 'tis impossible the object can at once exist conformable to both of them, their influence becomes mutually destructive, and the mind is determin'd to the superior only with that force, which remains after substracting the inferior.

I am sensible how abstruse all this reasoning must appear to the generality of readers, who not being accustom'd to such profound reflections on the intellectual faculties of the mind, will be apt to reject as chimerical whatever strikes not in with the common receiv'd notions, and with the easiest and most obvious principles of philosophy. And no doubt there are some pains requir'd to enter into these arguments; tho' perhaps very little are necessary to perceive the imperfection of every vulgar hypothesis on this subject, and the little light, which philosophy can yet afford us in such sublime and such curious speculations. Let men be once fully persuaded of these two principles, *That there is nothing in any object, consider'd in itself, which can afford us a reason for drawing a conclusion beyond it*; and, *That even after the observation of the frequent or constant conjunction of objects, we have no reason to draw any inference concerning any object beyond those of which we have had experience*; I say, let men be once fully convinc'd of these two principles, and this will throw them so loose from all common systems, that they will make no difficulty of receiving any, which may appear the most extraordinary. These principles we have found to be sufficiently convincing, even with regard to our most certain reasonings from causation: But I shall venture to affirm, that with regard to these conjectural or probable reasonings they still acquire a new degree of evidence.

First, 'Tis obvious, that in reasonings of this kind, 'tis

not the object presented to us, which, considered in itself, affords us any reason to draw a conclusion concerning any other object or event. For as this latter object is suppos'd uncertain, and as the uncertainty is deriv'd from a conceal'd contrariety of causes in the former, were any of the causes plac'd in the known qualities of that object, they wou'd no longer be conceal'd, nor wou'd our conclusion be uncertain.

But, *secondly*, 'tis equally obvious in this species of reasoning, that if the transference of the past to the future were founded merely on a conclusion of the understanding, it cou'd never occasion any belief of assurance. When we transfer contrary experiments to the future, we can only repeat these contrary experiments with their particular proportions; which cou'd not produce assurance in any single event, upon which we reason, unless the fancy melted together all those images that concur, and extracted from them one single idea or image, which is intense and lively in proportion to the number of experiments from which it is deriv'd, and their superiority above their antagonists. Our past experience presents no determinate object; and as our belief, however faint, fixes itself on a determinate object, 'tis evident that the belief arises not merely from the transference of past to future, but from some operation of the *fancy* conjoin'd with it. This may lead us to conceive the manner, in which that faculty enters into all our reasonings.

I shall conclude this subject with two reflections, which may deserve our attention. The *first* may be explain'd after this manner. When the mind forms a reasoning concerning any matter of fact, which is only probable, it casts its eye backward upon past experience, and transferring it to the future, is presented with so many contrary views of its object, of which those that are of the same kind uniting together, and running into one act of the mind, serve to fortify and inliven it. But suppose that this multitude of views or glimpses of an object proceeds not from experience, but from a voluntary act of the imagination; this effect does not follow, or at least, follows not in the same degree. For tho' custom and education produce belief by such a repetition, as is not deriv'd from experience, yet this requires a long tract of time, along with a very frequent and *undesign'd* repetition. In general we may pronounce, that a person, who wou'd* *voluntarily* repeat any idea in his mind, tho' supported by one past experience, wou'd be no more inclin'd to believe the existence of its object, than if he had contented himself with one survey of it. Beside the effect of design; each act of the mind, being separate and independent, has a separate influence, and joins not its force with that of its fellows. Not being united by any common object, producing them, they have no relation to each other; and consequently make no transition or union of forces. This phaenomenon we shall understand better afterwards.

My *second* reflection is founded on those large probabilities, which the mind can judge of, and the minute differences it can observe betwixt them. When the chances or experiments on one side amount to ten thousand, and on the other to ten thousand and one, the judgment gives the preference to the latter, upon account of that superiority; tho' 'tis plainly impossible for the mind to run over every particular view, and distinguish the superior vivacity of the image arising from the superior number, where the difference is so inconsiderable. We have a parallel instance in the affections. 'Tis evident, according to the principles above-mention'd, that when an object produces any passion in us, which varies according to the different quantity of the object; I say, 'tis evident, that the passion, properly speaking, is not a simple emotion, but a compounded one, of a great number of weaker passions, deriv'd from a view of each part of the object. For otherwise 'twere impossible the passion shou'd encrease by the encrease of these parts. Thus a man, who desires a thousand pound, has in reality a thousand or more desires, which uniting together, seem to make only one passion; tho' the composition evidently

* Pages 45, 46.

betrays itself upon every alteration of the object, by the preference he gives to the larger number, if superior only by an unite. Yet nothing can be more certain, than that so small a difference wou'd not be discernible in the passions, nor cou'd render them distinguishable from each other. The difference, therefore, of our conduct in preferring the greater number depends not upon our passions, but upon custom, and *general rules*. We have found in a multitude of instances, that the augmenting the numbers of any sum augments the passion, where the numbers are precise and the difference sensible. The mind can perceive from its immediate feeling, that three guineas produce a greater passion than two; and *this* it transfers to larger numbers, because of the resemblance; and by a general rule assigns to a thousand guineas, a stronger passion than to nine hundred and ninety nine. These general rules we shall explain presently.

But beside these two species of probability, which are deriv'd from an *imperfect* experience and from *contrary* causes, there is a third arising from ANALOGY, which differs from them in some material circumstances. According to the hypothesis above explain'd all kinds of reasoning from causes or effects are founded on two particulars, *viz.* the constant conjunction of any two objects in all past experience, and the resemblance of a present object to any one of them. The effect of these two particulars is, that the present object invigorates and inlivens the imagination; and the resemblance along with the constant union, conveys this force and vivacity to the related idea; which we are therefore said to believe, or assent to. If you weaken either the union or resemblance, you weaken the principle of transition, and of consequence that belief, which arises from it. The vivacity of the first impression cannot be fully convey'd to the related idea, either where the conjunction of their objects is not constant, or where the present impression does not perfectly resemble any of those, whose union we are accustom'd to observe. In those probabilities of chance and causes above-explain'd, 'tis the constancy of the union, which is diminish'd; and in the probability deriv'd from analogy, 'tis the resemblance only, which is affected. Without some degree of resemblance, as well as union, 'tis impossible there can be any reasoning: but as this resemblance admits of many different degrees, the reasoning becomes proportionately more or less firm and certain. An experiment loses of its force, when transferr'd to instances, which are not exactly resembling; tho' 'tis evident it may still retain as much as may be the foundation of probability, as long as there is any resemblance remaining.

SECT. XIII
Of unphilosophical probability

ALL these kinds of probability are receiv'd by philosophers, and allow'd to be reasonable foundations of belief and opinion. But there are others, that are deriv'd from the same principles, tho' they have not had the good fortune to obtain the same sanction. The *first* probability of this kind may be accounted for thus. The diminution of the union, and of the resemblance, as above explained, diminishes the facility of the transition, and by that means weakens the evidence; and we may farther observe, that the same diminution of the evidence will follow from a diminution of the impression, and from the shading of those colours, under which it appears to the memory or senses. The argument, which we found on any matter of fact we remember, is more or less convincing, according as the fact is recent or remote; and tho' the difference in these degrees of evidence be not receiv'd by philosophy as solid and legitimate; because in that case an argument must have a different force to day, from what it shall have a month hence; yet notwithstanding the opposition of philosophy, 'tis certain, this circumstance has a considerable influence on the understanding, and secretly changes the authority of the same argument, according to the different times, in which it is propos'd to us. A greater force and vivacity in the impression naturally conveys a greater to the related idea; and 'tis on the degrees of force and vivacity, that the belief depends, according to the foregoing system.

There is a *second* difference, which we may frequently observe in our degrees of belief and assurance, and which never fails to take place, tho' disclaim'd by philosophers. An experiment, that is recent and fresh in the memory, affects us more than one that is in some measure obliterated; and has a superior influence on the judgment, as well as on the passions. A lively impression produces more assurance than a faint one; because it has more original force to communicate to the related idea, which thereby acquires a greater force and vivacity. A recent observation has a like effect; because the custom and transition is there more entire, and preserves better the original force in the communication. Thus a drunkard, who has seen his companion die of a debauch, is struck with that instance for some time, and dreads a like accident for himself: But as the memory of it decays away by degrees, his former security returns, and the danger seems less certain and real.

I add, as a *third* instance of this kind, that tho' our reasonings from proofs and from probabilities be considerably different from each other, yet the former species of reasoning often degenerates insensibly into the latter, by nothing but the multitude of connected arguments. 'Tis certain, that when an inference is drawn immediately from an object, without any intermediate cause or effect, the conviction is much stronger, and the persuasion more lively, than when the imagination is carry'd thro' a long chain of connected arguments, however infallible the connexion of each link may be esteem'd. 'Tis from the original impression, that the vivacity of all the ideas is deriv'd, by means of the customary transition of the imagination; and 'tis evident this vivacity must gradually decay in proportion to the distance, and must lose somewhat in each transition. Sometimes this distance has a greater influence than even contrary experiments wou'd have; and a man may receive a more lively conviction from a probable reasoning, which is close and immediate, than from a long chain of consequences, tho' just and conclusive in each part. Nay 'tis seldom such reasonings produce any conviction; and one must have a very strong and firm imagination to preserve the evidence to the end, where it passes thro' so many stages.

But here it may not be amiss to remark a very curious phaenomenon, which the present subject suggests to us. 'Tis evident there is no point of ancient history, of which we can have any assurance, but by passing thro' many millions of causes and effects, and thro' a chain of arguments of almost an immeasurable length. Before the knowledge of the fact cou'd come to the first historian, it must be convey'd thro' many mouths; and after it is committed to writing, each new copy is a new object, of which the connexion with the foregoing is known only by experience and observation. Perhaps, therefore, it may be concluded from the precedent reasoning, that the evidence of all ancient history must now be lost; or at least, will be lost in time, as the chain of causes encreases, and runs on to a greater length. But as it seems contrary to common sense to think, that if the republic of letters, and the art of printing continue on the same footing as at present, our posterity, even after a thousand ages, can ever doubt if there has been such a man JULIUS CAESAR; this may be consider'd as an objection to the present system. If belief consisted only in a certain vivacity, convey'd from an original impression, it wou'd decay by the length of the transition, and must at last be utterly extinguish'd: And *vice versa,* if belief on some occasions be not capable of such an extinction; it must be something different from that vivacity.

Before I answer this objection I shall observe, that from this topic there has been borrow'd a very celebrated argument against the *Christian Religion*; but with this difference, that the connexion betwixt each link of the chain in human testimony has been there suppos'd not to go beyond probability, and to be liable to a degree of doubt and uncertainty. And indeed it must be confest, that in this manner of considering the subject, (which however is not a true one) there is no history or tradition, but what must in the end lose all its force and evidence. Every new probability diminishes the original conviction; and however great that conviction may be suppos'd, 'tis impossible it can subsist under such re-iterated diminutions. This is true in general; tho' we shall find * afterwards, that there is one very memorable exception, which is of vast consequence in the present subject of the understanding.

Mean while to give a solution of the preceding objection upon the supposition, that historical evidence amounts at first to an entire proof; let us consider, that tho' the links are innumerable, that connect any original fact with the present impression, which is the foundation of belief; yet they are all of the same kind, and depend on the fidelity of Printers and Copists. One edition passes into another, and that into a third, and so on, till we come to that volume we peruse at present. There is no variation in the steps. After we know one, we know all of them; and after we have made one, we can have no scruple as to the rest. This circumstance alone preserves the evidence of history, and will perpetuate the memory of the present age to the latest posterity. If all the long chain of causes and effects, which connect any past event with any volume of history, were compos'd of parts different from each other, and which 'twere necessary for the mind distinctly to conceive, 'tis impossible we shou'd preserve to the end any belief or evidence. But as most of these proofs are perfectly resembling, the mind runs easily along them, jumps from one part to another with facility, and forms but a confus'd and general notion of each link. By this means a long chain of argument, has as little effect in diminishing the original vivacity, as a much shorter wou'd have, if compos'd of parts, which

* Part IV. Sect. 1.

were different from each other, and of which each requir'd a distinct consideration.

A fourth unphilosophical species of probability is that deriv'd from *general rules*, which we rashly form to ourselves, and which are the source of what we properly call PREJUDICE. An *Irishman* cannot have wit, and a *Frenchman* cannot have solidity; for which reason, tho' the conversation of the former in any instance be visibly very agreeable, and of the latter very judicious, we have entertain'd such a prejudice against them, that they must be dunces or fops in spite of sense and reason. Human nature is very subject to errors of this kind; and perhaps this nation as much as any other.

Shou'd it be demanded why men form general rules, and allow them to influence their judgment, even contrary to present observation and experience, I shou'd reply, that in my opinion it proceeds from those very principles, on which all judgments concerning causes and effects depend. Our judgments concerning cause and effect are deriv'd from habit and experience; and when we have been accustom'd to see one object united to another, our imagination passes from the first to the second, by a natural transition, which precedes reflection, and which cannot be prevented by it. Now 'tis the nature of custom not only to operate with its full force, when objects are presented, that are exactly the same with those to which we have been accustom'd; but also to operate in an inferior degree, when we cover such as are similar; and tho' the habit loses somewhat of its force by every difference, yet 'tis seldom entirely destroy'd, where any considerable circumstances remain the same. A man, who has contracted a custom of eating fruit by the use of pears or peaches, will satisfy himself with melons, where he cannot find his favourite fruit; as one, who has become a drunkard by the use of red wines, will be carried almost with the same violence to white, if presented to him. From this principle I have accounted for that species of probability, deriv'd from analogy, where we transfer our experience in past instances to objects which are resembling, but are not exactly the same with those concerning which we have had experience. In proportion as the resemblance decays, the probability diminishes; but still has some force as long as there remain any traces of the resemblance.

This observation we may carry farther; and may remark, that tho' custom be the foundation of all our judgments, yet sometimes it has an effect on the imagination in opposition to the judgment, and produces a contrariety in our sentiments concerning the same object. I explain myself. In almost all kinds of causes there is a complication of circumstances, of which some are essential, and others superfluous; some are absolutely requisite to the production of the effect, and others are only conjoin'd by accident. Now we may observe, that when these superfluous circumstances are numerous, and remarkable, and frequently conjoin'd with the essential, they have such an influence on the imagination, that even in the absence of the latter they carry us on to the conception of the usual effect, and give to that conception a force and vivacity, which make it superior to the mere fictions of the fancy. We may correct this propensity by a reflection on the nature of those circumstances; but 'tis still certain, that custom takes the start, and gives a biass to the imagination.

To illustrate this by a familiar instance, let us consider the case of a man, who being hung out from a high tower in a cage of iron cannot forbear trembling, when he surveys the precipice below him, tho' he knows himself to be perfectly secure from falling, by his experience of the solidity of the iron, which supports him; and tho' the ideas of fall and descent, and harm and death, be deriv'd solely from custom and experience. The same custom goes beyond the instances, from which it is deriv'd, and to which it perfectly corresponds; and influences his ideas of such objects as are in some respect resembling, but fall not precisely under the same rule. The circumstances of depth and descent strike so strongly upon him, that their influence cannot be destroy'd by the contrary circumstances of support and solidity, which ought to give him a perfect security. His imagination runs away with its object, and excites a passion proportion'd to it. That passion returns back upon the imagination and inlivens the idea; which lively idea has a new influence on the passion, and in its turn augments its force and violence; and both his fancy and affections, thus mutually supporting each other, cause the whole to have a very great influence upon him.

But why need we seek for other instances, while the present subject of philosophical probabilities offers us so obvious an one, in the opposition betwixt the judgment and imagination arising from these effects of custom? According to my system, all reasonings are nothing but the effects of custom; and custom has no influence, but by inlivening the imagination, and giving us a strong conception of any object. It may, therefore, be concluded, that our judgment and imagination can never be contrary, and that custom cannot operate on the latter faculty after such a manner, as to render it opposite to the former. This difficulty we can remove after no other manner, than by supposing the influence of general rules. We shall afterwards * take notice of some general rules, by which we ought to regulate our judgment concerning causes and effects; and these rules are form'd on the nature of our understanding, and on our experience of its operations in the judgments we form concerning objects. By them we learn to distinguish the accidental circumstances from the efficacious causes; and when we find that an effect can be produc'd without the concurrence of any particular circumstance, we conclude that that circumstance makes not a part of the efficacious cause, however frequently conjoin'd with it. But as this frequent conjunction necessarily makes it have some effect on the imagination, in spite of the opposite conclusion from general rules, the opposition of these two principles produces a contrariety in our thoughts, and causes us to ascribe the one inference to our judgment, and the other to our imagination. The general rule is attributed to our judg-

* Sect. 15.

ment; as being more extensive and constant. The exception to the imagination; as being more capricious and uncertain.

Thus our general rules are in a manner set in opposition to each other. When an object appears, that resembles any cause in very considerable circumstances, the imagination naturally carries us to a lively conception of the usual effect, tho' the object be different in the most material and most efficacious circumstances from that cause. Here is the first influence of general rules. But when we take a review of this act of the mind, and compare it with the more general and authentic operations of the understanding, we find it to be of an irregular nature, and destructive of all the most establish'd principles of reasonings; which is the cause of our rejecting it. This is a second influence of general rules, and implies the condemnation of the former. Sometimes the one, sometimes the other prevails, according to the disposition and character of the person. The vulgar are commonly guided by the first, and wise men by the second. Mean while the sceptics may here have the pleasure of observing a new and signal contradiction in our reason, and of seeing all philosophy ready to be subverted by a principle of human nature, and again sav'd by a new direction of the very same principle. The following of general rules is a very unphilosophical species of probability; and yet 'tis only by following them that we can correct this, and all other unphilosophical probabilities.

Since we have instances, where general rules operate on the imagination even contrary to the judgment, we need not be surpriz'd to see their effects encrease, when conjoin'd with that latter faculty, and to observe that they bestow on the ideas they present to us a force superior to what attends any other. Every one knows, there is an indirect manner of insinuating praise or blame, which is much less shocking than the open flattery or censure of any person. However he may communicate his sentiments by such secret insinuations, and make them known with equal certainty as by the open discovery of them, 'tis certain that their influence is not equally strong and powerful. One who lashes me with conceal'd strokes of satire, moves not my indignation to such a degree, as if he flatly told me I was a fool and coxcomb; tho' I equally understand his meaning, as if he did. This difference is to be attributed to the influence of general rules.

Whether a person openly abuses me, or slyly intimates his contempt, in neither case do I immediately perceive his sentiment or opinion; and 'tis only by signs, that is, by its effects, I become sensible of it. The only difference, then, betwixt these two cases consists in this, that in the open discovery of his sentiments he makes use of signs, which are general and universal; and in the secret intimation employs such as are more singular and uncommon. The effect of this circumstance is, that the imagination, in running from the present impression to the absent idea, makes the transition with greater facility, and consequently conceives the object with greater force, where the connexion is common and universal, than where it is more rare and particular. Accordingly we may observe, that the open declaration of our sentiments is call'd the taking off the mask, as the secret intimation of our opinions is said to be the veiling of them. The difference betwixt an idea produc'd by a general connexion and that arising from a particular one is here compar'd to the difference betwixt an impression and an idea. This difference in the imagination has a suitable effect on the passions; and this effect is augmented by another circumstance. A secret intimation of anger or contempt shews that we still have some consideration for the person, and avoid the directly abusing him. This makes a conceal'd satire less disagreeable; but still this depends on the same principle. For if an idea were not more feeble, when only intimated, it wou'd never be esteem'd a mark of greater respect to proceed in this method than in the other.

Sometimes scurrility is less displeasing than delicate satire, because it revenges us in a manner for the injury at the very time it is committed, by affording us a just reason to blame and contemn the person, who injures us. But this phaenomenon likewise depends upon the same principle. For why do we blame all gross and injurious language, unless it be, because we esteem it contrary to good breeding and humanity? And why is it contrary, unless it be more shocking than any delicate satire? The rules of good-breeding condemn whatever is openly disobliging, and gives a sensible pain and confusion to those, with whom we converse. After this is once establish'd, abusive language is universally blam'd, and gives less pain upon account of its coarseness and incivility, which render the person despicable, that employs it. It becomes less disagreeable, merely because originally it is more so; and 'tis more disagreeable, because it affords an inference by general and common rules, that are palpable and undeniable.

To this explication of the different influence of open and conceal'd flattery or satire, I shall add the consideration of another phaenomenon, which is analogous to it. There are many particulars in the point of honour both of men and women, whose violations, when open and avow'd, the world never excuses, but which it is more apt to overlook, when the appearances are sav'd, and the transgression is secret and conceal'd. Even those, who know with equal certainty, that the fault is committed, pardon it more easily, when the proofs seem in some measure oblique and equivocal, than when they are direct and undeniable. The same idea is presented in both cases, and, properly speaking, is equally assented to by the judgment; and yet its influence is different, because of the different manner, in which it is presented.

Now if we compare these two cases, of the *open* and *conceal'd* violations of the laws of honour, we shall find, that the difference betwixt them consists in this, that in the first case the sign, from which we infer the blameable action, is single, and suffices alone to be the foundation of our reasoning and judgment; whereas in the latter the signs are numerous, and decide little or nothing when alone and unaccompany'd with many minute circumstances, which are almost imperceptible. But 'tis certainly true, that any reasoning is always the more convincing, the more single and united it is to the eye, and the less exercise it gives to the imagination to collect all its parts, and run from them to the correlative idea, which forms the conclusion. The labour of the thought disturbs the regular progress of the sentiments, as we shall observe presently *. The idea strikes not on us with such vivacity; and consequently has no such influence on the passion and imagination.

From the same principles we may account for those observations of the CARDINAL DE RETZ,[†] *that there are many things, in which the world wishes to be deceiv'd;* and *that it more easily excuses a person acting than in talking contrary to the decorum of his profession and character*. A fault in words is commonly more open and distinct than one in actions, which admit of many palliating excuses, and decide not so clearly concerning the intention and views of the actor.

Thus it appears upon the whole, that every kind of opinion or judgment, which amounts not to knowledge, is deriv'd entirely from the force and vivacity of the perception, and that these qualities constitute in the mind, what we call the BELIEF of the existence of any object. This force and this vivacity are most conspicuous in the memory; and therefore our confidence in the veracity of that faculty is the greatest imaginable, and equals in many respects the assurance of a demonstration. The next degree of these qualities is that deriv'd from the relation of cause and effect; and this too is very great, especially when the conjunction is found by experience to be perfectly constant, and when the object, which is present to us, exactly resembles those, of which we have had experience. But below this degree of evidence there are many others, which have an influence on the passions and imagination, proportion'd to that degree of force and vivacity, which they communicate to the ideas. 'Tis by habit we make the transition from cause to effect; and 'tis from some present impression we borrow that

* Part IV: Sect. 1.

[†*Mémoires* (Nancy 1717).]

vivacity, which we diffuse over the correlative idea. But when we have not observ'd a sufficient number of instances, to produce a strong habit; or when these instances are contrary to each other; or when the resemblance is not exact; or the present impression is faint and obscure; or the experience in some measure obliterated from the memory; or the connexion dependent on a long chain of objects; or the inference deriv'd from general rules, and yet not conformable to them: In all these cases the evidence diminishes by the diminution of the force and intenseness of the idea. This therefore is the nature of the judgment and probability.

What principally gives authority to this system is, beside the undoubted arguments, upon which each part is founded, the agreement of these parts, and the necessity of one to explain another. The belief, which attends our memory, is of the same nature with that, which is deriv'd from our judgments: Nor is there any difference betwixt that judgment, which is deriv'd from a constant and uniform connexion of causes and effects, and that which depends upon an interrupted and uncertain. 'Tis indeed evident, that in all determinations, where the mind decides from contrary experiments, 'tis first divided within itself, and has an inclination to either side in proportion to the number of experiments we have seen and remember. This contest is at last determin'd to the advantage of that side, where we observe a superior number of these experiments; but still with a diminution of force in the evidence correspondent to the number of the opposite experiments. Each possibility, of which the probability is compos'd, operates separately upon the imagination; and 'tis the larger collection of possibilities, which at last prevails, and that with a force proportionable to its superiority. All these phaenomena lead directly to the precedent system; nor will it ever be possible upon any other principles to give a satisfactory and consistent explication of them. Without considering these judgments as the effects of custom on the imagination, we shall lose ourselves in perpetual contradiction and absurdity.

SECT. XIV

Of the idea of necessary connexion

HAVING thus explain'd the manner, *in which we reason beyond our immediate impressions, and conclude[d] that such particular causes must have such particular effects;* we must now return upon our footsteps to examine that question, which * first occur'd to us, and which we dropt in our way, *viz. What is our idea of necessity, when we say that two objects are necessarily connected together.* Upon this head I repeat what I have often had occasion to observe, that as we have no idea, that is not deriv'd from an impression, we must find some impression, that gives rise to this idea of necessity, if we assert we have really such an idea. In order to this I consider, in what objects necessity is commonly suppos'd to lie; and finding that it is always ascrib'd to causes and effects, I turn my eye to two objects suppos'd to be plac'd in that relation: and examine them in all the situations, of which they are susceptible. I immediately perceive, that they are *contiguous* in time and place, and that the object we call cause *precedes* the other we call effect. In no one instance can I go any farther, nor is it possible for me to discover any third relation betwixt these objects. I therefore enlarge my view to comprehend several instances; where I find like objects always existing in like relations of contiguity and succession. At first sight this seems to serve but little to my purpose. The reflection on several instances only repeats the same objects; and therefore can never give rise to a new idea. But upon farther enquiry I find, that the repetition is not in every particular the same, but produces a new impression, and by that means the idea, which I at present examine. For after a frequent repetition, I find, that upon the appearance of one of the objects, the mind is *determin'd* by custom to consider its usual attendant, and to consider it in a stronger light upon

* Sect. 2.

account of its relation to the first object. 'Tis this impression, then, or *determination*, which affords me the idea of necessity.

I doubt not but these consequences will at first sight be receiv'd without difficulty, as being evident deductions from principles, which we have already establish'd, and which we have often employ'd in our reasonings. This evidence both in the first principles, and in the deductions, may reduce us unwarily into the conclusion, and make us imagine it contains nothing extraordinary, nor worthy of our curiosity. But tho' such an inadvertence may facilitate the reception of this reasoning, 'twill make it be the more easily forgot; for which reason I think it proper to give warning, that I have just now examin'd one of the most sublime questions in philosophy, *viz. that concerning the power and efficacy of causes*; where all the sciences seem so much interested. Such a warning will naturally rouze up the attention of the reader, and make him desire a more full account of my doctrine, as well as of the arguments, on which it is founded. This request is so reasonable, that I cannot refuse complying with it; especially as I am hopeful that these principles, the more they are examin'd, will acquire the more force and evidence.

There is no question, which on account of its importance, as well as difficulty, has caus'd more disputes both among antient and modern philosophers, than this concerning the efficacy of causes, or that quality which makes them be follow'd by their effects. But before they enter'd upon these disputes, methinks it wou'd not have been improper to have examin'd what idea we have of that efficacy, which is the subject of the controversy. This is what I find principally wanting in their reasonings, and what I shall here endeavour to supply.

I begin with observing that the terms of *efficacy, agency, power, force, energy, necessity, connexion*, and *productive quality*, are all nearly synonimous; and therefore 'tis an absurdity to employ any of them in defining the rest. By this observation we reject at once all the vulgar definitions which philosophers have given of power and efficacy; and instead of searching for the idea in these definitions, must look for it in the impressions, from which it is orginally deriv'd. If it be a compound idea, it must arise from compound impressions. If simple, from simple impressions.

I believe the most general and most popular explication of this matter, is to say, * that finding from experience, that there are several new productions in matter, such as the motions and variations of body, and concluding that there must somewhere be a power capable of producing them, we arrive at last by this reasoning at the idea of power and efficacy. But to be convinc'd that this explication is more popular than philosophical, we need but reflect on two very obvious principles. *First,* That reason alone can never give rise to any original idea, and *secondly,* that reason, as distinguish'd from experience, can never make us conclude, that a cause or productive quality is absolutely requisite to every beginning of existence. Both these considerations have been sufficiently explain'd; and therefore shall not at present be any farther insisted on.

I shall only infer from them, that since reason can never give rise to the idea of efficacy, that idea must be deriv'd from experience, and from some particular instances of this efficacy, which make their passage into the mind by the common channels of sensation or reflection. Ideas always represent their objects or impressions; and *vice versa,* there are some objects necessary to give rise to every idea. If we pretend, therefore, to have any just idea of this efficacy, we must produce some instance, wherein the efficacy is plainly discoverable to the mind, and its operations obvious to our consciousness or sensation. By the refusal of this, we acknowledge, that the idea is impossible and imaginary; since the principle of innate ideas, which alone can save us from this dilemma, has been already refuted, and is now almost universally rejected in the learned world. Our present business, then, must be to find some natural production, where the operation and efficacy of a cause can be clearly

* See Mr *Locke*; chapter of power.

conceiv'd and comprehended by the mind, without any danger of obscurity or mistake.

In this research we meet with very little encouragement from that prodigious diversity, which is found in the opinions of those philosophers, who have pretended to explain the secret force and energy of causes*. There are some, who maintain, that bodies operate by their substantial form; others, by their accidents or qualities; several, by their matter and form; some, by their form and accidents; others, by certain virtues and faculties distinct from all this. All these sentiments again are mix'd and vary'd in a thousand different ways; and form a strong presumption, that none of them have any solidity or evidence, and that the supposition of an efficacy in any of the known qualities of matter is entirely without foundation. This presumption must encrease upon us, when we consider, that these principles of substantial forms, and accidents, and faculties, are not in reality any of the known properties of bodies, but are perfectly unintelligible and inexplicable. For 'tis evident philosophers wou'd never have had recourse to such obscure and uncertain principles had they met with any satisfaction in such as are clear and intelligible; especially in such an affair as this, which must be an object of the simplest understanding, if not of the senses. Upon the whole, we may conclude, that 'tis impossible in any one instance to shew the principle, in which the force and agency of a cause is plac'd; and that the most refin'd and most vulgar understandings are equally at a loss in this particular. If any one think proper to refute this assertion, he need not put himself to the trouble of inventing any long reasonings; but may at once shew us an instance of a cause, where we discover the power or operating principle. This defiance we are oblig'd frequently to make use of, as being almost the only means of proving a negative in philosophy.

The small success, which has been met with in all the

*See Father *Malbranche*, Book vi. Part 2. chap. 3. and the illustrations upon it.

attempts to fix this power, has at last oblig'd philosophers to conclude, that the ultimate force and efficacy of nature is perfectly unknown to us, and that 'tis in vain we search for it in all the known qualities of matter. In this opinion they are almost unanimous; and 'tis only in the inference they draw from it, that they discover any difference in their sentiments. For some of them, as the *Cartesians* in particular, having establish'd it as a principle, that we are perfectly acquainted with the essence of matter, have very naturally inferr'd, that it is endow'd with no efficacy, and that 'tis impossible for it of itself to communicate motion, or produce any of those effects, which we ascribe to it. As the essence of matter consists in extension, and as extension implies not actual motion, but only mobility; they conclude, that the energy, which produces the motion, cannot lie in the extension.

This conclusion leads them into another, which they regard as perfectly unavoidable. Matter, say they, is in itself entirely unactive, and depriv'd of any power, by which it may produce, or continue, or communicate motion: But since these effects are evident to our senses, and since the power, that produces them, must be plac'd somewhere, it must lie in the Deity, or that divine being, who contains in his nature all excellency and perfection. 'Tis the deity, therefore, who is the prime mover of the universe, and who not only first created matter, and gave it its original impulse, but likewise by a continu'd exertion of omnipotence supports its existence, and successively bestows on it all those motions, and configurations, and qualities, with which it is endow'd.

This opinion is certainly very curious, and well worth our attention; but 'twill appear superflous to examine it in this place, if we reflect a moment on our present purpose in taking notice of it. We have establish'd it as a principle, that as all ideas are deriv'd from impressions, or some precedent *perceptions*, 'tis impossible we can have any idea of power and efficacy, unless some instances can be produc'd, wherein this power *is perceiv'd* to exert itself. Now as these instances can never be discover'd in body, the *Cartesians*, proceeding upon their principle of innate ideas, have had recourse to a supreme spirit or deity, whom they consider as the only active being in the universe, and as the immediate cause of every alteration in matter. But the principle of innate ideas being allow'd to be false, it follows, that the supposition of a deity can serve us in no stead, in accounting for that idea of agency, which we search for in vain in all the objects which are presented to our senses, or which we are internally conscious of in our own minds. For if every idea be deriv'd from an impression, the idea of a deity proceeds from the same origin; and if no impression, either of sensation or reflection, implies any force or efficacy, 'tis equally impossible to discover or even imagine any such active principle in the deity. Since these philosophers, therefore, have concluded, that matter cannot be endow'd with any efficacious principle, because 'tis impossible to discover in it such a principle; the same course of reasoning shou'd determine them to exclude it from the supreme being. Or if they esteem that opinion absurd and impious, as it really is, I shall tell them how they may avoid it; and that is, by concluding from the very first, that they have no adequate idea of power or efficacy in any object; since neither in body nor spirit, neither in superior nor inferior natures, are they able to discover one single instance of it.

The same conclusion is unavoidable upon the hypothesis of those, who maintain the efficacy of second causes, and attribute a derivative, but a real power and energy to matter. For as they confess, that this energy lies not in any of the known qualities of matter, the difficulty still remains concerning the origin of its idea. If we have really an idea of power, we may attribute power to an unknown quality: But as 'tis impossible, that that idea can be deriv'd from such a quality, and as there is nothing in known qualities, which can produce it; it follows that we deceive ourselves, when we imagine we are possest of any idea of this kind, after the manner we commonly understand it. All ideas are deriv'd from, and represent impressions. We never have any impression, that contains any power or efficacy. We never therefore have any idea of power.

[*] Some have asserted, that we feel an energy, or power, in our own mind; and that having in this manner acquir'd the idea of power, we transfer that quality to matter, where we are not able immediately to discover it. The motions of our body, and the thoughts and sentiments of our mind, (say they) obey the will; nor do we seek any farther to acquire a just notion of force or power. But to convince us how fallacious this reasoning is, we need only consider, that the will being here consider'd as a cause, has no more a discoverable connexion with its effects, than any material cause has with its proper effect. So far from perceiving the connexion betwixt an act of volition, and a motion of the body; 'tis allow'd that no effect is more inexplicable from the powers and essence of thought and matter. Nor is the empire of the will over our mind more intelligible. The effect is there distinguishable and separable from the cause, and cou'd not be foreseen without the experience of their constant conjunction. We have command over our mind to a certain degree, but beyond *that* lose all empire over it: And 'tis evidently impossible to fix any precise bounds to our authority, where we consult not experience. In short, the actions of the mind are, in this respect, the same with those of matter. We perceive only their constant conjunction; nor can we ever reason beyond it. No internal impression has an apparent energy, more than external objects have. Since, therefore, matter is confess'd by philosophers to operate by an unknown force, we shou'd in vain hope to attain an idea of force by consulting our own minds†.

[* The following paragraph is inserted from Hume's Appendix to Book III.]

† The same imperfection attends our ideas of the Deity; but this can have no effect either on religion or morals. The order of the universe proves an omnipotent mind; that is, a mind whose will is *constantly attended* with the obedience of every creature and being. Nothing more is requisite to give a foundation to all the articles of religion, nor is it necessary we shou'd form a distinct idea of the force and energy of the supreme Being.

It has been established as a certain principle, that general or abstract ideas are nothing but individual ones taken in a certain light, and that, in reflecting on any object, 'tis as impossible to exclude from our thought all particular degrees of quantity and quality as from the real nature of things. If we be possest, therefore, of any idea of power in general, we must also be able to conceive some particular species of it; and as power cannot subsist alone, but is always regarded as an attribute of some being or existence, we must be able to place this power in some particular being, and conceive that being as endow'd with real force and energy, by which such a particular effect necessarily results from its operation. We must distinctly and particularly conceive the connexion betwixt the cause and effect, and be able to pronounce, from a simple view of the one, that it must be follow'd or preceded by the other. This is the true manner of conceiving a particular power in a particular body: and a general idea being impossible without an individual; where the latter is impossible, 'tis certain the former can never exist. Now nothing is more evident, than that the human mind cannot form such an idea of two objects, as to conceive any connexion betwixt them, or comprehend distinctly that power or efficacy, by which they are united. Such a connexion wou'd amount to a demonstration, and wou'd imply the absolute impossibility for the one object not to follow, or to be conceiv'd not to follow upon the other: Which kind of connexion has already been rejected in all cases. If any one is of a contrary opinion, and thinks he has attain'd a notion of power in any particular object, I desire he may point out to me that object. But till I meet with such-a-one, which I despair of, I cannot forbear concluding, that since we can never distinctly conceive how any particular power can possibly reside in any particular object, we deceive ourselves in imagining we can form any such general idea.

Thus upon the whole we may infer, that when we talk of any being, whether of a superior or inferior nature, as endow'd with a power or force, proportion'd to any effect;

when we speak of a necessary connexion betwixt objects, and suppose, that this connexion depends upon an efficacy or energy, with which any of these objects are endow'd; in all these expressions, *so apply'd*, we have really no distinct meaning, and make use only of common words, without any clear and determinate ideas. But as 'tis more probable, that these expressions do here lose their true meaning by being *wrong apply'd*, than that they never have any meaning; 'twill be proper to bestow another consideration on this subject, to see if possibly we can discover the nature and origin of those ideas, we annex to them.

Suppose two objects to be presented to us, of which the one is the cause and the other the effect; 'tis plain, that from the simple consideration of one, or both these objects we never shall perceive the tie, by which they are united, or be able certainly to pronounce, that there is a connexion betwixt them. 'Tis not, therefore, from any one instance, that we arrive at the idea of cause and effect, of a necessary connexion of power, of force, of energy, and of efficacy. Did we never see any but particular conjunctions of objects, entirely different from each other, we should never be able to form any such ideas.

But again; suppose we observe several instances, in which the same objects are always conjoin'd together, we immediately conceive a connexion betwixt them, and begin to draw an inference from one to another. This multiplicity of resembling instances, therefore, constitutes the very essence of power or connexion, and is the source, from which the idea of it arises. In order, then, to understand the idea of power, we must consider that multiplicity; nor do I ask more to give a solution of that difficulty, which has so long perplex'd us. For thus I reason. The repetition of perfectly similar instances can never *alone* give rise to an original idea, different from what is to be found in any particular instance, as has been observ'd, and as evidently follows from our fundamental principle, *that all ideas are copy'd from impressions.* Since therefore the idea of power is a new original idea, not to be found in any one instance, and which yet arises from the repetition of several instances, it follows, that the repetition *alone* has not that effect, but must either *discover* or *produce* something new, which is the source of that idea. Did the repetition neither discover nor produce any thing new, our ideas might be multiply'd by it, but wou'd not be enlarg'd above what they are upon the observation of one single instance. Every enlargement, therefore, (such as the idea of power or connexion) which arises from the multiplicity of similar instances, is copy'd from some effects of the multiplicity, and will be perfectly understood by understanding these effects. Wherever we find any thing new to be discover'd or produc'd by the repetition, there we must place the power, and must never look for it in any other object.

But 'tis evident, in the first place, that the repetition of like objects in like relations of succession and contiguity *discovers* nothing new in any one of them; since we can draw no inference from it, nor make it a subject either of our demonstrative or probable reasonings; * as has been already prov'd. Nay suppose we cou'd draw an inference, 'twou'd be of no consequence in the present case; since no kind of reasoning can give rise to a new idea, such as this of power is; but wherever we reason, we must antecedently be possest of clear ideas, which may be the objects of our reasoning. The conception always precedes the understanding; and where the one is obscure, the other is uncertain; where the one fails, the other must fail also.

Secondly, 'Tis certain that this repetition of similar objects in similar situations *produces* nothing new either in these objects, or in any external body. For 'twill readily be allow'd, that the several instances we have of the conjunction of resembling causes and effects are in themselves entirely independent, and that the communication of motion, which I see result at present from the shock of two billiard-balls, is totally distinct from that which I saw result from such an impulse a twelve-month ago. These impulses have no influence on each other. They are entirely divided

* Sect. 6.

by time and place; and the one might have existed and communicated motion, tho' the other never had been in being.

There is, then, nothing new either discover'd or produc'd in any objects by their constant conjunction, and by the uninterrupted resemblance of their relations of succession and contiguity. But 'tis from this resemblance, that the ideas of necessity, of power, and of efficacy, are deriv'd. These ideas, therefore, represent not any thing, that does or can belong to the objects, which are constantly conjoin'd. This is an argument, which, in every view we can examine it, will be found perfectly unanswerable. Similar instances are still the first source of our idea of power or necessity; at the same time that they have no influence by their similarity either on each other, or on any external object. We must therefore, turn ourselves to some other quarter to seek the origin of that idea.

Tho' the several resembling instances, which give rise to the idea of power, have no influence on each other, and can never produce any new quality *in the object*, which can be the model of that idea, yet the *observation* of this resemblance produces a new impression *in the mind*, which is its real model. For after we have observ'd the resemblance in a sufficient number of instances, we immediately feel a determination of the mind to pass from one object to its usual attendant, and to conceive it in a stronger light upon account of that relation. This determination is the only effect of the resemblance; and therefore must be the same with power or efficacy, whose idea is deriv'd from the resemblance. The several instances of resembling conjunctions lead us into the notion of power and necessity. These instances are in themselves totally distinct from each other, and have no union but in the mind, which observes them, and collects their ideas. Necessity, then, is the effect of this observation, and is nothing but an internal impression of the mind, or a determination to carry our thoughts from one object to another. Without considering it in this view, we can never arrive at the most distant notion of it, or be able to attribute it either to external or internal objects, to spirit or body, to causes or effects.

The necessary connexion betwixt causes and effects is the foundation of our inference from one to the other. The foundation of our inference is the transition arising from the accustom'd union. These are, therefore, the same.

The idea of necessity arises from some impression. There is no impression convey'd by our senses, which can give rise to that idea. It must, therefore, be deriv'd from some internal impression, or impression of reflection. There is no internal impression, which has any relation to the present business, but that propensity, which custom produces, to pass from an object to the idea of its usual attendant. This therefore is the essence of necessity. Upon the whole, necessity is something, that exists in the mind, not in objects; nor is it possible for us ever to form the most distant idea of it, consider'd as a quality in bodies. Either we have no idea of necessity, or necessity is nothing but that determination of the thought to pass from causes to effects and from effects to causes, according to their experienc'd union.

Thus as the necessity, which makes two times two equal to four, or three angles of a triangle equal to two right ones, lies only in the act of understanding, by which we consider and compare these ideas; in like manner the necessity or power, which unites causes and effects, lies in the determination of the mind to pass from the one to the other. The efficacy or energy of causes is neither plac'd in the causes themselves, nor in the deity, nor in the concurrence of these two principles; but belongs entirely to the soul, which considers the union of two or more objects in all past instances. 'Tis here that the real power of causes is plac'd, along with their connexion and necessity.

I am sensible, that of all the paradoxes, which I have had, or shall hereafter have occasion to advance in the course of this treatise, the present one is the most violent, and that 'tis merely by dint of solid proof and reasoning I can ever hope it will have admission, and overcome the inveterate prejudices of mankind. Before we are reconcil'd to this doctrine, how often must we repeat to ourselves, *that* the simple view of any two objects or actions, however related, can never give us any idea of power, or of a connexion betwixt them: *that* this idea arises from the repetition of their union: *that* the repetition neither discovers nor causes any thing in the objects, but has an influence only on the mind, by that customary transition it produces: *that* this customary transition is, therefore, the same with the power and necessity; which are consequently qualities of perceptions, not of objects, and are internally felt by the soul, and not perceiv'd externally in bodies? There is commonly an astonishment attending every thing extraordinary; and this astonishment changes immediately into the highest degree of esteem or contempt, according as we approve or disapprove of the subject. I am much afraid, that tho' the foregoing reasoning appears to me the shortest and most decisive imaginable; yet with the generality of readers the biass of the mind will prevail, and give them a prejudice against the present doctrine.

This contrary biass is easily accounted for. 'Tis a common observation, that the mind has a great propensity to spread itself on external objects, and to conjoin with them any internal impressions, which they occasion, and which always make their appearance at the same time that these objects discover themselves to the senses. Thus as certain sounds and smells are always found to attend certain visible objects, we naturally imagine a conjunction, even in place, betwixt the objects and qualities, tho' the qualities be of such a nature as to admit of no such conjunction, and really exist no where. But of this more fully * hereafter. Mean while 'tis sufficient to observe, that the same propensity is the reason, why we suppose necessity and power to lie in the objects we consider, not in our mind, that considers them; notwithstanding it is not possible for us to form the most distant idea of that quality, when it is not taken for the determination of the mind, to pass from the idea of an object to that of its usual attendant.

* Part. IV. Sect. 5.

But tho' this be the only reasonable account we can give of necessity, the contrary notion is so riveted in the mind from the principles above-mention'd, that I doubt not but my sentiments will be treated by many as extravagant and ridiculous. What! the efficacy of causes lie in the determination of the mind! As if causes did not operate entirely independent of the mind, and wou'd not continue their operation, even tho' there was no mind existent to contemplate them, or reason concerning them. Thought may well depend on causes for its operation, but not causes on thought. This is to reverse the order of nature, and make that secondary, which is really primary. To every operation there is a power proportion'd; and this power must be plac'd on the body, that operates. If we remove the power from one cause, we must ascribe it to another: But to remove it from all causes, and bestow it on a being, that is no ways related to the cause or effect, but by perceiving them, is a gross absurdity, and contrary to the most certain principles of human reason.

I can only reply to all these arguments, that the case is here much the same, as if a blind man shou'd pretend to find a great many absurdities in the supposition, that the colour of scarlet is not the same with the sound of a trumpet, nor light the same with solidity. If we have really no idea of a power or efficacy in any object, or of any real connexion betwixt causes and effects, 'twill be to little purpose to prove, that an efficacy is necessary in all operations. We do not understand our own meaning in talking so, but ignorantly confound ideas, which are entirely distinct from each other. I am, indeed, ready to allow, that there may be several qualities both in material and immaterial objects, with which we are utterly unacquainted; and if we please to call these *power* or *efficacy*, 'twill be of little consequence to the world. But when, instead of meaning these unknown qualities, we make the terms of power and efficacy signify something, of which we have a clear idea, and which is incompatible with those objects, to which we apply it, obscurity and error begin then to take place, and we are led astray by a false philosophy. This is the case, when we transfer the determination of the thought to external objects, and suppose any real intelligible connexion betwixt them; that being a quality, which can only belong to the mind that considers them.

As to what may be said, that the operations of nature are independent of our thought and reasoning, I allow it; and accordingly have observ'd, that objects bear to each other the relations of contiguity and succession; that like objects may be observ'd in several instances to have like relations; and that all this is independent of, and antecedent to the operations of the understanding. But if we go any farther, and ascribe a power or necessary connexion to these objects; this is what we can never observe in them, but must draw the idea of it from what we feel internally in contemplating them. And this I carry so far, that I am ready to convert my present reasoning into an instance of it, by a subtility, which it will not be difficult to comprehend.

When any object is presented to us, it immediately conveys to the mind a lively idea of that object, which is usually found to attend it; and this determination of the mind forms the necessary connexion of these objects. But when we change the point of view, from the objects to the perceptions; in that case the impression is to be considered as the cause, and the lively idea as the effect; and their necessary connexion is that new determination, which we feel to pass from the idea of the one to that of the other. The uniting principle among our internal perceptions is as unintelligible as that among external objects, and is not known to us any other way than by experience. Now the nature and effects of experience have been already sufficiently examin'd and explain'd. It never gives us any insight into the internal structure or operating principle of objects, but only accustoms the mind to pass from one to another.

'Tis now time to collect all the different parts of this reasoning, and by joining them together form an exact definition of the relation of cause and effect, which makes the subject of the present enquiry. This order wou'd not have been excusable, of first examining our inference from the relation before we had explain'd the relation itself, had it been possible to proceed in a different method. But as the nature of the relation depends so much on that of the inference, we have been oblig'd to advance in this seemingly preposterous manner, and make use of terms before we were able exactly to define them, or fix their meaning. We shall now correct this fault by giving a precise definition of cause and effect.

There may two definitions be given of this relation, which are only different, by their presenting a different view of the same object, and making us consider it either as a *philosophical* or as a *natural* relation; either as a comparison of two ideas, or as an association betwixt them. We may define a CAUSE to be 'An object precedent and contiguous to another, and where all the objects resembling the former are plac'd in like relations of precedency and contiguity to those objects, that resemble the latter.' If this definition be esteemed defective, because drawn from objects foreign to the cause, we may substitute this other definition in its place, *viz.* 'A CAUSE is an object precedent and contiguous to another, and so united with it, that the idea of the one determines the mind to form the idea of the other, and the impression of the one to form a more lively idea of the other.' Shou'd this definition also be rejected for the same reason, I know no other remedy, than that the persons, who express this delicacy, shou'd substitute a juster definition in its place. But for my part I must own my incapacity for such an undertaking. When I examine with the utmost accuracy those objects, which are commonly denominated causes and effects, I find, in considering a single instance, that the one object is precedent and contiguous to the other; and in inlarging my view to consider several instances, I find only, that like objects are constantly plac'd in like relations of succession and contiguity. Again, when I consider the influence of this constant conjunction, I perceive, that such a relation can never be an object of reasoning, and can never operate upon the mind, but by means of custom, which determines the imagination to make a transition from the idea of one object to that of its usual attendant, and from the impression of one to a more lively idea of the other. However extraordinary these sentiments may appear, I think it fruitless to trouble myself with any farther enquiry or reasoning upon the subject, but shall repose myself on them as on establish'd maxims.

'Twill only be proper, before we leave this subject, to draw some corrollaries from it, by which we may remove several prejudices and popular errors, that have very much prevail'd in philosophy. First, We may learn from the foregoing doctrine, that all causes are of the same kind, and that in particular there is no foundation for that distinction, which we sometimes make betwixt efficient causes, and causes *sine qua non*; or betwixt efficient causes, and formal, and material, and exemplary, and final causes. For as our idea of efficiency is deriv'd from the constant conjunction of two objects, wherever this is observ'd, the cause is efficient; and where it is not, there can never be a cause of any kind. For the same reason we must reject the distinction betwixt *cause* and *occasion*, when suppos'd to signify any thing essentially different from each other. If constant conjunction be imply'd in what we call occasion, 'tis a real cause. If not, 'tis no relation at all, and cannot give rise to any argument or reasoning.

Secondly, The same course of reasoning will make us conclude, that there is but one kind of *necessity*, as there is but one kind of cause, and that the common distinction betwixt *moral* and *physical* necessity is without any foundation in nature. This clearly appears from the precedent explication of necessity. 'Tis the constant conjunction of objects, along with the determination of the mind, which constitutes a physical necessity: And the removal of these is the same thing with *chance*. As objects must either be conjoin'd or not, and as the mind must either be determin'd or not to pass from one object to another, 'tis impossible to admit of any medium betwixt chance and an absolute necessity. In weakening this conjunction and determination you do not change the nature of the necessity; since even in the operation of bodies, these have different degrees of constancy and force, without producing a different species of that relation.

The distinction, which we often make betwixt *power* and the *exercise* of it, is equally without foundation.

Thirdly, We may now be able fully to overcome all that repugnance, which 'tis so natural for us to entertain against the foregoing reasoning, by which we endeavour'd to prove, that the necessity of a cause to every beginning of existence is not founded on any arguments either demonstrative or intuitive. Such an opinion will not appear strange after the foregoing definitions. If we define a cause to be *an object precedent and contiguous to another, and where all the objects resembling the former are plac'd in a like relation of priority and contiguity to those objects, that resemble the latter*; we may easily conceive, that there is no absolute nor metaphysical necessity, that every beginning of existence shou'd be attended with such an object. If we define a cause to be, *An object precedent and contiguous to another and so united with it in the imagination, that the idea of the one determines the mind to form the idea of the other, and the impression of the one to form a more lively idea of the other*; we shall make still less difficulty of assenting to this opinion. Such an influence on the mind is in itself perfectly extraordinary and incomprehensible; nor can we be certain of its reality, but from experience and observation.

I shall add as a fourth corrollary, that we can never have reason to believe that any object exists, of which we cannot form an idea. For as all our reasonings concerning existence are deriv'd from causation, and as all our reasonings concerning causation are deriv'd from the experienc'd conjunction of objects, not from any reasoning or reflection, the same experience must give us a notion of these objects, and must remove all mystery from our conclusions. This is so evident, that 'twou'd scarce have merited our attention, were it not to obviate certain objections of this kind, which might arise against the following reasonings concerning *matter* and *substance*. I need not observe, that a full knowledge of the object is not requisite, but only of those qualities of it, which we believe to exist.

SECT. XV

Rules by which to judge of causes and effects

According to the precedent doctrine, there are no objects, which by the mere survey, without consulting experience, we can determine to be the causes of any other; and no objects, which we can certainly determine in the same manner not to be the causes. Any thing may produce any thing. Creation, annihilation, motion, reason, volition; all these may arise from one another, or from any other object we can imagine. Nor will this appear strange, if we compare two principles explain'd above, *that the constant conjunction of objects determines their causation, and* * *that properly speaking, no objects are contrary to each other, but existence and non-existence.* Where objects are not contrary, nothing hinders them from having that constant conjunction, on which the relation of cause and effect totally depends.

Since therefore 'tis possible for all objects to become causes or effects to each other, it may be proper to fix some general rules, by which we may know when they really are so.

(1) The cause and effect must be contiguous in space and time.

(2) The cause must be prior to the effect.

(3) There must be a constant union betwixt the cause and effect. 'Tis chiefly this quality, that constitutes the relation.

(4) The same cause always produces the same effect, and the same effect never arises but from the same cause. This principle we derive from experience, and is the source of most of our philosophical reasonings. For when by any clear

* Part I. Sect. 5.

experiment we have discover'd the causes or effects of any phaenomenon, we immediately extend our observation to every phaenomenon of the same kind, without waiting for that constant repetition, from which the first idea of this relation is deriv'd.

(5) There is another principle, which hangs upon this, *viz.* that where several different objects produce the same effect, it must be by means of some quality, which we discover to be common amongst them. For as like effects imply like causes, we must always ascribe the causation to the circumstance, wherein we discover the resemblance.

(6) The following principle is founded on the same reason. The difference in the effects of two resembling objects must proceed from that particular, in which they differ. For as like causes always produce like effects, when in any instance we find our expectation to be disappointed, we must conclude that this irregularity proceeds from some difference in the causes.

(7) When any object encreases or diminishes with the encrease or diminution of its cause, 'tis to be regarded as a compounded effect, deriv'd from the union of the several different effects, which arise from the several different parts of the cause. The absence or presence of one part of the cause is here suppos'd to be always attended with the absence or presence of a proportionable part of the effect. This constant conjunction sufficiently proves, that the one part is the cause of the other. We must, however, beware not to draw such a conclusion from a few experiments. A certain degree of heat gives pleasure; if you diminish that heat, the pleasure diminishes; but it does not follow, that if you augment it beyond a certain degree, the pleasure will likewise augment; for we find that it degenerates into pain.

(8) The eighth and last rule I shall take notice of is, that an object, which exists for any time in its full perfection without any effect, is not the sole cause of that effect, but requires to be assisted by some other principle, which may forward its influence and operation. For as like effects necessarily follow from like causes, and in a contiguous time and

place, their separation for a moment shews, that these causes are not compleat ones.

Here is all the LOGIC I think proper to employ in my reasoning; and perhaps even this was not very necessary, but might have been supply'd by the natural principles of our understanding. Our scholastic head-pieces and logicians shew no such superiority above the mere vulgar in their reason and ability, as to give us any inclination to imitate them in delivering a long system of rules and precepts to direct our judgment, in philosophy. All the rules of this nature are very easy in their invention, but extremely difficult in their application; and even experimental philosophy, which seems the most natural and simple of any, requires the utmost stretch of human judgment. There is no phaenomenon in nature, but what is compounded and modify'd by so many different circumstances, that in order to arrive at the decisive point, we must carefully separate whatever is superfluous, and enquire by new experiments, if every particular circumstance of the first experiment was essential to it. These new experiments are liable to a discussion of the same kind; so that the utmost constancy is requir'd to make us persevere in our enquiry, and the utmost sagacity to choose the right way among so many that present themselves. If this be the case even in natural philosophy, how much more in moral, where there is a much greater complication of circumstances, and where those views and sentiments, which are essential to any action of the mind, are so implicit and obscure, that they often escape our strictest attention, and are not only unaccountable in their causes, but even unknown in their existence? I am much afraid lest the small success I meet with in my enquiries will make this observation bear the air of an apology rather than of boasting.

If any thing can give me security in this particular, 'twill be the enlarging of the sphere of my experiments as much as possible; for which reason it may be proper in this place to examine the reasoning faculty of brutes, as well as that of human creatures.

SECT. XVI

Of the reason of animals

NEXT to the ridicule of denying an evident truth, is that of taking much pains to defend it; and no truth appears to me more evident, than that beasts are endow'd with thought and reason as well as men. The arguments are in this case so obvious, that they never escape the most stupid and ignorant.

We are conscious, that we ourselves, in adapting means to ends, are guided by reason and design, and that 'tis not ignorantly nor casually we perform those actions, which tend to self-preservation, to the obtaining pleasure, and avoiding pain. When therefore we see other creatures, in millions of instances, perform like actions, and direct them to like ends, all our principles of reason and probability carry us with an invincible force to believe the existence of a like cause. 'Tis needless in my opinion to illustrate this argument by the enumeration of particulars. The smallest attention will supply us with more than are requisite. The resemblance betwixt the actions of animals and those of men is so entire in this respect, that the very first action of the first animal we shall please to pitch on, will afford us an incontestable argument for the present doctrine.

This doctrine is as useful as it is obvious, and furnishes us with a kind of touchstone, by which we may try every system in this species of philosophy. 'Tis from the resemblance of the external actions of animals to those we ourselves perform, that we judge their internal likewise to resemble ours; and the same principle of reasoning, carry'd one step farther, will make us conclude that since our internal actions resemble each other, the causes, from which they are deriv'd, must also be resembling. When any hypothesis, therefore, is advanc'd to explain a mental operation, which is common to men and beasts, we must apply the same hypothesis to both; and as every true hypothesis will abide this trial, so I may venture to affirm, that no false one will ever be able to endure it. The common defect of those systems, which philosophers have employ'd to account for the actions of the mind, is, that they suppose such a subtility and refinement of thought, as not only exceeds the capacity of mere animals, but even of children and the common people in our own species; who are notwithstanding susceptible of the same emotions and affections as persons of the most accomplish'd genius and understanding. Such a subtility is a clear proof of the falshood, as the contrary simplicity of the truth, of any system.

Let us therefore put our present system concerning the nature of the understanding to this decisive trial, and see whether it will equally account for the reasonings of beasts as for these of the human species.

Here we must make a distinction betwixt those actions of animals, which are of a vulgar nature, and seem to be on a level with their common capacities, and those more extraordinary instances of sagacity, which they sometimes discover for their own preservation, and the propagation of their species. A dog, that avoids fire and precipices, that shuns strangers, and caresses his master, affords us an instance of the first kind. A bird, that chooses with such care and nicety the place and materials of her nest, and sits upon her eggs for a due time, and in suitable season, with all the precaution that a chymist is capable of in the most delicate projection, furnishes us with a lively instance of the second.

As to the former actions, I assert they proceed from a reasoning, that is not in itself different, nor founded on different principles, from that which appears in human nature. 'Tis necessary in the first place, that there be some impression immediately present to their memory or senses, in order to be the foundation of their judgment. From the tone of voice the dog infers his master's anger, and foresees his own punishment. From a certain sensation affecting his smell, he judges his game not to be far distant from him.

Secondly, The inference he draws from the present impression is built on experience, and on his observation of the conjunction of objects in past instances. As you vary this experience, he varies his reasoning. Make a beating follow upon one sign or motion for some time, and afterwards upon another; and he will successively draw different conclusions, according to his most recent experience.

Now let any philosopher make a trial, and endeavour to explain that act of the mind, which we call *belief*, and give an account of the principles, from which it is deriv'd, independent of the influence of custom on the imagination, and let his hypothesis be equally applicable to beasts as to the human species; and after he has done this, I promise to embrace his opinion. But at the same time I demand as an equitable condition, that if my system be the only one, which can answer to all these terms, it may be receiv'd as entirely satisfactory and convincing. And that 'tis the only one, is evident almost without any reasoning. Beasts certainly never perceive any real connexion among objects. 'Tis therefore by experience they infer one from another. They can never by any arguments form a general conclusion, that those objects, of which they have had no experience, resemble those of which they have. 'Tis therefore by means of custom alone, that experience operates upon them. All this was sufficiently evident with respect to man. But with respect to beasts there cannot be the least suspicion of mistake; which must be own'd to be a strong confirmation, or rather an invincible proof of my system.

Nothing shews more the force of habit in reconciling us to any phaenomenon, than this, that men are not astonish'd at the operations of their own reason, at the same time, that they admire the *instinct* of animals, and find a difficulty in explaining it, merely because it cannot be reduc'd to the very same principles. To consider the matter aright, reason is nothing but a wonderful and unintelligible instinct in our souls, which carries us along a certain train of ideas, and endows them with particular qualities, according to their particular situations and relations. This instinct, 'tis true, arises from past observation and experience; but can any one give the ultimate reason, why past experience and observation produces such an effect, any more than why nature alone shou'd produce it? Nature may certainly produce whatever can arise from habit: Nay, habit is nothing but one of the principles of nature, and derives all its force from that origin.

PART IV

Of the Sceptical and other systems of philosophy

SECT. I

Of scepticism with regard to reason

In all demonstrative sciences the rules are certain and infallible; but when we apply them, our fallible and uncertain faculties are very apt to depart from them, and fall into error. We must, therefore, in every reasoning form a new judgment, as a check or controul on our first judgment or belief; and must enlarge our view to comprehend a kind of history of all the instances, wherein our understanding has deceiv'd us, compar'd with those, wherein its testimony was just and true. Our reason must be consider'd as a kind of cause, of which truth is the natural effect; but such-a-one as by the irruption of other causes, and by the inconstancy of our mental powers, may frequently be prevented. By this means all knowledge degenerates into probability; and this probability is greater or less, according to our experience of the veracity or deceitfulness of our understanding, and according to the simplicity or intricacy of the question.

There is no Algebraist nor Mathematician so expert in his science, as to place entire confidence in any truth immediately upon his discovery of it, or regard it as any thing, but a mere probability. Every time he runs over his proofs, his confidence encreases; but still more by the approbation of his friends; and is rais'd to its utmost perfection by the universal assent and applauses of the learned world. Now 'tis evident, that this gradual encrease of assurance is nothing but the addition of new probabilities, and is deriv'd from the constant union of causes and effects, according to past experience and observation.

In accompts of any length or importance, Merchants seldom trust to the infallible certainty of numbers for their security; but by the artificial structure of the accompts, produce a probability beyond what is deriv'd from the skill and experience of the accomptant. For that is plainly of itself some degree of probability; tho' uncertain and variable, according to the degrees of his experience and length of the accompt. Now as none will maintain, that our assurance in a long numeration exceeds probability, I may safely affirm, that there scarce is any proposition concerning numbers, of which we can have a fuller security. For 'tis easily possible, by gradually diminishing the numbers, to reduce the longest series of addition to the most simple question, which can be form'd, to an addition of two single numbers; and upon this supposition we shall find it impracticable to shew the precise limits of knowledge and of probability, or discover that particular number, at which the one ends and the other begins. But knowledge and probability are of such contrary and disagreeing natures, that they cannot well run insensibly into each other, and that because they will not divide, but must be either entirely present, or entirely absent. Besides, if any single addition were certain, every one wou'd be so, and consequently the whole or total sum; unless the whole can be different from all its parts. I had almost said, that this was certain; but I reflect, that it must reduce *itself*, as well as every other reasoning, and from knowledge, degenerate into probability.

Since therefore all knowledge resolves itself into probability, and becomes at last of the same nature with that evidence, which we employ in common life, we must now examine this latter species of reasoning, and see on what foundation it stands.

In every judgment, which we can form concerning probability, as well as concerning knowledge, we ought always to correct the first judgment, deriv'd from the nature of the object, by another judgment, deriv'd from the nature of the understanding. 'Tis certain a man of solid sense and long experience ought to have, and usually has, a greater assurance in his opinions, than one that is foolish and ignorant, and that our sentiments have different degrees of authority, even with ourselves, in proportion to the degrees of our reason and experience. In the man of the best sense and longest experience, this authority is never entire; since even such-a-one must be conscious of many errors in the past, and must still dread the like for the future. Here then arises a new species of probability to correct and regulate the first, and fix its just standard and proportion. As demonstration is subject to the controul of probability, so is probability liable to a new correction by a reflex act of the mind, wherein the nature of our understanding, and our reasoning from the first probability become our objects.

Having thus found in every probability, beside the original uncertainty inherent in the subject, a new uncertainty deriv'd from the weakness of that faculty, which judges, and having adjusted these two together, we are oblig'd by our reason to add a new doubt deriv'd from the possibility of error in the estimation we make of the truth and fidelity of our faculties. This is a doubt, which immediately occurs to us, and of which, if we wou'd closely pursue our reason, we cannot avoid giving a decision. But this decision, tho' it shou'd be favourable to our preceeding judgment, being founded only on probability, must weaken still further our first evidence, and must itself be weaken'd by a fourth doubt of the same kind, and so on *in infinitum*; till at last there remain nothing of the original probability, however great we may suppose it to have been, and however small the diminution by every new uncertainty. No finite object can subsist under a decrease repeated *in infinitum*; and even the vastest quantity, which can enter into human imagination, must in this manner be reduc'd to nothing. Let our first belief be never so strong, it must infallibly perish by passing thro' so many new examinations, of which each diminishes somewhat of its force and vigour. When I reflect on the natural fallibility of my judgment, I have less confidence in my opinions, than when I only consider the objects concerning which I reason; and when I proceed still farther, to turn the scrutiny against every successive estimation I make of my faculties, all the rules of logic require a continual diminution, and at last a total extinction of belief and evidence.

Shou'd it here be ask'd me, whether I sincerely assent to this argument, which I seem to take such pains to inculcate, and whether I be really one of those sceptics, who hold that all is uncertain, and that our judgment is not in *any* thing possest of *any* measures of truth and falshood; I shou'd reply, that this question is entirely superfluous, and that neither I, nor any other person was ever sincerely and constantly of that opinion. Nature, by an absolute and uncontroulable necessity has determin'd us to judge as well as to breathe and feel; nor can we any more forbear viewing certain objects in a stronger and fuller light, upon account of their customary connexion with a present impression, than we can hinder ourselves from thinking as long as we are awake, or seeing the surrounding bodies, when we turn our eyes towards them in broad sunshine. Whoever has taken the pains to refute the cavils of this *total* scepticism, has really disputed without an antagonist, and endeavour'd by arguments to establish a faculty, which nature has antecedently implanted in the mind, and render'd unavoidable.

My intention then in displaying so carefully the arguments of that fantastic sect, is only to make the reader sensible of the truth of my hypothesis, *that all our reasonings concerning causes and effects are deriv'd from nothing but custom; and that belief is more properly an act of the sensitive, than of the cogitative part of our natures.* I have here prov'd, that the very same principles, which make us form a decision upon any subject, and correct that decision by the consideration of our genius and capacity, and of the situation of our mind, when we examin'd that subject; I say, I have prov'd, that these same principles, when carry'd farther, and apply'd to every new reflex judgment, must by continually diminishing the original evidence, at last reduce it to nothing, and utterly subvert all belief and opinion. If belief, therefore, were a simple act of the thought, without any peculiar manner of conception, or the addition of a force and vivacity, it must infallibly destroy itself, and in every case terminate in a total suspense of judgment. But as experience will sufficiently convince any one, who thinks it worth while to try, that tho' he can find no error in the foregoing arguments, yet he still continues to believe, and think, and reason as usual, he may safely conclude, that his reasoning and belief is some sensation or peculiar manner of conception, which 'tis impossible for mere ideas and reflections to destroy.

But here, perhaps, it may be demanded, how it happens, even upon my hypothesis, that these arguments above-explain'd produce not a total suspense of judgment, and after what manner the mind ever retains a degree of assurance in any subject? For as these new probabilities, which by their repetition perpetually diminish the original evidence, are founded on the very same principles, whether of thought or sensation, as the primary judgment, it may seem unavoidable, that in either case they must equally subvert it, and by the opposition, either of contrary thoughts or sensations, reduce the mind to a total uncertainty. I suppose, there is some question propos'd to me, and that after revolving over the impressions of my memory and senses, and carrying my thoughts from them to such objects, as are commonly conjoin'd with them, I feel a stronger and more forcible conception on the one side, than on the other. This strong conception forms my first decision. I suppose, that afterwards I examine my judgment itself, and observing from experience, that 'tis sometimes just and sometimes erroneous, I consider it as regulated by contrary principles or causes, of which some lead to truth, and some to error; and in ballancing these contrary causes, I diminish by a new probability the assurance of my first decision. This new probability is liable to the same diminution as the foregoing, and so on, *in infinitum*. 'Tis therefore demanded, *how it happens, that even after all we retain a degree of belief, which is sufficient for our purpose, either in philosophy or common life.*

I answer, that after the first and second decision; as the action of the mind becomes forc'd and unnatural, and the ideas faint and obscure; tho' the principles of judgment, and the ballancing of opposite causes be the same as at the very beginning; yet their influence on the imagination, and the vigour they add to, or diminish from the thought, is by no means equal. Where the mind reaches not its objects with easiness and facility, the same principles have not the same effect as in a more natural conception of the ideas; nor does the imagination feel a sensation, which holds any proportion with that which arises from its common judgments and opinions. The attention is on the stretch: The posture of the mind is uneasy; and the spirits being diverted from their natural course, are not govern'd in their movements by the same laws, at least not to the same degree, as when they flow in their usual channel.

If we desire similar instances, 'twill not be very difficult to find them. The present subject of metaphysics will supply us abundantly. The same argument, which wou'd have been esteem'd convincing in a reasoning concerning history or politics, has little or no influence in these abstruser subjects, even tho' it be perfectly comprehended; and that because there is requir'd a study and an effort of thought, in order to its being comprehended: And this effort of thought disturbs the operation of our sentiments, on which the belief depends. The case is the same in other subjects. The straining of the imagination always hinders the regular flowing of the passions and sentiments. A tragic poet, that wou'd represent his heroes as very ingenious and witty in their misfortunes, wou'd never touch the passions. As the emotions of the soul prevent any subtile reasoning and reflection, so these latter actions of the mind are equally prejudicial to the former. The mind, as well as the body, seems to be endow'd with a certain precise degree of force and activity, which it never employs in one action, but at the expence of all the rest. This is more evidently true, where the actions are of quite different natures; since in that case the force of the mind is not only diverted, but even the disposition chang'd, so as [to] render us incapable of a sudden transition from one action to the other, and still more of performing both at once. No wonder, then, the conviction, which arises from a subtile reasoning, diminishes in proportion to the efforts, which the imagination makes to enter into the reasoning, and to conceive it in all its parts. Belief, being a lively conception, can never be entire, where it is not founded on something natural and easy.

This I take to be the true state of the question, and cannot approve of that expeditious way, which some take with the sceptics, to reject at once all their arguments without enquiry or examination. If the sceptical reasonings be strong, say they, 'tis a proof, that reason may have some force and authority: if weak, they can never be sufficient to invalidate all the conclusions of our understanding. This argument is not just; because the sceptical reasonings, were it possible for them to exist, and were they not destroy'd by their subtility, wou'd be successively both strong and weak, according to the successive dispositions of the mind. Reason first appears in possession of the throne, prescribing laws, and imposing maxims, with an absolute sway and authority. Her enemy, therefore, is oblig'd to take shelter under her protection, and by making use of rational arguments to prove the fallaciousness and imbecility of reason, produces, in a manner, a patent under his hand and seal. This patent has at first an authority proportion'd to the present and immediate authority of reason, from which it is deriv'd. But as it is supposed to be contradictory to reason, it gradually diminishes the force of that governing power, and its own at the same time; till at last they both vanish away into nothing, by a regular and just diminution. The sceptical and dogmatical reasons are of the same kind, tho' contrary in their operation and tendency; so that where the latter is strong, it has an enemy of equal force in the former to encounter: and as their forces were at first equal, they still continue so, as long as either of them subsists; nor does one of them lose any force in the contest, without taking as much from its antagonist. 'Tis happy, therefore, that nature breaks the force of all sceptical arguments in time, and keeps them from having any considerable influence on the understanding. Were we to trust entirely to their self-destruction, that can never take place, 'till they have first subverted all conviction, and have totally destroy'd human reason.

SECT. II

Of scepticism with regard to the senses

THUS the sceptic still continues to reason and believe, even tho' he asserts, that he cannot defend his reason by reason; and by the same rule he must assent to the principle concerning the existence of body, tho' he cannot pretend by any arguments of philosophy to maintain its veracity. Nature has not left this to his choice, and has doubtless esteem'd it an affair of too great importance to be trusted to our uncertain reasonings and speculations. We may well ask, *What causes induce us to believe in the existence of body?* but 'tis in vain to ask, *Whether there be body or not?* That is a point, which we must take for granted in all our reasonings.

The subject, then, of our present enquiry is concerning the *causes* which induce us to believe in the existence of body: And my reasonings on this head I shall begin with a distinction, which at first sight may seem superfluous, but which will contribute very much to the perfect understanding of what follows. We ought to examine apart those two questions, which are commonly confounded together, *viz.* Why we attribute a CONTINUED existence to objects, even when they are not present to the senses; and why we suppose them to have an existence DISTINCT from the mind and perception. Under this last head I comprehend their situation as well as relations, their *external* position as well as the *independence* of their existence and operation. These two questions concerning the continu'd and distinct existence of body are intimately connected together. For if the objects of our senses continue to exist, even when they are not perceiv'd, their existence is of course independent of and distinct from the perception; and *vice versa*, if their existence be independent of the perception and distinct from it, they must continue to exist, even tho' they be not perceiv'd. But tho' the decision of the one question decides the other; yet that we may the more easily discover the principles of human nature, from whence the decision arises, we shall carry along with us this distinction, and shall consider, whether it be the *senses, reason*, or the *imagination*, that produces the opinion of a *continu'd* or of a *distinct* existence. These are the only questions, that are intelligible on the present subject. For as to the notion of external existence, when taken for something specifically different from our perceptions,* we have already shewn its absurdity.

To begin with the SENSES, *'tis evident these faculties* are incapable of giving rise to the notion of the *continu'd* existence of their objects, after they no longer appear to the senses. For that is a contradiction in terms, and supposes that the senses continue to operate, even after they have ceas'd all manner of operation. These faculties, therefore, if they have any influence in the present case, must produce the opinion of a distinct, not of a continu'd existence; and in order to that, must present their impressions either as images and representations, or as these very distinct and external existences.

That our senses offer not their impressions as the images of something *distinct*, or *independent*, and *external*, is evident; because they convey to us nothing but a single perception, and never give us the least intimation of any thing beyond. A single perception can never produce the idea of a double existence, but by some inference either of the reason or imagination. When the mind looks farther than what immediately appears to it, its conclusions can never be put

*Part. II. Sect. 6.

to the account of the senses; and it certainly looks farther, when from a single perception it infers a double existence, and supposes the relations of resemblance and causation betwixt them.

If our senses, therefore, suggest any idea of distinct existences, they must convey the impressions as those very existences, by a kind of fallacy and illusion. Upon this head we may observe, that all sensations are felt by the mind, such as they really are, and that when we doubt, whether they present themselves as distinct objects, or as mere impressions, the difficulty is not concerning their nature, but concerning their relations and situation. Now if the senses presented our impressions as external to, and independent of ourselves, both the objects and ourselves must be obvious to our senses, otherwise they cou'd not be compar'd by these faculties. The difficulty, then, is how far we are *ourselves* the objects of our senses.

'Tis certain there is no question in philosophy more abstruse than that concerning identity, and the nature of the uniting principle, which constitutes a person. So far from being able by our senses merely to determine this question, we must have recourse to the most profound metaphysics to give a satisfactory answer to it; and in common life 'tis evident these ideas of self and person are never very fix'd nor determinate. 'Tis absurd, therefore, to imagine the senses can ever distinguish betwixt ourselves and external objects.

Add to this, that every impression, external and internal, passions, affections, sensations, pains, and pleasures are originally on the same footing; and that whatever other differences we may observe among them, they appear, all of them, in their true colours, as impressions or perceptions. And indeed, if we consider the matter aright, 'tis scarce possible it shou'd be otherwise, nor is it conceivable that our senses shou'd be more capable of deceiving us in the situation and relations than in the nature of our impressions. For since all actions and sensations of the mind are known to us by consciousness, they must necessarily appear in every particular what they are, and be what they appear. Every thing that enters the mind, being in *reality* a perception, 'tis impossible any thing shou'd to *feeling* appear different. This were to suppose, that even where we are most intimately conscious, we might be mistaken.

But not to lose time in examining, whether 'tis possible for our senses to deceive us, and represent our perceptions as distinct from ourselves, that is as *external* to and *independent* of us; let us consider whether they really do so, and whether this error proceeds from an immediate sensation or from some other causes.

To begin with the question concerning *external* existence, it may perhaps be said, that setting aside the metaphysical question of the identity of a thinking substance, our own body evidently belongs to us; and, as several impressions appear exterior to the body, we suppose them also exterior to ourselves. The paper, on which I write at present, is beyond my hand. The table is beyond the paper. The walls of the chamber beyond the table. And in casting my eye towards the window, I perceive a great extent of fields and buildings beyond my chamber. From all this it may be infer'd, that no other faculty is requir'd, beside the senses, to convince us of the external existence of body. But to prevent this inference, we need only weigh the three following considerations. *First,* That, properly speaking, 'tis not our body we perceive, when we regard our limbs and members, but certain impressions, which enter by the senses; so that the ascribing a real and corporeal existence to these impressions, or to their objects, is an act of the mind as difficult to explain, as that which we examine at present. *Secondly*, Sounds, and tastes, and smells, tho' commonly regarded by the mind as continu'd independent qualities, appear not to have any existence in extension, and consequently cannot appear to the senses as situated externally to the body. The reason, why we ascribe a place to them, shall be consider'd * afterwards. *Thirdly*, Even our sight informs us not of distance or outness (so to speak) immediately and without a certain reasoning

* Sect. 5.

and experience, as is acknowledg'd by the most rational philosophers.

As to the *independency* of our perceptions on ourselves, this can never be an object of the senses; but any opinion we form concerning it, must be deriv'd from experience and observation: And we shall see afterwards, that our conclusions from experience are far from being favourable to the doctrine of the independency of our perceptions. Mean while we may observe that when we talk of real distinct existences, we have commonly more in our eye their independency than external situation in place, and think an object has a sufficient reality, when its Being is uninterrupted, and independent of the incessant revolutions, which we are conscious of in ourselves.

Thus to resume what I have said concerning the senses; they give us no notion of continu'd existence, because they cannot operate beyond the extent, in which they really operate. They as little produce the opinion of a distinct existence, because they neither can offer it to the mind as represented, nor as original. To offer it as represented, they must present both an object and an image. To make it appear as original, they must convey a falshood; and this falshood must lie in the relations and situation: In order to which they must be able to compare the object with ourselves; and even in that case they do not, nor is it possible they shou'd, deceive us. We may, therefore, conclude with certainty, that the opinion of a continu'd and of a distinct existence never arises from the senses.

To confirm this we may observe, that there are three different kinds of impressions convey'd by the senses. The first are those of the figure, bulk, motion and solidity of bodies. The second those of colours, tastes, smells, sounds, heat and cold. The third are the pains and pleasures, that arise from the application of objects to our bodies, as by the cutting of our flesh with steel, and such like. Both philosophers and the vulgar suppose the first of these to have a distinct continu'd existence. The vulgar only regard the second as on the same footing. Both philosophers and the vulgar again, esteem the third to be merely perceptions; and consequently interrupted and dependent beings.

Now 'tis evident, that, whatever may be our philosophical opinion, colours, sounds, heat and cold, as far as appears to the senses, exist after the same manner with motion and solidity, and that the difference we make betwixt them in this respect, arises not from the mere perception. So strong is the prejudice for the distinct continu'd existence of the former qualities, that when the contrary opinion is advanc'd by modern philosophers, people imagine they can almost refute it from their feeling and experience, and that their very senses contradict this philosophy. 'Tis also evident, that colours, sounds, *&c.* are originally on the same footing with the pain that arises from steel, and pleasure that proceeds from a fire; and that the difference betwixt them is founded neither on perception nor reason, but on the imagination. For as they are confest to be, both of them, nothing but perceptions arising from the particular configurations and motions of the parts of body, wherein possibly can their difference consist? Upon the whole, then, we may conclude, that as far as the senses are judges, all perceptions are the same in the manner of their existence.

We may also observe in this instance of sounds and colours, that we can attribute a distinct continu'd existence to objects without ever consulting REASON or weighing our opinions by any philosophical principles. And indeed, whatever convincing arguments philosophers may fancy they can produce to establish the belief of objects independent of the mind, 'tis obvious these arguments are known but to very few, and that 'tis not by them, that children, peasants, and the greatest part of mankind are induc'd to attribute objects to some impressions, and deny them to others. Accordingly we find, that all the conclusions, which the vulgar form on this head, are directly contrary to those, which are confirm'd by philosophy. For philosophy informs us, that every thing, which appears to the mind, is nothing but a perception, and is interrupted, and dependent on the mind; whereas the vulgar confound perceptions and objects, and attribute a distinct continu'd existence to the very things they feel or see. This sentiment, then, as it is entirely unreasonable, must proceed from some other faculty than the understanding. To which we may add, that as long as we take our perceptions and objects to be the same, we can never infer the existence of the one from that of the other, nor form any argument from the relation of cause and effect; which is the only one that can assure us of matter of fact. Even after we distinguish our perceptions from our objects, 'twill appear presently, that we are still incapable of reasoning from the existence of one to that of the other: So that upon the whole our reason neither does, nor is it possible it ever shou'd, upon any supposition give us an assurance of the continu'd and distinct existence of body. That opinion must be entirely owing to the IMAGINATION: which must now be the subject of our enquiry.

Since all impressions are internal and perishing existences, and appear as such, the notion of their distinct and continu'd existence must arise from a concurrence of some of their qualities with the qualities of the imagination; and since this notion does not extend to all of them, it must arise from certain qualities peculiar to some impressions. 'Twill therefore be easy for us to discover these qualities by a comparison of the impressions, to which we attribute a distinct and continu'd existence, with those, which we regard as internal and perishing.

We may observe, then, that 'tis neither upon account of the involuntariness of certain impressions, as is commonly suppos'd, nor of their superior force and violence, that we attribute to them a reality, and continu'd existence, which we refuse to others, that are voluntary or feeble. For 'tis evident our pains and pleasures, our passions and affections, which we never suppose to have any existence beyond our perception, operate with greater violence, and are equally involuntary, as the impressions of figure and extension, colour and sound, which we suppose to be permanent beings. The heat of a fire, when moderate, is suppos'd to exist in the fire; but the pain, which it causes upon a near approach, is not taken to have any being except in the perception.

These vulgar opinions, then, being rejected, we must search for some other hypothesis, by which we may discover those peculiar qualities in our impressions, which makes us attribute to them a distinct and continu'd existence.

After a little examination, we shall find, that all those objects, to which we attribute a continu'd existence, have a peculiar *constancy*, which distinguishes them from the impressions, whose existence depends upon our perception. These mountains, and houses and trees, which lie at present under my eye, have always appear'd to me in the same order; and when I lose sight of them by shutting my eyes or turning my head, I soon after find them return upon me without the least alteration. My bed and table, my books and papers, present themselves in the same uniform manner, and change not upon account of any interruption in my feeling or perceiving them. This is the case with all the impressions, whose objects are suppos'd to have an external existence; and is the case with no other impressions, whether gentle or violent, voluntary or involuntary.

This constancy, however, is not so perfect as not to admit of very considerable exceptions. Bodies often change their position and qualities, and after a little absence or interruption may become hardly knowable. But here 'tis observable, that even in these changes they preserve a *coherence*, and have a regular dependence on each other; which is the foundation of a kind of reasoning from causation, and produces the opinion of their continu'd existence. When I return to my chamber after an hour's absence, I find not my fire in the same situation, in which I left it: But then I am accustom'd in other instances to see a like alteration produc'd in a like time, whether I am present or absent, near or remote. This coherence, therefore, in their changes is one of the characteristics of external objects, as well as their constancy.

Having found that the opinion of the continu'd existence of body depends on the COHERENCE and constancy of certain impressions, I now proceed to examine after what manner these qualities give rise to so extraordinary an opinion. To begin with the coherence; we may observe, that tho' those internal impressions, which we regard as fleeting and perishing, have also a certain coherence or regularity in their appearances, yet 'tis of somewhat a different nature, from that which we discover in bodies. Our passions are found by experience to have a mutual connexion with and dependance on each other; but on no occasion is it necessary to suppose, that they have existed and operated, when they were not perceiv'd, in order to preserve the same dependance and connexion, of which we have had experience. The case is not the same with relation to external objects. Those require a continu'd existence, or otherwise lose, in a great measure, the regularity of their operation. I am here seated in my chamber with my face to the fire; and all the objects, that strike my senses, are contain'd in a few yards around me. My memory, indeed, informs me of the existence of many objects; but then this information extends not beyond their past existence, nor do either my senses or memory give any testimony to the continuance of their being. When therefore I am thus seated, and revolve over these thoughts, I hear on a sudden a noise as of a door turning upon its hinges; and a little after see a porter, who advances towards me. This gives occasion to many new reflections and reasonings. First, I never have observ'd, that this noise cou'd proceed from any thing but the motion of a door; and therefore conclude, that the present phaenomenon is a contradiction to all past experience, unless the door, which I remember on t'other side the chamber, be still in being. Again, I have always found, that a human body was possest of a quality, which I call gravity, and which hinders it from mounting in the air, as this porter must have done to arrive at my chamber, unless the stairs I remember be not annihilated by my absence. But this is not all. I receive a letter, which upon opening it I perceive by the hand-writing and subscription to have come from a friend, who says he is two hundred leagues distant. 'Tis evident I can never account for this phaenomenon, conformable to my experience in other instances, without spreading out in my mind the whole sea and continent between us, and supposing the effects and continu'd existence of posts and ferries, according to my memory and observation. To consider these phaenomena of the porter and letter in a certain light, they are contradictions to common experience, and may be regarded as objections to those maxims, which we form concerning the connexions of causes and effects. I am accustom'd to hear such a sound, and see such an object in motion at the same time. I have not receiv'd in this particular instance both these perceptions. These observations are contrary, unless I suppose that the door still remains, and that it was open'd without my perceiving it: And this supposition, which was at first entirely arbitrary and hypothetical, acquires a force and evidence by its being the only one, upon which I can reconcile these contradictions. There is scarce a moment of my life, wherein there is not a similar instance presented to me, and I have not occasion to suppose the continu'd existence of objects, in order to connect their past and present appearances, and give them such an union with each other, as I have found by experience to be suitable to their particular natures and circumstances. Here then I am naturally led to regard the world, as something real and durable, and as preserving its existence, even when it is no longer present to my perception.

But tho' this conclusion from the coherence of appearances may seem to be of the same nature with our reasonings concerning causes and effects; as being deriv'd from custom, and regulated by past experience; we shall find upon examination, that they are at the bottom considerably different from each other, and that this inference arises from the understanding, and from custom in an indirect and oblique manner. For 'twill readily be allow'd, that since nothing is ever really present to the mind, besides its own perceptions, 'tis not only impossible, that any habit shou'd ever be acquir'd otherwise than by the regular succession of these perceptions, but also that any habit shou'd ever exceed that degree of regularity. Any degree, therefore, of regularity in our perceptions, can never be a foundation for us to infer a greater degree of regularity in some objects, which are not perceiv'd; since this supposes a contradiction, *viz.* a habit acquir'd by what was never present to the mind. But 'tis evident, that whenever we infer the continu'd existence of the objects of sense from their coherence, and the frequency of their union, 'tis in order to bestow on the objects greater regularity than what is observ'd in our mere perceptions. We remark a connexion betwixt two kinds of objects in their past appearance to the senses, but are not able to observe this connexion to be perfectly constant, since the turning about of our head, or the shutting of our eyes is able to break it. What then do we suppose in this case, but that these objects still continue their usual connexion, notwithstanding their apparent interruption, and that the irregular appearances are join'd by something, of which we are insensible? But as all reasoning concerning matters of fact arises only from custom, and custom can only be the effect of repeated perceptions, the extending of custom and reasoning beyond the perceptions can never be the direct and natural effect of the constant repetition and connexion, but must arise from the co-operation of some other principles.

I have already * observ'd, in examining the foundation of mathematics, that the imagination, when set into any train of thinking, is apt to continue, even when its object fails it, and like a galley put in motion by the oars, carries on its course without any new impulse. This I have assign'd for the reason, why, after considering several loose standards of equality, and correcting them by each other, we proceed to imagine so correct and exact a standard of that relation, as is not liable to the least error or variation. The same

* Part. II. Sect. 4.

principle makes us easily entertain this opinion of the continu'd existence of body. Objects have a certain coherence even as they appear to our senses; but this coherence is much greater and more uniform, if we suppose the objects to have a continu'd existence; and as the mind is once in the train of observing an uniformity among objects, it naturally continues, till it renders the uniformity as compleat as possible. The simple supposition of their continu'd existence suffices for this purpose, and gives us a notion of a much greater regularity among objects, than what they have when we look no farther than our senses.

But whatever force we may ascribe to this principle, I am afraid 'tis too weak to support alone so vast an edifice, as is that of the continu'd existence of all external bodies; and that we must join the *constancy* of their appearance to the *coherence*, in order to give a satisfactory account of that opinion. As the explication of this will lead me into a considerable compass of very profound reasoning; I think it proper, in order to avoid confusion, to give a short sketch or abridgment of my system, and afterwards draw out all its parts in their full compass. This inference from the constancy of our perceptions, like the precedent from their coherence, gives rise to the opinion of the *continu'd* existence of body, which is prior to that of its *distinct* existence, and produces that latter principle.

When we have been accustom'd to observe a constancy in certain impressions, and have found, that the perception of the sun or ocean, for instance, returns upon us after an absence or annihilation with like parts and in a like order, as at its first appearance, we are not apt to regard these interrupted perceptions as different, (which they really are) but on the contrary consider them as individually the same, upon account of their resemblance. But as this interruption of their existence is contrary to their perfect identity, and makes us regard the first impression as annihilated, and the second as newly created, we find ourselves somewhat at a loss, and are involv'd in a kind of contradiction. In order to free ourselves from this difficulty, we disguise, as much as possible, the interruption, or rather remove it entirely, by supposing that these interrupted perceptions are connected by a real existence, of which we are insensible. This supposition, or idea of continu'd existence, acquires a force and vivacity from the memory of these broken impressions, and from that propensity, which they give us, to suppose them the same; and according to the precedent reasoning, the very essence of belief consists in the force and vivacity of the conception.

In order to justify this system, there are four things requisite. *First,* To explain the *principium individuationis,* or principle of identity. *Secondly,* Give a reason, why the resemblance of our broken and interrupted perceptions induces us to attribute an identity to them. *Thirdly,* Account for that propensity, which this illusion gives, to unite these broken appearances by a continu'd existence. *Fourthly* and lastly, Explain that force and vivacity of conception, which arises from the propensity.

First, As to the principle of individuation; we may observe, that the view of any one object is not sufficient to convey the idea of identity. For in that proposition, *an object is the same with itself,* if the idea express'd by the word, *object,* were no ways distinguish'd from that meant by *itself*; we really shou'd mean nothing, nor wou'd the proposition contain a predicate and a subject, which however are imply'd in this affirmation. One single object conveys the idea of unity, not that of identity.

On the other hand, a multiplicity of objects can never convey this idea, however resembling they may be suppos'd. The mind always pronounces the one not to be the other, and considers them as forming two, three, or any determinate number of objects, whose existences are entirely distinct and independent.

Since then both number and unity are incompatible with the relation of identity, it must lie in something that is neither of them. But to tell the truth, at first sight this seems utterly impossible. Betwixt unity and number there can be no medium; no more than betwixt existence and non-existence. After one object is suppos'd to exist, we must either suppose another also to exist; in which case we have the idea of number: Or we must suppose it not to exist; in which case the first object remains at unity.

To remove this difficulty, let us have recourse to the idea of time or duration. I have already observ'd, * that time, in a strict sense, implies succession, and that when we apply its idea to any unchangeable object, 'tis only by a fiction of the imagination, by which the unchangeable object is suppos'd to participate of the changes of the co-existent objects, and in particular of that of our perceptions. This fiction of the imagination almost universally takes place; and 'tis by means of it, that a single object, plac'd before us, and survey'd for any time without our discovering in it any interruption or variation, is able to give us a notion of identity. For when we consider any two points of this time, we may place them in different lights: We may either survey them at the very same instant; in which case they give us the idea of number, both by themselves and by the object; which must be multiply'd, in order to be conceiv'd at once, as existent in these two different points of time: Or on the other hand, we may trace the succession of time by a like succession of ideas, and conceiving first one moment, along with the object then existent, imagine afterwards a change in the time without any *variation* or *interruption* in the object; in which case it gives us the idea of unity. Here then is an idea, which is a medium betwixt unity and number; or more properly speaking, is either of them, according to the view, in which we take it: And this idea we call that of identity. We cannot, in any propriety of speech, say, that an object is the same with itself, unless we mean, that the object existent at one time is the same with itself existent at another. By this means we make a difference, betwixt the idea meant by the word, *object*, and that meant by *itself*, without going the length of number, and at the same time without restraining ourselves to a strict and absolute unity.

* Part II. Sect. 5.

Thus the principle of individuation is nothing but the *invariableness* and *uninterruptedness* of any object, thro' a suppos'd variation of time, by which the mind can trace it in the different periods of its existence, without any break of the view, and without being oblig'd to form the idea of multiplicity or number.

I now proceed to explain the *second* part of my system, and shew why the constancy of our perceptions makes us ascribe to them a perfect numerical identity, tho' there be very long intervals betwixt their appearance, and they have only one of the essential qualities of identity, *viz. invariableness.* That I may avoid all ambiguity and confusion on this head, I shall observe, that I here account for the opinions and belief of the vulgar with regard to the existence of body; and therefore must entirely conform myself to their manner of thinking and of expressing themselves. Now we have already observ'd, that however philosophers may distinguish betwixt the objects and perceptions of the senses; which they suppose co-existent and resembling; yet this is a distinction, which is not comprehended by the generality of mankind, who as they perceive only one being, can never assent to the opinion of a double existence and representation. Those very sensations, which enter by the eye or ear, are with them the true objects, nor can they readily conceive that this pen or paper, which is immediately perceiv'd, represents another, which is different from, but resembling it. In order, therefore, to accommodate myself to their notions, I shall at first suppose; that there is only a single existence, which I shall call indifferently *object* or *perception*, according as it shall seem best to suit my purpose, understanding by both of them what any common man means by a hat, or shoe, or stone, or any other impression, convey'd to him by his senses. I shall be sure to give warning, when I return to a more philosophical way of speaking and thinking.

To enter, therefore, upon the question concerning the source of the error and deception with regard to identity, when we attribute it to our resembling perceptions, notwithstanding their interruption; I must here recal an observation, which I have already prov'd and explain'd *. Nothing is more apt to make us mistake one idea for another, than any relation betwixt them, which associates them together in the imagination, and makes it pass with facility from one to the other. Of all relations, that of resemblance is in this respect the most efficacious; and that because it not only causes an association of ideas, but also of dispositions, and makes us conceive the one idea by an act or operation of the mind, similar to that by which we conceive the other. This circumstance I have observ'd to be of great moment; and we may establish it for a general rule, that whatever ideas place the mind in the same disposition or in similar ones, are very apt to be confounded. The mind readily passes from one to the other, and perceives not the change without a strict attention, of which, generally speaking, 'tis wholly incapable.

In order to apply this general maxim, we must first examine the disposition of the mind in viewing any object which preserves a perfect identity, and then find some other object, that is confounded with it, by causing a similar disposition. When we fix our thought on any object, and suppose it to continue the same for some time; 'tis evident we suppose the change to lie only in the time, and never exert ourselves to produce any new image or idea of the object. The faculties of the mind repose themselves in a manner, and take no more exercise, than what is necessary to continue that idea, of which we were formerly possest, and which subsists without variation or interruption. The passage from one moment to another is scarce felt, and distinguishes not itself by a different perception or idea, which may require a different direction of the spirits, in order to its conception.

Now what other objects, beside identical ones, are capable of placing the mind in the same disposition, when it considers them, and of causing the same uninterrupted passage of the imagination from one idea to another? This question

* Part II. Sect. 5.

is of the last importance. For if we can find any such objects, we may certainly conclude, from the foregoing principle, that they are very naturally confounded with identical ones, and are taken for them in most of our reasonings. But tho' this question be very important, 'tis not very difficult nor doubtful. For I immediately reply, that a succession of related objects places the mind in this disposition, and is consider'd with the same smooth and uninterrupted progress of the imagination, as attends the view of the same invariable object. The very nature and essence of relation is to connect our ideas with each other, and upon the appearance of one, to facilitate the transition to its correlative. The passage betwixt related ideas is, therefore, so smooth and easy, that it produces little alteration on the mind, and seems like the continuation of the same action; and as the continuation of the same action is an effect of the continu'd view of the same object, 'tis for this reason we attribute sameness to every succession of related objects. The thought slides along the succession with equal facility, as if it consider'd only one object; and therefore confounds the succession with the identity.

We shall afterwards see many instances of this tendency of relation to make us ascribe an *identity* to *different* objects; but shall here confine ourselves to the present subject. We find by experience, that there is such a *constancy* in almost all the impressions of the senses, that their interruption produces no alteration on them, and hinders them not from returning the same in appearance and in situation as at their first experience. I survey the furniture of my chamber; I shut my eyes, and afterwards open them; and find the new perceptions to resemble perfectly those, which formerly struck my senses. This resemblance is observ'd in a thousand instances, and naturally connects together our ideas of these interrupted perceptions by the strongest relation, and conveys the mind with an easy transition from one to another. An easy transition or passage of the imagination, along the ideas of these different and interrupted perceptions, is almost the same disposition of mind with that in which we consider one constant and uninterrupted perception. 'Tis therefore very natural for us to mistake the one for the other *.

The persons, who entertain this opinion concerning the identity of our resembling perceptions, are in general all the unthinking and unphilosophical part of mankind, (that is, all of us, at one time or other) and consequently such as suppose their perceptions to be their only objects, and never think of a double existence internal and external, representing and represented. The very image, which is present to the senses, is with us the real body; and 'tis to these interrupted images we ascribe a perfect identity. But as the interruption of the appearance seems contrary to the identity, and naturally leads us to regard these resembling perceptions as different from each other, we here find ourselves at a loss how to reconcile such opposite opinions. The smooth passage of the imagination along the ideas of the resembling perceptions makes us ascribe to them a perfect identity. The interrupted manner of their appearance makes us consider them as so many resembling, but still distinct beings, which appear after certain intervals. The perplexity arising from this contradiction produces a propension to unite these broken appearances by the fiction of a continu'd existence, which is the *third* part of that hypothesis I propos'd to explain.

Nothing is more certain from experience, than that any contradiction either to the sentiments or passions gives a sensible uneasiness, whether it proceeds from without or

* This reasoning, it must be confest, is somewhat abstruse, and difficult to be comprehended; but it is remarkable, that this very difficulty may be converted into a proof of the reasoning. We may observe, that there are two relations, and both of them resemblances, which contribute to our mistaking the succession of our interrupted perceptions for an identical object. The first is, the resemblance of the perceptions: The second is the resemblance, which the act of the mind in surveying a succession of resembling objects bears to that in surveying an identical object. Now these resemblances we are apt to confound with each other; and 'tis natural we shou'd, according to this very reasoning. But let us keep them distinct, and we shall find no difficulty in conceiving the precedent argument.

from within; from the opposition of external objects, or from the combat of internal principles. On the contrary, whatever strikes in with the natural propensities, and either externally forwards their satisfaction, or internally concurs with their movements, is sure to give a sensible pleasure. Now there being here an opposition betwixt the notion of the identity of resembling perceptions, and the interruption of their appearance, the mind must be uneasy in that situation, and will naturally seek relief from the uneasiness. Since the uneasiness arises from the opposition of two contrary principles, it must look for relief by sacrificing the one to the other. But as the smooth passage of our thought along our resembling perceptions makes us ascribe to them an identity, we can never without reluctance yield up that opinion. We must, therefore, turn to the other side, and suppose that our perceptions are no longer interrupted, but preserve a continu'd as well as an invariable existence, and are by that means entirely the same. But here the interruptions in the appearance of these perceptions are so long and frequent, that 'tis impossible to overlook them; and as the *appearance* of a perception in the mind and its *existence* seem at first sight entirely the same, it may be doubted, whether we can ever assent to so palpable a contradiction, and suppose a perception to exist without being present to the mind. In order to clear up this matter, and learn how the interruption in the appearance of a perception implies not necessarily an interruption in its existence, 'twill be proper to touch upon some principles, which we shall have occasion to explain more fully afterwards *.

We may begin with observing, that the difficulty in the present case is not concerning the matter of fact, or whether the mind forms such a conclusion concerning the continu'd existence of its perceptions, but only concerning the manner in which the conclusion is form'd, and principles from which it is deriv'd. 'Tis certain, that almost all mankind, and even philosophers themselves, for the greatest part of their lives, take their perceptions to be their

* Sect. 6.

only objects, and suppose, that the very being, which is intimately present to the mind, is the real body or material existence. 'Tis also certain, that this very perception or object is suppos'd to have a continu'd uninterrupted being, and neither to be annihilated by our absence, nor to be brought into existence by our presence. When we are absent from it, we say it still exists, but that we do not feel, we do not see it. When we are present, we say we feel, or see it. Here then may arise two questions; *First*, How we can satisfy ourselves in supposing a perception to be absent from the mind without being annihilated. *Secondly*, After what manner we conceive an object to become present to the mind, without some new creation of a perception or image; and what we mean by this *seeing*, and *feeling*, and *perceiving*.

As to the first question; we may observe, that what we call a *mind*, is nothing but a heap or collection of different perceptions, united together by certain relations, and suppos'd, tho' falsely, to be endow'd with a perfect simplicity and identity. Now as every perception is distinguishable from another, and may be consider'd as separately existent; it evidently follows, that there is no absurdity in separating any particular perception from the mind; that is, in breaking off all its relations, with that connected mass of perceptions, which constitute a thinking being.

The same reasoning affords us an answer to the second question. If the name of *perception* renders not this separation from a mind absurd and contradictory, the name of *object*, standing for the very same thing, can never render their conjunction impossible. External objects are seen, and felt, and become present to the mind; that is, they acquire such a relation to a connected heap of perceptions, as to influence them very considerably in augmenting their number by present reflections and passions, and in storing the memory with ideas. The same continu'd and uninterrupted Being may, therefore, be sometimes present to the mind, and sometimes absent from it, without any real or essential change in the Being itself. An interrupted appearance to the senses implies not necessarily an interruption in the existence. The supposition of the continu'd existence of sensible objects or perceptions involves no contradiction. We may easily indulge our inclination to that supposition. When the exact resemblance of our perceptions makes us ascribe to them an identity, we may remove the seeming interruption by feigning a continu'd being, which may fill those intervals, and preserve a perfect and entire identity to our perceptions.

But as we here not only *feign* but *believe* this continu'd existence, the question is, *from whence arises such a belief*; and this question leads us to the *fourth* member of this system. It has been prov'd already, that belief in general consists in nothing, but the vivacity of an idea; and that an idea may acquire this vivacity by its relation to some present impression. Impressions are naturally the most vivid perceptions of the mind; and this quality is in part convey'd by the relation to every connected idea. The relation causes a smooth passage from the impression to the idea, and even give a propensity to that passage. The mind falls so easily from the one perception to the other, that it scarce perceives the change, but retains in the second a considerable share of the vivacity of the first. It is excited by the lively impression; and this vivacity is convey'd to the related idea, without any great diminution in the passage, by reason of the smooth transition and the propensity of the imagination.

But suppose, that this propensity arises from some other principle, besides that of relation; 'tis evident it must still have the same effect, and convey the vivacity from the impression to the idea. Now this is exactly the present case. Our memory presents us with a vast number of instances of perceptions perfectly resembling each other, that return at different distances of time, and after considerable interruptions. This resemblance gives us a propension to consider these interrupted perceptions as the same; and also a propension to connect them by a continu'd existence, in order to justify this identity, and avoid the contradiction, in which the interrupted appearance of these perceptions seems necessarily to involve us. Here then we have a propensity to feign the continu'd existence of all sensible objects; and as this propensity arises from some lively impressions of the memory, it bestows a vivacity on that fiction; or in other words, makes us believe the continu'd existence of body. If sometimes we ascribe a continu'd existence to objects, which are perfectly new to us, and of whose constancy and coherence we have no experience, 'tis because the manner, in which they present themselves to our senses, resembles that of constant and coherent objects; and this resemblance is a source of reasoning and analogy, and leads us to attribute the same qualities to the similar objects.

I believe an intelligent reader will find less difficulty to assent to this system, than to comprehend it fully and distinctly, and will allow, after a little reflection, that every part carries its own proof along with it. 'Tis indeed evident, that as the vulgar *suppose* their perceptions to be their only objects, and at the same time *believe* the continu'd existence of matter, we must account for the origin of the belief upon that supposition. Now upon that supposition, 'tis a false opinion that any of our objects, or perceptions, are identically the same after an interruption; and consequently the opinion of their identity can never arise from reason, but must arise from the imagination. The imagination is seduc'd into such an opinion only by means of the resemblance of certain perceptions; since we find they are only our resembling perceptions, which we have a propension to suppose the same. This propension to bestow an identity on our resembling perceptions, produces the fiction of a continu'd existence; since that fiction, as well as the identity, is really false, as is acknowledg'd by all philosophers, and has no other effect than to remedy the interruption of our perceptions, which is the only circumstance that is contrary to their identity. In the last place this propension causes belief by means of the present impressions of the memory; since without the remembrance of former sensations, 'tis plain we never shou'd have any belief of the continu'd existence of body. Thus in examining all these parts, we find that each of them is supported by the strongest proofs; and that all of them together form a consistent system, which is perfectly convincing. A strong propensity or inclination alone, without any present impression, will sometimes cause a belief or opinion. How much more when aided by that circumstance?

But tho' we are led after this manner, by the natural propensity of the imagination, to ascribe a continu'd existence to those sensible objects or perceptions; which we find to resemble each other in their interrupted appearance; yet a very little reflection and philosophy is sufficient to make us perceive the fallacy of that opinion. I have already observ'd, that there is an intimate connexion betwixt those two principles, of a *continu'd* and of a *distinct* or *independent* existence, and that we no sooner establish the one than the other follows, as a necessary consequence. 'Tis the opinion of a continu'd existence, which first takes place, and without much study or reflection draws the other along with it, wherever the mind follows its first and most natural tendency. But when we compare experiments, and reason a little upon them, we quickly perceive, that the doctrine of the independent existence of our sensible perceptions is contrary to the plainest experience. This leads us backward upon our footsteps to perceive our error in attributing a continu'd existence to our perceptions, and is the origin of many very curious opinions, which we shall here endeavour to account for.

'Twill first be proper to observe a few of those experiments, which convince us, that our perceptions are not possest of any independent existence. When we press one eye with a finger, we immediately perceive all the objects to become double, and one half of them to be remov'd from their common and natural position. But as we do not attribute a continu'd existence to both these perceptions, and as they are both of the same nature, we clearly perceive, that all our perceptions are dependent on our organs, and the disposition of our nerves and animal spirits. This opinion is confirm'd by the seeming encrease and diminution of objects, according to their distance; by the apparent alterations in their figure; by the changes in their colour and other qualities from our sickness and distempers; and by an infinite number of other experiments of the same kind; from all which we learn, that our sensible perceptions are not possest of any distinct or independent existence.

The natural consequence of this reasoning shou'd be, that our perceptions have no more a continu'd than an independent existence; and indeed philosophers have so far run into this opinion, that they change their system, and distinguish, (as we shall do for the future) betwixt perceptions and objects, of which the former are suppos'd to be interrupted, and perishing, and different at every different return; the latter to be uninterrupted, and to preserve a continu'd existence and identity. But however philosophical this new system may be esteem'd, I assert that 'tis only a palliative remedy, and that it contains all the difficulties of the vulgar system, with some others, that are peculiar to itself. There are no principles either of the understanding or fancy, which lead us directly to embrace this opinion of the double existence of perceptions and objects, nor can we arrive at it but by passing thro' the common hypothesis of the identity and continuance of our interrupted perceptions. Were we not first persuaded, that our perceptions are our only objects, and continue to exist even when they no longer make their appearance to the senses, we shou'd never be led to think, that our perceptions and objects are different, and that our objects alone preserve a continu'd existence. 'The latter hypothesis has no primary recommendation either to reason or the imagination, but acquires all its influence on the imagination from the former'. This proposition contains two parts, which we shall endeavour to prove as distinctly and clearly, as such abstruse subjects will permit.

As to the first part of the proposition, *that this philosophical hypothesis has no primary recommendation, either to reason or the imagination,* we may soon satisfy ourselves with regard to reason by the following reflections. The only existences, of which we are certain, are perceptions, which being immediately present to us by consciousness, command our strongest assent, and are the first foundation of all our conclusions. The only conclusion we can draw from the existence of one thing to that of another, is by means of the relation of cause and effect, which shews, that there is a connexion betwixt them, and that the existence of one is dependent on that of the other. The idea of this relation is deriv'd from past experience, by which we find, that two beings are constantly conjoin'd together, and are always present at once to the mind. But as no beings are ever present to the mind but perceptions; it follows that we may observe a conjunction or a relation of cause and effect between different perceptions, but can never observe it between perceptions and objects. 'Tis impossible, therefore, that from the existence or any of the qualities of the former, we can ever form any conclusion concerning the existence of the latter, or ever satisfy our reason in this particular.

'Tis no less certain, that this philosophical system has no primary recommendation to the *imagination*, and that that faculty wou'd never, of itself, and by its original tendency, have fallen upon such a principle. I confess it will be somewhat difficult to prove this to the full satisfaction of the reader; because it implies a negative, which in many cases will not admit of any positive proof. If any one wou'd take the pains to examine this question, and wou'd invent a system, to account for the direct origin of this opinion from the imagination, we shou'd be able, by the examination of that system, to pronounce a certain judgment in the present subject. Let it be taken for granted, that our perceptions are broken, and interrupted, and however like, are still different from each other; and let any one upon this supposition shew why the fancy, directly and immediately, proceeds to the belief of another existence, resembling these perceptions in their nature, but yet continu'd, and uninterrupted, and identical; and after he has done this to my satisfaction, I promise to renounce my present opinion. Mean while I cannot forbear concluding, from the very abstractedness and difficulty of the first supposition, that 'tis an improper subject for the fancy to work upon. Whoever wou'd explain the origin of the *common* opinion concerning the continu'd and distinct existence of body, must take the mind in its *common* situation, and must proceed upon the supposition, that our perceptions are our only objects, and continue to exist even when they are not perceiv'd. Tho' this opinion be false, 'tis the most natural of any, and has alone any primary recommendation to the fancy.

As to the second part of the proposition, *that the philosophical system acquires all its influence on the imagination from the vulgar one*; we may observe, that this is a natural and unavoidable consequence of the foregoing conclusion, *that it has no primary recommendation to reason or the imagination.* For as the philosophical system is found by experience to take hold of many minds, and in particular of all those, who reflect ever so little on this subject, it must derive all its authority from the vulgar system; since it has no original authority of its own. The manner, in which these two systems, tho' directly contrary, are connected together, may be explain'd, as follows.

The imagination naturally runs on in this train of thinking. Our perceptions are our only objects: Resembling perceptions are the same, however broken or uninterrupted in their appearance: This appearing interruption is contrary to the identity: The interruption consequently extends not beyond the appearance, and the perception or object really continues to exist, even when absent from us: Our sensible perceptions have, therefore, a continu'd and uninterrupted existence. But as a little reflection destroys this conclusion, that our perceptions have a continu'd existence, by shewing that they have a dependent one, 'twou'd naturally be expected, that we must altogether reject the opinion, that there is such a thing in nature as a continu'd existence, which is preserv'd even when it no longer appears to the senses. The case, however, is otherwise. Philosophers are so far from rejecting the opinion of a continu'd existence upon rejecting that of the independence and continuance of our sensible perceptions, that tho' all sects agree in the latter sentiment, the former, which is, in a manner, its necessary consequence, has been peculiar to a few extravagant sceptics; who after all maintain'd that opinion in words only, and were never able to bring themselves sincerely to believe it.

There is a great difference betwixt such opinions as we form after a calm and profound reflection, and such as we embrace by a kind of instinct or natural impulse, on account of their suitableness and conformity to the mind. If these opinions become contrary, 'tis not difficult to foresee which of them will have the advantage. As long as our attention is bent upon the subject, the philosophical and study'd principle may prevail; but the moment we relax our thoughts, nature will display herself, and draw us back to our former opinion. Nay she has sometimes such an influence, that she can stop our progress, even in the midst of our most profound reflections, and keep us from running on with all the consequences of any philosophical opinion. Thus tho' we clearly perceive the dependence and interruption of our perceptions, we stop short in our carreer, and never upon that account reject the notion of an independent and continu'd existence. That opinion has taken such deep root in the imagination, that 'tis impossible ever to eradicate it, nor will any strain'd metaphysical conviction of the dependence of our perceptions be sufficient for that purpose.

But tho' our natural and obvious principles here prevail above our study'd reflections, 'tis certain there must be some struggle and opposition in the case; at least so long as these reflections retain any force or vivacity. In order to set ourselves at ease in this particular, we contrive a new hypothesis, which seems to comprehend both these principles of reason and imagination. This hypothesis is the philosophical one of the double existence of perceptions and objects; which pleases our reason, in allowing, that our dependent perceptions are interrupted and different; and at the same time is agreeable to the imagination in attributing a continu'd existence to something else, which we call *objects.*

This philosophical system, therefore, is the monstrous offspring of two principles, which are contrary to each other, which are both at once embrac'd by the mind, and which are unable mutually to destroy each other. The imagination tells us, that our resembling perceptions have a continu'd and uninterrupted existence, and are not annihilated by their absence. Reflection tells us, that even our resembling perceptions are interrupted in their existence, and different from each other. The contradiction betwixt these opinions we elude by a new fiction, which is conformable to the hypothesis both of reflection and fancy, by ascribing these contrary qualities to different existences; the *interruption* to perceptions, and the *continuance* to objects. Nature is obstinate, and will not quit the field, however strongly attack'd by reason; and at the same time reason is so clear in the point, that there is no possibility of disguising her. Not being able to reconcile these two enemies, we endeavour to set ourselves at ease as much as possible, by successively granting to each whatever it demands, and by feigning a double existence, where each may find something, that has all the conditions it desires. Were we fully convinc'd, that our resembling perceptions are continu'd, and identical, and independent, we shou'd never run into this opinion of a double existence, since we shou'd find satisfaction in our first supposition, and wou'd not look beyond. Again, were we fully convinc'd, that our perceptions are dependent, and interrupted, and different, we shou'd be inclined to embrace the opinion of a double existence; since in that case we shou'd clearly perceive the error of our first supposition of a continu'd existence, and wou'd never regard it any farther. 'Tis therefore from the intermediate situation of the mind, that this opinion arises, and from such an adherence to these two contrary principles, as makes us seek some pretext to justify our receiving both; which happily at last is found in the system of a double existence.

Another advantage of this philosophical system is its similarity to the vulgar one; by which means we can humour our reason for a moment, when it becomes troublesome and sollicitous; and yet upon its least negligence or inattention, can easily return to our vulgar and natural notions. Accordingly we find, that philosophers neglect not this advantage; but immediately upon leaving their closets, mingle with the rest of mankind in those exploded opinions, that our perceptions are our only objects, and continue identically and uninterruptedly the same in all their interrupted appearances.

There are other particulars of this system, wherein we may remark its dependence on the fancy, in a very conspicuous manner. Of these, I shall observe the two following. *First*, We suppose external objects to resemble internal perceptions. I have already shewn, that the relation of cause and effect can never afford us any just conclusion from the existence or qualities of our perceptions to the existence of external continu'd objects: And I shall farther add, that even tho' they cou'd afford such a conclusion, we shou'd never have any reason to infer, that our objects resemble our perceptions. That opinion, therefore, is deriv'd from nothing but the quality of the fancy above-explain'd, *that it borrows all its ideas from some precedent perception.* We never can conceive any thing but perceptions, and therefore must make every thing resemble them.

Secondly, As we suppose our objects in general to resemble our perceptions, so we take it for granted, that every particular object resembles that perception, which it causes. The relation of cause and effect determines us to join the other of resemblance; and the ideas of these existences being already united together in the fancy by the former relation, we naturally add the latter to compleat the union. We have a strong propensity to compleat every union by joining new relations to those which we have before observ'd betwixt any ideas, as we shall have occasion to observe presently *.

Having thus given an account of all the systems both popular and philosophical, with regard to external existences, I cannot forbear giving vent to a certain sentiment,

* Sect. 5.

which arises upon reviewing those systems. I begun this subject with premising, that we ought to have an implicit faith in our senses, and that this wou'd be the conclusion, I shou'd draw from the whole of my reasoning. But to be ingenuous, I feel myself *at present* of a quite contrary sentiment, and am more inclin'd to repose no faith at all in my senses, or rather imagination, than to place in it such an implicit confidence. I cannot conceive how such trivial qualities of the fancy, conducted by such false suppositions, can ever lead to any solid and rational system. They are the coherence and constancy of our perceptions, which produce the opinion of their continu'd existence; tho' these qualities of perceptions have no perceivable connexion with such an existence. The constancy of our perceptions has the most considerable effect, and yet is attended with the greatest difficulties. 'Tis a gross illusion to suppose, that our resembling perceptions are numerically the same; and 'tis this illusion, which leads us into the opinion, that these perceptions are uninterrupted, and are still existent, even when they are not present to the senses. This is the case with our popular system. And as to our philosophical one, 'tis liable to the same difficulties; and is over-and-above loaded with this absurdity, that it at once denies and establishes the vulgar supposition. Philosophers deny our resembling perceptions to be identically the same, and uninterrupted; and yet have so great a propensity to believe them such, that they arbitrarily invent a new set of perceptions, to which they attribute these qualities. I say, a new set of perceptions: For we may well suppose in general, but 'tis impossible for us distinctly to conceive, objects to be in their nature any thing but exactly the same with perceptions. What then can we look for from this confusion of groundless and extraordinary opinions but error and falshood? And how can we justify to ourselves any belief we repose in them?

This sceptical doubt, both with respect to reason and the senses, is a malady, which can never be radically cur'd, but must return upon us every moment, however we may chace it away, and sometimes may seem entirely free from it. 'Tis impossible upon any system to defend either our understanding or senses; and we but expose them farther when we endeavour to justify them in that manner. As the sceptical doubt arises naturally from a profound and intense reflection on those subjects, it always encreases, the farther we carry our reflections, whether in opposition or conformity to it. Carelessness and in-attention alone can afford us any remedy. For this reason I rely entirely upon them; and take it for granted, whatever may be the reader's opinion at this present moment, that an hour hence he will be persuaded there is both an external and internal world; and going upon that supposition, I intend to examine some general systems both ancient and modern, which have been propos'd of both, before I proceed to a more particular enquiry concerning our impressions. This will not, perhaps, in the end be found foreign to our present purpose.

SECT. III

Of the antient philosophy

SEVERAL moralists have recommended it as an excellent method of becoming acquainted with our own hearts, and knowing our progress in virtue, to recollect our dreams in a morning, and examine them with the same rigour, that we wou'd our most serious and most deliberate actions. Our character is the same throughout, say they, and appears best where artifice, fear, and policy have no place, and men can neither be hypocrites with themselves nor others. The generosity, or baseness of our temper, our meekness or cruelty, our courage or pusillanimity, influence the fictions of the imagination with the most unbounded liberty, and discover themselves in the most glaring colours. In like manner, I am persuaded, there might be several useful discoveries made from a criticism of the fictions of the antient philosophy, concerning *substances, and substantial forms, and accidents, and occult qualities;* which, however unreasonable and capricious, have a very intimate connexion with the principles of human nature.

'Tis confest by the most judicious philosophers, that our ideas of bodies are nothing but collections form'd by the mind of the ideas of the several distinct sensible qualities, of which objects are compos'd, and which we find to have a constant union with each other. But however these qualities may in themselves be entirely distinct, 'tis certain we commonly regard the compound, which they form, as ONE thing, and as continuing the SAME under very considerable alterations. The acknowledg'd composition is evidently contrary to this suppos'd *simplicity* and the variation to the *identity*. It may, therefore, be worth while to consider the *causes*, which make us almost universally fall into such evident contradictions, as well as the *means* by which we endeavour to conceal them.

'Tis evident, that as the ideas of the several distinct *successive* qualities of objects are united together by a very close relation, the mind, in looking along the succession, must be carry'd from one part of it to another by an easy transition, and will no more perceive the change, than if it contemplated the same unchangeable object. This easy transition is the effect, or rather essence of relation; and as the imagination readily takes one idea for another, where their influence on the mind is similar; hence it proceeds, that any such succession of related qualities is readily consider'd as one continued object, existing without any variation. The smooth and uninterrupted progress of the thought, being alike in both cases, readily deceives the mind, and makes us ascribe an identity to the changeable succession of connected qualities.

But when we alter our method of considering the succession, and instead of traceing it gradually thro' the successive points of time, survey at once any two distinct periods of its duration, and compare the different conditions of the successive qualities; in that case the variations, which were insensible when they arose gradually, do now appear of consequence, and seem entirely to destroy the identity. By this means there arises a kind of contrariety in our method of thinking, from the different points of view, in which we survey the object, and from the nearness or remoteness of those instants of time, which we compare together. When we gradually follow an object in its successive changes, the smooth progress of the thought makes us ascribe an identity to the succession; because 'tis by a similar act of the mind we consider an unchangeable object. When we compare its situation after a considerable change the progress of the thought is broke; and consequently we are presented with the idea of diversity: In order to reconcile which contradictions the imagination is apt to feign something unknown and invisible, which it supposes to continue the same under all these variations; and this unintelligible something it calls a *substance, or original and first matter*.

We entertain a like notion with regard to the *simplicity* of substances, and from like causes. Suppose an object perfectly simple and indivisible to be presented, along with another object, whose *co-existent* parts are connected together by a strong relation, 'tis evident the actions of the mind, in considering these two objects, are not very different. The imagination conceives the simple object at once, with facility, by a single effort of thought, without change or variation. The connexion of parts in the compound object has almost the same effect, and so unites the object within itself, that the fancy feels not the transition in passing from one part to another. Hence the colour, taste, figure, solidity, and other qualities, combin'd in a peach or melon, are conceiv'd to form *one thing*; and that on account of their close relation, which makes them affect the thought in the same manner, as if perfectly uncompounded. But the mind rests not here. Whenever it views the object in another light, it finds that all these qualities are different, and distinguishable, and separable from each other; which view of things being destructive of its primary and more natural notions, obliges the imagination to feign an unknown something, or *original* substance and matter, as a principle of union or cohesion among these qualities, and as what may give the compound object a title to be call'd one thing, notwithstanding its diversity and composition.

The peripatetic philosophy asserts the *original* matter to be perfectly homogeneous in all bodies, and considers fire, water, earth, and air, as of the very same substance; on account of their gradual revolutions and changes into each other. At the same time it assigns to each of these species of objects a distinct *substantial form*, which it supposes to be the source of all those different qualities they possess, and to be a new foundation of simplicity and identity to each particular species. All depends on our manner of viewing the objects. When we look along the insensible changes of bodies, we suppose all of them to be of the same substance or essence. When we consider their sensible differences, we attribute to each of them a substantial and essential difference. And in order to indulge ourselves in both these ways of considering our objects, we suppose all bodies to have at once a substance and a substantial form.

The notion of *accidents* is an unavoidable consequence of this method of thinking with regard to substances and substantial forms; nor can we forbear looking upon colours, sounds, tastes, figures, and other properties of bodies, as existences, which cannot subsist apart, but require a subject of inhesion to sustain and support them. For having never discover'd any of these sensible qualities, where, for the reasons above mention'd, we did not likewise fancy a substance to exist; the same habit, which makes us infer a connexion betwixt cause and effect, makes us here infer a dependance of every quality on the unknown substance. The custom of imagining a dependance has the same effect as the custom of observing it wou'd have. This conceit, however, is no more reasonable than any of the foregoing. Every quality being a distinct thing from another, may be conceiv'd to exist apart, and may exist apart, not only from every other quality, but from that unintelligible chimera of a substance.

But these philosophers carry their fictions still farther in their sentiments concerning *occult qualities*, and both suppose a substance supporting, which they do not understand, and an accident supported, of which they have as imperfect an idea. The whole system, therefore, is entirely incomprehensible, and yet is deriv'd from principles as natural as any of these above-explain'd.

In considering this subject we may observe a gradation of three opinions, that rise above each other, according as the persons, who form them, acquire new degrees of reason and knowledge. These opinions are that of the vulgar, that of a false philosophy, and that of the true; where we shall find upon enquiry, that the true philosophy approaches nearer to the sentiments of the vulgar, than to those of a mistaken knowledge. 'Tis natural for men, in their common and careless way of thinking, to imagine they perceive a connexion betwixt such objects as they have constantly found united together; and because custom has render'd it difficult to separate the ideas, they are apt to fancy such a separation to be in itself impossible and absurd. But philosophers, who abstract from the effects of custom, and compare the ideas of objects, immediately perceive the falsehood of these vulgar sentiments, and discover that there is no known connexion among objects. Every different object appears to them entirely distinct and separate; and they perceive, that 'tis not from a view of the nature and qualities of objects we infer one from another, but only when in several instances we observe them to have been constantly conjoin'd. But these philosophers, instead of drawing a just inference from this observation, and concluding, that we have no idea of power or agency, separate from the mind, and belonging to causes; I say, instead of drawing this conclusion, they frequently search for the qualities, in which this agency consists, and are displeas'd with every system, which their reason suggests to them, in order to explain it. They have sufficient force of genius to free them from the vulgar error, that there is a natural and perceivable connexion betwixt the several sensible qualities and actions of matter; but not sufficient to keep them from ever seeking for this connexion in matter, or causes. Had they fallen upon the just conclusion, they wou'd have return'd back to the situation of the vulgar, and wou'd have regarded all these disquisitions with indolence and indifference. At present they seem to be in a very lamentable condition, and such as the poets have given us but a faint notion of in their descriptions of the punishment of *Sisyphus* and *Tantalus*. For what can be imagin'd more tormenting, than to seek with eagerness, what for ever flies us; and seek for it in a place, where 'tis impossible it can ever exist?

But as nature seems to have observ'd a kind of justice and compensation in every thing, she has not neglected philosophers more than the rest of the creation; but has reserv'd them a consolation amid all their disappointments and afflictions. This consolation principally consists in their invention of the words *faculty* and *occult quality*. For it being usual, after the frequent use of terms, which are really significant and intelligible, to omit the idea, which we wou'd express by them, and to preserve only the custom, by which we recal the idea at pleasure; so it naturally happens, that after the frequent use of terms, which are wholly insignificant and unintelligible, we fancy them to be on the same footing with the precedent, and to have a secret meaning, which we might discover by reflection. The resemblance of their appearance deceives the mind, as is usual, and makes us imagine a thorough resemblance and conformity. By this means these philosophers set themselves at ease, and arrive at last, by an illusion, at the same indifference, which the people attain by their stupidity, and true philosophers by their moderate scepticism. They need only say, that any phaenomenon, which puzzles them, arises from a faculty or an occult quality, and there is an end of all dispute and enquiry upon the matter.

But among all the instances, wherein the Peripatetics have shewn they were guided by every trivial propensity of the imagination, no one is more remarkable than their *sympathies, antipathies, and horrors of a vacuum*. There is a very remarkable inclination in human nature, to bestow on external objects the same emotions, which it observes in itself; and to find every where those ideas, which are most present to it. This inclination, 'tis true, is suppress'd by a little reflection, and only takes place in children, poets, and the antient philosophers. It appears in children, by their desire of beating the stones, which hurt them: In poets, by their readiness to personify every thing: And in the antient philosophers, by these fictions of sympathy and antipathy. We must pardon children, because of their age; poets, because they profess to follow implicitly the suggestions of their fancy: But what excuse shall we find to justify our philosophers in so signal a weakness?

SECT. IV

Of the modern philosophy

BUT here it may be objected, that the imagination, according to my own confession, being the ultimate judge of all systems of philosophy, I am unjust in blaming the antient philosophers for makeing use of that faculty, and allowing themselves to be entirely guided by it in their reasonings. In order to justify myself, I must distinguish in the imagination betwixt the principles which are permanent, irresistable, and universal; such as the customary transition from causes to effects, and from effects to causes: And the principles, which are changeable, weak, and irregular; such as those I have just now taken notice of. The former are the foundation of all our thoughts and actions, so that upon their removal human nature must immediately perish and go to ruin. The latter are neither unavoidable to mankind, nor necessary, or so much as useful in the conduct of life; but on the contrary are observ'd only to take place in weak minds, and being opposite to the other principles of custom and reasoning, may easily be subverted by a due contrast and opposition. For this reason the former are received by philosophy, and the latter rejected. One who concludes somebody to be near him, when he hears an articulate voice in the dark, reasons justly and naturally; tho' that conclusion be deriv'd from nothing but custom, which infixes and inlivens the idea of a human creature, on account of his usual conjunction with the present impression. But one, who is tormented he knows not why, with the apprehension of spectres in the dark, may, perhaps, be said to reason, and to reason naturally too: But then it must be in the same sense, that a malady is said to be natural; as arising from natural causes, tho' it be contrary to health, the most agreeable and most natural situation of man.

The opinions of the antient philosophers, their fictions of substance and accident, and their reasonings concerning substantial forms and occult qualities, are like the spectres in the dark, and are deriv'd from principles, which, however common, are neither universal nor unavoidable in human nature. The *modern philosophy* pretends to be entirely free from this defect, and to arise only from the solid, permanent, and consistent principles of the imagination. Upon what grounds this pretension is founded must now be the subject of our enquiry.

The fundamental principle of that philosophy is the opinion concerning colours, sounds, tastes, smells, heat and cold; which it asserts to be nothing but impressions in the mind, deriv'd from the operation of external objects, and without any resemblance to the qualities of the objects. Upon examination, I find only one of the reasons commonly produc'd for this opinion to be satisfactory, *viz.* that deriv'd from the variations of those impressions, even while the external object, to all appearance, continues the same. These variations depend upon several circumstances. Upon the different situations of our health: A man in a malady feels a disagreeable taste in meats, which before pleas'd him the most. Upon the different complexions and constitutions of men: That seems bitter to one, which is sweet to another. Upon the difference of their external situation and position: Colours reflected from the clouds change according to the distance of the clouds, and according to the angle they make with the eye and luminous body. Fire also communicates the sensation of pleasure at one distance, and that of pain at another. Instances of this kind are very numerous and frequent.

The conclusion drawn from them, is likewise as satisfactory as can possibly be imagin'd. 'Tis certain, that when different impressions of the same sense arise from any object, every one of these impressions has not a resembling quality existent in the object. For as the same object cannot, at the same time, be endow'd with different qualities of the same sense, and as the same quality cannot resemble impressions entirely different; it evidently follows, that many of our impressions have no external model or archetype. Now from like effects we presume like causes. Many of the impressions of colour, sound *&c.* are confest to be nothing but internal existences, and to arise from causes, which no ways resemble them. These impressions are in appearance nothing different from the other impressions of colour, sound, *&c.* We conclude therefore that they are, all of them, deriv'd from a like origin.

This principle being once admitted, all the other doctrines of that philosophy seem to follow by an easy consequence. For upon the removal of sounds, colours, heat, cold, and other sensible qualities, from the rank of continu'd independent existences, we are reduc'd merely to what are called primary qualities, as the only *real* ones, of which we have any adequate notion. These primary qualities are extension and solidity, with their different mixtures and modifications; figure, motion, gravity, and cohesion. The generation, encrease, decay, and corruption of animals and vegetables, are nothing but changes of figure and motion; as also the operations of all bodies on each other; of fire, of light, water, air, earth, and of all the elements and powers of nature. One figure and motion produces another figure and motion; nor does there remain in the material universe any other principle, either active or passive, of which we can form the most distant idea.

I believe many objections might be made to this system:

But at present I shall confine myself to one, which is in my opinion very decisive. I assert, that instead of explaining the operations of external objects by its means, we utterly annihilate all these objects, and reduce ourselves to the opinions of the most extravagant scepticism concerning them. If colours, sounds, tastes, and smells be merely perceptions, nothing we can conceive is possest of a real, continu'd, and independent existence; not even motion, extension and solidity, which are the primary qualities chiefly insisted on.

To begin with the examination of motion; 'tis evident this is a quality altogether inconceivable alone, and without a reference to some other object. The idea of motion necessarily supposes that of a body moving. Now what is our idea of the moving body, without which motion is incomprehensible? It must resolve itself into the idea of extension or of solidity; and consequently the reality of motion depends upon that of these other qualities.

This opinion, which is universally acknowledg'd concerning motion, I have prov'd to be true with regard to extension; and have shewn that 'tis impossible to conceive extension, but as compos'd of parts, endow'd with colour or solidity. The idea of extension is a compound idea; but as it is not compounded of an infinite number of parts or inferior ideas, it must at last resolve itself into such as are perfectly simple and indivisible. These simple and indivisible parts, not being ideas of extension, must be non-entities, unless conceiv'd as colour'd or solid. Colour is excluded from any real existence. The reality, therefore, of our idea of extension depends upon the reality of that of solidity, nor can the former be just while the latter is chimerical. Let us, then, lend our attention to the examination of the idea of solidity.

The idea of solidity is that of two objects, which being impell'd by the utmost force, cannot penetrate each other; but still maintain a separate and distinct existence. Solidity, therefore, is perfectly incomprehensible alone, and without the conception of some bodies, which are solid, and maintain this separate and distinct existence. Now what idea have we of these bodies? The ideas of colours, sounds, and other secondary qualities are excluded. The idea of motion depends on that of extension, and the idea of extension on that of solidity. 'Tis impossible, therefore, that the idea of solidity can depend on either of them. For that wou'd be to run in a circle, and make one idea depend on another, while at the same time the latter depends on the former. Our modern philosophy, therefore, leaves us no just nor satisfactory idea of solidity; nor consequently of matter.

This argument will appear entirely conclusive to every one that comprehends it; but because it may seem abstruse and intricate to the generality of readers, I hope to be excus'd, if I endeavour to render it more obvious by some variation of the expression. In order to form an idea of solidity, we must conceive two bodies pressing on each other without any penetration; and 'tis impossible to arrive at this idea, when we confine ourselves to one object, much more without conceiving any. Two non-entities cannot exclude each other from their places; because they never possess any place, nor can be endow'd with any quality. Now I ask, what idea do we form of these bodies or objects, to which we suppose solidity to belong? To say, that we conceive them merely as solid, is to run on *in infinitum*. To affirm, that we paint them out to ourselves as extended, either resolves all into a false idea, or returns in a circle. Extension must necessarily be consider'd either as colour'd, which is a false idea; or as solid, which brings us back to the first question. We may make the same observation concerning mobility and figure; and upon the whole must conclude, that after the exclusion of colours, sounds, heat and cold from the rank of external existences, there remains nothing, which can afford us a just and consistent idea of body.

Add to this, that, properly speaking, solidity or impenetrability is nothing, but an impossibility of annihilation, as * has been already observ'd: For which reason 'tis the

* Part II. Sect. 4.

more necessary for us to form some distinct idea of that object, whose annihilation we suppose impossible. An impossibility of being annihilated cannot exist, and can never be conceived to exist, by itself; but necessarily requires some object or real existence, to which it may belong. Now the difficulty still remains, how to form an idea of this object or existence, without having recourse to the secondary and sensible qualities.

Nor must we omit on this occasion our accustom'd method of examining ideas by considering those impressions, from which they are deriv'd. The impressions, which enter by the sight and hearing, the smell and taste, are affirm'd by modern philosophy to be without any resembling objects; and consequently the idea of solidity, which is suppos'd to be real, can never be deriv'd from any of these senses. There remains, therefore, the feeling as the only sense, that can convey the impression, which is original to the idea of solidity; and indeed we naturally imagine, that we feel the solidity of bodies, and need but touch any object in order to perceive this quality. But this method of thinking is more popular than philosophical; as will appear from the following reflections.

First, 'Tis easy to observe, that tho' bodies are felt by means of their solidity, yet the feeling is a quite different thing from the solidity; and that they have not the least resemblance to each other. A man, who has the palsey in one hand, has as perfect an idea of impenetrability, when he observes that hand to be supported by the table, as when he feels the same table with the other hand. An object, that presses upon any of our members, meets with resistance; and that resistance, by the motion it gives to the nerves and animal spirits, conveys a certain sensation to the mind; but it does not follow, that the sensation, motion, and resistance are any ways resembling.

Secondly, The impressions of touch are simple impressions, except when consider'd with regard to their extension; which makes nothing to the present purpose: And from this simplicity I infer, that they neither represent solidity, nor any real object. For let us put two cases, *viz.* that of a man, who presses a stone, or any solid body, with his hand, and that of two stones, which press each other; 'twill readily be allow'd, that these two cases are not in every respect alike, but that in the former there is conjoin'd with the solidity, a feeling or sensation, of which there is no appearance in the latter. In order, therefore, to make these two cases alike, 'tis necessary to remove some part of the impression, which the man feels by his hand, or organ of sensation; and that being impossible in a simple impression, obliges us to remove the whole, and proves that this whole impression has no archetype or model in external objects. To which we may add, that solidity necessarily supposes two bodies, along with contiguity and impulse; which being a compound object, can never be represented by a simple impression. Not to mention, that tho' solidity continues always invariably the same, the impressions of touch change every moment upon us; which is a clear proof that the latter are not representations of the former.

Thus there is a direct and total opposition betwixt our reason and our senses; or more properly speaking, betwixt those conclusions we form from cause and effect, and those that persuade us of the continu'd and independent existence of body. When we reason from cause and effect, we conclude, that neither colour, sound, taste, nor smell have a continu'd and independent existence. When we exclude these sensible qualities there remains nothing in the universe, which has such an existence.

SECT. V

Of the immateriality of the soul

HAVING found such contradictions and difficulties in every system concerning external objects, and in the idea of matter, which we fancy so clear and determinate, we shall naturally expect still greater difficulties and contradictions in every hypothesis concerning our internal perceptions, and the nature of the mind, which we are apt to imagine so much more obscure, and uncertain. But in this we shou'd deceive ourselves. The intellectual world, tho' involv'd in infinite obscurities, is not perplex'd with any such contradictions, as those we have discover'd in the natural. What is known concerning it, agrees with itself; and what is unknown, we must be contented to leave so.

'Tis true, wou'd we hearken to certain philosophers, they promise to diminish our ignorance; but I am afraid 'tis at the hazard of running us into contradictions, from which the subject is of itself exempted. These philosophers are the curious reasoners concerning the material or immaterial substances, in which they suppose our perceptions to inhere. In order to put a stop to these endless cavils on both sides, I know no better method, than to ask these philosophers in a few words, *What they mean by substance and inhesion*? And after they have answer'd this question, 'twill then be reasonable, and not till then, to enter seriously into the dispute.

This question we have found impossible to be answer'd with regard to matter and body: But besides that in the case of the mind, it labours under all the same difficulties, 'tis burthen'd with some additional ones, which are peculiar to that subject. As every idea is deriv'd from a precedent impression, had we any idea of the substance of our minds, we must also have an impression of it; which is very difficult, if not impossible, to be conceiv'd. For how can an impression represent a substance, otherwise than by resembling it? And how can an impression resemble a substance, since, according to this philosophy, it is not a substance, and has none of the peculiar qualities or characteristics of a substance?

But leaving the question *of what may or may not be*, for that other *what actually is*, I desire those philosophers, who pretend that we have an idea of the substance of our minds, to point out the impression that produces it, and tell distinctly after what manner that impression operates, and from what object it is deriv'd. Is it an impression of sensation or of reflection? Is it pleasant, or painful, or indifferent? Does it attend us at all times, or does it only return at intervals? If at intervals, at what times principally does it return, and by what causes is it produc'd?

If instead of answering these questions, any one shou'd evade the difficulty, by saying, that the definition of a substance is *something which may exist by itself*; and that this definition ought to satisfy us: Shou'd this be said, I shou'd observe, that this definition agrees to every thing, that can possibly be conceiv'd; and never will serve to distinguish substance from accident, or the soul from its perceptions. For thus I reason. Whatever is clearly conceiv'd may exist; and whatever is clearly conceiv'd, after any manner, may exist after the same manner. This is one principle, which has been already acknowledg'd. Again, every thing, which is different, is distinguishable, and every thing which is distinguishable, is separable by the imagination. This is another principle. My conclusion from both is, that since all our perceptions are different from each other, and from everything else in the universe, they are also distinct and separable, and may be consider'd as separately existent, and may exist separately, and have no need of any thing else to support their existence. They are, therefore, substances, as far as this definition explains a substance.

Thus neither by considering the first origin of ideas, nor by means of a definition are we able to arrive at any satisfactory notion of substance; which seems to me a sufficient reason for abandoning utterly that dispute concerning the materiality and immateriality of the soul, and makes me absolutely condemn even the question itself. We have no perfect idea of any thing but of a perception. A substance is entirely different from a perception. We have, therefore, no idea of a substance. Inhesion in something is suppos'd to be requisite to support the existence of our perceptions. Nothing appears requisite to support the existence of a perception. We have, therefore, no idea of inhesion. What possibility then of answering that question, *Whether perceptions inhere in a material or immaterial substance,* when we do not so much as understand the meaning of the question?

There is one argument commonly employ'd for the immateriality of the soul, which seems to me remarkable. Whatever is extended consists of parts; and whatever consists of parts is divisible, if not in reality, at least in the imagination. But 'tis impossible any thing divisible can be *conjoin'd* to a thought or perception, which is a being altogether inseparable and indivisible. For supposing such a conjunction, wou'd the indivisible thought exist on the left or on the right hand of this extended divisible body? On the surface or in the middle? On the back- or fore-side of it? If it be conjoin'd with the extension, it must exist somewhere within its dimensions. If it exist within its dimensions, it must either exist in one particular part; and then that particular part is indivisible, and the perception is conjoin'd only with it, not with the extension: Or if the thought exists in every part, it must also be extended, and separable, and divisible, as well as the body; which is utterly absurd and contradictory. For can any one conceive a passion of a yard in length, a foot in breadth, and an inch in thickness? Thought, therefore, and extension are qualities wholly incompatible, and never can incorporate together into one subject.

This argument affects not the question concerning the *substance* of the soul, but only that concerning its *local conjunction* with matter; and therefore it may not be improper to consider in general what objects are, or are not susceptible of a local conjunction. This is a curious question, and may lead us to some discoveries of considerable moment.

The first notion of space and extension is deriv'd solely from the senses of sight and feeling; nor is there any thing, but what is colour'd or tangible, that has parts dispos'd after such a manner, as to convey that idea. When we diminish or encrease a relish, 'tis not after the same manner that we diminish or increase any visible object; and when several sounds strike our hearing at once, custom and reflection alone make us form an idea of the degrees of the distance and contiguity of those bodies, from which they are deriv'd. What ever marks the place of its existence either must be extended, or must be a mathematical point, without parts or composition. What is extended must have a particular figure, as square, round, triangular; none of which will agree to a desire, or indeed to any impression or idea, except of these two senses above-mention'd. Neither ought a desire, tho' indivisible, to be consider'd as a mathematical point. For in that case 'twou'd be possible, by the tradition of others, to make two, three, four desires, and these dispos'd and situated in such a manner, as to have a determinate length, breadth and thickness; which is evidently absurd.

'Twill not be surprizing after this, if I deliver a maxim, which is condemn'd by several metaphysicians, and is esteem'd contrary to the most certain principles of human reason. This maxim is *that an object may exist, and yet be no where*: and I assert, that this is not only possible, but that the greatest part of beings do and must exist after this manner. An object may be said to be no where, when its parts are not so situated with respect to each other, as to form any figure or quantity; nor the whole with respect to other bodies so as to answer to our notions of contiguity or distance. Now this is evidently the case with all our perceptions and objects, except those of the sight and feeling. A moral reflection cannot be plac'd on the right or on the left hand of a passion, nor can a smell or sound be either of a circular or a square figure. These objects and perceptions, so far from requiring any particular place, are absolutely incompatible with it, and even the imagination cannot attribute it to them. And as to the absurdity of supposing them to be no where, we may consider, that if the passions and sentiments appear to the perception to have any particular place, the idea of extension might be deriv'd from them, as well as from the sight and touch; contrary to what we have already establish'd. If they *appear* not to have any particular place, they may possibly *exist* in the same manner; since whatever we conceive is possible.

'Twill not now be necessary to prove, that those perceptions, which are simple, and exist no where, are incapable of any conjunction in place with matter or body, which is extended and divisible; since 'tis impossible to found a relation * but on some common quality. It may be better worth our while to remark, that this question of the local conjunction of objects does not only occur in metaphysical disputes concerning the nature of the soul, but that even in common life we have every moment occasion to examine it. Thus supposing we consider a fig at one end of the table, and an olive at the other, 'tis evident, that in forming the complex ideas of these substances, one of the most obvious is that of their different relishes; and 'tis as evident, that we incorporate and conjoin these qualities with such as are colour'd and tangible. The bitter taste of the one, and sweet of the other are suppos'd to lie in the very visible body, and to be separated from each other by the whole length of the table. This is so notable and so natural an illusion, that it may be proper to consider the principles, from which it is deriv'd.

Tho' an extended object be incapable of a conjunction in place with another, that exists without any place or extension, yet are they susceptible of many other relations. Thus the taste and smell of any fruit are inseparable from its other qualities of colour and tangibility; and which-ever of them be the cause or effect, 'tis certain they are always co-existent. Nor are they only co-existent in general, but also co-temporary in their appearance in the mind; and 'tis upon the application of the extended body to our senses we perceive its particular taste and smell. These relations, then, of *causation, and contiguity in the time of their appearance* betwixt the extended object and the quality, which exists without any particular place, must have such an effect on the mind, that upon the appearance

* Part I. Sect. 5.

of one it will immediately turn its thought to the conception of the other. Nor is this all. We not only turn our thought from one to the other upon account of their relation, but likewise endeavour to give them a new relation, *viz.* that of *a conjunction in place*, that we may render the transition more easy and natural. For 'tis a quality, which I shall often have occasion to remark in human nature, and shall explain more fully in its proper place, that when objects are united by any relation, we have a strong propensity to add some new relation to them, in order to compleat the union. In our arrangement of bodies we never fail to place such as are resembling, in contiguity to each other, or at least in correspondent points of view: Why? but because we feel a satisfaction in joining the relation of contiguity to that of resemblance, or the resemblance of situation to that of qualities. The effects of this propensity have been * already observ'd in that resemblance, which we so readily suppose betwixt particular impressions and their external causes. But we shall not find a more evident effect of it, than in the present instance, where from the relations of causation and contiguity in time betwixt two objects, we feign likewise that of a conjunction in place, in order to strengthen the connexion.

But whatever confus'd notions we may form of an union in place betwixt an extended body, as a fig, and its particular taste, 'tis certain that upon reflection we must observe in this union something altogether unintelligible and contradictory. For shou'd we ask ourselves one obvious question, *viz.* if the taste, which we conceive to be contain'd in the circumference of the body, is in every part of it or in one only, we must quickly find ourselves at a loss, and perceive the impossibility of ever giving a satisfactory answer. We cannot reply, that 'tis only in one part: For experience convinces us, that every part has the same relish. We can as little reply, that it exists in every part: For then we must suppose it figur'd and extended; which is absurd

* Sect. 2. towards the end.

and incomprehensible. Here then we are influenc'd by two principles directly contrary to each other, *viz.* that *inclination* of our fancy by which we are determin'd to incorporate the taste with the extended object, and our *reason,* which shows us the impossibility of such an union. Being divided betwixt these opposite principles, we renounce neither one nor the other, but involve the subject in such confusion and obscurity, that we no longer perceive the opposition. We suppose, that the taste exists within the circumference of the body, but in such a manner, that it fills the whole without extension, and exists entire in every part without separation. In short, we use in our most familiar way of thinking, that scholastic principle, which, when crudely propos'd, appears so shocking, of *totum in toto & totum in qualibet parte*: Which is much the same, as if we shou'd say, that a thing is in a certain place, and yet is not there.

All this absurdity proceeds from our endeavouring to bestow a place on what is utterly incapable of it; and that endeavour again arises from our inclination to compleat an union, which is founded on causation, and a contiguity of time, by attributing to the objects a conjunction in place. But if ever reason be of sufficient force to overcome prejudice, 'tis certain, that in the present case it must prevail. For we have only this choice left, either to suppose that some beings exist without any place; or that they are figur'd and extended; or that when they are incorporated with extended objects, the whole is in the whole, and the whole in every part. The absurdity of the two last suppositions proves sufficiently the veracity of the first. Nor is there any fourth opinion. For as to the supposition of their existence in the manner of mathematical points, it resolves itself into the second opinion, and supposes, that several passions may be plac'd in a circular figure, and that a certain number of smells, conjoin'd with a certain number of sounds, may make a body of twelve cubic inches; which appears ridiculous upon the bare mentioning of it.

But tho' in this view of things we cannot refuse to condemn the materialists, who conjoin all thought with extension; yet a little reflection will show us equal reason for blaming their antagonists, who conjoin all thought with a simple and indivisible substance. The most vulgar philosophy informs us, that no external object can make itself known to the mind immediately, and without the interposition of an image or perception. That table, which just now appears to me, is only a perception, and all its qualities are qualities of a perception. Now the most obvious of all its qualities is extension. The perception consists of parts. These parts are so situated, as to afford us the notion of distance and contiguity; of length, breadth, and thickness. The termination of these three dimensions is what we call figure. This figure is moveable, separable, and divisible. Mobility, and separability are the distinguishing properties of extended objects. And to cut short all disputes, the very idea of extension is copy'd from nothing but an impression, and consequently must perfectly agree to it. To say the idea of extension agrees to any thing, is to say it is extended.

The free-thinker may now triumph in his turn; and having found there are impressions and ideas really extended, may ask his antagonists, how they can incorporate a simple and indivisible subject with an extended perception? All the arguments of Theologians may here be retorted upon them. Is the indivisible subject, or immaterial substance, if you will, on the left or on the right hand of the perception? Is it in this particular part, or in that other? Is it in every part without being extended? Or is it entire in any one part without deserting the rest? 'Tis impossible to give any answer to these questions, but what will both be absurd in itself, and will account for the union of our indivisible perceptions with an extended substance.

This gives me an occasion to take a-new into consideration the question concerning the substance of the soul; and tho' I have condemn'd that question as utterly unintelligible, yet I cannot forbear proposing some farther reflections concerning it. I assert, that the doctrine of the immateriality, simplicity, and indivisibility of a thinking substance is a true atheism, and will serve to justify all those sentiments, for which *Spinoza* is so universally infamous. From this topic, I hope at least to reap one advantage, that my adversaries will not have any pretext to render the present doctrine odious by their declamations, when they see that they can be so easily retorted on them.

The fundamental principle of the atheism of *Spinoza* is the doctrine of the simplicity of the universe, and the unity of that substance, in which he supposes both thought and matter to inhere. There is only one substance, says he, in the world; and that substance is perfectly simple and indivisible, and exists every where, without any local presence. Whatever we discover externally by sensation; whatever we feel internally by reflection; all these are nothing but modifications of that one, simple, and necessarily existent being, and are not possest of any separate or distinct existence. Every passion of the soul; every configuration of matter, however different and various, inhere in the same substance, and preserve in themselves their characters of distinction, without communicating them to that subject, in which they inhere. The same *substratum*, if I may so speak, supports the most different modifications, without any difference in itself; and varies them, without any variation. Neither time, nor place, nor all the diversity of nature are able to produce any composition or change in its perfect simplicity and identity.

I believe this brief exposition of the principles of that famous atheist will be sufficient for the present purpose, and that without entering farther into these gloomy and obscure regions, I shall be able to shew, that this hideous hypothesis is almost the same with that of the immateriality of the soul, which has become so popular. To make this evident, let us * remember, that as every idea is deriv'd from a preceding perception, 'tis impossible our idea of a perception, and that of an object or external existence can ever represent what are specifically different from each

* Part II. Sect. 6.

other. Whatever difference we may suppose betwixt them, 'tis still incomprehensible to us; and we are oblig'd either to conceive an external object merely as a relation without a relative, or to make it the very same with a perception or impression.

The consequence I shall draw from this may, at first sight, appear a mere sophism; but upon the least examination will be found solid and satisfactory. I say then, that since we may suppose, but never can conceive a specific difference betwixt an object and impression; any conclusion we form concerning the connexion and repugnance of impressions, will not be known certainly to be applicable to objects; but that on the other hand, whatever conclusions of this kind we form concerning objects, will most certainly be applicable to impressions. The reason is not difficult. As an object is suppos'd to be different from an impression, we cannot be sure, that the circumstance, upon which we found our reasoning, is common to both, supposing we form the reasoning upon the impression. 'Tis still possible, that the object may differ from it in that particular. But when we first form our reasoning concerning the object, 'tis beyond doubt, that the same reasoning must extend to the impression: And that because the quality of the object, upon which the argument is founded, must at least be conceiv'd by the mind; and cou'd not be conceiv'd, unless it were common to an impression; since we have no idea but what is deriv'd from that origin. Thus we may establish it as a certain maxim, that we can never by any principle, but by an irregular kind * of reasoning from experience, discover a connexion or repugnance betwixt objects, which extends not to impressions; tho' the inverse proposition may not be equally true, that all the discoverable relations of impressions are common to objects.

To apply this to the present case; there are two different systems of beings presented, to which I suppose myself under a necessity of assigning some substance, or ground of inhesion. I observe first the universe of objects or of body;

* Such as that of Sect. 2. form the coherence of our perceptions.

The sun, moon and stars; the earth, seas, plants, animals, men, ships, houses, and other productions either of art or nature. Here *Spinoza* appears, and tells me, that these are only modifications; and that the subject, in which they inhere, is simple, incompounded, and indivisible. After this I consider the other system of beings, *viz.* the universe of thought, or my impressions and ideas. There I observe another sun, moon and stars; an earth, and seas, cover'd and inhabited by plants and animals; towns, houses, mountains, rivers; and in short every thing I can discover or conceive in the first system. Upon my enquiring concerning these, Theologians present themselves, and tell me, that these also are modifications, and modifications of one simple, uncompounded, and indivisible substance. Immediately upon which I am deafen'd with the noise of a hundred voices, that treat the first hypothesis with detestation and scorn, and the second with applause and veneration. I turn my attention to these hypotheses to see what may be the reason of so great a partiality; and find that they have the same fault of being unintelligible, and that as far as we can understand them, they are so much alike, that 'tis impossible to discover any absurdity in one, which is not common to both of them. We have no idea of any quality in an object, which does not agree to, and may not represent a quality in an impression; and that because all our ideas are deriv'd from our impressions. We can never, therefore, find any repugnance betwixt an extended object as a modification, and a simple uncompounded essence, as its substance, unless that repugnance takes place equally betwixt the perception or impression of that extended object, and the same uncompounded essence. Every idea of a quality in an object passes thro' an impression; and therefore every *perceivable* relation, whether of connexion or repugnance, must be common both to objects and impressions.

But tho' this argument, consider'd in general, seems evident beyond all doubt and contradiction, yet to make it more clear and sensible, let us survey it in detail; and see whether all the absurdities, which have been found in the system of *Spinoza*, may not likewise be discover'd in that of Theologians *.

First, It has been said against *Spinoza*, according to the scholastic way of talking, rather than thinking, that a mode, not being any distinct or separate existence, must be the very same with its substance, and consequently the extension of the universe, must be in a manner identify'd with that simple, uncompounded essence, in which the universe is suppos'd to inhere. But this, it may be pretended, is utterly impossible and inconceivable unless the indivisible substance expand itself so as to correspond to the extension, or the extension contract itself, so as to answer to the indivisible substance. This argument seems just, as far as we can understand it; and 'tis plain nothing is requir'd, but a change in the terms, to apply the same argument to our extended perceptions, and the simple essence of the soul; the ideas of objects and perceptions being in every respect the same, only attended with the supposition of a difference, that is unknown and incomprehensible.

Secondly, It has been said, that we have no idea of substance, which is not applicable to matter; nor any idea of a distinct substance, which is not applicable to every distinct portion of matter. Matter, therefore, is not a mode but a substance, and each part of matter is not a distinct mode, but a distinct substance. I have already prov'd, that we have no perfect idea of substance; but that taking it *for something, that can exist by itself*, 'tis evident every perception is a substance, and every distinct part of a perception a distinct substance: And consequently the one hypothesis labours under the same difficulties in this respect with the other.

Thirdly, It has been objected to the system of one simple substance in the universe, that this substance being the support or *substratum* of every thing, must at the very same instant be modify'd into forms, which are contrary and incompatible. The round and square figures are incompat-

* See *Bayle*'s dictionary, article of *Spinoza*.

ible in the same substance at the same time. How then is it possible, that the same substance can at once be modify'd into that square table, and into this round one? I ask the same question concerning the impressions of these tables; and find that the answer is no more satisfactory in one case than in the other.

It appears, then, that to whatever side we turn, the same difficulties follow us, and that we cannot advance one step towards the establishing the simplicity and immateriality of the soul, without preparing the way for a dangerous and irrecoverable atheism. 'Tis the same case, if instead of calling thought a modification of the soul, we shou'd give it the more antient, and yet more modish name of an *action*. By an action we mean much the same thing, as what is commonly call'd an abstract mode; that is, something, which, properly speaking, is neither distinguishable, nor separable from its substance, and is only conceiv'd by a distinction of reason, or an abstraction. But nothing is gain'd by this change of the term of modification, for that of action; nor do we free ourselves from one single difficulty by its means; as will appear from the two following reflections.

First, I observe, that the word, action, according to this explication of it, can never justly be apply'd to any perception, as deriv'd from a mind or thinking substance. Our perceptions are all really different, and separable, and distinguishable from each other, and from every thing else, which we can imagine; and therefore 'tis impossible to conceive, how they can be the action or abstract mode of any substance. The instance of motion, which is commonly made use of to shew after what manner perception depends, as an action, upon its substance, rather confounds than instructs us. Motion to all appearance induces no real nor essential change on the body, but only varies its relation to other objects. But betwixt a person in the morning walking in a garden with company, agreeable to him; and a person in the afternoon inclos'd in a dungeon, and full of terror, despair, and resentment, there seems to be a radical difference, and of quite another kind, than what is produc'd on a body by the change of its situation. As we conclude from the distinction and separability of their ideas, that external objects have a separate existence from each other; so when we make these ideas themselves our objects, we must draw the same conclusion concerning *them*, according to the precedent reasoning. At least it must be confest, that having no idea of the substance of the soul, 'tis impossible for us to tell how it can admit of such differences, and even contrarieties of perception without any fundamental change; and consequently can never tell in what sense perceptions are actions of that substance. The use, therefore, of the word, *action*, unaccompany'd with any meaning, instead of that of modification, makes no addition to our knowledge, nor is of any advantage to the doctrine of the immateriality of the soul.

I add in the second place, that if it brings any advantage to that cause, it must bring an equal to the cause of atheism. For do our Theologians pretend to make a monopoly of the word, *action*, and may not the atheists likewise take possession of it, and affirm that plants, animals, men &c. are nothing but particular actions of one simple universal substance, which exerts itself from a blind and absolute necessity? This you'll say is utterly absurd. I own 'tis unintelligible; but at the same time assert, according to the principles above-explain'd, that 'tis impossible to discover any absurdity in the supposition, that all the various objects in nature are actions of one simple substance, which absurdity will not be applicable to a like supposition concerning impressions and ideas.

From these hypotheses concerning the *substance* and *local conjunction* of our perceptions, we may pass to another, which is more intelligible than the former, and more important than the latter, *viz*. concerning the *cause* of our perceptions. Matter and motion, 'tis commonly said in the schools, however vary'd, are still matter and motion, and produce only a difference in the position and situation of objects. Divide a body as often as you please, 'tis still body. Place it in any figure, nothing ever results but figure, or the relation of parts. Move it in any manner, you still find motion or a change of relation. 'Tis absurd to imagine, that motion in a circle, for instance, shou'd be nothing but merely motion in a circle; while motion in another direction, as in an ellipse, shou'd also be a passion or moral reflection: That the shocking of two globular particles shou'd become a sensation of pain, and that the meeting of two triangular ones shou'd afford a pleasure. Now as these different shocks, and variations, and mixtures are the only changes, of which matter is susceptible, and as these never afford us any idea of thought or perception, 'tis concluded to be impossible, that thought can ever be caus'd by matter.

Few have been able to withstand the seeming evidence of this argument; and yet nothing in the world is more easy than to refute it. We need only reflect on what has been prov'd at large, that we are never sensible of any connexion betwixt causes and effects, and that 'tis only by our experience of their constant conjunction, we can arrive at any knowledge of this relation. Now as all objects, which are not contrary, are susceptible of a constant conjunction, and as no real objects are contrary; * I have inferr'd from these principles, that to consider the matter *a priori*, any thing may produce any thing, and that we shall never discover a reason, why any object may or may not be the cause of any other, however great, or however little the resemblance may be betwixt them. This evidently destroys the precedent reasoning concerning the cause of thought or perception. For tho' there appear no manner of connexion betwixt motion or thought, the case is the same with all the other causes and effects. Place one body of a pound weight on one end of a lever, and another body of the same weight on another end; you will never find in these bodies any principle of motion dependent on their distances from the center, more than of thought and perception. If you pretend, therefore, to prove *a priori*, that such a

* Part III. Sect. 15.

position of bodies can never cause thought; because turn it which way you will, 'tis nothing but a position of bodies; you must by the same course of reasoning conclude, that it can never produce motion; since there is no more apparent connexion in the one case than in the other. But as this latter conclusion is contrary to evident experience, and as 'tis possible we may have a like experience in the operations of the mind, and may perceive a constant conjunction of thought and motion; you reason too hastily, when from the mere consideration of the ideas you conclude that 'tis impossible motion can ever produce thought, or a different position of parts give rise to a different passion or reflection. Nay 'tis not only possible we may have such an experience, but 'tis certain we have it; since every one may perceive, that the different dispositions of his body change his thoughts and sentiments. And shou'd it be said that this depends on the union of soul and body; I wou'd answer, that we must separate the question concerning the substance of the mind from that concerning the cause of its thought; and that confining ourselves to the latter question we find by the comparing their ideas, that thought and motion are different from each other, and by experience, that they are constantly united; which being all the circumstances, that enter into the idea of cause and effect, when apply'd to the operations of matter, we may certainly conclude, that motion may be, and actually is, the cause of thought and perception.

There seems only this dilemma left us in the present case; either to assert, that nothing can be the cause of another, but where the mind can perceive the connexion in its idea of the objects: Or to maintain, that all objects, which we find constantly conjoin'd, are upon that account to be regarded as causes and effects. If we choose the first part of the dilemma, these are the consequences. *First,* We in reality affirm, that there is no such thing in the universe as a cause or productive principle, not even the deity himself; since our idea of that supreme Being is deriv'd from particular impressions none of which contain any efficacy, nor seem to have *any* connexion with *any* other existence. As to what may be said, that the connexion betwixt the idea of an infinitely powerful being, and that of any effect, which he wills, is necessary and unavoidable; I answer, that we have no idea of being endow'd with any power, much less of one endow'd with infinite power. But if we will change expressions, we can only define power by connexion; and then in saying, that the idea of an infinitely powerful being is connected with that of every effect, which he wills, we really do no more than assert, that a being, whose volition is connected with every effect, is connected with every effect; which is an identical proposition, and gives us no insight into the nature of this power or connexion. But, *secondly*, supposing, that the deity were the great and efficacious principle, which supplies the deficiency of all causes, this leads us into the grossest impieties and absurdities. For upon the same account, that we have recourse to him in natural operations, and assert that matter cannot of itself communicate motion, or produce thought, *viz.* because there is no apparent connexion betwixt these objects; I say, upon the very same account, we must acknowledge that the deity is the author of all our volitions and perceptions; since they have no more apparent connexion either with one another, or with the suppos'd but unknown substance of the soul. This agency of the supreme Being we know to have been asserted by * several philosophers with relation to all the actions of the mind, except volition, or rather an inconsiderable part of volition; tho' 'tis easy to perceive, that this exception is a mere pretext, to avoid the dangerous consequences of that doctrine. If nothing be active but what has an apparent power, thought is in no case any more active than matter; and if this inactivity must make us have recourse to a deity, the supreme being is the real cause of all our actions, bad as well as good, vicious as well as virtuous.

Thus we are necessarily reduc'd to the other side of the dilemma, *viz.* that all objects, which are found to be

* As father *Malebranche* and other *Cartesians.*

constantly conjoin'd are upon that account only to be regarded as causes and effects. Now as all objects, which are not contrary, are susceptible of a constant conjunction, and as no real objects are contrary; it follows, that for ought we can determine by the mere ideas, any thing may be the cause or effect of any thing; which evidently gives the advantage to the materialists above their antagonists.

To pronounce, then, the final decision upon the whole; the question concerning the substance of the soul is absolutely unintelligible: All our perceptions are not susceptible of a local union, either with what is extended or unextended; there being some of them of the one kind, and some of the other: And as the constant conjunction of objects constitutes the very essence of cause and effect, matter and motion may often be regarded as the causes of thought, as far as we have any notion of that relation.

'Tis certainly a kind of indignity to philosophy, whose sovereign authority ought every where to be acknowledg'd, to oblige her on every occasion to make apologies for her conclusions, and justify herself to every particular art and science, which may be offended at her. This puts one in mind of a king arraign'd for high-treason against his subjects. There is only one occasion, when philosophy will think it necessary and even honourable to justify herself, and that is, when religion may seem to be in the least offended; whose rights are as dear to her as her own, and are indeed the same. If any one, therefore, shou'd imagine that the foregoing arguments are any ways dangerous to religion, I hope the following apology will remove his apprehensions.

There is no foundation for any conclusion *a priori*, either concerning the operations or duration of any object, of which 'tis possible for the human mind to form a conception. Any object may be imagin'd to become entirely inactive, or to be annihilated in a moment; and 'tis an evident principle, *that whatever we can imagine, is possible*. Now this is no more true of matter, than of spirit; of an extended compounded substance, than of a simple and unextended.

In both cases the metaphysical arguments for the immortality of the soul are equally inconclusive; and in both cases the moral arguments and those deriv'd from the analogy of nature are equally strong and convincing. If my philosophy, therefore, makes no addition to the arguments for religion, I have at least the satisfaction to think it takes nothing from them, but that every thing remains precisely as before.

SECT. VI

Of personal identity

THERE are some philosophers, who imagine we are every moment intimately conscious of what we call our SELF; that we feel its existence and its continuance in existence; and are certain, beyond the evidence of a demonstration, both of its perfect identity and simplicity. The strongest sensation, the most violent passion, say they, instead of distracting us from this view, only fix it the more intensely, and make us consider their influence on *self* either by their pain or pleasure. To attempt a farther proof of this were to weaken its evidence; since no proof can be deriv'd from any fact, of which we are so intimately conscious; nor is there any thing, of which we can be certain, if we doubt of this.

Unluckily all these positive assertions are contrary to that very experience, which is pleaded for them, nor have we any idea of *self*, after the manner it is here explain'd. For from what impression cou'd this idea be deriv'd? This question 'tis impossible to answer without a manifest contradiction and absurdity; and yet 'tis a question, which must necessarily be answer'd, if we wou'd have the idea of self pass for clear and intelligible. It must be some one impression, that gives rise to every real idea. But self or person is not any one impression, but that to which our several impressions and ideas are suppos'd to have a reference. If any impression gives rise to the idea of self, that impression must continue invariably the same, thro' the whole course of our lives; since self is suppos'd to exist after that manner. But there is no impression constant and invariable. Pain and pleasure, grief and joy, passions and sensations succeed each other, and never all exist at the same time. It cannot, therefore, be from any of these impressions, or from any other, that the idea of self is deriv'd; and consequently there is no such idea.

But farther, what must become of all our particular perceptions upon this hypothesis? All these are different, and distinguishable, and separable from each other, and may be separately consider'd, and may exist separately, and have no need of any thing to support their existence. After what manner, therefore, do they belong to self; and how are they connected with it? For my part, when I enter most intimately into what I call *myself*, I always stumble on some particular perception or other, of heat or cold, light or shade, love or hatred, pain or pleasure. I never can catch *myself* at any time without a perception, and never can observe any thing but the perception. When my perceptions are remov'd for any time, as by sound-sleep; so long am I insensible of *myself*, and may truly be said not to exist. And were all my perceptions remov'd by death, and cou'd I neither think, nor feel, nor see, nor love, nor hate after the dissolution of my body, I shou'd be entirely annihilated, nor do I conceive what is farther requisite to make me a perfect non-entity. If any one upon serious and unprejudic'd reflection, thinks he has a different notion of *himself*, I must confess I can reason no longer with him. All I can allow him is, that he may be in the right as well as I, and that we are essentially different in this particular. He may perhaps, perceive something simple and continu'd, which he calls *himself;* tho' I am certain there is no such principle in me.

But setting aside some metaphysicians of this kind, I may venture to affirm of the rest of mankind, that they are nothing but a bundle or collection of different perceptions, which succeed each other with an inconceivable rapidity, and are in a perpetual flux and movement. Our eyes cannot turn in their sockets without varying our perceptions. Our thought is still more variable than our sight, and all our other senses and faculties contribute to this change; nor is there any single power of the soul, which remains unalterably the same, perhaps for one moment. The mind is a kind of theatre, where several perceptions successively make their apperance; pass, re-pass, glide away, and mingle in an infinite variety of postures and situations. There is properly no *simplicity* in it at one time, nor *identity* in different; whatever natural propension we may have to imagine that simplicity and identity. The comparison of the theatre must not mislead us. They are the successive perceptions only, that constitute the mind; nor have we the most distant notion of the place, where these scenes are represented, or of the materials, of which it is compos'd.

What then gives us so great a propension to ascribe an identity to these successive perceptions, and to suppose ourselves possest of an invariable and uninterrupted existence thro' the whole course of our lives? In order to answer this question, we must distinguish betwixt personal identity, as it regards our thought or imagination, and as it regards our passions or the concern we take in ourselves. The first is our present subject; and to explain it perfectly we must take the matter pretty deep, and account for that identity, which we attribute to plants and animals; there being a great analogy betwixt it, and the identity of a self or person.

We have a distinct idea of an object, that remains invariable and uninterrupted thro' a suppos'd variation of time; and this idea we call that of *identity* or *sameness*. We have also a distinct idea of several different objects existing in succession, and connected together by a close relation; and this to an accurate view affords as perfect a notion of *diversity*, as if there was no manner of relation among the objects. But tho' these two ideas of identity, and a succession of related objects be in themselves perfectly distinct, and even contrary, yet 'tis certain, that in our common way of thinking they are generally confounded with each other. That action of the imagination, by which we consider the uninterrupted and invariable object, and that by which we reflect on the succession of related objects, are almost the same to the feeling, nor is there much more effort of thought requir'd in the latter case than in the former. The relation facilitates the transition of the mind from one object to another, and renders its passage as smooth as if it contemplated one continu'd object. This resemblance is the cause of the confusion and mistake, and makes us substitute the notion of identity, instead of that of related objects. However at one instant we may consider the related succession as variable or interrupted, we are sure the next to ascribe to it a perfect identity, and regard it as invariable and uninterrupted. Our propensity to this mistake is so great from the resemblance above-mention'd, that we fall into it before we are aware; and tho' we incessantly correct ourselves by reflection, and return to a more accurate method of thinking, yet we cannot long sustain our philosophy, or take off this bias from the imagination. Our last resource is to yield to it, and boldly assert that these different related objects are in effect the same, however interrupted and variable. In order to justify to ourselves this absurdity, we often feign some new and unintelligible principle, that connects the objects together, and prevents their interruption or variation. Thus we feign the continu'd existence of the perceptions of our senses, to remove the interruption, and run into the notion of a *soul*, and *self*, and *substance*, to disguise the variation. But we may farther observe, that where we do not give rise to such a fiction, our propension to confound identity with relation is so great, that we are apt to imagine * something unknown and mysterious, connecting the parts, beside their relation; and this I take to be the case with regard to the identity we ascribe to plants and vegetables. And even

* If the reader is desirous to see how a great genius may be influenc'd by these seemingly trivial principles of the imagination, as well as the mere vulgar, let him read my Lord *Shaftsbury*'s reasonings concerning the uniting principle of the universe, and the identity of plants and animals. See his *Moralists: or, Philosophical rhapsody.*

when this does not take place, we still feel a propensity to confound these ideas, tho' we are not able fully to satisfy ourselves in that particular, nor find any thing invariable and uninterrupted to justify our notion of identity.

Thus the controversy concerning identity is not merely a dispute of words. For when we attribute identity, in an improper sense, to variable or interrupted objects, our mistake is not confin'd to the expression, but is commonly attended with a fiction, either of something invariable and uninterrupted, or of something mysterious and inexplicable, or at least with a propensity to such fictions. What will suffice to prove this hypothesis to the satisfaction of every fair enquirer, is to shew from daily experience and observation, that the objects, which are variable or interrupted, and yet are suppos'd to continue the same, are such only as consist of a succession of parts, connected together by resemblance, contiguity, or causation. For as such a succession answers evidently to our notion of diversity, it can only be by mistake we ascribe to it an identity; and as the relation of parts, which leads us into this mistake, is really nothing but a quality, which produces an association of ideas, and an easy transition of the imagination from one to another, it can only be from the resemblance, which this act of the mind bears to that, by which we contemplate one continu'd object, that the error arises. Our chief business, then, must be to prove, that all objects, to which we ascribe identity, without observing their invariableness and uninterruptedness, are such as consist of a succession of related objects.

In order to this, suppose any mass of matter, of which the parts are contiguous and connected, to be plac'd before us; 'tis plain we must attribute a perfect identity to this mass, provided all the parts continue uninterruptedly and invariably the same, whatever motion or change of place we may observe either in the whole or in any of the parts. But supposing some very *small* or *inconsiderable* part to be added to the mass, or subtracted from it; tho' this absolutely destroys the identity of the whole, strictly speaking;

yet as we seldom think so accurately, we scruple not to pronounce a mass of matter the same, where we find so trivial an alteration. The passage of the thought from the object before the change to the object after it, is so smooth and easy, that we scarce perceive the transition, and are apt to imagine, that 'tis nothing but a continu'd survey of the same object.

There is a very remarkable circumstance, that attends this experiment; which is, that tho' the change of any considerable part in a mass of matter destroys the identity of the whole, yet we must measure the greatness of the part, not absolutely, but by its *proportion* to the whole. The addition or diminution of a mountain wou'd not be sufficient to produce a diversity in a planet; tho' the change of a very few inches wou'd be able to destroy the identity of some bodies. 'Twill be impossible to account for this, but by reflecting that objects operate upon the mind, and break or interrupt the continuity of its actions not according to their real greatness, but according to their proportion to each other: And therefore, since this interruption makes an object cease to appear the same, it must be the uninterrupted progress of the thought, which constitutes the imperfect identity.

This may be confirm'd by another phaenomenon. A change in any considerable part of a body destroys its identity; but 'tis remarkable, that where the change is produc'd *gradually* and *insensibly* we are less apt to ascribe to it the same effect. The reason can plainly be no other, than that the mind, in following the successive changes of the body, feels an easy passage from the surveying its condition in one moment to the viewing of it in another, and at no particular time perceives any interruption in its actions. From which continu'd perception, it ascribes a continu'd existence and identity to the object.

But whatever precaution we may use in introducing the changes gradually, and making them proportionable to the whole, 'tis certain, that where the changes are at last observ'd to become considerable, we make a scruple of ascribing identity to such different objects. There is, however, another artifice, by which we may induce the imagination to advance a step farther; and that is, by producing a reference of the parts to each other, and a combination to some *common end* or purpose. A ship, of which a considerable part has been chang'd by frequent reparations, is still consider'd as the same; nor does the difference of the materials hinder us from ascribing an identity to it. The common end, in which the parts conspire, is the same under all their variations, and affords an easy transition of the imagination from one situation of the body to another.

But this is still more remarkable, when we add a *sympathy* of parts to their *common end*, and suppose that they bear to each other, the reciprocal relation of cause and effect in all their actions and operations. This is the case with all animals and vegetables; where not only the several parts have a reference to some general purpose, but also a mutual dependance on, and connexion with each other. The effect of so strong a relation is, that tho' every one must allow, that in a very few years both vegetables and animals endure a *total* change, yet we still attribute identity to them, while their form, size, and substance are entirely alter'd. An oak, that grows from a small plant to a large tree, is still the same oak; tho' there be not one particle of matter, or figure of its parts the same. An infant becomes a man, and is sometimes fat, sometimes lean, without any change in his identity.

We may also consider the two following phaenomena, which are remarkable in their kind. The first is, that tho' we commonly be able to distinguish pretty exactly betwixt numerical and specific identity, yet it sometimes happens, that we confound them, and in our thinking and reasoning employ the one for the other. Thus a man, who hears a noise, that is frequently interrupted and renew'd says it is still the same noise; tho' 'tis evident the sounds have only a specific identity or resemblance, and there is nothing numerically the same, but the cause, which produc'd them. In like manner it may be said without breach of the propriety of language, that such a church, which was formerly of brick, fell to ruin, and that the parish rebuilt the same church of free-stone, and according to modern architecture. Here neither the form nor materials are the same, nor is there any thing common to the two objects, but their relation to the inhabitants of the parish; and yet this alone is sufficient to make us denominate them the same. But we must observe, that in these cases the first object is in a manner annihilated before the second comes into existence; by which means, we are never presented in any one point of time with the idea of difference and multiplicity; and for that reason are less scrupulous in calling them the same.

Secondly, We may remark, that tho' in a succession of related objects, it be in a manner requisite, that the change of parts be not sudden nor entire, in order to preserve the identity, yet where the objects are in their nature changeable and inconstant, we admit of a more sudden transition, than wou'd otherwise be consistent with that relation. Thus as the nature of a river consists in the motion and change of parts; tho' in less than four and twenty hours these be totally alter'd; this hinders not the river from continuing the same during several ages. What is natural and essential to any thing is, in a manner, expected; and what is expected makes less impression, and appears of less moment, than what is unusual and extraordinary. A considerable change of the former kind seems really less to the imagination, than the most trivial alteration of the latter; and by breaking less the continuity of the thought, has less influence in destroying the identity.

We now proceed to explain the nature of *personal identity*, which has become so great a question in philosophy, especially of late years in *England*, where all the abstruser sciences are study'd with a peculiar ardour and application. And here 'tis evident, the same method of reasoning must be continu'd, which has so successfully explain'd the identity of plants, and animals, and ships, and houses, and of all the compounded and changeable productions either of art or nature. The identity, which we ascribe to the mind of man, is only a fictitious one, and of a like kind with that which we ascribe to vegetables and animal bodies. It cannot, therefore, have a different origin, but must proceed from a like operation of the imagination upon like objects.

But lest this argument shou'd not convince the reader; tho' in my opinion perfectly decisive; let him weigh the following reasoning, which is still closer and more immediate. 'Tis evident, that the identity, which we attribute to the human mind, however perfect we may imagine it to be, is not able to run the several different perceptions into one, and make them lose their characters of distinction and difference, which are essential to them. 'Tis still true, that every distinct perception, which enters into the composition of the mind, is a distinct existence, and is different, and distinguishable, and separable from every other perception, either contemporary or successive. But, as, notwithstanding this distinction and separability, we suppose the whole train of perceptions to be united by identity, a question naturally arises concerning this relation of identity; whether it be something that really binds our several perceptions together, or only associates their ideas in the imagination. That is, in other words, whether in pronouncing concerning the identity of a person, we observe some real bond among his perceptions, or only feel one among the ideas we form of them. This question we might easily decide, if we wou'd recollect what has been already prov'd at large, that the understanding never observes any real connexion among objects, and that even the union of cause and effect, when strictly examin'd, resolves itself into a customary association of ideas. For from thence it evidently follows, that identity is nothing really belonging to these different perceptions, and uniting them together; but is merely a quality, which we attribute to them, because of the union of their ideas in the imagination, when we reflect upon them. Now the only qualities, which can give ideas an union in the imagination, are these three relations above-mentioned. These are the uniting principles in the ideal world, and without them every distinct object is separable by the mind, and may be separately consider'd, and appears not to have any more connexion with any other object, than if disjoin'd by the greatest difference and remoteness. 'Tis, therefore, on some of these three relations of resemblance, contiguity and causation, that identity depends; and as the very essence of these relations consists in their producing an easy transition of ideas; it follows, that our notions of personal identity, proceed entirely from the smooth and uninterrupted progress of the thought along a train of connected ideas, according to the principles above-explain'd.

The only question, therefore, which remains, is, by what relations this uninterrupted progress of our thought is produc'd, when we consider the successive existence of a mind or thinking person. And here 'tis evident we must confine ourselves to resemblance and causation, and must drop contiguity, which has little or no influence in the present case. [*]

To begin with *resemblance*; suppose we cou'd see clearly into the breast of another, and observe that succession of perceptions, which constitutes his mind or thinking principle, and suppose that he always preserves the memory of a considerable part of past perceptions; 'tis evident that nothing cou'd more contribute to the bestowing a relation on this succession amidst all its variations. For what is memory, but a faculty, by which we raise up the images of past perceptions? And as an image necessarily resembles its object, must not the frequent placing of these resembling perceptions in the chain of thought, convey the imagination more easily from one link to another, and make the whole seem like the continuance of one object? In this particular, then, the memory not only discovers the identity, but also contributes to its production, by producing the relation of resemblance among the perceptions. The case is the same whether we consider ourselves or others.

As to *causation*; we may observe, that the true idea of the human mind, is to consider it as a sytsem of different perceptions or different existences, which are link'd together by the relation of cause and effect, and mutually produce, de-

[* See Appendix, p. 677, for further comment.]

stroy, influence, and modify each other. Our impressions give rise to their correspondent ideas; and these ideas in their turn produce other impressions. One thought chaces another, and draws after it a third, by which it is expell'd in its turn. In this respect, I cannot compare the soul more properly to any thing than to a republic or commonwealth, in which the several members are united by the reciprocal ties of government and subordination, and give rise to other persons, who propagate the same republic in the incessant changes of its parts. And as the same individual republic may not only change its members, but also its laws and constitutions; in like manner the same person may vary his character and disposition, as well as his impressions and ideas, without losing his identity. Whatever changes he endures, his several parts are still connected by the relation of causation. And in this view our identity with regard to the passions serves to corroborate that with regard to the imagination, by the making our distant perceptions influence each other, and by giving us a present concern for our past or future pains or pleasures.

As memory alone acquaints us with the continuance and extent of this succession of perceptions, 'tis to be consider'd, upon that account chiefly, as the source of personal identity. Had we no memory, we never shou'd have any notion of causation, nor consequently of that chain of causes and effects, which constitute our self or person. But having once acquir'd this notion of causation from the memory, we can extend the same chain of causes, and consequently the identity of our persons beyond our memory, and can comprehend times, and circumstances, and actions, which we have entirely forgot, but suppose in general to have existed. For how few of our past actions are there, of which we have any memory? Who can tell me, for instance, what were his thoughts and actions on the first of *January* 1715, the 11th of *March* 1719, and the 3rd of *August* 1733? Or will he affirm, because he has entirely forgot the incidents of these days, that the present self is not the same person with the self of that time; and by that means overturn all the most establish'd notions of personal identity? In this view, therefore, memory does not so much *produce* as *discover* personal identity, by shewing us the relation of cause and effect among our different perceptions. 'Twill be incumbent on those, who affirm that memory produces entirely our personal identity, to give a reason why we can thus extend our identity beyond our memory.

The whole of this doctrine leads us to a conclusion, which is of great importance in the present affair, *viz.* that all the nice and subtle questions concerning personal identity can never possibly be decided, and are to be regarded rather as grammatical than as philosophical difficulties. Identity depends on the relations of ideas; and these relations produce identity, by means of that easy transition they occasion. But as the relations, and the easiness of the transition may diminish by insensible degrees, we have no just standard, by which we can decide any dispute concerning the time, when they acquire or lose a title to the name of identity. All the disputes concerning the identity of connected objects are merely verbal, except so far as the relation of parts gives rise to some fiction or imaginary principle of union, as we have already observ'd.

What I have said concerning the first origin and uncertainty of our notion of identity, as apply'd to the human mind, may be extended with little or no variation to that of *simplicity*. An object, whose different co-existent parts are bound together by a close relation, operates upon the imagination after much the same manner as one perfectly simple and indivisible, and requires not a much greater stretch of thought in order to its conception. From this similarity of operation we attribute a simplicity to it, and feign a principle of union as the support of this simplicity, and the center of all the different parts and qualities of the object.

Thus we have finish'd our examination of the several systems of philosophy, both of the intellectual and natural world; and in our miscellaneous way of reasoning have been led into several topics; which will either illustrate and confirm some preceding part of this discourse, or prepare the way for our following opinions. 'Tis now time to return to a more close examination of our subject, and to proceed in the accurate anatomy of human nature, having fully explain'd the nature of our judgment and understanding.

SECT. VII

Conclusion of this book

But before I launch out into these immense depths of philosophy, which lie before me, I find myself inclin'd to stop a moment in my present station, and to ponder that voyage, which I have undertaken, and which undoubtedly requires the utmost art and industry to be brought to a happy conclusion. Methinks I am like a man, who having struck on many shoals, and having narrowly escap'd shipwreck in passing a small frith, has yet the temerity to put out to sea in the same leaky weather-beaten vessel, and even carries his ambition so far as to think of compassing the globe under these disadvantageous circumstances. My memory of past errors and perplexities, makes me diffident for the future. The wretched condition, weakness, and disorder of the faculties, I must employ in my enquiries, encrease my apprehensions. And the impossibility of amending or correcting these faculties, reduces me almost to despair, and makes me resolve to perish on the barren rock, on which I am at present, rather than venture myself upon that boundless ocean, which runs out into immensity. This sudden view of my danger strikes me with melancholy; and as 'tis usual for that passion, above all others, to indulge itself; I cannot forbear feeding my despair, with all those desponding reflections, which the present subject furnishes me with in such abundance.

I am first affrighted and confounded with that forelorn solitude, in which I am plac'd in my philosophy, and fancy myself some strange uncouth monster, who not being able to mingle and unite in society, has been expell'd all human commerce, and left utterly abandon'd and disconsolate. Fain wou'd I run into the crowd for shelter and warmth; but cannot prevail with myself to mix with such deformity. I call upon others to join me, in order to make a company apart; but no one will hearken to me. Every one keeps at a distance, and dreads that storm, which beats upon me from every side. I have expos'd myself to the enmity of all metaphysicians, logicians, mathematicians, and even theologians; and can I wonder at the insults I must suffer? I have declar'd my dis-approbation of their systems; and can I be surpriz'd, if they shou'd express a hatred of mine and of my person? When I look abroad, I foresee on every side, dispute, contradiction, anger, calumny and detraction. When I turn my eye inward, I find nothing but doubt and ignorance. All the world conspires to oppose and contradict me; tho' such is my weakness, that I feel all my opinions loosen and fall of themselves, when unsupported by the approbation of others. Every step I take is with hesitation, and every new reflection makes me dread an error and absurdity in my reasoning.

For with what confidence can I venture upon such bold enterprizes, when beside those numberless infirmities peculiar to myself, I find so many which are common to human nature? Can I be sure, that in leaving all establish'd opinions I am following truth; and by what criterion shall I distinguish her, even if fortune shou'd at last guide me on her foot-steps? After the most accurate and exact of my reasonings, I can give no reason why I shou'd assent to it; and feel nothing but a *strong* propensity to consider objects *strongly* in that view, under which they appear to me. Experience is a principle, which instructs me in the several conjunctions of objects for the past. Habit is another principle, which determines me to expect the same for the future; and both of them conspiring to operate upon the imagination, make me form certain ideas in a more intense and lively manner, than others, which are not attended with the same advantages. Without this quality, by which the mind enlivens some ideas beyond others (which seemingly is so trivial, and so little founded on reason) we cou'd never assent to any argument, nor carry our view beyond those few objects, which are present to our senses. Nay, even to these objects we cou'd never attribute any existence, but what was dependent on the senses; and must comprehend them entirely in that succession of perceptions, which constitutes our self or person. Nay, farther, even with relation to that succession, we cou'd only admit of those perceptions, which are immediately present to our consciousness, nor cou'd those lively images, with which the memory presents us, be ever receiv'd as true pictures of past perceptions. The memory, senses, and understanding are, therefore, all of them founded on the imagination, or the vivacity of our ideas.

No wonder a principle so inconstant and fallacious shou'd lead us into errors, when implicitly follow'd (as it must be) in all its variations. 'Tis this principle, which makes us reason from causes and effects; and 'tis the same principle, which convinces us of the continu'd existence of external objects, when absent from the senses. But tho' these two operations be equally natural and necessary in the human mind, yet in some circumstances they are * directly contrary, nor is it possible for us to reason justly and regularly from causes and effects, and at the same time believe the continu'd existence of matter. How then shall we adjust those principles together? Which of them shall we prefer? Or in case we prefer neither of them, but successively assent to both, as is usual among philosophers, with what confidence can we afterwards usurp that glorious title, when we thus knowingly embrace a manifest contradiction?

This † contradiction wou'd be more excusable, were it compensated by any degree of solidity and satisfaction in the other parts of our reasoning. But the case is quite contrary. When we trace up the human understanding to its first principles, we find it to lead us into such sentiments, as seem to turn into ridicule all our past pains and industry, and to discourage us from future enquiries. Nothing is more

* Sect. 4. † Part III. Sect. 14.

curiously enquir'd after by the mind of man, than the causes of every phaenomenon; nor are we content with knowing the immediate causes, but push on our enquiries, till we arrive at the original and ultimate principle. We wou'd not willingly stop before we are acquainted with that energy in the cause, by which it operates on its effect; that tie, which connects them together; and that efficacious quality, on which the tie depends. This is our aim in all our studies and reflections: And how must we be disappointed, when we learn, that this connexion, tie, or energy lies merely in ourselves, and is nothing but that determination of the mind, which is acquir'd by custom, and causes us to make a transition from an object to its usual attendant, and from the impression of one to the lively idea of the other? Such a discovery not only cuts off all hope of ever attaining satisfaction, but even prevents our very wishes; since it appears, that when we say we desire to know the ultimate and operating principle, as something, which resides in the external object, we either contradict ourselves, or talk without a meaning.

This deficiency in our ideas is not, indeed, perceiv'd in common life, nor are we sensible, that in the most usual conjunctions of cause and effect we are as ignorant of the ultimate principle, which binds them together, as in the most unusual and extraordinary. But this proceeds merely from an illusion of the imagination; and the question is, how far we ought to yield to these illusions. This question is very difficult, and reduces us to a very dangerous dilemma, which-ever way we answer it. For if we assent to every trivial suggestion of the fancy; beside that these suggestions are often contrary to each other; they lead us into such errors, absurdities, and obscurities, that we must at last become asham'd of our credulity. Nothing is more dangerous to reason than the flights of the imagination, and nothing has been the occasion of more mistakes among philosophers. Men of bright fancies may in this respect be compar'd to those angels, whom the scripture represents as covering their eyes with their wings. This has already appear'd in so many instances, that we may spare ourselves the trouble of enlarging upon it any farther.

But on the other hand, if the consideration of these instances makes us take a resolution to reject all the trivial suggestions of the fancy, and adhere to the understanding, that is, to the general and more establish'd properties of the imagination; even this resolution, if steadily executed, wou'd be dangerous, and attended with the most fatal consequences. For I have already shewn, * that the understanding, when it acts alone, and according to its most general principles, entirely subverts itself, and leaves not the lowest degree of evidence in any proposition, either in philosophy or common life. We save ourselves from this total scepticism only by means of that singular and seemingly trivial property of the fancy, by which we enter with difficulty into remote views of things, and are not able to accompany them with so sensible an impression, as we do those, which are more easy and natural. Shall we, then, establish it for a general maxim, that no refin'd or elaborate reasoning is ever to be receiv'd? Consider well the consequences of such a principle. By this means you cut off entirely all science and philosophy: You proceed upon one singular quality of the imagination, and by a parity of reason must embrace all of them: And you expressly contradict yourself; since this maxim must be built on the preceding reasoning, which will be allow'd to be sufficiently refin'd and metaphysical. What party, then, shall we choose among these difficulties? If we embrace this principle, and condemn all refin'd reasoning, we run into the most manifest absurdities. If we reject it in favour of these reasonings, we subvert entirely the human understanding. We have, therefore, no choice left but betwixt a false reason and none at all. For my part, I know not what ought to be done in the present case. I can only observe what is commonly done; which is, that this difficulty is seldom or never thought of; and even where it has once been present to the mind, is quickly forgot, and leaves but a small impression behind it. Very refin'd reflections have little or

* Sect. 1.

no influence upon us; and yet we do not, and cannot establish it for a rule, that they ought not to have any influence; which implies a manifest contradiction.

But what have I here said, that reflections very refin'd and metaphysical have little or no influence upon us? This opinion I can scarce forbear retracting, and condemning from my present feeling and experience. The *intense* view of these manifold contradictions and imperfections in human reason has so wrought upon me, and heated my brain, that I am ready to reject all belief and reasoning, and can look upon no opinion even as more probable or likely than another. Where am I, or what? From what causes do I derive my existence, and to what condition shall I return? Whose favour shall I court, and whose anger must I dread? What beings surround me? and on whom have I any influence, or who have any influence on me? I am confounded with all these questions, and begin to fancy myself in the most deplorable condition imaginable, inviron'd with the deepest darkness, and utterly depriv'd of the use of every member and faculty.

Most fortunately it happens, that since reason is incapable of dispelling these clouds, nature herself suffices to that purpose, and cures me of this philosophical melancholy and delirium, either by relaxing this bent of mind, or by some avocation, and lively impression of my senses, which obliterate all these chimeras. I dine, I play a game of backgammon, I converse, and am merry with my friends; and when after three or four hour's amusement, I wou'd return to these speculations, they appear so cold, and strain'd, and ridiculous, that I cannot find in my heart to enter into them any farther.

Here then I find myself absolutely and necessarily determin'd to live, and talk, and act like other people in the common affairs of life. But notwithstanding that my natural propensity, and the course of my animal spirits and passions reduce me to this indolent belief in the general maxims of the world, I still feel such remains of my former disposition, that I am ready to throw all my books and papers into the fire, and resolve never more to renounce the pleasures of life for the sake of reasoning and philosophy. For these are my sentiments in that splenetic humour, which governs me at present. I may, nay I must yield to the current of nature, in submitting to my senses and understanding; and in this blind submission I shew most perfectly my sceptical disposition and principles. But does it follow, that I must strive against the current of nature, which leads me to indolence and pleasure; that I must seclude myself, in some measure, from the commerce and society of men, which is so agreeable; and that I must torture my brain with subtilities and sophistries, at the very time that I cannot satisfy myself concerning the reasonableness of so painful an application, nor have any tolerable prospect of arriving by its means at truth and certainty. Under what obligation do I lie of making such an abuse of time? And to what end can it serve either for the service of mankind, or for my own private interest? No: If I must be a fool, as all those who reason or believe any thing *certainly* are, my follies shall at least be natural and agreeable. Where I strive against my inclination, I shall have a good reason for my resistance; and will no more be led a wandering into such dreary solitudes, and rough passages, as I have hitherto met with.

These are the sentiments of my spleen and indolence; and indeed I must confess, that philosophy has nothing to oppose to them, and expects a victory more from the returns of a serious good-humour'd disposition, than from the force of reason and conviction. In all the incidents of life we ought still to preserve our scepticism. If we believe, that fire warms, or water refreshes, 'tis only because it costs us too much pains to think otherwise. Nay if we are philosophers, it ought only to be upon sceptical principles, and from an inclination, which we feel to the employing ourselves after that manner. Where reason is lively, and mixes itself with some propensity, it ought to be assented to. Where it does not, it never can have any title to operate upon us.

At the time, therefore, that I am tir'd with amusement

and company, and have indulg'd a *reverie* in my chamber, or in a solitary walk by a river-side, I feel my mind all collected within itself, and am naturally *inclin'd* to carry my view into all those subjects, about which I have met with so many disputes in the course of my reading and conversation. I cannot forbear having a curiosity to be acquainted with the principles of moral good and evil, the nature and foundation of government, and the cause of those several passions and inclinations, which actuate and govern me. I am uneasy to think I approve of one object, and disapprove of another; call one thing beautiful, and another deform'd; decide concerning truth and falshood, reason and folly, without knowing upon what principles I proceed. I am concern'd for the condition of the learned world, which lies under such a deplorable ignorance in all these particulars. I feel an ambition to arise in me of contributing to the instruction of mankind, and of acquiring a name by my inventions and discoveries. These sentiments spring up naturally in my present disposition; and shou'd I endeavour to banish them, by attaching myself to any other business or diversion, I *feel* I shou'd be a loser in point of pleasure; and this is the origin of my philosophy.

But even suppose this curiosity and ambition shou'd not transport me into speculations without the sphere of common life, it would necessarily happen, that from my very weakness I must be led into such enquiries. 'Tis certain, that superstition is much more in its systems and hypotheses than philosophy; and while the latter contents itself with assigning new causes and principles to the phaenomena, which appear in the visible world, the former opens a world of its own, and presents us with scenes, and beings, and objects, which are altogether new. Since therefore 'tis almost impossible for the mind of man to rest, like those of beasts, in that narrow circle of objects, which are the subject of daily conversation and action, we ought only to deliberate concerning the choice of our guide, and ought to prefer that which is safest and most agreeable. And in this respect I make bold to recommend philosophy, and shall not scruple to give it the preference to superstition of every kind or denomination. For as superstition arises naturally and easily from the popular opinions of mankind, it seizes more strongly on the mind, and is often able to disturb us in the conduct of our lives and actions. Philosophy on the contrary, if just, can present us only with mild and moderate sentiments; and if false and extravagant, its opinions are merely the objects of a cold and general speculation, and seldom go so far as to interrupt the course of our natural propensities. The CYNICS are an extraordinary instance of philosophers, who from reasonings purely philosophical ran into as great extravagancies of conduct as any *Monk* or *Dervise* that ever was in the world. Generally speaking, the errors in religion are dangerous; those in philosophy only ridiculous.

I am sensible, that these two cases of the strength and weakness of the mind will not comprehend all mankind, and that there are in *England*, in particular, many honest gentlemen, who being always employ'd in their domestic affairs, or amusing themselves in common recreations, have carried their thoughts very little beyond those objects, which are every day expos'd to their senses. And indeed, of such as these I pretend not to make philosophers, nor do I expect them either to be associates in these researches or auditors of these discoveries. They do well to keep themselves in their present situation; and instead of refining them into philosophers, I wish we cou'd communicate to our founders of systems, a share of this gross earthy mixture, as an ingredient, which they commonly stand much in need of, and which wou'd serve to temper those fiery particles, of which they are compos'd. While a warm imagination is allow'd to enter into philosophy, and hypotheses embrac'd merely for being specious and agreeable, we can never have any steady principles, nor any sentiments, which will suit with common practice and experience. But were these hypotheses once remov'd, we might hope to establish a system or set of opinions, which if not true (for that, perhaps, is too much to be hop'd for) might at least be satisfactory to the human mind, and might stand the test of the most critical examination. Nor shou'd we despair of attaining this end, because of the many chimerical systems, which have successively arisen and decay'd away among men, wou'd we consider the shortness of that period, wherein these questions have been the subjects of enquiry and reasoning. Two thousand years with such long interruptions, and under such mighty discouragements are a small space of time to give any tolerable perfection to the sciences; and perhaps we are still in too early an age of the world to discover any principles which will bear the examination of the latest posterity. For my part, my only hope is, that I may contribute a little to the advancement of knowledge, by giving in some particulars a different turn to the speculations of philosophers, and pointing out to them more distinctly those subjects, where alone they can expect assurance and conviction. Human Nature is the only science of man; and yet has been hitherto the most neglected. 'Twill be sufficient for me, if I can bring it a little more into fashion; and the hope of this serves to compose my temper from that spleen, and invigorate it from that indolence, which sometimes prevail upon me. If the reader finds himself in the same easy disposition, let him follow me in my future speculations. If not, let him follow his inclination, and wait the returns of application and good humour. The conduct of a man, who studies philosophy in this careless manner, is more truly sceptical than that of one, who feeling in himself an inclination to it, is yet so over-whelm'd with doubts and scruples, as totally to reject it. A true sceptic will be diffident of his philosophical doubts, as well as of his philosophical conviction; and will never refuse any innocent satisfaction, which offers itself, upon account of either of them.

Nor is it only proper we shou'd in general indulge our inclination in the most elaborate philosophical researches, notwithstanding our sceptical principles, but also that we shou'd yield to that propensity, which inclines us to be positive and certain in *particular points*, according to the light, in which we survey them in any *particular instant.* 'Tis easier to forbear all examination and enquiry, than to check ourselves in so natural a propensity, and guard against that assurance, which always arises from an exact and full survey of an object. On such an occasion we are apt not only to forget our scepticism, but even our modesty too; and make use of such terms as these, *'tis evident, 'tis certain, 'tis undeniable*; which a due deference to the public ought, perhaps, to prevent. I may have fallen into this fault after the example of others; but I here enter a *caveat* against any objections, which may be offer'd on that head; and declare that such expressions were extorted from me by the present view of the object, and imply no dogmatical spirit, nor conceited idea of my own judgment, which are sentiments that I am sensible can become no body, and a sceptic still less than any other.

A

TREATISE

OF

Human Nature:

BEING

An ATTEMPT to introduce the experimental Method of Reasoning

INTO

MORAL SUBJECTS.

by David Hume Esqr.

Rara temporum felicitas, ubi sentire, quæ velis; & quæ sentias, dicere licet. TACIT.

VOL. II.

OF THE

PASSIONS.

LONDON:
Printed for JOHN NOON, at the *White-Hart*, near *Mercers-Chapel*, in *Cheapside*.
MDCCXXXIX.

BOOK II

OF THE PASSIONS

PART I

Of pride and humility

SECT. I

Division of the subject

As all the perceptions of the mind may be divided into *impressions* and *ideas*, so the impressions admit of another division into *original* and *secondary*. This division of the impressions is the same with that which * I formerly made use of when I distinguish'd them into impressions of *sensation* and *reflection*. Original impressions or impressions of sensation are such as without any antecedent perception arise in the soul, from the constitution of the body, from the animal spirits, or from the application of objects to the external organs. Secondary, or reflective impressions are such as proceed from some of these original ones, either immediately or by the interposition of its idea. Of the first kind are all the impressions of the senses, and all bodily pains and pleasures: Of the second are the passions, and other emotions resembling them.

'Tis certain, that the mind, in its perceptions, must begin somewhere; and that since the impressions precede their correspondent ideas, there must be some impressions, which without any introduction make their appearance in the soul. As these depend upon natural and physical causes, the examination of them wou'd lead me too far from my present subject, into the sciences of anatomy and natural philosophy. For this reason I shall here confine myself to those other impressions, which I have call'd secondary and reflective, as arising either from the original impressions, or

* Book I. Part I. Sect. 2.

from their ideas. Bodily pains and pleasures are the source of many passions, both when felt and consider'd by the mind; but arise originally in the soul, or in the body, whichever you please to call it, without any preceding thought or perception. A fit of the gout produces a long train of passions, as grief, hope, fear; but is not deriv'd immediately from any affection or idea.

The reflective impressions may be divided into two kinds, *viz*. the *calm* and the *violent*. Of the first kind is the sense of beauty and deformity in action, composition, and external objects. Of the second are the passions of love and hatred, grief and joy, pride and humility. This division is far from being exact. The raptures of poetry and music frequently rise to the greatest height; while those other impressions, properly call'd *passions*, may decay into so soft an emotion, as to become, in a manner, imperceptible. But as in general the passions are more violent than the emotions arising from beauty and deformity, these impressions have been commonly distinguish'd from each other. The subject of the human mind being so copious and various, I shall here take advantage of this vulgar and spacious division, that I may proceed with the greater order; and having said all I thought necessary concerning our ideas, shall now explain those violent emotions or passions, their nature, origin, causes, and effects.

When we take a survey of the passions, there occurs a division of them into *direct* and *indirect*. By direct passions I understand such as arise immediately from good or evil, from pain or pleasure. By indirect such as proceed from the same principles, but by the conjunction of other qualities. This distinction I cannot at present justify or explain any farther. I can only observe in general, that under the indirect passions I comprehend pride, humility, ambition, vanity, love, hatred, envy, pity, malice, generosity, with their dependants. And under the direct passions, desire, aversion, grief, joy, hope, fear, despair and security. I shall begin with the former.

SECT. II

Of pride and humility; their objects and causes

THE passions of PRIDE and HUMILITY being simple and uniform impressions, 'tis impossible we can ever, by a multitude of words, give a just definition of them, or indeed of any of the passions. The utmost we can pretend to is a description of them, by an enumeration of such circumstances, as attend them: But as these words, *pride* and *humility*, are of general use, and the impressions they represent the most common of any, every one, of himself, will be able to form a just idea of them, without any danger of mistake. For which reason, not to lose time upon preliminaries, I shall immediately enter upon the examination of these passions.

'Tis evident, that pride and humility, tho' directly contrary, have yet the same OBJECT. This object is self, or that succession of related ideas and impressions, of which we have an intimate memory and consciousness. Here the view always fixes when we are actuated by either of these passions. According as our idea of ourself is more or less advantageous, we feel either of those opposite affections, and are elated by pride, or dejected with humility. Whatever other objects may be comprehended by the mind, they are always consider'd with a view to ourselves; otherwise they would never be able either to excite these passions, or produce the smallest encrease or diminution of them. When self enters not into the consideration, there is no room either for pride or humility.

But tho' that connected succession of perceptions, which we call *self*, be always the object of these two passions, 'tis impossible it can be their CAUSE, or be sufficient alone to excite them. For as these passions are directly contrary, and have the same object in common; were their object also their cause; it cou'd never produce any degree of the one passion, but at the same time it must excite an equal degree of the other; which opposition and contrariety must destroy both. 'Tis impossible a man can at the same time be both proud and humble; and where he has different reasons for these passions, as frequently happens, the passions either take place alternately; or if they encounter, the one annihilates the other, as far as its strength goes, and the remainder only of that, which is superior, continues to operate upon the mind. But in the present case neither of the passions cou'd ever become superior; because supposing it to be the view only of ourself, which excited them, that being perfectly indifferent to either, must produce both in the very same proportion; or in other words, can produce neither. To excite any passion, and at the same time raise an equal share of its antagonist, is immediately to undo what was done, and must leave the mind at last perfectly calm and indifferent.

We must, therefore, make a distinction betwixt the cause and the object of these passions; betwixt that idea, which excites them, and that to which they direct their view, when excited. Pride and humility, being once rais'd, immediately turn our attention to ourself, and regard that as their ultimate and final object; but there is something farther requisite in order to raise them: Something, which is peculiar to one of the passions, and produces not both in the very same degree. The first idea, that is presented to the mind, is that of the cause or productive principle. This excites the passion, connected with it; and that passion, when excited, turns our view to another idea, which is that of self. Here then is a passion plac'd betwixt two ideas, of which the one produces it, and the other is produc'd by it. The first idea, therefore, represents the *cause*, the second the *object* of the passion.

To begin with the causes of pride and humility; we may observe, that their most obvious and remarkable property is the vast variety of *subjects*, on which they may be plac'd. Every valuable quality of the mind, whether of the imagination, judgment, memory or disposition; wit, good-sense, learning, courage, justice, integrity; all these are the cause of pride; and their opposites of humility. Nor are these passions confin'd to the mind but extend their view to the body likewise. A man may be proud of his beauty, strength, agility, good mein, address in dancing, riding, and of his dexterity in any manual business or manufacture. But this is not all. The passions looking farther, comprehend whatever objects are in the least ally'd or related to us. Our country, family, children, relations, riches, houses, gardens, horses, dogs, cloaths; any of these may become a cause either of pride or of humility.

From the consideration of these causes, it appears necessary we shou'd make a new distinction in the causes of the passion, betwixt that *quality*, which operates, and the *subject*, on which it is plac'd. A man, for instance, is vain of a beautiful house, which belongs to him, or which he has himself built and contriv'd. Here the object of the passion is himself, and the cause is the beautiful house: Which cause again is sub-divided into two parts, *viz.* the quality, which operates upon the passion, and the subject, in which the quality inheres. The quality is the beauty, and the subject is the house, consider'd as his property or contrivance. Both these parts are essential, nor is the distinction vain and chimerical. Beauty, consider'd merely as such, unless plac'd upon something related to us, never produces any pride or vanity; and the strongest relation alone, without beauty, or something else in its place, has as little influence on that passion. Since, therefore, these two particulars are easily separated, and there is a necessity for their conjunction, in order to produce the passion, we ought to consider them as component parts of the cause; and infix in our minds an exact idea of this distinction.

SECT. III

Whence these objects and causes are deriv'd

BEING so far advanc'd as to observe a difference betwixt the *object* of the passions and their *cause*, and to distinguish in the cause the *quality*, which operates on the passions, from the *subject*, in which it inheres; we now proceed to examine what determines each of them to be what it is, and assigns such a particular object, and quality, and subject to these affections. By this means we shall fully understand the origin of pride and humility.

'Tis evident in the first place, that these passions are determin'd to have self for their *object*, not only by a natural but also by an original property. No one can doubt but this property is *natural* from the constancy and steadiness of its operations. 'Tis always self, which is the object of pride and humility; and whenever the passions look beyond, 'tis still with a view to ourselves, nor can any person or object otherwise have any influence upon us.

That this proceeds from an *original* quality or primary impulse, will likewise appear evident, if we consider that 'tis the distinguishing characteristic of these passions. Unless nature had given some original qualities to the mind, it cou'd never have any secondary ones; because in that case it wou'd have no foundation for action, nor cou'd ever begin to exert itself. Now these qualities, which we must consider as original, are such as are most inseparable from the soul, and can be resolv'd into no other: And such is the quality, which determines the object of pride and humility.

We may, perhaps, make it a greater question, whether the *causes*, that produce the passion, be as *natural* as the object, to which it is directed, and whether all that vast variety proceeds from caprice or from the constitution of the mind. This doubt we shall soon remove, if we cast our eye upon human nature, and consider that in all nations and ages, the same objects still give rise to pride and humility; and that upon the view even of a stranger, we can know pretty nearly, what will either encrease or diminish his passions of this kind. If there be any variation in this particular, it proceeds frcm nothing but a difference in the tempers and complexions of men; and is besides very inconsiderable. Can we imagine it possible, that while human nature remains the same, men will ever become entirely indifferent to their power, riches, beauty or personal merit, and that their pride and vanity will not be affected by these advantages?

But tho' the causes of pride and humility be plainly *natural*, we shall find upon examination, that they are not *original*, and that 'tis utterly impossible they shou'd each of them be adapted to these passions by a particular provision, and primary constitution of nature. Beside their prodigious number, many of them are the effects of art, and arise partly from the industry, partly from the caprice, and partly from the good fortune of men. Industry produces houses, furniture, cloaths. Caprice determines their particular kinds and qualities. And good fortune frequently contributes to all this, by discovering the effects that result from the different mixtures and combinations of bodies. 'Tis absurd, therefore, to imagine, that each of these was foreseen and provided for by nature, and that every new production of art, which causes pride or humility; instead of adapting itself to the passion by partaking of some general quality, that naturally operates on the mind; is itself the object of an original principle, which till then lay conceal'd in the soul, and is only by accident at last brought to light. Thus the first mechanic, that invented a fine scritoire, produc'd pride in him, who became possest of it, by principles different from those, which made him proud of handsome chairs and tables. As this appears evidently ridiculous, we must conclude, that each cause of pride and humility is not adapted to the passions by a distinct original quality; but that there are some one or more circumstances common to all of them, on which their efficacy depends.

Besides, we find in the course of nature, that tho' the

effects be many, the principles, from which they arise, are commonly but few and simple, and that 'tis the sign of an unskilful naturalist to have recourse to a different quality, in order to explain every different operation. How much more must this be true with regard to the human mind, which being so confin'd a subject may justly be thought incapable of containing such a monstrous heap of principles, as wou'd be necessary to excite the passions of pride and humility, were each distinct cause adapted to the passion by a distinct set of principles?

Here, therefore, moral philosophy is in the same condition as natural, with regard to astronomy before the time of *Copernicus.* The antients, tho' sensible of that maxim, *that nature does nothing in vain*, contriv'd such intricate systems of the heavens, as seem'd inconsistent with true philosophy, and gave place at last to something more simple and natural. To invent without scruple a new principle to every new phaenomenon, instead of adapting it to the old; to overload our hypotheses with a variety of this kind; are certain proofs, that none of these principles is the just one, and that we only desire, by a number of falsehoods, to cover our ignorance of the truth.

SECT. IV

Of the relations of impressions and ideas

THUS we have establish'd two truths without any obstacle or difficulty, *that 'tis from natural principles this variety of causes excites pride and humility*, and *that 'tis not by a different principle each different cause is adapted to its passion.* We shall now proceed to enquire how we may reduce these principles to a lesser number, and find among the causes something common, on which their influence depends.

In order to this we must reflect on certain properties of human nature, which tho' they have a mighty influence on every operation both of the understanding and passions, are not commonly much insisted on by philosophers. The *first* of these is the association of ideas, which I have so often observ'd and explain'd. 'Tis impossible for the mind to fix itself steadily upon one idea for any considerable time; nor can it by its utmost efforts ever arrive at such a constancy. But however changeable our thoughts may be, they are not entirely without rule and method in their changes. The rule, by which they proceed, is to pass from one object to what is resembling, contiguous to, or produc'd by it. When one idea is present to the imagination, any other, united by these relations, naturally follows it, and enters with more facility by means of that introduction.

The *second* property I shall observe in the human mind is a like association of impressions. All resembling impressions are connected together, and no sooner one arises than the rest immediately follow. Grief and disappointment give rise to anger, anger to envy, envy to malice, and malice to grief again, till the whole circle be compleated. In like manner our temper, when elevated with joy, naturally throws itself into love, generosity, pity, courage, pride, and the other resembling affections. 'Tis difficult for the mind, when actuated by any passion, to confine itself to that passion alone, without any change or variation. Human nature is too inconstant to admit of any such regularity. Changeableness is essential to it. And to what can it so naturally change as to affections or emotions, which are suitable to the temper, and agree with that set of passions, which then prevail? 'Tis evident, then, there is an attraction or association among impressions, as well as among ideas; tho' with this remarkable difference, that ideas are associated by resemblance, contiguity, and causation; and impressions only by resemblance.

In the *third* place, 'tis observable of these two kinds of association, that they very much assist and forward each other, and that the transition is more easily made where they both concur in the same object. Thus a man, who, by any injury from another, is very much discompos'd and ruffled in his temper, is apt to find a hundred subjects of discontent, impatience, fear, and other uneasy passions; especially if he can discover these subjects in or near the person, who was the cause of his first passion. Those principles, which forward the transition of ideas, here concur with those, which operate on the passions; and both uniting in one action, bestow on the mind a double impulse. The new passion, therefore, must arise with so much greater violence, and the transition to it must be render'd so much more easy and natural.

Upon this occasion I may cite the authority of an elegant writer, [*] who expresses himself in the following manner.

'As the fancy delights in every thing that is great, strange, or beautiful, and is still more pleas'd the more it finds of these perfections in the *same* object, so it is capable of receiving a new satisfaction by the assistance of another sense. Thus any continu'd sound, as the music of birds, or a fall of waters, awakens every moment the mind of the beholder, and makes him more attentive to the several beauties of the place, that lie before him. Thus if there arises a fragrancy of smells or perfumes, they heighten the pleasure of the imagination, and make even the colours and verdure of the landschape appear more agreeable; for the ideas of both senses recommend each other, and are pleasanter together than when they enter the mind separately: As the different colours of a picture, when they are well disposed, set off one another, and receive an additional beauty from the advantage of the situation.'

In this phaenomenon we may remark the association both of impressions and ideas, as well as the mutual assistance they lend each other.

SECT. V

Of the influence of these relations on pride and humility

THESE principles being establish'd on unquestionable experience, I begin to consider how we shall apply them, by revolving over all the causes of pride and humility, whether

[* Addison, *Spectator* 412, final paragraph.]

these causes be regarded, as the qualities, that operate, or as the subjects, on which the qualities are plac'd. In examining these *qualities* I immediately find many of them to concur in producing the sensation of pain and pleasure, independent of those affections, which I here endeavour to explain. Thus the beauty of our person, of itself, and by its very appearance, gives pleasure, as well as pride; and its deformity, pain as well as humility. A magnificent feast delights us, and a sordid one displeases. What I discover to be true in some instances, I *suppose* to be so in all; and take it for granted at present, without any farther proof, that every cause of pride, by its peculiar qualities, produces a separate pleasure, and of humility a separate uneasiness.

Again, in considering the *subjects,* to which these qualities adhere, I make a new *supposition*, which also appears probable from many obvious instances, *viz.* that these subjects are either parts of ourselves, or something nearly related to us. Thus the good and bad qualities of our actions and manners constitute virtue and vice, and determine our personal character, than which nothing operates more strongly on these passions. In like manner, 'tis the beauty or deformity of our person, houses, equipage, or furniture, by which we are render'd either vain or humble. The same qualities, when transfer'd to subjects, which bear us no relation, influence not in the smallest degree either of these affections.

Having thus in a manner suppos'd two properties of the causes of these affections, *viz.* that the *qualities* produce a separate pain or pleasure, and that the *subjects,* on which the qualities are plac'd, are related to self; I proceed to examine the passions themselves, in order to find something in them, correspondent to the suppos'd properties of their causes. *First,* I find, that the peculiar object of pride and humility is determin'd by an original and natural instinct, and that 'tis absolutely impossible, from the primary constitution of the mind, that these passions shou'd ever look beyond self, or that individual person, of whose actions and sentiments each of us is intimately conscious. Here at last the view always rests, when we are actuated by either of these passions; nor can we, in that situation of mind, ever lose sight of this object. For this I pretend not to give any reason; but consider such a peculiar direction of the thought as an original quality.

The *second* quality, which I discover in these passions, and which I likewise consider an an original quality, is their sensations, or the peculiar emotions they excite in the soul, and which constitute their very being and essence. Thus pride is a pleasant sensation, and humility a painful; and upon the removal of the pleasure and pain, there is in reality no pride nor humility. Of this our very feeling convinces us; and beyond our feeling, 'tis here in vain to reason or dispute.

If I compare, therefore, these two *establish'd* properties of the passions, *viz.* their object, which is self, and their sensation, which is either pleasant or painful, to the two *suppos'd* properties of the causes, *viz.* their relation to self, and their tendency to produce a pain or pleasure, independent of the passion; I immediately find, that taking these suppositions to be just, the true system breaks in upon me with an irresistible evidence. That cause, which excites the passion, is related to the object, which nature has attributed to the passion; the sensation, which the cause separately produces, is related to the sensation of the passion: From this double relation of ideas and impressions, the passion is deriv'd. The one idea is easily converted into its correlative; and the one impression into that, which resembles and corresponds to it: With how much greater facility must this transition be made, where these movements mutually assist each other, and the mind receives a double impulse from the relations both of its impressions and ideas?

That we may comprehend this the better, we must suppose, that nature has given to the organs of the human mind, a certain disposition fitted to produce a peculiar impression or emotion, which we call *pride*: To this emotion she has assign'd a certain idea, *viz.* that of *self*, which it never fails to produce. This contrivance of nature is easily conceiv'd. We have many instances of such a situation of affairs. The nerves of the nose and palate are so dispos'd, as in certain circumstances to convey such peculiar sensations to the mind: The sensations of lust and hunger always produce in us the idea of those peculiar objects, which are suitable to each appetite. These two circumstances are united in pride. The organs are so dispos'd as to produce the passion; and the passion, after its production, naturally produces a certain idea. All this needs no proof. 'Tis evident we never shou'd be possest of that passion, were there not a disposition of mind proper for it; and 'tis as evident, that the passion always turns our view to ourselves, and makes us think of our own qualities and circumstances.

This being fully comprehended, it may now be ask'd, *Whether nature produces the passion immediately, of herself; or whether she must be assisted by the co-operation of other causes?* For 'tis observable, that in this particular her conduct is different in the different passions and sensations. The palate must be excited by an external object, in order to produce any relish: But hunger arises internally, without the concurrence of any external object. But however the case may stand with other passions and impressions, 'tis certain, that pride requires the assistance of some foreign object, and that the organs, which produce it, exert not themselves like the heart and arteries, by an original internal movement. For *first*, daily experience convinces us, that pride requires certain causes to excite it, and languishes when unsupported by some excellency in the character, in bodily accomplishments, in cloaths, equipage or fortune. *Secondly*, 'tis evident pride wou'd be perpetual, if it arose immediately from nature; since the object is always the same, and there is no disposition of body peculiar to pride, as there is to thirst and hunger. *Thirdly*, Humility is in the very same situation with pride; and therefore, either must, upon this supposition, be perpetual likewise, or must destroy the contrary passion from the very first moment; so that none of them cou'd ever make its appearance. Upon the whole, we may rest satisfy'd with the foregoing conclusion, that pride must have a cause, as well as an object, and that the one has no influence without the other.

The difficulty, then, is only to discover this cause, and find what it is that gives the first motion to pride, and sets those organs in action, which are naturally fitted to produce that emotion. Upon my consulting experience, in order to resolve this difficulty, I immediately find a hundred different causes, that produce pride; and upon examining these causes, I suppose, what at first I perceive to be probable, that all of them concur in two circumstances; which are, that of themselves they produce an impression, ally'd to the passion, and are plac'd on a subject, ally'd to the object of the passion. When I consider after this the nature of *relation*, and its effects both on the passions and ideas, I can no longer doubt, upon these suppositions, that 'tis the very principle, which gives rise to pride, and bestows motion on those organs, which being naturally dispos'd to produce that affection, require only a first impulse or beginning to their action. Any thing, that gives a pleasant sensation, and is related to self, excites the passion of pride, which is also agreeable, and has self for its object.

What I have said of pride is equally true of humility. The sensation of humility is uneasy, as that of pride is agreeable; for which reason the separate sensation, arising from the causes, must be revers'd, while the relation to self continues the same. Tho' pride and humility are directly contrary in their effects, and in their sensations, they have notwithstanding the same object; so that 'tis requisite only to change the relation of impressions, without making any change upon that of ideas. Accordingly we find, that a beautiful house, belonging to ourselves, produces pride; and that the same house, still belonging to ourselves, produces humility, when by any accident its beauty is chang'd into deformity, and thereby the sensation of pleasure, which corresponded to pride, is transform'd into pain, which is related to humility. The double relation between the ideas and impressions subsists in both cases, and produces an easy transition from the one emotion to the other.

In a word, nature has bestow'd a kind of attraction on certain impressions and ideas, by which one of them, upon its appearance, naturally introduces its correlative. If these two attractions or associations of impressions and ideas concur on the same object, they mutually assist each other, and the transition of the affections and of the imagination is made with the greatest ease and facility. When an idea produces an impression, related to an impression, which is connected with an idea, related to the first idea, these two impressions must be in a manner inseparable, nor will the one in any case be unattended with the other. 'Tis after this manner, that the particular causes of pride and humility are determin'd. The quality, which operates on the passion, produces separately an impression resembling it; the subject, to which the quality adheres, is related to self, the object of the passion: No wonder the whole cause, consisting of a quality and of a subject, does so unavoidably give rise to the passion.

To illustrate this hypothesis, we may compare it to that, by which I have already explain'd the belief attending the judgments, which we form from causation. I have observ'd, that in all judgments of this kind, there is always a present impression, and a related idea; and that the present impression gives a vivacity to the fancy, and the relation conveys this vivacity, by an easy transition, to the related idea. Without the present impression, the attention is not fix'd, nor the spirits excited. Without the relation, this attention rests on its first object, and has no farther consequence. There is evidently a great analogy betwixt that hypothesis, and our present one of an impression and idea, that transfuse themselves into another impression and idea by means of their double relation: Which analogy must be allow'd to be no despicable proof of both hypotheses.

SECT. VI

Limitations of this system

BUT before we proceed farther in this subject, and examine particularly all the causes of pride and humility, 'twill be proper to make some limitations to the general system, *that all agreeable objects, related to ourselves, by an association of ideas and of impressions, produce pride, and disagreeable ones, humility*: And these limitations are deriv'd from the very nature of the subject.

I. Suppose an agreeable object to acquire a relation to self, the first passion, that appears on this occasion, is joy; and this passion discovers itself upon a slighter relation than pride and vain-glory. We may feel joy upon being present at a feast, where our senses are regal'd with delicacies of every kind: But 'tis only the master of the feast, who, beside the same joy, has the additional passion of self-applause and vanity. 'Tis true, men sometimes boast of a great entertainment, at which they have only been present; and by so small a relation convert their pleasure into pride: But however, this must in general be own'd, that joy arises from a more inconsiderable relation than vanity, and that many things, which are too foreign to produce pride, are yet able to give us a delight and pleasure. The reason of the difference may be explain'd thus. A relation is requisite to joy, in order to approach the object to us, and make it give us any satisfaction. But beside this, which is common to both passions, 'tis requisite to pride, in order to produce a transition from one passion to another, and convert the falsification into vanity. As it has a double task to perform, it must be endow'd with double force and energy. To which we may add, that where agreeable objects bear not a very close relation to ourselves, they commonly do to some other person; and this latter relation not only excels, but even diminishes, and sometimes destroys the former, as we shall see afterwards*.

* Part II. Sect. 4.

Here then is the first limitation, we must make to our general position, *that every thing related to us, which produces pleasure or pain, produces likewise pride or humility.* There is not only a relation requir'd, but a close one, and a closer than is requir'd to joy.

II. The second limitation is, that the agreeable or disagreeable object be not only closely related, but also peculiar to ourselves, or at least common to us with a few persons. 'Tis a quality observable in human nature, and which we shall endeavour to explain afterwards, that every thing, which is often presented, and to which we have been long accustom'd, loses its value in our eyes, and is in a little time despis'd and neglected. We likewise judge of objects more from comparison than from their real and intrinsic merit; and where we cannot by some contrast enhance their value, we are apt to overlook even what is essentially good in them. These qualities of the mind have an effect upon joy as well as pride; and 'tis remarkable, that goods, which are common to all mankind, and have become familiar to us by custom, give us little satisfaction; tho' perhaps of a more excellent kind, than those on which, for their singularity, we set a much higher value. But tho' this circumstance operates on both these passions, it has a much greater influence on vanity. We are rejoic'd for many goods, which, on account of their frequency, give us no pride. Health, when it returns after a long absence, affords us a very sensible satisfaction; but is seldom regarded as a subject of vanity, because 'tis shar'd with such vast numbers.

The reason, why pride is so much more delicate in this particular than joy, I take to be, as follows. In order to excite pride, there are always two objects we must contemplate, *viz.* the *cause* or that object which produces pleasure; and self, which is the real object of the passion. But joy has only one object necessary to its production, *viz.* that which gives pleasure; and tho' it be requisite, that this bear some relation to self, yet that is only requisite in order to render it agreeable; nor is self, properly speaking, the object of this passion. Since, therefore, pride has in a manner two objects, to which it directs our view; it follows, that where neither of them have any singularity, the passion must be more weaken'd upon that account, than a passion, which has only one object. Upon comparing ourselves with others, as we are every moment apt to do, we find we are not in the least distinguish'd; and upon comparing the object we possess, we discover still the same unlucky circumstance. By two comparisons so disadvantageous the passion must be entirely destroy'd.

III. The third limitation is, that the pleasant or painful object be very discernible and obvious, and that not only to ourselves, but to others also. This circumstance, like the two foregoing, has an effect upon joy, as well as pride. We fancy ourselves more happy, as well as more virtuous or beautiful, when we appear so to others; but are still more ostentatious of our virtues than of our pleasures. This proceeds from causes, which I shall endeavour to explain afterwards.

IV. The fourth limitation is deriv'd from the inconstancy of the cause of these passions, and from the short duration of its connexion with ourselves. What is casual and inconstant gives but little joy, and less pride. We are not much satisfy'd with the thing itself; and are still less apt to feel any new degrees of self-satisfaction upon its account. We foresee and anticipate its change by the imagination; which makes us little satisfy'd with the thing: We compare it to ourselves, whose existence is more durable; by which means its inconstancy appears still greater. It seems ridiculous to infer an excellency in ourselves from an object, which is of so much shorter duration, and attends us during so small a part of our existence. 'Twill be easy to comprehend the reason, why this cause operates not with the same force in joy as in pride; since the idea of self is not so essential to the former passion as to the latter.

V. I may add as a fifth limitation, or rather enlargement of this system, that *general rules* have a great influence upon pride and humility, as well as on all the other passions. Hence we form a notion of different ranks of men, suitable to the power of riches they are possest of; and this notion we change not upon account of any peculiarities of the health or temper of the persons, which may deprive them of all enjoyment in their possessions. This may be accounted for from the same principles, that explain'd the influence of general rules on the understanding. Custom readily carries us beyond the just bounds in our passions, as well as in our reasonings.

It may not be amiss to observe on this occasion, that the influence of general rules and maxims on the passions very much contributes to facilitate the effects of all the principles, which we shall explain in the progress of this treatise. For 'tis evident, that if a person full-grown, and of the same nature with ourselves, were on a sudden transported into our world, he wou'd be very much embarrass'd with every object, and wou'd not readily find what degree of love or hatred, pride or humility, or any other passion he ought to attribute to it. The passions are often vary'd by very inconsiderable principles; and these do not always play with a perfect regularity, especially on the first trial. But as custom and practice have brought to light all these principles, and have settled the just value of every thing; this must certainly contribute to the easy production of the passions, and guide us, by means of general establish'd maxims, in the proportions we ought to observe in preferring one object to another. This remark may, perhaps, serve to obviate difficulties, that may arise concerning some causes, which I shall hereafter ascribe to particular passions, and which may be esteem'd too refin'd to operate so universally and certainly, as they are found to do.

I shall close this subject with a reflection deriv'd from these five limitations. This reflection is, that the persons, who are proudest, and who in the eye of the world have most reason for their pride, are not always the happiest; nor the most humble always the most miserable, as may at first sight be imagin'd from this system. An evil may be real, tho' its cause has no relation to us: It may be real, without being peculiar: It may be real, without shewing itself to others: It may be real, without being constant: And it may be real, without falling under the general rules. Such evils as these will not fail to render us miserable, tho' they have little tendency to diminish pride: And perhaps the most real and the most solid evils of life will be found of this nature.

SECT. VII

Of vice and virtue

TAKING these limitations along with us, let us proceed to examine the causes of pride and humility; and see, whether in every case we can discover the double relations, by which they operate on the passions. If we find that all these causes are related to self, and produce a pleasure or uneasiness separate from the passion, there will remain no farther scruple with regard to the present system. We shall principally endeavour to prove the latter point; the former being in a manner self-evident.

To begin with VICE and VIRTUE, which are the most obvious causes of these passions; 'twou'd be entirely foreign to my present purpose to enter upon the controversy, which of late years has so much excited the curiosity of the publick, *whether these moral distinctions be founded on natural and original principles, or arise from interest and education.* The examination of this I reserve for the following book; and in the mean time I shall endeavour to show, that my system maintains its ground upon either of these hypotheses; which will be a strong proof of its solidity.

For granting that morality had no foundation in nature, it must still be allow'd, that vice and virtue, either from self-interest or the prejudices of education, produce in us a real pain and pleasure; and this we may observe to be strenuously asserted by the defenders of that hypothesis. Every passion, habit, or turn of character (say they) which has a tendency to our advantage or prejudice, gives a delight or uneasiness; and 'tis from thence the approbation or disapprobation arises. We easily gain from the liberality of others, but are always in danger of losing by their avarice: Courage defends us, but cowardice lays us open to every attack: Justice is the support of society, but injustice, unless check'd wou'd quickly prove its ruin: Humility exalts; but pride mortifies us. For these reasons the former qualities are esteem'd virtues, and the latter regarded as vices. Now since 'tis granted there is a delight or uneasiness still attending merit or demerit of every kind, this is all that is requisite for my purpose.

But I go farther, and observe, that this moral hypothesis and my present system not only agree together, but also that, allowing the former to be just, 'tis an absolute and invincible proof of the latter. For if all morality be founded on the pain or pleasure, which arises from the prospect of any loss or advantage, that may result from our own characters, or from those of others, all the effects of morality must be deriv'd from the same pain or pleasure, and among the rest, the passions of pride and humility. The very essence of virtue, according to this hypothesis, is to produce pleasure and that of vice to give pain. The virtue and vice must be part of our character in order to excite pride or humility. What farther proof can we desire for the double relation of impressions and ideas?

The same unquestionable argument may be deriv'd from the opinion of those, who maintain that morality is something real, essential, and founded on nature. The most probable hypothesis, which has been advanc'd to explain the distinction betwixt vice and virtue, and the origin of moral rights and obligations, is, that from a primary constitution of nature certain characters and passions, by the very view and contemplation, produce a pain, and others in like manner excite a pleasure. The uneasiness and satisfaction are not only inseparable from vice and virtue, but constitute their very nature and essence. To approve of a character is to feel an original delight upon its appearance. To disapprove of it is to be sensible of an uneasiness. The pain and pleasure, therefore, being the primary causes of vice and virtue, must also be the causes of all their effects, and consequently of pride and humility, which are the unavoidable attendants of that distinction.

But supposing this hypothesis of moral philosophy shou'd be allow'd to be false, 'tis still evident, that pain and pleasure, if not the causes of vice and virtue, are at least inseparable from them. A generous and noble character affords a satisfaction even in the survey; and when presented to us, tho' only in a poem or fable, never fails to charm and delight us. On the other hand cruelty and treachery displease from their very nature; nor is it possible ever to reconcile us to these qualities, either in ourselves or others. Thus one hypothesis of morality is an undeniable proof of the foregoing system, and the other at worst agrees with it.

But pride and humility arise not from these qualities alone of the mind, which, according to the vulgar systems of ethicks, have been comprehended as parts of moral duty, but from any other that has a connexion with pleasure and uneasiness. Nothing flatters our vanity more than the talent of pleasing by our wit, good humour, or any other accomplishment; and nothing gives us a more sensible mortification than a disappointment in any attempt of that nature. No one has ever been able to tell what *wit* is, and to shew why such a system of thought must be receiv'd under that denomination, and such another rejected. 'Tis only by taste we can decide concerning it, nor are we possest of any other standard, upon which we can form a judgment of this kind. Now what is this *taste*, from which true and false wit in a manner receive their being, and without which no thought can have a title to either of these denominations? 'Tis plainly nothing but a sensation of pleasure from true wit, and of uneasiness from false, without our being able to tell the reasons of that pleasure or uneasiness. The power of bestowing these opposite sensations is, therefore, the very essence of true and false wit; and consequently the cause of that pride or humility, which arises from them.

There may, perhaps, be some, who being accustom'd to the style of the schools and pulpit, and having never consider'd human nature in any other light, than that in which *they* place it, may here be surpriz'd to hear me talk of virtue as exciting pride, which they look upon as a vice; and of vice as producing humility, which they have been taught to consider as a virtue. But not to dispute about words, I observe, that by *pride* I understand that agreeable impression, which arises in the mind, when the view either of our virtue, beauty, riches or power makes us satisfy'd with ourselves: and that by *humility* I mean the opposite impression. 'Tis evident the former impression is not always vicious, nor the latter virtuous. The most rigid morality allows us to receive a pleasure from reflecting on a generous action; and 'tis by none esteem'd a virtue to feel any fruitless remorses upon the thoughts of past villainy and baseness. Let us, therefore, examine these impressions, consider'd in themselves; and enquire into their causes, whether plac'd on the mind or body, without troubling ourselves at present with that merit or blame, which may attend them.

SECT. VIII

Of beauty and deformity

Whether we consider the body as a part of ourselves, or assent to those philosophers, who regard it as something external, it must still be allow'd to be near enough connected with us to form one of these double relations, which I have asserted to be necessary to the causes of pride and humility. Wherever, therefore, we can find the other relation of impressions to join to this of ideas, we may expect with assurance either of these passions, according as the impression is pleasant or uneasy. But *beauty* of all kinds gives us a peculiar delight and satisfaction; as *deformity* produces pain, upon whatever subject it may be plac'd, and whether survey'd in an animate or inanimate object. If the beauty or deformity, therefore, be plac'd upon our own bodies, this pleasure or uneasiness must be converted into pride or humility, as having in this case all the circumstances requisite to produce a perfect transition of impressions and ideas. These opposite sensations are related to the opposite passions. The beauty or deformity is closely related to self, the object of both these passions. No wonder, then our own beauty becomes an object of pride, and deformity of humility.

But this effect of personal and bodily qualities is not only a proof of the present system, by shewing that the passions arise not in this case without all the circumstances I have requir'd, but may be employ'd as a stronger and more convincing argument. If we consider all the hypotheses, which have been form'd either by philosophy or common reason, to explain the difference betwixt beauty and deformity, we shall find that all of them resolve into this, that beauty is such an order and construction of parts, as either by the *primary constitution* of our nature, by *custom*, or by *caprice*, is fitted to give a pleasure and satisfaction to the soul. This is the distinguishing character of beauty, and forms all the difference betwixt it and deformity, whose natural tendency is to produce uneasiness. Pleasure and pain, therefore, are not only necessary attendants of beauty and deformity, but constitute their very essence. And indeed, if we consider, that a great part of the beauty, which we admire either in animals or in other objects, is deriv'd from the idea of convenience and utility, we shall make no scruple to assent to this opinion. That shape, which produces strength, is beautiful in one animal; and that which is a sign of agility in another. The order and convenience of a palace are no less essential to its beauty, than its mere figure and appearance. In like manner the rules of architecture require, that the top of a pillar shou'd be more slender than its base, and that because such a figure conveys to us the idea of security, which is pleasant; whereas the contrary form gives us the apprehension of danger, which is uneasy. From innumerable instances of this kind, as well as from considering that beauty like wit, cannot be defin'd, but is discern'd only by a taste or sensation, we may conclude, that beauty is nothing but a form, which produces pleasure, as deformity is a structure of parts, which conveys pain; and since the power of producing pain and pleasure make in this manner the essence of beauty and deformity, all the effects of these qualities must be deriv'd from the sensation; and among the rest pride and humility, which of all their effects are the most common and remarkable.

This argument I esteem just and decisive; but in order to give greater authority to the present reasoning, let us suppose it false for a moment, and see what will follow. 'Tis certain, then, that if the power of producing pleasure and pain forms not the essence of beauty and deformity, the sensations are at least inseparable from the qualities, and 'tis even difficult to consider them apart. Now there is nothing common to natural and moral beauty, (both of which are the causes of pride) but this power of producing pleasure; and as a common effect supposes always a common cause, 'tis plain the pleasure must in both cases be the real and influencing cause of the passion. Again; there is nothing originally different betwixt the beauty of our bodies and the beauty of external and foreign objects, but that the one has a near relation to ourselves, which is wanting in the other. This original difference, therefore, must be the cause of all their other differences, and among the rest, of their different influence upon the passion of pride, which is excited by the beauty of our person, but is not affected in the least by that of foreign and external objects. Placing, then, these two conclusions together, we find they compose the preceding system betwixt them, *viz.* that pleasure, as a related or resembling impression, when plac'd on a related object, by a natural transition, produces pride; and its contrary, humility. This system, then, seems already sufficiently confirm'd by experience; tho' we have not yet exhausted all our arguments.

'Tis not the beauty of the body alone that produces pride, but also its strength and force. Strength is a kind of power; and therefore the desire to excel in strength is to be consider'd as an inferior species of *ambition*. For this reason the present phaenomenon will be sufficiently accounted for, in explaining that passion.

Concerning all other bodily accomplishments we may observe in general, that whatever in ourselves is either useful, beautiful, or surprising, is an object of pride; and it's contrary, of humility. Now 'tis obvious, that every thing useful, beautiful or surprising, agrees in producing a separate pleasure and agrees in nothing else. The pleasure, therefore, with the relation to self must be the cause of the passion.

Tho' it shou'd be question'd, whether beauty be not something real, and different from the power of producing pleasure, it can never be disputed, that as surprize is nothing but a pleasure arising from novelty, it is not, properly speaking, a quality in any object, but merely a passion or impression in the soul. It must, therefore, be from that impression, that pride by a natural transition arises. And it arises so naturally, that there is nothing *in us or belonging to us*, which produces surprize, that does not at the same time excite that other passion. Thus we are vain of the surprising adventures we have met with, the escapes we have made, and dangers we have been expos'd to. Hence the origin of vulgar lying; where men without any interest, and merely out of vanity, heap up a number of extraordinary events, which are either the fictions of their brain, or if true, have at least no connexion with themselves. Their fruitful invention supplies them with a variety of adventures; and where that talent is wanting, they appropriate such as belong to others, in order to satisfy their vanity.

In this phaenomenon are contain'd two curious experiments, which if we compare them together, according to the known rules, by which we judge of cause and effect in anatomy, natural philosophy, and other sciences, will be an undeniable argument for that influence of the double relations above-mention'd. By one of these experiments we find, that an object produces pride merely by the interposition of pleasure; and that because the quality, by which it produces pride, is in reality nothing but the power of producing pleasure. By the other experiment we find, that the pleasure produces the pride by a transition along related ideas; because when we cut off that relation the passion is immediately destroy'd. A surprising adventure, in which we have been ourselves engag'd, is related to us, and by that means produces pride: But the adventures of others, tho' they may cause pleasure, yet for want of this relation of ideas, never excite that passion. What farther proof can be desired for the present system?

There is only one objection to this system with regard to our body; which is, that tho' nothing be more agreeable than health, and more painful than sickness, yet commonly men are neither proud of the one, nor mortify'd with the other. This will easily be accounted for, if we consider the *second* and *fourth* limitations, propos'd to our general system. It was observ'd, that no object ever produces pride or humility, if it has not something *peculiar* to ourself; as also, that every cause of that passion must be in some measure *constant*, and hold some proportion to the duration of our self, which is its object. Now as health and sickness vary incessantly to all men, and there is none, who is *solely* or certainly fix'd in either, these accidental blessings and calamities are in a manner separated from us, and are never consider'd as connected with our being and existence. And that this account is just appears hence, that wherever a malady of any kind is so rooted in our constitution, that we no longer entertain any hopes of recovery, from that moment it becomes an object of humility; as is evident in old men, whom nothing mortifies more than the consideration of their age and infirmities. They endeavour, as long as possible, to conceal their blindness and deafness, their rheums and gouts; nor do they ever confess them without reluctance and uneasiness. And tho' young men are not asham'd of every head-ach or cold they fall into, yet no topic is so proper to mortify human pride, and make us entertain a mean opinion of our nature, than this, that we are every moment of our lives subject to such infirmities. This sufficiently proves that bodily pain and sickness are in themselves proper causes of humility; tho' the custom of estimating every thing by comparison more than by its intrinsic worth and value, makes us overlook these calamities, which we find to be incident to every one, and causes us to form an idea of our merit and character independent of them.

We are asham'd of such maladies as affect others, and are either dangerous or disagreeable to them. Of the epilepsy; because it gives a horror to every one present: Of the itch; because it is infectious: Of the king's-evil; because it commonly goes to posterity. Men always consider the sentiments of others in their judgment of themselves. This has evidently appear'd in some of the foregoing reasonings; and will appear still more evidently, and be more fully explain'd afterwards.

SECT. IX
Of external advantages and disadvantages

But tho' pride and humility have the qualities of our mind and body, that is *self*, for their natural and more immediate causes, we find by experience, that there are many other objects, which produce these affections, and that the primary one is, in some measure, obscur'd and lost by the multiplicity of foreign and extrinsic. We found a vanity upon houses, gardens, equipages, as well as upon personal merit and accomplishments; and tho' these external advantages be in themselves widely distant from thought or a person, yet they considerably influence even a passion, which is directed to that as its ultimate object. This happens when external objects acquire any particular relation to ourselves, and are associated or connected with us. A beautiful fish in the ocean, an animal in a desart, and indeed any thing that neither belongs, nor is related to us, has no manner of influence on our vanity, whatever extraordinary qualities it may be endow'd with, and whatever degree of surprize and admiration it may naturally occasion. It must be some way associated with us in order to touch our pride. Its idea must hang in a manner, upon that of ourselves; and the transition from the one to the other must be easy and natural.

But here 'tis remarkable, that tho' the relation of ***resemblance*** operates upon the mind in the same manner as contiguity and causation, in conveying us from one idea to another, yet 'tis seldom a foundation either of pride or of humility. If we resemble a person in any of the valuable parts of his character, we must, in some degree, possess the quality, in which we resemble him; and this quality we always chuse to survey directly in ourselves rather than by reflexion in another person, when we wou'd found upon it any degree of vanity. So that tho' a likeness may occasionally produce that passion by suggesting a more advantageous idea of ourselves, 'tis there the view fixes at last, and the passion finds its ultimate and final cause.

There are instances, indeed, wherein men shew a vanity in resembling a great man in his countenance, shape, air, or other minute circumstances, that contribute not in any degree to his reputation; but it must be confess'd, that this extends not very far, nor is of any considerable moment in these affections. For this I assign the following reason. We can never have a vanity of resembling in trifles any person, unless he be possess'd of very shining qualities, which give us a respect and veneration for him. These qualities, then, are, properly speaking, the causes of our vanity, by means of their relation to ourselves. Now after what manner are they related to ourselves? They are parts of the person we value, and consequently connected with these trifles; which are also suppos'd to be parts of him. These trifles are connected with the resembling qualities in us; and these qualities in us, being parts, are connected with the whole; and by that means form a chain of several links of the person we resemble. But besides that this multitude of relations must weaken the connexion; 'tis evident the mind, in passing from the shining qualities to the trivial ones, must by that contrast the better perceive the minuteness of the latter, and be in some measure asham'd of the comparison and resemblance.

The relation, therefore, of contiguity, or that of causation, betwixt the cause and object of pride and humility, is alone requisite to give rise to these passions; and these relations are nothing else but qualities, by which the imagination is convey'd from one idea to another. Now let us consider what effect these can possibly have upon the mind, and by what means they become so requisite to the production of the passions. 'Tis evident, that the association of ideas operates in so silent and imperceptible a manner, that we are scarce sensible of it, and discover it more by its effects than by any immediate feeling or perception. It produces no emotion, and gives rise to no new impression of any kind, but only modifies those ideas, of which the mind was formerly possess'd, and which it cou'd recal upon occasion. From this reasoning, as well as from undoubted experience, we may conclude, that an association of ideas, however necessary, is not alone sufficient to give rise to any passion.

'Tis evident, then, that when the mind feels the passion either of pride or humility upon the appearance of a related object, there is, beside the relation or transition of thought, an emotion or original impression produc'd by some other principle. The question is, whether the emotion first produc'd be the passion itself, or some other impression related to it. This question we cannot be long in deciding. For besides all the other arguments, with which this subject abounds, it must evidently appear, that the relation of ideas, which experience shews to be so requisite a circumstance to the production of the passion, wou'd be entirely superfluous, were it not to second a relation of affections, and facilitate the transition from one impression to another. If nature produc'd immediately the passion of pride or humility, it wou'd be compleated in itself, and wou'd require no farther addition or encrease from any other affection. But supposing the first emotion to be only related to pride or humility, 'tis easily conceiv'd to what purpose the relation of objects may serve, and how the two different associations, of impressions and ideas, by uniting their forces, may assist each other's operation. This is not only easily conceiv'd, but I will venture to affirm 'tis the only manner, in which we can conceive this subject. An easy transition of ideas, which, of itself, causes no emotion, can never be necessary, or even useful to the passions, but by forwarding the transition betwixt some related impressions. Not to mention, that the same object causes a greater or smaller degree of pride, not only in proportion to the encrease or decrease of its qualities, but also to the distance or nearness of the relation; which is a clear argument for the transition of affections along the relation of ideas; since every change in the relation produces a proportionable change in the passion. Thus one part of the preceding system, concerning the relations of ideas is a sufficient proof of the other, concerning that of impressions; and is itself so evidently founded on experience, that 'twou'd be lost time to endeavour farther to prove it.

This will appear still more evidently in particular instances. Men are vain of the beauty of their country, of their county, of their parish. Here the idea of beauty plainly produces a pleasure. This pleasure is related to pride. The object or cause of this pleasure is, by the supposition, related to self, or the object of pride. By this double relation of impressions and ideas, a transition is made from the one impression to the other.

Men are also vain of the temperature of the climate, in which they were born; of the fertility of their native soil; of the goodness of the wines, fruits or victuals, produc'd by it; of the softness or force of their language; with other particulars of that kind. These objects have plainly a reference to the pleasures of the senses, and are originally consider'd as agreeable to the feeling, taste or hearing. How is it possible they cou'd ever become objects of pride, except by means of that transition above-explain'd?

There are some, that discover a vanity of an opposite kind, and affect to depreciate their own country, in comparison of those, to which they have travell'd. These persons find, when they are at home, and surrounded with their countrymen, that the strong relation betwixt them and their own nation is shar'd with so many, that 'tis in a manner lost to them; whereas their distant relation to a foreign country, which is form'd by their having seen it and liv'd in it, is augmented by their considering how few there are who have done the same. For this reason they always admire the beauty, utility and rarity of what is abroad, above what is at home.

Since we can be vain of a country, climate or any inanimate object, which bears a relation to us, 'tis no wonder we are vain of the qualities of those, who are connected with us by blood or friendship. Accordingly we find, that the very same qualities, which in ourselves produce pride, produce also in a lesser degree the same affection, when discover'd in persons related to us. The beauty, address, merit, credit and honours of their kindred are carefully display'd by the proud, as some of their most considerable sources of their vanity.

As we are proud of riches in ourselves, so to satisfy our vanity we desire that every one, who has any connexion with us, shou'd likewise be possest of them, and are asham'd of any one, that is mean or poor, among our friends and relations. For this reason we remove the poor as far from us as possible; and as we cannot prevent poverty in some distant collaterals, and our forefathers are taken to be our nearest relations; upon this account every one affects to be of a good family, and to be descended from a long succession of rich and honourable ancestors.

I have frequently observ'd, that those, who boast of the antiquity of their families, are glad when they can join this circumstance, that their ancestors for many generations have been uninterrupted proprietors of the same portion of land, and that their family has never chang'd its possessions, or been transplanted into any other county or province. I have also observ'd, that 'tis an additional subject of vanity, when they can boast, that these possessions have been transmitted thro' a descent compos'd entirely of males, and that the honours and fortune have never past thro' any female. Let us endeavour to explain these phaenomena by the foregoing system.

'Tis evident, that when any one boasts of the antiquity

of his family, the subjects of his vanity are not merely the extent of time and number of ancestors, but also their riches and credit, which are suppos'd to reflect a lustre on himself on account of his relation to them. He first considers these objects; is affected by them in an agreeable manner; and then returning back to himself, thro' the relation of parent and child, is elevated with the passion of pride, by means of the double relation of impressions and ideas. Since therefore the passion depends on these relations, whatever strengthens any of the relations must also encrease the passion, and whatever weakens the relations must diminish the passion. Now 'tis certain the identity of the possession strengthens the relation of ideas arising from blood and kindred, and conveys the fancy with greater facility from one generation to another, from the remote ancestors to their posterity, who are both their heirs and their descendants. By this facility the impression is transmitted more entire, and excites a greater degree of pride and vanity.

The case is the same with the transmission of the honours and fortune thro' a succession of males without their passing thro' any female. 'Tis a quality of human nature, which we shall consider * afterwards, that the imagination naturally turns to whatever is important and considerable; and where two objects are presented to it, a small and a great one, usually leaves the former, and dwells entirely upon the latter. As in the society of marriage, the male sex has the advantage above the female, the husband first engages our attention; and whether we consider him directly, or reach him by passing thro' related objects, the thought both rests upon him with greater satisfaction, and arrives at him with greater facility than his consort. 'Tis easy to see, that this property must strengthen the child's relation to the father, and weaken that to the mother. For as all relations are nothing but a propensity to pass from one idea to another, whatever strengthens the propensity strengthens the relation; and as we have a stronger propensity to pass from the idea of the children to that of the father, than from the same

* Part II. Sect. 2.

idea to that of the mother, we ought to regard the former relation as the closer and more considerable. This is the reason why children commonly bear their father's name, and are esteem'd to be of nobler or baser birth, according to *his* family. And tho' the mother shou'd be possest of a superior spirit and genius to the father, as often happens, the *general rule* prevails, notwithstanding the exception, according to the doctrine above-explain'd. Nay even when a superiority of any kind is so great, or when any other reasons have such an effect, as to make the children rather represent the mother's family than the father's, the general rule still retains such an efficacy that it weakens the relation, and makes a kind of break in the line of ancestors. The imagination runs not along them with facility, nor is able to transfer the honour and credit of the ancestors to their posterity of the same name and family so readily, as when the transition is conformable to the general rules, and passes from father to son, or from brother to brother.

SECT. X
Of property and riches

BUT the relation, which is esteem'd the closest, and which of all others produces most commonly the passion of pride, is that of *property*. This relation 'twill be impossible for me fully to explain before I come to treat of justice and the other moral virtues. 'Tis sufficient to observe on this occasion, that property may be defin'd, *such a relation betwixt a person and an object as permits him, but forbids any other, the free use and possession of it, without violating the laws of justice and moral equity*. If justice, therefore, be a virtue, which has a natural and original influence on the human mind, property may be look'd upon as a particular species of *causation*; whether we consider the liberty it gives the proprietor to operate as he please upon the object, or the advantages, which he reaps from it. 'Tis the same case, if justice, according to the system of certain philosophers, shou'd be esteemed an artificial and not a natural virtue. For then honour, and custom, and civil laws supply the place of natural conscience, and produce, in some degree, the same effects. This in the mean time is certain, that the mention of the property naturally carries our thought to the proprietor, and of the proprietor to the property; which being a proof of a perfect relation of ideas is all that is requisite to our present purpose. A relation of ideas, join'd to that of impressions, always produces a transition of affections; and therefore, whenever any pleasure or pain arises from an object, connected with us by property, we may be certain, that either pride or humility must arise from this conjunction of relations; if the foregoing system be solid and satisfactory. And whether it be so or not, we may soon satisfy ourselves by the most cursory view of human life.

Every thing belonging to a vain man is the best that is any where to be found. His houses, equipage, furniture, cloaths, horses, hounds, excel all others in his conceit; and 'tis easy to observe, that from the least advantage in any of these, he draws a new subject of pride and vanity. His wine, if you'll believe him, has a finer flavour than any other; his cookery is more exquisite; his table more orderly; his servants more expert; the air, in which he lives, more healthful; the soil he cultivates more fertile; his fruits ripen earlier and to greater perfection: Such a thing is remarkable for its novelty; such another for its antiquity: This is the workmanship of a famous artist; that belong'd once to such a prince or great man: All objects, in a word, that are useful, beautiful or surprizing, or are related to such, may, by means of property, give rise to this passion. These agree in giving pleasure, and agree in nothing else. This alone is common to them; and therefore must be the quality that produces the passion, which is their common effect. As every new instance is a new argument, and as the instances are here without number, I may venture to affirm, that scarce any system was ever so fully prov'd by experience, as that which I have here advanc'd.

If the property of any thing, that gives pleasure either by its utility, beauty or novelty, produces also pride by a double relation of impressions and ideas; we need not be surpriz'd, that the power of acquiring this property, shou'd have the same effect. Now riches are to be consider'd as the power of acquiring the property of what pleases; and 'tis only in this view they have any influence on the passions. Paper will, on many occasions, be consider'd as riches, and that because it may convey the power of acquiring money: And money is not riches, as it is a metal endow'd with certain qualities of solidity, weight and fusibility; but only as it has a relation to the pleasures and conveniences of life. Taking then this for granted, which is in itself so evident, we may draw from it one of the strongest arguments I have yet employ'd to prove the influence of the double relations on pride and humility.

It has been observ'd in treating of the understanding, that the distinction, which we sometimes make betwixt a *power* and the *exercise* of it, is entirely frivolous, and that neither man nor any other being ought ever to be thought possest of any ability, unless it be exerted and put in action. But tho' this be strictly true in a just and *philosophical* way of thinking, 'tis certain it is not *the philosophy* of our passions; but that many things operate upon them by means of the idea and supposition of power, independent of its actual exercise. We are pleas'd when we acquire an ability of procuring pleasure, and are displeas'd when another acquires a power of giving pain. This is evident from experience; but in order to give a just explication of the matter, and account for this satisfaction and uneasiness, we must weigh the following reflections.

'Tis evident the error of distinguishing power from its exercise proceeds not entirely from the scholastic doctrine of *free-will*, which, indeed, enters very little into common life, and has but small influence on our vulgar and popular ways of thinking. According to that doctrine, motives deprive us not of free-will, nor take away our power of performing or forbearing any action. But according to common notions a man has no power, where very considerable motives lie betwixt him and the satisfaction of his desires, and determine him to forbear what he wishes to perform. I do not think I have fallen into my enemy's power, when I see him pass me in the streets with a sword by his side, while I am unprovided of any weapon. I know that the fear of the civil magistrate is as strong a restraint as any of iron, and that I am in as perfect safety as if he were chain'd or imprison'd. But when a person acquires such an authority over me, that not only there is no external obstacle to his actions; but also that he may punish or reward me as he pleases, without any dread of punishment in his turn, I then attribute a full power to him, and consider myself as his subject or vassal.

Now if we compare these two cases, that of a person, who has very strong motives of interest or safety to forbear any action, and that of another, who lies under no such obligation, we shall find, according to the philosophy explain'd in the foregoing book, that the only *known* difference betwixt them lies in this, that in the former case we conclude from *past experience*, that the person never will perform that action, and in the latter, that he possibly or probably will perform it. Nothing is more fluctuating and inconstant on many occasions, than the will of man; nor is there any thing but strong motives, which can give us an absolute certainty in pronouncing concerning any of his future actions. When we see a person free from these motives, we suppose a possibility either of his acting or forbearing; and tho' in general we may conclude him to be determin'd by motives and causes, yet this removes not the uncertainty of our judgment concerning these causes, nor the influence of that uncertainty on the passions. Since therefore we ascribe a power of performing an action to every one, who has no very powerful motive to forbear it, and refuse it to such as have; it may justly be concluded, that *power* has always a reference to its *exercise*, either actual or probable, and that we consider a person as endow'd with any ability when we find from past experience, that 'tis probable, or at least possible he may exert it. And indeed, as our passions always regard the real existence of objects, and we always judge of this reality from past instances; nothing can be more likely of itself, without any farther reasoning, than that power consists in the possibility or probability of any action, as discover'd by experience and the practice of the world.

Now 'tis evident, that wherever a person is in such a situation with regard to me, that there is no very powerful motive to deter him from injuring me, and consequently 'tis *uncertain* whether he will injure me or not, I must be uneasy in such a situation, and cannot consider the possibility or probability of that injury without a sensible concern. The passions are not only affected by such events as are certain and infallible, but also in an inferior degree by such as are possible and contingent. And tho' perhaps I never really feel any harm, and discover by the event, that, philosophically speaking, the person never had any power of harming me; since he did not exert any; this prevents not my uneasiness from the preceding uncertainty. The agreeable passions may here operate as well as the uneasy, and convey a pleasure when I perceive a good to become either possible or probable by the possibility or probability of another's bestowing it on me, upon the removal of any strong motives, which might formerly have hinder'd him.

But we may farther observe, that this satisfaction encreases, when any good approaches in such a manner that it is in one's *own* power to take or leave it, and there neither is any physical impediment, nor any very strong motive to hinder our enjoyment. As all men desire pleasure, nothing can be more probable, than its existence when there is no external obstacle to the producing it, and men perceive no danger in following their inclinations. In that case their imagination easily anticipates the satisfaction, and conveys the same joy, as if they were persuaded of its real and actual existence.

But this accounts not sufficiently for the satisfaction, which attends riches. A miser receives delight from his money; that is, from the *power* it affords him of procuring all the pleasures and conveniences of life, tho' he knows he has enjoy'd his riches for forty years without ever employing them; and consequently cannot conclude by any species of reasoning, that the real existence of these pleasures is nearer, than if he were entirely depriv'd of all his possessions. But tho' he cannot form any such conclusion in a way of reasoning concerning the nearer approach of the pleasure, 'tis certain he *imagines* it to approach nearer, whenever all external obstacles are remov'd, along with the more powerful motives of interest and danger, which oppose it. For farther satisfaction on this head I must refer to my account of the will, where I shall * explain that false sensation of liberty, which makes us imagine we can perform any thing, that is not very dangerous or destructive. Whenever any other person is under no strong obligations of interest to forbear any pleasure, we judge from *experience*, that the pleasure will exist, and that he will probably obtain it. But when ourselves are in that situation, we judge from an *illusion of the fancy*, that the pleasure is still closer and more immediate. The will seems to move easily every way, and casts a shadow or image of itself, even to that side, on which it did not settle. By means of this image the enjoyment seems to approach nearer to us, and gives us the same lively satisfaction, as if it were perfectly certain and unavoidable.

'Twill now be easy to draw this whole reasoning to a point, and to prove, that when riches produce any pride or vanity in their possessors, as they never fail to do, 'tis only by means of a double relation of impressions and ideas. The very essence of riches consists in the power of procuring the pleasures and conveniences of life. The very essence of this consists in the probability of its exercise, and in its causing us to anticipate, by a *true* or *false* reasoning, the real existence of the pleasure. This anticipation of pleasure is, in itself, a very considerable pleasure; and as its cause is some possession or property, which we enjoy, and which is thereby related to us, we here clearly see all the parts of the forego-

* Part III. Sect. 2.

ing system most exactly and distinctly drawn out before us.

For the same reason, that riches cause pleasure and pride, and poverty excites uneasiness and humility, power must produce the former emotions, and slavery the latter. Power or an authority over others makes us capable of satisfying all our desires; as slavery, by subjecting us to the will of others, exposes us to a thousand wants, and mortifications.

'Tis here worth observing, that the vanity of power, or shame of slavery, are much augmented by the consideration of the persons, over whom we exercise our authority, or who exercise it over us. For supposing it possible to frame statues of such an admirable mechanism, that they cou'd move and act in obedience to the will; 'tis evident the possession of them wou'd give pleasure and pride, but not to such a degree, as the same authority, when exerted over sensible and rational creatures, whose condition, being compar'd to our own, makes it seem more agreeable and honourable. Comparison is in every case a sure method of augmenting our esteem of any thing. A rich man feels the felicity of his condition better by opposing it to that of a beggar. But there is a peculiar advantage in power, by the contrast, which is, in a manner, presented to us, betwixt ourselves and the person we command. The comparison is obvious and natural: The imagination finds it in the very subject: The passage of the thought to its conception is smooth and easy. And that this circumstance has a considerable effect in augmenting its influence, will appear afterwards in examining the nature of *malice* and *envy*.

SECT. XI

Of the love of fame

But beside these original causes of pride and humility, there is a secondary one in the opinions of others, which has an equal influence on the affections. Our reputation, our character, our name are considerations of vast weight and importance; and even the other causes of pride; virtue, beauty and riches; have little influence, when not seconded by the opinions and sentiments of others. In order to account for this phaenomenon 'twill be necessary to take some compass, and first explain the nature of *sympathy*.

No quality of human nature is more remarkable, both in itself and in its consequences, than that propensity we have to sympathize with others, and to receive by communication their inclinations and sentiments, however different from, or even contrary to our own. This is not only conspicuous in children, who implicitly embrace every opinion propos'd to them; but also in men of the greatest judgment and understanding, who find it very difficult to follow their own reason or inclination, in opposition to that of their friends and daily companions. To this principle we ought to ascribe the great uniformity we may observe in the humours and turn of thinking of those of the same nation; and 'tis much more probable, that this resemblance arises from sympathy, than from any influence of the soil and climate, which, tho' they continue invariably the same, are not able to preserve the character of a nation the same for a century together. A good-natur'd man finds himself in an instant of the same humour with his company; and even the proudest and most surly take a tincture from their countrymen and acquaintance. A chearful countenance infuses a sensible complacency and serenity into my mind; as an angry or sorrowful one throws a sudden dump upon me. Hatred, resentment, esteem, love, courage, mirth and melancholy; all these passions I feel more from communication than from my own natural temper and disposition. So remarkable a phaenomenon merits our attention, and must be trac'd up to its first principles.

When any affection is infus'd by sympathy, it is at first known only by its effects, and by those external signs in the countenance and conversation, which convey an idea of it. This idea is presently converted into an impression, and acquires such a degree of force and vivacity, as to become the very passion itself, and produce an equal emotion, as any original affection. However instantaneous this change of the idea into an impression may be, it proceeds from certain views and reflections, which will not escape the strict scrutiny of a philosopher, tho' they may the person himself, who makes them.

'Tis evident, that the idea, or rather impression of ourselves is always intimately present with us, and that our consciousness gives us so lively a conception of our own person, that 'tis not possible to imagine, that any thing can in this particular go beyond it. Whatever object, therefore, is related to ourselves must be conceived with a little vivacity of conception, according to the foregoing principles; and tho' this relation shou'd not be so strong as that of causation, it must still have a considerable influence. Resemblance and contiguity are relations not to be neglected; especially when by an inference from cause and effect, and by the observation of external signs, we are inform'd of the real existence of the object, which is resembling or contiguous.

Now 'tis obvious, that nature has preserv'd a great resemblance among all human creatures, and that we never remark any passion or principle in others, of which, in some degree or other, we may not find a parallel in ourselves. The case is the same with the fabric of the mind, as with that of the body. However the parts may differ in shape or size, their structure and composition are in general the same. There is a very remarkable resemblance, which preserves itself amidst all their variety; and this resemblance must very much contribute to make us enter into the sentiments of others, and embrace them with facility and pleasure. Accordingly we find, that where, beside the general resemblance of our natures, there is any peculiar similarity in our manners, or character, or country, or language, it facilitates the sympathy. The stronger the relation is betwixt ourselves and any object, the more easily does the imagination make the transition, and convey to the related idea the vivacity of conception, with which we always form the idea of our own person.

Nor is resemblance the only relation, which has this effect, but receives new force from other relations, that may accompany it. The sentiments of others have little influence, when far remov'd from us, and require the relation of contiguity, to make them communicate themselves entirely. The relations of blood, being a species of causation, may sometimes contribute to the same effect; as also acquaintance, which operates in the same manner with education and custom; as we shall see more fully * afterwards. All these relations, when united together, convey the impression or consciousness of our own person to the idea of the sentiments or passions of others, and makes us conceive them in the strongest and most lively manner.

It has been remark'd in the beginning of this treatise, that all ideas are borrow'd from impressions, and that these two kinds of perceptions differ only in the degrees of force and vivacity, with which they strike upon the soul. The component parts of ideas and impressions are precisely alike. The manner and order of their appearance may be the same. The different degrees of their force and vivacity are, therefore, the only particulars, that distinguish them: And as this difference may be remov'd, in some measure, by a relation betwixt the impressions and ideas, 'tis no wonder an idea of a sentiment or passion, may by this means be so inliven'd as to become the very sentiment or passion. The lively idea of any object always approaches its impression; and 'tis certain we may feel sickness and pain from the mere force of imagination, and make a malady real by often thinking of it. But this is most remarkable in the opinions and affections; and 'tis there principally that a lively idea is converted into an impression. Our affections depend more upon ourselves, and the internal operations of the mind, than any other impressions; for which reason they arise more naturally from the imagination, and from every lively idea we form of them. This is the nature and cause of sympathy; and 'tis after this manner we enter so deep into the opinions and affections of others, whenever we discover them.

* Part II. Sect. 4.

What is principally remarkable in this whole affair is the strong confirmation these phaenomena give to the foregoing system concerning the understanding, and consequently to the present one concerning the passions; since these are analogous to each other. 'Tis indeed evident, that when we sympathize with the passions and sentiments of others, these movements appear at first in *our* mind as mere ideas, and are conceiv'd to belong to another person, as we conceive any other matter of fact. 'Tis also evident, that the ideas of the affections of others are converted into the very impressions they represent, and that the passions arise in conformity to the images we form of them. All this is an object of the plainest experience, and depends not on any hypothesis of philosophy. That science can only be admitted to explain the phaenomena; tho' at the same time it must be confest, they are so clear of themselves, that there is but little occasion to employ it. For besides the relation of cause and effect, by which we are convinc'd of the reality of the passion, with which we sympathize; besides this, I say, we must be assisted by the relations of resemblance and contiguity, in order to feel the sympathy in its full perfection. And since these relations can entirely convert an idea into an impression, and convey the vivacity of the latter into the former, so perfectly as to lose nothing of it in the transition, we may easily conceive how the relation of cause and effect alone, may serve to strengthen and inliven an idea. In sympathy there is an evident conversion of an idea into an impression. This conversion arises from the relation of objects to ourself. Ourself is always intimately present to us. Let us compare all these circumstances, and we shall find, that sympathy is exactly correspondent to the operations of our understanding; and even contains something more surprizing and extraordinary.

'Tis now time to turn our view from the general consideration of sympathy, to its influence on pride and humility, when these passions arise from praise and blame, from reputation and infamy. We may observe, that no person is ever prais'd by another for any quality, which wou'd not, if real, produce, of itself, a pride in the person possest of it. The elogiums either turn upon his power, or riches, or family, or virtue; all of which are subjects of vanity, that we have already explain'd and accounted for. 'Tis certain, then, that if a person consider'd himself in the same light, in which he appears to his admirer, he wou'd first receive a separate pleasure, and afterwards a pride or self-satisfaction, according to the hypothesis above explain'd. Now nothing is more natural than for us to embrace the opinions of others in this particular; both from *sympathy*, which renders all their sentiments intimately present to us; and from *reasoning*, which makes us regard their judgment, as a kind of argument for what they affirm. These two principles of authority and sympathy influence almost all our opinions; but must have a peculiar influence, when we judge of our own worth and character. Such judgments are always attended with passion * ; and nothing tends more to disturb our understanding, and precipitate us into any opinions, however unreasonable, than their connexion with passion; which diffuses itself over the imagination, and gives an additional force to every related idea. To which we may add, that being conscious of great partiality in our own favour, we are peculiarly pleas'd with any thing, that confirms the good opinion we have of ourselves, and are easily shock'd with whatever opposes it.

All this appears very probable in theory; but in order to bestow a full certainty on this reasoning, we must examine the phaenomena of the passions, and see if they agree with it.

Among these phaenomena we may esteem it a very favourable one to our present purpose, that tho' fame in general be agreeable, yet we receive a much greater satisfaction from the approbation of those, whom we ourselves esteem and approve of, than of those, whom we hate and despise. In like measure we are principally mortify'd with the contempt of persons, upon whose judgment we set some value, and are, in a great measure, indifferent about the

* Book I. Part III. Sect. 10.

opinions of the rest of mankind. But if the mind receiv'd from any original instinct a desire of fame and aversion to infamy, fame and infamy wou'd influence us without distinction; and every opinion, according as it were favourable or unfavourable, wou'd equally excite that desire or aversion. The judgment of a fool is the judgment of another person, as well as that of a wise man, and is only inferior in its influence on our own judgment.

We are not only better pleas'd with the approbation of a wise man than with that of a fool, but receive an additional satisfaction from the former, when 'tis obtain'd after a long and intimate acquaintance. This is accounted for after the same manner.

The praises of others never give us much pleasure, unless they concur with our own opinion, and extol us for those qualities, in which we chiefly excel. A mere soldier little values the character of eloquence: A gownman of courage: A bishop of humour: Or a merchant of learning. Whatever esteem a man may have for any quality, abstractedly consider'd; when he is conscious he is not possest of it; the opinions of the whole world will give him little pleasure in that particular, and that because they never will be able to draw his own opinion after them.

Nothing is more usual than for men of good families, but narrow circumstances, to leave their friends and country, and rather seek their livelihood by mean and mechanical employments among strangers, than among those, who are acquainted with their birth and education. We shall be unknown, say they, where we go. No body will suspect from what family we are sprung. We shall be remov'd from all our friends and acquaintance, and our poverty and meanness will by that means sit more easy upon us. In examining these sentiments, I find they afford many very convincing arguments for my present purpose.

First, We may infer from them, that the uneasiness of being contemn'd depends on sympathy, and that sympathy depends on the relation of objects to ourselves; since we are most uneasy under the contempt of persons, who are both related to us by blood, and contiguous in place. Hence we seek to diminish this sympathy and uneasiness by separating these relations, and placing ourselves in a contiguity to strangers, and at a distance from relations.

Secondly, We may conclude, that relations are requisite to sympathy, not absolutely consider'd as relations, but by their influence in converting our ideas of the sentiments of others into the very sentiments, by means of the association betwixt the idea of their persons, and that of our own. For here the relations of kindred and contiguity both subsist; but not being united in the same persons, they contribute in a less degree to the sympathy.

Thirdly, This very circumstance of the diminution of sympathy by the separation of relations is worthy of our attention. Suppose I am plac'd in a poor condition among strangers, and consequently am but lightly treated; I yet find myself easier in that situation, than when I was every day expos'd to the contempt of my kindred and countrymen. Here I feel a double contempt; from my relations, but they are absent; from those about me, but they are strangers. This double contempt is likewise strengthen'd by the two relations of kindred and contiguity. But as the persons are not the same, who are connected with me by those two relations, this difference of ideas separates the impressions arising from the contempt, and keeps them from running into each other. The contempt of my neighbours has a certain influence; as has also that of my kindred: But these influences are distinct, and never unite; as when the contempt proceeds from persons who are at once both my neighbours and kindred. This phaenomenon is analogous to the system of pride and humility above-explain'd, which may seem so extraordinary to vulgar apprehensions.

Fourthly, A person in these circumstances naturally conceals his birth from those among whom he lives, and is very uneasy, if any one suspects him to be of a family, much superior to his present fortune and way of living. Every thing in this world is judg'd of by comparison. What is an immense fortune for a private gentleman is beggary for a prince. A peasant wou'd think himself happy in what cannot afford necessaries for a gentleman. When a man has either been acustom'd to a more splendid way of living, or thinks himself intitled to it by his birth and quality, every thing below is disagreeable and even shameful; and 'tis with the greatest industry he conceals his pretensions to a better fortune. Here he himself knows his misfortunes; but as those, with whom he lives, are ignorant of them, he has the disagreeable reflection and comparison suggested only by his own thoughts, and never receives it by a sympathy with others; which must contribute very much to his ease and satisfaction.

If there be any objections to this hypothesis, *that the pleasure, which we receive from praise, arises from a communication of sentiments*, we shall find, upon examination, that these objections, when taken in a proper light, will serve to confirm it. Popular fame may be agreeable even to a man, who despises the vulgar; but 'tis because their multitude gives them additional weight and authority. Plagiaries are delighted with praises, which they are conscious they do not deserve; but this is a kind of castle-building, where the imagination amuses itself with its own fictions, and strives to render them firm and stable by a sympathy with the sentiments of others. Proud men are most shock'd with contempt, tho' they do not most readily assent to it; but 'tis because of the opposition betwixt the passion, which is natural to them, and that receiv'd by sympathy. A violent lover in like manner is very much displeas'd when you blame and condemn his love; tho' 'tis evident your opposition can have no influence, but by the hold it takes of himself, and by his sympathy with you. If he despises you, or perceives you are in jest, whatever you say has no effect upon him.

SECT. XII

Of the pride and humility of animals

THUS in whatever light we consider this subject, we may still observe, that the causes of pride and humility correspond exactly to our hypothesis, and that nothing can excite either of these passions, unless it be both related to ourselves, and produces a pleasure or pain independent of the passion. We have not only prov'd, that a tendency to produce pleasure or pain is common to all the causes of pride or humility, but also that 'tis the only thing, which is common; and consequently is the quality, by which they operate. We have farther prov'd, that the most considerable causes of these passions are really nothing but the power of producing either agreeable or uneasy sensations; and therefore that all their effects, and amongst the rest, pride and humility, are deriv'd solely from that origin. Such simple and natural principles, founded on such solid proofs, cannot fail to be receiv'd by philosophers, unless oppos'd by some objections, that have escaped me.

'Tis usual with anatomists to join their observations and experiments on human bodies to those on beasts, and from the agreement of these experiments to derive an additional argument for any particular hypothesis. 'Tis indeed certain, that where the structure of parts in brutes is the same as in men, and the operation of these parts also the same, the causes of that operation cannot be different, and that whatever we discover to be true of the one species, may be concluded without hesitation to be certain of the other. Thus tho' the mixture of humours and the composition of minute parts may justly be presum'd to be somewhat different in men from what it is in mere animals; and therefore any experiment we make upon the one concerning the effects of medicines will not always apply to the other; yet as the structure of the veins and muscles, the fabric and situation of the heart, of the lungs, the stomach, the liver and other parts, are the same or nearly the same in all animals, the very same hypothesis, which in one species explains muscular motion, the progress of the chyle, the circulation of the blood, must be applicable to every one; and according as it agrees or disagrees with the experiments we may make in any species of creatures, we may draw a proof of its truth or falshood on the whole. Let us, therefore, apply this method of enquiry, which is found so just and useful in reasonings concerning the body, to our present anatomy of the mind, and see what discoveries we can make by it.

In order to this we must first shew the correspondence of *passions* in men and animals, and afterwards compare the *causes*, which produce these passions.

'Tis plain, that almost in every species of creatures, but especially of the nobler kind, there are many evident marks of pride and humility. The very port and gait of a swan, or turkey, or peacock show the high idea he has entertain'd of himself, and his contempt of all others. This is the more remarkable, that in the two last species of animals, the pride always attends the beauty, and is discover'd in the male only. The vanity and emulation of nightingales in singing have been commonly remark'd; as likewise that of horses in swiftness, of hounds in sagacity and smell, of the bull and cock in strength, and of every other animal in his particular excellency. Add to this, that every species of creatures, which approach so often to man, as to familiarize themselves with him, show an evident pride in his approbation, and are pleas'd with his praises and caresses, independent of every other consideration. Nor are they the caresses of every one without distinction, which give them this vanity, but those principally of the persons they know and love; in the same manner as that passion is excited in mankind. All these are evident proofs, that pride and humility are not merely human passions, but extend themselves over the whole animal creation.

The *causes* of these passions are likewise much the same in beasts as in us, making a just allowance for our superior knowledge and understanding. Thus animals have little or no sense of virtue or vice; they quickly lose sight of the relations of blood; and are incapable of that of right and property: For which reason the causes of their pride and humility must lie solely in the body, and can never be plac'd either in the mind or external objects. But so far as regards the body, the same qualities cause pride in the animal as in the human kind; and 'tis on beauty, strength, swiftness or some other useful or agreeable quality that this passion is always founded.

The next question is, whether, since those passions are the same, and arise from the same causes thro' the whole creation, the *manner*, in which the causes operate, be also the same. According to all rules of analogy, this is justly to be expected; and if we find upon trial, that the explication of these phaenomena, which we make use of in one species, will not apply to the rest, we may presume that that explication, however specious, is in reality without foundation.

In order to decide this question, let us consider, that there is evidently the same *relation* of ideas, and deriv'd from the same causes, in the minds of animals as in those of men. A dog, that has hid a bone, often forgets the place; but when brought to it, his thought passes easily to what he formerly conceal'd, by means of the contiguity, which produces a relation among his ideas. In like manner, when he has been heartily beat in any place, he will tremble on his approach to it, even tho' he discover no signs of any present danger. The effects of resemblance are not so remarkable; but as that relation makes a considerable ingredient in causation, of which all animals shew so evident a judgment, we may conclude that the three relations of resemblance, contiguity and causation operate in the same manner upon beasts as upon human creatures.

There are also instances of the relation of impressions, sufficient to convince us, that there is an union of certain affections with each other in the inferior species of creatures as well as in the superior, and that their minds are frequently convey'd thro' a series of connected emotions. A dog, when elevated with joy, runs naturally into love and kindness, whether of his master or of the sex. In like manner, when full of pain and sorrow, he becomes quarrelsome and ill-natur'd; and that passion, which at first was grief, is by the smallest occasion converted into anger.

Thus all the internal principles, that are necessary in us to produce either pride or humility, are common to all creatures; and since the causes, which excite these passions, are likewise the same, we may justly conclude, that these causes operate after the same *manner* thro' the whole animal creation. My hypothesis is so simple, and supposes so little reflection and judgment, that 'tis applicable to every sensible creature; which must not only be allow'd to be a convincing proof of its veracity, but, I am confident, will be found an objection to every other system.

PART II

Of love and hatred

SECT. I

Of the object and causes of love and hatred

'Tis altogether impossible to give any definition of the passions of *love* and *hatred*; and that because they produce merely a simple impression, without any mixture or composition. 'Twou'd be as unnecessary to attempt any description of them, drawn from their nature, origin, causes and objects; and that both because these are the subjects of our present enquiry, and because these passions of themselves are sufficiently known from our common feeling and experience. This we have already observ'd concerning pride and humility, and here repeat it concerning love and hatred; and indeed there is so great a resemblance betwixt these two sets of passions, that we shall be oblig'd to begin with a kind of abridgment of our reasonings concerning the former, in order to explain the latter.

As the immediate *object* of pride and humility is self or that identical person, of whose thoughts, actions, and sensations we are intimately conscious; so the *object* of love and hatred is some other person, of whose thoughts, actions, and sensations we are not conscious. This is sufficiently evident from experience. Our love and hatred are always directed to some sensible being external to us; and when we talk of *self-love,* 'tis not in a proper sense, nor has the sensation it produces any thing in common with that tender emotion, which is excited by a friend or mistress. 'Tis the same case with hatred. We may be mortified by our own faults and follies; but never feel any anger or hatred, except from the injuries of others.

But tho' the object of love and hatred be always some other person, 'tis plain that the object is not, properly speaking, the *cause* of these passions, or alone sufficient to excite them. For since love and hatred are directly contrary in their sensation, and have the same object in common, if that object were also their cause, it wou'd produce these opposite passions in an equal degree; and as they must, from the very first moment, destroy each other, none of them wou'd ever be able to make its appearance. There must, therefore, be some cause different from the object.

If we consider the causes of love and hatred, we shall find they are very much diversify'd, and have not many things in common. The virtue, knowledge, wit, good sense, good humour of any person, produce love and esteem; as the opposite qualities, hatred and contempt. The same passions arise from bodily accomplishments, such as beauty, force, swiftness, dexterity; and from their contraries; as likewise from the external advantages and disadvantages of family, possession, cloaths, nation and climate. There is not one of these objects, but what by its different qualities may produce love and esteem, or hatred and contempt.

From the view of these causes we may derive a new distinction betwixt the *quality* that operates, and the *subject* on which it is plac'd. A prince, that is possess'd of a stately palace, commands the esteem of the people upon that account; and that *first*, by the beauty of the palace, and *secondly*, by the relation of property, which connects it with him. The removal of either of these destroys the passion; which evidently proves that the cause is a compounded one.

'Twou'd be tedious to trace the passions of love and hatred, thro' all the observations which we have form'd concerning pride and humility, and which are equally applicable to both sets of passions. 'Twill be sufficient to *remark* in general, that the object of love and hatred is evidently some thinking person; and that the sensation of the former passion is always agreeable, and of the latter uneasy. We may also *suppose* with some shew of probability, *that the cause of both these passions is always related to a thinking being,* and *that the cause of the former produce a separate pleasure, and of the latter a separate uneasiness.*

One of these suppositions, *viz.* that the cause of love and hatred must be related to a person or thinking being, in order to produce these passions, is not only probable, but too evident to be contested. Virtue and vice, when consider'd in the abstract; beauty and deformity, when plac'd on inanimate objects; poverty and riches when belonging to a third person, excite no degree of love or hatred, esteem or contempt towards those, who have no relation to them. A person looking out at a window, sees me in the street, and beyond me a beautiful palace, with which I have no concern: I believe none will pretend, that this person will pay me the same respect, as if I were owner of the palace.

'Tis not so evident at first sight, that a relation of impressions is requisite to these passions, and that because in the transition the one impression is so much confounded with the other, that they become in a manner undistinguishable. But as in pride and humility, we have easily been able to make the separation, and to prove, that every cause of these passions produces a separate pain or pleasure, I might here observe the same method with the same success, in examining particularly the several causes of love and hatred. But as I hasten to a full and decisive proof of these systems, I delay this examination for a moment: And in the mean time shall endeavour to convert to my present purpose all my reasonings concerning pride and humility, by an argument that is founded on unquestionable experience.

There are few persons, that are satisfy'd with their own character, or genius, or fortune, who are not desirous of shewing themselves to the world, and of acquiring the love and approbation of mankind. Now 'tis evident, that the very same qualities and circumstances, which are the causes of pride or self-esteem, are also the causes of vanity or the desire of reputation; and that we always put to view those particulars with which in ourselves we are best satisfy'd. But if love and esteem were not produc'd by the same qualities as pride, according as these qualities are related to ourselves or others, this method of proceeding wou'd be very absurd, nor cou'd men expect a correspondence in the sentiments of every other person, with those themselves have entertain'd. 'Tis true, few can form exact systems of the passions, or make reflections on their general nature and resemblances. But without such a progress in philosophy, we are not subject to many mistakes in this particular, but are sufficiently guided by common experience, as well as by a kind of *presentation*; which tells us what will operate on others, by what we feel immediately in ourselves. Since then the same qualities that produce pride or humility, cause love or hatred; all the arguments that have been employ'd to prove, that the causes of the former passions excite a pain or pleasure independent of the passion, will be applicable with equal evidence to the causes of the latter.

SECT. II

Experiments to confirm this system

Upon duly weighing these arguments, no one will make any scruple to assent to that conclusion I draw from them, concerning the transition along related impressions and ideas, especially as 'tis a principle, in itself, so easy and natural. But that we may place this system beyond doubt both with regard to love and hatred, pride and humility, 'twill be proper to make some new experiments upon all these passions, as well as to recal a few of these observations, which I have formerly touch'd upon.

In order to make these experiments, let us suppose I am in company with a person, whom I formerly regarded without any sentiments either of friendship or enmity. Here I have the natural and ultimate object of all these four passions plac'd before me. Myself am the proper object of pride or humility; the other person of love or hatred.

Regard now with attention the nature of these passions, and their situation with respect to each other. 'Tis evident here are four affections, plac'd, as it were, in a square or regular connexion with, and distance from each other. The passions of pride and humility, as well as those of love and hatred, are connected together by the identity of their object, which to the first set of passions is self, to the second some other person. These two lines of communication or connexion form two opposite sides of the square. Again, pride and love are agreeable passions; hatred and humility uneasy. This similitude of sensation betwixt pride and love, and that betwixt humility and hatred form a new connexion, and may be consider'd as the other two sides of the square. Upon the whole, pride is connected with humility, love with hatred, by their objects or ideas: Pride with love, humility with hatred, by their sensations or impressions.

I say then, that nothing can produce any of these passions without bearing it a double relation, *viz.* of ideas to the object of the passion, and of sensation to the passion itself. This we must prove by our experiments.

First Experiment. To proceed with the greater order in these experiments, let us first suppose, that being plac'd in the situation above-mentioned, *viz.* in company with some other person, there is an object presented, that has no relation either of impressions or ideas to any of these passions. Thus suppose we regard together an ordinary stone, or other common object, belonging to neither of us, and causing of itself no emotion, or independent pain and pleasure: 'Tis evident such an object will produce none of these four passions. Let us try it upon each of them successively. Let us apply it to love, to hatred, to humility, to pride; none of them ever arises in the smallest degree imaginable. Let us change the object, as oft as we please; provided still we choose one, that has neither of these two relations. Let us repeat the experiment in all the dispositions, of which the mind is susceptible. No object, in the vast variety of nature, will, in any disposition, produce any passion without these relations.

Second Experiment. Since an object, that wants both these relations can never produce any passion, let us bestow on it only one of these relations; and see what will follow. Thus suppose, I regard a stone or any common object, that belongs either to me or my companion, and by that means acquires a relation of ideas to the object of the passions: 'Tis plain, that to consider the matter *a priori*, no emotion of any kind can reasonably be expected. For besides, that a relation of ideas operates secretly and calmly on the mind, it bestows an equal impulse towards the opposite passions of pride and humility, love and hatred, according as the object belongs to ourselves or others; which opposition of the passions must destroy both, and leave the mind perfectly free from any affection or emotion. This reasoning *a priori* is confirm'd by experience. No trivial or vulgar object, that causes not a pain or pleasure, independent of the passion, will ever, by its property or other relations either to ourselves or others, be able to produce the affections of pride or humility, love or hatred.

Third Experiment. 'Tis evident, therefore, that a relation of ideas is not able alone to give rise to these affections. Let us now remove this relation, and in its stead place a relation of impressions, by presenting an object, which is agreeable or disagreeable, but has no relation either to ourself or companion; and let us observe the consequences. To consider the matter first *a priori*, as in the preceding experiment; we may conclude, that the object will have a small, but an uncertain connexion with these passions. For besides, that this relation is not a cold and imperceptible one, it has not the inconvenience of the relation of ideas, nor directs us with equal force to two contrary passions, which by their opposition destroy each other. But if we consider, on the other hand, that this transition from the sensation to the affection is not forwarded by any principle, that produces a transition of ideas; but, on the contrary, that tho' the one impression be easily transfus'd into the other, yet the change of objects is suppos'd contrary to all the principles, that cause a transition of that kind; we may from thence infer, that nothing will ever be a steady or durable cause of any passion, that is connected with the passion merely by a relation of impressions. What our reason wou'd conclude from analogy, after balancing these arguments, wou'd be, that an object, which produces pleasure or uneasiness, but has no manner of connexion either with ourselves or others, may give such a turn to the disposition, as that may naturally fall into pride or love, humility or hatred, and search for other objects, upon which by a double relation, it can found these affections; but that an object, which has only one of these relations, tho' the most advantageous one, can never give rise to any constant and establish'd passion.

Most fortunately all this reasoning is found to be exactly conformable to experience, and the phaenomena of the passions. Suppose I were travelling with a companion thro' a country, to which we are both utter strangers; 'tis evident, that if the prospects be beautiful, the roads agreeable, and the inns commodious, this may put me into good humour both with myself and fellow-traveller. But as we suppose, that this country has no relation either to myself or friend, it can never be the immediate cause of pride or love; and therefore if I found not the passion on some other object, that bears either of us a closer relation, my emotions are rather to be consider'd as the overflowings of an elevate or humane disposition, than as an establish'd passion. The case is the same where the object produces uneasiness.

Fourth Experiment. Having found, that neither an object without any relation of ideas or impressions, nor an object, that has only one relation, can ever cause pride or humility, love or hatred; reason alone may convince us, without any farther experiment, that whatever has a double relation must necessarily excite these passions; since 'tis evident they must have some cause. But to leave as little room for doubt as possible, let us renew our experiments, and see whether the event in this case answers our expectation. I choose an object, such as virtue, that causes a separate satisfaction: On this object I bestow a relation to self; and find, that from this disposition of affairs, there immediately arises a passion. But what passion? That very one of pride, to which this object bears a double relation. Its idea is related to that of self, the object of the passion: The sensation it causes resembles the sensation of the passion. That I may be sure I am not mistaken in this experiment, I remove first one relation; then another; and find, that each removal destroys the passion, and leaves the object perfectly indifferent. But I am not content with this. I make a still farther trial; and instead of removing the relation, I only change it for one of a different kind. I suppose the virtue to belong to my companion, not to myself; and observe what follows from this alteration. I immediately perceive the affections wheel to about, and leaving pride, where there is only one relation, *viz.* of impressions, fall to the side of love, where they are attracted by a double relation of impressions and ideas. By repeating the same experiment, in changing anew the relation of ideas, I bring the affections back to pride; and by a new repetition I again place them at love or kindness. Being fully convinc'd of the influence of this relation, I try the effects of the other; and by changing virtue for vice, convert the pleasant impression, which arises from the former, into the disagreeable one, which proceeds from the latter. The effect still answers expectation. Vice, when plac'd on another, excites, by means of its double relations, the passion of hatred, instead of love, which for the same reason arises from virtue. To continue the experiment, I change anew the relation of ideas, and suppose the vice to belong to myself. What follows? What is usual. A subsequent change of the passion from hatred to humility. This humility I convert into pride by a new change of the impression; and find after all that I have compleated the round, and have by these changes brought back the passion to that very situation, in which I first found it.

But to make the matter still more certain, I alter the object; and instead of vice and virtue, make the trial upon beauty and deformity, riches and poverty, power and servitude. Each of these objects runs the circle of the passions in the same manner, by a change of their relations: And in whatever order we proceed, whether thro' pride, love, hatred, humility, or thro' humility, hatred, love, pride, the experiment is not in the least diversify'd. Esteem and contempt, indeed, arise on some occasions instead of love and hatred; but these are at the bottom the same passions, only diversify'd by some causes, which we shall explain afterwards.

Fifth Experiment. To give greater authority to these experiments, let us change the situation of affairs as much as possible, and place the passions and objects in all the different positions, of which they are susceptible. Let us suppose, beside the relations above-mention'd, that the person, along with whom I make all these experiments, is closely connected with me either by blood or friendship. He is, we shall suppose, my son or brother, or is united to me by a long and familiar acquaintance. Let us next suppose, that the cause of the passion acquires a double relation of impressions and ideas to this person; and let us see what the effects are of all these complicated attractions and relations.

Before we consider what they are in fact, let us determine what they ought to be, conformable to my hypothesis. 'Tis plain, that, according as the impression is either pleasant or uneasy, the passion of love or hatred must arise towards the person, who is thus connected to the cause of the impression by these double relations, which I have all along requir'd. The virtue of a brother must make me love him; as his vice or infamy must excite the contrary passion. But to judge only from the situation of affairs, I shou'd not expect, that the affections wou'd rest there, and never transfuse themselves into any other impression. As there is here a person, who by means of a double relation is the object of my passion, the very same reasoning leads me to think the passion will be carry'd farther. The person has a relation of ideas to myself, according to the supposition; the passion, of which he is the object, by being either agreeable or uneasy, has a relation of impressions to pride or humility. 'Tis evident, then, that one of these passions must arise from the love or hatred.

This is the reasoning I form in conformity to my hypothesis; and am pleas'd to find upon trial that every thing answers exactly to my expectation. The virtue or vice of a son or brother not only excites love or hatred, but by a new transition, from similar causes, gives rise to pride or humility. Nothing causes greater vanity than any shining quality in our relations; as nothing mortifies us more than their vice or infamy. This exact conformity of experience to our reasoning is a convincing proof of the solidity of that hypothesis, upon which we reason.

Sixth Experiment. This evidence will be still augmented, if we reverse the experiment, and preserving still the same relations, begin only with a different passion. Suppose, that instead of the virtue or vice of a son or brother, which causes first love or hatred, and afterwards pride or humility, we place these good or bad qualities on ourselves, without any immediate connexion with the person, who is related to us: Experience shews us, that by this change of situation the whole chain is broke, and that the mind is not convey'd from one passion to another, as in the preceding instance. We never love or hate a son or brother for the virtue or vice we discern in ourselves; tho' 'tis evident the same qualities in him give us a very sensible pride or humility. The transition from pride or humility to love or hatred is not so natural as from love or hatred to pride or humility. This may at first sight be esteem'd contrary to my hypothesis; since the relations of impressions and ideas are in both cases precisely the same. Pride and humility are impressions related to love and hatred. Myself am related to the person. It shou'd, therefore, be expected, that like causes must produce like effects, and a perfect transition arise from the double relation, as in all other cases. This difficulty we may easily solve by the following reflections.

'Tis evident, that as we are at all times intimately conscious of ourselves, our sentiments and passions, their ideas must strike upon us with greater vivacity than the ideas of the sentiments and passions of any other person. But every thing, that strikes upon us with vivacity, and appears in a full and strong light, forces itself, in a manner, into our consideration, and becomes present to the mind on the smallest hint and most trivial relation. For the same reason, when it is once present, it engages the attention, and keeps it from wandering to other objects, however strong may be their relation to our first object. The imagination passes easily from obscure to lively ideas, but with difficulty from lively to obscure. In the one case the relation is aided by another principle: In the other case, 'tis oppos'd by it.

Now I have observ'd, that those two faculties of the mind, the imagination and passions, assist each other in their operation, when their propensities are similar, and when they act upon the same object. The mind has always a propensity to pass from a passion to any other related to it; and this propensity is forwarded when the object of the one passion is related to that of the other. The two impulses concur with each other, and render the whole transition more smooth and easy. But if it shou'd happen, that while the relation of ideas, strictly speaking, continues the same, its influence, in causing a transition of the imagination, shou'd no longer take place, 'tis evident its influence on the passions must also cease, as being dependent entirely on that transition. This is the reason why pride or humility is not transfus'd into love or hatred with the same ease, that the latter passions are chang'd into the former. If a person be my brother I am his likewise: but tho' the relations be reciprocal they have very different effects on the imagination. The passage is smooth and open from the consideration of any person related to us to that of ourself, of whom we are every moment conscious. But when the affections are once directed to ourself, the fancy passes not with the same facility from that object to any other person, how closely so ever connected with us. This easy or difficult transition of the imagination operates upon the passions, and facilitates or retards their transition, which is a clear proof, that these two faculties of the passions and imagination are connected together, and that the relations of ideas have an influence upon the affections. Besides innumerable experiments that prove this, we here find, that even when the relation remains; if by any particular circumstance its usual effect upon the fancy in producing an association or transition of ideas, is prevented; its usual effect upon the passions, in conveying us from one to another, is in like manner prevented.

Some may, perhaps, find a contradiction betwixt this phaenomenon and that of sympathy, where the mind passes easily from the idea of ourselves to that of any other object related to us. But this difficulty will vanish, if we consider that in sympathy our own person is not the object of any passion, nor is there any thing, that fixes our attention on ourselves; as in the present case, where we are suppos'd to be actuated with pride or humility. Ourself, independent of the perception of every other object, is in reality nothing: For which reason we must turn our view to external objects; and 'tis natural for us to consider with most attention such as lie contiguous to us, or resemble us. But when self is the object of a passion, 'tis not natural to quit the consideration of it, till the passion be exhausted; in which case the double relations of impressions and ideas can no longer operate.

Seventh Experiment. To put this whole reasoning to a farther trial, let us make a new experiment; and as we have already seen the effects of related passions and ideas, let us here suppose an identity of passions along with a relation of ideas; and let us consider the effects of this new situation. 'Tis evident a transition of the passions from the one object to the other is here in all reason to be expected; since the relation of ideas is suppos'd still to continue, and identity of impressions must produce a stronger connexion, than the most perfect resemblance, that can be imagin'd. If a double relation, therefore, of impressions and ideas is able to produce a transition from one to the other, much more an identity of impressions with a relation of ideas. Accordingly we find, that when we either love or hate any person, the passions seldom continue within their first bounds; but extend themselves towards all the contiguous objects, and comprehend the friends and relations of him we love or hate. Nothing is more natural than to bear a kindness to one brother on account of our friendship for another, without any farther examination of his character. A quarrel with one person gives us a hatred for the whole family, tho' entirely innocent of that, which displeases us. Instances of this kind are every where to be met with.

There is only one difficulty in this experiment, which it will be necessary to account for, before we proceed any farther. 'Tis evident, that tho' all passions pass easily from one object to another related to it, yet this transition is made with greater facility, where the more considerable object is first presented, and the lesser follows it, than where this order is revers'd, and the lesser takes the precedence. Thus 'tis more natural for us to love the son upon account of the father, than the father upon account of the son; the servant for the master, than the master for the servant; the subject for the prince, than the prince for the subject. In like manner we more readily contract a hatred against a whole family, where our first quarrel is with the head of it, than where we are displeas'd with a son, or servant, or some inferior member. In short, our passions, like other objects, descend with greater facility than they ascend.

That we may comprehend, wherein consists the difficulty of explaining this phaenomenon, we must consider, that the very same reason, which determines the imagination to pass from remote to contiguous objects, with more facility than from contiguous to remote, causes it likewise to change with more ease, the less for the greater, than the greater for the less. Whatever has the greatest influence is most taken notice of; and whatever is most taken notice of, presents itself most readily to the imagination. We are more apt to over-look in any subject, what is trivial, than what appears of considerable moment; but especially if the latter takes the precedence, and first engages our attention. Thus if any accident makes us consider the *Satellites* of *Jupiter*, our fancy is naturally determin'd to form the idea of that planet; but if we first reflect on the principal planet, 'tis more natural for us to overlook its attendants. The mention of the provinces of any empire conveys our thought to the seat of the empire; but the fancy returns not with the same facility to the consideration of the provinces. The idea of the servant makes us think of the master; that of the subject carries our view to the prince. But the same relation has not an equal influence in conveying us back again. And on this is founded that reproach of *Cornelia* to her sons, that they ought to be asham'd she shou'd be more known by the title of the daughter of *Scipio* than by that of the mother of the *Gracchi*. This was, in other words, exhorting them to render themselves as illustrious and famous as their grandfather, otherwise the imagination of the people, passing from her who was intermediate, and plac'd in an equal relation to both, wou'd always leave them, and denominate her by what was more considerable and of greater moment. On the same principle is founded that common custom of making wives bear the name of their husbands, rather than husbands that of their wives; as also the ceremony of giving the precedency to those, whom we honour and respect. We might find many other instances to confirm this principle, were it not already sufficiently evident.

Now since the fancy finds the same facility in passing from the lesser to the greater, as from remote to contiguous, why does not this easy transition of ideas assist the transition of passions in the former case, as well as in the latter? The virtues of a friend or brother produce first love, and then pride; because in that case the imagination passes from remote to contiguous, according to its propensity. Our own virtues produce not first pride, and then love to a friend or brother; because the passage in that case wou'd be from contiguous to remote, contrary to its propensity. But the love or hatred of an inferior causes not readily any passion to the superior, tho' that be the natural propensity of the imagination: While the love or hatred of a superior, causes a passion to the inferior, contrary to its propensity. In short, the same facility of transition operates not in the same manner upon superior and inferior as upon contiguous and remote. These two phaenomena appear contradictory, and require some attention to be reconcil'd.

As the transition of ideas is here made contrary to the natural propensity of the imagination, that faculty must be overpower'd by some stronger principle of another kind; and as there is nothing ever present to the mind but impressions and ideas, this principle must necessarily lie in the impressions. Now it has been observ'd, that impressions or passions are connected only by their resemblance, and that where any two passions place the mind in the same or in similar dispositions, it very naturally passes from the one to the other: As on the contrary, a repugnance in the dispositions produces a difficulty in the transition of the passions. But 'tis observable, that this repugnance may arise from a difference of degree as well as of kind; nor do we experience a greater difficulty in passing suddenly from a small degree of love to a small degree of hatred, than from a small to a great degree of either of these affections. A man, when calm or only moderately agitated, is so different, in every respect, from himself, when disturbed with a violent passion, that no two persons can be more unlike; nor is it easy to pass from the one extreme to the other, without a considerable interval betwixt them.

The difficulty is not less, if it be not rather greater, in passing from the strong passion to the weak, than in passing from the weak to the strong, provided the one passion upon its appearance destroys the other, and they do not both of them exist at once. But the case is entirely alter'd, when the passions unite together, and actuate the mind at the same time. A weak passion, when added to a strong, makes not so considerable a change in the disposition, as a strong when added to a weak; for which reason there is a closer connexion betwixt the great degree and the small, than betwixt the small degree and the great.

The degree of any passion depends upon the nature of its object; and an affection directed to a person, who is considerable in our eyes, fills and possesses the mind much more than one, which has for its object a person we esteem of less consequence. Here then the contradiction betwixt the propensities of the imagination and passion displays itself. When we turn our thought to a great and a small object, the imagination finds more facility in passing from the small to the great, than from the great to the small; but the affections find a greater difficulty: And as the affections are a more powerful principle than the imagination, no wonder they prevail over it, and draw the mind to their side. In spite of the difficulty of passing from the idea of great to that of little, a passion directed to the former, produces always a similar passion towards the latter; when the great and little are related together. The idea of the servant conveys our thought most readily to the master; but the hatred or love of the master produces with greater facility anger or good-will to the servant. The strongest passion in this case takes the precedence; and the addition of the weaker making no considerable change on the disposition, the passage is by that means render'd more easy and natural betwixt them.

As in the foregoing experiment we found, that a relation of ideas, which, by any particular circumstance, ceases to produce its usual effect of facilitating the transition of ideas, ceases likewise to operate on the passions; so in the present experiment we find the same property of the impressions. Two different degrees of the same passion are surely related together; but if the smaller be first present, it has little or no tendency to introduce the greater; and that because the addition of the great to the little, produces a more sensible alteration on the temper, than the addition of the little to the great. These phaenomena, when duly weigh'd, will be found convincing proofs of this hypothesis.

And these proofs will be confirm'd, if we consider the manner in which the mind here reconciles the contradiction, I have observ'd betwixt the passions and the imagination. The fancy passes with more facility from the less to the greater, than from the greater to the less: But on the contrary a violent passion produces more easily a feeble, than that does a violent. In this opposition the passion in the end prevails over the imagination; but 'tis commonly by complying with it, and by seeking another quality, which may counter-ballance that principle, from whence the opposition arises. When we love the father or master of a family, we little think of his children or servants. But when these are present with us, or when it lies any ways in our power to serve them, the nearness and contiguity in this case encreases their magnitude, or at least removes that opposition, which the fancy makes to the transition of the affections. If the imagination finds a difficulty in passing from greater to less, it finds an equal facility in passing from remote to contiguous, which brings the matter to an equality, and leaves the way open from the one passion to the other.

Eighth Experiment. I have observ'd that the transition from love or hatred to pride or humility, is more easy than from pride or humility to love or hatred; and that the difficulty, which the imagination finds in passing from contiguous to remote, is the cause why we scarce have any instance of the latter transition of the affections. I must, however, make one exception, *viz.* when the very cause of the pride and humility is plac'd in some other person. For in that case the imagination is necessitated to consider the person, nor can it possibly confine its view to ourselves. Thus nothing more readily produces kindness and affection to any person, than his approbation of our conduct and character: As on the other hand, nothing inspires us with a stronger hatred, than his blame or contempt. Here 'tis evident, that the original passion is pride or humility, whose object is self; and that this passion is transfus'd into love or hatred, whose object is some other person, notwithstanding the rule I have already establish'd, *that the imagination passes with difficulty from contiguous to remote.* But the transition in this case is not made merely on account of the relation betwixt ourselves and the person; but because that very person is the real cause of our first passion, and of consequence is intimately connected with it. 'Tis his approbation that produces pride; and disapprobation, humility. No wonder, then, the imagination returns back again attended with the related passions of love and hatred. This is not a contradiction, but an exception to the rule; and an exception that arises from the same reason with the rule itself.

Such an exception as this is, therefore, rather a confirmation of the rule. And indeed, if we consider all the eight experiments I have explain'd, we shall find that the same principle appears in all of them, and that 'tis by means of a transition arising from a double relation of impressions and ideas, pride and humility, love and hatred are produc'd. An object without * a relation, or † with but one, never produces either of these passions; and 'tis ‡ found that the passion always varies in conformity to the relation. Nay we may observe, that where the relation, by any particular circumstance, has not its usual effect of producing a transition either of ** ideas or of impressions, it ceases to operate upon the passions, and gives rise neither to pride nor love, humility nor hatred. This rule we find still to hold good ††, even under the appearance of its contrary; and as relation is frequently experienc'd to have no effect; which upon examination is found to proceed from some particular circumstance, that prevents the transition; so even in instances, where that circumstance, tho' present, prevents not the transition, 'tis found to arise from some other circumstance, which counter-balances it. Thus not only the varia-

* First Experiment.

† Second and Third Experiments. ‡ Fourth Experiment.

** Sixth Experiment. †† Seventh and Eighth Experiments.

tions resolve themselves into the general principle, but even the variations of these variations.

SECT. III
Difficulties solv'd

AFTER so many and such undeniable proofs drawn from daily experience and observation, it may seem superfluous to enter into a particular examination of all the causes of love and hatred. I shall, therefore, employ the sequel of this part, *First*, In removing some difficulties, concerning particular causes of these passions. *Secondly*, In examining the compound affections, which arise from the mixture of love and hatred with other emotions.

Nothing is more evident, than that any person acquires our kindness, or is expos'd to our ill-will, in proportion to the pleasure or uneasiness we receive from him, and that the passions keep pace exactly with the sensations in all their changes and variations. Whoever can find the means either by his services, his beauty, or his flattery, to render himself useful or agreeable to us, is sure of our affections: As on the other hand, whoever harms or displeases us never fails to excite our anger or hatred. When our own nation is at war with any other, we detest them under the character of cruel, perfidious, unjust and violent: But always esteem ourselves and allies equitable, moderate, and merciful. If the general of our enemies be successful, 'tis with difficulty we allow him the figure and character of a man. He is a sorcerer: He has a communication with daemons; as is reported of *Oliver Cromwell*, and the *Duke of Luxembourg:* He is bloody-minded, and takes a pleasure in death and destruction. But if the success be on our side, our commander has all the opposite good qualities, and is a pattern of virtue, as well as of courage and conduct. His treachery we call policy: His cruelty is an evil inseparable from war. In short, every one of his faults we either endeavour to extenuate, or dignify it with the name of that virtue, which approaches it. 'Tis evident the same method of thinking runs thro' common life.

There are some, who add another condition, and require not only that the pain and pleasure arise from the person, but likewise that it arise knowingly, and with a particular design and intention. A man, who wounds and harms us by accident, becomes not our enemy upon that account, nor do we think ourselves bound by any ties of gratitude to one, who does us any service after the same manner. By the intention we judge of the actions, and according as that is good or bad, they become causes of love or hatred.

But here we must make a distinction. If that quality in another, which pleases or displeases, be constant and inherent in his person and character, it will cause love or hatred independent of the intention: But otherwise a knowledge and design is requisite, in order to give rise to these passions. One that is disagreeable by his deformity or folly is the object of our aversion, tho' nothing be more certain, than that he has not the least intention of displeasing us by these qualities. But if the uneasiness proceed not from a quality, but an action, which is produc'd and annihilated in a moment, 'tis necessary, in order to produce some relation, and connect this action sufficiently with the person, that it be deriv'd from a particular fore-thought and design. 'Tis not enough, that the action arise from the person, and have him for its immediate cause and author. This relation alone is too feeble and inconstant to be a foundation for these passions. It reaches not the sensible and thinking part, and neither proceeds from any thing *durable* in him, nor leaves any thing behind it; but passes in a moment, and is as if it had never been. On the other hand, an intention shews certain qualities, which remaining after the action is perform'd, connect it with the person, and facilitate the transition of ideas from one to the other. We can never think of him without reflecting on these qualities; unless repentance and a change of life have produc'd an alteration in that respect: In which case the passion is likewise alter'd. This therefore is one reason, why an intention is requisite to excite either love or hatred.

But we must farther consider, that an intention, besides its strengthening the relation of ideas, is often necessary to produce a relation of impressions, and give rise to pleasure and uneasiness. For 'tis observable, that the principal part of an injury is the contempt and hatred, which it shews in the person, that injures us; and without that, the mere harm gives us a less sensible uneasiness. In like manner, a good office is agreeable, chiefly because it flatters our vanity, and is a proof of the kindness and esteem of the person, who performs it. The removal of the intention, removes the mortification in the one case, and vanity in the other; and must of course cause a remarkable diminution in the passions of love and hatred.

I grant, that these effects of the removal of design, in diminishing the relations of impressions and ideas, are not entire, nor able to remove every degree of these relations. But then I ask, if the removal of design be able entirely to remove the passion of love and hatred? Experience, I am sure, informs us of the contrary, nor is there any thing more certain, than that men often fall into a violent anger for injuries, which they themselves must own to be entirely involuntary and accidental. This emotion, indeed, cannot be of long continuance; but still is sufficient to shew, that there is a natural connexion betwixt uneasiness and anger, and that the relation of impressions will operate upon a very small relation of ideas. But when the violence of the impression is once a little abated, the defect of the relation begins to be better felt; and as the character of a person is no wise interested in such injuries as are casual and involuntary, it seldom happens that on their account, we entertain a lasting enmity.

To illustrate this doctrine by a parallel instance, we may observe, that not only the uneasiness, which proceeds from another by accident, has but little force to excite our passion, but also that which arises from an acknowledg'd necessity and duty. One that has a real design of harming us, proceeding not from hatred and ill-will, but from justice and equity, draws not upon him our anger, if we be in any degree reasonable; notwithstanding he is both the cause, and the knowing cause of our sufferings. Let us examine a little this phaenomenon.

'Tis evident in the first place, that this circumstance is not decisive; and tho' it may be able to diminish the passions, 'tis seldom it can entirely remove them. How few criminals are there, who have no ill-will to the person, that accuses them, or to the judge, that condemns them, even tho' they be conscious of their own deserts? In like manner our antagonist in a law-suit, and our competitor for any office, are commonly regarded as our enemies; tho' we must acknowledge, if we wou'd but reflect a moment, that their motive is entirely as justifiable as our own.

Besides we may consider, that when we receive harm from any person, we are apt to imagine him criminal, and 'tis with extreme difficulty we allow of his justice and innocence. This is a clear proof, that, independent of the opinion of iniquity, any harm or uneasiness has a natural tendency to excite our hatred, and that afterwards we seek for reasons upon which we may justify and establish the passion. Here the idea of injury produces not the passion, but arises from it.

Nor is it any wonder that passion shou'd produce the opinion of injury; since otherwise it must suffer a considerable diminution, which all the passions avoid as much as possible. The removal of injury may remove the anger, without proving that the anger arises only from the injury. The harm and the justice are two contrary objects, of which the one has a tendency to produce hatred, and the other love; and 'tis according to their different degrees, and our particular turn of thinking, that either of the objects prevails, and excites its proper passion.

SECT. IV

Of the love of relations

HAVING given a reason, why several actions, that cause a real pleasure or uneasiness, excite not any degree, or but a small one, of the passion of love or hatred towards the actors; 'twill be necessary to shew, wherein consists the pleasure or uneasiness of many objects, which we find by experience to produce these passions.

According to the preceding system there is always requir'd a double relation of impressions and ideas betwixt the cause and effect, in order to produce either love or hatred. But tho' this be universally true, 'tis remarkable that the passion of love may be excited by only one *relation* of a different kind, *viz.* betwixt ourselves and the object; or more properly speaking, that this relation is always attended with both the others. Whoever is united to us by any connexion is always sure of a share of our love, proportion'd to the connexion, without enquiring into his other qualities. Thus the relation of blood produces the strongest tie the mind is capable of in the love of parents to their children, and a lesser degree of the same affection, as the relation lessens. Nor has consanguinity alone this effect, but any other relation without exception. We love our country-men, our neighbours, those of the same trade, profession, and even name with ourselves. Every one of these relations is esteem'd some tie, and gives a title to a share of our affection.

There is another phaenomenon, which is parallel to this, *viz.* that *acquaintance*, without any kind of relation, gives rise to love and kindness. When we have contracted a habitude and intimacy with any person; tho' in frequenting his company we have not been able to discover any very valuable quality, of which he is possess'd; yet we cannot forebear preferring him to strangers, of whose superior merit we are fully convinc'd. These two phaenomena of the effects of relation and acquaintance will give mutual light to each other, and may be both explain'd from the same principle.

Those, who take a pleasure in declaiming against human nature, have observ'd, that man is altogether insufficient to support himself; and that when you loosen all the holds, which he has of external objects, he immediately drops down into the deepest melancholy and despair. From this, say they, proceeds that continual search after amusement in gaming, in hunting, in business; by which we endeavour to forget ourselves, and excite our spirits from the languid state, into which they fall, when not sustain'd by some brisk and lively emotion. To this method of thinking I so far agree, that I own the mind to be insufficient, of itself, to its own entertainment, and that it naturally seeks after foreign objects, which may produce a lively sensation, and agitate the spirits. On the appearance of such an object it awakes, as it were, from a dream: The blood flows with a new tide: The heart is elevated: And the whole man acquires a vigour, which he cannot command in his solitary and calm moments. Hence company is naturally so rejoicing, as presenting the liveliest of all objects, *viz.* a rational and thinking Being like ourselves, who communicates to us all the actions of his mind; makes us privy to his inmost sentiments and affections; and lets us see, in the very instant of their production, all the emotions, which are caus'd by any object. Every lively idea is agreeable, but especially that of a passion, because such an idea becomes a kind of passion, and gives a more sensible agitation to the mind, than any other image or conception.

This being once admitted, all the rest is easy. For as the company of strangers is agreeable to us for *a short time*, by inlivening our thought; so the company of our relations and acquaintance must be peculiarly agreeable, because it has this effect in a greater degree, and is of more *durable* influence. Whatever is related to us is conceiv'd in a lively manner by the easy transition from ourselves to the related object. Custom also, or acquaintance facilitates the entrance, and strengthens the conception of any object. The first case is parallel to our reasonings from cause and effect; the second to education. And as reasoning and education concur only in producing a lively and strong idea of any object; so is this the only particular, which is common to relation and acquaintance. This must, therefore, be the influencing quality, by which they produce all their common effects; and love or kindness being one of these effects, it must be from the force and liveliness of conception, that the passion is deriv'd. Such a conception is peculiarly agreeable, and makes us have an affectionate regard for every thing, that produces it, when the proper object of kindness and good-will.

'Tis obvious, that people associate together according to their particular tempers and dispositions, and that men of gay tempers naturally love the gay; as the serious bear an affection to the serious. This not only happens, where they remark this resemblance betwixt themselves and others, but also by the natural course of the disposition, and by a certain sympathy, which always arises betwixt similar characters. Where they remark the resemblance, it operates after the manner of a relation, by producing a connexion of ideas. Where they do not remark it, it operates by some other principle; and if this latter principle be similar to the former, it must be receiv'd as a confirmation of the foregoing reasoning.

The idea of ourselves is always intimately present to us, and conveys a sensible degree of vivacity to the idea of any other object, to which we are related. This lively idea changes by degrees into a real impression; these two kinds of perception being in a great measure the same, and differing only in their degrees of force and vivacity. But this change must be produc'd with the greater ease, that our natural temper gives us a propensity to the same impression, which we observe in others, and makes it arise upon any slight occasion. In that case resemblance converts the idea into an impression, not only by means of the relation, and by transfusing the original vivacity into the related idea; but also by presenting such materials as take fire from the least spark. And as in both cases a love or affection arises from the resemblance, we may learn that a sympathy with others is agreeable only by giving an emotion to the spirits, since an easy sympathy and correspondent emotions are alone common to *relation*, *acquaintance*, and *resemblance*.

The great propensity men have to pride may be consider'd as another similar phaenomenon. It often happens, that after we have liv'd a considerable time in any city; however at first it might be disagreeable to us; yet as we become familiar with the objects, and contact an acquaintance, tho' merely with the streets and buildings, the aversion diminishes by degrees, and at last changes into the opposite passion. The mind finds a satisfaction and ease in the view of objects, to which it is accustom'd, and naturally prefers them to others, which, tho', perhaps, in themselves more valuable, are less known to it. By the same quality of the mind we are seduc'd into a good opinion of ourselves, and of all objects, that belong to us. They appear in a stronger light; are more agreeable; and consequently fitter subjects of pride and vanity, than any other.

It may not be amiss, in treating of the affection we bear our acquaintance and relations, to observe some pretty curious phaenomena, which attend it. 'Tis easy to remark in common life, that children esteem their relation to their mother to be weaken'd, in a great measure, by her second marriage, and no longer regard her with the same eye, as if she had continu'd in her state of widow-hood. Nor does this happen only, when they have felt any inconveniences from her second marriage, or when her husband is much her inferior; but even without any of these considerations, and merely because she has become part of another family. This also takes place with regard to the second marriage of a father; but in a much less degree: And 'tis certain the ties of blood are not so much loosen'd in the latter case as by the marriage of a mother. These two phaenomena are remarkable in themselves, but much more so when compared.

In order to produce a perfect relation betwixt two objects,

'tis requisite, not only that the imagination be convey'd from one to the other by resemblance, contiguity or causation, but also that it return back from the second to the first with the same ease and facility. At first sight this may seem a necessary and unavoidable consequence. If one object resemble another, the latter object must necessarily resemble the former. If one object be the cause of another, the second object is effect to its cause. 'Tis the same case with contiguity: And therefore the relation being always reciprocal, it may be thought, that the return of the imagination from the second to the first must also, in every case, be equally natural as its passage from the first to the second. But upon farther examination we shall easily discover our mistake. For supposing the second object, beside its reciprocal relation to the first, to have also a strong relation to a third object; in that case the thought, passing from the first object to the second, returns not back with the same facility, tho' the relation continues the same; but is readily carry'd on to the third object, by means of the new relation, which presents itself, and gives a new impulse to the imagination. This new relation, therefore, weakens the tie betwixt the first and second objects. The fancy is by its very nature wavering and inconstant; and considers always two objects as more strongly related together, where it finds the passage equally easy both in going and returning, than where the transition is easy only in one of these motions. The double motion is a kind of a double tie, and binds the objects together in the closest and most intimate manner.

The second marriage of a mother breaks not the relation of child and parent; and that relation suffices to convey my imagination from myself to her with the greatest ease and facility. But after the imagination is arriv'd at this point of view, it finds its object to be surrounded with so many other relations, which challenge its regard, that it knows not which to prefer, and is at a loss what new object to pitch upon. The ties of interest and duty bind her to another family, and prevent that return of the fancy from her to myself, which is necessary to support the union. The thought has no longer the vibration, requisite to set it perfectly at ease, and indulge its inclination to change. It goes with facility, but returns with difficulty; and by that interruption finds the relation much weaken'd from what it wou'd be were the passage open and easy on both sides.

Now to give a reason, why this effect follows not in the same degree upon the second marriage of a father: we may reflect on what has been prov'd already, that tho' the imagination goes easily from the view of a lesser object to that of a greater, yet it returns not with the same facility from the greater to the less. When my imagination goes from myself to my father, it passes not so readily from him to his second wife, nor considers him as entering into a different family, but as continuing the head of that family, of which I am myself a part. His superiority prevents the easy transition of the thought from him to his spouse, but keeps the passage still open for a return to myself along the same relation of child and parent. He is not sunk in the new relation he acquires; so that the double motion or vibration of thought is still easy and natural. By this indulgence of the fancy in its inconstancy, the tie of child and parent still preserves its full force and influence.

A mother thinks not her tie to a son weaken'd, because 'tis shar'd with her husband: Nor a son his with a parent, because 'tis shar'd with a brother. The third object is here related to the first, as well as to the second; so that the imagination goes and comes along all of them with the greatest facility.

SECT. V

Of our esteem for the rich and powerful

NOTHING has a greater tendency to give us an esteem for any person, than his power and riches; or a contempt, than his poverty and meanness: And as esteem and contempt are to be consider'd as species of love and hatred, 'twill be proper in this place to explain these phaenomena.

Here it happens most fortunately, that the greatest difficulty is not to discover a principle capable of producing such an effect, but to choose the chief and predominant among several, that present themselves. The *satisfaction* we take in the riches of others, and the *esteem* we have for the possessors may be ascrib'd to three different causes. *First*, To the objects they possess; such as houses, gardens, equipages; which, being agreeable in themselves, necessarily produce a sentiment of pleasure in every one, that either considers or surveys them. *Secondly*, To the expectation of advantage from the rich and powerful by our sharing their possessions. *Thirdly*, To sympathy, which makes us partake of the satisfaction of every one, that approaches us. All these principles may concur in producing the present phaenomenon. The question is, to which of them we ought principally to ascribe it.

'Tis certain, that the first principle, *viz*. the reflection on agreeable objects, has a greater influence, than what, at first sight, we may be apt to imagine. We seldom reflect on what is beautiful or ugly, agreeable or disagreeable, without an emotion of pleasure or uneasiness; and tho' these sensations appear not much in our common indolent way of thinking, 'tis easy, either in reading or conversation, to discover them. Men of wit always turn the discourse on subjects that are entertaining to the imagination; and poets never present any objects but such as are of the same nature. Mr *Philips* has chosen *Cyder* for the subject of an excellent poem. Beer wou'd not have been so proper, as being neither so agreeable to the taste nor eye. But he wou'd certainly have preferr'd wine to either of them, cou'd his native country have afforded him so agreeable a liquor. We may learn from thence, that every thing, which is agreeable to the senses, is also in some measure agreeable to the fancy, and conveys to the thought an image of that satisfaction, which it gives by its real application to the bodily organs.

But tho' these reasons may induce us to comprehend this delicacy of the imagination among the causes of the respect, which we pay the rich and powerful, there are many other reasons, that may keep us from regarding it as the sole or principal. For as the ideas of pleasure can have an influence only by means of their vivacity, which makes them approach impressions, 'tis most natural those ideas shou'd have that influence, which are favour'd by most circumstances, and have a natural tendency to become strong and lively; such as our ideas of the passions and sensations of any human creature. Every human creature resembles ourselves, and by that means has an advantage above any other object, in operating on the imagination.

Besides, if we consider the nature of that faculty, and the great influence which all relations have upon it, we shall easily be persuaded, that however the ideas of the pleasant wines, music, or gardens, which the rich man enjoys, may become lively and agreeable, the fancy will not confine itself to them, but will carry its view to the related objects; and in particular, to the person, who possesses them. And this is the more natural, that the pleasant idea or image produces here a passion towards the person, by means of his relation to the object; so that 'tis unavoidable but he must enter into the original conception, since he makes the object of the derivative passion. But if he enters into the original conception, and is consider'd as enjoying these agreeable objects, 'tis *sympathy*, which is properly the cause of the affection; and the *third* principle is more powerful and universal than the *first*.

Add to this, that riches and power alone, even tho' unemploy'd, naturally cause esteem and respect: And consequently these passions arise not from the idea of any beautiful or agreeable objects. 'Tis true; money implies a kind of representation of such objects, by the power it affords of obtaining them; and for that reason may still be esteem'd proper to convey those agreeable images, which may give rise to the passion. But as this prospect is very distant, 'tis more natural for us to take a contiguous object, *viz.* the satisfaction, which this power affords the person, who is possest of it. And of this we shall be farther satisfy'd, if we consider, that riches represent the goods of life, only by means of the will; which employs them; and therefore imply in their very nature an idea of the person, and cannot be consider'd without a kind of sympathy with his sensations and enjoyments.

This we may confirm by a reflection, which to some will, perhaps, appear too subtile and refin'd. I have already observ'd, that power, as distinguish'd from its exercise, has either no meaning at all, or is nothing but a possibility or probability of existence; by which any object approaches to reality, and has a sensible influence on the mind. I have also observ'd, that this approach, by an illusion of the fancy, appears much greater, when we ourselves are possest of the power, than when it is enjoy'd by another; and that in the former case the objects seem to touch upon the very verge of reality, and convey almost an equal satisfaction, as if actually in our possession. Now I assert, that where we esteem a person upon account of his riches, we must enter into this sentiment of the proprietor, and that without such a sympathy the idea of the agreeable objects, which they give him the power to produce, wou'd have but a feeble influence upon us. An avaritious man is respected for his money, tho' he scarce is possest of a *power*; that is, there scarce is a *probability* or even *possibility* of his employing it in the acquisition of the pleasures and conveniences of life. To himself alone this power seems perfect and entire; and therefore we must receive his sentiments by sympathy, before we can have a strong intense idea of these enjoyments, or esteem him upon account of them.

Thus we have found, that the *first* principle, *viz. the agreeable idea of those objects, which riches afford the enjoyment of*; resolves itself in a great measure into the *third*, and becomes a *sympathy* with the person we esteem or love. Let us now examine the *second* principle, *viz. the agreeable expectation of advantage*, and see what force we may justly attribute to it.

'Tis obvious, that tho' riches and authority undoubtedly give their owner a power of doing us service, yet this power is not to be consider'd as on the same footing with that, which they afford him, of pleasing himself, and satisfying his own appetites. Self-love approaches the power and exercise very near each other in the latter case; but in order to produce a similar effect in the former, we must suppose a friendship and good-will to be conjoin'd with the riches. Without that circumstance 'tis difficult to conceive on what we can found our hope of advantage from the riches of others, tho' there is nothing more certain, than that we naturally esteem and respect the rich, even before we discover in them any such favourable disposition towards us.

But I carry this farther, and observe, not only that we respect the rich and powerful, where they shew no inclination to serve us, but also when we lie so much out of the sphere of their activity, that they cannot even be suppos'd to be endow'd with that power. Prisoners of war are always treated with a respect suitable to their condition; and 'tis certain riches go very far towards fixing the condition of any person. If birth and quality enter for a share, this still affords us an argument of the same kind. For what is it we call a man of birth, but one who is descended from a long succession of rich and powerful ancestors, and who acquires our esteem by his relation to persons whom we esteem? His ancestors, therefore, tho' dead, are respected, in some measure, on account of their riches, and consequently without any kind of expectation.

But not to go so far as prisoners of war and the dead to find instances of this disinterested esteem for riches, let us observe with a little attention those phaenomena that occur to us in common life and conversation. A man, who is himself of a competent fortune, upon coming into a company of strangers, naturally treats them with different degrees of respect and deference, as he is inform'd of their different fortunes and conditions; tho' 'tis impossible he can ever propose, and perhaps wou'd not accept of any advantage from them. A traveller is always admitted into company, and meets with civility, in proportion as his train and equipage speak him a man of great or moderate fortune. In short, the different ranks of men are, in a great measure, regulated by riches, and that with regard to superiors as well as inferiors, strangers as well as acquaintance.

There is, indeed, an answer to these arguments, drawn from the influence of *general rules.* It may be pretended, that being accustom'd to expect succour and protection from the rich and powerful, and to esteem them upon that account, we extend the same sentiments to those, who resemble them in their fortune, but from whom we can never hope for any advantage. The general rule still prevails, and by giving a bent to the imagination draws along the passion, in the same manner as if its proper object were real and existent.

But that this principle does not here take place, will easily appear, if we consider, that in order to establish a general rule, and extend it beyond its proper bounds, there is requir'd a certain uniformity in our experience, and a great superiority of those instances, which are conformable to the rule, above the contrary. But here the case is quite otherwise. Of a hundred men of credit and fortune I meet with, there is not, perhaps, one from whom I can expect advantage; so that 'tis impossible any custom can ever prevail in the present case.

Upon the whole, there remains nothing, which can give us an esteem for power and riches, and a contempt for meanness and poverty, except the principle of *sympathy*, by which we enter into the sentiments of the rich and poor, and partake of their pleasure and uneasiness. Riches give satisfaction to their possessor; and this satisfaction is convey'd to the beholder by the imagination, which produces an idea resembling the original impression in force and vivacity. This agreeable idea or impression is connected with love, which is an agreeable passion. It proceeds from a thinking conscious being, which is the very object of love. From this relation of impressions, and identity of ideas, the passion arises, according to my hypothesis.

The best method of reconciling us to this opinion is to take a general survey of the universe, and observe the force of sympathy thro' the whole animal creation, and the easy communication of sentiments from one thinking being to another. In all creatures, that prey not upon others, and are not agitated with violent passions, there appears a remarkable desire of company, which associates them together, without any advantages they can ever propose to reap from their union. This is still more conspicuous in man, as being the creature of the universe, who has the most ardent desire of society, and is fitted for it by the most advantages. We can form no wish, which has not a reference to society. A perfect solitude is, perhaps, the greatest punishment we can suffer. Every pleasure languishes when enjoy'd a-part from company, and every pain becomes more cruel and intolerable. Whatever other passions we may be actuated by; pride, ambition, avarice, curiosity, revenge or lust; the soul or animating principle of them all is sympathy; nor wou'd they have any force, were we to abstract entirely from the thoughts and sentiments of others. Let all the powers and elements of nature conspire to serve and obey one man: Let the sun rise and set at his command: The sea and rivers roll as he pleases, and the earth furnish spontaneously whatever may be useful or agreeable to him: He will still be miserable, till you give him some one person at least, with whom he may share his happiness, and whose esteem and friendship he may enjoy.

This conclusion from a general view of human nature, we may confirm by particular instances, wherein the force of sympathy is very remarkable. Most kinds of beauty are deriv'd from this origin; and tho' our first object be some senseless inanimate piece of matter, 'tis seldom we rest there, and carry not our view to its influence on sensible and raional creatures. A man, who shews us any house or building, takes particular care among other things to point out the convenience of the apartments, the advantages of their situation, and the little room lost in the stairs, antichambers and passages; and indeed 'tis evident, the chief part of the beauty consists in these particulars. The observation of convenience gives pleasure, since convenience is a beauty. But after what manner does it give pleasure? 'Tis certain our own interest is not in the least concern'd; and as this is a beauty of interest, not of form, so to speak, it must delight us merely by communication, and by our sympathizing with the proprietor of the lodging. We enter into his interest by the force of imagination, and feel the same satisfaction, that the objects naturally occasion in him.

This observation extends to tables, chairs, scritoires, chimneys, coaches, sadles, ploughs, and indeed to every work of art; it being an universal rule, that their beauty is chiefly deriv'd from their utility, and from their fitness for that purpose, to which they are destined. But this is an advantage, that concerns only the owner, nor is there any thing but sympathy, which can interest the spectator.

'Tis evident, that nothing renders a field more agreeable than its fertility, and that scarce any advantages of ornament or situation will be able to equal this beauty. 'Tis the same case with particular trees and plants, as with the field on which they grow. I know not but a plain, overgrown with furze and broom, may be, in itself, as beautiful as a hill cover'd with vines or olive-trees; tho' it will never appear so to one, who is acquainted with the value of each. But this is a beauty merely of imagination, and has no foundation in what appears to the senses. Fertility and value have a plain reference to use; and that to riches, joy, and plenty; in which tho' we have no hope of partaking, yet we enter into them by the vivacity of the fancy, and share them, in some measure, with the proprietor.

There is no rule in painting more reasonable than that of ballancing the figures, and placing them with the greatest exactness on their proper centers of gravity. A figure, which is not justly ballanc'd, is disagreeable; and that because it conveys the ideas of its fall, of harm, and of pain: Which ideas are painful, when by sympathy they acquire any degree of force and vivacity.

Add to this, that the principal part of personal beauty is an air of health and vigour, and such a construction of members as promises strength and activity. This idea of beauty cannot be accounted for but by sympathy.

In general we may remark, that the minds of men are mirrors to one another, not only because they reflect each others emotions, but also because those rays of passions, sentiments and opinions may be often reverberated, and may decay away by insensible degrees. Thus the pleasure, which a rich man receives from his possessions, being thrown upon the beholder, causes a pleasure and esteem; which sentiments again, being perceiv'd and sympathiz'd with, encrease the pleasure of the possessor; and being once more reflected, become a new foundation for pleasure and esteem in the beholder. There is certainly an original satisfaction in riches deriv'd from that power, which they bestow, of enjoying all the pleasures of life; and as this is their very nature and essence, it must be the first source of all the passions, which arise from them. One of the most considerable of these passions is that of love or esteem in others, which therefore proceeds from a sympathy with the pleasure of the possessor. But the possessor has also a secondary satisfaction in riches arising from the love and esteem he acquires by them, and this satisfaction is nothing but a second reflexion of that original pleasure, which proceeded from himself. This secondary satisfaction or vanity becomes one of the principal recommendations of riches, and is the chief reason, why we either desire them for ourselves, or esteem them in others. Here then is a third rebound of the original pleasure; after which 'tis difficult to distinguish the images and reflexions, by reason of their faintness and confusion.

SECT. VI

Of benevolence and anger

IDEAS may be compar'd to the extension and solidity of matter, and impressions, especially reflective ones, to colours, tastes, smells and other sensible qualities. Ideas never admit of a total union, but are endow'd with a kind of impenetrability, by which they exclude each other, and are capable of forming a compound by their conjunction, not by their mixture. On the other hand, impressions and passions are susceptible of an entire union; and like colours, may be blended so perfectly together, that each of them may lose itself, and contribute only to vary that uniform impression, which arises from the whole. Some of the most curious phaenomena of the human mind are deriv'd from this property of the passions.

In examining those ingredients, which are capable of uniting with love and hatred, I begin to be sensible, in some measure, of a misfortune, that has attended every system of philosophy, with which the world has been yet acquainted. 'Tis commonly found, that in accounting for the operations of nature by any particular hypothesis; among a number of experiments, that quadrate exactly with the principles we wou'd endeavour to establish; there is always some phaenomenon, which is more stubborn, and will not so easily bend to our purpose. We need not be surpriz'd, that this shou'd happen in natural philosophy. The essence and composition of external bodies are so obscure, that we must necessarily, in our reasonings, or rather conjectures concerning them, involve ourselves in contradictions and absurdities. But as the perceptions of the mind are perfectly known, and I have us'd all imaginable caution in forming conclusions concerning them, I have always hop'd to keep clear of those contradictions, which have attended every other system. Accordingly the difficulty, which I have at present in my eye, is no-wise contrary to my system; but only departs a little from that simplicity, which has been hitherto its principal force and beauty.

The passions of love and hatred are always follow'd by, or rather conjoin'd with benevolence and anger. 'Tis this conjunction, which chiefly distinguishes these affections from pride and humility. For pride and humility are pure emotions in the soul, unattended with any desire, and not immediately exciting us to action. But love and hatred are not compleated within themselves, nor rest in that emotion, which they produce, but carry the mind to something farther. Love is always follow'd by a desire of the happiness of the person belov'd, and an aversion to his misery: As hatred produces a desire of the misery and an aversion to the happiness of the person hated. So remarkable a difference betwixt these two sets of passions of pride and humility, love and hatred, which in so many other particulars correspond to each other, merits our attention.

The conjunction of this desire and aversion with love and hatred may be accounted for by two different hypotheses. The first is, that love and hatred have not only a *cause*, which excites them, *viz.* pleasure and pain; and an *object*, to which they are directed, *viz.* a person or thinking being; but likewise an *end*, which they endeavour to attain, *viz.* the happiness or misery of the person belov'd or hated; all which views, mixing together, make only one passion. According to this system, love is nothing but the desire of happiness to another person, and hatred that of misery. The desire and aversion constitute the very nature of love and hatred. They are not only inseparable but the same.

But this is evidently contrary to experience. For tho' 'tis certain we never love any person without desiring his happiness, nor hate any without wishing his misery, yet these desires arise only upon the ideas of the happiness or misery of our friend or enemy being presented by the imagination, and are not absolutely essential to love and hatred. They are the most obvious and natural sentiments of these affections, but not the only ones. The passions may express themselves in a hundred ways, and may subsist a considerable time, without our reflecting on the happiness or misery of their objects; which clearly proves, that these desires are not the same with love and hatred, nor make any essential part of them.

We may, therefore, infer, that benevolence and anger are passions different from love and hatred, and only conjoin'd with them, by the original constitution of the mind. As nature has given to the body certain appetites and inclinations, which she encreases, diminishes, or changes according to the situation of the fluids or solids; she has proceeded in the same manner with the mind. According as we are possess'd with love or hatred, the correspondent desire of the happiness or misery of the person, who is the object of these passions, arises in the mind, and varies with each variation of these opposite passions. This order of things, abstractedly consider'd, is not necessary. Love and hatred might have been unattended with any such desires, or their particular connexion might have been entirely revers'd. If nature had so pleas'd, love might have had the same effect as hatred, and hatred as love. I see no contradiction in supposing a desire of producing misery annex'd to love, and of happiness to hatred. If the sensation of the passion and desire be opposite, nature cou'd have alter'd the sensation without altering the tendency of the desire, and by that means made them compatible with each other.

SECT. VII

Of compassion

But tho' the desire of the happiness or misery of others, according to the love or hatred we bear them, be an arbitrary and original instinct implanted in our nature, we find it may be counterfeited on many occasions, and may arise from secondary principles. *Pity* is a concern for, and *malice* a joy in the misery of others, without any friendship or enmity to occasion this concern or joy. We pity even strangers, and such as are perfectly indifferent to us: And if our ill-will to another proceed from any harm or injury, it is not, properly speaking, malice, but revenge. But if we examine these affections of pity and malice we shall find them to be secondary ones, arising from original affections, which are varied by some particular turn of thought and imagination.

'Twill be easy to explain the passion of *pity*, from the precedent reasoning concerning *sympathy*. We have a lively idea of every thing related to us. All human creatures are related to us by resemblance. Their persons, therefore, their interests, their passions, their pains and pleasures must strike upon us in a lively manner, and produce an emotion similar to the original one; since a lively idea is easily converted into an impression. If this be true in general, it must be more so of affliction and sorrow. These have always a stronger and more lasting influence than any pleasure or enjoyment.

A spectator of a tragedy passes thro' a long train of grief, terror, indignation, and other affections, which the poet represents in the persons he introduces. As many tragedies end happily, and no excellent one can be compos'd without some reverses of fortune, the spectator must sympathize with all these changes, and receive the fictitious joy as well as every other passion. Unless, therefore, it be asserted, that every distinct passion is communicated by a distinct original quality, and is not deriv'd from the general principle of sympathy above-explain'd, it must be allow'd, that all of them arise from that principle. To except any one in particular must appear highly unreasonable. As they are all first present in the mind of one person, and afterwards appear in the mind of another; and as the manner of their appearance, first as an idea, then as an impression, is in every case the same, the transition must arise from the same principle. I am at least sure, that this method of reasoning wou'd be consider'd as certain, either in natural philosophy or common life.

Add to this, that pity depends, in a great measure, on the contiguity, and even sight of the object; which is a proof, that 'tis deriv'd from the imagination. Not to mention that women and children are most subject to pity, as being most guided by that faculty. The same infirmity, which makes them faint at the sight of a naked sword, tho' in the hands of their best friend, makes them pity extremely those, whom they find in any grief or affliction. Those philosophers, who derive this passion from I know not what subtile reflections on the instability of fortune, and our being liable to the same miseries we behold, will find this observation contrary to them among a great many others, which it were easy to produce.

There remains only to take notice of a pretty remarkable phaenomenon of this passion; which is, that the communicated passion of sympathy sometimes acquires strength from the weakness of its original, and even arises by a transition from affections, which have no existence. Thus when a person obtains any honourable office, or inherits a great fortune, we are always the more rejoic'd for his prosperity, the less sense he seems to have of it, and the greater equanimity and indifference he shews in its enjoyment. In like manner a man, who is not dejected by misfortunes, is the more lamented on account of his patience; and if that virtue extends so far as utterly to remove all sense of uneasiness, it still farther encreases our compassion. When a person of merit falls into what is vulgarly esteem'd a great misfortune, we form a notion of his condition; and carrying our fancy from the cause to the usual effect, first conceive a lively idea of his sorrow, and then feel an impression of it, entirely over-looking that greatness of mind, which elevates him above such emotions, or only considering it so far as to encrease our admiration, love and tenderness for him. We find from experience, that such a degree of passion is usually connected with such a misfortune; and tho' there be an exception in the present case, yet the imagination is affected by the *general rule*, and makes us conceive a lively idea of the passion, or rather feel the passion itself, in the same manner, as if the person were really actuated by it. From the same principles we blush for the conduct of those, who behave themselves foolishly before us; and that tho' they shew no sense of shame, nor seem in the least conscious of their folly. All this proceeds from sympathy; but 'tis of a partial kind, and views its objects only on one side, without considering the other, which has a contrary effect, and wou'd entirely destroy that emotion, which arises from the first appearance.

We have also instances, wherein an indifference and insensibility under misfortune encreases our concern for the misfortunate, even tho' the indifference proceed not from any virtue and magnanimity. 'Tis an aggravation of a murder, that it was committed upon persons asleep and in perfect security; as historians readily observe of any infant prince, who is captive in the hands of his enemies, that he is the more worthy of compassion the less sensible he is of his miserable condition. As we ourselves are here acquainted with the wretched situation of the person, it gives us a lively idea and sensation of sorrow, which is the passion that *generally* attends it; and this idea becomes still more lively, and the sensation more violent by a contrast with that security and indifference, which we observe in the person himself. A contrast of any kind never fails to affect the imagination, especially when presented by the subject; and 'tis on the imagination that pity entirely depends*.

SECT. VIII
Of malice and envy

We must now proceed to account for the passion of *malice*, which imitates the effects of hatred, as pity does those of love; and gives us a joy in the sufferings and miseries of others, without any offence or injury on their part.

So little are men govern'd by reason in their sentiments and opinions, that they always judge more of objects by comparison than from their intrinsic worth and value. When the mind considers, or is accustom'd to, any degree of perfection, whatever falls short of it, tho' really esteemable, has notwithstanding the same effect upon the passions; as what is defective and ill. This is an *original* quality of the soul, and similar to what we have every day experience of in our bodies. Let a man heat one hand and cool the other; the same water will, at the same time, seem both hot and cold, according to the disposition of the different organs. A

* To prevent all ambiguity, I must observe, that where I oppose the imagination to the memory, I mean in general the faculty that presents our fainter ideas. In all other places, and particularly when it is oppos'd to the understanding, I understand the same faculty, excluding only our demonstrative and probable reasonings.

small degree of any quality, succeeding a greater, produces the same sensation, as if less than it really is, and even sometimes as the opposite quality. Any gentle pain, that follows a violent one, seems as nothing, or rather becomes a pleasure; as on the other hand a violent pain, succeeding a gentle one, is doubly grievous and uneasy.

This no one can doubt of with regard to our passions and sensations. But there may arise some difficulty with regard to our ideas and objects. When an object augments or diminishes to the eye or imagination from a comparison with others, the image and idea of the object are still the same, and are equally extended in the *retina*, and in the brain or organ of perception. The eyes refract the rays of light, and the optic nerves convey the images to the brain in the very same manner, whether a great or small object has preceded; nor does even the imagination alter the dimensions of its object on account of a comparison with others. The question then is, how from the same impression and the same idea we can form such different judgments concerning the same object, and at one time admire its bulk, and at another despise its littleness. This variation in our judgments must certainly proceed from a variation in some perception; but as the variation lies not in the immediate impression or idea of the object, it must lie in some other impression, that accompanies it.

In order to explain this matter, I shall just touch upon two principles, one of which shall be more fully explain'd in the progress of this treatise; the other has been already accounted for. I believe it may safely be establish'd for a general maxim, that no object is presented to the senses, nor image form'd in the fancy, but what is accompany'd with some emotion or movement of spirits proportion'd to it; and however custom may make us insensible of this sensation and cause us to confound it with the object or idea, 'twill be easy, by careful and exact experiments, to separate and distinguish them. For to instance only in the cases of extension and number; 'tis evident, that any very bulky object, such as the ocean, an extended plain, a vast chain of mountains, a wide forest; or any very numerous collection of objects, such as an army, a fleet, a crowd, excite in the mind a sensible emotion; and that the admiration, which arises on the appearance of such objects, is one of the most lively pleasures, which human nature is capable of enjoying. Now as this admiration encreases or diminishes by the encrease or diminution of the objects, we may conclude, according to our foregoing * principles, that 'tis a compound effect, proceeding from the conjunction of the several effects, which arise from each part of the cause. Every part, then, of extension, and every unite of number has a separate emotion attending it; and tho' that emotion be not always agreeable, yet by its conjunction with others, and by its agitating the spirits to a just pitch, it contributes to the production of admiration, which is always agreeable. If this be allow'd with respect to extension and number, we can make no difficulty with respect to virtue and vice, wit and folly, riches and poverty, happiness and misery, and other objects of that kind, which are always attended with an evident emotion.

The second principle I shall take notice of is that of our adherence to *general rules*; which has such a mighty influence on the actions and understanding, and is able to impose on the very senses. When an object is found by experience to be always accompany'd with another; whenever the first object appears, tho' chang'd in very material circumstances; we naturally fly to the conception of the second, and form an idea of it in as lively and strong a manner, as if we had infer'd its existence by the justest and most authentic conclusion of our understanding. Nothing can undeceive us, not even our senses, which, instead of correcting this false judgment, are often perverted by it, and seem to authorize its errors.

The conclusion I draw from these two principles, join'd to the influence of comparison above-mention'd, is very short and decisive. Every object is attended with some emotion proportion'd to it; a great object with a great emotion, a small object with a small emotion. A great *object*, therefore,

* Book I. Part III. Sect. 15.

succeeding a small one makes a great *emotion* succeed a small one. Now a great emotion succeeding a small one becomes still greater, and rises beyond its ordinary proportion. But as there is a certain degree of an emotion, which commonly attends every magnitude of an object; when the emotion encreases, we naturally imagine that the object has likewise encreas'd. The effect conveys our view to its usual cause, a certain degree of emotion to a certain magnitude of the object; nor do we consider, that comparison may change the emotion without changing anything in the object. Those who are acquainted with the metaphysical part of optics and know how we transfer the judgments and conclusions of the understanding to the senses, will easily conceive this whole operation.

But leaving this new discovery of an impression, that secretly attends every idea; we must at least allow of that principle, from whence the discovery arose, *that objects appear greater or less by a comparison with others.* We have so many instances of this, that it is impossible we can dispute its veracity; and 'tis from this principle I derive the passions of malice and envy.

'Tis evident we must receive a greater or less satisfaction or uneasiness from reflecting on our own condition and circumstances, in proportion as they appear more or less fortunate or unhappy, in proportion to the degrees of riches, and power, and merit, and reputation, which we think ourselves possest of. Now as we seldom judge of objects from their intrinsic value, but form our notions of them from a comparison with other objects; it follows, that according as we observe a greater or less share of happiness or misery in others, we must make an estimate of our own, and feel a consequent pain or pleasure. The misery of another gives us a more lively idea of our happiness, and his happiness of our misery. The former, therefore, produces delight; and the latter uneasiness.

Here then is a kind of pity reverst, or contrary sensations arising in the beholder, from those which are felt by the person, whom he considers. In general we may observe, that in all kinds of comparison an object makes us always receive from another, to which it is compar'd, a sensation contrary to what arises from itself in its direct and immediate survey. A small object makes a great one appear still greater. A great object makes a little one appear less. Deformity of itself produces uneasiness; but makes us receive new pleasure by its contrast with a beautiful object, whose beauty is augmented by it; as on the other hand, beauty, which of itself produces pleasure, makes us receive a new pain by the contrast with any thing ugly, whose deformity it augments. The case, therefore, must be the same with happiness and misery. The direct survey of another's pleasure naturally gives us pleasure, and therefore produces pain when compar'd with our own. His pain, consider'd in itself, is painful to us, but augments the idea of our own happiness, and gives us pleasure.

Nor will it appear strange, that we may feel a reverst sensation from the happiness and misery of others; since we find the same comparison may give us a kind of malice against ourselves, and make us rejoice for our pains, and grieve for our pleasures. Thus the prospect of past pain is agreeable, when we are satisfy'd with our present condition; as on the other hand our past pleasures give us uneasiness, when we enjoy nothing at present equal to them. The comparison being the same, as when we reflect on the sentiments of others, must be attended with the same effects.

Nay a person may extend this malice against himself, even to his present fortune, and carry it so far as designedly to seek affliction, and encrease his pains and sorrows. This may happen upon two occasions. *First,* Upon the distress and misfortune of a friend, or person dear to him. *Secondly,* Upon the feeling any remorses for a crime, of which he has been guilty. 'Tis from the principle of comparison that both these irregular appetites for evil arise. A person, who indulges himself in any pleasure, while his friend lies under affliction, feels the reflected uneasiness from his friend more sensibly by a comparison with the original pleasure, which he himself enjoys. This contrast, indeed, ought also to inliven the present pleasure. But as grief is here suppos'd to be the predominant passion, every addition falls to that side, and is swallow'd up in it, without operating in the least upon the contrary affection. 'Tis the same case with those penances, which men inflict on themselves for their past sins and failings. When a criminal reflects on the punishment he deserves, the idea of it is magnify'd by a comparison with his present ease and satisfaction; which forces him, in a manner, to seek uneasiness, in order to avoid so disagreeable a contrast.

This reasoning will account for the origin of *envy* as well as of malice. The only difference betwixt these passions lies in this, that envy is excited by some present enjoyment of another, which by comparison diminishes our idea of our own: Whereas malice is the unprovok'd desire of producing evil to another, in order to reap a pleasure from the comparison. The enjoyment, which is the object of envy, is commonly superior to our own. A superiority naturally seems to overshade us, and presents a disagreeable comparison. But even in the case of an inferiority, we still desire a greater distance, in order to augment still more the idea of ourself. When this distance diminishes, the comparison is less to our advantage; and consequently gives us less pleasure, and is even disagreeable. Hence arises that species of envy, which men feel, when they perceive their inferiors approaching or overtaking them in the pursuits of glory or happiness. In this envy we may see the effects of comparison twice repeated. A man, who compares himself to his inferior, receives a pleasure from the comparison: And when the inferiority decreases by the elevation of the inferior, what shou'd only have been a decrease of pleasure, becomes a real pain, by a new comparison with its preceding condition.

'Tis worthy of observation concerning that envy, which arises from a superiority in others, that 'tis not the great disproportion betwixt ourself and another, which produces it; but on the contrary, our proximity. A common soldier bears no such envy to his general as to his sergeant or corporal;

nor does an eminent writer meet with so great jealousy in common hackney scriblers, as in authors, that more nearly approach him. It may, indeed, be thought, that the greater the disproportion is, the greater must be the uneasiness from the comparison. But we may consider on the other hand, that the great disproportion cuts off the relation, and either keeps us from comparing ourselves with what is remote from us, or diminishes the effects of the comparison. Resemblance and proximity always produce a relation of ideas; and where you destroy these ties, however other accidents may bring two ideas together; as they have no bond or connecting quality to join them in the imagination; 'tis impossible they can remain long united, or have any considerable influence on each other.

I have observ'd in considering the nature of ambition, that the great feel a double pleasure in authority from the comparison of their own condition with that of their slaves; and that this comparison has a double influence, because 'tis natural, and presented by the subject. When the fancy, in the comparison of objects, passes not easily from the one object to the other, the action of the mind is, in a great measure, broke, and the fancy, in considering the second object, begins, as it were, upon a new footing. The impression, which attends every object, seems not greater in that case by succeeding a less of the same kind; but these two impressions are distinct, and produce their distinct effects, without any communication together. The want of relation in the ideas breaks the relation of the impressions, and by such a separation prevents their mutual operation and influence.

To confirm this we may observe, that the proximity in the degree of merit is not alone sufficient to give rise to envy, but must be assisted by other relations. A poet is not apt to envy a philosopher, or a poet of a different kind, of a different nation, or of a different age. All these differences prevent or weaken the comparison, and consequently the passion.

This too is the reason, why all objects appear great or

little, merely by a comparison with those of the same species. A mountain neither magnifies nor diminishes a horse in our eyes; but when a *Flemish* and a *Welsh* horse are seen together, the one appears greater and the other less, than when view'd apart.

From the same principle we may account for that remark of historians, that any party in a civil war always choose to call in a foreign enemy at any hazard rather than submit to their fellow-citizens. *Guicciardin* applies this remark to the wars in *Italy*, where the relations betwixt the different states are, properly speaking, nothing but of name, language, and contiguity. Yet even these relations, when join'd with superiority, by making the comparison more natural, make it likewise more grievous, and cause men to search for some other superiority, which may be attended with no relation, and by that means may have a less sensible influence on the imagination. The mind quickly perceives its several advantages and disadvantages; and finding its situation to be most uneasy, where superiority is conjoin'd with other relations, seeks its repose as much as possible, by their separation, and by breaking that association of ideas, which renders the comparison so much more natural and efficacious. When it cannot break the association, it feels a stronger desire to remove the superiority; and this is the reason why travellers are commonly so lavish of their praises to the *Chinese* and *Persians*, at the same time, that they depreciate those neighbouring nations, which may stand upon a foot of rivalship with their native country.

These examples from history and common experience are rich and curious; but we may find parallel ones in the arts, which are no less remarkable. Shou'd an author compose a treatise, of which one part was serious and profound, another light and humorous, every one wou'd conaemn so strange a mixture, and wou'd accuse him of the neglect of all rules of art and criticism. These rules of art are founded on the qualities of human nature; and the quality of human nature, which requires a consistency in every performance, is that which renders the mind incapable of passing in a moment from one passion and disposition to a quite different one. Yet this makes us not blame Mr *Prior* for joining his *Alma* and his *Solomon* in the same volume; tho' that admirable poet has succeeded perfectly well in the gaiety of the one, as well as in the melancholy of the other. Even supposing the reader shou'd peruse these two compositions without any interval, he wou'd feel little or no difficulty in the change of passions: Why, but because he considers these performances as entirely different, and by this break in the ideas, breaks the progress of the affections, and hinders the one from influencing or contradicting the other?

An heroic and burlesque design, united in one picture, wou'd be monstrous; tho' we place two pictures of so opposite a character in the same chamber, and even close by each other, without any scruple or difficulty.

In a word, no ideas can affect each other, either by comparison, or by the passions they separately produce, unless they be united together by some relation, which may cause an easy transition of the ideas, and consequently of the emotions or impressions, attending the ideas; and may preserve the one impression in the passage of the imagination to the object of the other. This principle is very remarkable, because it is analogous to what we have observ'd both concerning the *understanding* and the *passions*. Suppose two objects to be presented to me, which are not connected by any kind of relation. Suppose that each of these objects separately produces a passion; and that these two passions are in themselves contrary: We find from experience, that the want of relation in the objects or ideas hinders the natural contrariety of the passions, and that the break in the transition of the thought removes the affections from each other, and prevents their opposition. 'Tis the same case with comparison; and from both these phaenomena we may safely conclude, that the relation of ideas must forward the transition of impressions; since its absence alone is able to prevent it, and to separate what naturally shou'd have operated upon each other. When the absence of an object or quality removes any usual or natural effect, we may certainly conclude that its presence contributes to the production of the effect.

SECT. IX

Of the mixture of benevolence and anger with compassion and malice

THUS we have endeavour'd to account for *pity* and *malice*. Both these affections arise from the imagination, according to the light, in which it places its object. When our fancy considers directly the sentiments of others, and enters deep into them, it makes us sensible of all the passions it surveys, but in a particular manner of grief or sorrow. On the contrary, when we compare the sentiments of others to our own, we feel a sensation directly opposite to the original one, *viz.* a joy from the grief of others, and a grief from their joy. But these are only the first foundations of the affections of pity and malice. Other passions are afterwards confounded with them. There is always a mixture of love or tenderness with pity, and of hatred or anger with malice. But it must be confess'd, that this mixture seems at first sight to be contradictory to my system. For as pity is an uneasiness, and malice a joy, arising from the misery of others, pity shou'd naturally, as in all other cases, produce hatred; and malice, love. This contradiction I endeavour to reconcile, after the following manner.

In order to cause a transition of passions, there is requir'd a double relation of impressions and ideas, nor is one relation sufficient to produce this effect. But that we may understand the full force of this double relation, we must consider, that 'tis not the present sensation alone or momentary pain or pleasure, which determines the character of any passion, but the whole bent or tendency of it from the beginning to the end. One impression may be related to another, not only when their sensations are resembling, as we have all along suppos'd in the preceding cases; but also when their impulses or directions are similar and correspondent. This cannot take place with regard to pride and humility; because these are only pure sensations, without any direction or tendency to action. We are, therefore, to look for instances of this peculiar relation of impressions only in such affections, as are attended with a certain appetite or desire; such as those of love and hatred.

Benevolence or the appetite, which attends love, is a desire of the happiness of the person belov'd, and an aversion to his misery; as anger or the appetite, which attends hatred, is a desire of the misery of the person hated, and an aversion to his happiness. A desire, therefore, of the happiness of another, and aversion to his misery, are similar to benevolence; and a desire of his misery and aversion to his happiness are correspondent to anger. Now pity is a desire of happiness to another, and aversion to his misery; as malice is the contrary appetite. Pity, then, is related to benevolence; and malice to anger: And as benevolence has been already found to be connected with love, by a natural and original quality, and anger with hatred; 'tis by this chain the passions of pity and malice are connected with love and hatred.

This hypothesis is founded on sufficient experience. A man, who from any motives has entertain'd a resolution of performing an action, naturally runs into every other view or motive, which may fortify that resolution, and give it authority and influence on the mind. To confirm us in any design, we search for motives drawn from interest, from honour, from duty. What wonder, then, that pity and benevolence, malice, and anger, being the same desires arising from different principles, shou'd so totally mix together as to be undistinguishable? As to the connexion betwixt benevolence and love, anger and hatred, being *original* and primary, it admits of no difficulty.

We may add to this another experiment, *viz.* that benevolence and anger, and consequently love and hatred, arise when our happiness or misery have any dependance on the happiness or misery of another person, without any farther relation. I doubt not but this experiment will appear so singular as to excuse us for stopping a moment to consider it.

Suppose, that two persons of the same trade shou'd seek employment in a town, that is not able to maintain both, 'tis plain the success of one is perfectly incompatible with that of the other, and that whatever is for the interest of either is contrary to that of his rival, and so *vice versa.* Suppose again, that two merchants, tho' living in different parts of the world, shou'd enter into co-partnership together, the advantage or loss of one becomes immediately the advantage or loss of his partner, and the same fortune necessarily attends both. Now 'tis evident, that in the first case, hatred always follows upon the contrariety of interests; as in the second, love arises from their union. Let us consider to what principle we can ascribe these passions.

'Tis plain they arise not from the double relations of impressions and ideas, if we regard only the present sensation. For takeing the first case of rivalship; tho' the pleasure and advantage of an antagonist necessarily causes my pain and loss, yet to counter-ballance this, his pain and loss causes my pleasure and advantage; and supposing him to be unsuccessful, I may by this means receive from him a superior degree of satisfaction. In the same manner the success of a partner rejoices me, but then his misfortunes afflict me in an equal proportion; and 'tis easy to imagine, that the latter sentiment may in many cases preponderate. But whether the fortune of a rival or partner be good or bad, I always hate the former and love the latter.

This love of a partner cannot proceed from the relation or connexion betwixt us; in the same manner as I love a brother or countryman. A rival has almost as close a relation to me as a partner. For as the pleasure of the latter causes my pleasure, and his pain my pain; so the pleasure of the former causes my pain, and his pain my pleasure. The connexion, then, of cause and effect is the same in both cases; and if in the one case, the cause and effect have a farther relation of resemblance, they have that of contrariety in the other; which, being also a species of resemblance, leaves the matter pretty equal.

The only explication, then, we can give of this phaenomenon is deriv'd from that principle of a parallel direction above-mention'd. Our concern for our own interest gives us a pleasure in the pleasure, and a pain in the pain of a partner, after the same manner as by sympathy we feel a sensation correspondent to those, which appear in any person, who is present with us. On the other hand, the same concern for our interest makes us feel a pain in the pleasure, and a pleasure in the pain of a rival; and in short the same contrariety of sentiments as arises from comparison and malice. Since, therefore, a parallel direction of the affections, proceeding from interest, can give rise to benevolence or anger, no wonder the same parallel direction, deriv'd from sympathy and from comparison, shou'd have the same effect.

In general we may observe, that 'tis impossible to do good to others, from whatever motive, without feeling some touches of kindness and good-will towards 'em; as the injuries we do, not only cause hatred in the person, who suffers them, but even in ourselves. These phaenomena, indeed, may in part be accounted for from other principles.

But here there occurs a considerable objection, which 'twill be necessary to examine before we proceed any farther. I have endeavour'd to prove, that power and riches, or poverty and meanness; which give rise to love or hatred, without producing any original pleasure or uneasiness; operate upon us by means of a secondary sensation deriv'd from a sympathy with that pain or satisfaction, which they produce in the person, who possesses them. From a sympathy with his pleasure there arises love; from that with his uneasiness, hatred. But 'tis a maxim, which I have just now establish'd, and which is absolutely necessary to the explication of the phaenomena of pity and malice, 'That 'tis not the present sensation or momentary pain or pleasure, which determines the character of any passion, but the general bent or tendency of it from the beginning to the end.' For this reason, pity or a sympathy with pain produces love, and that because it interests us in the fortunes of others, good or bad, and gives us a secondary sensation correspondent to the primary; in which it has the same influence with love and benevolence. Since then this rule holds good in one case, why does it not prevail throughout, and why does sympathy in uneasiness ever produce any passion beside good-will and kindness? Is it becoming a philosopher to alter his method of reasoning, and run from one principle to its contrary, according to the particular phaenomenon, which he wou'd explain?

I have mention'd two different causes, from which a transition of passion may arise, *viz.* a double relation of ideas and impressions, and what is similar to it, a conformity in the tendency and direction of any two desires, which arise from different principles. Now I assert, that when a sympathy with uneasiness is weak, it produces hatred or contempt by the former cause; when strong, it produces love or tenderness by the latter. This is the solution of the foregoing difficulty, which seems so urgent; and this is a principle founded on such evident arguments, that we ought to have establish'd it, even tho' it were not necessary to the explication of any phaenomenon.

'Tis certain, that sympathy is not always limited to the present moment, but that we often feel by communication the pains and pleasures of others, which are not in being, and which we only anticipate by the force of imagination. For supposing I saw a person perfectly unknown to me, who, while asleep in the fields, was in danger of being trod under foot by horses, I shou'd immediately run to his assistance; and in this I shou'd be actuated by the same principle of sympathy, which makes me concern'd for the present sorrows of a stranger. The bare mention of this is sufficient. Sympathy being nothing but a lively idea converted into an impression, 'tis evident, that, in considering the future possible or probable condition of any person, we may enter into it with so vivid a conception as to make it our own concern; and by that means be sensible of pains and pleasures, which neither belong to ourselves, nor at the present instant have any real existence.

But however we may look forward to the future in sympathizing with any person, the extending of our sympathy depends in a great measure upon our sense of his present condition. 'Tis a great effort of imagination, to form such lively ideas even of the present sentiments of others as to feel these very sentiments; but 'tis impossible we cou'd extend this sympathy to the future, without being aided by some circumstance in the present, which strikes upon us in a lively manner. When the present misery of another has any strong influence upon me, the vivacity of the conception is not confin'd merely to its immediate object, but diffuses its influence over all the related ideas, and gives me a lively notion of all the circumstances of that person, whether past, present, or future; possible, probable or certain. By means of this lively notion I am interested in them; take part with them; and feel a sympathetic motion in my breast, conformable to whatever I imagine in his. If I diminish the vivacity of the first conception, I diminish that of the related ideas; as pipes can convey no more water than what arises at the fountain. By this diminution I destroy the future prospect, which is necessary to interest me perfectly in the fortune of another. I may feel the present impression, but carry my sympathy no farther, and never transfuse the force of the first conception into my ideas of the related objects. If it be another's misery, which is presented in this feeble manner, I receive it by communication, and am affected with all the passions related to it: But as I am not so much interested as to concern myself in his good fortune, as well as his bad, I never feel the extensive sympathy, nor the passions related to *it*.

Now in order to know what passions are related to these different kinds of sympathy, we must consider, that benevolence is an original pleasure arising from the pleasure of the person belov'd, and a pain proceeding from his pain: From which correspondence of impressions there arises a subsequent desire of his pleasure, and aversion to his pain.

In order, then, to make a passion run parallel with benevolence, 'tis requisite we shou'd feel these double impressions, correspondent to those of the person, whom we consider; nor is any one of them alone sufficient for that purpose. When we sympathize only with one impression, and that a painful one, this sympathy is related to anger and to hatred, upon account of the uneasiness it conveys to us. But as the extensive or limited sympathy depends upon the force of the first sympathy; it follows, that the passion of love or hatred depends upon the same principle. A strong impression, when communicated, gives a double tendency of the passions; which is related to benevolence and love by a similarity of direction; however painful the first impression might have been. A weak impression, that is painful, is related to anger and hatred by the resemblance of sensations. Benevolence, therefore, arises from a great degree of misery, or any degree strongly sympathiz'd with: Hatred or contempt from a small degree, or one weakly sympathiz'd with; which is the principle I intended to prove and explain.

Nor have we only our reason to trust to for this principle, but also experience. A certain degree of poverty produces contempt; but a degree beyond causes compassion and good-will. We may under-value a peasant or servant; but when the misery of a beggar appears very great, or is painted in very lively colours, we sympathize with him in his afflictions; and feel in our heart evident touches of pity and benevolence. The same object causes contrary passions according to its different degrees. The passions, therefore, must depend upon principles, that operate in such certain degrees, according to my hypothesis. The encrease of the sympathy has evidently the same effect as the encrease of the misery.

A barren or desolate country always seems ugly and disagreeable, and commonly inspires us with contempt for the inhabitants. This deformity, however, proceeds in a great measure from a sympathy with the inhabitants, as has been already observ'd; but it is only a weak one, and reaches no farther than the immediate sensation, which is disagreeable. The view of a city in ashes conveys benevolent sentiments; because we there enter so deep into the interests of the miserable inhabitants, as to wish for their prosperity, as well as feel their adversity.

But tho' the force of the impression generally produces pity and benevolence, 'tis certain, that by being carry'd too far it ceases to have that effect. This, perhaps, may be worth our notice. When the uneasiness is either small in itself, or remote from us, it engages not the imagination, nor is able to convey an equal concern for the future and contingent good, as for the present and real evil. Upon its acquiring greater force, we become so interested in the concerns of the person, as to be sensible both of his good and bad fortune; and from that compleat sympathy there arises pity and benevolence. But 'twill easily be imagin'd, that where the present evil strikes with more than ordinary force, it may entirely engage our attention, and prevent that double sympathy, above-mention'd. Thus we find, that tho' every one, but especially women, are apt to contract a kindness for criminals, who go to the scaffold, and readily imagine them to be uncommonly handsome and well-shaped; yet one, who is present at the cruel execution of the rack, feels no such tender emotions; but is in a manner overcome with horror, and has no leisure to temper this uneasy sensation by any opposite sympathy.

But the instance, which makes the most clearly for my hypothesis, is that wherein by a change of the objects we separate the double sympathy even from a midling degree of the passion; in which case we find, that pity, instead of producing love and tenderness as usual, always gives rise to the contrary affection. When we observe a person in misfortunes, we are affected with pity and love; but the author of that misfortune becomes the object of our strongest hatred, and is the more detested in proportion to the degree of our compassion. Now for what reason shou'd the same passion of pity produce love to the person, who suffers the misfortune, and hatred to the person, who causes it;

unless it be because in the latter case the author bears a relation only to the misfortune; whereas in considering the sufferer we carry our view on every side, and wish for his prosperity, as well as are sensible of his affliction?

I shall just observe, before I leave the present subject, that this phaenomenon of the double sympathy, and its tendency to cause love, may contribute to the production of the kindness, which we naturally bear our relations and acquaintance. Custom and relation make us enter deeply into the sentiments of others; and whatever fortune we suppose to attend them, is render'd present to us by the imagination, and operates as if originally our own. We rejoice in their pleasures, and grieve for their sorrows, merely from the force of sympathy. Nothing that concerns them is indifferent to us; and as this correspondence of sentiments is the natural attendant of love, it readily produces that affection.

SECT. X

Of respect and contempt

THERE now remains only to explain the passion of *respect* and *contempt*, along with the *amorous* affection, in order to understand all the passions which have any mixture of love or hatred. Let us begin with respect and contempt.

In considering the qualities and circumstances of others, we may either regard them as they really are in themselves; or may make a comparison betwixt them and our own qualities and circumstances; or may join these two methods of consideration. The good qualities of others, from the first point of view, produce love; from the second, humility; and from the third, respect; which is a mixture of these two passions. Their bad qualities, after the same manner, cause either hatred, or pride, or contempt, according to the light in which we survey them.

That there is a mixture of pride in contempt, and of humility in respect, is, I think, too evident, from their very feeling or appearance, to require any particular proof. That this mixture arises from a tacit comparison of the person contemn'd or respected with ourselves is no less evident. The same man may cause either respect, love, or contempt by his condition and talents, according as the person, who considers him, from his inferior becomes his equal or superior. In changing the point of view, tho' the object may remain the same, its proportion to ourselves entirely alters; which is the cause of an alteration in the passions. These passions, therefore, arise from our observing the proportion; that is, from a comparison.

I have already observ'd, that the mind has a much stronger propensity to pride than to humility, and have endeavour'd, from the principles of human nature, to assign a cause for this phaenomenon. Whether my reasoning be receiv'd or not, the phaenomenon is undisputed, and appears in many instances. Among the rest, 'tis the reason why there is a much greater mixture of pride in contempt, than of humility in respect, and why we are more elevated with the view of one below us, than mortify'd with the presence of one above us. Contempt or scorn has so strong a tincture of pride, that there scarce is any other passion discernable: Whereas in esteem or respect, love makes a more considerable ingredient than humility. The passion of vanity is so prompt, that it rouzes at the least call; while humility requires a stronger impulse to make it exert itself.

But here it may reasonably be ask'd, why this mixture takes place only in some cases, and appears not on every occasion. All those objects, which cause love, when plac'd on another person, are the causes of pride, when transfer'd to ourselves; and consequently ought to be causes of humility, as well as love, while they belong to others, and are only compar'd to those, which we ourselves possess. In like manner every quality, which, by being directly consider'd, produces hatred, ought always to give rise to pride by comparison, and by a mixture of these passions of hatred and pride ought to excite contempt or scorn. The difficulty then is, why any objects ever cause pure love or hatred, and produce not always the mixt passions of respect and contempt.

I have suppos'd all along, that the passions of love and pride, and those of humility and hatred are similar in their sensations, and that the two former are always agreeable, and the two latter painful. But tho' this be universally true, 'tis observable, that the two agreeable, as well as the two painful passions, have some difference, and even contrarieties, which distinguish them. Nothing invigorates and exalts the mind equally with pride and vanity; tho' at the same time love or tenderness is rather found to weaken and infeeble it. The same difference is observable betwixt the uneasy passions. Anger and hatred bestow a new force on all our thoughts and actions; while humility and shame deject and discourage us. Of these qualities of the passions, 'twill be necessary to form a distinct idea. Let us remember, that pride and hatred invigorate the soul; and love and humility infeeble it.

From this it follows, that tho' the conformity betwixt love and hatred in the agreeableness of their sensation makes them always be excited by the same objects, yet this other contrariety is the reason, why they are excited in very different degrees. Genius and learning are *pleasant* and *magnificent* objects, and by both these circumstances are adapted to pride and vanity; but have a relation to love by their pleasure only. Ignorance and simplicity are *disagreeable* and *mean*, which in the same manner gives them a double connexion with humility, and a single one with hatred. We may, therefore, consider it as certain, that tho' the same object always produces love and pride, humility and hatred, according to its different situations, yet it seldom produces either the two former or the two latter passions, in the same proportion.

'Tis here we must seek for a solution of the difficulty above-mention'd, why any object ever excites pure love or hatred, and does not always produce respect or contempt, by a mixture of humility or pride. No quality in another gives rise to humility by comparison, unless it wou'd have produc'd pride by being plac'd in ourselves; and *vice versa* no object excites pride by comparison, unless it wou'd have produc'd humility by the direct survey. This is evident, objects always produce by *comparison* a sensation directly contrary to their *original* one. Suppose, therefore, an object to be presented, which is peculiarly fitted to produce love, but imperfectly to excite pride; this object, belonging to another, gives rise directly to a great degree of love, but to a small one of humility by comparison; and consequently that latter passion is scarce felt in the compound, nor is able to convert the love into respect. This is the case with good nature, good humour, facility, generosity, beauty, and many other qualities. These have a peculiar aptitude to produce love in others; but not so great a tendency to excite pride in ourselves: For which reason the view of them, as belonging to another person, produces pure love, with but a small mixture of humility and respect. 'Tis easy to extend the same reasoning to the opposite passions.

Before we leave this subject, it may not be amiss to account for a pretty curious phaenomenon, *viz.* why we commonly keep at a distance such as we contemn, and allow not our inferiors to approach too near even in place and situation. It has already been observ'd, that almost every kind of idea is attended with some emotion, even the ideas of number and extension, much more those of such objects as are esteem'd of consequence in life, and fix our attention. 'Tis not with entire indifference we can survey either a rich man or a poor one, but must feel some faint touches at least, of respect in the former case, and of contempt in the latter. These two passions are contrary to each other; but in order to make this contrariety be felt, the objects must be someway related; otherwise the affections are totally separate and distinct, and never encounter. The relation takes place wherever the persons become contiguous; which is a general reason why we are uneasy at seeing such disproportion'd objects, as a rich man and a poor one, a nobleman and a porter, in that situation.

This uneasiness, which is common to every spectator, must be more sensible to the superior; and that because the near approach of the inferior is regarded as a piece of ill-breeding, and shews that he is not sensible of the disproportion, and is no way affected by it. A sense of superiority in another breeds in all men an inclination to keep themselves at a distance from him, and determines them to redouble the marks of respect and reverence, when they are oblig'd to approach him; and where they do not observe that conduct, 'tis a proof they are not sensible of his superiority. From hence too it proceeds, that any great *difference* in the degrees of any quality is call'd a *distance* by a common metaphor, which, however trivial it may appear, is founded on natural principles of the imagination. A great difference inclines us to produce a distance. The ideas of distance and difference are, therefore, connected together. Connected ideas are readily taken for each other; and this is in general the source of the metaphor, as we shall have occasion to observe afterwards.

SECT. XI

Of the amorous passion, or love betwixt the sexes

Of all the compound passions, which proceed from a mixture of love and hatred with other affections, no one better deserves our attention, than that love, which arises betwixt the sexes, as well on account of its force and violence, as those curious principles of philosophy, for which it affords us an uncontestable argument. 'Tis plain, that this affection, in its most natural state, is deriv'd from the conjunction of three different impressions or passions, *viz.* The pleasing sensation arising from beauty; the bodily appetite for generation; and a generous kindness or good-will. The origin of kindness from beauty may be explain'd from the foregoing reasoning. The question is how the bodily appetite is excited by it.

The appetite of generation, when confin'd to a certain degree, is evidently of the pleasant kind, and has a strong connexion with all the agreeable emotions. Joy, mirth, vanity, and kindness are all incentives to this desire; as well as music, dancing, wine, and good cheer. On the other hand, sorrow, melancholy, poverty, humility are destructive of it. From this quality 'tis easily conceiv'd why it shou'd be connected with the sense of beauty.

But there is another principle that contributes to the same effect. I have observ'd that the parallel direction of the desires is a real relation, and no less than a resemblance in their sensation, produces a connexion among them. That we may fully comprehend the extent of this relation, we must consider, that any principal desire may be attended with subordinate ones, which are connected with it, and to which if other desires are parallel, they are by that means related to the principal one. Thus hunger may oft be consider'd as the primary inclination of the soul, and the desire of approaching the meat as the secondary one; since 'tis absolutely necessary to the satisfying that appetite. If an object, therefore, by any separate qualities, inclines us to approach the meat, it naturally encreases our appetite; as on the contrary, whatever inclines us to set our victuals at a distance, is contradictory to hunger, and diminishes our inclination to them. Now 'tis plain that beauty has the first effect, and deformity the second: Which is the reason why the former gives us a keener appetite for our victuals, and the latter is sufficient to disgust us at the most savoury dish, that cookery has invented. All this is easily applicable to the appetite for generation.

From these two relations, *viz.* resemblance and a parallel desire, there arises such a connexion betwixt the sense of beauty, the bodily appetite, and benevolence, that they become in a manner inseparable: And we find from experience that 'tis indifferent which of them advances first; since any of them is almost sure to be attended with the related affections. One, who is inflam'd with lust, feels at least a momentary kindness towards the object of it, and at the same time fancies her more beautiful than ordinary; as there are many, who begin with kindness and esteem for the wit and merit of the person, and advance from that to the other passions. But the most common species of love is that which first arises from beauty, and afterwards diffuses itself into kindness and into the bodily appetite. Kindness or esteem, and the appetite to generation, are too remote to unite easily together. The one is, perhaps, the most refin'd passion of the soul; the other the most gross and vulgar. The love of beauty is plac'd in a just medium betwixt them, and partakes of both their natures: From whence it proceeds, that 'tis so singularly fitted to produce both.

This account of love is not peculiar to my system, but is unavoidable on any hypothesis. The three affections, which compose this passion, are evidently distinct, and has each of them its distinct object. 'Tis certain, therefore, that 'tis only by their relation they produce each other. But the relation of passions is not alone sufficient. 'Tis likewise necessary, there shou'd be a relation of ideas. The beauty of one person never inspires us with love for another. This then is a sensible proof of the double relation of impressions and ideas. From one instance so evident as this we may form a judgment of the rest.

This may also serve in another view to illustrate what I have insisted on concerning the origin of pride and humility; love and hatred. I have observ'd, that tho' self be the object of the first set of passions, and some other person of the second, yet these objects cannot alone be the causes of the passions; as having each of them a relation to two contrary affections, which must from the very first moment destroy each other. Here then is the situation of the mind, as I have already describ'd it. It has certain organs naturally fitted to produce a passion; that passion, when produc'd, naturally turns the view to a certain object. But this not being sufficient to produce the passion, there is requir'd some other emotion, which by a double relation of impressions and ideas may set these principles in action, and bestow on them their first impulse. This situation is still more remarkable with regard to the appetite of generation. Sex is not only the object, but also the cause of the appetite. We not only turn our view to it, when actuated by that appetite; but the reflecting on it suffices to excite the appetite. But as this cause loses its force by too great frequency, 'tis necessary it shou'd be quicken'd by some new impulse; and that impulse we find to arise from the *beauty* of the *person*; that is, from a double relation of impressions and ideas. Since this double relation is necessary where an affection has both a distinct cause, and object, how much more so, where it has only a distinct object, without any determinate cause?

SECT. XII

Of the love and hatred of animals

But to pass from the passions of love and hatred, and from their mixtures and compositions, as they appear in man, to the same affections, as they display themselves in brutes; we may observe, not only that love and hatred are common to the whole sensitive creation, but likewise that their causes, as above-explain'd, are of so simple a nature, that they may easily be suppos'd to operate on mere animals. There is no force of reflection or penetration requir'd. Every thing is conducted by springs and principles, which are not peculiar to man, or any one species of animals. The conclusion from this is obvious in favour of the foregoing system.

Love in animals, has not for its only object animals of the same species, but extends itself farther, and comprehends almost every sensible and thinking being. A dog naturally loves a man above his own species, and very commonly meets with a return of affection.

As animals are but little susceptible either of the pleasures or pains of the imagination, they can judge of objects only by the sensible good or evil, which they produce, and from *that* must regulate their affections towards them. Accordingly we find, that by benefits or injuries we produce their love or hatred; and that by feeding and cherishing any animal, we quickly acquire his affections; as by beating and abusing him we never fail to draw on us his enmity and ill-will.

Love in beasts is not caus'd so much by relation, as in our species; and that because their thoughts are not so active as to trace relations, except in very obvious instances. Yet 'tis easy to remark, that on some occasions it has a considerable influence upon them. Thus acquaintance, which has the same effect as relation, always produces love in animals either to men or to each other. For the same reason any likeness among them is the source of affection. An ox confin'd to a park with horses, will naturally join their company, if I may so speak, but always leaves it to enjoy that of his own species, where he has the choice of both.

The affection of parents to their young proceeds from a peculiar instinct in animals, as well as in our species.

'Tis evident, that *sympathy*, or the communication of passions, takes place among animals, no less than among men. Fear, anger, courage, and other affections are frequently communicated from one animal to another, without their knowledge of that cause, which produc'd the original passion. Grief likewise is receiv'd by sympathy; and produces almost all the same consequences, and excites the same emotions as in our species. The howlings and lamentations of a dog produce a sensible concern in his fellows. And 'tis remarkable, that tho' almost all animals use in play the same member, and nearly the same action as in fighting; a lion, a tyger, a cat their paws; an ox his horns; a dog his teeth; a horse his heels: Yet they most carefully avoid harming their companion, even tho' they have nothing to fear from his resentment; which is an evident proof of the sense brutes have of each other's pain and pleasure.

Every one has observ'd how much more dogs are animated when they hunt in a pack, than when they pursue their game apart; and 'tis evident this can proceed from nothing but from sympathy. 'Tis also well known to hunters, that this effect follows in a greater degree, and even in too great a degree, where two packs, that are strangers to each other, are join'd together. We might, perhaps, be at a loss to explain this phaenomenon, if we had not experience of a similar in ourselves.

Envy and malice are passions very remarkable in animals. They are perhaps more common than pity; as requiring less effort of thought and imagination.

PART III

Of the will and direct passions

SECT. I

Of liberty and necessity

WE come now to explain the *direct* passions, or the impressions, which arise immediately from good or evil, from pain or pleasure. Of this kind are, *desire and aversion, grief and joy, hope and fear.*

Of all the immediate effects of pain and pleasure, there is none more remarkable than the WILL; and tho' properly speaking, it be not comprehended among the passions, yet as the full understanding of its nature and properties, is necessary to the explanation of them, we shall here make it the subject of our enquiry. I desire it may be observ'd, that by the *will,* I mean nothing but *the internal impression we feel and are conscious of, when we knowingly give rise to any new motion of our body, or new perception of our mind.* This impression, like the preceding ones of pride and humility, love and hatred, 'tis impossible to define, and needless to describe any farther; for which reason we shall cut off all those definitions and distinctions, with which philosophers are wont to perplex rather than clear up this question; and entering at first upon the subject, shall examine that long disputed question concerning *liberty and necessity*; which occurs so naturally in treating of the will.

'Tis universally acknowledg'd, that the operations of external bodies are necessary, and that in the communication of their motion, in their attraction, and mutual cohesion, there are not the least traces of indifference or liberty. Every object is determin'd by an absolute fate to a certain degree and direction of its motion, and can no more depart from that precise line, in which it moves, than it can convert itself into an angel, or spirit, or any superior substance. The actions, therefore, of matter are to be regarded as instances of necessary actions; and whatever is in this respect on the same footing with matter, must be acknowledg'd to be necessary. That we may know whether this be the case with the actions of the mind, we shall begin with examining matter, and considering on what the idea of a necessity in its operations are founded, and why we conclude one body or action to be the infallible cause of another.

It has been observ'd already, that in no single instance the ultimate connexion of any objects is discoverable, either by our senses or reason, and that we can never penetrate so far into the essence and construction of bodies, as to perceive the principle, on which their mutual influence depends. 'Tis their constant union alone, with which we are acquainted; and 'tis from the constant union the necessity arises. If objects had not an uniform and regular conjunction with each other, we shou'd never arrive at any idea of cause and effect; and even after all, the necessity, which enters into that idea, is nothing but a determination of the mind to pass from one object to its usual attendant, and infer the existence of one from that of the other. Here then are two particulars, which we are to consider as essential to necessity, *viz.* the constant *union* and the *inference* of the mind; and wherever we discover these we must acknowledge a necessity. As the actions of matter have no necessity, but what is deriv'd from these circumstances, and it is not by any insight into the essence of bodies we discover their connexion, the absence of this insight, while the union and inference remain, will never, in any case, remove the necessity. 'Tis the observation of the union, which produces the inference; for which reason it might be thought sufficient, if we prove a constant union in the actions of the mind, in order to establish the inference, along with the necessity of these actions. But that I may bestow a greater force on my reasoning, I shall examine these particulars apart, and shall first prove from experience that our actions have a constant union with our motives, tempers, and circumstances, before I consider the inferences we draw from it.

To this end a very slight and general view of the common course of human affairs will be sufficient. There is no light, in which we can take them, that does not confirm this principle. Whether we consider mankind according to the difference of sexes, ages, governments, conditions, or methods of education; the same uniformity and regular operation of natural principles are discernible. Like causes still produce like effects; in the same manner as in the mutual action of the elements and powers of nature.

There are different trees, which regularly produce fruit, whose relish is different from each other; and this regularity will be admitted as an instance of necessity and causes in external bodies. But are the products of *Guienne* and of *Champagne* more regularly different than the sentiments, actions, and passions of the two sexes, of which the one are distinguish'd by their force and maturity, the other by their delicacy and softness?

Are the changes of our body from infancy to old age more regular and certain than those of our mind and conduct? And wou'd a man be more ridiculous, who wou'd expect that an infant of four years old will raise a weight of three hundred pound, than one, who from a person of the same age, wou'd look for a philosophical reasoning, or a prudent and well-concerted action?

We must certainly allow, that the cohesion of the parts of matter arises from natural and necessary principles, whatever difficulty we may find in explaining them: And for a reason we must allow, that human society is founded on like principles; and our reason in the latter case, is better than even that in the former; because we not only observe, that men *always* seek society, but can also explain the principles, on which this universal propensity is founded.

For is it more certain, that two flat pieces of marble will unite together, than that two young savages of different sexes will copulate? Do the children arise from this copulation more uniformly, than does the parents care for their safety and preservation? And after they have arriv'd at years of discretion by the care of their parents, are the inconveniencies attending their separation more certain than their foresight of these inconveniencies and their care of avoiding them by a close union and confederacy?

The skin, pores, muscles, and nerves of a day-labourer are different from those of a man of quality: So are his sentiments, actions and manners. The different stations of life influence the whole fabric, external and internal; and different stations arise necessarily, because uniformly, from the necessary and uniform principles of human nature. Men cannot live without society, and cannot be associated without government. Government makes a distinction of property, and establishes the different ranks of men. This produces industry, traffic, manufactures, law-suits, war, leagues, alliances, voyages, travels, cities, fleets, ports, and all those other actions and objects, which cause such a diversity, and at the same time maintain such an uniformity in human life.

Shou'd a traveller, returning from a far country, tell us, that he had seen a climate in the fiftieth degree of northern latitude, where all the fruits ripen and come to perfection in the winter, and decay in the summer, after the same manner as in *England* they are produc'd and decay in the contrary seasons, he wou'd find few so credulous as to believe him. I am apt to think a travellar wou'd meet with as little credit, who shou'd inform us of people exactly of the same character with those in *Plato*'s republic on the one hand, or those in *Hobbes*'s *Leviathan* on the other. There is a general course of nature in human actions, as well as in the operations of the sun and the climate. There are also characters peculiar to different nations and particular persons, as well as common to mankind. The knowledge of these characters is founded on the observation of an uniformity in the actions, that flow from them; and this uniformity forms the very essence of necessity.

I can imagine only one way of eluding this argument, which is by denying that uniformity of human actions, on which it is founded. As long as actions have a constant union and connexion with the situation and temper of the agent, however we may in words refuse to acknowledge the necessity, we really allow the thing. Now some may, perhaps, find a pretext to deny this regular union and connexion. For what is more capricious than human actions? What more inconstant than the desires of man? And what creature departs more widely, not only from right reason, but from his own character and disposition? An hour, a moment is sufficient to make him change from one extreme to another, and overturn what cost the greatest pain and labour to establish. Necessity is regular and certain. Human conduct is irregular and uncertain. The one, therefore, proceeds not from the other.

To this I reply, that in judging of the actions of men we must proceed upon the same maxims, as when we reason concerning external objects. When any phaenomena are constantly and invariably conjoin'd together, they acquire such a connexion in the imagination, that it passes from one to the other, without any doubt or hesitation. But below this there are many inferior degrees of evidence and probability, nor does one single contrariety of experiment entirely destroy all our reasoning. The mind ballances the contrary experiments, and deducting the inferior from the superior, proceeds with that degree of assurance or evidence, which remains. Even when these contrary experiments are entirely equal, we remove not the notion of causes and necessity; but supposing that the usual contrariety proceeds from the operation of contrary and conceal'd causes, we conclude, that the chance or indifference lies only in our judgment on account of our imperfect knowledge, not in the things themselves, which are in every case equally necessary, tho' to appearance not equally constant or certain. No union can be more constant and certain, than that of some actions with some motives and characters; and if in other cases the union is uncertain, 'tis no more than what happens in the operations of body, nor can we conclude any thing from the one irregularity, which will not follow equally from the other.

'Tis commonly allow'd that mad-men have no liberty. But were we to judge by their actions, these have less regularity and constancy than the actions of wise-men, and consequently are farther remov'd from necessity. Our way of thinking in this particular is, therefore, absolutely inconsistent; but is a natural consequence of these confus'd ideas and undefin'd terms, which we so commonly make use of in our reasonings, especially on the present subject.

We must now shew, that as the *union* betwixt motives and actions has the same constancy, as that in any natural operations, so its influence on the understanding is also the same, in *determining* us to infer the existence of one from that of another. If this shall appear, there is no known circumstance, that enters into the connexion and production of the actions of matter, that is not to be found in all the operations of the mind; and consequently we cannot, without a manifest absurdity, attribute necessity to the one, and refuse it to the other.

There is no philosopher, whose judgment is so riveted to this fantastical system of liberty, as not to acknowledge the force of *moral evidence*, and both in speculation and practice proceed upon it, as upon a reasonable foundation. Now moral evidence is nothing but a conclusion concerning the actions of men, deriv'd from the consideration of their motives, temper and situation. Thus when we see certain characters or figures describ'd upon paper, we infer that the person, who produc'd them, wou'd affirm such facts, the death of *Caesar*, the success of *Augustus*, the cruelty of *Nero*; and remembering many other concurrent testimonies we conclude, that those facts were once really existant, and that so many men, without any interest, wou'd never conspire to deceive us; especially since they must, in the attempt, expose themselves to the derision of all their contemporaries, when these facts were asserted to be recent and universally known. The same kind of reasoning runs thro' politics, war, commerce, economy, and indeed mixes itself so entirely in human life, that 'tis impossible to act or subsist a moment without having recourse to it. A prince, who imposes a tax upon his subjects, expects their compliance. A general, who conducts an army, makes account of a certain degree of courage. A merchant looks for fidelity and skill in his factor or super-cargo. A man, who gives orders for his dinner, doubts not of the obedience of his servants. In short, as nothing more nearly interests us than our own actions and those of others, the greatest part of our reasonings is employ'd in judgments concerning them. Now I assert, that whoever reasons after this manner, does *ipso facto* believe the actions of the will to arise from necessity, and that he knows not what he means, when he denies it.

All those objects, of which we call the one *cause* and the other *effect*, consider'd in themselves, are as distinct and separate from each other, as any two things in nature, nor can we ever, by the most accurate survey of them, infer the existence of the one from that of the other. 'Tis only from experience and the observation of their constant union, that we are able to form this inference; and even after all, the inference is nothing but the effects of custom on the imagination. We must not here be content with saying, that the idea of cause and effect arises from objects constantly united; but must affirm, that 'tis the very same with the idea of those objects, and that the *necessary connexion* is not discover'd by a conclusion of the understanding, but is merely a perception of the mind. Wherever, therefore, we observe the same union, and wherever the union operates in the same manner upon the belief and opinion, we have the idea of causes and necessity, tho' perhaps we may avoid those expressions. Motion in one body in all past instances, that have fallen under our observation, is follow'd upon impulse by motion in another. 'Tis impossible for the mind to penetrate farther. From this constant union it *forms* the idea of cause and effect, and by its influence *feels* the necessity. As there is the same constancy, and the same influence in what we call moral evidence, I ask no more. What remains can only be a dispute of words.

And indeed, when we consider how aptly *natural* and *moral* evidence cement together, and form only one chain of argument betwixt them, we shall make no scruple to allow, that they are of the same nature, and deriv'd from the same principles. A prisoner, who has neither money nor interest, discovers the impossibility of his escape, as well from the obstinacy of the goaler, as from the walls and bars with which he is surrounded; and in all attempts for his freedom chuses rather to work upon the stone and iron of the one, than upon the inflexible nature of the other. The same prisoner, when conducted to the scaffold, foresees his death as certainly from the constancy and fidelity of his guards as from the operation of the ax or wheel. His mind runs along a certain train of ideas: The refusal of the soldiers to consent to his escape, the action of the executioner; the separation of the head and body; bleeding, convulsive motions, and death. Here is a connected chain of natural causes and voluntary actions; but the mind feels no difference betwixt them in passing from one link to another; nor is less certain of the future event than if it were connected with the present impressions of the memory and senses by a train of causes cemented together by what we are pleas'd to call a *physical necessity*. The same experienc'd union has the same effect on the mind, whether the united objects be motives, volitions and actions; or figure and motion. We may change the names of things; but their nature and their operation on the understanding never change.

I dare be positive no one will ever endeavour to refute these reasonings otherwise than by altering my definitions, and assigning a different meaning to the terms of *cause, and effect, and necessity, and liberty, and chance*. According to my definitions, necessity makes an essential part of causation; and consequently liberty, by removing necessity, removes also causes, and is the very same thing with chance. As chance is commonly thought to imply a contradiction, and is at least directly contrary to experience, there are always the same arguments against liberty or free-will. If any one alters the definitions, I cannot pretend to argue with him, 'till I know the meaning he assigns to these terms.

SECT. II

The same subject continu'd

I BELIEVE we may assign the three following reasons for the prevalance of the doctrine of liberty, however absurd it may be in one sense, and unintelligible in any other. First, After we have perform'd any action; tho' we confess we were influenc'd by particular views and motives; 'tis difficult for us to persuade ourselves we were govern'd by necessity, and that 'twas utterly impossible for us to have acted otherwise; the idea of necessity seeming to imply something of force, and violence, and constraint, of which we are not sensible. Few are capable of distinguishing betwixt the liberty of *spontaniety*, as it is call'd in the schools, and the liberty of *indifference*; betwixt that which is oppos'd to violence, and that which means a negation of necessity and causes. The first is even the most common sense of the word; and as 'tis only that species of liberty, which it concerns us to preserve, our thoughts have been principally turn'd towards it, and have almost universally confounded it with the other.

Secondly, There is a *false sensation or experience* even of the liberty of indifference; which is regarded as an argument for its real existence. The necessity of any action, whether of matter or of the mind, is not properly a quality in the agent, but in any thinking or intelligent being, who may consider the action, and consists in the determination of his thought to infer its existence from some preceding objects: As liberty or chance, on the other hand, is nothing but the want of that determination, and a certain looseness, which we feel in passing or not passing from the idea of one to that of the other. Now we may observe, that tho' in reflecting on human actions we seldom feel such a looseness or indifference, yet it very commonly happens, that in performing the actions themselves we are sensible of something like it: And as all related or resembling objects are readily taken for each other, this has been employ'd as a demonstrative or even an intuitive proof of human liberty. We feel that our actions are subject to our will on most occasions, and imagine we feel that the will itself is subject to nothing; because when by a denial of it we are provok'd to try, we feel that it moves easily every way, and produces an image of itself even on that side, on which it did not settle. This image or faint motion, we persuade ourselves, cou'd have been compleated into the thing itself; because, shou'd that be deny'd, we find, upon a second trial, that it can. But these efforts are all in vain; and whatever capricious and irregular actions we may perform; as the desire of showing our liberty is the sole motive of our actions; we can never free ourselves from the bonds of necessity. We may imagine we feel a liberty within ourselves; but a spectator can commonly infer our actions from our motives and character; and even where he cannot, he concludes in general, that he might, were he perfectly acquainted with every circumstance of our situation and temper, and the most secret springs of our complexion and disposition. Now this is the very essence of necessity, according to the foregoing doctrine.

A third reason why the doctrine of liberty has generally been better receiv'd in the world, than its antagonist, proceeds from *religion*, which has been very unnecessarily interested in this question. There is no method of reasoning more common, and yet none more blameable, than in philosophical debates to endeavour to refute any hypothesis by a pretext of its dangerous consequences to religion and morality. When any opinion leads us into absurdities, 'tis certainly false; but 'tis not certain an opinion is false, because 'tis of dangerous consequence. Such topics, therefore, ought entirely to be foreborn, as serving nothing to the discovery of truth, but only to make the person of an antagonist odious. This I observe in general, without pretending to draw any advantage from it. I submit myself frankly to an examination of this kind, and dare venture to affirm, that the doctrine of necessity, according to my explication of it, is not only innocent, but even advantageous to religion and morality.

I define necessity two ways, conformable to the two definitions of cause, of which it makes an essential part. I place it either in the constant union and conjunction of like objects, or in the inference of the mind from the one to the other. Now necessity, in both these senses, has universally, tho' tacitely, in the schools, in the pulpit, and in common life, been allow'd to belong to the will of man, and no one has ever pretended to deny, that we can draw inferences concerning human actions, and that those inferences are founded on the experienc'd union of like actions with like motives and circumstances. The only particular in which any one can differ from me, is either, that perhaps he will refuse to call this necessity. But as long as the meaning is understood, I hope the word can do no harm. Or that he will maintain there is something else in the operations of matter. Now whether it be so or not is of no consequence to religion, whatever it may be to natural philosophy. I may be mistaken in asserting, that we have no idea of any other connexion in the actions of body, and shall be glad to be farther instructed on that head: But sure I am, I ascribe nothing to the actions of the mind, but what must readily be allow'd of. Let no one, therefore, put an invidious construction on my words, by saying simply, that I assert the necessity of human actions, and place them on the same footing with the operations of senseless matter. I do not ascribe to the will that unintelligible necessity, which is suppos'd to lie in matter. But I ascribe to matter, that intelligible quality, call it necessity or not, which the most rigorous orthodoxy does or must allow to belong to the will. I change, therefore, nothing in the receiv'd systems, with regard to the will, but only with regard to material objects.

Nay I shall go farther, and assert, that this kind of necessity is so essential to religion and morality, that without it there must ensue an absolute subversion of both, and that every other supposition is entirely destructive to all laws both *divine* and *human*. 'Tis indeed certain, that as all human laws are founded on rewards and punishments, 'tis suppos'd as a fundamental principle, that these motives have an influence on the mind, and both produce the good and prevent the evil actions. We may give to this influence what name we please; but as 'tis usually conjoin'd with the action, common sense requires it shou'd be esteem'd a cause, and be look'd upon as an instance of that necessity, which I wou'd establish.

This reasoning is equally solid, when apply'd to *divine* laws, so far as the deity is consider'd as a legislator, and is suppos'd to inflict punishment and bestow rewards with a design to produce obedience. But I also maintain, that even where he acts not in his magisterial capacity, but is regarded as the avenger of crimes merely on account of their odiousness and deformity, not only 'tis impossible, without the necessary connexion of cause and effect in human actions, that punishments cou'd be inflicted compatible with justice and moral equity; but also that it cou'd ever enter into the thoughts of any reasonable being to inflict them. The constant and universal object of hatred or anger is a person or creature endow'd with thought and consciousness; and when any criminal or injurious actions excite that passion, 'tis only by their relation to the person or connexion with him. But according to the doctrine of liberty or chance, this connexion is reduc'd to nothing, nor are men more accountable for those actions, which are design'd and premeditated, than for such as are the most casual and accidental. Actions are by their very nature temporary and perishing; and where they proceed not from some cause in the characters and disposition of the person, who perform'd them, they infix not themselves upon him, and can neither redound to his honour, if good, nor infamy, if evil. The action itself may be blameable; it may be contrary to all the rules of morality and religion: But the person is not responsible for it; and as it proceeded from nothing in him, that is durable or constant, and leaves nothing of that nature behind it, 'tis impossible he can, upon its account, become the object of punishment or vengeance. According to the hypothesis of liberty, therefore, a man is as pure and untainted, after having committed the most horrid crimes, as at the first moment of his birth, nor is his character any way concern'd in his actions; since they are not deriv'd from it, and the wickedness of the one can never be us'd as a proof of the depravity of the other. 'Tis only upon the principles of necessity, that a person acquires any merit or demerit from his actions, however the common opinion may incline to the contrary.

But so inconsistent are men with themselves, that tho' they often assert, that necessity utterly destroys all merit and demerit either towards mankind or superior powers, yet they continue still to reason upon these very principles of necessity in all their judgments concerning this matter. Men are not blam'd for such evil actions as they perform ignorantly and casually, whatever may be their consequences. Why? but because the causes of these actions are only momentary, and terminate in them alone. Men are less blam'd for such evil actions, as they perform hastily and unpremeditately, than for such as proceed from thought and deliberation. For what reason? but because a hasty temper, tho' a constant cause in the mind, operates only by intervals, and infects not the whole character. Again, repentance wipes off every crime, especially if attended with an evident reformation of life and manners. How is this to be accounted for? But by asserting that actions render a person criminal, merely as they are proofs of criminal passions or principles in the mind; and when by any alteration of these principles they cease to be just proofs, they likewise cease to be criminal. But according to the doctrine of *liberty* or *chance* they never were just proofs, and consequently never were criminal.

Here then I turn to my adversary, and desire him to free his own system from these odious consequences before he charge them upon others. Or if he rather chuses, that this question shou'd be decided by fair arguments before philosophers, than by declamations before the people, let him return to what I have advanc'd to prove that liberty and chance are synonimous; and concerning the nature of moral evidence and the regularity of human actions. Upon a review of these reasonings, I cannot doubt of an entire victory; and therefore having prov'd, that all actions of the will have particular causes, I proceed to explain what these causes are, and how they operate.

SECT. III

Of the influencing motives of the will

NOTHING is more usual in philosophy, and even in common life, than to talk of the combat of passion and reason, to give the preference to reason, and assert that men are only so far virtuous as they conform themselves to its dictates. Every rational creature, 'tis said, is oblig'd to regulate his actions by reason; and if any other motive or principle challenge the direction of his conduct, he ought to oppose it, 'till it be entirely subdu'd, or at least brought to a conformity with that superior principle. On this method of thinking the greatest part of moral philosophy, antient and modern, seems to be founded; nor is there an ampler field, as well for metaphysical arguments, as popular declamations, than this suppos'd pre-eminence of reason above passion. The eternity, invariableness, and divine origin of the former have been display'd to the best advantage: The blindness, unconstancy, and deceitfulness of the latter have been as strongly insisted on. In order to shew the fallacy of all this philosophy, I shall endeavour to prove *first*, that reason alone can never be a motive to any action of the will; and *secondly,* that it can never oppose passion in the direction of the will.

The understanding exerts itself after two different ways, as it judges from demonstration or probability; as it regards the abstract relations of our ideas, or those relations of objects, of which experience only gives us information. I believe it scarce will be asserted, that the first species of reasoning alone is ever the cause of any action. As its proper province is the world of ideas, and as the will always places us in that of realities, demonstration and volition seem, upon that account, to be totally remov'd, from each other. Mathematics, indeed, are useful in all mechanical operations, and arithmetic in almost every art and profession: But 'tis not of themselves they have any influence: Mechanics are the art of regulating the motions of bodies to *some design'd end or purpose*; and the reason why we employ arithmetic in fixing the proportions of numbers, is only that we may discover the proportions of their influence and operation. A merchant is desirous of knowing the sum total of his accounts with any person: Why? but that he may learn what sum will have the same *effects* in paying his debt, and going to market, as all the particular articles taken together. Abstract or demonstrative reasoning, therefore, never influences any of our actions, but only as it directs our judgment concerning causes and effects; which leads us to the second operation of the understanding.

'Tis obvious, that when we have the prospect of pain or pleasure from any object, we feel a consequent emotion of aversion or propensity, and are carry'd to avoid or embrace what will give us this uneasines or satisfaction. 'Tis also obvious, that this emotion rests not here, but making us cast our view on every side, comprehends whatever objects are connected with its original one by the relation of cause and effect. Here then reasoning takes place to discover this relation; and according as our reasoning varies, our actions receive a subsequent variation. But 'tis evident in this case that the impulse arises not from reason, but is only directed by it. 'Tis from the prospect of pain or pleasure that the aversion or propensity arises towards any object: And these emotions extend themselves to the causes and effects of that object, as they are pointed out to us by reason and experience. It can never in the least concern us to know, that such objects are causes, and such others effects, if both the causes and effects be indifferent to us. Where the objects themselves do not affect us, their connexion can never give them any influence; and 'tis plain, that as reason is nothing but the discovery of this connexion, it cannot be by its means that the objects are able to affect us.

Since reason alone can never produce any action, or give rise to volition, I infer, that the same faculty is as incapable of preventing volition, or of disputing the preference with any passion or emotion. This consequence is necessary. 'Tis impossible reason cou'd have the latter effect of preventing volition, but by giving an impulse in a contrary direction to our passion; and that impulse, had it operated alone, wou'd have been able to produce volition. Nothing can oppose or retard the impulse of passion, but a contrary impulse; and if this contrary impulse ever arises from reason, that latter faculty must have an original influence on the will, and must be able to cause, as well as hinder any act of volition. But if reason has no original influence, 'tis impossible it can withstand any principle, which has such an efficacy, or ever keep the mind in suspence a moment. Thus it appears, that the principle, which opposes our passion, cannot be the same with reason, and is only call'd so in an improper sense. We speak not strictly and philosophically when we talk of the combat of passion and of reason. Reason is, and ought only to be the slave of the passions, and can never pretend to any other office than to serve and obey them. As this opinion may appear somewhat extraordinary, it may not be improper to confirm it by some other considerations.

A passion is an original existence, or, if you will, modification of existence, and contains not any representative quality, which renders it a copy of any other existence or modification. When I am angry, I am actually possest with the passion, and in that emotion have no more a reference to any other object, than when I am thirsty, or sick, or more than five foot high. 'Tis impossible, therefore, that this passion can be oppos'd by, or be contradictory to truth and reason; since this contradiction consists in the disagreement of ideas, consider'd as copies, with those objects, which they represent.

What may at first occur on this head, is, that as nothing can be contrary to truth or reason, except what has a reference to it, and as the judgments of our understanding only have this reference, it must follow, that passions can be contrary to reason only so far as they are *accompany'd* with some judgment or opinion. According to this principle, which is so obvious and natural, 'tis only in two senses, that any affection can be call'd unreasonable. First, When a passion, such as hope or fear, grief or joy, despair or security, is founded on the supposition or the existence of objects, which really do not exist. Secondly, When in exerting any passion in action, we chuse means insufficient for the design'd end, and deceive ourselves in our judgment of causes and effects. Where a passion is neither founded on false suppositions, nor chuses means insufficient for the end, the understanding can neither justify nor condemn it. 'Tis not contrary to reason to prefer the destruction of the whole world to the scratching of my finger. 'Tis not contrary to reason for me to chuse my total ruin, to prevent the least uneasiness of an *Indian* or person wholly unknown to me. 'Tis as little contrary to reason to prefer even my own acknowledge'd lesser good to my greater, and have a more ardent affection for the former than the latter. A trivial good may, from certain circumstances, produce a desire superior to what arises from the greatest and most valuable enjoyment; nor is there any thing more extraordinary in this, than in mechanics to see one pound weight raise up a hundred by the advantage of its situation. In short, a passion must be accompany'd with some false judgment, in order to its being unreasonable; and even then 'tis not the passion, properly speaking, which is unreasonable, but the judgment.

The consequences are evident. Since a passion can never, in any sense, be call'd unreasonable, but when founded on a false supposition, or when it chuses means insufficient for the design'd end, 'tis impossible, that reason and passion can ever oppose each other, or dispute for the government of the will and actions. The moment we perceive the falshood of any supposition, or the insufficiency of any means our passions yield to our reason without any opposition. I may desire any fruit as of an excellent relish; but whenever you convince me of my mistake, my longing ceases. I may will the performance of certain actions as means of obtaining any desir'd good; but as my willing of these actions is only secondary, and founded on the supposition, that they are causes of the propos'd effect; as soon as I discover the falshood of that supposition, they must become indifferent to me.

'Tis natural for one, that does not examine objects with a strict philosophic eye, to imagine, that those actions of the mind are entirely the same, which produce not a different sensation, and are not immediately distinguishable to the feeling and perception. Reason, for instance, exerts itself without producing any sensible emotion; and except in the more sublime disquisitions of philosophy, or in the frivolous subtilties of the school, scarce ever conveys any pleasure or uneasiness. Hence it proceeds, that every action of the mind, which operates with the same calmness and tranquillity, is confounded with reason by all those, who judge of things from the first view and appearance. Now 'tis certain, there are certain calm desires and tendencies, which, tho' they be real passions, produce little emotion in the mind, and are more known by their effects than by the immediate feeling or sensation. These desires are of two kinds; either certain instincts originally implanted in our natures, such as benevolence and resentment, the love of life, and kindness to children; or the general appetite to good, and aversion to evil, consider'd merely as such. When any of these passions are calm, and cause no disorder in the soul, they are very readily taken for the determinations of reason, and are suppos'd to proceed from the same faculty, with that, which judges of truth and falshood. Their nature and principles have been suppos'd the same, because their sensations are not evidently different.

Beside these calm passions, which often determine the will, there are certain violent emotions of the same kind, which have likewise a great influence on that faculty. When I receive any injury from another, I often feel a violent passion of resentment, which makes me desire his evil and punishment, independent of all considerations of pleasure and advantage to myself. When I am immediately threaten'd with any grievous ill, my fears, apprehensions, and aversions rise to a great height, and produce a sensible emotion.

The common error of metaphysicians has lain in ascribing the direction of the will entirely to one of these principles, and supposing the other to have no influence. Men often act knowingly against their interest: For which reason the view of the greatest possible good does not always influence them. Men often counter-act a violent passion in prosecution of their interests and designs: 'Tis not therefore the present uneasiness alone, which determines them. In general we may observe, that both these principles operate on the will; and where they are contrary, that either of them prevails, according to the *general* character or *present* disposition of the person. What we call strength of mind, implies the prevalence of the calm passions above the violent; tho' we may easily observe, there is no man so constantly possess'd of this virtue, as never on any occasion to yield to the sollicitations of passion and desire. From these variations of temper proceeds the great difficulty of deciding concerning the actions and resolutions of men, where there is any contrariety of motives and passions.

SECT. IV

Of the causes of the violent passions

THERE is not in philosophy a subject of more nice speculation than this of the different *causes* and *effects* of the calm and violent passions. 'Tis evident passions influence not the will in proportion to their violence, or the disorder they occasion in the temper; but on the contrary, that when a passion has once become a settled principle of action, and is the predominant inclination of the soul, it commonly produces no longer any sensible agitation. As repeated custom and its own force have made every thing yield to it, it directs the actions and conduct without that opposition and emotion, which so naturally attend every momentary gust of passion. We must, therefore, distinguish betwixt a calm and a weak passion; betwixt a violent and a strong one. But notwithstanding this, 'tis certain, that when we wou'd govern a man, and push him to any action, 'twill commonly be better policy to work upon the violent than the calm passions, and rather take him by his inclination, than what is vulgarly call'd his *reason*. We ought to place the object in such particular situations as are proper to encrease the violence of the passion. For we may observe, that all depends upon the situation of the object, and that a variation in this particular will be able to change the calm and the violent passions into each other. Both these kinds of passions pursue good, and avoid evil; and both of them are encreas'd or diminish'd by the encrease or diminution of the good or evil. But herein lies the difference betwixt them: The same good, when near, will cause a violent passion, which, when remote, produces only a calm one. As this subject belongs very properly to the present question concerning the will, we shall here examine it to the bottom, and shall consider some of those circumstances and situations of objects, which render a passion either calm or violent.

'Tis a remarkable property of human nature, that any emotion, which attends a passion, is easily converted into it, tho' in their natures they be originally different from, and even contrary to each other. 'Tis true; in order to make a perfect union among passions, there is always requir'd a double relation of impressions and ideas; nor is one relation sufficient for that purpose. But tho' this be confirmed by undoubted experience, we must understand it with its proper limitations, and must regard the double relation, as requisite only to make one passion produce another. When two passions are already produc'd by their separate causes, and are both present in the mind, they readily mingle and unite, tho' they have but one relation, and sometimes without any. The predominant passion swallows up the inferior, and converts it into itself. The spirits, when once excited, easily receive a change in their direction; and 'tis natural to imagine this change will come from the prevailing affection. The connexion is in many respects closer betwixt any two passions, than betwixt any passion and indifference.

When a person is once heartily in love, the little faults and caprices of his mistress, the jealousies and quarrels, to which that commerce is so subject; however unpleasant and related to anger and hatred; are yet found to give additional force to the prevailing passion. 'Tis a common artifice of politicians, when they wou'd affect any person very much by a matter of fact, of which they intend to inform him, first to excite his curiosity; delay as long as possible the satisfying it; and by that means raise his anxiety and impatience to the utmost, before they give him a full insight into the business. They know that his curiosity will precipitate him into the passion they design to raise, and assist the object in its influence on the mind. A soldier advancing to the battle, is naturally inspir'd with courage and confidence, when he thinks on his friends and fellow-soldiers; and is struck with fear and terror, when he reflects on the enemy. Whatever new emotion, therefore, proceeds from the former naturally encreases the courage; as the same emotion, proceeding from the latter, augments the fear; by the relation of ideas, and the conversion of the inferior emotion into the predominant. Hence it is that in martial discipline, the uniformity and lustre of our habit, the regularity of our figures and motions, with all the pomp and majesty of war, encourage ourselves and allies; while the same objects in the enemy strike terror into us, tho' agreeable and beautiful in themselves.

Since passions, however independent, are naturally transfus'd into each other, if they are both present at the same time; it follows, that when good or evil is plac'd in such a situation, as to cause any particular emotion, beside its direct passion of desire or aversion, that latter passion must acquire new force and violence.

This happens, among other cases, whenever any object excites contrary passions. For 'tis observable that an opposition of passions commonly causes a new emotion in the spirits, and produces more disorder, than the concurrence of any two affections of equal force. This new emotion is easily converted into the predominant passion, and encreases its violence, beyond the pitch it wou'd have arriv'd at had it met with no opposition. Hence we naturally desire what is forbid, and take a pleasure in performing actions, merely because they are unlawful. The notion of duty, when opposite to the passions, is seldom able to overcome them; and when it fails of that effect, is apt rather to encrease them, by producing an opposition in our motives and principles.

The same effect follows whether the opposition arises from internal motives or external obstacles. The passion commonly acquires new force and violence in both cases. The efforts, which the mind makes to surmount the obstacle, excite the spirits and inliven the passion.

Uncertainty has the same influence as opposition. The agitation of the thought; the quick turns it makes from one view to another; the variety of passions, which succeed each other, according to the different views; All these produce an agitation in the mind, and transfuse themselves into the predominant passion.

There is not in my opinion any other natural cause, why security diminishes the passions, than because it removes that uncertainty, which encreases them. The mind, when left to itself, immediately languishes; and in order to preserve its ardour, must be every moment supported by a new flow of passion. For the same reason, despair, tho' contrary to security, has a like influence.

'Tis certain nothing more powerfully animates any affection, than to conceal some part of its object by throwing it into a kind of shade, which at the same time that it shews enough to pre-possess us in favour of the object, leaves still some work for the imagination. Besides that obscurity is always attended with a kind of uncertainty; the effort, which the fancy makes to compleat the idea, rouzes the spirits, and gives an additional force to the passion.

As despair and security, tho' contrary to each other, produce the same effects; so absence is observ'd to have contrary effects, and in different circumstances either encreases or diminishes our affections. The *Duc de la Rochefoucault* has very well observ'd, that absence destroys weak passions, but encreases strong; as the wind extinguishes a candle, but blows up a fire. Long absence naturally weakens our idea, and diminishes the passion: But where the idea is so strong and lively as to support itself, the uneasiness, arising from absence, encreases the passion, and gives it new force and violence.

SECT. V

Of the effects of custom

But nothing has a greater effect both to encrease and diminish our passions, to convert pleasure into pain, and pain into pleasure, than custom and repetition. Custom has two *original* effects upon the mind, in bestowing a *facility* in the performance of any action or the conception of any object; and afterwards a *tendency or inclination* towards it; and from these we may account for all its other effects, however extraordinary.

When the soul applies itself to the performance of any action, or the conception of any object, to which it is not accustom'd, there is a certain unpliableness in the faculties, and a difficulty of the spirit's moving in their new direction. As this difficulty excites the spirits, 'tis the source of wonder, surprize, and of all the emotions, which arise from novelty; and is in itself very agreeable, like every thing, which inlivens the mind to a moderate degree. But tho' surprize be agreeable in itself, yet as it puts the spirits in agitation, it not only augments our agreeable affections, but also our painful, according to the foregoing principle, *that every emotion, which precedes or attends a passion, is easily converted into it.* Hence every thing, that is new, is most affecting, and gives us either more pleasure or pain, than what, strictly speaking, naturally belongs to it. When it often returns upon us, the novelty wears off; the passions subside; the hurry of the spirits is over; and we survey the objects with greater tranquillity.

By degrees the repetition produces a facility of the human mind, and an infallible source of pleasure, where the facility goes not beyond a certain degree. And here 'tis remarkable that the pleasure, which arises from a moderate facility, has not the same tendency with that which arises from novelty, to augment the painful, as well as the agreeable affections. The pleasure of facility does not so much consist in any ferment of the spirits, as in their orderly motion; which will sometimes be so powerful as even to convert pain into pleasure, and give us a relish in time what at first was most harsh and disagreeable.

But again, as facility converts pain into pleasure, so it often converts pleasure into pain, when it is too great, and renders the actions of the mind so faint and languid, that they are no longer able to interest and support it. And indeed, scarce any other objects become disagreeable thro' custom; but such as are naturally attended with some emotion or affection, which is destroy'd by the too frequent repetition.

One can consider the clouds, and heavens, and trees, and stones, however frequently repeated, without ever feeling any aversion. But when the fair sex, or music, or good cheer, or any thing, that naturally ought to be agreeable, becomes indifferent, it easily produces the opposite affection.

But custom not only gives a facility to perform any action, but likewise an inclination and tendency towards it, where it is not entirely disagreeable, and can never be the object of inclination. And this is the reason why custom encreases all *active* habits, but diminishes *passive*, according to the observation of a late eminent philosopher. The facility takes off from the force of the passive habits by rendering the motion of the spirits faint and languid. But as in the active, the spirits are sufficiently supported of themselves, the tendency of the mind gives them new force, and bends them more strongly to the action.

SECT. VI

Of the influence of the imagination on the passions

'Tis remarkable, that the imagination and affections have close union together, and that nothing, which affects the former, can be entirely indifferent to the latter. Wherever our ideas of good or evil acquire a new vivacity, the passions become more violent; and keep pace with the imagination in all its variations. Whether this proceeds from the principle above-mention'd, *that any attendant emotion is easily converted into the predominant*, I shall not determine. 'Tis sufficient for my present purpose, that we have many instances to confirm this influence of the imagination upon the passions.

Any pleasure, with which we are acquainted, affects us more than any other, which we own to be superior, but of whose nature we are wholly ignorant. Of the one we can form a particular and determinate idea: The other we conceive under the general notion of pleasure; and 'tis certain, that the more general and universal any of our ideas are, the less influence they have upon the imagination. A general idea, tho' it be nothing but a particular one consider'd in a certain view, is commonly more obscure; and that because no particular idea, by which we represent a general one, is ever fix'd or determinate, but may easily be chang'd for other particular ones, which will serve equally in the representation.

There is a noted passage in the history of *Greece*, which may serve for our present purpose. *Themistocles* told the *Athenians*, that he had form'd a design, which wou'd be highly useful to the public, but which 'twas impossible for him to communicate to them without ruining the execution, since its success depended entirely on the secrecy with which it shou'd be conducted. The *Athenians*, instead of granting him full power to act as he thought fitting, order'd him to communicate his design to *Aristides*, in whose prudence they had an entire confidence, and whose opinion they were resolv'd blindly to submit to. The design of *Themistocles* was secretly to set fire to the fleet of all the *Grecian* commonwealths, which was assembled in a neighbouring port, and which being once destroy'd wou'd give the *Athenians* the empire of the sea without any rival. *Aristides* return'd to the assembly, and told them, that nothing cou'd be more advantageous than the design of *Themistocles*; but at the same time that nothing cou'd be more unjust: Upon which the people unanimously rejected the project.

A late celebrated * historian admires this passage of antient history, as one of the most singular that is any where to be met.

'Here,' says he, 'they are not philosophers, to whom 'tis easy in their schools to establish the finest maxims and most sublime rules of morality, who decide that interest ought never to prevail above justice. 'Tis a whole people interested in the proposal, which is made to them, who consider it as of importance to the

* Mons. *Rollin* [Charles Rollin, *Histoire Ancienne* (*Paris* 1730–38)].

public good, and who notwithstanding reject it unanimously, and without hesitation, merely because it is contrary to justice.'

For my part I see nothing so extraordinary in this proceeding of the *Athenians*. The same reasons, which render it so easy for philosophers to establish these sublime maxims, tend, in part, to diminish the merit of such a conduct in that people. Philosophers never ballance betwixt profit and honesty, because their decisions are general, and neither their passions nor imaginations are interested in the objects. And tho' in the present case the advantage was immediate to the *Athenians*, yet as it was known only under the general notion of advantage, without being conceiv'd by any particular idea, it must have had a less considerable influence on their imaginations, and have been a less violent temptation, than if they had been acquainted with all its circumstances: Otherwise 'tis difficult to conceive, that a whole people, unjust and violent as men commonly are, shou'd so unanimously have adher'd to justice, and rejected any considerable advantage.

Any satisfaction, which we lately enjoy'd, and of which the memory is fresh and recent, operates on the will with more violence, than another of which the traces are decay'd, and almost obliterated. From whence does this proceed, but that the memory in the first case assists the fancy, and gives an additional force and vigour to its conceptions? The image of the past pleasure being strong and violent, bestows these qualities on the idea of the future pleasure, which is connected with it by the relation of resemblance.

A pleasure, which is suitable to the way of life, in which we are engag'd, excites more our desires and appetites than another, which is foreign to it. This phaenomenon may be explain'd from the same principle.

Nothing is more capable of infusing any passion into the mind, than eloquence, by which objects are represented in their strongest and most lively colours. We may of ourselves acknowledge, that such an object is valuable, and such another odious; but 'till an orator excites the imagination, and gives force to these ideas, they may have but a feeble influence either on the will or the affections.

But eloquence is not always necessary. The bare opinion of another, especially when inforc'd with passion, will cause an idea of good or evil to have an influence upon us, which wou'd otherwise have been entirely neglected. This proceeds from the principle of sympathy or communication; and sympathy, as I have already observ'd, is nothing but the conversion of an idea into an impression by the force of imagination.

'Tis remarkable, that lively passions commonly attend a lively imagination. In this respect, as well as others, the force of the passion depends as much on the temper of the person, as the nature or situation of the object.

I have already observ'd, that belief is nothing but a lively idea related to a present impression. This vivacity is a requisite circumstance to the exciting all our passions, the calm as well as the violent; nor has a mere fiction of the imagination any considerable influence upon either of them. 'Tis too weak to take hold of the mind, or be attended with emotion.

SECT. VII

Of contiguity and distance in space and time

THERE is an easy reason, why every thing contiguous to us, either in space or time, shou'd be conceiv'd with a peculiar force and vivacity, and excel every other object, in its influence on the imagination. Ourself is intimately present to us, and whatever is related to self must partake of that quality. But where an object is so far remov'd as to have lost the advantage of this relation, why, as it is farther remov'd, its idea becomes still fainter and more obscure, wou'd, perhaps, require a more particular examination.

'Tis obvious, that the imagination can never totally forget the points of space and time, in which we are existent; but receives such frequent advertisements of them from the passions and senses, that however it may turn its attention to foreign and remote objects, it is necessitated every moment to reflect on the present. 'Tis also remarkable, that in the conception of those objects, which we regard as real and existent, we take them in their proper order and situation, and never leap from one object to another, which is distant from it, without running over, at least in a cursory manner, all those objects, which are interpos'd betwixt them. When we reflect, therefore, on any object distant from ourselves, we are oblig'd not only to reach it at first by passing thro' all the intermediate space betwixt ourselves and the object, but also to renew our progress every moment; being every moment recall'd to the consideration of ourselves and our present situation. 'Tis easily conceiv'd, that this interruption must weaken the idea by breaking the action of the mind, and hindering the conception from being so intense and continu'd, as when we reflect on a nearer object. The *fewer* steps we make to arrive at the object, and the *smoother* the road is, this diminution of vivacity is less sensibly felt, but still may be observ'd more or less in proportion to the degrees of distance and difficulty.

Here then we are to consider two kinds of objects, the contiguous and remote; of which the former, by means of their relation to ourselves, approach an impression in force and vivacity; the latter by reason of the interruption in our manner of conceiving them, appear in a weaker and more imperfect light. This is their effect on the imagination. If my reasoning be just, they must have a proportionable effect on the will and passions. Contiguous objects must have an influence much superior to the distant and remote. Accordingly we find in common life, that men are principally concern'd about those objects, which are not much remov'd either in space or time, enjoying the present, and leaving what is afar off to the care of chance and fortune. Talk to a man of his condition thirty years hence, and he will not regard you. Speak of what is to happen tomorrow, and he will lend you attention. The breaking of a mirror gives us more concern when at home, than the burning of a house, when abroad, and some hundred leagues distant.

But farther; tho' distance both in space and time has a considerable effect on the imagination, and by that means on the will and passions, yet the consequence of a removal in *space* are much inferior to those of a removal in *time*. Twenty years are certainly but a small distance of time in comparison of what history and even the memory of some may inform them of, and yet I doubt if a thousand leagues, or even the greatest distance of place this globe can admit of, will so remarkably weaken our ideas, and diminish our passions. A *West-Indian* merchant will tell you, that he is not without concern about what passes in *Jamaica*; tho' few extend their views so far into futurity, as to dread very remote accidents.

The cause of this phaenomenon must evidently lie in the different properties of space and time. Without having recourse to metaphysics, any one may easily observe, that space or extension consists of a number of co-existent parts dispos'd in a certain order, and capable of being at once present to the sight or feeling. On the contrary, time or succession, tho' it consists likewise of parts, never presents to us more than one at once; nor is it possible for any two of them ever to be co-existent. These qualities of the objects have a suitable effect on the imagination. The parts of extension being susceptible of an union to the senses, acquire an union in the fancy; and as the appearance of one part excludes not another, the transition or passage of the thought thro' the contiguous parts is by that means render'd more smooth and easy. On the other hand, the incompatibility of the parts of time in their real existence separates them in the imagination, and makes it more *difficult* for that faculty to trace any long succession or series of events. Every part must appear single and alone, nor can regularly have entrance into the fancy without banishing what is suppos'd to have been immediately precedent. By this means any distance in time causes a greater interruption in the thought than an equal distance in space, and consequently weakens more considerably the idea, and consequently the passions; which depend in a great measure, on the imagination, according to my system.

There is another phaenomenon of a like nature with the foregoing, viz, *the superior effects of the same distance in futurity above that in the past.* This difference with respect to the will is easily accounted for. As none of our actions can alter the past, 'tis not strange it shou'd never determine the will. But with respect to the passions the question is yet entire, and well worth the examining.

Besides the propensity to a gradual progression thro' the points of space and time, we have another peculiarity in our method of thinking, which concurs in producing this phaenomenon. We always follow the succession of time in placing our ideas, and from the consideration of any object pass more easily to that, which follows immediately after it, than to that which went before it. We may learn this, among other instances, from the order, which is always observ'd in historical narrations. Nothing but an absolute necessity can oblige an historian to break the order of time, and in his *narration* give the precedence to an event, which was in *reality* posterior to another.

This will easily be apply'd to the question in hand, if we reflect on what I have before observ'd, that the present situation of the person is always that of the imagination, and that 'tis from thence we proceed to the conception of any distant object. When the object is past, the progression of the thought in passing to it from the present is contrary to nature, as proceeding from one point of time to that which is preceding, and from that to another preceding, in opposition to the natural course of the succession. On the other hand, when we turn our thought to a future object, our fancy flows along the stream of time, and arrives at the object by an order, which seems most natural, passing always from one point of time to that which is immediately posterior to it. This *easy* progression of ideas favours the imagination, and makes it conceive its object in a stronger and fuller light, than when we are continually oppos'd in our passage, and are oblig'd to overcome the difficulties arising from the natural propensity of the fancy. A small degree of distance in the past has, therefore, a greater effect, in interupting and weakening the conception, than a much greater in the future. From this effect of it on the imagination is deriv'd its influence on the will and passions.

There is another cause, which both contributes to the same effect, and proceeds from the same quality of the fancy, by which we are determin'd to trace the succession of time by a similar succession of ideas. When from the present instant we consider two points of time equally distant in the future and in the past, 'tis evident, that, abstractedly consider'd, their relation to the present is almost equal. For as the future will *sometime* be present, so the past was *once* present. If we cou'd, therefore, remove this quality of the imagination, an equal distance in the past and in the future, wou'd have a similar influence. Nor is this only true, when the fancy remains fix'd, and from the present instant surveys the future and the past; but also when it changes its situation, and places us in different periods of time. For as on the one hand, in supposing ourselves existent in a point of time interpos'd betwixt the present instant and the future object, we find the future object approach to us, and the past retire, and become more distant: so on the other hand, in supposing ourselves existent in a point of time interpos'd betwixt the present and the past, the past approaches to us, and the future becomes more distant. But from the property of the fancy above-mention'd we rather chuse to fix our thought on the point of time interposed betwixt the present and the future, than on that betwixt the present and the past. We advance, rather than retard our existence; and following what seems the natural succession of time, proceed from past to present, and from present to future. By which means we conceive the future as flowing every moment nearer us, and the past as retiring. An equal distance, therefore, in the past and in the future, has not the same effect on the imagination; and that because we consider the one as continually encreasing, and the other as continually diminishing. The fancy anticipates the course of things, and surveys the object in that condition, to which it tends, as well as in that, which is regarded as the present.

SECT. VIII

The same subject continu'd

THUS we have accounted for three phaenomena, which seem pretty remarkable. Why distance weakens the conception and passion: Why distance in time has a greater effect than that in space: And why distance in past time has still a greater effect than that in future. We must now consider three phaenomena, which seem to be, in a manner, the reverse of these: Why a very great distance encreases our esteem and admiration for an object; Why such a distance in time encreases it more than that in space: And a distance in past time more than that in future. The curiousness of the subject will, I hope, excuse my dwelling on it for some time.

To begin with the first phaenomenon, why a great distance encreases our esteem and admiration for an object; 'tis evident that the mere view and contemplation of any greatness, whether successive or extended, enlarges the soul, and give it a sensible delight and pleasure. A wide plain, the ocean, eternity, a succession of several ages; all these are entertaining objects, and excel every thing, however beautiful, which accompanies not its beauty with a suitabie greatness. Now when any very distant object is presented to the imagination, we naturally reflect on the interpos'd distance, and by that means, conceiving something great and magnificent, receive the usual satisfaction. But as the fancy passes easily from one idea to another related to it, and transports to the second all the passions excited by the first, the admiration, which is directed to the distance, naturally diffuses itself over the distant object. Accordingly we find, that 'tis not necessary the object shou'd be actually distant from us, in order to cause our admiration; but that 'tis sufficient, if, by the natural association of ideas, it conveys our view to any considerable distance. A great traveller, tho' in the same chamber, will pass for a very extraordinary person; as a *Greek* medal, even in our cabinet, is always esteem'd a valuable curiosity. Here the object, by a natural transition, conveys our views to the distance; and the admiration, which arises from that distance, by another natural transition, returns back to the object.

But tho' every great distance produces an admiration for the distant object, a distance in time has a more considerable effect than that in space. Antient busts and inscriptions are more valu'd than *Japan* tables: And not to mention the *Greeks* and *Romans*, 'tis certain we regard with more veneration the old *Chaldeans* and *Egyptians*, than the modern *Chinese* and *Persians*, and bestow more fruitless pains to clear up the history and chronology of the former, than it wou'd cost us to make a voyage, and be certainly inform'd of the character, learning and government of the latter. I shall be oblig'd to make a digression in order to explain this phaenomenon.

'Tis a quality very observable in human nature, that any opposition, which does not entirely discourage and intimidate us, has rather a contrary effect, and inspires us with a more than ordinary grandeur and magnanimity. In collecting our force to overcome the opposition, we invigorate the soul, and give it an elevation with which otherwise it wou'd never have been acquainted. Compliance, by rendering our strength useless, makes us insensible of it: but opposition awakens and employs it.

This is also true in the universe. Opposition not only enlarges the soul; but the soul, when full of courage and magnanimity, in a manner seeks opposition.

Spumantemque dari pecora inter inertia votis
Optat aprum, aut fulvum descendere monte leonem.

[And, among the tamer beasts, [he] longs to be granted, in answer to his prayers, a slavering boar, or to have a tawny lion come down from the mountain.]

Whatever supports and fills the passions is agreeable to us; as on the contrary, what weakens and infeebles them is uneasy. As opposition has the first effect, and facility the second, no wonder the mind, in certain dispositions, desires the former, and is averse to the latter.

These principles have an effect on the imagination as well as on the passions. To be convinc'd of this we need only consider the influence of *heights* and *depths* on that faculty. Any great elevation of place communicates a kind of pride or sublimity of imagination, and gives a fancy'd superiority over those that lie below; and, *vice versa,* a sublime and strong imagination conveys the idea of ascent and elevation. Hence it proceeds, that we associate, in a manner, the idea of whatever is good with that of height, and evil with lowness. Heaven is suppos'd to be above, and hell below. A noble genius is call'd an elevate and sublime one. *Atque udam spernit humum fugiente penna.* [Spurns the dank soil in winged flight.] On the contrary, a vulgar and trivial conception is stil'd indifferently low or mean. Prosperity is denominated ascent, and adversity descent. Kings and princes are suppos'd to be plac'd at the top of human affairs; as peasants and day-labourers are said to be in the lowest stations. These methods of thinking, and of expressing ourselves, are not of so little consequence as they may appear at first sight.

'Tis evident to common sense, as well as philosophy, that there is no natural nor essential difference betwixt high and low, and that this distinction arises only from the gravitation of matter, which produces a motion from the one to the other. The very same direction, which in this part of the globe is call'd *ascent*, is denominated *descent* in our antipodes; which can proceed from nothing but the contrary tendency of bodies. Now 'tis certain, that the tendency of bodies, continually operating upon our senses, must produce, from custom, a like tendency in the fancy, and that when we consider any object situated in an ascent, the idea of its weight gives us a propensity to transport it from the place, in which it is situated, to the place immediately below it, and so on, 'till we come to the ground, which equally stops the body and our imagination. For a like reason we feel a difficulty in mounting, and pass not without a kind of reluctance from the inferior to that which is situated above it; as if our ideas acquir'd a kind of gravity from their objects. As a proof of this, do we not find, that the facility, which is so much study'd in music and poetry, is call'd the fall or cadency of the harmony or period; the idea of facility communicating to us that of descent, in the same manner as descent produces a facility?

Since the imagination, therefore, in running from low to high, finds an opposition in its internal qualities and principles, and since the soul, when elevated with joy and courage, in a manner seeks opposition, and throws itself with alacrity into any scene of thought or action, where its courage meets with matter to nourish and employ it; it follows, that everything, which invigorates and inlivens the soul, whether by touching the passions or imagination, naturally conveys to the fancy this inclination for ascent, and determines it to run against the natural stream of its thoughts and conceptions. This aspiring progress of the imagination suits the present disposition of the mind; and the difficulty, instead of extinguishing its vigour and alacrity, has the contrary affect, of sustaining and encreasing it. Virtue, genius, power, and riches are for this reason associated with height and sublimity; as poverty, slavery, and folly are conjoin'd with descent and lowness. Were the case the same with us as *Milton* represents it to be with the angels, to whom *descent is adverse*, and who *cannot sink without labour and compulsion*, this order of things wou'd be entirely inverted; as appears hence, that the very nature of ascent and descent is deriv'd from the difficulty and propensity, and consequently every one of their effects proceeds from that origin.

All this is easily apply'd to the present question, why a considerable distance in time produces a greater veneration for the distant objects than a like removal in space. The imagination moves with more difficulty in passing from one portion of time to another, than in a transition thro' the parts of space; and that because space or extension appears united to our senses, while time or succession is always broken and divided. This difficulty, when join'd with a small distance, interrupts and weakens the fancy: But has a contrary effect in a great removal. The mind, elevated by the vastness of its object, is still farther elevated by the difficulty of the conception; and being oblig'd every moment to renew its efforts in the transition from one part of time to another, feels a more vigorous and sublime disposition, than in a transition thro' the parts of space, where the ideas flow along with easiness and facility. In this disposition, the imagination, passing, as is usual, from the consideration of the distance to the view of the distant objects, gives us a proportionable veneration for it; and this is the reason why all the relicts of antiquity are so precious in our eyes, and appear more valuable than what is brought even from the remotest parts of the world.

The third phaenomenon I have remark'd will be a full confirmation of this. 'Tis not every removal in time, which has the effect of producing veneration and esteem. We are not apt to imagine our posterity will excel us, or equal our ancestors. This phaenomenon is the more remarkable, because any distance in futurity weakens not our ideas so much as an equal removal in the past. Tho' a removal in the past, when very great, encreases our passions beyond a like removal in the future, yet a small removal has a greater influence in diminishing them.

In our common way of thinking we are plac'd in a kind of middle station betwixt the past and future; and as our imagination finds a kind of difficulty in running along the former, and a facility in following the course of the latter, the difficulty conveys the notion of ascent, and the facility of the contrary. Hence we imagine our ancestors to be, in a manner, mounted above us, and our posterity to lie below us. Our fancy arrives not at the one without effort, but easily reaches the other: Which effort weakens the conception, where the distance is small; but enlarges and elevates the imagination, when attended with a suitable object. As on the other hand, the facility assists the fancy in a small removal, but takes off from its force when it contemplates any considerable distance.

It may not be improper, before we leave this subject of the will, to resume, in a few words, all that has been said concerning it, in order to set the whole more distinctly before the eyes of the reader. What we commonly understand by *passion* is a violent and sensible emotion of mind, when any good or evil is presented, or any object, which, by the original formation of our faculties, is fitted to excite an appetite. By *reason* we mean affections of the very same kind with the former; but such as operate more calmly, and cause no disorder in the temper: Which tranquillity leads us into a mistake concerning them, and causes us to regard them as conclusions only of our intellectual faculties. Both the *causes* and *effects* of these violent and calm passions are pretty variable, and depend, in a great measure, on the peculiar temper and disposition of every individual. Generally speaking, the violent passions have a more powerful influence on the will; tho' 'tis often found, that the calm ones, when corroborated by reflection, and seconded by resolution, are able to controul them in their most furious movements. What makes this whole affair more uncertain, is, that a calm passion may easily be chang'd into a violent one, either by a change of temper, or of the circumstances and situation of the object, as by the borrowing of force from any attendant passion, by custom, or by exciting the imagination. Upon the whole, this struggle of passion and of reason, as it is call'd, diversifies human life, and makes men so different not only from each other, but also from themselves in different times. Philosophy can only account for a few of the greater and more sensible events of this war; but must leave all the smaller and more delicate revolutions, as dependent on principles too fine and minute for her comprehension.

SECT. IX

Of the direct passions

'TIS easy to observe, that the passions, both direct and indirect, are founded on pain and pleasure, and that in order to produce an affection of any kind, 'tis only requisite to present some good or evil. Upon the removal of pain and pleasure there immediately follows a removal of love and hatred, pride and humility, desire and aversion, and of most of our reflective or secondary impressions.

The impressions, which arise from good and evil most naturally, and with the least preparation are the *direct* passions of desire and aversion, grief and joy, hope and fear, along with volition. The mind by an *original* instinct tends to unite itself with the good, and to avoid the evil, tho' they be conceiv'd merely in idea, and be consider'd as to exist in any future period of time.

But supposing that there is an immediate impression of pain or pleasure, and *that* arising from an object related to ourselves or others, this does not prevent the propensity or aversion, with the consequent emotions, but by concurring with certain dormant principles of the human mind, excites the new impressions of pride or humility, love or hatred. That propensity, which unites us to the object, or separates us from it, still continues to operate, but in conjunction with the *indirect* passions, which arise from a double relation of impressions and ideas.

These indirect passions, being always agreeable or uneasy, give in their turn additional force to the direct passions, and encrease our desire and aversion to the object. Thus a suit of fine cloaths produces pleasure from their beauty; and this pleasure produces the direct passions, or the impressions of volition and desire. Again, when these cloaths are consider'd as belonging to ourself, the double relation conveys to us the sentiment of pride, which is an indirect passion; and the pleasure, which attends that passion, returns back to the direct affections, and gives new force to our desire or volition, joy or hope.

When good is certain or probable, it produces JOY. When evil is in the same situation there arises GRIEF or SORROW.

When either good or evil is uncertain, it gives rise to FEAR or HOPE, according to the degrees of uncertainty on the one side or the other.

DESIRE arises from good consider'd simply, and AVERSION is deriv'd from evil. The WILL exerts itself, when either the good or the absence of the evil may be attain'd by any action of the mind or body.

Beside good and evil, or in other words, pain and pleasure, the direct passions frequently arise from a natural impulse or instinct, which is perfectly unaccountable. Of this kind is the desire of punishment to our enemies, and of happiness to our friends; hunger, lust, and a few other bodily appetites. These passions, properly speaking, produce good and evil, and proceed not from them, like the other affections.

None of the direct affections seem to merit our particular attention, except hope and fear, which we shall here endeavour to account for. 'Tis evident that the very same event, which by its certainty wou'd produce grief or joy, gives always rise to fear or hope, when only probable and uncertain. In order, therefore, to understand the reason why this circumstance makes such a considerable difference, we must reflect on what I have already advanc'd in the preceding book concerning the nature of probability.

Probability arises from an opposition of contrary chances or causes, by which the mind is not allow'd to fix on either side, but is incessantly tost from one to another, and at one moment is determin'd to consider an object as existent, and at another moment as the contrary. The imagination or understanding, call it which you please, fluctuates betwixt the opposite views; and tho' perhaps it may be oftner turn'd to the one side than the other, 'tis impossible for it, by reason of the opposition of causes or chances, to rest on either. The *pro* and *con* of the question alternately prevail; and the mind, surveying the object in its opposite principles, finds such a contrariety as utterly destroys all certainty and establish'd opinion.

Suppose, then, that the object, concerning whose reality we are doubtful, is an object either of desire or aversion, 'tis evident, that, according as the mind turns itself either to the one side or the other, it must feel a momentary impression of joy or sorrow. An object, whose existence we desire, gives satisfaction, when we reflect on those causes, which produce it; and for the same reason excites grief or uneasiness from the opposite consideration: So that as the understanding, in all probable questions, is divided betwixt the contrary points of view, the affections must in the same manner be divided betwixt opposite emotions.

Now if we consider the human mind, we shall find, that with regard to the passions, 'tis not the nature of a wind-instrument of music, which in running over all the notes immediately loses the sound after the breath ceases; but rather resembles a string-instrument, where after each stroke the vibrations still retain some sound, which gradually and insensibly decays. The imagination is extreme quick and agile; but the passions are slow and restive: For which reason, when any object is presented, that affords a variety of views to the one, and emotions to the other; tho' the fancy may change its views with great celerity; each stroke will not produce a clear and distinct note of passion, but the one passion will always be mixt and confounded with the other. According as the probability inclines to good or evil, the passion of joy or sorrow predominates in the composition: Because the nature of probability is to cast a superior number of views or chances on one side; or, which is the same thing, a superior number of returns of one passion; or since the dispers'd passions are collected into one, a superior degree of that passion. That is, in other words, the grief and joy being intermingled with each other, by means of the contrary views of the imagination, produce by their union the passions of hope and fear.

Upon this head there may be started a very curious question concerning that contrariety of passions, which is our present subject. 'Tis observable, that where the objects of contrary passions are presented at once, beside the encrease of the predominant passion (which has been already explain'd, and commonly arises at their first shock or rencounter) it sometimes happens, that both the passions exist successively, and by short intervals; sometimes, that they destroy each other, and neither of them takes place; and sometimes that both of them remain united in the mind. It may, therefore, be ask'd, by what theory we can explain these variations, and to what general principle we can reduce them.

When the contrary passions arise from objects entirely different, they take place alternately, the want of relation in the ideas separating the impressions from each other, and preventing their opposition. Thus when a man is afflicted for the loss of a law-suit, and joyful for the birth of a son, the mind running from the agreeable to the calamitous object, with whatever celerity it may perform this motion, can scarcely temper the one affection with the other, and remain betwixt them in a state of indifference.

It more easily attains that calm situation, when the same event is of a mixt nature, and contains something adverse and something prosperous in its different circumstances. For in that case, both the passions, mingling with each other by means of the relation, become mutually destructive, and leave the mind in perfect tranquility.

But suppose, in the third place, that the object is not a compound of good or evil, but is consider'd as probable or improbable in any degree; in that case I assert, that the contrary passions will both of them be present at once in the soul, and instead of destroying and tempering each other, will subsist together, and produce a third impression or affection by their union. Contrary passions are not capable of destroying each other, except when their contrary movements exactly rencounter, and are opposite in their direction, as well as in the sensation they produce. This exact rencounter depends upon the relations of those ideas, from which they are deriv'd, and is more or less perfect, according to the degrees of the relation. In the case of probability the contrary chances are so far related, that they determine concerning the existence or non-existence of the same object. But this relation is far from being perfect; since some of the chances lie on the side of existence, and others on that of non-existence; which are objects altogether incompatible. 'Tis impossible by one steady view to survey the opposite chances, and the events dependent on them; but 'tis necessary, that the imagination shou'd run alternately from the one to the other. Each view of the imagination produces its peculiar passion, which decays away by degrees, and is follow'd by a sensible vibration after the stroke. The incompatibility of the views keeps the passions from shocking in a direct line, if that expression may be allow'd; and yet their relation is sufficient to mingle their fainter emotions. 'Tis after this manner that hope and fear arise from the different mixture of these opposite passions of grief and joy, and from their imperfect union and conjunction.

Upon the whole, contrary passions succeed each other alternately, when they arise from different objects: They mutually destroy each other, when they proceed from different parts of the same: And they subsist both of them, and mingle together, when they are deriv'd from the contrary and incompatible chances or possibilities, on which any one object depends. The influence of the relations of ideas is plainly seen in this whole affair. If the objects of the contrary passions be totally different, the passions are like two opposite liquors in different bottles, which have no influence on each other. If the objects be intimately connected, the passions are like an *alcali* and an *acid,* which, being mingled, destroy each other. If the relation be more imperfect, and consists in the contradictory views of the same object, the passions are like oil and vinegar, which, however mingled, never perfectly unite and incorporate.

As the hypothesis concerning hope and fear carries its

own evidence along with it, we shall be the more concise in our proofs. A few strong arguments are better than many weak ones.

The passions of fear and hope may arise when the chances are equal on both sides, and no superiority can be discover'd in the one above the other. Nay, in this situation the passions are rather the strongest, as the mind has then the least foundation to rest upon, and is toss'd with the greatest uncertainty. Throw in a superior degree of probability to the side of grief, you immediately see that passion diffuse itself over the composition, and tincture it into fear. Encrease the probability, and by that means the grief, the fear prevails still more and more, till at last it runs insensibly, as the joy continually diminishes, into pure grief. After you have brought it to this situation, diminish the grief, after the same manner that you encreas'd it; by diminishing the probability on that side, and you'll see the passion clear every moment, 'till it changes insensibly into hope; which again runs, after the same manner, by slow degrees, into joy, as you encrease that part of the composition by the encrease of the probability. Are not these as plain proofs, that the passions of fear and hope are mixtures of grief and joy, as in optics 'tis a proof, that a colour'd ray of the sun passing thro' a prism, is a composition of two others, when, as you diminish or encrease the quantity of either, you find it prevail proportionably more or less in the composition? I am sure neither natural nor moral philosophy admits of stronger proofs.

Probability is of two kinds, either when the object is really in itself uncertain, and to be determin'd by chance; or when, tho' the object be already certain, yet 'tis uncertain to our judgment, which finds a number of proofs on each side of the question. Both these kinds of probabilities cause fear and hope; which can only proceed from that property, in which they agree, *viz.* the uncertainty and fluctuation they bestow on the imagination by that contrariety of views, which is common to both.

'Tis a probable good or evil, that commonly produces

hope or fear; because probability, being a wavering and unconstant method of surveying an object, causes naturally a like mixture and uncertainty of passion. But we may observe, that wherever from other causes this mixture can be produc'd, the passions of fear and hope will arise, even tho' there be no probability; which must be allow'd to be a convincing proof of the present hypothesis.

We find that an evil, barely conceiv'd as *possible*, does sometimes produce fear; especially if the evil be very great. A man cannot think of excessive pains and tortures without trembling, if he be in the least danger of suffering them. The smallness of the probability is compensated by the greatness of the evil; and the sensation is equally lively, as if the evil were more probable. One view or glimpse of the former, has the same effect as several of the latter.

But they are not only possible evils, that cause fear, but even some allow'd to be *impossible*; as when we tremble on the brink of a precipice, tho' we know ourselves to be in perfect security, and have it in our choice whether we will advance a step farther. This proceeds from the immediate presence of the evil, which influences the imagination in the same manner as the certainty of it wou'd do; but being encounter'd by the reflection on our security, is immediately retracted, and causes the same kind of passion, as when from a contrariety of chances contrary passions are produc'd.

Evils, that are *certain*, have sometimes the same effect in producing fear, as the possible or impossible. Thus a man in a strong prison well-guarded, without the least means of escape, trembles at the thought of the rack, to which he is sentenc'd. This happens only when the certain evil is terrible and confounding; in which case the mind continually rejects it with horror, while it continually presses in upon the thought. The evil is there fix'd and establish'd, but the mind cannot endure to fix upon it; from which fluctuation and uncertainty there arises a passion of much the same appearance with fear.

But 'tis not only where good or evil is uncertain, as to its *existence*, but also as to its *kind*, that fear or hope arises. Let one be told by a person, whose veracity he cannot doubt of, that one of his sons is suddenly kill'd, 'tis evident the passion this event wou'd occasion, wou'd not settle into pure grief, till he got certain information, which of his sons he had lost. Here there is an evil certain, but the kind of it uncertain. Consequently the fear we feel on this occasion is without the least mixture of joy, and arises merely from the fluctuation of the fancy betwixt its objects. And tho' each side of the question produces here the same passion, yet that passion cannot settle, but receives from the imagination a tremulous and unsteady motion, resembling in its cause, as well as in its sensation, the mixture and contention of grief and joy.

From these principles we may account for a phaenomenon in the passions, which at first sight seems very extraordinary, *viz.* that surprize is apt to change into fear, and every thing that is unexpected affrights us. The most obvious conclusion from this is, that human nature is in general pusillanimous; since upon the sudden appearance of any object we immediately conclude it to be an evil, and without waiting till we can examine its nature, whether it be good or bad, are at first affected with fear. This I say is the most obvious conclusion; but upon farther examination we shall find that the phaenomenon is otherwise to be accounted for. The suddenness and strangeness of an appearance naturally excite a commotion in the mind, like every thing for which we are not prepar'd, and to which we are not accustom'd. This commotion, again, naturally produces a curiosity or inquisitiveness, which being very violent, from the strong and sudden impulse of the object, becomes uneasy, and resembles in its fluctuation and uncertainty, the sensation of fear or the mix'd passions of grief and joy. This image of fear naturally converts into the thing itself, and gives us a real apprehension of evil, as the mind always forms its judgments more from its present disposition than from the nature of its objects.

Thus all kinds of uncertainty have a strong connexion

with fear, even tho' they do not cause any opposition of passions by the opposite views and considerations they present to us. A person, who has left his friend in any malady, will feel more anxiety upon his account, than if he were present, tho' perhaps he is not only incapable of giving him assistance, but likewise of judging of the event of his sickness. In this case, tho' the principal object of the passion, *viz.* the life or death of his friend, be to him equally uncertain when present as when absent; yet there are a thousand little circumstances of his friend's situation and condition, the knowledge of which fixes the idea, and prevents that fluctuation and uncertainty so near ally'd to fear. Uncertainty is, indeed, in one respect as near ally'd to hope as to fear, since it makes an essential part in the composition of the former passion; but the reason, why it inclines not to that side, is, that uncertainty alone is uneasy, and has a relation of impressions to the uneasy passions.

'Tis thus our uncertainty concerning any minute circumstance relating to a person encreases our apprehensions of his death or misfortune. *Horace* has remark'd this phaenomenon.

Ut assidens implumibus pullus avis
Serpentium allapsus timet,
Magis relictis; non, ut adsit, auxili
Latura plus presentibus.

[As a bird, watching over her fledgelings, is more afraid of their being attacked by snakes if she were to leave them – even though, were she to stay, she would not be any more capable of helping them, when they were with her.]

But this principle of the connexion of fear with uncertainty I carry farther, and observe that any doubt produces that passion, even tho' it presents nothing to us on any side but what is good and desireable. A virgin, on her bridal-night goes to bed full of fears and apprehensions, tho' she expects nothing but pleasure of the highest kind, and what she has long wish'd for. The newness and greatness of the event, the confusion of wishes and joys so embarrass the mind, that it knows not on what passion to fix itself; from whence arises a fluttering or unsettledness of the spirits, which being, in some degree, uneasy, very naturally degenerates into fear.

Thus we still find, that whatever causes any fluctuation or mixture of passions, with any degree of uneasiness, always produces fear, or at least a passion so like it, that they are scarcely to be distinguish'd.

I have here confin'd myself to the examination of hope and fear in their most simple and natural situation, without considering all the variations they may receive from the mixture of different views and reflections. *Terror, consternation, astonishment, anxiety*, and other passions of that kind, are nothing but different species and degrees of fear. 'Tis easy to imagine how a different situation of the object, or a different turn of thought, may change even the sensation of a passion; and this may in general account for all the particular sub-divisions of the other affections, as well as of fear. Love may shew itself in the shape of *tenderness, friendship, intimacy, esteem, good-will*, and in many other appearances; which at the bottom are the same affections; and arise from the same causes, tho' with a small variation, which it is not necessary to give any particular account of. 'Tis for this reason I have all along confin'd myself to the principal passion.

The same care of avoiding prolixity is the reason why I wave the examination of the will and direct passions, as they appear in animals; since nothing is more evident, than that they are of the same nature, and excited by the same causes as in human creatures. I leave this to the reader's own observation; desiring him at the same time to consider the additional force this bestows on the present system.

SECT. X

Of curiosity, or the love of truth

But methinks we have been not a little inattentive to run over so many different parts of the human mind, and examine so many passions, without taking once into the consideration that love of truth, which was the first source of all our enquiries. 'Twill therefore be proper, before we leave this subject, to bestow a few reflections on that passion, and shew its origin in human nature. 'Tis an affection of so peculiar a kind, that 'twould have been impossible to have treated of it under any of those heads, which we have examin'd, without danger of obscurity and confusion.

Truth is of two kinds, consisting either in the discovery of the proportions of ideas, consider'd as such, or in the conformity of our ideas of objects to their real existence. 'Tis certain, that the former species of truth, is not desir'd merely as truth, and that 'tis not the justness of our conclusions, which alone gives the pleasure. For these conclusions are equally just, when we discover the equality of two bodies by a pair of compasses, as when we learn it by a mathematical demonstration; and tho' in the one case the proofs be demonstrative, and in the other only sensible, yet generally speaking, the mind acquiesces with equal assurance in the one as in the other. And in an arithmetical operation, where both the truth and the assurance are of the same nature, as in the most profound algebraical problem, the pleasure is very inconsiderable, if rather it does not degenerate into pain: Which is an evident proof, that the satisfaction, which we sometimes receive from the discovery of truth, proceeds not from it, merely as such, but only as endow'd with certain qualities.

The first and most considerable circumstance requisite to render truth agreeable, is the genius and capacity, which is employ'd in its invention and discovery. What is easy and obvious is never valu'd; and even what is *in itself* difficult, if we come to the knowledge of it without difficulty, and without any stretch of thought or judgment, is but little regarded. We love to trace the demonstrations of mathematicians; but shou'd receive small entertainment from a person, who shou'd barely inform us of the proportions of lines and angles, tho' we repos'd the utmost confidence both in his judgment and veracity. In this case 'tis sufficient to have ears to learn the truth. We never are oblig'd to fix our attention or exert our genius; which of all other exercises of the mind is the most pleasant and agreeable.

But tho' the exercise of genius be the principal source of that satisfaction we receive from the sciences, yet I doubt, if it be alone sufficient to give us any considerable enjoyment. The truth we discover must also be of some importance. 'Tis easy to multiply algebraical problems to infinity, nor is there any end in the discovery of the proportions of conic sections; tho' few mathematicians take any pleasure in these researches, but turn their thoughts to what is more useful and important. Now the question is, after what manner this utility and importance operate upon us? The difficulty on this head arises from hence, that many philosophers have consum'd their time, have destroy'd their health, and neglected their fortune, in the search of such truths, as they esteem'd important and useful to the world, tho' it appear'd from their whole conduct and behaviour, that they were not endow'd with any share of public spirit, nor had any concern for the interests of mankind. Were they convinc'd, that their discoveries were of no consequence, they wou'd entirely lose all relish for their studies, and that tho' the consequences be entirely indifferent to them; which seems to be a contradiction.

To remove this contradiction, we must consider, that there are certain desires and inclinations, which go no farther than the imagination, and are rather the faint shadows and images of passions, than any real affections. Thus, suppose a man, who takes a survey of the fortifications of any city; considers their strength and advantages, natural or acquir'd; observes the disposition and contrivance of the bastions, ramparts, mines, and other military works; 'tis plain, that in proportion as all these are fitted to attain their ends he will receive a suitable pleasure and satisfaction. This pleasure, as it arises from the utility, not the form of the objects, can be no other than a sympathy with the inhabitants, for whose security all this art is employ'd; tho' 'tis possible, that this person, as a stranger or an enemy, may in his heart have no kindness for them, or may even entertain a hatred against them.

It may indeed be objected, that such a remote sympathy is a very slight foundation for a passion, and that so much industry and application, as we frequently observe in philosophers, can never be deriv'd from so inconsiderable an original. But here I return to what I have already remark'd, that the pleasure of study conflicts chiefly in the action of the mind, and the exercise of the genius and understanding in the discovery or comprehension of any truth. If the importance of the truth be requisite to compleat the pleasure, 'tis not on account of any considerable addition, which of itself it brings to our enjoyment, but only because 'tis, in some measure, requisite to fix our attention. When we are careless and inattentive, the same action of the understanding has no effect upon us, nor is able to convey any of that satisfaction, which arises from it, when we are in another disposition.

But beside the action of the mind, which is the principal foundation of the pleasure, there is likewise requir'd a degree of success in the attainment of the end, or the discovery of that truth we examine. Upon this head I shall make a general remark, which may be useful on many occasions, *viz.* that where the mind pursues any end with passion; tho' that passion be not deriv'd originally from the end, but merely from the action and pursuit; yet by the natural course of the affections, we acquire a concern for the end itself, and are uneasy under any disappointment we meet with in the pursuit of it. This proceeds from the relation and parallel direction of the passions above-mention'd.

To illustrate all this by a similar instance, I shall observe, that there cannot be two passions more nearly resembling each other, than those of hunting and philosophy, whatever disproportion may at first sight appear betwixt them. 'Tis evident, that the pleasure of hunting conflicts in the action of the mind and body; the motion, the attention, the difficulty, and the uncertainty. 'Tis evident likewise, that these actions must be attended with an idea of utility, in order to their having any effect upon us. A man of the greatest fortune, and the farthest remov'd from avarice, tho' he takes a pleasure in hunting after patridges and pheasants, feels no satisfaction in shooting crows and magpies; and that because he considers the first as fit for the table, and the other as entirely useless. Here 'tis certain, that the utility or importance of itself causes no real passion, but is only requisite to support the imagination; and the same person, who over-looks a ten times greater profit in any other subject, is pleas'd to bring home half a dozen woodcocks or plovers, after having employ'd several hours in hunting after them. To make the parallel betwixt hunting and philosophy more compleat, we may observe, that tho' in both cases the end of our action may in itself be despis'd, yet in the heat of the action we acquire such an attention to this end, that we are very uneasy under any disappointments, and are sorry when we either miss our game, or fall into any error in our reasoning.

If we want another parallel to these affections, we may consider the passion of gaming, which affords a pleasure from the same principles as hunting and philosophy. It has been remark'd, that the pleasure of gaming arises not from interest alone; since many leave a sure gain for this entertainment: Neither is it deriv'd from the game alone; since the same persons have no satisfaction, when they play for nothing: But proceeds from both these causes united, tho' separately they have no effect. 'Tis here, as in certain chymical preparations, where the mixture of two clear and transparent liquids produces a third, which is opaque and colour'd.

The interest, which we have in any game, engages our

attention, without which we can have no enjoyment, either in that or in any other action. Our attention being once engag'd, the difficulty, variety, and sudden reverses of fortune, still farther interest us; and 'tis from that concern our satisfaction arises. Human life is so tiresome a scene, and men generally are of such indolent dispositions, that whatever amuses them, tho' by a passion mixt with pain, does in the main give them a sensible pleasure. And this pleasure is here encreas'd by the nature of the objects, which being sensible, and of a narrow compass, are enter'd into with facility, and are agreeable to the imagination.

The same theory, that accounts for the love of truth in mathematics and algebra, may be extended to morals, politics, natural philosophy, and other studies, where we consider not the other abstract relations of ideas, but their real connexions and existence. But beside the love of knowledge, which displays itself in the sciences, there is a certain curiosity implanted in human nature, which is a passion deriv'd from a quite different principle. Some people have an insatiable desire of knowing the actions and circumstances of their neighbours, tho' their interest be no way concern'd in them, and they must entirely depend on others for their information; in which case there is no room for study or application. Let us search for the reason of this phaenomenon.

It has been prov'd at large, that the influence of belief is at once to inliven and infix any idea in the imagination, and prevent all kind of hesitation and uncertainty about it. Both these circumstances are advantageous. By the vivacity of the idea we interest the fancy, and produce, tho' in a lesser degree, the same pleasure, which arises from a moderate passion. As the vivacity of the idea gives pleasure, so its certainty prevents uneasiness, by fixing one particular idea in the mind, and keeping it from wavering in the choice of its objects. 'Tis a quality of human nature, which is conspicuous on many occasions, and is common both to the mind and body, that too sudden and violent a change is unpleasant to us, and that however any objects may in themselves be indifferent, yet their alteration gives uneasiness. As 'tis the nature of doubt to cause a variation in the thought, and transport us suddenly from one idea to another, it must of consequence be the occasion of pain. This pain chiefly takes place, where interest, relation, or the greatness and novelty of any event interests us in it. 'Tis not every matter of fact, of which we have a curiosity to be inform'd; neither are they such only as we have an interest to know. 'Tis sufficient if the idea strikes on us with such force, and concerns us so nearly, as to give us an uneasiness in its instability and inconstancy. A stranger, when he arrives first at any town, may be entirely indifferent about knowing the history and adventures of the inhabitants; but as he becomes farther acquainted with them, and has liv'd any considerable time among them, he acquires the same curiosity as the natives. When we are reading the history of a nation, we may have an ardent desire of clearing up any doubt or difficulty, that occurs in it; but become careless in such researches, when the ideas of these events are, in a great measure, obliterated.

Facsimile of the title-page of the first edition of Book III (1740). The quotation means 'Constant lover of stern virtue, inquire what virtue is, and demand a pattern of honour.'

A

TREATISE

OF

Human Nature:

BEING

An ATTEMPT to introduce the experimental Method of Reasoning

INTO

MORAL SUBJECTS.

——— *Duræ semper virtutis amator,*
Quære quid est virtus, et posce exemplar honesti.

LUCAN.

WITH AN

APPENDIX.

Wherein some Passages of the foregoing Volumes are illustrated and explain'd.

VOL. III.

OF

MORALS.

LONDON,
Printed for THOMAS LONGMAN, at the *Ship* in *Pater-noster-Row*, MDCCXL.

ADVERTISEMENT

I think it proper to inform the public, that tho' this be a third volume of the Treatise of Human Nature, *yet 'tis in some measure independent of the other two, and requires not that the reader shou'd enter into all the abstract reasonings contain'd in them. I am hopeful it may be understood by ordinary readers, with as little attention as is usually given to any books of reasoning. It must only be observ'd, that I continue to make use of the terms,* impressions *and* ideas, *in the same sense as formerly; and that by impressions I mean our stronger perceptions, such as our sensations, affections and sentiments; and by ideas the fainter perceptions, or the copies of these in the memory and imagination.*

BOOK III

OF MORALS

PART I

Of virtue and vice in general

SECT. I

Moral distinctions not deriv'd from reason

THERE is an inconvenience which attends all abstruse reasoning, that it may silence, without convincing an antagonist, and requires the same intense study to make us sensible of its force, that was at first requisite for its invention. When we leave our closet, and engage in the common affairs of life, its conclusions seem to vanish, like the phantoms of the night on the appearance of the morning; and 'tis difficult for us to retain even that conviction, which we had attain'd with difficulty. This is still more conspicuous in a long chain of reasoning, where we must preserve to the end the evidence of the first propositions, and where we often lose sight of all the most receiv'd maxims, either of philosophy or common life. I am not, however, without hopes, that the present system of philosophy will acquire new force as it advances; and that our reasonings concerning morals will corroborate whatever has been said concerning the *understanding* and the *passions*. Morality is a subject that interests us above all others: We fancy the peace of society to be at stake in every decision concerning it; and 'tis evident, that this concern must make our speculations appear more real and solid, than where the subject is, in a great measure, indifferent to us. What affects us, we conclude can never be a chimera; and as our passion is engag'd on the one side or the other, we naturally think that the question lies within human comprehension; which, in other cases of this nature, we are apt to entertain some doubt of. Without this advantage I never should have ventur'd upon a third volume of such abstruse philosophy, in an age, wherein the greatest part of men seem agreed to convert reading into an amusement, and to reject every thing that requires any considerable degree of attention to be comprehended.

It has been observ'd, that nothing is ever present to the mind but its perceptions; and that all the actions of seeing, hearing, judging, loving, hating, and thinking, fall under this denomination. The mind can never exert itself in any action, which we may not comprehend under the term of *perception;* and consequently that term is no less applicable to those judgments, by which we distinguish moral good and evil, than to every other operation of the mind. To approve of one character, to condemn another, are only so many different perceptions.

Now as perceptions resolve themselves into two kinds, viz. *impressions* and *ideas*, this distinction gives rise to a question, with which we shall open up our present enquiry concerning morals. *Whether 'tis by means of our* ideas *or* impressions *we distinguish betwixt vice and virtue, and pronounce an action blameable or praiseworthy?* This will immediately cut off all loose discourses and declamations, and reduce us to something precise and exact on the present subject.

Those who affirm that virtue is nothing but a conformity to reason; that there are eternal fitnesses and unfitnesses of things, which are the same to every rational being that considers them; that the immutable measures of right and wrong impose an obligation, not only on human creatures, but also on the Deity himself: All these systems concur in the opinion, that morality, like truth, is discern'd merely by ideas, and by their juxta-position and comparison. In order, therefore, to judge of these systems, we need only consider, whether it be possible, from reason alone, to distinguish betwixt moral good and evil, or whether there must concur some other principles to enable us to make that distinction.

If morality had naturally no influence on human passions and actions, 'twere in vain to take such pains to inculcate it; and nothing wou'd be more fruitless than that multitude of rules and precepts, with which all moralists abound. Philosophy is commonly divided into *speculative* and *practical;* and as morality is always comprehended under the latter division, 'tis supposed to influence our passions and actions, and to go beyond the calm and indolent judgments of the understanding. And this is confirm'd by common experience, which informs us, that men are often govern'd by their duties, and are deter'd from some actions by the opinion of injustice, and impell'd to others by that of obligation.

Since morals, therefore, have an influence on the actions and affections, it follows, that they cannot be deriv'd from reason; and that because reason alone, as we have already prov'd, can never have any such influence. Morals excite passions, and produce or prevent actions. Reason of itself is utterly impotent in this particular. The rules of morality, therefore, are not conclusions of our reason.

No one, I believe, will deny the justness of this inference; nor is there any other means of evading it, than by denying that principle, on which it is founded. As long as it is allow'd, that reason has no influence on our passions and actions, 'tis in vain to pretend, that morality is discover'd only by a deduction of reason. An active principle can never be founded on an inactive; and if reason be inactive in itself, it must remain so in all its shapes and appearances, whether it exerts itself in natural or moral subjects, whether it considers the powers of external bodies, or the actions of rational beings.

It would be tedious to repeat all the arguments, by which I have prov'd,* that reason is perfectly inert, and can never either prevent or produce any action or affection. 'Twill be easy to recollect what has been said upon that subject. I shall only recal on this occasion one of these arguments,

*Book II. Part III. Sect. 3.

which I shall endeavour to render still more conclusive, and more applicable to the present subject.

Reason is the discovery of truth or falshood. Truth or falshood consists in an agreement or disagreement either to the *real* relations of ideas, or to *real* existence and matter of fact. Whatever, therefore, is not susceptible of this agreement or disagreement, is incapable of being true or false, and can never be an object of our reason. Now 'tis evident our passions, volitions, and actions, are not susceptible of any such agreement or disagreement; being original facts and realities, compleat in themselves, and implying no reference to other passions, volitions, and actions. 'Tis impossible, therefore, they can be pronounced either true or false, and be either contrary or conformable to reason.

This argument is of double advantage to our present purpose. For it proves *directly*, that actions do not derive their merit from a conformity to reason, nor their blame from a contrariety to it; and it proves the same truth more *indirectly*, by shewing us, that as reason can never immediately prevent or produce any action by contradicting or approving of it, it cannot be the source of moral good and evil, which are found to have that influence. Actions may be laudable or blameable; but they cannot be reasonable: Laudable or blameable, therefore, are not the same with reasonable or unreasonable. The merit and demerit of actions frequently contradict, and sometimes controul our natural propensities. But reason has no such influence. Moral distinctions, therefore, are not the offspring of reason. Reason is wholly inactive, and can never be the source of so active a principle as conscience, or a sense of morals.

But perhaps it may be said, that tho' no will or action can be immediately contradictory to reason, yet we may find such a contradiction in some of the attendants of the action, that is, in its causes or effects. The action may cause a judgment, or may be *obliquely* caus'd by one, when the judgment concurs with a passion; and by an abusive way of speaking, which philosophy will scarce allow of, the same contrariety may, upon that account, be ascrib'd to the action. How far this truth or falshood may be the source of morals, 'twill now be proper to consider.

It has been observ'd, that reason, in a strict and philosophical sense, can have influence on our conduct only after two ways: Either when it excites a passion by informing us of the existence of something which is a proper object of it; or when it discovers the connexion of causes and effects, so as to afford us means of exerting any passion. These are the only kinds of judgment, which can accompany our actions, or can be said to produce them in any manner; and it must be allow'd, that these judgments may often be false and erroneous. A person may be affected with passion, by supposing a pain or pleasure to lie in an object, which has no tendency to produce either of these sensations, or which produces the contrary to what is imagin'd. A person may also take false measures for the attaining his end, and may retard, by his foolish conduct, instead of forwarding the execution of any project. These false judgments may be thought to affect the passions and actions, which are connected with them, and may be said to render them unreasonable, in a figurative and improper way of speaking. But tho' this be acknowledg'd, 'tis easy to observe, that these errors are so far from being the source of all immorality, that they are commonly very innocent, and draw no manner of guilt upon the person who is so unfortunate as to fall into them. They extend not beyond a mistake of *fact*, which moralists have not generally suppos'd criminal, as being perfectly involuntary. I am more to be lamented than blam'd, if I am mistaken with regard to the influence of objects in producing pain or pleasure, or if I know not the proper means of satisfying my desires. No one can ever regard such errors as a defect in my moral character. A fruit, for instance, that is really disagreeable, appears to me at a distance, and thro' mistake I fancy it to be pleasant and delicious. Here is one error. I choose certain means of reaching this fruit, which are not proper for my end. Here is a second error; nor is there any third one, which can ever possibly enter into our reasonings concerning actions. I ask, therefore, if a man, in this situation, and guilty of these two errors, is to be regarded as vicious and criminal, however unavoidable they might have been? Or if it be possible to imagine, that such errors are the sources of all immorality?

And here it may be proper to observe, that if moral distinctions be deriv'd from the truth or falshood of those judgments, they must take place wherever we form the judgments; nor will there be any difference, whether the question be concerning an apple or a kingdom, or whether the error be avoidable or unavoidable. For as the very essence of morality is suppos'd to consist in an agreement or disagreement to reason, the other circumstances are entirely arbitrary, and can never either bestow on any action the character of virtuous or vicious, or deprive it of that character. To which we may add, that this agreement or disagreement, not admitting of degrees, all virtues and vices wou'd of course be equal.

Shou'd it be pretended, that tho' a mistake of *fact* be not criminal, yet a mistake of *right* often is; and that this may be the source of immorality: I would answer, that 'tis impossible such a mistake can ever be the original source of immorality, since it supposes a real right and wrong; that is, a real distinction in morals, independent of these judgments. A mistake, therefore, of right may become a species of immorality; but 'tis only a secondary one, and is founded on some other, antecedent to it.

As to those judgments which are the *effects* of our actions, and which, when false, give occasion to pronounce the actions contrary to truth and reason; we may observe, that our actions never cause any judgment, either true or false, in ourselves, and that 'tis only on others they have such an influence. 'Tis certain, that an action, on many occasions, may give rise to false conclusions in others; and that a person, who thro' a window sees any lewd behaviour of mine with my neighbour's wife, may be so simple as to imagine she is certainly my own. In this respect my action resembles somewhat a lye or falshood; only with this difference, which is material, that I perform not the action with any intention of giving rise to a false judgment in another, but merely to satisfy my lust and passion. It causes, however, a mistake and false judgment by accident; and the falshood of its effects may be ascribed, by some odd figurative way of speaking, to the action itself. But still I can see no pretext of reason for asserting, that the tendency to cause such an error is the first spring or original source of all immorality*.

* One might think it were entirely superfluous to prove this, if a late author [William Wollaston, *The Religion of Nature Delineated* (London 1722)], who has had the good fortune to obtain some reputation, had not seriously affirmed, that such a falshood is the foundation of all guilt and moral deformity. That we may discover the fallacy of his hypothesis, we need only consider, that a false conclusion is drawn from an action, only by means of an obscurity of natural principles, which makes a cause be secretly interrupted in its operation, by contrary causes, and renders the connexion betwixt two objects uncertain and variable. Now, as a like uncertainty and variety of causes take place, even in natural objects, and produce a like error in our judgment, if that tendency to produce error were the very essence of vice and immorality, it shou'd follow, that even inanimate objects might be vicious and immoral.

'Tis in vain to urge, that inanimate objects act without liberty and choice. For as liberty and choice are not necessary to make an action produce in us an erroneous conclusion, they can be, in no respect, essential to morality; and I do not readily perceive, upon this system, how they can ever come to be regarded by it. If the tendency to cause error be the origin of immorality, that tendency and immorality wou'd in every case be inseparable.

Add to this, that if I had used the precaution of shutting the windows, while I indulg'd myself in those liberties with my neighbour's wife, I should have been guilty of no immorality; and that because my action, being perfectly conceal'd, wou'd have had no tendency to produce any false conclusion.

For the same reason, a thief, who steals in by a ladder at a window, and takes all imaginable care to cause no disturbance, is in no respect criminal. For either he will not be perceiv'd, or if he be, 'tis impossible he can produce any error, nor will any one, from these circumstances, take him to be other than what he really is.

'Tis well known, that those who are squint-sighted, do very readily cause mistakes in others, and that we imagine they salute or are talking to one person, while they address themselves to another. Are they therefore, upon that account, immoral?

Besides, we may easily observe, that in all those arguments there is an evident reasoning in a circle. A person who takes possession of

Thus upon the whole, 'tis impossible, that the distinction betwixt moral good and evil, can be made to reason; since that distinction has an influence upon our actions, of which reason alone is incapable. Reason and judgment may, indeed, be the mediate cause of an action, by prompting, or by directing a passion: But it is not pretended, that a judgment of this kind, either in its truth or falshood, is attended with virtue or vice. And as to the judgments, which are caused by our judgments, they can still less bestow those moral qualities on the actions, which are their causes.

But to be more particular, and to shew, that those eternal immutable fitnesses and unfitnesses of things cannot be defended by sound philosophy, we may weigh the following considerations.

---

another's goods, and uses them as his *own*, in a manner declares them to be his own; and this falshood is the source of the immorality of injustice. But is property, or right, or obligation, intelligible, without an antecedent morality?

A man that is ungrateful to his benefactor, in a manner affirms, that he never received any favours from him. But in what manner? Is it because 'tis his duty to be grateful? But this supposes, that there is some antecedent rule of duty and morals. Is it because human nature is generally grateful, and makes us conclude, that a man who does any harm never received any favour from the person he harm'd? But human nature is not so generally grateful, as to justify such a conclusion. Or if it were, is an exception to a general rule in every case criminal, for no other reason than because it is an exception?

But what may suffice entirely to destroy this whimsical system is, that it leaves us under the same difficulty to give a reason why truth is virtuous and falshood vicious, as to account for the merit or turpitude of any other action. I shall allow, if you please, that all immorality is derived from this supposed falshood in action, provided you can give me any plausible reason, why such a falshood is immoral. If you consider rightly of the matter, you will find yourself in the same difficulty as at the beginning.

This last argument is very conclusive; because, if there be not an evident merit or turpitude annex'd to this species of truth or falshood, it can never have any influence upon our actions. For, who ever thought of forbearing any action, because others might possibly draw false conclusions from it? Or, who ever perform'd any, that he might give rise to true conclusions?

If the thought and understanding were alone capable of fixing the boundaries of right and wrong, the character of virtuous and vicious either must lie in some relations of objects, or must be a matter of fact, which is discovered by our reasoning. This consequence is evident. As the operations of human understanding divide themselves into two kinds, the comparing of ideas, and the inferring of matter of fact; were virtue discover'd by the understanding; it must be an object of one of these operations, nor is there any third operation of the understanding, which can discover it. There has been an opinion very industriously propagated by certain philosophers, that morality is susceptible of demonstration; and tho' no one has ever been able to advance a single step in those demonstrations; yet 'tis taken for granted, that this science may be brought to an equal certainty with geometry or algebra. Upon this supposition, vice and virtue must consist in some relations; since 'tis allow'd on all hands, that no matter of fact is capable of being demonstrated. Let us, therefore, begin with examining this hypothesis, and endeavour, if possible, to fix those moral qualities, which have been so long the objects of our fruitless researches. Point out distinctly the relations, which constitute morality or obligation, that we may know wherein they consist, and after what manner we must judge of them.

If you assert, that vice and virtue consist in relations susceptible of certainty and demonstration, you must confine yourself to those *four* relations, which alone admit of that degree of evidence; and in that case you run into absurdities, from which you will never be able to extricate yourself. For as you make the very essence of morality to lie in the relations, and as there is no one of these relations but what is applicable, not only to an irrational, but also to an inanimate object; it follows, that even such objects must be susceptible of merit or demerit. *Resemblance, contrariety, degrees in quality*, and *proportions in quantity and number;* all these relations belong as properly to matter, as to our actions, passions, and volitions. 'Tis unquestionable, therefore, that morality lies not in any of these relations, nor the sense of it in their discovery *.

Shou'd it be asserted, that the sense of morality consists in the discovery of some relation, distinct from these, and that our enumeration was not compleat, when we comprehended all demonstrable relations under four general heads: To this I know not what to reply, till some one be so good as to point out to me this new relation. 'Tis impossible to refute a system, which has never yet been explain'd. In such a manner of fighting in the dark, a man loses his blows in the air, and often places them where the enemy is not present.

I must, therefore, on this occasion, rest contented with requiring the two following conditions of any one that wou'd undertake to clear up this system. *First*, As moral good and evil belong only to the actions of the mind, and are deriv'd from our situation with regard to external objects, the relations, from which these moral distinctions arise, must lie only betwixt internal actions, and external objects, and must not be applicable either to internal actions, compared among themselves, or to external objects, when placed in opposition to other external objects. For as morality is supposed to attend certain relations, if these re-

* As a proof, how confus'd our way of thinking on this subject commonly is, we may observe, that those who assert, that morality is demonstrable, do not say, that morality lies in the relations, and that the relations are distinguishable by reason. They only say, that reason can discover such an action, in such relations, to be virtuous, and such another vicious. It seems they thought it sufficient, if they cou'd bring the word, Relation, into the proposition, without troubling themselves whether it was to the purpose or not. But here, I think, is plain argument. Demonstrative reason discovers only relations. But that reason, according to this hypothesis, discovers also vice and virtue. These moral qualities, therefore, must be relations. When we blame any action, in any situation, the whole complicated object, of action and situation, must form certain relations, wherein the essence of vice consists. This hypothesis is not otherwise intelligible. For what does reason discover, when it pronounces any action vicious? Does it discover a relation or a matter of fact? These questions are decisive, and must not be eluded.

lations cou'd belong to internal actions consider'd singly, it wou'd follow, that we might be guilty of crimes in ourselves, and independent of our situation, with respect to the universe: And in like manner, if these moral relations cou'd be apply'd to external objects, it wou'd follow, that even inanimate beings wou'd be susceptible of moral beauty and deformity. Now it seems difficult to imagine, that any relation can be discover'd betwixt our passions, volitions and actions, compared to external objects, which relation might not belong either to these passions and volitions, or to these external objects, compar'd among *themselves*.

But it will be still more difficult to fulfil the *second* condition, requisite to justify this system. According to the principles of those who maintain an abstract rational difference betwixt moral good and evil, and a natural fitness and unfitness of things, 'tis not only suppos'd, that these relations, being eternal and immutable, are the same, when consider'd by every rational creature, but their *effects* are also suppos'd to be necessarily the same; and 'tis concluded they have no less, or rather a greater, influence in directing the will of the deity, than in governing the rational and virtuous of our own species. These two particulars are evidently distinct. 'Tis one thing to know virtue, and another to conform the will to it. In order, therefore, to prove, that the measures of right and wrong are eternal laws, *obligatory* on every rational mind, 'tis not sufficient to shew the relations upon which they are founded: We must also point out the connexion betwixt the relation and the will; and must prove that this connexion is so necessary, that in every well-disposed mind, it must take place and have its influence; tho' the difference betwixt these minds be in other respects immense and infinite. Now besides what I have already prov'd, that even in human nature no relation can ever alone produce any action: besides this, I say, it has been shewn, in treating of the understanding, that there is no connexion of cause and effect, such as this is suppos'd to be, which is discoverable otherwise than by experience, and of which we can pretend to have any security by the simple consideration of the objects. All beings in the universe, consider'd in themselves, appear entirely loose and independent of each other. 'Tis only by experience we learn their influence and connexion; and this influence we ought never to extend beyond experience.

Thus it will be impossible to fulfil the *first* condition required to the system of eternal measures of right and wrong; because it is impossible to shew those relations, upon which such a distinction may be founded: And 'tis as impossible to fulfil the *second* condition; because we cannot prove *a priori,* that these relations, if they really existed and were perceiv'd, wou'd be universally forcible and obligatory.

But to make these general reflections more clear and convincing, we may illustrate them by some particular instances, wherein this character of moral good or evil is the most universally acknowledged. Of all crimes that human creatures are capable of committing, the most horrid and unnatural is ingratitude, especially when it is committed against parents, and appears in the more flagrant instances of wounds and death. This is acknowledg'd by all mankind, philosophers as well as the people; the question only arises among philosophers, whether the guilt or moral deformity of this action be discover'd by demonstrative reasoning, or be felt by an internal sense, and by means of some sentiment, which the reflecting on such an action naturally occasions. This question will soon be decided against the former opinion, if we can shew the same relations in other objects, without the notion of any guilt or iniquity attending them. Reason or science is nothing but the comparing of ideas, and the discovery of their relations; and if the same relations have different characters, it must evidently follow, that those characters are not discover'd merely by reason. To put the affair, therefore, to this trial, let us chuse any inanimate object, such as an oak or elm; and let us suppose, that by the dropping of its seed, it produces a sapling below it, which springing up by degrees, at last overtops and destroys the parent tree: I ask, if in this instance there be wanting any relation, which is discoverable in parricide or ingratitude? Is not the one tree the cause of the other's existence; and the latter the cause of the destruction of the former, in the same manner as when a child murders his parent? 'Tis not sufficient to reply, that a choice or will is wanting. For in the case of parricide, a will does not give rise to any *different* relations, but is only the cause from which the action is deriv'd; and consequently produces the *same* relations, that in the oak or elm arise from some other principles. 'Tis a will or choice, that determines a man to kill his parent; and they are the laws of matter and motion, that determine a sapling to destroy the oak, from which it sprung. Here then the same relations have different causes; but still the relations are the same: And as their discovery is not in both cases attended with a notion of immorality, it follows, that that notion does not arise from such a discovery.

But to chuse an instance, still more resembling; I would fain ask any one, why incest in the human species is criminal, and why the very same action, and the same relations in animals have not the smallest moral turpitude and deformity? If it be answer'd, that this action is innocent in animals, because they have not reason sufficient to discover its turpitude; but that man, being endow'd with that faculty which *ought* to restrain him to his duty, the same action instantly becomes criminal to him; should this be said, I would reply, that this is evidently arguing in a circle. For before reason can perceive this turpitude, the turpitude must exist; and consequently is independent of the decisions of our reason, and is their object more properly than their effect. According to this system, then, every animal, that has sense, and appetite, and will; that is, every animal must be susceptible of all the same virtues and vices, for which we ascribe praise and blame to human creatures. All the difference is, that our superior reason may serve to discover the vice or virtue, and by that means may augment the blame or praise: But still this discovery supposes a separate being in these moral distinctions, and a being, which depends only on the will and appetite, and which, both in thought and reality, may be distinguish'd from the reason. Animals are susceptible of the same relations, with respect to each other, as the human species, and therefore wou'd also be susceptible of the same morality, if the essence of morality consisted in these relations. Their want of a sufficient degree of reason may hinder them from perceiving the duties and obligations of morality, but can never hinder these duties from existing; since they must antecedently exist, in order to their being perceiv'd. Reason must find them, and can never produce them. This argument deserves to be weigh'd, as being, in my opinion, entirely decisive.

Nor does this reasoning only prove, that morality consists not in any relations, that are the objects of science; but if examin'd, will prove with equal certainty, that it consists not in any *matter of fact*, which can be discover'd by the understanding. This is the *second* part of our argument; and if it can be made evident, we may conclude, that morality is not an object of reason. But can there be any difficulty in proving, that vice and virtue are not matters of fact, whose existence we can infer by reason? Take any action allow'd to be vicious: Wilful murder, for instance. Examine it in all lights, and see if you can find that matter of fact, or real existence, which you call *vice*. In which-ever way you take it, you find only certain passions, motives, volitions and thoughts. There is no other matter of fact in the case. The vice entirely escapes you, as long as you consider the object. You never can find it, till you turn your reflection into your own breast, and find a sentiment of disapprobation, which arises in you, towards this action. Here is a matter of fact; but 'tis the object of feeling, not of reason. It lies in yourself, not in the object. So that when you pronounce any action or character to be vicious, you mean nothing, but that from the constitution of your nature you have a feeling or sentiment of blame from the contemplation of it. Vice and virtue, therefore, may be compar'd to sounds, colours, heat and cold, which, according to modern philosophy, are not qualities in objects, but perceptions in the mind: And this discovery in morals, like that other in physics, is to be regarded as a considerable advancement of the speculative sciences; tho', like that too, it has little or no influence on practice. Nothing can be more real, or concern us more, than our own sentiments of pleasure and uneasiness; and if these be favourable to virtue, and unfavourable to vice, no more can be requisite to the regulation of our conduct and behaviour.

I cannot forbear adding to these reasonings an observation, which may, perhaps, be found of some importance. In every system of morality, which I have hitherto met with, I have always remark'd, that the author proceeds for some time in the ordinary way of reasoning, and establishes the being of a God, or makes observations concerning human affairs; when of a sudden I am surpriz'd to find, that instead of the usual copulations of propositions, *is*, and *is not*, I meet with no proposition that is not connected with an *ought*, or an *ought not*. This change is imperceptible; but is, however, of the last consequence. For as this *ought*, or *ought not*, expresses some new relation or affirmation, 'tis necessary that it shou'd be observ'd and explain'd; and at the same time that a reason should be given, for what seems altogether inconceivable, how this new relation can be a deduction from others, which are entirely different from it. But as authors do not commonly use this precaution, I shall presume to recommend it to the readers; and am persuaded, that this small attention wou'd subvert all the vulgar systems of morality, and let us see, that the distinction of vice and virtue is not founded merely on the relations of objects, nor is perceiv'd by reason.

SECT. II

Moral distinctions deriv'd from a moral sense

THUS the course of the argument leads us to conclude, that since vice and virtue are not discoverable merely by reason, or the comparison of ideas, it must be by means of some impression or sentiment they occasion, that we are able to mark the difference betwixt them. Our decisions concerning moral rectitude and depravity are evidently perceptions; and as all perceptions are either impressions or ideas, the exclusion of the one is a convincing argument for the other. Morality, therefore, is more properly felt than judg'd of; tho' this feeling or sentiment is commonly so soft and gentle, that we are apt to confound it with an idea, according to our common custom of taking all things for the same, which have any near resemblance to each other.

The next question is, Of what nature are these impressions, and after what manner do they operate upon us? Here we cannot remain long in suspense, but must pronounce the impression arising from virtue, to be agreeable, and that proceding from vice to be uneasy. Every moment's experience must convince us of this. There is no spectacle so fair and beautiful as a noble and generous action; nor any which gives us more abhorrence than one that is cruel and treacherous. No enjoyment equals the satisfaction we receive from the company of those we love and esteem; as the greatest of all punishments is to be oblig'd to pass our lives with those we hate or contemn. A very play or romance may afford us instances of this pleasure, which virtue conveys to us; and pain, which arises from vice.

Now since the distinguishing impressions, by which moral good or evil is known, are nothing but *particular* pains or pleasures; it follows, that in all enquiries concerning these moral distinctions, it will be sufficient to shew the principles, which make us feel a satisfaction or uneasiness from the survey of any character, in order to satisfy us why the character is laudable or blameable. An action, or sentiment, or character is virtuous or vicious; why? because its view causes a pleasure or uneasiness of a particular kind. In giving a reason, therefore, for the pleasure or uneasiness, we sufficiently explain the vice or virtue. To have the sense of virtue, is nothing but to *feel* a satisfaction of a particular kind from the contemplation of a character. The very *feeling* constitutes our praise or admiration. We go no farther; nor do we enquire into the cause of the satisfaction. We do not infer a character to be virtuous, because it pleases: But in feeling that it pleases after such a particular manner, we in effect feel that it is virtuous. The case is the same as in our judgments concerning all kinds of beauty, and tastes, and sensations. Our approbation is imply'd in the immediate pleasure they convey to us.

I have objected to the system, which establishes eternal rational measures of right and wrong, that 'tis impossible to shew, in the actions of reasonable creatures, any relations, which are not found in external objects; and therefore, if morality always attended these relations, 'twere possible for inanimate matter to become virtuous or vicious. Now it may, in like manner, be objected to the present system, that if virtue and vice be determin'd by pleasure and pain, these qualities must, in every case, arise from the sensations; and consequently any object, whether animate or inanimate, rational or irrational, might become morally good or evil, provided it can excite a satisfaction or uneasiness. But tho' this objection seems to be the very same, it has by no means the same force, in the one case as in the other. For, *first,* 'tis evident, that under the term *pleasure*, we comprehend sensations, which are very different from each other, and which have only such a distant resemblance, as is requisite to make them be express'd by the same abstract term. A good composition of music and a bottle of good wine equally produce pleasure; and what is more, their goodness is determin'd merely by the pleasure. But shall we say upon that account, that the wine is harmonious, or the music of a good flavour? In like manner an inanimate object, and the character or sentiments of any person may, both of them, give satisfaction; but as the satisfaction is different, this keeps our sentiments concerning them from being confounded, and makes us ascribe virtue to the one, and not to the other. Nor is every sentiment of pleasure or pain, which arises from characters and actions, of that *peculiar* kind, which makes us praise or condemn. The good qualities of an enemy are hurtful to us; but may still command our esteem and respect. 'Tis only when a character is considered in general, without reference to our particular interest, that it causes such a feeling or sentiment, as denominates it morally good or evil. 'Tis true, those sentiments, from interest and morals, are apt to be confounded, and naturally run into one another. It seldom happens, that we do not think an enemy vicious, and can distinguish betwixt his opposition to our interest and real villainy or baseness. But this hinders not, but that the sentiments are, in themselves, distinct; and a man of temper and judgment may preserve himself from these illusions. In like manner, tho' 'tis certain a musical voice is nothing but one that naturally gives a *particular* kind of pleasure; yet 'tis difficult for a man to be sensible, that the voice of an enemy is agreeable, or to allow it to be musical. But a person of a fine ear, who has the command of himself, can separate these feelings, and give praise to what deserves it.

Secondly, We may call to remembrance the preceding system of the passions, in order to remark a still more considerable difference among our pains and pleasures. Pride and humility, love and hatred are excited, when there is any thing presented to us, that both bears a relation to the object of the passion, and produces a separate sensation related to the sensation of the passion. Now virtue and vice are attended with these circumstances. They must necessarily be plac'd either in ourselves or others, and excite either pleasure or uneasiness; and therefore must give rise to one of these four passions; which clearly distinguishes them from the pleasure and pain arising from inanimate objects, that often bear no relation to us: And this is, perhaps, the most considerable effect that virtue and vice have upon the human mind.

It may now be ask'd *in general*, concerning this pain or pleasure, that distinguishes moral good and evil, *From what principles is it derived,andwhence does it arise in the human mind?* To this I reply, *first*, that 'tis absurd to imagine, that in every particular instance, these sentiments are produc'd by an *original* quality and *primary* constitution. For as the number of our duties is, in a manner, infinite, 'tis impossible that our original instincts should extend to each of them, and from our very first infancy impress on the human mind all that multitude of precepts, which are contain'd in the compleatest system of ethics. Such a method of proceeding is not conformable to the usual maxims, by which nature is conducted, where a few principles produce all that variety we observe in the universe, and every thing is carry'd on in the easiest and most simple manner. 'Tis necessary, therefore, to abridge these primary impulses, and find some more general principles, upon which all our notions of morals are founded.

But in the *second* place, should it be ask'd, Whether we ought to search for these principles in *nature*, or whether we must look for them in some other origin? I wou'd reply, that our answer to this question depends upon the definition of the word, Nature, than which there is none more ambiguous and equivocal. If *nature* be oppos'd to miracles, not only the distinction betwixt vice and virtue is natural, but also every event, which has ever happen'd in the world, *excepting those miracles, on which our religion is founded.* In saying, then, that the sentiments of vice and virtue are natural in this sense, we make no very extraordinary discovery.

But *nature* may also be opposed to rare and unusual; and in this sense of the word, which is the common one, there may often arise disputes concerning what is natural or unnatural; and one may in general affirm, that we are not possess'd of any very precise standard, by which these disputes can be decided. Frequent and rare depend upon the number of examples we have observ'd; and as this number may gradually encrease or diminish, 'twill be impossible to fix any exact boundaries betwixt them. We may only affirm on this head, that if ever there was any thing, which cou'd be call'd natural in this sense, the sentiments of morality certainly may; since there never was any nation of the world, nor any single person in any nation, who was utterly depriv'd of them, and who never, in any instance, shew'd the least approbation or dislike of manners. These sentiments are so rooted in our constitution and temper, that without entirely confounding the human mind by disease or madness, 'tis impossible to extirpate and destroy them.

But *nature* may also be opposed to artifice, as well as to what is rare and unusual; and in this sense it may be disputed, whether the notions of virtue be natural or not. We readily forget, that the designs, and projects, and views of men are principles as necessary in their operation as heat and cold, moist and dry: But taking them to be free and entirely our own, 'tis usual for us to set them in opposition to the other principles of nature. Shou'd it, therefore, be demanded, whether the sense of virtue be natural or artificial, I am of opinion, that 'tis impossible for me at present to give any precise answer to this question. Perhaps it will appear afterwards, that our sense of some virtues is artificial, and that of others natural. The discussion of this question will be more proper, when we enter upon an exact detail of each particular vice and virtue*.

Mean while it may not be amiss to observe from these definitions of *natural* and *unnatural*, that nothing can be more unphilosophical than those systems, which assert, that virtue is the same with what is natural, and vice with what is unnatural. For in the first sense of the word, Nature, as opposed to miracles, both vice and virtue are equally natural; and in the second sense, as oppos'd to what is unusual, perhaps virtue will be found to be the most unnatural. At

*In the following discourse *natural* is also opposed sometimes to *civil*, sometimes to *moral*. The opposition will always discover the sense, in which it is taken.

least it must be own'd, that heroic virtue, being as unusual, is as little natural as the most brutal barbarity. As to the third sense of the word, 'tis certain, that both vice and virtue are equally artificial, and out of nature. For however it may be disputed, whether the notion of a merit or demerit in certain actions be natural or artificial, 'tis evident, that the actions themselves are artificial, and are perform'd with a certain design and intention; otherwise they cou'd never be rank'd under any of these denominations. 'Tis impossible, therefore, that the character of natural and unnatural can ever, in any sense, mark the boundaries of vice and virtue.

Thus we are still brought back to our first position, that virtue is distinguished by the pleasure, and vice by the pain, that any action, sentiment or character gives us by the mere view and contemplation. This decision is very commodious; because it reduces us to this simple question, *Why any action or sentiment upon the general view or survey, gives a certain satisfaction or uneasiness*, in order to shew the origin of its moral rectitude or depravity, without looking for any incomprehensible relations and qualities, which never did exist in nature, nor even in our imagination, by any clear and distinct conception. I flatter myself I have executed a great part of my present design by a state of the question, which appears to me so free from ambiguity and obscurity.

PART II

Of justice and injustice

SECT. I

Justice, whether a natural or artificial virtue?

I HAVE already hinted, that our sense of every kind of virtue is not natural; but that there are some virtues, that produce pleasure and approbation by means of an artifice or contrivance, which arises from the circumstances and necessity of mankind. Of this kind I assert *justice* to be; and shall endeavour to defend this opinion by a short, and, I hope, convincing argument, before I examine the nature of the artifice, from which the sense of that virtue is derived.

'Tis evident, that when we praise any actions, we regard only the motives that produced them, and consider the actions as signs or indications of certain principles in the mind and temper. The external performance has no merit. We must look within to find the moral quality. This we cannot do directly; and therefore fix our attention on actions, as on external signs. But these actions are still considered as signs; and the ultimate object of our praise and approbation is the motive, that produc'd them.

After the same manner, when we require any action, or blame a person for not performing it, we always suppose, that one in that situation shou'd be influenc'd by the proper motive of that action, and we esteem it vicious in him to be regardless of it. If we find, upon enquiry, that the virtuous motive was still powerful over his breast, tho' check'd in its operation by some circumstances unknown to us, we retract our blame, and have the same esteem for him, as if he had actually perform'd the action, which we require of him.

It appears, therefore, that all virtuous actions derive their merit only from virtuous motives, and are consider'd merely as signs of those motives. From this principle I conclude, that the first virtuous motive, which bestows a merit on any action, can never be a regard to the virtue of that action, but must be some other natural motive or principle. To suppose, that the mere regard to the virtue of the action, may be the first motive, which produc'd the action, and render'd it virtuous, is to reason in a circle. Before we can have such a regard, the action must be really virtuous; and this virtue must be deriv'd from some virtuous motive: And consequently the virtuous motive must be different from the regard to the virtue of the action. A virtuous motive is requisite to render an action virtuous. An action must be virtuous, before we can have a regard to its virtue. Some virtuous motive, therefore, must be antecedent to that regard.

Nor is this merely a metaphysical subtilty; but enters into all our reasonings in common life, tho' perhaps we may not be able to place it in such distinct philosophical terms. We blame a father for neglecting his child. Why? because it shews a want of natural affection, which is the duty of every parent. Were not natural affection a duty, the care of children cou'd not be a duty; and 'twere impossible we cou'd have the duty in our eye in the attention we give to our offspring. In this case, therefore, all men suppose a motive to the action distinct from a sense of duty.

Here is a man, that does many benevolent actions; relieves the distress'd, comforts the afflicted, and extends his bounty even to the greatest strangers. No character can be more amiable and virtuous. We regard these actions as proofs of the greatest humanity. This humanity bestows a merit on the actions. A regard to this merit is, therefore, a secondary consideration, and deriv'd from the antecedent principle of humanity, which is meritorious and laudable.

In short, it may be establish'd as an undoubted maxim,

that no action can be virtuous, or morally good, unless there be in human nature some motive to produce it, distinct from the sense of its morality.

But may not the sense of morality or duty produce an action, without any other motive? I answer, It may: But this is no objection to the present doctrine. When any virtuous motive or principle is common in human nature, a person, who feels his heart devoid of that motive, may hate himself upon that account, and may perform the action without the motive, from a certain sense of duty, in order to acquire by practice, that virtuous principle, or at least, to disguise to himself, as much as possible, his want of it. A man that really feels no gratitude in his temper, is still pleas'd to perform grateful actions, and thinks he has, by that means, fulfill'd his duty. Actions are at first only consider'd as signs of motives: But 'tis usual, in this case, as in all others, to fix our attention on the signs, and neglect, in some measure, the thing signify'd. But tho', on some occasions, a person may perform an action merely out of regard to its moral obligation, yet still this supposes in human nature some distinct principles, which are capable of producing the action, and whose moral beauty renders the action meritorious.

Now to apply all this to the present case; I suppose a person to have lent me a sum of money, on condition that it be restor'd in a few days; and also suppose, that after the expiration of the term agreed on, he demands the sum: I ask, *What reason or motive have I to restore the money?* It will, perhaps, be said, that my regard to justice, and abhorrence of villainy and knavery, are sufficient reasons for me, if I have the least grain of honesty, or sense of duty and obligation. And this answer, no doubt, is just and satisfactory to man in his civiliz'd state, and when train'd up according to a certain discipline and education. But in his rude and more *natural* condition, if you are pleas'd to call such a condition natural, this answer wou'd be rejected as perfectly unintelligible and sophistical. For one in that situation wou'd immediately ask you, *Wherein consists this honesty and justice, which you find in restoring a loan, and abstaining from the property of others?* It does not surely lie in the external action. It must, therefore be plac'd in the motive, from which the external action is deriv'd. This motive can never be a regard to the honesty of the action. For 'tis a plain fallacy to say, that a virtuous motive is requisite to render an action honest, and at the same time that a regard to the honesty is the motive of the action. We can never have a regard to the virtue of an action, unless the action be antecedently virtuous. No action can be virtuous, but so far as it proceeds from a virtuous motive. A virtuous motive, therefore, must precede the regard to the virtue; and 'tis impossible, that the virtuous motive and the regard to the virtue can be the same.

'Tis requisite, then, to find some motive to acts of justice and honesty, distinct from our regard to the honesty; and in this lies the great difficulty. For shou'd we say, that a concern for our private interest or reputation is the legitimate motive to all honest actions; it wou'd follow, that wherever that concern ceases, honesty can no longer have place. But 'tis certain, that self-love, when it acts at its liberty, instead of engaging us to honest actions, is the source of all injustice and violence; nor can a man ever correct those vices, without correcting and restraining the *natural* movements of that appetite.

But shou'd it be affirm'd, that the reason or motive of such actions is the *regard to publick interest*, to which nothing is more contrary than examples of injustice and dishonesty; shou'd this be said, I wou'd propose the three following considerations, as worthy of our attention. *First*, public interest is not naturally attach'd to the observation of the rules of justice; but is only connected with it, after an artificial convention for the establishment of these rules, as shall be shewn more at large hereafter. *Secondly*, if we suppose, that the loan was secret, and that it is necessary for the interest of the person, that the money be restor'd in the same manner (as when the lender wou'd conceal his riches) in that case the example ceases, and the public is no longer interested in the actions of the borrower; tho' I suppose there is no moralist, who will affirm, that the duty and obligation ceases. *Thirdly,* experience sufficiently proves, that men, in the ordinary conduct of life, look not so far as the public interest, when they pay their creditors, perform their promises, and abstain from theft, and robbery, and injustice of every kind. That is a motive too remote and too sublime to affect the generality of mankind, and operate with any force in actions so contrary to private interest as are frequently those of justice and common honesty.

In general, it may be affirm'd, that there is no such passion in human minds, as the love of mankind, merely as such, independent of personal qualities, of services, or of relation to ourself. 'Tis true, there is no human, and indeed no sensible, creature, whose happiness or misery does not, in some measure, affect us when brought near to us, and represented in lively colours: But this proceeds merely from sympathy, and is no proof of such an universal affection to mankind, since this concern extends itself beyond our own species. An affection betwixt the sexes is a passion evidently implanted in human nature; and this passion not only appears in its peculiar symptoms, but also in inflaming every other principle of affection, and raising a stronger love from beauty, wit, kindness, than what wou'd otherwise flow from them. Were there an universal love among all human creatures, it wou'd appear after the same manner. Any degree of a good quality wou'd cause a stronger affection than the same degree of a bad quality wou'd cause hatred; contrary to what we find by experience. Men's tempers are different, and some have a propensity to the tender, and others to the rougher, affections: But in the main, we may affirm, that man in general, or human nature, is nothing but the object both of love and hatred, and requires some other cause, which by a double relation of impressions and ideas, may excite these passions. In vain wou'd we endeavour to elude this hypothesis. There are no phaenomena that point out any such kind affection to men, independent of their merit, and every other circumstance. We love company in general; but 'tis as we love any other amusement. An *Englishman* in *Italy* is a friend: A *Europaean* in *China*; and perhaps a man wou'd be belov'd as such, were we to meet him in the moon. But this proceeds only from the relation to ourselves; which in these cases gathers force by being confined to a few persons.

If public benevolence, therefore, or a regard to the interests of mankind, cannot be the original motive to justice, much less can *private benevolence*, or a *regard to the interests of the party concern'd*, be this motive. For what if he be my enemy, and has given me just cause to hate him? What if he be a vicious man, and deserves the hatred of all mankind? What if he be a miser, and can make no use of what I wou'd deprive him of? What if he be a profligate debauchee, and wou'd rather receive harm than benefit from large possessions? What if I be in necessity, and have urgent motives to acquire something to my family? In all these cases, the original motive to justice wou'd fail; and consequently the justice itself, and along with it all property, right, and obligation.

A rich man lies under a moral obligation to communicate to those in necessity a share of his superfluities. Were private benevolence the original motive to justice, a man wou'd not be oblig'd to leave others in the possession of more than he is oblig'd to give them. At least the difference wou'd be very inconsiderable. Men generally fix their affections more on what they are possess'd of, than on what they never enjoy'd: For this reason, it wou'd be greater cruelty to dispossess a man of any thing, than not to give it him. But who will assert, that this is the only foundation of justice?

Besides, we must consider, that the chief reason, why men attach themselves so much to their possessions is, that they consider them as their property, and as secur'd to them inviolably by the laws of society. But this is a secondary consideration, and dependent on the preceding notions of justice and property.

A man's property is suppos'd to be fenc'd against every

mortal, in every possible case. But private benevolence is, and ought to be, weaker in some persons, than in others: And in many, or indeed in most persons, must absolutely fail. Private benevolence, therefore, is not the original motive of justice.

From all this it follows, that we have no real or universal motive for observing the laws of equity, but the very equity and merit of that observance; and as no action can be equitable or meritorious, where it cannot arise from some separate motive, there is here an evident sophistry and reasoning in a circle. Unless, therefore, we will allow, that nature has establish'd a sophistry, and render'd it necessary and unavoidable, we must allow, that the sense of justice and injustice is not deriv'd from nature, but arises artificially, tho' necessarily from education, and human conventions.

I shall add, as a corollary to this reasoning, that since no action can be laudable or blameable, without some motives or impelling passions, distinct from the sense of morals, these distinct passions must have a great influence on that sense. 'Tis according to their general force in human nature, that we blame or praise. In judging of the beauty of animal bodies, we always carry in our eye the oeconomy of a certain species; and where the limbs and features observe that proportion, which is common to the species, we pronounce them handsome and beautiful. In like manner we always consider the *natural* and *usual* force of the passions, when we determine concerning vice and virtue; and if the passions depart very much from the common measures on either side, they are always disapprov'd as vicious. A man naturally loves his children better than his nephews, his nephews better than his cousins, his cousins better than strangers, where every thing else is equal. Hence arise our common measures of duty, in preferring the one to the other. Our sense of duty always follows the common and natural course of our passions.

To avoid giving offence, I must here observe, that when I deny justice to be a natural virtue, I make use of the word, *natural*, only as oppos'd to *artificial*. In another sense of the word; as no principle of the human mind is more natural than a sense of virtue; so no virtue is more natural than justice. Mankind is an inventive species; and where an invention is obvious and absolutely necessary, it may as properly be said to be natural as any thing that proceeds immediately from original principles, without the intervention of thought or reflection. Tho' the rules of justice be *artificial*, they are not *arbitrary*. Nor is the expression improper to call them *Laws of Nature*; if by natural we understand what is common to any species, or even if we confine it to mean what is inseparable from the species.

SECT. II

Of the origin of justice and property

We now proceed to examine two questions, viz. *concerning the manner, in which the rules of justice are establish'd by the artifice of men;* and *concerning the reasons, which determine us to attribute to the observance or neglect of these rules a moral beauty and deformity*. These questions will appear afterwards to be distinct. We shall begin with the former.

Of all the animals, with which this globe is peopled, there is none towards whom nature seems, at first sight, to have exercis'd more cruelty than towards man, in the numberless wants and necessities, with which she has loaded him, and in the slender means, which she affords to the relieving these necessities. In other creatures these two particulars generally compensate each other. If we consider the lion as a voracious and carnivorous animal, we shall easily discover him to be very necessitous; but if we turn our eye to his make and temper, his agility, his courage, his arms, and his force, we shall find, that his advantages hold proportion with his wants. The sheep and ox are depriv'd of all these advantages; but their appetites are moderate, and their food is of easy purchase. In man alone, this unnatural conjunction of infirmity, and of necessity, may be observ'd in its greatest perfection. Not only the food, which is requir'd for his sustenance, flies his search and approach, or at least requires his labour to be produc'd, but he must be possess'd of cloaths and lodging, to defend him against the injuries of the weather; tho' to consider him only in himself, he is provided neither with arms, nor force, nor other natural abilities, which are in any degree answerable to so many necessities.

'Tis by society alone he is able to supply his defects, and raise himself up to an equality with his fellow-creatures, and even acquire a superiority above them. By society all his infirmities are compensated; and tho' in that situation his wants multiply every moment upon him, yet his abilities are still more augmented, and leave him in every respect more satisfied and happy, than 'tis possible for him, in his savage and solitary condition, ever to become. When every individual person labours a-part, and only for himself, his force is too small to execute any considerable work; his labour being employ'd in supplying all his different necessities, he never attains a perfection in any particular art; and as his force and success are not at all times equal, the least failure in either of these particulars must be attended with inevitable ruin and misery. Society provides a remedy for these *three* inconveniences. By the conjunction of forces, our power is augmented: By the partition of employments, our ability encreases: And by mutual succour we are less expos'd to fortune and accidents. 'Tis by this additional *force*, *ability*, and *security*, that society becomes advantageous.

But in order to form society, 'tis requisite not only that it be advantageous, but also that men be sensible of these advantages; and 'tis impossible, in their wild uncultivated state, that by study and reflection alone, they should ever be able to attain this knowledge. Most fortunately, therefore, there is conjoin'd to those necessities, whose remedies are remote and obscure, another necessity, which having a present and more obvious remedy, may justly be regarded as the first and original principle of human society. This necessity is no other than that natural appetite betwixt the sexes, which unites them together, and preserves their union, till a new tye takes place in their concern for their common offspring. This new concern becomes also a principle of union betwixt the parents and offspring, and forms a more numerous society; where the parents govern by the advantage of their superior strength and wisdom, and at the same time are restrain'd in the exercise of their authority by that natural affection, which they bear their children. In a little time, custom and habit operating on the tender minds of the children, makes them sensible of the advantages, which they may reap from society, as well as fashions them by degrees for it, by rubbing off those rough corners and untoward affections, which prevent their coalition.

For it must be confest, that however the circumstances of human nature may render an union necessary, and however those passions of lust and natural affection may seem to render it unavoidable; yet there are other particulars in our *natural temper*, and in our *outward circumstances*, which are very incommodious, and are even contrary to the requisite conjunction. Among the former, we may justly esteem our *selfishness* to be the most considerable. I am sensible, that generally speaking, the representations of this quality have been carried much too far; and that the descriptions, which certain philosophers delight so much to form of mankind in this particular, are as wide of nature as any accounts of monsters, which we meet with in fables and romances. So far from thinking, that men have no affection for any thing beyond themselves, I am of opinion, that tho' it be rare to meet with one, who loves any single person better than himself; yet 'tis as rare to meet with one, in whom all the kind affections, taken together, do not overbalance all the selfish. Consult common experience: Do you not see, that tho' the whole expence of the family be generally under the direction of the master of it, yet there are few that do not bestow the largest part of their fortunes on the pleasures of their wives, and the education of their children, reserving the smallest portion for their own proper use and entertainment. This is what we may observe concerning such as have those endearing ties; and may presume, that the case would be the same with others, were they plac'd in a like situation.

But tho' this generosity must be acknowledg'd to the honour of human nature, we may at the same time remark, that so noble an affection, instead of fitting men for large societies, is almost as contrary to them, as the most narrow selfishness. For while each person loves himself better than any other single person, and in his love to others bears the greatest affection to his relations and acquaintance, this must necessarily produce an oppositon of passions, and a consequent opposition of actions; which cannot but be dangerous to the new-establish'd union.

'Tis however worth while to remark, that this contrariety of passions wou'd be attended with but small danger, did it not concur with a peculiarity in our *outward circumstances*, which affords it an opportunity of exerting itself. There are different species of goods, which we are possess'd of; the internal satisfaction of our minds, the external advantages of our body, and the enjoyment of such possessions as we have acquir'd by our industry and good fortune. We are perfectly secure in the enjoyment of the first. The second may be ravish'd from us, but can be of no advantage to him who deprives us of them. The last only are both expos'd to the violence of others, and may be transferr'd without suffering any loss or alteration; while at the same time, there is not a sufficient quantity of them to supply every one's desires and necessities. As the improvement, therefore, of these goods is the chief advantage of society, so the *instability* of their possession, along with their *scarcity*, is the chief impediment.

In vain shou'd we expect to find, in *uncultivated nature*, a remedy to this inconvenience; or hope for any inartificial principle of the human mind, which might controul those partial affections, and make us overcome the temptations arising from our circumstances. The idea of justice can never serve to this purpose, or be taken for a natural principle, capable of inspiring men with an equitable conduct towards each other. That virtue, as it is now understood, wou'd never have been dream'd of among rude and savage men. For the notion of injury or injustice implies an immorality or vice committed against some other person: And as every immorality is deriv'd from some defect or unsoundness of the passions, and as this defect must be judg'd of, in a great measure, from the ordinary course of nature in the constitution of the mind; 'twill be easy to know, whether we be guilty of any immorality, with regard to others, by considering the natural, and usual force of those several affections, which are directed towards them. Now it appears, that in the original frame of our mind, our strongest attention is confin'd to ourselves; our next is extended to our relations and acquaintance; and 'tis only the weakest which reaches to strangers and indifferent persons. This partiality, then, and unequal affection, must not only have an influence on our behaviour and conduct in society, but even on our ideas of vice and virtue; so as to make us regard any remarkable transgression of such a degree of partiality, either by too great an enlargement, or contraction of the affections, as vicious and immoral. This we may observe in our common judgments concerning actions, where we blame a person, who either centers all his affections in his family, or is so regardless of them, as, in any opposition of interest, to give the preference to a stranger, or mere chance acquaintance. From all which it follows, that our natural uncultivated ideas of morality, instead of providing a remedy for the partiality of our affections, do rather conform themselves to that partiality, and give it an additional force and influence.

The remedy, then, is not deriv'd from nature, but from *artifice*; or more properly speaking, nature provides a remedy in the judgment and understanding, for what is irregular and incommodious in the affections. For when men, from their early education in society, have become sensible of the infinite advantages that result from it, and have besides acquir'd a new affection to company and conversation; and when they have observ'd, that the principal disturbance in society arises from those goods, which we call external, and from their looseness and easy transition from one person to another; they must seek for a remedy by putting these goods, as far as possible, on the same footing with the fix'd and constant advantages of the mind and body. This can be done after no other manner, than by a convention enter'd into by all the members of the society to bestow stability on the possession of those external goods, and leave every one in the peaceable enjoyment of what he may acquire by his fortune and industry. By this means, every one knows what he may safely possess; and the passions are restrain'd in their partial and contradictory motions. Nor is such a restraint contrary to these passions; for if so, it cou'd never be enter'd into, nor maintain'd; but it is only contrary to their heedless and impetuous movement. Instead of departing from our own interest, or from that of our nearest friends, by abstaining from the possessions of others, we cannot better consult both these interests, than by such a convention; because it is by that means we maintain society, which is so necessary to their well-being and subsistence, as well as to our own.

This convention is not of the nature of a *promise*: For even promises themselves, as we shall see afterwards, arise from human conventions. It is only a general sense of common interest; which sense all the members of the society express to one another, and which induces them to regulate their conduct by certain rules. I observe, that it will be for my interest to leave another in the possession of his goods, *provided* he will act in the same manner with regard to me. He is sensible of a like interest in the regulation of his conduct. When this common sense of interest is mutually express'd, and is known to both, it produces a suitable resolution and behaviour. And this may properly enough be call'd a convention or agreement betwixt us, tho' without the interposition of a promise; since the actions of each of us have a reference to those of the other, and are perform'd upon the supposition, that something is to be perform'd on the other part. Two men, who pull the oars of a boat, do it by an agreement or convention, tho' they have never given promises to each other. Nor is the rule concerning the stability of possession the less deriv'd from human conventions, that it arises gradually, and acquires force by a slow progression, and by our repeated experience of the inconveniences of transgressing it. On the contrary, this experience assures us still more, that the sense of interest has become common to all our fellows, and gives us a confidence of the future regularity of their conduct: And 'tis only on the expectation of this, that our moderàtion and abstinence are founded. In like manner are languages gradually establish'd by human conventions without any promise. In like manner do gold and silver become the common measures of exchange, and are esteem'd sufficient payment for what is of a hundred times their value.

After this convention, concerning abstinence from the possessions of others, is enter'd into, and every one has acquir'd a stability in his possessions, there immediately arise the ideas of justice and injustice; as also those of *property*, *right*, and *obligation*. The latter are altogether unintelligible without first understanding the former. Our property is nothing but those goods, whose constant possession is establish'd by the laws of society; that is, by the laws of justice. Those, therefore, who make use of the words *property*, or *right*, or *obligation*, before they have explain'd the origin of justice, or even make use of them in that explication, are guilty of a very gross fallacy, and can never reason upon any solid foundation. A man's property is some object related to him. This relation is not natural, but moral, and founded on justice. 'Tis very preposterous, therefore, to imagine, that we can have any idea of property, without fully comprehending the nature of justice, and shewing its origin in the artifice and contrivance of man. The origin of justice explains that of property. The same artifice gives rise to both. As our first and most natural sentiment of morals is founded on the nature of our passions, and gives the preference to ourselves and friends, above strangers; 'tis impossible there can be naturally any such thing as a fix'd right or property, while the opposite passions of men impel them in contrary directions, and are not restrain'd by any convention or agreement.

No one can doubt, that the convention for the distinction of property, and for the stability of possession, is of all circumstances the most necessary to the establishment of human society, and that after the agreement for the fixing and observing of this rule, there remains little or nothing to be done towards settling a perfect harmony and concord. All the other passions, besides this of interest, are either easily restrain'd, or are not of such pernicious consequence, when indulg'd. *Vanity* is rather to be esteem'd a social passion, and a bond of union among men. *Pity* and *love* are to be consider'd in the same light. And as to *envy* and *revenge*, tho' pernicious, they operate only by intervals, and are directed against particular persons, whom we consider as our superiors or enemies. This avidity alone, of acquiring goods and possessions for ourselves and our nearest friends, is insatiable, perpetual, universal, and directly destructive of society. There scarce is any one, who is not actuated by it; and there is no one, who has not reason to fear from it, when it acts without any restraint, and gives way to its first and most natural movements. So that upon the whole, we are to esteem the difficulties in the establishment of society, to be greater or less, according to those we encounter in regulating and restraining this passion.

'Tis certain, that no affection of the human mind has both a sufficient force, and a proper direction to counterbalance the love of gain, and render men fit members of society, by making them abstain from the possessions of others. Benevolence to strangers is too weak for this purpose; and as to the other passions, they rather inflame this avidity, when we observe, that the larger our possessions are, the more ability we have of gratifying all our appetites. There is no passion, therefore, capable of controlling the interested affection, but the very affection itself, by an alteration of its direction. Now this alteration must necessarily take place upon the least reflection; since 'tis evident, that the passion is much better satisfy'd by its restraint, than by its liberty, and that in preserving society, we make much greater advances in the acquiring possessions, than in the solitary and forlorn condition, which must follow upon violence and an universal licence. The question, therefore, concerning the wickedness or goodness of human nature, enters not in the least into that other question concerning the origin of society; nor is there any thing to be consider'd but the degrees of men's sagacity or folly. For whether the passion of self-interest be esteemed vicious or virtuous, 'tis all a case; since itself alone restrains it: So that if it be virtuous, men become social by their virtue; if vicious, their vice has the same effect.

Now as 'tis by establishing the rule for the stability of possession, that this passion restrains itself; if that rule be very abstruse, and of difficult invention; society must be esteem'd, in a manner, accidental, and the effect of many ages. But if it be found, that nothing can be more simple and obvious than that rule; that every parent, in order to preserve peace among his children, must establish it; and that these first rudiments of justice must every day be improv'd, as the society enlarges: If all this appear evident, as it certainly must, we may conclude, that 'tis utterly impossible for men to remain any considerable time in that savage condition, which precedes society; but that his very first state and situation may justly be esteem'd social. This, however, hinders not, but that philosophers may, if they please, extend their reasoning to the suppos'd *state of nature*; provided they allow it to be a mere philosophical fiction, which never had, and never cou'd have any reality. Human nature being compos'd of two principal parts, which are requisite in all its actions, the affections and understanding; 'tis certain, that the blind motions of the former, without the direction of the latter, incapacitate men for society:

And it may be allow'd us to consider separately the effects, that result from the separate operations of these two component parts of the mind. The same liberty may be permitted to moral, which is allow'd to natural philosophers; and 'tis very usual with the latter to consider any motion as compounded and consisting of two parts separate from each other, tho' at the same time they acknowledge it to be in itself uncompounded and inseparable.

This *state of nature*, therefore, is to be regarded as a mere fiction, not unlike that of the *golden age*, which poets have invented; only with this difference, that the former is describ'd as full of war, violence and injustice; whereas the latter is pointed out to us, as the most charming and most peaceable condition, that can possibly be imagin'd. The seasons, in that first age of nature, were so temperate, if we may believe the poets, that there was no necessity for men to provide themselves with cloaths and houses as a security against the violence of heat and cold. The rivers flow'd with wine and milk: The oaks yielded honey; and nature spontaneously produc'd her greatest delicacies. Nor were these the chief advantages of that happy age. The storms and tempests were not alone remov'd from nature; but those more furious tempests were unknown to human breasts, which now cause such uproar, and engender such confusion. Avarice, ambition, cruelty, selfishness, were never heard of: Cordial affection, compassion, sympathy, were the only movements, with which the human mind was yet acquainted. Even the distinction of *mine* and *thine* was banish'd from that happy race of mortals, and carry'd with them the very notions of property and obligation, justice and injustice.

This, no doubt, is to be regarded as an idle fiction; but yet deserves our attention, because nothing can more evidently shew the origin of those virtues, which are the subjects of our present enquiry. I have already observ'd, that justice takes its rise from human conventions; and that these are intended as a remedy to some inconveniences, which proceed from the concurrence of certain *qualities* of the human mind with the *situation* of external objects. The qualities of the mind are *selfishness* and *limited generosity*: And the situation of external objects is their *easy change*, join'd to their *scarcity* in comparison of the wants and desires of men. But however philosophers may have been bewilder'd in those speculations, poets have been guided more infallibly, by a certain taste or common instinct, which in most kinds of reasoning goes farther than any of that art and philosophy, with which we have been yet acquainted. They easily perceiv'd, if every man had a tender regard for another, or if nature supplied abundantly all our wants and desires, that the jealousy of interest, which justice supposes, could no longer have place; nor would there be any occasion for those distinctions and limits of property and possession, which at present are in use among mankind. Encrease to a sufficient degree the benevolence of men, or the bounty of nature, and you render justice useless, by supplying its place with much nobler virtues, and more valuable blessings. The selfishness of men is animated by the few possessions we have, in proportion to our wants; and 'tis to restrain this selfishness, that men have been oblig'd to separate themselves from the community, and to distinguish betwixt their own goods and those of others.

Nor need we have recourse to the fictions of poets to learn this; but beside the reason of the thing, may discover the same truth by common experience and observation. 'Tis easy to remark, that a cordial affection renders all things common among friends; and that married people in particular mutually lose their property, and are unacquainted with the *mine* and *thine*, which are so necessary, and yet cause such disturbance in human society. The same effect arises from any alteration in the circumstances of mankind; as when there is such a plenty of any thing as satisfies all the desires of men: In which case the distinction of property is entirely lost, and every thing remains in common. This we may observe with regard to air and water, tho' the most valuable of all external objects; and may easily conclude, that if men were supplied with every thing in the same abundance, or if *every one* had the same affection and tender regard for *every one* as for himself; justice and injustice would be equally unknown among mankind.

Here then is a proposition, which, I think, may be regarded as certain, *that 'tis only from the selfishness and confin'd generosity of men, along with the scanty provision nature has made for his wants, that justice derives its origin.* If we look backward we shall find, that this proposition bestows an additional force on some of those observations, which we have already made on this subject.

First, we may conclude from it, that a regard to public interest, or a strong extensive benevolence, is not our first and original motive for the observation of the rules of justice; since 'tis allow'd, that if men were endow'd with such a benevolence, these rules would never have been dreamt of.

Secondly, we may conclude from the same principle, that the sense of justice is not founded on reason, or on the discovery of certain connexions and relations of ideas, which are eternal, immutable, and universally obligatory. For since it is confest, that such an alteration as that above-mention'd, in the temper and circumstances of mankind, wou'd entirely alter our duties and obligations, 'tis necessary upon the common system, *that the sense of virtue is deriv'd from reason*, to shew the change which this must produce in the relations and ideas. But 'tis evident, that the only cause, why the extensive generosity of man, and the perfect abundance of every thing, wou'd destroy the very idea of justice, is because they render it useless; and that, on the other hand, his confin'd benevolence, and his necessitous condition, give rise to that virtue, only by making it requisite to the publick interest, and to that of every individual. 'Twas therefore a concern for our own, and the publick interest, which made us establish the laws of justice; and nothing can be more certain, than that it is not any relation of ideas, which gives us this concern, but our impressions and sentiments, without which every thing in nature is perfectly indifferent to us, and can never in the least affect us. The sense of justice, therefore, is not founded on our ideas, but on our impressions.

Thirdly, we may farther confirm the foregoing proposition, *that those impressions, which give rise to this sense of justice, are not natural to the mind of man, but arise from artifice and human conventions.* For since any considerable alteration of temper and circumstances destroys equally justice and injustice; and since such an alteration has an effect only by changing our own and the publick interest; it follows, that the first establishment of the rules of justice depends on these different interests. But if men pursu'd the publick interest naturally, and with a hearty affection, they wou'd never have dream'd of restraining each other by these rules; and if they pursu'd their own interest, without any precaution, they wou'd run head-long into every kind of injustice and violence. These rules, therefore, are artificial, and seek their end in an oblique and indirect manner; nor is the interest, which gives rise to them, of a kind that cou'd be pursu'd by the natural and inartificial passions of men.

To make this more evident, consider, that tho' the rules of justice are establish'd merely by interest, their connexion with interest is somewhat singular, and is different from what may be observ'd on other occasions. A single act of justice is frequently contrary to *public interest*; and were it to stand alone, without being follow'd by other acts, may, in itself, be very prejudicial to society. When a man of merit, of a beneficent disposition, restores a great fortune to a miser, or a seditious bigot, he has acted justly and laudably, but the public is a real sufferer. Nor is every single act of justice, consider'd apart, more conducive to private interest, than to public; and 'tis easily conceiv'd how a man may impoverish himself by a signal instance of integrity, and have reason to wish, that with regard to that single act, the laws of justice were for a moment suspended in the universe. But however single acts of justice may be contrary, either to public or private interest, 'tis certain, that the whole plan or scheme is highly conducive, or indeed absolutely requisite, both to the support of society, and the well-being of every individual. 'Tis impossible to separate the good from the ill. Property must be stable, and must be fix'd by general rules. Tho' in one instance the public be a sufferer, this momentary ill is amply compensated by the steady prosecution of the rule, and by the peace and order, which it establishes in society. And even every individual person must find himself a gainer, on ballancing the account; since, without justice, society must immediately dissolve, and every one must fall into that savage and solitary condition, which is infinitely worse than the worst situation that can possibly be suppos'd in society. When therefore men have had experience enough to observe, that whatever may be the consequence of any single act of justice, perform'd by a single person, yet the whole system of actions, concurr'd in by the whole society, is infinitely advantageous to the whole, and to every part; it is not long before justice and property take place. Every member of society is sensible of this interest: Every one expresses this sense to his fellows, along with the resolution he has taken of squaring his actions by it, on condition that others will do the same. No more is requisite to induce any one of them to perform an act of justice, who has the first opportunity. This becomes an example to others. And thus justice establishes itself by a kind of convention or agreement; that is, by a sense of interest, suppos'd to be common to all, and where every single act is perform'd in expectation that others are to perform the like. Without such a convention, no one wou'd ever have dream'd, that there was such a virtue as justice, or have been induc'd to conform his actions to it. Taking any single act, my justice may be pernicious in every respect; and 'tis only upon the supposition, that others are to imitate my example, that I can be induc'd to embrace that virtue; since nothing but this combination can render justice advantageous, or afford me any motives to conform my self to its rules.

We come now to the *second* question we propos'd, *viz. Why we annex the idea of virtue to justice, and of vice to injustice.* This question will not detain us long after the principles, which we have already establish'd. All we can say of it at present will be dispatch'd in a few words: And for farther satisfaction, the reader must wait till we come to the *third* part of this book. The *natural* obligation to justice, *viz.* interest, has been fully explain'd; but as to the *moral* obligation, or the sentiment of right and wrong, 'twill first be requisite to examine the natural virtues, before we can give a full and satisfactory account of it.

After men have found by experience, that their selfishness and confin'd generosity, acting at their liberty, totally incapacitate them for society; and at the same time have observ'd, that society is necessary to the satisfaction of those very passions, they are naturally induc'd to lay themselves under the restraint of such rules, as may render their commerce more safe and commodious. To the imposition then, and observance of these rules, both in general, and in every particular instance, they are at first induc'd only by a regard to interest; and this motive, on the first formation of society, is sufficiently strong and forcible. But when society has become numerous, and has encreas'd to a tribe or nation, this interest is more remote; nor do men so readily perceive, that disorder and confusion follow upon every breach of these rules, as in a more narrow and contracted society. But tho' in our own actions we may frequently lose sight of that interest, which we have in maintaining order, and may follow a lesser and more present interest, we never fail to observe the prejudice we receive, either mediately or immediately, from the injustice of others; as not being in that case either blinded by passion, or byass'd by any contrary temptation. Nay when the injustice is so distant from us, as no way to affect our interest, it still displeases us; because we consider it as prejudicial to human society, and pernicious to every one that approaches the person guilty of it. We partake of their uneasiness by *sympathy*; and as every thing, which gives uneasiness in human actions, upon the general survey, is call'd Vice, and whatever produces satisfaction, in the same manner, is denominated Virtue; this is the reason why the sense of moral good and evil follows upon justice and injustice. And tho' this sense, in the present case, be deriv'd only from contemplating the actions of others, yet we fail not to extend it even to our own actions. The *general rule* reaches beyond those instances, from which it arose; while at the same time we naturally *sympathize* with others in the sentiments they entertain of us. *Thus self-interest is the original motive to the* establishment *of justice: but a* sympathy *with public interest is the source of the* moral approbation, *which attends that virtue.*

Tho' this progress of the sentiments be *natural*, and even necessary, 'tis certain, that it is here forwarded by the artifice of politicians, who, in order to govern men more easily, and preserve peace in human society, have endeavour'd to produce an esteem for justice, and an abhorrence of injustice. This, no doubt, must have its effect; but nothing can be more evident, than that the matter has been carry'd too far by certain writers on morals, who seem to have employ'd their utmost efforts to extirpate all sense of virtue from among mankind. Any artifice of politicians may assist nature in the producing of those sentiments, which she suggests to us, and may even on some occasions, produce alone an approbation or esteem for any particular action; but 'tis impossible it should be the sole cause of the distinction we make betwixt vice and virtue. For if nature did not aid us in this particular, 'twou'd be in vain for politicians to talk of *honourable* or *dishonourable*, *praiseworthy* or *blameable*. These words wou'd be perfectly unintelligible, and wou'd no more have any idea annex'd to them, than if they were of a tongue perfectly unknown to us. The utmost politicians can perform, is, to extend the natural sentiments beyond their original bounds; but still nature must furnish the materials, and give us some notion of moral distinctions.

As publick praise and blame encrease our esteem for justice; so private education and instruction contribute to the same effect. For as parents easily observe, that a man is the more useful, both to himself and others, the greater degree of probity and honour he is endow'd with; and that those principles have greater force, when custom and education assist interest and reflection: For these reasons they are induc'd to inculcate on their children, from their earliest infancy, the principles of probity, and teach them to regard the observance of those rules, by which society is maintain'd, as worthy and honourable, and their violation as base and infamous. By this means the sentiments of honour may take root in their tender minds, and acquire such firmness and solidity, that they may fall little short of those principles, which are the most essential to our natures, and the most deeply radicated in our internal constitution.

What farther contributes to encrease their solidity, is the interest of our reputation, after the opinion, *that a merit or demerit attends justice or injustice*, is once firmly establish'd among mankind. There is nothing, which touches us more nearly than our reputation, and nothing on which our reputation more depends than our conduct, with relation to the property of others. For this reason, every one, who has any regard to his character, or who intends to live on good terms with mankind, must fix an inviolable law to himself, never, by any temptation, to be induc'd to violate those principles, which are essential to a man of probity and honour.

I shall make only one observation before I leave this subject, *viz.* that tho' I assert, that in the *state of nature*, or that imaginary state, which preceded society, there be neither justice nor injustice, yet I assert not, that it was allowable, in such a state, to violate the property of others. I only maintain, that there was no such thing as property; and consequently cou'd be no such thing as justice or injustice. I shall have occasion to make a similar reflection with regard to *promises*, when I come to treat of them; and I hope this reflection, when duly weigh'd, will suffice to remove all odium from the foregoing opinions, with regard to justice and injustice.

SECT. III

Of the rules, which determine property

THO' the establishment of the rule, concerning the stability of possession, be not only useful, but even absolutely necessary to human society, it can never serve to any purpose, while it remains in such general terms. Some method must be shewn, by which we may distinguish what particular goods are to be assign'd to each particular person, while the rest of mankind are excluded from their possession and enjoyment. Our next business, then, must be to discover the reasons which modify this general rule, and fit it to the common use and practice of the world.

'Tis obvious, that those reasons are not deriv'd from any utility or advantage, which either the *particular* person or the public may reap from his enjoyment of any particular goods, beyond what wou'd result from the possession of them by any other person. 'Twere better, no doubt, that every one were possess'd of what is most suitable to him, and proper for his use: But besides, that this relation of fitness may be common to several at once, 'tis liable to so many controversies, and men are so partial and passionate in judging of these controversies, that such a loose and uncertain rule wou'd be absolutely incompatible with the peace of human society. The convention concerning the stability of possession is enter'd into, in order to cut off all occasions of discord and contention; and this end wou'd never be attain'd, were we allow'd to apply this rule differently in every particular case, according to every particular utility, which might be discover'd in such an application. Justice, in her decisions, never regards the fitness or unfitness of objects to particular persons, but conducts herself by more extensive views. Whether a man be generous, or a miser, he is equally well receiv'd by her, and obtains with the same facility a decision in his favours, even for what is entirely useless to him.

It follows therefore, that the general rule, *that possession must be stable,* is not apply'd by particular judgments, but by other general rules, which must extend to the whole society, and be inflexible either by spite or favour. To illustrate this, I propose the following instance. I first consider men in their savage and solitary condition; and suppose, that being sensible of the misery of that state, and foreseeing the advantages that wou'd result from society, they seek each other's company, and make an offer of mutual protection and assistance. I also suppose, that they are endow'd with such sagacity as immediately to perceive, that the chief impediment to this project of society and partnership lies in the avidity and selfishness of their natural temper; to remedy which, they enter into a convention for the stability of possession, and for mutual restraint and forbearance. I am sensible, that this method of proceeding is not altogether natural; but besides that I here only suppose those reflections to be form'd at once, which in fact arise insensibly and by degrees; besides this, I say, 'tis very possible, that several persons, being by different accidents separated from the societies, to which they formerly belong'd, may be oblig'd to form a new society among themselves; in which case they are entirely in the situation abovemention'd.

'Tis evident, then, that their first difficulty, in this situation, after the general convention for the establishment of society, and for the constancy of possession, is, how to separate their possessions, and assign to each his particular portion, which he must for the future inalterably enjoy. This difficulty will not detain them long; but it must immediately occur to them, as the most natural expedient, that every one continue to enjoy what he is at present master of, and that property or constant possession be conjoin'd to the immediate possession. Such is the effect of custom, that it not only reconciles us to any thing we have long enjoy'd, but even gives us an affection for it, and makes us prefer it to other objects, which may be more valuable, but are less known to us. What has long lain under our eye, and has often been employ'd to our advantage, *that* we are always the most unwilling to part with; but can easily live without possessions, which we never have enjoy'd, and are not accustom'd to. 'Tis evident, therefore, that men wou'd easily acquiesce in this expedient, *that every one continue to enjoy what he is at present possess'd of*; and this is the reason, why they wou'd so naturally agree in preferring it*.

* No questions in philosophy are more difficult, than when a number of causes present themselves for the same phaenomenon, to determine which is the principal and predominant. There seldom is any very precise argument to fix our choice, and men must be contented to be guided by a kind of taste or fancy, arising from analogy, and a comparison of familiar instances. Thus, in the present case, there are, no doubt, motives of public interest for most of the rules, which determine property; but still I suspect, that these rules are principally fix'd by the imagination, or the more frivolous properties of our thought and conception. I shall continue to explain these causes, leaving it to the reader's choice, whether he will prefer those deriv'd from publick utility, or those deriv'd from the imagination. We shall begin with the right of the present possessor.

'Tis a quality, which (*a*) I have already observ'd in human nature, that when two objects appear in a close relation to each other, the mind is apt to ascribe to them any additional relation, in order to compleat the union; and this inclination is so strong, as often to make us run into errors (such as that of the conjunction of thought and matter) if we find that they can serve to that purpose. Many of our impressions are incapable of place or local position; and yet those very impressions we suppose to have a local conjunction with the impressions of sight and touch, merely because they are conjoin'd by causation, and are already united in the imagination. Since, therefore, we can feign a new relation, and even an absurd one, in order to compleat any union, 'twill easily be imagin'd, that if there be any relations, which depend on the mind, 'twill readily conjoin them to any preceding relation, and unite, by a new bond, such objects as have already an union in the fancy. Thus for instance, we never fail, in our arrangement of bodies, to place those which are *resembling* in *contiguity* to each other, or at least in *correspondent* points of view; because we feel a satisfaction in joining the relation of contiguity to that of resemblance, or the resemblance of situation to that of qualities. And this is easily accounted for from the known properties of human nature. When the mind is determin'd to join certain objects,

(*a*) *Book* I. *Part* IV. *Sect.* 5.

But we may observe, that tho' the rule of the assignment of property to the present possessor be natural, and by that means useful, yet its utility extends not beyond the first formation of society; nor wou'd any thing be more pernicious, than the constant observance of it; by which restitution wou'd be excluded, and every injustice wou'd be authoriz'd and rewarded. We must, therefore, seek for some other circumstance, that may give rise to property after society is once establish'd; and of this kind, I find four most considerable, *viz.* Occupation, Prescription, Accession, and Succession. We shall briefly examine each of these, beginning with *Occupation.*

The possession of all external goods is changeable and uncertain; which is one of the most considerable impediments to the establishment of society, and is the reason why, by universal agreement, express or tacite, men restrain themselves by what we now call the rules of justice and equity. The misery of the condition, which precedes this restraint, is the cause why we submit to that remedy as quickly as possible; and this affords us an easy reason, why we annex the idea of property to the first possession, or to *occupation.* Men are unwilling to leave property in suspense,

---

but undetermin'd in its choice of the particular objects, it naturally turns its eye to such as are related together. They are already united in the mind: They present themselves at the same time to the conception; and instead of requiring any new reason for their conjunction, it wou'd require a very powerful reason to make us over-look this natural affinity. This we shall have occasion to explain more fully afterwards, when we come to treat of *beauty.* In the mean time, we may content ourselves with observing, that the same love of order and uniformity, which arranges the books in a library, and the chairs in a parlour, contribute to the formation of society, and to the well-being of mankind, by modifying the general rule concerning the stability of possession. And as property forms a relation betwixt a person and an object, 'tis natural to found it on some preceding relation; and as property is nothing but a constant possession, secur'd by the laws of society, 'tis natural to add it to the present possession, which is a relation that resembles it. For this also has its influence. If it be natural to conjoin all sorts of relations, 'tis more so, to conjoin such relations as are resembling, and are related together.

even for the shortest time, or open the least door to violence and disorder. To which we may add, that the first possession always engages the attention most; and did we neglect it, there wou'd be no colour of reason for assigning property to any succeeding possession*.

There remains nothing, but to determine exactly, what is meant by possession; and this is not so easy as may at first sight be imagin'd. We are said to be in possession of any thing, not only when we immediately touch it, but also when we are so situated with respect to it, as to have it in our power to use it; and may move, alter, or destroy it, according to our present pleasure or advantage. This relation, then, is a species of cause and effect; and as property is nothing but a stable possession, deriv'd from the rules of justice, or the conventions of men, 'tis to be consider'd as the same species of relation. But here we may observe, that as the power of using any object becomes more or less certain, according as the interruptions we may meet with are more or less probable; and as this probability may increase by insensible degrees; 'tis in many cases impossible to determine when possession begins or ends; nor is there any certain standard, by which we can decide such controversies. A wild boar, that falls into our snares, is deem'd to be in our possession, if it be impossible for him to escape. But what do we mean by impossible? How do we separate this impossibility from an improbability? And how distinguish that exactly from a probability? Mark the precise limits of the one and the other, and shew the standard, by which

*Some philosophers account for the right of occupation, by saying, that every one has a property in his own labour; and when he joins that labour to any thing, it gives him the property of the whole: But, 1. There are several kinds of occupation, where we cannot be said to join our labour to the object we acquire: As when we possess a meadow by grazing our cattle upon it. 2. This accounts for the matter by means of *accession*; which is taking a needless circuit. 3. We cannot be said to join our labour to any thing but in a figurative sense. Properly speaking, we only make an alteration on it by our labour. This forms a relation betwixt us and the object; and thence arises the property, according to the preceding principles.

we may decide all disputes that may arise, and, as we find by experience, frequently do arise upon this subject*.

But such disputes may not only arise concerning the real existence of property and possession, but also concerning their extent; and these disputes are often susceptible of no decision, or can be decided by no other faculty than the imagination. A person who lands on the shore of a small island, that is desart and uncultivated, is deem'd its possessor from the very first moment, and acquires the property of the whole; because the object is there bounded and circumscrib'd in the fancy, and at the same time is proportion'd to the new possessor. The same person landing on a desart island, as large as *Great Britain*, extends his property no farther than his immediate possession; tho' a numerous colony are esteem'd the proprietors of the whole from the instant of their debarkment.

But it often happens, that the title of first possession becomes obscure thro' time; and that 'tis impossible to determine many controversies, which may arise concerning it. In that case long possession or *prescription* naturally takes

*If we seek a solution of these difficulties in reason and public interest, we never shall find satisfaction; and if we look for it in the imagination, 'tis evident, that the qualities, which operate upon that faculty, run so insensibly and gradually into each other, that 'tis impossible to give them any precise bounds or termination. The difficulties on this head must encrease, when we consider, that our judgment alters very sensibly, according to the subject, and that the same power and proximity will be deem'd possession in one case, which is not esteem'd such in another. A person, who has hunted a hare to the last degree of weariness, wou'd look upon it as an injustice for another to rush in before him, and seize his prey. But the same person, advancing to pluck an apple, that hangs within his reach, has no reason to complain, if another, more alert, passes him, and takes possession. What is the reason of this difference, but that immobility, not being natural to the hare, but the effect of industry, forms in that case a strong relation with the hunter, which is wanting in the other?

Here then it appears, that a certain and infallible power of enjoyment, without touch or some other sensible relation, often produces not property: And I farther observe, that a sensible relation, without any present power, is sometimes sufficient to give a title to any object. The sight of a thing is seldom a considerable relation, and is only regarded as such, when the object is hidden, or very obscure; in which case we find, that the view alone conveys a property; according to that maxim, *that even a whole continent belongs to the nation, which first discover'd it.* 'Tis however remarkable that both in the case of discovery and that of possession, the first discoverer and possessor must join to the relation an intention of rendering himself proprietor, otherwise the relation will not have its effect; and that because the connexion in our fancy betwixt the property and the relation is not so great, but that it requires to be help'd by such an intention.

From all these circumstances, 'tis easy to see how perplex'd many questions may become concerning the acquisition of property by occupation; and the least effort of thought may present us with instances, which are not susceptible of any reasonable decision. If we prefer examples, which are real, to such as are feign'd, we may consider the following one, which is to be met with in almost every writer, that has treated of the laws of nature. Two *Grecian* colonies, leaving their native country, in search of new feats, were inform'd that a city near them was deserted by its inhabitants. To know the truth of this report, they dispatch'd at once two messengers, one from each colony; who finding on their approach, that their information was true, begun a race together with an intention to take possession of the city, each of them for his countrymen. One of these messengers, finding that he was not an equal match for the other, launch'd his spear at the gates of the city, and was so fortunate as to fix it there before the arrival of his companion. This produc'd a dispute betwixt the two colonies, which of them was the proprietor of the empty city; and this dispute still subsists among philosophers. For my part I find the dispute impossible to be decided, and that because the whole question hangs upon the fancy, which in this case is not possess'd of any precise or determinate standard, upon which it can give sentence. To make this evident, let us consider, that if these two persons had been simply members of the colonies, and not messengers or deputies, their actions wou'd not have been of any consequence; since in that case their relation to the colonies wou'd have been but feeble and imperfect. Add to this, that nothing determin'd them to run to the gates rather than the walls, or any other part of the city, but that the gates, being the most obvious and remarkable part, satisfy the fancy best in taking them for the whole; as we find by the poets, who frequently draw their images and metaphors from them. Besides we may consider, that the touch or contact of the one messenger is not properly possession, no more than the piercing the gates with a spear; but only forms a relation; and there is a relation, in the other case, equally obvious, tho' not, perhaps, of equal force. Which of these relations, then, conveys a right and property, or whether any of them be sufficient for that effect, I leave to the decision of such as are wiser than myself.

place, and gives a person a sufficient property in any thing he enjoys. The nature of human society admits not of any great accuracy; nor can we always remount to the first origin of things, in order to determine their present condition. Any considerable space of time sets objects at such a distance, that they seem, in a manner, to lose their reality, and have as little influence on the mind, as if they never had been in being. A man's title, that is clear and certain at present, will seem obscure and doubtful fifty years hence, even tho' the facts, on which it is founded, shou'd be prov'd with the greatest evidence and certainty. The same facts have not the same influence after so long an interval of time. And this may be receiv'd as a convincing argument for our preceding doctrine with regard to property and justice. Possession during a long tract of time conveys a title to any object. But as 'tis certain, that, however every thing be produc'd in time, there is nothing real that is produc'd by time; it follows, that property being produc'd by time, is not any thing real in the objects, but is the off-spring of the sentiments, on which alone time is found to have any influence *.

We acquire the property of objects by *accession*, when they are connected in an intimate manner with objects that are already our property, and at the same time are inferior to them. Thus the fruits of our garden, the offspring of our cattle, and the work of our slaves, are all of them esteem'd our property, even before possession. Where objects are connected together in the imagination, they are apt to be put on the same footing, and are commonly suppos'd to be endow'd with the same qualities. We readily pass from one to the other, and make no difference in our judgments concern-

* Present possession is plainly a relation betwixt a person and an object; but is not sufficient to counter-ballance the relation of first possession, unless the former be long and uninterrupted: In which case the relation is encreas'd on the side of the present possession, by the extent of time, and diminish'd on that of first possession, by the distance. This change in the relation produces a consequent change in the property.

ing them; especially if the latter be inferior to the former*.

The right of *succession* is a very natural one, from the presum'd consent of the parent or near relation, and from the general interest of mankind, which requires, that men's possessions shou'd pass to those, who are dearest to them, in order to render them more industrious and frugal. Perhaps these causes are seconded by the influence of *relation*, or the association of ideas, by which we are naturally directed to consider the son after the parent's decease, and ascribe to him a title to his father's possessions. Those goods must become the property of some body: But *of whom* is the question. Here 'tis evident the persons children naturally present themselves to the mind; and being already

*This source of property can never be explain'd but from the imaginations; and one may affirm, that the causes are here unmix'd. We shall proceed to explain them more particularly, and illustrate them by examples from common life and experience.

It has been observed above, that the mind has a natural propensity to join relations, especially resembling ones, and finds a kind of fitness and uniformity in such an union. From this propensity are deriv'd these laws of nature, *that upon the first formation of society, property always follows the present possession*; and afterwards, *that it arises from first or from long possession.* Now we may easily observe, that relation is not confin'd merely to one degree; but that from an object, that is related to us, we acquire a relation to every other object, which is related to it, and so on, till the thought loses the chain by too long a progress. However the relation may weaken by each remove, 'tis not immediately destroy'd; but frequently connects two objects by means of an intermediate one, which is related to both. And this principle is of such force as to give rise to the right of *accession*, and causes us to acquire the property not only of such objects as we are immediately possess'd of, but also of such as are closely connected with them.

Suppose a *German*, a *Frenchman*, and a *Spaniard* to come into a room, where there are plac'd upon the table three bottles of wine, *Rhenish, Burgundy* and *Port*; and suppose they shou'd fall a quarrelling about the division of them; a person, who was chosen for umpire, wou'd naturally, to shew his impartiality, give every one the product of his own country: And this from a principle, which, in some measure, is the source of those laws of nature, that ascribe property to occupation, prescription and accession.

In all these cases, and particularly that of accession, there is first a *natural* union betwixt the idea of the person and that of the object, and afterwards a new and *moral* union produc'd by that right or property, which we ascribe to the person. But here there occurs a difficulty, which merits our attention, and may afford us an opportunity of putting to tryal that singular method of reasoning, which has been employ'd on the present subject. I have already observ'd that the imagination passes with greater facility from little to great, than from great to little, and that the transition of ideas is always easier and smoother in the former case than in the latter. Now as the right of accession arises from the easy transition of ideas, by which related objects are connected together, it shou'd naturally be imagin'd, that the right of accession must encrease in strength, in proportion as the transition of ideas is perform'd with greater facility. It may, therefore, be thought, that when we have acquir'd the property of any small object, we shall readily consider any great object related to it as an accession, and as belonging to the proprietor of the small one; since the transition is in that case very easy from the small object to the great one, and shou'd connect them together in the closest manner. But in fact the case is always found to be otherwise. The empire of *Great Britain* seems to draw along with it the dominion of the *Orkneys*, the *Hebrides*, the isle of *Man*, and the isle of *Wight*; but the authority over those lesser islands does not naturally imply any title to *Great Britain*. In short, a small object naturally follows a great one as its accession; but a great one is never suppos'd to belong to the proprietor of a small one related to it, merely on account of that property and relation. Yet in this latter case the transition of ideas is smoother from the proprietor to the small object, which is his property, and from the small object to the great one, than in the former case from the proprietor to the great object, and from the great one to the small. It may therefore be thought, that these phaenomena are objections to the foregoing hypothesis, *that the ascribing of property to accession is nothing but an affect of the relations of ideas, and of the smooth transition of the imagination.*

'Twill be easy to solve this objection, if we consider the agility and unsteadiness of the imagination, with the different views, in which it is continually placing its objects. When we attribute to a person a property in two objects, we do not always pass from the person to one object, and from that to the other related to it. The objects being here to be consider'd as the property of the person, we are apt to join them together, and place them in the same light. Suppose, therefore, a great and a small object to be related together; if a person be strongly related to the great object, he will likewise be strongly related to both the objects, consider'd together, because he is related to the most considerable part. On the contrary, if he be only related to the small object, he will not be strongly related to both, consider'd together, since his relation lies only with the most trivial part, which is not apt to strike us in any great degree, when we consider the whole. And this is the reason, why small objects become accessions to great ones, and not great to small.

'Tis the general opinion of philosophers and civilians, that the sea is incapable of becoming the property of any nation; and that because 'tis impossible to take possession of it, or form any such distinct relation with it, as may be the foundation of property. Where this reason ceases, property immediately takes place. Thus the most strenuous advocates for the liberty of the seas universally allow, that friths and bays naturally belong as an accession to the proprietors of the surrounding continent. These have properly no more bond or union with the land, than the *pacific* ocean wou'd have; but having an union in the fancy, and being at the same time *inferior*, they are of course regarded as an accession.

The property of rivers, by the laws of most nations, and by the natural turn of our thought, is attributed to the proprietors of their banks, excepting such vast rivers as the *Rhine* or the *Danube*, which seem too large to the imagination to follow as an accession the property of the neighbouring fields. Yet even these rivers are consider'd as the property of that nation, thro' whose dominions they run; the idea of a nation being of a suitable bulk to correspond with them, and bear them such a relation in the fancy.

The accessions, which are made to lands bordering upon rivers, follow the land, say the civilians, provided it be made by what they call *alluvion*, that is, insensibly and imperceptibly; which are circumstances that mightily assist the imagination in the conjunction. Where there is any considerable portion torn at once from one bank, and join'd to another, it becomes not his property, whose land it falls on, till it unite with the land, and till the trees or plants have spread their roots into bcth. Before that, the imagination does not sufficiently join them.

There are other cases, which somewhat resemble this of accession, but which, at the bottom, are considerably different, and merit our attention. Of this kind is the conjunction of the properties of different persons, after such a manner as not to admit of *separation*. The question is, to whom the united mass must belong.

Where this conjunction is of such a nature as to admit of *division*, but not of *separation*, the decision is natural and easy. The whole mass must be suppos'd to be common betwixt the proprietors of the several parts, and afterwards must be divided according to the proportions of these parts. But here I cannot forbear taking notice of a remarkable subtilty of the *Roman* law, in distinguishing betwixt *confusion* and *commixtion*. Confusion is an union of two bodies, such as different liquors, where the parts become entirely undistinguishable. Commixtion is the blending of two bodies, such as two bushels of corn, where the parts remain separate in an obvious and visible manner. As in the latter case the imagination discovers not so entire an union as in the former, but is able to trace and preserve a distinct idea of the property of each; this is the reason, why the *civil* law, tho' it establish'd an entire community in the case of *confusion*, and after that a proportional division, yet in the case of *commixtion*, supposes each of the proprietors to maintain a distinct right; however necessity may at last force them to submit to the same division.

Quod si frumentum Titii frumento tuo mistum fuerit: siquidem ex voluntate vestra, commune est: quia singula corpora, id est, singula grana, quae cujusque propria fuerunt, ex consensu vestro communicata sunt. Quod si casu id mistum fuerit, vel Titius id miscuerit sine tua voluntate, non videtur id commune esse; quia singula corpora in sua substantia durant. Sed nec magis istis casibus commune sit frumentum quam grex intelligitur esse communis, si pecora Titii tuis pecoribus mista fuerint. Sed si ab alterutro vestrûm totum id frumentum retineatur, in rem quidem actio pro modo frumenti cujusque competit. Arbitrio autem judicis, ut ipse aestimet quale cujusque frumentum fuerit. Inst. Lib. II. Tit. 1. § 28.

[In the case that your grain was mixed with that of Titius, if it was done voluntarily on the part of both of you, it is common property, inasmuch as the individual items, i.e., the single grains, which were the peculiar property of either of you, were combined with your joint consent. If, however, the mixture was accidental, or if Titius mixed it without your consent, it does not appear that it is common property, inasmuch as the several components retain their original identity. Rather, in circumstances of this sort the grain does not become common property, any more than a herd of cattle is regarded as common property, if Titius' beasts should have become mixed up with yours.

However, if all of the aforesaid corn is kept by either of you, this gives rise to a suit to determine the ownership of property, in respect of the amount of corn belonging to each. It is in the discretion of the judge to determine which is the corn belonging to either party.]

Where the properties of two persons are united after such a manner as neither to admit of *division* nor *separation*, as when one builds a house on another's ground, in that case, the whole must belong to one of the proprietors: And here I assert, that it naturally is conceiv'd to belong to the proprietor of the most considerable part. For however the compound object may have a relation to two different persons, and carry our view at once to both of them, yet as the most considerable part principally engages our attention, and by the strict union draws the inferior along it; for this reason, the whole bears a relation to the proprietor of that part, and is regarded as his property. The only difficulty is, what we shall be pleas'd to call the most considerable part, and most attractive to the imagination.

connected to those possessions by means of their deceas'd parent, we are apt to connect them still farther by the relation of property. Of this there are many parallel instances*.

This quality depends on several different circumstances, which have little connexion with each other. One part of a compound object may become more considerable than another, either because it is more constant and durable; because it is of greater value; because it is more obvious and remarkable; because it is of greater extent; or because its existence is more separate and independent. 'Twill be easy to conceive, that, as these circumstances may be conjoin'd and oppos'd in all the different ways, and according to all the different degrees, which can be imagin'd, there will result many cases, where the reasons on both sides are so equally ballanc'd, that 'tis impossible for us to give any satisfactory decision. Here then is the proper business of municipal laws, to fix what the principles of human nature have left undetermin'd.

The superficies yields to the soil, says the civil law: The writing to the paper: The canvas to the picture. These decisions do not well agree together, and are a proof of the contrariety of those principles, from which they are deriv'd.

But of all the questions of this kind the most curious is that, which for so many ages divided the disciples of *Proculus* and *Sabinus*. Suppose a person shou'd make a cup from the metal of another, or a ship from his wood, and suppose the proprietor of the metal or wood shou'd demand his goods, the question is, whether he acquires a title to the cup or ship. *Sabinus* maintain'd the affirmative, and asserted that the substance or matter is the foundation of all the qualities; that it is incorruptible and immortal, and therefore superior to the form, which is casual and dependent. On the other hand, *Proculus* observ'd, that the form is the most obvious and remarkable part, and that from it bodies are denominated of this or that particular species. To which he might have added, that the matter or substance is in most bodies so fluctuating and uncertain, that 'tis utterly impossible to trace it in all its changes. For my part, I know not from what principles such a controversy can be certainly determin'd. I shall therefore content my self with observing, that the decision of *Trebonian* seems to me pretty ingenious; that the cup belongs to the proprietor of the metal, because it can be brought back to its first form: But that the ship belongs to the author of its form for a contrary reason. But however ingenious this reason may seem, it plainly depends upon the fancy, which by the possibility of such a reduction, finds a closer connexion and relation betwixt a cup and the proprietor of its metal, than betwixt a ship and the proprietor of its wood, where the substance is more fix'd and unalterable.

*In examining the different titles to authority in government, we

SECT. IV

Of the transference of property by consent

HOWEVER useful, or even necessary, the stability of possession may be to human society, 'tis attended with very considerable inconveniences. The relation of fitness or suitableness ought never to enter into consideration, in distributing the properties of mankind; but we must govern ourselves by rules, which are more general in their application, and more free from doubt and uncertainty. Of this kind is *present* possession upon the first establishment of society; and afterwards *occupation, prescription, accession,* and *succession.* As these depend very much on chance, they must frequently prove contradictory both to men's wants and desires; and persons and possessions must often be very ill adjusted. This is a grand inconvenience, which calls for a remedy. To apply one directly, and allow every man to seize by violence what he judges to be fit for him, wou'd destroy society; and therefore the rules of justice seek some medium betwixt a rigid stability, and this changeable and uncertain adjustment. But there is no medium better than that obvious one, that possession and property shou'd always be stable, except when the proprietor consents to bestow them on some other

---

shall meet with many reasons to convince us, that the right of succession depends, in a great measure on the imagination. Mean while I shall rest contented with observing one example, which belongs to the present subject. Suppose that a person die without children, and that a dispute arises among his relations concerning his inheritance; 'tis evident, that if his riches be deriv'd partly from his father, partly from his mother, the most natural way of determining such a dispute, is, to divide his possessions, and ássign each part to the family, from whence it is deriv'd. Now as the person is suppos'd to have been once the full and entire proprietor of those goods; I ask, what is it makes us find a certain equity and natural reason in this partition, except it be the imagination? His affection to these families does not depend upon his possessions; for which reason his consent can never be presum'd precisely for such a partition. And as to the public interest, it seems not to be in the least concern'd on the one side or the other.

person. This rule can have no ill consequence, in occasioning wars and dissentions; since the proprietor's consent, who alone is concern'd, is taken along in the alienation: And it may serve to many good purposes in adjusting property to persons. Different parts of the earth produce different commodities; and not only so, but different men both are by nature fitted for different employments, and attain to greater perfection in any one, when they confine themselves to it alone. All this requires a mutual exchange and commerce; for which reason the translation of property by consent is founded on a law of nature, as well as its stability without such a consent.

So far is determin'd by a plain utility and interest. But perhaps 'tis from more trivial reasons, that *delivery*, or a sensible transference of the object is commonly requir'd by civil laws, and also by the laws of nature, according to most authors, as a requisite circumstance in the translation of property. The property of an object, when taken for something real, without any reference to morality, or the sentiments of the mind, is a quality perfectly insensible, and even inconceivable; nor can we form any distinct notion, either of its stability or translation. This imperfection of our ideas is less sensibly felt with regard to its stability, as it engages less our attention, and is easily past over by the mind, without any scrupulous examination. But as the translation of property from one person to another is a more remarkable event, the defect of our ideas becomes more sensible on that occasion, and obliges us to turn ourselves on every side in search of some remedy. Now as nothing more enlivens any idea than a present impression, and a relation betwixt that impression and the idea; 'tis natural for us to seek some false light from this quarter. In order to aid the imagination in conceiving the transference of property, we take the sensible object, and actually transfer its possession to the person, on whom we wou'd bestow the property. The suppos'd resemblance of the actions, and the presence of this sensible delivery, deceive the mind, and make it fancy, that it conceives the mysterious transition of the property. And that this explication of the matter is just, appears hence, that men have invented a *symbolical* delivery, to satisfy the fancy, where the real one is impracticable. Thus the giving the keys of a granary is understood to be the delivery of the corn contain'd in it: The giving of stone and earth represents the delivery of a mannor. This is a kind of superstitious practice in civil laws, and in the laws of nature, resembling the *Roman catholic* superstitions in religion. As the *Roman catholics* represent the inconceivable mysteries of the *Christian* religion, and render them more present to the mind, by a taper, or habit, or grimace, which is suppos'd to resemble them; so lawyers and moralists have run into like inventions for the same reason, and have endeavour'd by those means to satisfy themselves concerning the transference of property by consent.

SECT. V

Of the obligation of promises

THAT the rule of morality, which enjoins the performance of promises, is not *natural,* will sufficiently appear from these two propositions, which I proceed to prove, viz. *that a promise wou'd not be intelligible, before human conventions had establish'd it*; and *that even if it were intelligible, it wou'd not be attended with any moral obligation.*

I say, *first,* that a promise is not intelligible naturally, nor antecedent to human conventions; and that a man, unacquainted with society, could never enter into any engagements with another, even tho' they could perceive each other's thoughts by intuition. If promises be natural and intelligible, there must be some act of the mind attending these words, *I promise*; and on this act of the mind must the obligation depend. Let us, therefore, run over all the faculties of the soul, and see which of them is exerted in our promises.

The act of the mind, exprest by a promise, is not a *resolution* to perform any thing: For that alone never imposes any obligation. Nor is it a *desire* of such a performance: For we may bind ourselves without such a desire, or even with an aversion, declar'd and avow'd. Neither is it the *willing* of that action, which we promise to perform: For a promise always regards some future time, and the will has an influence only on present actions. It follows, therefore, that since the act of the mind, which enters into a promise, and produces its obligation, is neither the resolving, desiring, nor willing any particular performance, it must necessarily be the *willing* of that *obligation*, which arises from the promise. Nor is this only a conclusion of philosophy; but is entirely conformable to our common ways of thinking and of expressing ourselves, when we say that we are bound by our own consent, and that the obligation arises from our mere will and pleasure. The only question then is, whether there be not a manifest absurdity in supposing this act of the mind, and such an absurdity as no man cou'd fall into, whose ideas are not confounded with prejudice and the fallacious use of language.

All morality depends upon our sentiments; and when any action, or quality of the mind, pleases us *after a certain manner*, we say it is virtuous; and when the neglect, or non-performance of it, displeases us *after a like manner*, we say that we lie under an obligation to perform it. A change of the obligation supposes a change of the sentiment; and a creation of a new obligation supposes some new sentiment to arise. But 'tis certain we can naturally no more change our own sentiments, than the motions of the heavens; nor by a single act of our will, that is, by a promise, render any action agreeable or disagreeable, moral or immoral; which, without that act, wou'd have produc'd contrary impressions, or have been endow'd with different qualities. It wou'd be absurd, therefore, to will any new obligation, that is, any new sentiment of pain or pleasure; nor is it possible, that men cou'd naturally fall into so gross an absurdity. A promise, therefore, is *naturally* something altogether unintelligible, nor is there any act of the mind belonging to it *.

But, *secondly*, if there was any act of the mind belonging to it, it could not *naturally* produce any obligation. This appears evidently from the foregoing reasoning. A promise creates a new obligation. A new obligation supposes new sentiments to arise. The will never creates new sentiments. There could not naturally, therefore, arise any obligation from a promise, even supposing the mind could fall into the absurdity of willing that obligation.

The same truth may be prov'd still more evidently by that reasoning, which prov'd justice in general to be an artificial virtue. No action can be requir'd of us as our duty, unless there be implanted in human nature some actuating passion or motive, capable of producing the action. This motive cannot be the sense of duty. A sense of duty supposes an antecedent obligation: And where an action is not requir'd by any natural passion, it cannot be requir'd by any natural

* Were morality discoverable by reason, and not by sentiment, 'twou'd be still more evident, that promises cou'd make no alteration upon it. Morality is suppos'd to consist in relation. Every new imposition of morality, therefore, must arise from some new relation of objects; and consequently the will cou'd not produce *immediately* any change in morals, but cou'd have that effect only by producing a change upon the objects. But as the moral obligation of a promise is the pure effect of the will, without the least change in any part of the universe; it follows, that promises have no *natural* obligation.

Shou'd it be said, that this act of the will being in effect a new object, produces new relations and new duties; I wou'd answer, that this is a pure sophism, which may be detected by a very moderate share of accuracy and exactness. To will a new obligation, is to will a new relation of objects; and therefore, if this new relation of objects were form'd by the volition itself, we should in effect will the volition; which is plainly absurd and impossible. The will has here no object to which it cou'd tend; but must return upon itself *in infinitum*. The new obligation depends upon new relations. The new relations depend upon a new volition. The new volition has for object a new obligation, and consequently new relations, and consequently a new volition; which volition again has in view a new obligation, relation and volition, without any termination. 'Tis impossible, therefore, we cou'd ever will a new obligation; and consequently 'tis impossible the will cou'd ever accompany a promise, or produce a new obligation of morality.

obligation; since it may be omitted without proving any defect or imperfection in the mind and temper, and consequently without any vice. Now 'tis evident we have no motive leading us to the performance of promises, distinct from a sense of duty. If we thought, that promises had no moral obligation, we never shou'd feel any inclination to observe them. This is not the case with the natural virtues. Tho' there was no obligation to relieve the miserable, our humanity wou'd lead us to it; and when we omit that duty, the immorality of the omission arises from its being a proof, that we want the natural sentiments of humanity. A father knows it to be his duty to take care of his children: But he has also a natural inclination to it. And if no human creature had that inclination, no one cou'd lie under any such obligation. But as there is naturally no inclination to observe promises, distinct from a sense of their obligation; it follows, that fidelity is no natural virtue, and that promises have no force, antecedent to human conventions.

If any one dissent from this, he must give a regular proof of these two propositions, viz. *that there is a peculiar act of the mind, annext to promises*; and *that consequent to this act of the mind, there arises an inclination to perform, distinct from a sense of duty*. I presume, that it is impossible to prove either of these two points; and therefore I venture to conclude that promises are human inventions, founded on the necessities and interests of society.

In order to discover these necessities and interests, we must consider the same qualities of human nature, which we have already found to give rise to the preceding laws of society. Men being naturally selfish, or endow'd only with a confin'd generosity, they are not easily induc'd to perform any action for the interest of strangers, except with a view to some reciprocal advantage, which they had no hope of obtaining but by such a performance. Now as it frequently happens, that these mutual performances cannot be finish'd at the same instant, 'tis necessary, that one party be contented to remain in uncertainty, and depend upon the gratitude of the other for a return of kindness. But so much corruption is there among men, that, generally speaking, this becomes but a slender security; and as the benefactor is here suppos'd to bestow his favours with a view to self-interest, this both takes off from the obligation, and sets an example to selfishness, which is the true mother of ingratitude. Were we, therefore, to follow the natural course of our passions and inclinations, we shou'd perform but few actions for the advantage of others, from distinterested views; because we are naturally very limited in our kindness and affection: And we shou'd perform as few of that kind, out of a regard to interest; because we cannot depend upon their gratitude. Here then is the mutual commerce of good offices in a manner lost among mankind, and every one reduc'd to his own skill and industry for his well-being and subsistence. The invention of the law of nature, concerning the *stability* of possession, has already render'd men tolerable to each other; that of the *transference* of property and possession by consent has begun to render them mutually advantageous: But still these laws of nature, however strictly observ'd, are not sufficient to render them so serviceable to each other, as by nature they are fitted to become. Tho' possession be *stable,* men may often reap but small advantage from it, while they are possess'd of a greater quantity of any species of goods than they have occasion for, and at the same time suffer by the want of others. The *transference* of property, which is the proper remedy for this inconvenience, cannot remedy it entirely; because it can only take place with regard to such objects as are *present* and *individual,* but not to such as are *absent* or *general.* One cannot transfer the property of a particular house, twenty leagues distant; because the consent cannot be attended with delivery, which is a requisite circumstance. Neither can one transfer the property of ten bushels of corn, or five hogsheads of wine, by the mere expression and consent; because these are only general terms, and have no direct relation to any particular heap of corn, or barrels of wine. Besides, the commerce of mankind is not confin'd to the barter of commodities, but may extend to services and actions, which we may exchange to our mutual interest and advantage. Your corn is ripe to-day; mine will be so to-morrow. 'Tis profitable for us both, that I shou'd labour with you to-day, and that you shou'd aid me to-morrow. I have no kindness for you, and know you have as little for me. I will not, therefore, take any pains upon your account; and shou'd I labour with you upon my own account, in expectation of a return, I know I shou'd be disappointed, and that I shou'd in vain depend upon your gratitude. Here then I leave you to labour alone: You treat me in the same manner. The seasons change; and both of us lose our harvests for want of mutual confidence and security.

All this is the effect of the natural and inherent principles and passions of human nature; and as these passions and principles are inalterable, it may be thought, that our conduct, which depends on them, must be so too, and that 'twou'd be in vain, either for moralists or politicians, to tamper with us, or attempt to change the usual course of our actions, with a view to public interest. And indeed, did the success of their designs depend upon their success in correcting the selfishness and ingratitude of men, they wou'd never make any progress, unless aided by omnipotence, which is alone able to new-mould the human mind, and change its character in such fundamental articles. All they can pretend to, is, to give a new direction to those natural passions, and teach us that we can better satisfy our appetites in an oblique and artificial manner, than by their headlong and impetuous motion. Hence I learn to do a service to another, without bearing him any real kindness; because I forsee, that he will return my service, in expectation of another of the same kind, and in order to maintain the same correspondence of good offices with me or with others. And accordingly, after I have serv'd him, and he is in possession of the advantage arising from my action, he is induc'd to perform his part, as foreseeing the consequences of his refusal.

But tho' this self-interested commerce of man begins to take place, and to predominate in society, it does not entirely abolish the more generous and noble intercourse of friendship and good offices. I may still do services to such persons as I love, and am more particularly acquainted with, without any prospect of advantage; and they may make me a return in the same manner, without any view but that of recompensing my past services. In order, therefore, to distinguish those two different sorts of commerce, the interested and the disinterested, there is a *certain form of words* invented for the former, by which we bind ourselves to the performance of any action. This form of words constitutes what we call a *promise*, which is the sanction of the interested commerce of mankind. When a man says *he promises any thing*, he in effect expresses a *resolution* of performing it; and along with that, by making use of this *form of words*, subjects himself to the penalty of never being trusted again in case of failure. A resolution is the natural act of the mind, which promises express: But were there no more than a resolution in the case, promises wou'd only declare our former motives, and wou'd not create any new motive or obligation. They are the conventions of men, which create a new motive, when experience has taught us, that human affairs wou'd be conducted much more for mutual advantage, were there certain *symbols* or *signs* instituted, by which we might give each other security of our conduct in any particular incident. After these signs are instituted, whoever uses them is immediately bound by his interest to execute his engagements, and must never expect to be trusted any more, if he refuse to perform what he promis'd.

Nor is that knowledge, which is requisite to make mankind sensible of this interest in the *institution* and *observance* of promises, to be esteem'd superior to the capacity of human nature, however savage and uncultivated. There needs but a very little practice of the world, to make us perceive all these consequences and advantages. The shortest experience of society discovers them to every mortal; and when each individual perceives the same sense of interest in all his fellows, he immediately performs his part of any contract, as being assur'd, that they will not be wanting in theirs. All of them, by concert, enter into a scheme of actions, calculated for common benefit, and agree to be true to their word; nor is there any thing requisite to form this concert or convention, but that every one have a sense of interest in the faithful fulfilling of engagements, and express that sense to other members of the society. This immediately causes that interest to operate upon them; and interest is the *first* obligation to the performance of promises.

Afterwards a sentiment of morals concurs with interest, and becomes a new obligation upon mankind. This sentiment of morality, in the performance of promises, arises from the same principles as that in the abstinence from the property of others. *Public interest, education,* and *the artifices of politicians,* have the same effect in both cases. The difficulties, that occur to us, in supposing a moral obligation to attend promises, we either surmount or elude. For instance; the expression of a resolution is not commonly suppos'd to be obligatory; and we cannot readily conceive how the making use of a certain form of words shou'd be able to cause any material difference. Here, therefore, we *feign* a new act of the mind, which we call the *willing* an obligation; and on this we suppose the morality to depend. But we have prov'd already, that there is no such act of the mind, and consequently that promises impose no natural obligation.

To confirm this, we may subjoin some other reflections concerning that will, which is suppos'd to enter into a promise, and to cause its obligation. 'Tis evident, that the will alone is never suppos'd to cause the obligation, but must be express'd by words or signs, in order to impose a tye upon any man. The expression being once brought in as subservient to the will, soon becomes the principal part of the promise; nor will a man be less bound by his word, tho' he secretly give a different direction to his intention, and with-hold himself both from a resolution, and from willing an obligation. But tho' the expression makes on most occasions the whole of the promise, yet it does not always so; and one, who shou'd make use of any expression, of which he knows not the meaning, and which he uses without any intention of binding himself, wou'd not certainly be bound by it. Nay, tho' he knows its meaning, yet if he uses it in jest only, and with such signs as shew evidently he has no serious intention of binding himself, he wou'd not lie under any obligation of performance; but 'tis necessary, that the words be a perfect expression of the will, without any contrary signs. Nay, even this we must not carry so far as to imagine, that one, whom, by our quickness of understanding, we conjecture, from certain signs, to have an intention of deceiving us, is not bound by his expression or verbal promise, if we accept of it; but must limit this conclusion to those cases, where the signs are of a different kind from those of deceit. All these contradictions are easily accounted for, if the obligation of promises be merely a human invention for the convenience of society; but will never be explain'd, if it be something *real* and *natural*, arising from any action of the mind or body.

I shall farther observe, that since every new promise imposes a new obligation of morality on the person who promises, and since this new obligation arises from his will; 'tis one of the most mysterious and incomprehensible operations that can possibly be imagin'd, and may even be compar'd to *transubstantiation*, or *holy orders* *, where a certain form of words, along with a certain intention, changes entirely the nature of an external object, and even of a human nature. But tho' these mysteries be so far alike, 'tis very remarkable, that they differ widely in other particulars, and that this difference may be regarded as a strong proof of the difference of their origins. As the obligation of promises is an invention for the interest of society, 'tis warp'd into as many different forms as that interest requires, and even runs into direct contradictions, rather than lose sight of its object. But as those other monstrous doc-

*I mean so far, as holy orders are suppos'd to produce the *indelible character*. In other respects they are only a legal qualification.

trines are mere priestly inventions, and have no public interest in view, they are less disturb'd in their progress by new obstacles; and it must be own'd, that, after the first absurdity, they follow more directly the current of reason and good sense. Theologians clearly perceiv'd, that the external form of words, being mere sound, require an intention to make them have any efficacy; and that this intention being once consider'd as a requisite circumstance, its absence must equally prevent the effect, whether avow'd or conceal'd, whether sincere or deceitful. Accordingly they have commonly determin'd, that the intention of the priest makes the sacrament, and that when he secretly withdraws his intention, he is highly criminal in himself; but still destroys the baptism, or communion, or holy orders. The terrible consequences of this doctrine were not able to hinder its taking place; as the inconvenience of a similar doctrine, with regard to promises, have prevented that doctrine from establishing itself. Men are always more concern'd about the present life than the future; and are apt to think the smallest evil, which regards the former, more important than the greatest, which regards the latter.

We may draw the same conclusion, concerning the origin of promises, from the *force*, which is suppos'd to invalidate all contracts, and to free us from their obligation. Such a principle is a proof, that promises have no natural obligation, and are mere artificial contrivances for the convenience and advantage of society. If we consider aright of the matter, force is not essentially different from any other motive of hope or fear, which may induce us to engage our word, and lay ourselves under any obligation. A man, dangerously wounded, who promises a competent sum to a surgeon to cure him, wou'd certainly be bound to performance; tho' the case be not so much different from that of one, who promises a sum to a robber, as to produce so great a difference in our sentiments of morality, if these sentiments were not built entirely on public interest and convenience.

SECT. VI

Some farther reflections concerning justice and injustice

WE have now run over the three fundamental laws of nature, *that of the stability of possession, of its transference by consent*, and *of the performance of promises*. 'Tis on the strict observance of those three laws, that the peace and security of human society entirely depend; nor is there any possibility of establishing a good correspondence among men, where these are neglected. Society is absolutely necessary for the well-being of men; and these are as necessary to the support of society. Whatever restraint they may impose on the passions of men, they are the real offspring of those passions, and are only a more artful and more refin'd way of satisfying them. Nothing is more vigilant and inventive than our passions; and nothing is more obvious, than the convention for the observance of these rules. Nature has, therefore, trusted this affair entirely to the conduct of men, and has not plac'd in the mind any peculiar original principles, to determine us to a set of actions, into which the other principles of our frame and constitution were sufficient to lead us. And to convince us the more fully of this truth, we may here stop a moment, and from a review of the preceding reasonings may draw some new arguments, to prove that those laws, however necessary, are entirely artificial, and of human invention; and consequently that justice is an artificial, and not a natural virtue.

(1) The first argument I shall make use of is deriv'd from the vulgar definition of justice. Justice is commonly defin'd to be *a constant and perpetual will of giving every one his due*. In this definition 'tis suppos'd, that there are such things as right and property, independent of justice, and antecedent to it; and that they wou'd have subsisted, tho' men had never dreamt of practising such a virtue. I have

already observ'd, in a cursory manner, the fallacy of this opinion, and shall here continue to open up a little more distinctly my sentiments on that subject.

I shall begin with observing, that this quality, which we shall call *property*, is like many of the imaginary qualities of the *peripatetic* philosophy, and vanishes upon a more accurate inspection into the subject, when consider'd a-part from our moral sentiments. 'Tis evident property does not consist in any of the sensible qualities of the object. For these may continue invariably the same, while the property changes. Property, therefore, must consist in some relation of the object. But 'tis not in its relation with regard to other external and inanimate objects. For these may also continue invariably the same, while the property changes. This quality, therefore, consists in the relations of objects to intelligent and rational beings. But 'tis not the external and corporeal relation, which forms the essence of property. For that relation may be the same betwixt inanimate objects, or with regard to brute creatures; tho' in those cases it forms no property. 'Tis, therefore, in some internal relation, that the property consists; that is, in some influence, which the external relations of the object have on the mind and actions. Thus the external relation, which we call *occupation* or first possession, is not of itself imagin'd to be the property of the object, but only to cause its property. Now 'tis evident, this external relation causes nothing in external objects, and has only an influence on the mind, by giving us a sense of duty in abstaining from that object, and in restoring it to the first possessor. These actions are properly what we call *justice*; and consequently 'tis on that virtue that the nature of property depends, and not the virtue on the property.

If any one, therefore, wou'd assert, that justice is a natural virtue, and injustice a natural vice, he must assert, that abstracting from the nations of *property*, and *right* and *obligation*, a certain conduct and train of actions, in certain external relations of objects, has naturally a moral beauty or deformity, and causes an original pleasure or uneasiness.

Thus the restoring a man's goods to him is consider'd as virtuous, not because nature has annex'd a certain sentiment of pleasure to such a conduct, with regard to the property of others, but because she has annex'd that sentiment to such a conduct, with regard to those external objects, of which others have had the first or long possession, or which they have receiv'd by the consent of those, who have had first or long possession. If nature has given us no such sentiment, there is not, naturally, nor antecedent to human conventions, any such thing as property. Now, tho' it seems sufficiently evident, in this dry and accurate consideration of the present subject, that nature has annex'd no pleasure or sentiment of approbation to such a conduct; yet that I may leave as little room for doubt as possible, I shall subjoin a few more arguments to confirm my opinion.

First, If nature had given us a pleasure of this kind, it wou'd have been as evident and discernible as on every other occasion; nor shou'd we have found any difficulty to perceive, that the consideration of such actions, in such a situation, gives a certain pleasure and sentiment of approbation. We shou'd not have been oblig'd to have recourse to notions of property in the definition of justice, and at the same time make use of the notions of justice in the definition of property. This deceitful method of reasoning is a plain proof, that there are contain'd in the subject some obscurities and difficulties, which we are not able to surmount, and which we desire to evade by this artifice.

Secondly, Those rules, by which properties, rights, and obligations are determin'd, have in them no marks of a natural origin but many of artifice and contrivance. They are too numerous to have proceeded from nature: They are changeable by human laws: And have all of them a direct and evident tendency to public good, and the support of civil society. This last circumstance is remarkable upon two accounts. *First*, because, tho' the cause of the establishment of these laws had been a *regard* for the public good, as much as the public good is their natural tendency, they wou'd still have been artificial, as being purposely contriv'd and directed to a certain end. *Secondly*, because, if men had been endow'd with such a strong regard for public good, they wou'd never have restrain'd themselves by these rules; so that the laws of justice arise from natural principles in a manner still more oblique and artificial. 'Tis self-love which is their real origin; and as the self-love of one person is naturally contrary to that of another, these several interested passions are oblig'd to adjust themselves after such a manner as to concur in some system of conduct and behaviour. This system, therefore, comprehending the interest of each individual, is of course advantageous to the public; tho' it be not intended for that purpose by the inventors.

(2) In the second place we may observe, that all kinds of vice and virtue run insensibly into each other, and may approach by such imperceptible degrees as will make it very difficult, if not absolutely impossible, to determine when the one ends, and the other begins; and from this observation we may derive a new argument for the foregoing principle. For whatever may be the case, with regard to all kinds of vice and virtue, 'tis certain, that rights, and obligations, and property, admit of no such insensible gradation, but that a man either has a full and perfect property, or none at all; and is either entirely oblig'd to perform any action, or lies under no manner of obligation. However civil laws may talk of a perfect *dominion*, and of an imperfect, 'tis easy to observe, that this arises from a fiction, which has no foundation in reason, and can never enter into our notions of natural justice and equity. A man that hires a horse, tho' but for a day, has as full a right to make use of it for that time, as he whom we call its proprietor has to make use of it any other day; and 'tis evident, that however the use may be bounded in time or degree, the right itself is not susceptible of any such gradation, but is absolute and entire, so far as it extends. Accordingly we may observe, that this right both arises and perishes in an instant; and that a man entirely acquires the property of any

object by occupation, or the consent of the proprietor; and loses it by his own consent; without any of that insensible gradation, which is remarkable in other qualities and relations. Since, therefore, this is the case with regard to property, and rights, and obligations, I ask, how it stands with regard to justice and injustice? After whatever manner you answer this question, you run into inextricable difficulties. If you reply, that justice and injustice admit of degree, and run insensibly into each other, you expressly contradict the foregoing position, that obligation and property are not susceptible of such a gradation. These depend entirely upon justice and injustice, and follow them in all their variations. Where the justice is entire, the property is also entire: Where the justice is imperfect, the property must also be imperfect. And *vice versa,* if the property admit of no such variations, they must also be incompatible with justice. If you assent, therefore, to this last proposition, and assert, that justice and injustice are not susceptible of degrees, you in effect assert, that they are not *naturally* either vicious or virtuous; since vice and virtue, moral good and evil, and indeed all *natural* qualities, run insensibly into each other, and are, on many occasions, undistinguishable.

And here it may be worth while to observe, that tho' abstract reasoning, and the general maxims of philosophy and law establish this position, *that property, and right, and obligation admit not of degrees,* yet in our common and negligent way of thinking, we find great difficulty to entertain that opinion, and do even *secretly* embrace the contrary principle. An object must either be in the possession of one person or another. An action must either be perform'd or not. The necessity there is of choosing one side in these dilemmas, and the impossibility there often is of finding any just medium, oblige us, when we reflect on the matter, to acknowledge, that all property and obligations are entire. But on the other hand, when we consider the origin of property and obligation, and find that they depend on public utility, and sometimes on the propensities of the imagination, which are seldom entire on any side; we are naturally inclin'd to imagine, that these moral relations admit of an insensible gradation. Hence it is, that in references, where the consent of the parties leave the referees entire masters of the subject, they commonly discover so much equity and justice on both sides, as induces them to strike a medium, and divide the difference betwixt the parties. Civil judges, who have not this liberty, but are oblig'd to give a decisive sentence on some one side, are often at a loss how to determine, and are necessitated to proceed on the most frivolous reasons in the world. Half rights and obligations, which seem so natural in common life, are perfect absurdities in their tribunal; for which reason they are often oblig'd to take half arguments for whole ones, in order to terminate the affair one way or other.

(3) The third argument of this kind I shall make use of may be explain'd thus. If we consider the ordinary course of human actions, we shall find, that the mind restrains not itself by any general and universal rules; but acts on most occasions as it is determin'd by its present motives and inclination. As each action is a particular individual event, it must proceed from particular principles, and from our immediate situation within ourselves, and with respect to the rest of the universe. If on some occasions we extend our motives beyond those very circumstances, which gave rise to them, and form something like *general rules* for our conduct, 'tis easy to observe, that these rules are not perfectly inflexible, but allow of many exceptions. Since, therefore, this is the ordinary course of human actions, we may conclude, that the laws of justice, being universal and perfectly inflexible, can never be deriv'd from nature, nor be the immediate offspring of any natural motive or inclination. No action can be either morally good or evil, unless there be some natural passion or motive to impel us to it, or deter us from it; and 'tis evident, that the morality must be susceptible of all the same variations, which are natural to the passion. Here are two persons, who dispute for an estate; of whom one is rich, a fool, and a batchelor; the other poor, a

man of sense, and has a numerous family: The first is my enemy; the second my friend. Whether I be actuated in this affair by a view to public or private interest, by friendship or enmity, I must be induc'd to do my utmost to procure the estate to the latter. Nor wou'd any consideration of the right and property of the persons be able to restrain me, were I actuated only by natural motives, without any combination or convention with others. For as all property depends on morality; and as all morality depends on the ordinary course of our passions and actions; and as these again are only directed by particular motives; 'tis evident, such a partial conduct must be suitable to the strictest morality, and cou'd never be a violation of property. Were men, therefore, to take the liberty of acting with regard to the laws of society, as they do in every other affair, they wou'd conduct themselves, on most occasions, by particular judgments, and wou'd take into consideration the characters and circumstances of the persons, as well as the general nature of the question. But 'tis easy to observe, that this wou'd produce an infinite confusion in human society, and that the avidity and partiality of men wou'd quickly bring disorder into the world, if not restrain'd by some general and inflexible principles. 'Twas, therefore, with a view to this inconvenience, that men have establish'd those principles, and have agreed to restrain themselves by general rules, which are unchangeable by spite and favour, and by particular views of private or public interest. These rules, then, are artificially invented for a certain purpose, and are contrary to the common principles of human nature, which accommodate themselves to circumstances, and have no stated invariable method of operation.

Nor do I perceive how I can easily be mistaken in this matter. I see evidently, that when any man imposes on himself general inflexible rules in his conduct with others, he considers certain objects as their property, which he supposes to be sacred and inviolable. But no proposition can be more evident, than that property is perfectly unintelligible without first supposing justice and injustice; and that these virtues and vices are as unintelligible, unless we have motives, independent of the morality, to impel us to just actions, and deter us from unjust ones. Let those motives, therefore, be what they will, they must accommodate themselves to circumstances, and must admit of all the variations, which human affairs, in their incessant revolutions, are susceptible of. They are consequently a very improper foundation for such rigid inflexible rules as the laws of nature; and 'tis evident these laws can only be deriv'd from human conventions, when men have perceiv'd the disorders that result from following their natural and variable principles.

Upon the whole, then, we are to consider this distinction betwixt justice and injustice, as having two different foundations, *viz.* that of *interest*, when men observe, that 'tis impossible to live in society without restraining themselves by certain rules; and that of *morality*, when this interest is once observ'd, and men receive a pleasure from the view of such actions as tend to the peace of society, and an uneasiness from such as are contrary to it. 'Tis the voluntary convention and artifice of men, which makes the first interest take place; and therefore those laws of justice are so far to be consider'd as *artificial*. After that interest is once establish'd and acknowledg'd, the sense of morality in the observance of these rules follows *naturally*, and of itself; tho' 'tis certain, that it is also augmented by a new *artifice*, and that the public instructions of politicians, and the private education of parents, contribute to the giving us a sense of honour and duty in the strict regulation of our actions with regard to the properties of others.

SECT. VII

Of the origin of government

NOTHING is more certain, than that men are, in a great measure, govern'd by interest, and that even when they extend their concern beyond themselves, 'tis not to any great distance; nor is it usual for them, in common life, to look farther than their nearest friends and acquaintance. 'Tis no less certain, that 'tis impossible for men to consult their interest in so effectual a manner, as by an universal and inflexible observance of the rules of justice, by which alone they can preserve society, and keep themselves from falling into that wretched and savage condition, which is commonly represented as the *state of nature.* And as this interest, which all men have in the upholding of society, and the observation of the rules of justice, is great, so is it palpable and evident, even to the most rude and uncultivated of human race; and 'tis almost impossible for any one, who has had experience of society, to be mistaken in this particular. Since, therefore, men are so sincerely attach'd to their interest, and their interest is so much concern'd in the observance of justice, and this interest is so certain and avow'd; it may be ask'd, how any disorder can ever arise in society, and what principle there is in human nature so *powerful* as to overcome so strong a passion, or so *violent* as to obscure so clear a knowledge?

It has been observ'd, in treating of the passions, that men are mightily govern'd by the imagination, and proportion their affections more to the light, under which any object appears to them, than to its real and intrinsic value. What strikes upon them with a strong and lively idea commonly prevails above what lies in a more obscure light; and it must be a great superiority of value, that is able to compensate this advantage. Now as every thing, that is contiguous to us, either in space or time, strikes upon us with such an idea, it has a proportional effect on the will and passions, and commonly operates with more force than any object, that lies in a more distant and obscure light. Tho' we may be fully convinc'd, that the latter object excels the former, we are not able to regulate our actions by this judgment; but yield to the sollicitations of our passions, which always plead in favour of whatever is near and contiguous.

This is the reason why men so often act in contradiction to their known interest; and in particular why they prefer any trivial advantage, that is present, to the maintenance of order in society, which so much depends on the observance of justice. The consequences of every breach of equity seem to lie very remote, and are not able to counter-ballance any immediate advantage, that may be reap'd from it. They are, however, never the less real for being remote; and as all men are, in some degree, subject to the same weakness, it necessarily happens, that the violations of equity must become very frequent in society, and the commerce of men, by that means, be render'd very dangerous and uncertain. You have the same propension, that I have, in favour of what is contiguous above what is remote. You are, therefore, naturally carried to commit acts of injustice as well as me. Your example both pushes me forward in this way by imitation, and also affords me a new reason for any breach of equity, by shewing me, that I should be the cully of my integrity, if I alone shou'd impose on myself a severe restraint amidst the licentiousness of others.

This quality, therefore, of human nature, not only is very dangerous to society, but also seems, on a cursory view, to be incapable of any remedy. The remedy can only come from the consent of men; and if men be incapable of themselves to prefer remote to contiguous, they will never consent to any thing, which wou'd oblige them to such a choice, and contradict, in so sensible a manner, their natural principles and propensities. Whoever chuses the means, chuses also the end; and if it be impossible for us to prefer what is remote, 'tis equally impossible for us to submit to any necessity, which wou'd oblige us to such a method of acting.

But here 'tis observable, that this infirmity of human nature becomes a remedy to itself, and that we provide against our negligence about remote objects, merely because we are naturally inclin'd to that negligence. When we consider any objects at a distance, all their minute distinctions vanish, and we always give the preference to whatever is in itself preferable, without considering its situation and circumstances. This gives rise to what in an improper sense we call *reason,* which is a principle, that is often contradictory to those propensities that display themselves upon the approach of the object. In reflecting on any action, which I am to perform a twelve-month hence, I always resolve to prefer the greater good, whether at that time it will be more contiguous or remote; nor does any difference in that particular make a difference in my present intentions and resolutions. My distance from the final determination makes all those minute differences vanish, nor am I affected by any thing, but the general and more discernible qualities of good and evil. But on my nearer approach, those circumstances, which I at first over-look'd, begin to appear, and have an influence on my conduct and affections. A new inclination to the present good springs up, and makes it difficult for me to adhere inflexibly to my first purpose and resolution. This natural infirmity I may very much regret, and I may endeavour, by all possible means, to free my self from it. I may have recourse to study and reflection within myself; to the advice of friends; to frequent meditation, and repeated resolution: And having experienc'd how ineffectual all these are, I may embrace with pleasure any other expedient, by which I may impose a restraint upon myself, and guard against this weakness.

The only difficulty, therefore, is to find out this expedient, by which men cure their natural weakness, and lay themselves under the necessity of observing the laws of justice and equity, notwithstanding their violent propension to prefer contiguous to remote. 'Tis evident such a remedy can never be effectual without correcting this propensity; and as 'tis impossible to change or correct any thing material in our nature, the utmost we can do is to change our circumstances and situation, and render the observance of the laws of justice our nearest interest, and their violation our most remote. But this being impracticable with respect to all mankind, it can only take place with respect to a few, whom we thus immediately interest in the execution of justice. There are the persons, whom we call civil magistrates, kings and their ministers, our governors and rulers, who being indifferent persons to the greatest part of the state, have no interest, or but a remote one, in any act of injustice; and being satisfied with their present condition, and with their part in society, have an immediate interest in every execution of justice, which is so necessary to the upholding of society. Here then is the origin of civil government and society. Men are not able radically to cure, either in themselves or others, that narrowness of soul, which makes them prefer the present to the remote. They cannot change their natures. All they can do is to change their situation, and render the observance of justice the immediate interest of some particular persons, and its violation their more remote. These persons, then, are not only induc'd to observe those rules in their own conduct, but also to constrain others to a like regularity, and inforce the dictates of equity thro' the whole society. And if it be necessary, they may also interest others more immediately in the execution of justice, and create a number of officers, civil and military, to assist them in their government.

But this execution of justice, tho' the principal, is not the only advantage of government. As violent passion hinder men from seeing distinctly the interest they have in an equitable behaviour towards others; so it hinders them from seeing that equity itself, and gives them a remarkable partiality in their own favours. This inconvenience is corrected in the same manner as that above-mention'd. The same persons, who execute the laws of justice, will also decide all controversies concerning them; and being indifferent to the greatest part of the society, will decide them more equitably than every one wou'd in his own case.

By means of these two advantages, in the *execution* and *decision* of justice, men acquire a security against each others weakness and passion, as well as against their own, and under the shelter of their governors, begin to taste at ease the sweets of society and mutual assistance. But government extends farther its beneficial influence; and not contented to protect men in those conventions they make for their mutual interest, it often obliges them to make such conventions, and forces them to seek their own advantage, by a concurrence in some common end or purpose. There is no quality in human nature, which causes more fatal errors in our conduct, than that which leads us to prefer whatever is present to the distant and remote, and makes us desire objects more according to their situation than their intrinsic value. Two neighbours may agree to drain a meadow, which they possess in common; because 'tis easy for them to know each others mind; and each must perceive, that the immediate consequence of his failing in his part, is, the abandoning the whole project. But 'tis very difficult, and indeed impossible, that a thousand persons shou'd agree in any such action; it being difficult for them to concert so complicated a design, and still more difficult for them to execute it; while each seeks a pretext to free himself of the trouble and expence, and wou'd lay the whole burden on others. Political society easily remedies both these inconveniences. Magistrates find an immediate interest in the interest of any considerable part of their subjects. They need consult no body but themselves to form any scheme for the promoting of that interest. And as the failure of any one piece in the execution is connected, tho' not immediately, with the failure of the whole, they prevent that failure, because they find no interest in it, either immediate or remote. Thus bridges are built; harbours open'd; ramparts rais'd; canals form'd; fleets equip'd; and armies disciplin'd every where, by the care of government, which, tho' compos'd of men subject to all human infirmities, becomes, by one of the finest and most subtle inventions imaginable, a composition, which is, in some measure, exempted from all these infirmities.

SECT. VIII

Of the source of allegiance

THOUGH government be an invention very advantageous, and even in some circumstances absolutely necessary to mankind; it is not necessary in all circumstances, nor is it impossible for men to preserve society for some time, without having recourse to such an invention. Men, 'tis true, are always much inclin'd to prefer present interest to distant and remote; nor is it easy for them to resist the temptation of any advantage, that they may immediately enjoy, in apprehension of an evil that lies at a distance from them: But still this weakness is less conspicuous where the possessions, and the pleasures of life are few, and of little value, as they always are in the infancy of society. An *Indian* is but little tempted to dispossess another of his hut, or to steal his bow, as being already provided of the same advantages; and as to any superior fortune, which may attend one above another in hunting and fishing, 'tis only casual and temporary, and will have but small tendency to disturb society. And so far am I from thinking with some philosophers, that men are utterly incapable of society without government, that I assert the first rudiments of government to arise from quarrels, not among men of the same society, but among those of different societies. A less degree of riches will suffice to this latter effect, than is requisite for the former. Men fear nothing from public war and violence but the resistance they meet with, which, because they share it in common, seems less terrible; and because it comes from strangers, seems less pernicious in its consequences, than when they are expos'd singly against one whose commerce is advantageous to them, and without whose society 'tis impossible they can subsist. Now foreign war to a society without government necessarily produces civil war. Throw any considerable goods among men, they instantly fall a quarrelling, while each strives to get possession of what pleases him, without regard to the consequences. In a foreign war the most considerable of all goods, life and limbs, are at stake; and as every one shuns dangerous ports, seizes the best arms, seeks excuse for the slightest wounds, the laws, which may be well enough observ'd while men were calm, can now no longer take place, when they are in such commotion.

This we find verified in the *American* tribes, where men live in concord and amity among themselves without any establish'd government and never pay submission to any of their fellows, except in time of war, when their captain enjoys a shadow of authority, which he loses after their return from the field, and the establishment of peace with the neighbouring tribes. This authority, however, instructs them in the advantages of government, and teaches them to have recourse to it, when either by the pillage of war, by commerce, or by any fortuitous inventions, their riches and possessions have become so considerable as to make them forget, on every emergence, the interest they have in the preservation of peace and justice. Hence we may give a plausible reason, among others, why all governments are at first monarchical, without any mixture and variety; and why republics arise only from the abuses of monarchy and despotic power. Camps are the true mothers of cities; and as war cannot be administered, by reason of the suddenness of every exigency, without some authority in a single person, the same kind of authority naturally takes place in that civil government, which succeeds the military. And this reason I take to be more natural, than the common one deriv'd from patriarchal government, or the authority of a father, which is said first to take place in one family, and to accustom the members of it to the government of a single person. The state of society without government is one of the most natural states of men, and must submit with the conjunction of many families, and long after the first generation. Nothing but an encrease of riches and possessions cou'd oblige men to quit it; and so barbarous and uninstructed are all societies on their first formation, that many years must elapse before these can encrease to such a degree, as to disturb men in the enjoyment of peace and concord.

But tho' it be possible for men to maintain a small uncultivated society without government, 'tis impossible they shou'd maintain a society of any kind without justice, and the observance of those three fundamental laws concerning the stability of possession, its translation by consent, and the performance of promises. These are, therefore, antecedent to government, and are suppos'd to impose an obligation before the duty of allegiance to civil magistrates has once been thought of. Nay, I shall go farther, and assert, that government, *upon its first establishment*, wou'd naturally be suppos'd to derive its obligation from those laws of nature, and, in particular, from that concerning the performance of promises. When men have once perceiv'd the necessity of government to maintain peace, and execute justice, they wou'd naturally assemble together, wou'd chuse magistrates, determine power, and *promise* them obedience. As a promise is suppos'd to be a bond or security already in use, and attended with a moral obligation, 'tis to be consider'd as the original sanction of government, and as the source of the first obligation to obedience. This reasoning appears so natural, that it has become the foundation of our fashionable system of politics, and is in a manner the creed of a party amongst us, who pride themselves, with reason, on the soundness of their philosophy, and their liberty of thought. *All men*, say they, *are born free and equal: Government and superiority can only be establish'd by consent: The consent of men, in establishing government, imposes on them a new obligation, unknown to the laws of nature. Men, therefore, are bound to obey their magistrates, only because they promise it; and if they had not given their word, either expressly or tacitly, to preserve allegiance, it would never have become a part of their moral duty.* This conclusion, however, when carried so far as to comprehend government in all its ages and situations, is entirely erroneous; and I maintain, that tho' the duty of allegiance be at first grafted on the obligation of promises, and be for some time supported by that obligation, yet it quickly takes root of itself, and has an original obligation and authority, independent of all contracts. This is a principle of moment, which we must examine with care and attention, before we proceed any farther.

'Tis reasonable for those philosophers, who assert justice to be a natural virtue, and antecedent to human conventions, to resolve all civil allegiance into the obligation of a promise, and assert that 'tis our own consent alone, which binds us to any submission to magistracy. For as all government is plainly an invention of men, and the origin of most governments is known in history, 'tis necessary to mount higher, in order to find the source of our political duties, if we wou'd assert them to have any *natural* obligation of morality. These philosophers, therefore, quickly observe, that society is as antient as the human species, and those three fundamental laws of nature as antient as society: So that taking advantage of the antiquity, and obscure origin of these laws, they first deny them to be artificial and voluntary inventions of men, and then seek to ingraft on them those other duties, which are more plainly artificial. But being once undeceiv'd in this particular, and having found that *natural*, as well as *civil* justice, derives its origin from human conventions, we shall quickly perceive, how fruitless it is to resolve the one into the other, and seek, in the laws of nature, a stronger foundation for our political duties than interest, and human conventions; while these laws themselves are built on the very same foundation. On which ever side we turn this subject, we shall find, that these two kinds of duty are exactly on the same footing, and have the same source both of their *first invention* and *moral obligation*. They are contriv'd to remedy like inconveniences, and acquire their moral sanction in the same manner, from their remedying those inconveniences. These are two points, which we shall endeavour to prove as distinctly as possible.

We have already shewn, that men *invented* the three fundamental laws of nature, when they observ'd the necessity of society to their mutual subsistance, and found, that 'twas impossible to maintain any correspondence together, without some restraint on their natural appetites. The same self-love, therefore, which renders men so incommodious to each other, taking a new and more convenient direction, produces the rules of justice, and is the *first* motive of their observance. But when men have observ'd, that tho' the rules of justice be sufficient to maintain any society, yet 'tis impossible for them, of themselves, to observe those rules, in large and polish'd societies; they establish government, as a new invention to attain their ends, and preserve the old, or procure new advantages, by a more strict execution of justice. So far, therefore, our *civil* duties are connected with our *natural*, that the former are invented chiefly for the sake of the latter; and that the principal object of government is to constrain men to observe the laws of nature. In this respect, however, that law of nature, concerning the performance of promises, is only compriz'd along with the rest; and its exact observance is to be consider'd as an effect of the institution of government, and not the obedience to government as an effect of the obligation of a promise. Tho' the object of our civil duties be the enforcing of our natural, yet the * *first* motive of the invention, as well as performance of both, is nothing but self-interest: And since there is a separate interest in the obedience to government, from that in the performance of promises, we must also allow of a separate obligation. To obey the civil magistrate is requisite to preserve order and concord in society. To perform promises is requisite to beget mutual trust and confidence in the common offices of life. The ends, as well as the means, are perfectly distinct; nor is the one subordinate to the other.

To make this more evident, let us consider, that men will often bind themselves by promises to the performance of what it wou'd have been their interest to perform, independent of these promises; as when they wou'd give others a fuller security, by super-adding a new obligation of interest to that which they formerly lay under. The interest in the performance of promises, besides its moral obligation, is general, avow'd, and of the last consequence in life. Other interests may be more particular and doubtful; and we are apt to entertain a greater suspicion, that men may indulge their humour, or passion, in acting contrary to them. Here, therefore, promises come naturally in play, and are often requir'd for fuller satisfaction and security. But supposing those other interests to be as general and avow'd as the interest in the performance of a promise, they will be regarded as on the same footing, and men will begin to

* First in time, not in dignity or force.

repose the same confidence in them. Now this is exactly the case with regard to our civil duties, or obedience to the magistrate; without which no government cou'd subsist, nor any peace or order be maintain'd in large societies, where there are so many possessions on the one hand, and so many wants, real or imaginary, on the other. Our civil duties, therefore, must soon detach themselves from our promises, and acquire a separate force and influence. The interest in both is of the very same kind: 'Tis general, avow'd, and prevails in all times and places. There is, then, no pretext of reason for founding the one upon the other; while each of them has a foundation peculiar to itself. We might as well resolve the obligation to abstain from the possessions of others, into the obligation of a promise, as that of allegiance. The interests are not more distinct in the one case than the other. A regard to property is not more necessary to natural society, than obedience is to civil society or government; nor is the former society more necessary to the being of mankind, than the latter to their well-being and happiness. In short, if the performance of promises be advantageous, so is obedience to government: If the former interest be general, so is the latter: If the one interest be obvious and avow'd, so is the other. And as these two rules are founded on like obligations of interest, each of them must have a peculiar authority, independent of the other.

But 'tis not only the *natural* obligations of interest, which are distinct in promises and allegiance; but also the *moral* obligations of honour and conscience: Nor does the merit or demerit of the one depend in the least upon that of the other. And indeed, if we consider the close connexion there is betwixt the natural and moral obligations, we shall find this conclusion to be entirely unavoidable. Our interest is always engag'd on the side of obedience to magistracy; and there is nothing but a great present advantage, that can lead us to rebellion, by making us over-look the remote interest, which we have in the preserving of peace and order in society. But tho' a present interest may thus blind us with regard to our own actions, it takes not place with regard to those of others; nor hinders them from appearing in their true colours, as highly prejudicial to public interest, and to our own in particular. This naturally gives us an uneasiness, in considering such seditious and disloyal actions, and makes us attach to them the idea of vice and moral deformity. 'Tis the same principle, which causes us to disapprove of all kinds of private injustice, and in particular of the breach of promises. We blame all treachery and breach of faith; because we consider, that the freedom and extent of human commerce depend entirely on a fidelity with regard to promises. We blame all disloyalty to magistrates; because we perceive, that the execution of justice, in the stability of possession, its translation by consent, and the performance of promises, is impossible, without submission to government. As there are here two interests entirely distinct from each other, they must give rise to two moral obligations, equally separate and independent. Tho' there was no such thing as a promise in the world, government wou'd still be necessary in all large and civiliz'd societies; and if promises had only their own proper obligation, without the separate sanction of government, they wou'd have but little efficacy in such societies. This separates the boundaries of our public and private duties, and shews that the latter are more dependant on the former, than the former on the latter. *Education*, and *the artifice of politicians*, concur to bestow a farther morality on loyalty, and to brand all rebellion with a greater degree of guilt and infamy. Nor is it a wonder, that politicians shou'd be very industrious in inculcating such notions, where their interest is so particularly concern'd.

Lest those arguments shou'd not appear entirely conclusive (as I think they are) I shall have recourse to authority, and shall prove, from the universal consent of mankind, that the obligation of submission to government is not deriv'd from any promise of the subjects. Nor need any one wonder, that tho' I have all along endeavour'd to establish my system on pure reason, and have scarce ever cited the judgment even of philosophers or historians on any article, I shou'd now appeal to popular authority, and oppose the sentiments of the rabble to any philosophical reasoning. For it must be observ'd, that the opinions of men, in this case, carry with them a peculiar authority, and are, in a great measure, infallible. The distinction of moral good and evil is founded on the pleasure or pain, which results from the view of any sentiment, or character; and as that pleasure or pain cannot be unknown to the person who feels it, it follows,* that there is just so much vice or virtue in any character, as every one places in it, and that 'tis impossible in this particular we can ever be mistaken. And tho' our judgments concerning the *origin* of any vice or virtue, be not so certain as those concerning their *degrees*; yet, since the question in this case regards not any philosophical origin of an obligation, but a plain matter of fact, 'tis not easily conceiv'd how we can fall into an error. A man, who acknowledges himself to be bound to another, for a certain sum, must certainly know whether it be by his own bond, or that of his father; whether it be of his mere good-will, or for money lent him; and under what conditions, and for what purposes he has bound himself. In like manner, it being certain, that there is a moral obligation to submit to government, because every one thinks so; it must be as certain, that this obligation arises not from a promise; since no one, whose judgment has not been led astray by too strict adherence to a system of philosophy, has ever yet dreamt of ascribing it to that origin. Neither magistrates nor subjects have form'd this idea of our civil duties.

We find, that magistrates are so far from deriving their authority, and the obligation to obedience in their subjects, from the foundation of a promise or original contract,

*This proposition must hold strictly true, with regard to every quality, that is determin'd merely by sentiment. In what sense we can talk either of a *right* or a *wrong* taste in morals, eloquence, or beauty, shall be consider'd afterwards. In the mean time, it may be observ'd, that there is such an uniformity in the *general* sentiments of mankind, as to render such questions of but small importance.

that they conceal, as far as possible, from their people, especially from the vulgar, that they have their origin from thence. Were this the sanction of government, our rulers wou'd never receive it tacitly, which is the utmost that can be pretended; since what is given tacitly and insensibly can never have such influence on mankind, as what is perform'd expressly and openly. A tacit promise is, where the will is signified by other more diffuse signs than those of speech; but a will there must certainly be in the case, and that can never escape the person's notice, who exerted it, however silent or tacit. But were you to ask the far greatest part of the nation, whether they had ever consented to the authority of their rulers, or promis'd to obey them, they wou'd be inclin'd to think very strangely of you; and wou'd certainly reply, that the affair depended not on their consent, but that they were born to such an obedience. In consequence of this opinion, we frequently see them imagine such persons to be their natural rulers, as are at that time depriv'd of all power and authority, and whom no man, however foolish, wou'd voluntarily chuse; and this merely because they are in that line, which rul'd before, and in that degree of it, which us'd to succeed; tho' perhaps in so distant a period, that scarce any man alive cou'd ever have given any promise of obedience. Has a government, then, no authority over such as these, because they never consented to it, and wou'd esteem the very attempt of such a free choice a piece of arrogance and impiety? We find by experience, that it punishes them very freely for what it calls treason and rebellion, which, it seems, according to this system, reduces itself to common injustice. If you say, that by dwelling in its dominions, they in effect consented to the establish'd government; I answer, that this can only be, where they think the affair depends on their choice, which few or none, beside those philosophers, have ever yet imagin'd. It never was pleaded as an excuse for a rebel, that the first act he perform'd, after he came to years of discretion, was to levy war against the sovereign of the state; and that while he was a child he cou'd not bind himself by his own consent, and having become a man, show'd plainly, by the first act he perform'd, that he had no design to impose on himself any obligation to obedience. We find, on the contrary, that civil laws punish this crime at the same age as any other, which is criminal, of itself, without our consent; that is, when the person is come to the full use of reason: Whereas to this crime they ought in justice to allow some intermediate time, in which a tacit consent at least might be suppos'd. To which we may add, that a man living under an absolute government, wou'd owe it no allegiance; since, by its very nature, it depends not on consent. But as that is as *natural* and *common* a government as any, it must certainly occasion some obligation; and 'tis plain from experience, that men, who are subjected to it, do always think so. This is a clear proof, that we do not commonly esteem our allegiance to be deriv'd from our consent or promise; and a farther proof is, that when our promise is upon any account expressly engag'd, we always distinguish exactly betwixt the two obligations, and believe the one to add more force to the other, than in a repetition of the same promise. Where no promise is given, a man looks not on his faith as broken in private matters, upon account of rebellion; but keeps those two duties of honour and allegiance perfectly distinct and separate. As the uniting of them was thought by these philosophers a very subtile invention, this is a convincing proof, that 'tis not a true one; since no man can either give a promise, or be restrain'd by its sanction and obligation unknown to himself.

SECT. IX

Of the measures of allegiance

THOSE political writers, who have had recourse to a promise, or original contract, as the source of our allegiance to government, intended to establish a principle, which is perfectly just and reasonable; tho' the reasoning, upon which they endeavour'd to establish it, was fallacious and sophistical. They wou'd prove, that our submission to government admits of exceptions, and that an egregious tyranny in the rulers is sufficient to free the subjects from all ties of allegiance. Since men enter into society, say they, and submit themselves to government, by their free and voluntary consent, they must have in view certain advantages, which they propose to reap from it, and for which they are contented to resign their native liberty. There is, therefore, something mutual engag'd on the part of the magistrate, *viz.* protection and security; and 'tis only by the hopes he affords of these advantages, that he can ever persuade men to submit to him. But when instead of protection and security, they meet with tyranny and oppression, they are free'd from their promises, (as happens in all conditional contracts) and return to that state of liberty, which preceded the institution of government. Men wou'd never be so foolish as to enter into such engagements as shou'd turn entirely to the advantage of others, without any view of bettering their own condition. Whoever proposes to draw any profit from our submission, must engage himself, either expressly or tacitly, to make us reap some advantage from his authority; nor ought he to expect, that without the performance of his part we will ever continue in obedience.

I repeat it: This conclusion is just, tho' the principles be erroneous; and I flatter myself, that I can establish the same conclusion on more reasonable principles. I shall not take such a compass, in establishing our political duties, as to assert, that men perceive the advantages of government; that they institute government with a view to those advantages; that this institution requires a promise of obedience; which imposes a moral obligation to a certain degree, but being conditional, ceases to be binding, whenever the other contracting party performs not his part of the engagement. I perceive, that a promise itself arises entirely from human conventions, and is invented with a view to a certain interest. I seek, therefore, some such interest more immediately connected with government, and which may be at once the original motive to its institution, and the source of our obedience to it. This interest I find to consist in the security and protection, which we enjoy in political society, and which we can never attain, when perfectly free and independent. As interest, therefore, is the immediate sanction of government, the one can have no longer being than the other; and whenever the civil magistrate carries his oppression so far as to render his authority perfectly intolerable, we are no longer bound to submit to it. The cause ceases; the effect must cease also.

So far the conclusion is immediate and direct, concerning the *natural* obligation which we have to allegiance. As to the *moral* obligation, we may observe, that the maxim wou'd here be false, that *when the cause ceases, the effect must cease also*. For there is a principle of human nature, which we have frequently taken notice of, that men are mightily addicted to *general rules*, and that we often carry our maxims beyond those reasons, which first induc'd us to establish them. Where cases are similar in many circumstances, we are apt to put them on the same footing, without considering, that they differ in the most material circumstances, and that the resemblance is more apparent than real. It may, therefore, be thought, that in the case of allegiance our moral obligation of duty will not cease, even tho' the natural obligation of interest, which is its cause, has ceas'd; and that men may be bound by *conscience* to submit to a tyrannical government against their own and the public interest. And indeed, to the force of this argument I so far submit, as to acknowledge, that general rules commonly extend beyond the principles, on which they are founded; and that we seldom make any exception to them, unless that exception have the qualities of a general rule, and be founded on very numerous and common instances. Now this I assert to be entirely the present case. When men submit to the authority of others, 'tis to procure themselves some security against the wickedness and injustice of men, who are perpetually carried, by their unruly passions, and by their present and immediate interest, to the violation of all the laws of society. But as this imperfection is inherent in human nature, we know that it must attend men in all their states and conditions; and that those, whom we chuse for rulers, do not immediately become of a superior nature to the rest of mankind, upon account of their superior power and authority. What we expect from them depends not on a change of their nature but of their situation, when they acquire a more immediate interest in the preservation of order and the execution of justice. But besides that this interest is only more immediate in the execution of justice among their subjects; besides this, I say, we may often expect, from the irregularity of human nature, that they will neglect even this immediate interest, and be transported by their passions into all the excesses of cruelty and ambition. Our general knowledge of human nature, our observation of the past history of mankind, our experience of present times; all these causes must induce us to open the door to exceptions, and must make us conclude, that we may resist the more violent effects of supreme power, without any crime or injustice.

Accordingly we may observe, that this is both the general practice and principle of mankind, and that no nation, that cou'd find any remedy, ever yet suffer'd the cruel ravages of a tyrant, or were blam'd for their resistance. Those who took up arms against *Dionysius* or *Nero*, or *Philip the second*, have the favour of every reader in the perusal of their history; and nothing but the most violent perversion of common sense can ever lead us to condemn them. 'Tis certain, therefore, that in all our notions of morals we never entertain such an absurdity as that of passive obedience, but make allowances for resistance in the more flagrant instances of tyranny and oppression. The general opinion of mankind has some authority in all cases; but in this of morals 'tis perfectly infallible. Nor is it less infallible, because men cannot distinctly explain the principles, on which it is founded. Few persons can carry on this train of reasoning:

'Government is a mere human invention for the interest of society. Where the tyranny of the governor removes this interest, it also removes the natural obligation to obedience. The moral obligation is founded on the natural, and therefore must cease where *that* ceases; especially where the subject is such as makes us foresee very many occasions wherein the natural obligation may cease, and causes us to form a kind of general rule for the regulation of our conduct in such occurrences.'

But tho' this train of reasoning be too subtile for the vulgar, 'tis certain, that all men have an implicit notion of it, and are sensible, that they owe obedience to government merely on account of the public interest; and at the same time, that human nature is so subject to frailties and passions, as may easily pervert this institution, and change their governors into tyrants and public enemies. If the sense of common interest were not our original motive to obedience, I wou'd fain ask, what other principle is there in human nature capable of subduing the natural ambition of men, and forcing them to such a submission? Imitation and custom are not sufficient. For the question still recurs, what motive first produces those instances of submission, which we imitate, and that train of actions, which produces the custom? There evidently is no other principle than public interest; and if interest first produces obedience to government, the obligation to obedience must cease, whenever the interest ceases, in any great degree, and in a considerable number of instances.

SECT. X

Of the objects of allegiance

BUT tho', on some occasions, it may be justifiable, both in sound politics and morality, to resist supreme power, 'tis certain, that in the ordinary course of human affairs nothing can be more pernicious and criminal; and that besides the convulsions, which always attend revolutions, such a practice tends directly to the subversion of all government, and the causing an universal anarchy and confusion among mankind. As numerous and civiliz'd societies cannot subsist without government, so government is entirely useless without an exact obedience. We ought always to weigh the advantages, which we reap from authority, against the disadvantages; and by this means we shall become more scrupulous of putting in practice the doctrine of resistance. The common rule requires submission; and 'tis only in cases of grievous tyranny and oppression, that the exception can take place.

Since then such a blind submission is commonly due to magistracy, the next question is, *to whom it is due, and whom we are to regard as our lawful magistrates?* In order to answer this question, let us recollect what we have already establish'd concerning the origin of government and political society. When men have once experienc'd the impossibility of preserving any steady order in society, while every one is his own master, and violates or observes the laws of society, according to his present interest or pleasure, they naturally run into the invention of government, and put it out of their own power, as far as possible, to transgress the laws of society. Government, therefore, arises from the same voluntary conversation of men; and 'tis evident, that the same convention, which establishes government, will also determine the persons who are to govern, and will remove all doubt and ambiguity in this particular. And the voluntary consent of men must here have the greater efficacy, that the authority of the magistrate does *at first* stand upon the foundation of a promise of the subjects, by which they bind themselves to obedience; as in every other contract or engagement. The same promise, then, which binds them to obedience, ties them down to a particular person, and makes him the object of their allegiance.

But when government has been establish'd on this footing for some considerable time, and the separate interest, which we have in submission, has produc'd a separate sentiment of morality, the case is entirely alter'd, and a promise is no longer able to determine the particular magistrate;

since it is no longer consider'd as the foundation of government. We naturally suppose ourselves born to submission; and imagine, that such particular persons have a right to command, as we on our part are bound to obey. These notions of right and obligation are deriv'd from nothing but the *advantage* we reap from government, which gives us a repugnance to practise resistance ourselves, and makes us displeas'd with any instance of it in others. But here 'tis remarkable, that in this new state of affairs, the original sanction of government, which is *interest*, is not admitted to determine the persons, whom we are to obey, as the original sanction did at first, when affairs were on the footing of a *promise*. A *promise* fixes and determines the persons, without any uncertainty: But 'tis evident, that if men were to regulate their conduct in this particular, by the view of a peculiar *interest*, either public or private, they wou'd involve themselves in endless confusion, and wou'd render all government, in a great measure, ineffectual. The private interest of every one is different; and tho' the public interest in itself be always one and the same, yet it becomes the source of as great dissentions, by reason of the different opinions of particular persons concerning it. The same interest, therefore, which causes us to submit to magistracy, makes us renounce itself in the choice of our magistrates, and binds us down to a certain form of government, and to particular persons, without allowing us to aspire to the utmost perfection in either. The case is here the same as in that law of nature concerning the stability of possession. 'Tis highly advantageous, and even absolutely necessary to society, that possession shou'd be stable; and this leads us to the establishment of such a rule: But we find, that were we to follow the same advantage, in assigning particular possessions to particular persons, we shou'd disappoint our end, and perpetuate the confusion, which that rule is intended to prevent. We must, therefore, proceed by general rules, and regulate ourselves by general interests, in modifying the law of nature concerning the stability of possession. Nor need we fear, that our attachment to this law will diminish upon account of the seeming frivolousness of those interests, by which it is determin'd. The impulse of the mind is deriv'd from a very strong interest; and those other more minute interests serve only to direct the motion, without adding any thing to it, or diminishing from it. 'Tis the same case with government. Nothing is more advantageous to society than such an invention; and this interest is sufficient to make us embrace it with ardour and alacrity; tho' we are oblig'd afterwards to regulate and direct our devotion to government by several considerations, which are not of the same importance, and to chuse our magistrates without having in view any particular advantage from the choice.

The *first* of those principles I shall take notice of, as a foundation of the right of magistracy, is that which gives authority to all the most establish'd governments of the world without exception: I mean, *long possession* in any one form of government, or succession of princes. 'Tis certain, that if we remount to the first origin of every nation, we shall find, that there scarce is any race of kings, or form of a commonwealth, that is not primarily founded on usurpation and rebellion, and whose title is not at first worse than doubtful and uncertain. Time alone gives solidity to their right; and operating gradually on the minds of men, reconciles them to any authority, and makes it seem just and reasonable. Nothing causes any sentiment to have a greater influence upon us than custom, or turns our imagination more strongly to any object. When we have been long accustom'd to obey any set of men, that general instinct or tendency, which we have to suppose a moral obligation attending loyalty, takes easily this direction, and chuses that set of men for its objects. 'Tis interest which gives the general instinct; but 'tis custom which gives the particular direction.

And here 'tis observable, that the same length of time has a different influence on our sentiments of morality, according to its different influence on the mind. We naturally judge of every thing by comparison; and since in considering the fate of kingdoms and republics, we embrace a long extent of time, a small duration has not in this case a like influence on our sentiments, as when we consider any other object. One thinks he acquires a right to a horse, or a suit of cloaths, in a very short time; but a century is scarce sufficient to establish any new government, or remove all scruples in the minds of the subjects concerning it. Add to this, that a shorter period of time will suffice to give a prince a title to any additional power he may usurp, than will serve to fix his right, where the whole is an usurpation. The kings of *France* have not been possess'd of absolute power for above two reigns; and yet nothing will appear more extravagant to *Frenchmen* than to talk of their liberties. If we consider what has been said concerning *accession*, we shall easily account for this phaenomenon.

When there is no form of government establish'd by *long* possession, the *present* possession is sufficient to supply its place, and may be regarded as the *second* source of all public authority. Right to authority is nothing but the constant possession of authority, maintain'd by the laws of society and the interests of mankind; and nothing can be more natural than to join this constant possession to the present one, according to the principles above-mention'd. If the same principles did not take place with regard to the property of private persons, 'twas because these principles were counter-ballanc'd by very strong considerations of interest; when we observ'd, that all restitution wou'd by that means be prevented, and every violence be authoriz'd and protected. And tho' the same motives may seem to have force, with regard to public authority, yet they are oppos'd by a contrary interest; which consists in the preservation of peace, and the avoiding of all changes, which, however they may be easily produc'd in private affairs, are unavoidably attended with bloodshed and confusion, where the public is interested.

Any one, who finding the impossibility of accounting for the right of the present possessor, by any receiv'd system of ethics, shou'd resolve to deny absolutely that right, and assert, that it is not authoriz'd by morality, wou'd be justly thought to maintain a very extravagant paradox, and to shock the common sense and judgment of mankind. No maxim is more conformable, both to prudence and morals, than to submit quietly to the government, which we find establish'd in the country where we happen to live, without enquiring too curiously into its origin and first establishment. Few governments will bear being examin'd so rigorously. How many kingdoms are there at present in the world, and how many more do we find in history, whose governors have no better foundation for their authority than that of present possession? To confine ourselves to the *Roman* and *Grecian* empire; is it not evident, that the long succession of emperors, from the dissolution of the *Roman* liberty, to the final extinction of that empire by the *Turks*, cou'd not so much as pretend to any other title to the empire? The election of the senate was a mere form, which always follow'd the choice of the legions; and these were almost always divided in the different provinces, and nothing but the sword was able to terminate the difference. 'Twas by the sword, therefore, that every emperor acquir'd, as well as defended his right; and we must either say, that all the known world, for so many ages, had no government, and ow'd no allegiance to any one, or must allow, that the right of the stronger, in public affairs, is to be receiv'd as legitimate, and authoriz'd by morality, when not oppos'd by any other title.

The right of *conquest* may be consider'd as a *third* source of the title of sovereigns. This right resembles very much that of present possession; but has rather a superior force, being seconded by the notions of glory and honour, which we ascribe to *conquerors*, instead of the sentiments of hatred and detestation, which attend *usurpers*. Men naturally favour those they love; and therefore are more apt to ascribe a right to successful violence, betwixt one sovereign and another, than to the successful rebellion of a subject against his sovereign*.

*It is not here asserted, that *present possession* or *conquest* are sufficient to give a title against *long possession* and *positive laws*;

When neither long possession, nor present possession, nor conquest take place, as when the first sovereign, who founded any monarchy, dies; in that case, the right of *succession* naturally prevails in their stead, and men are commonly induc'd to place the son of their late monarch on the throne, and suppose him to inherit his father's authority. The presum'd consent of the father, the imitation of the succession to private families, the interest, which the state has in chusing the person, who is most powerful, and has the most numerous followers; all these reasons lead men to prefer the son of their late monarch to any other person*.

These reasons have some weight; but I am persuaded, that to one, who considers impartially of the matter, 'twill appear, that there concur some principles of the imagination, along with those views of interest. The royal authority seems to be connected with the young prince even in his father's life-time, by the natural transition of the thought; and still more after his death: So that nothing is more natural than to compleat this union by a new relation, and by putting him actually in possession of what seems so naturally to belong to him.

To confirm this we may weigh the following phaenomena, which are pretty curious in their kind. In elective monarchies the right of succession has no place by the laws and settled custom; and yet its influence is so natural, that 'tis impossible entirely to exclude it from the imagination, and render the subjects indifferent to the son of their deceas'd

---

But only that they have some force, and will be able to call the ballance where the titles are otherwise equal, and will even be sufficient *sometimes* to sanctify the weaker title. What degree of force they have is difficult to determine. I believe all moderate men will allow, that they have great force in all disputes concerning the rights of princes.

* To prevent mistakes I must observe, that this case of succession is not the same with that of hereditary monarchies, where custom has fix'd the right of succession. These depend upon the principle of long possession above explain'd.

monarch. Hence in some governments of this kind, the choice commonly falls on one or other of the royal family; and in some governments they are all excluded. Those contrary phaenomena proceed from the same principle. Where the royal family is excluded, 'tis from a refinement in politics, which makes people sensible of their propensity to chuse a sovereign in that family, and gives them a jealousy of their liberty, lest their new monarch, aided by this propensity, shou'd establish his family, and destroy the freedom of elections for the future.

The history of *Artaxerxes*, and the younger *Cyrus*, may furnish us with some reflections to the same purpose. *Cyrus* pretended a right to the throne above his elder brother, because he was born after his father's accession. I do not pretend, that this reason was valid. I wou'd only infer from it, that he wou'd never have made use of such a pretext, were it not for the qualities of the imagination above-mention'd, by which we are naturally inclin'd to unite by a new relation whatever objects we find already united. *Artaxerxes* had an advantage above his brother, as being the eldest son, and the first in succession: But *Cyrus* was more closely related to the royal authority, as being begot after his father was invested with it.

Shou'd it here be pretended, that the view of convenience may be the source of all the right of succession, and that men gladly take advantage of any rule, by which they can fix the successor of their late sovereign, and prevent that anarchy and confusion, which attends all new elections: To this I wou'd answer, that I readily allow, that this motive may contribute something to the effect; but at the same time I assert, that without another principle, 'tis impossible such a motive shou'd take place. The interest of a nation requires, that the succession to the crown shou'd be fix'd one way or other; but 'tis the same thing to its interest in what way it be fix'd: So that if the relation of blood had not an effect independent of public interest, it wou'd never have been regarded, without a positive law; and 'twou'd have been impossible, that so many positive laws of different nations cou'd ever have concur'd precisely in the same views and intentions.

This leads us to consider the *fifth* source of authority, viz. *positive laws*; when the legislature establishes a certain form of government and succession of princes. At first sight it may be thought, that this must resolve into some of the preceding titles of authority. The legislative power, whence the positive law is deriv'd, must either be establish'd by original contract, long possession, present possession, conquest, or succession; and consequently the positive law must derive its force from some of those principles. But here 'tis remarkable, that tho' a positive law can only derive its force from these principles, yet it acquires not all the force of the principle from whence it is deriv'd, but loses considerably in the transition; as it is natural to imagine. For instance; a government is establish'd for many centuries on a certain system of laws, forms, and methods of succession. The legislative power, establish'd by this long succession, changes all on a sudden the whole system of government, and introduces a new constitution in its stead. I believe few of the subjects will think themselves bound to comply with this alteration, unless it have an evident tendency to the public good: But will think themselves still at liberty to return to the antient government. Hence the notion of *fundamental laws;* which are suppos'd to be inalterable by the will of the sovereign: And of this nature the *Salic* law is understood to be in *France*. How far these fundamental laws extend is not determin'd in any government; nor is it possible it ever shou'd. There is such an indefensible gradation from the most material laws to the most trivial, and from the most antient laws to the most modern, that 'twill be impossible to set bounds to the legislative power, and determine how far it may innovate in the principles of government. That is the work more of imagination and passion than of reason.

Whoever considers the history of the several nations of the world; their revolutions, conquests, increase, and diminution; the manner in which their particular governments are establish'd, and the successive right transmitted from one person to another, will soon learn to treat very lightly all disputes concerning the rights of princes, and will be convinc'd, that a strict adherence to any general rules, and the rigid loyalty to particular persons and families, on which some people set so high a value, are virtues that hold less of reason, than of bigotry and superstition. In this particular, the study of history confirms the reasonings of true philosophy; which, shewing us the original qualities of human nature, teaches us to regard the controversies in politics as incapable of any decision in most cases, and as entirely subordinate to the interests of peace and liberty. Where the public good does not evidently demand a change; 'tis certain, that the concurrence of all those titles, *original contract, long possession, present possession, succession,* and *positive laws,* forms the strongest title to sovereignty, and is justly regarded as sacred and inviolable. But when these titles are mingled and oppos'd in different degrees, they often occasion perplexity; and are less capable of solution from the arguments of lawyers and philosophers, than from the swords of the soldiery. Who shall tell me, for instance, whether *Germanicus,* or *Drufus,* ought to have succeeded *Tiberius,* had he died while they were both alive, without naming any of them for his successor? Ought the right of adoption to be receiv'd as equivalent to that of blood in a nation, where it had the same effect in private families, and had already, in two instances, taken place in the public? Ought *Germanicus* to be esteem'd the eldest son, because he was born before *Drufus*; or the younger, because he was adopted after the birth of his brother? Ought the right of the elder to be regarded in a nation, where the eldest brother had no advantage in the succession to private families? Ought the *Roman* empire at that time to be esteem'd hereditary, because of two examples; or ought it, even so early, to be regarded as belonging to the stronger, or the present possessor, as being founded on so recent an usurpation? Upon whatever principles we may pretend to answer these and such like questions, I am afraid we shall never be able to satisfy an impartial enquirer, who adopts no party in political controversies, and will be satisfied with nothing but sound reason and philosophy.

But here an *English* reader will be apt to enquire concerning that famous *revolution*, which has had such a happy influence on our constitution, and has been attended with such mighty consequences. We have already remark'd, that in the case of enormous tyranny and oppression, 'tis lawful to take arms even against supreme power; and that as government is a mere human invention for mutual advantage and security, it no longer imposes any obligation, either natural or moral, when once it ceases to have that tendency. But tho' this *general* principle be authoriz'd by common sense, and the practice of all ages, 'tis certainly impossible for the laws, or even for philosophy, to establish any *particular* rules, by which we may know when resistance is lawful; and decide all controversies, which may arise on that subject. This may not only happen with regard to supreme power; but 'tis possible, even in some constitutions, where the legislative authority is not lodg'd in one person, that there may be a magistrate so eminent and powerful, as to oblige the laws to keep silence in this particular. Nor wou'd this silence be an effect only of their *respect*, but also of their *prudence*; since 'tis certain, that in the vast variety of circumstances, which occur in all governments, an exercise of power, in so great a magistrate, may at one time be beneficial to the public, which at another time wou'd be pernicious and tyrannical. But notwithstanding this silence of the laws in limited monarchies, 'tis certain, that the people still retain the right of resistance; since 'tis impossible, even in the most despotic governments, to deprive them of it. The same necessity of self-preservation, and the same motive of public good, give them the same liberty in the one case as in the other. And we may farther observe, that in such mix'd governments, the cases, wherein resistance is lawful, must occur much oftener, and greater indulgence be given to the subjects to defend themselves by force of arms, than in arbitrary governments. Not only where the chief magistrate enters into measures, in themselves, extremely pernicious to the public, but even when he wou'd encroach on the other parts of the constitution, and extend his power beyond the legal bounds, it is allowable to resist and dethrone him; tho' such resistance and violence may, in the general tenor of the laws, be deem'd unlawful and rebellious. For besides that nothing is more essential to public interest, than the preservation of public liberty; 'tis evident, that if such a mix'd government be once suppos'd to be established, every part or member of the constitution must have a right of self-defence, and of maintaining its antient bounds against the encroachment of every other authority. As matter wou'd have been created in vain, were it depriv'd of a power of resistance, without which no part of it cou'd preserve a distinct existence, and the whole might be crowded up into a single point: So 'tis a gross absurdity to suppose, in any government, a right without a remedy, or allow, that the supreme power is shar'd with the people, without allowing, that 'tis lawful for them to defend their share against every invader. Those, therefore, who wou'd seem to respect our free government, and yet deny the right of resistance, *have* renounc'd all pretensions to common sense, and do not merit a serious answer.

It does not belong to my present purpose to shew, that these general principles are applicable to the late *revolution*; and that all the rights and privileges, which ought to be sacred to a free nation, were at that time threaten'd with the utmost danger. I am better pleas'd to leave this controverted subject, if it really admits of controversy; and to indulge myself in some philosophical reflections, which naturally arise from that important event.

First, We may observe, that shou'd the *lords* and *commons* in our constitution, without any reason from public interest, either depose the king in being, or after his death exclude the prince, who, by laws and settled custom, ought to succeed, no one wou'd esteem their proceedings legal, or think themselves bound to comply with them. But shou'd the king, by his unjust practices, or his attempts for a tyrannical and despotic power, justly forfeit his legal, it then not only becomes morally lawful and suitable to the nature of political society to dethrone him; but what is more, we are apt likewise to think, that the remaining members of the constitution acquire a right of excluding his next heir, and of chusing whom they please for his successor. This is founded on a very singular quality of our thought and imagination. When a king forfeits his authority, his heir ought naturally to remain in the same situation, as if the king were remov'd by death; unless by mixing himself in the tyranny, he forfeit it for himself. But tho' this may seem reasonable, we easily comply with the contrary opinion. The deposition of a king, in such a government as ours, is certainly an act beyond all common authority, and an illegal assuming a power for public good, which, in the ordinary course of government, can belong to no member of the constitution. When the public good is so great and so evident as to justify the action, the commendable use of this licence causes us naturally to attribute to the *parliament* a right of using farther licences; and the antient bounds of the laws being once transgressed with approbation, we are not apt to be so strict in confining ourselves precisely within their limits. The mind naturally runs on with any train of action, which it has begun; nor do we commonly make any scruple concerning our duty, after the first action of any kind, which we perform. Thus at the *revolution*, no one who thought the deposition of the father justifiable, esteem'd themselves to be confin'd to his infant son; tho' had that unhappy monarch died innocent at that time, and had his son, by any accident, been convey'd beyond seas, there is no doubt but a regency wou'd have been appointed till he shou'd come to age, and cou'd be restored to his dominions. As the slightest properties of the imagination have an effect on the judgments of the people, it shews the wisdom of the laws and of the parliament to take advantage of such properties, and to chuse the magistrates either in or out of a line, according as the vulgar will most naturally attribute authority and right to them.

Secondly, Tho' the accession of the *Prince of Orange* to the throne might at first give occasion to many disputes, and his title be contested, it ought not now to appear doubtful, but must have acquir'd a sufficient authority from those three princes, who have succeeded him upon the same title. Nothing is more usual, tho' nothing may, at first sight, appear more unreasonable, than this way of thinking. Princes often *seem* to acquire a right from their successors, as well as from their ancestors; and a king, who during his life-time might justly be deem'd an usurper, will be regarded by posterity as a lawful prince, because he has had the good fortune to settle his family on the throne, and entirely change the antient form of government. *Julius Caesar* is regarded as the first *Roman* emperor; while *Sylla* and *Marius,* whose titles were really the same as his, are treated as tyrants and usurpers. Time and custom give authority to all forms of government, and all successions of princes; and that power, which at first was founded only on injustice and violence, becomes in time legal and obligatory. Nor does the mind rest there; but returning back upon its footsteps, transfers to their predecessors and ancestors that right, which it naturally ascribes to the posterity, as being related together, and united in the imagination. The present *king* of *France* makes *Hugh Capet* a more lawful prince than *Cromwell*; as the establish'd liberty of the *Dutch* is no inconsiderable apology for their obstinate resistance to *Philip* the second.

SECT. XI

Of the laws of nations

WHEN civil government has been established over the greatest part of mankind, and different societies have been form'd contiguous to each other, there arises a new set of duties among the neighbouring states, suitable to the nature of that commerce, which they carry on with each other. Political writers tell us, that in every kind of intercourse, a body politic is to be consider'd as one person; and indeed this assertion is so far just, that different nations, as well as private persons, require mutual assistance; at the same time that their selfishness and ambition are perpetual sources of war and discord. But tho' nations in this particular resemble individuals, yet as they are very different in other respects, no wonder they regulate themselves by different maxims, and give rise to a new set of rules, which we call *the laws of nations.* Under this head we may comprize the sacredness of the persons of ambassadors, the declaration of war, the abstaining from poison'd arms, with other duties of that kind, which are evidently calculated for the commerce, that is peculiar to different societies.

But tho' these rules be super-added to the laws of nature, the former do not entirely abolish the latter; and one may safely affirm, that the three fundamental rules of justice, the stability of possession, its transference by consent, and the performance of promises, are duties of princes, as well as of subjects. The same interest produces the same effect in both cases. Where possession has no stability, there must be perpetual war. Where property is not transferr'd by consent, there can be no commerce. Where promises are not observ'd, there can be no leagues nor alliances. The advantages, therefore, of peace, commerce, and mutual succour, make us extend to different kingdoms the same notions of justice, which take place among individuals.

There is a maxim very current in the world, which few politicians are willing to avow, but which has been authoriz'd by the practice of all ages, *that there is a system of morals calculated for princes, much more free than that which ought to govern private persons.* 'Tis evident this is not to be understood of the lesser *extent* of public duties and obligations; nor will any one be so extravagant as to assert, that the most solemn treaties ought to have no force among princes. For as princes do actually form treaties among themselves, they must propose some advantage from the execution of them; and the prospect of such advantage for the future must engage them to perform their part, and must establish that law of nature. The meaning, therefore, of this political maxim is, that tho' the morality of princes has the same *extent,* yet it has not the same *force* as that of private persons, and may lawfully be trangress'd from a more trivial motive. However shocking such a proposition may appear to certain philosophers, 'twill be easy to defend it upon those principles, by which we have accounted for the origin of justice and equity.

When men have found by experience, that 'tis impossible to subsist without society, and that 'tis impossible to maintain society, while they give free course to their appetites; so urgent an interest quickly restrains their actions, and imposes an obligation to observe those rules, which we call *the laws of justice.* This obligation of interest rests not here; but by the necessary course of the passions and sentiments, gives rise to the moral obligation of duty; while we approve of such actions as tend to the peace of society, and disapprove of such as tend to its disturbance. The same *natural* obligation of interest takes place among independent kingdoms, and gives rise to the same *morality*; so that no one of ever so corrupt morals will approve of a prince, who voluntarily, and of his own accord, breaks his word, or violates any treaty. But here we may observe, that tho' the intercourse of different states be advantageous, and even sometimes necessary, yet it is not so necessary nor advantageous as that among individuals, without which 'tis utterly impossible for human nature ever to subsist. Since, therefore, the *natural* obligation to justice, among different states, is not so strong as among individuals, the *moral* obligation, which arises from it, must partake of its weakness; and we must necessarily give a greater indulgence to a prince or minister, who deceives another; than to a private gentleman, who breaks his word of honour.

Shou'd it be ask'd, *what proportion these two species of morality bear to each other?* I wou'd answer, that this is a question, to which we can never give any precise answer; nor is it possible to reduce to numbers the proportion, which we ought to fix betwixt them. One may safely affirm, that this proportion finds itself, without any art or study of men; as we may observe on many other occasions. The practice of the world goes farther in teaching us the degrees of our duty, than the most subtile philosophy, which was ever yet invented. And this may serve as a convincing proof, that all men have an implicit notion of the foundation of those moral rules concerning natural and civil justice, and are sensible, that they arise merely from human conventions, and from the interest, which we have in the preservation of peace and order. For otherwise the diminution of the interest wou'd never produce a relaxation of the morality, and reconcile us more easily to any transgression of justice among princes and republics, than in the private commerce of one subject with another.

SECT. XII

Of chastity and modesty

IF any difficulty attend this system concerning the laws of nature and nations, 'twill be with regard to the universal approbation or blame, which follows their observance or transgression, and which some may not think sufficiently explain'd from the general interests of society. To remove, as far as possible, all scruples of this kind, I shall here consider another set of duties, *viz.* the *modesty* and *chastity* which belong to the fair sex: And I doubt not but these virtues will be found to be still more conspicuous instances of the operation of those principles, which I have insisted on.

There are some philosophers, who attack the female virtues with great vehemence, and fancy they have gone very far in detecting popular errors, when they can show, that there is no foundation in nature for all that exterior modesty, which we require in the expressions, and dress, and behaviour of the fair sex. I believe I may spare myself the trouble of insisting on so obvious a subject, and may proceed, without farther preparation, to examine after what manner such notions arise from education, from the voluntary conventions of men, and from the interest of society.

Whoever considers the length and feebleness of human infancy, with the concern which both sexes naturally have for their offspring, will easily perceive, that there must be an union of male and female for the education of the young, and that this union must be of considerable duration. But in order to induce the men to impose on themselves this restraint, and undergo chearfully all the fatigues and expences, to which it subjects them, they must believe, that the children are their own, and that their natural instinct is not directed to a wrong object, when they give a loose to love and tenderness. Now if we examine the structure of the human body, we shall find, that this security is very difficult to be attain'd on our part; and that since, in the copulation of the sexes, the principle of generation goes from the man to the woman, an error may easily take place on the side of the former, tho' it be utterly impossible with regard to the latter. From this trivial and anatomical observation is deriv'd that vast difference betwixt the education and duties of the two sexes.

Were a philosopher to examine the matter *a priori*, he wou'd reason after the following manner. Men are induc'd to labour for the maintenance and education of their children, by the persuasion that they are really their own; and therefore 'tis reasonable, and even necessary, to give them some security in this particular. This security cannot consist entirely in the imposing of severe punishments on any transgressions of conjugal fidelity on the part of the wife; since these public punishments cannot be inflicted without legal proof, which 'tis difficult to meet with in this subject. What restraint, therefore, shall we impose on women, in order to counter-balance so strong a temptation as they have to infidelity[*]? There seems to be no restraint possible, but in the punishment of bad fame or reputation; a punishment, which has a mighty influence on the human mind, and at the same time is inflicted by the world upon surmizes, and conjectures, and proofs, that wou'd never be receiv'd in any court of judicature. In order, therefore, to impose a due restraint on the female sex, we must attach a peculiar degree of shame to their infidelity, above what arises merely from its injustice, and must bestow proportionable praises on their chastity.

But tho' this be a very strong motive to fidelity, our philosopher wou'd quickly discover, that it wou'd not alone be sufficient to that purpose. All human creatures, especially of the female sex, are apt to over-look remote motives in favour of any present temptation: The temptation is here the strongest imaginable: Its approaches are insensible and seducing: And a woman easily finds, or flatters herself she shall find, certain means of securing her reputation, and preventing all the pernicious consequences of her pleasures. 'Tis necessary, therefore, that, beside the infamy attending such licences, there shou'd be some preceding backwardness or dread, which may prevent their first approaches, and may give the female sex a repugnance to all expressions, and postures, and liberties, that have an immediate relation to that enjoyment.

Such wou'd be the reasonings of our speculative philosopher: But I am persuaded, that if he had not a perfect knowledge of human nature, he wou'd be apt to regard them as mere chimerical speculations, and wou'd consider the infamy attending infidelity, and backwardness to all its approaches, as principles that were rather to be wish'd than hop'd for in the world. For what means, wou'd he say, of persuading mankind, that the transgressions of conjugal duty are more infamous than any other kind of injustice, when 'tis evident they are more excusable, upon account of the greatness of the temptation? And what possibility of giving a backwardness to the approaches of a pleasure, to

[* 'Fidelity' in the original altered to 'infidelity' by editor.]

which nature has inspir'd so strong a propensity; and a propensity that 'tis absolutely necessary in the end to comply with, for the support of the species?

But speculative reasonings, which cost so much pains to philosophers, are often form'd by the world naturally, and without reflection: As difficulties, which seem unsurmountable in theory, are easily got over in practice. Those, who have an interest in the fidelity of women, naturally disapprove of their infidelity, and all the approaches to it. Those, who have no interest, are carried along with the stream. Education takes possession of the ductile minds of the fair sex in their infancy. And when a general rule of this kind is once establish'd, men are apt to extend it beyond those principles, from which it first arose. Thus batchelors, however debauch'd, cannot chuse but be shock'd with any instance of lewdness or impudence in women. And tho' all these maxims have a plain reference to generation, yet women past child-bearing have no more privilege in this respect, than those who are in the flower of their youth and beauty. Men have undoubtedly an implicit notion, that all those ideas of modesty and decency have a regard to generation; since they impose not the same laws, *with the same force*, on the male sex, where that reason takes not place. The exception is there obvious and extensive, and founded on a remarkable difference, which produces a clear separation and disjunction of ideas. But as the case is not the same with regard to the different ages of women, for this reason, tho' men know, that these notions are founded on the public interest, yet the general rule carries us beyond the original principle, and makes us extend the notions of modesty over the whole sex, from their earliest infancy to their extremest old-age and infirmity.

Courage, which is the point of honour among men, derives its merit, in a great measure, from artifice, as well as the chastity of women; tho' it has also some foundation in nature, as we shall see afterwards.

As to the obligations which the male sex lie under, with regard to chastity, we may observe, that according to the general notions of the world, they bear nearly the same proportion to the obligations of women, as the obligations of the law of nations do to those of the law of nature. 'Tis contrary to the interest of civil society, that men shou'd have an *entire* liberty of indulging their appetites in venereal enjoyment: But as this interest is weaker than in the case of the female sex, the moral obligation, arising from it, must be proportionably weaker. And to prove this we need only appeal to the practice and sentiments of all nations and ages.

PART III

Of the other virtues and vices

SECT. I

Of the origin of the natural virtues and vices

WE come now to the examination of such virtues and vices as are entirely natural, and have no dependance on the artifice and contrivance of men. The examination of these will conclude this system of morals.

The chief spring or actuating principle of the human mind is pleasure or pain; and when these sensations are remov'd, both from our thought and feeling, we are, in a great measure, incapable of passion or action, of desire or volition. The most immediate effects of pleasure and pain are the propense and averse motions of the mind; which are diversified into volition, into desire and aversion, grief and joy, hope and fear, according as the pleasure or pain changes its situation, and becomes probable or improbable, certain or uncertain, or is consider'd as out of our power for the present moment. But when along with this, the objects, that cause pleasure or pain, acquire a relation to ourselves or others; they still continue to excite desire and aversion, grief and joy: But cause, at the same time, the indirect passions of pride or humility, love or hatred, which in this case have a double relation of impressions and ideas to the pain or pleasure.

We have already observ'd, that moral distinctions depend entirely on certain peculiar sentiments of pain and pleasure, and that whatever mental quality in ourselves or others gives us a satisfaction, by the survey or reflection, is of course virtuous; as every thing of this nature, that gives uneasiness, is vicious. Now since every quality in ourselves or others, which gives pleasure, always causes pride or love; as every one, that produces uneasiness, excites humility or hatred: It follows, that these two particulars are to be consider'd as equivalent, with regard to our mental qualities, *virtue* and the power of producing love or pride, *vice* and the power of producing humility or hatred. In every case, therefore, we must judge of the one by the other; and may pronounce any *quality* of the mind virtuous, which causes love or pride; and any one vicious, which causes hatred or humility.

If any *action* be either virtuous or vicious, 'tis only as a sign of some quality or character. It must depend upon durable principles of the mind, which extend over the whole conduct, and enter into the personal character. Actions themselves, not proceeding from any constant principle, have no influence on love or hatred, pride or humility; and consequently are never consider'd in morality.

This reflection is self-evident, and deserves to be attended to, as being of the utmost importance in the present subject. We are never to consider any single action in our enquiries concerning the origin of morals; but only the quality or character from which the action proceeded. These alone are *durable* enough to affect our sentiments concerning the person. Actions are, indeed, better indications of a character than words, or even wishes and sentiments; but 'tis only so far as they are such indications, that they are attended with love or hatred, praise or blame.

To discover the true origin of morals, and of that love or hatred, which arises from mental qualities, we must take the matter pretty deep, and compare some principles, which have been already examin'd and explain'd.

We may begin with considering a-new the nature and force of *sympathy*. The minds of all men are similar in their feelings and operations; nor can any one be actuated by any affection, of which all others are not, in some degree, susceptible. As in strings equally wound up, the motion of one communicates itself to the rest; so all the affections readily pass from one person to another, and beget correspondent movements in every human creature. When I see the *effects* of passion in the voice and gesture of any person, my mind immediately passes from these effects to their causes, and forms such a lively idea of the passion, as is presently converted into the passion itself. In like manner, when I perceive the *causes of* any emotion, my mind is convey'd to the effects, and is actuated with a like emotion. Were I present at any of the more terrible operations of surgery, 'tis certain, that even before it begun, the preparation of the instruments, the laying of the bandages in order, the heating of the irons, with all the signs of anxiety and concern in the patient and assistants, wou'd have a great effect upon my mind, and excite the strongest sentiments of pity and terror. No passion of another discovers itself immediately to the mind. We are only sensible of its causes or effects. From *these* we infer the passion: And consequently *these* give rise to our sympathy.

Our sense of beauty depends very much on this principle; and where any object has a tendency to produce pleasure in its possessor, it is always regarded as beautiful; as every object, that has a tendency to produce pain, is disagreeable and deform'd. Thus the conveniency of a house, the fertility of a field, the strength of a horse, the capacity, security, and swift-sailing of a vessel, form the principal beauty of these several objects. Here the object, which is denominated beautiful, pleases only by its tendency to produce a certain effect. That effect is the pleasure or advantage of some other person. Now the pleasure of a stranger, for whom we have no friendship, pleases us only by sympathy. To this principle, therefore, is owing the beauty, which we find in every thing that is useful. How considerable a part this is of beauty will easily appear upon reflection. Wherever an object has a tendency to produce pleasure in the possessor, or in other words, is the proper *cause* of pleasure, it is sure to please the spectator, by a delicate sympathy with the possessor. Most of the works of art are esteem'd beautiful, in proportion to their fitness for the use of man, and even many of the productions of nature derive their beauty from that source. Handsome and beautiful, on most occasions, is not an absolute but a relative quality, and pleases us by nothing but its tendency to produce an end that is agreeable*.

The same principle produces, in many instances, our sentiments of morals, as well as those of beauty. No virtue is more esteem'd than justice, and no vice more detested than injustice; nor are there any qualities, which go farther to the fixing the character, either as amiable or odious. Now justice is a moral virtue, merely because it has that tendency to the good of mankind; and, indeed, is nothing but an artificial invention to that purpose. The same may be said of allegiance, of the laws of nations, of modesty, and of good-manners. All these are mere human contrivances for the interest of society. And since there is a very strong sentiment of morals, which in all nations, and all ages, has attended them, we must allow, that the reflecting on the tendency of characters and mental qualities, is sufficient to give us the sentiments of approbation and blame. Now as the means to an end can only be agreeable, where the end is agreeable; and as the good of society, where our own interest is not concern'd, or that of our friends, pleases only by sympathy: It follows, that sympathy is the source of the esteem, which we pay to all the artificial virtues.

Thus it appears, *that* sympathy is a very powerful principle in human nature, *that* it has a great influence on our taste of beauty, and *that* it produces our sentiment of morals in all the artificial virtues. From thence we may presume, that it also gives rise to many of the other virtues; and

* Decentior equus cujus astricta sunt ilia; sed idem velocior. Pulcher aspectu sit athleta, cujus lacertos exercitatio expressit; idem certamini paratior. Nunquam vero *species* ab *utilitate* dividitur. Sed hoc quidem discernere, modici judicii est. *Quinct.* lib. 8.

[A horse with narrow flanks looks more comely; it also moves faster. An athlete whose muscles have been developed by training presents a handsome appearance; he is also better prepared for the contest. Attractive appearance is invariably associated with efficient functioning. Yet it takes no outstanding powers of judgement to make this distinction.]

that qualities acquire our approbation, because of their tendency to the good of mankind. This presumption must become a certainty, when we find that most of those qualities, which we *naturally* approve of, have actually that tendency, and render a man a proper member of society: While the qualities, which we *naturally* disapprove of, have a contrary tendency, and render any intercourse with the person dangerous or disagreeable. For having found, that such tendencies have force enough to produce the strongest sentiment of morals, we can never reasonably, in these cases, look for any other cause of approbation or blame; it being an inviolable maxim in philosophy, that where any particular cause is sufficient for an effect, we ought to rest satisfied with it, and ought not to multiply causes without necessity. We have happily attain'd experiments in the artificial virtues, where the tendency of qualities to the good of society, is the *sole* cause of our approbation, without any suspicion of the concurrence of another principle. From thence we learn the force of that principle. And where that principle may take place, and the quality approv'd of is really beneficial to society, a true philosopher will never require any other principle to account for the strongest approbation and esteem.

That many of the natural virtues have this tendency to the good of society, no one can doubt of. Meekness, beneficence, charity, generosity, clemency, moderation, equity bear the greatest figure among the moral qualities, and are commonly denominated the *social* virtues, to mark their tendency to the good of society. This goes so far, that some philosophers have represented all moral distinctions as the effect of artifice and education, when skilful politicians endeavour'd to restrain the turbulent passions of men, and make them operate to the public good, by the notions of honour and shame. This system, however, is not consistent with experience. For, *first*, there are other virtues and vices beside those which have this tendency to the public advantage and loss. *Secondly*, had not men a natural sentiment of approbation and blame, it cou'd never be excited by politicians; nor wou'd the words *laudable* and *praise-worthy, blameable* and *odious* be any more intelligible, than if they were a language perfectly known to us, as we have already observ'd. But tho' this system be erroneous, it may teach us, that moral distinctions arise, in a great measure, from the tendency of qualities and characters to the interests of society, and that 'tis our concern for that interest, which makes us approve or disapprove of them. Now we have no such extensive concern for society but from sympathy; and consequently 'tis that principle, which takes us so far out of ourselves, as to give us the same pleasure or uneasiness in the characters of others, as if they had a tendency to our own advantage or loss.

The only difference betwixt the natural virtues and justice lies in this, that the good, which results from the former, arises from every single act, and is the object of some natural passion: Whereas a single act of justice, consider'd in itself, may often be contrary to the public good; and 'tis only the concurrence of mankind, in a general scheme or system of action, which is advantageous. When I relieve persons in distress, my natural humanity is my motive; and so far as my succour extends, so far have I promoted the happiness of my fellow-creatures. But if we examine all the questions, that come before any tribunal of justice, we shall find, that, considering each case apart, it wou'd as often be an instance of humanity to decide contrary to the laws of justice as conformable them. Judges take from a poor man to give to a rich; they bestow on the dissolute the labour of the industrious; and put into the hands of the vicious the means of harming both themselves and others. The whole scheme, however, of law and justice is advantageous to the society; and 'twas with a view to this advantage, that men, by their voluntary conventions, establish'd it. After it is once establish'd by these conventions, it is *naturally* attended with a strong sentiment of morals; which can proceed from nothing but our sympathy with the interests of society. We need no other explication of that esteem, which attends such of the natural virtues, as have a tendency to the public good.

I must farther add, that there are several circumstances, which render this hypothesis much more probable with regard to the natural than the artificial virtues. 'Tis certain, that the imagination is more affected by what is particular, than by what is general; and that the sentiments are always mov'd with difficulty, where their objects are, in any degree, loose and undetermin'd: Now every particular act of justice is not beneficial to society, but the whole scheme or system: And it may not, perhaps, be any individual person, for whom we are concern'd, who receives benefit from justice, but the whole society alike. On the contrary, every particular act of generosity, or relief of the industrious and indigent, is beneficial; and is beneficial to a particular person, who is not undeserving of it. 'Tis more natural, therefore, to think, that the tendencies of the latter virtue will affect our sentiments, and command our approbation, than those of the former; and therefore, since we find, that the approbation of the former arises from their tendencies, we may ascribe, with better reason, the same cause to the approbation of the latter. In any number of similar effects, if a cause can be discover'd for one, we ought to extend that cause to all the other effects, which can be accounted for by it: But much more, if these other effects be attended with peculiar circumstances, which facilitate the operation of that cause.

Before I proceed farther, I must observe two remarkable circumstances in this affair, which may seem objections to the present system. The first may be thus explain'd. When any quality, or character, has a tendency to the good of mankind, we are pleas'd with it, and approve of it; because it presents the lively idea of pleasure; which idea affects us by sympathy, and is itself a kind of pleasure. But as this sympathy is very variable, it may be thought, that our sentiments of morals must admit of all the same variations. We sympathize more with persons contiguous to us, than with persons remote from us: With our acquaintance, than with strangers: With our countrymen, than with foreigners. But notwithstanding this variation of our sympathy, we give the same approbation to the same moral qualities in *China* as in *England*. They appear equally virtuous, and recommend themselves equally to the esteem of a judicious spectator. The sympathy varies without a variation in our esteem. Our esteem, therefore, proceeds not from sympathy.

To this I answer: The approbation of moral qualities most certainly is not deriv'd from reason, or any comparison of ideas; but proceeds entirely from a moral taste, and from certain sentiments of pleasure or disgust, which arise upon the contemplation and view of particular qualities or characters. Now 'tis evident, that those sentiments, whence-ever they are deriv'd, must vary according to the distance or contiguity of the objects; nor can I feel the same lively pleasure from the virtues of a person, who liv'd in *Greece* two thousand years ago, that I feel from the virtues of a familiar friend and acquaintance. Yet I do not say, that I esteem the one more than the other: And therefore, if the variation of the sentiment, without a variation of the esteem, be an objection, it must have equal force against every other system, as against that of sympathy. But to consider the matter a-right, it has no force at all; and 'tis the easiest matter in the world to account for it. Our situation, with regard both to persons and things, is in continual fluctuation; and a man, that lies at a distance from us, may, in a little time, become a familiar acquaintance. Besides, every particular man has a peculiar position with regard to others; and 'tis impossible we cou'd ever converse together on any reasonable terms, were each of us to consider characters and persons, only as they appear from his peculiar point of view. In order, therefore, to prevent those continual *contradictions*, and arrive at a more *stable* judgment of things, we fix on some *steady* and *general* points of view; and always, in our thoughts, place ourselves in them, whatever may be our present situation. In like manner, external beauty is determin'd merely by pleasure; and 'tis evident, a beautiful countenance cannot give so much pleasure, when seen at the distance of twenty paces, as when it is brought nearer us. We say not, however, that it appears to us less beautiful: Because we know what effect it will have in such a position, and by that reflection we correct its momentary appearance.

In general, all sentiments of blame or praise are variable, according to our situation of nearness or remoteness, with regard to the person blam'd or prais'd, and according to the present disposition of our mind. But these variations we regard not in our general decision, but still apply the terms expressive of our liking or dislike, in the same manner, as if we remain'd in one point of view. Experience soon teaches us this method of correcting our sentiments, or at least, of correcting our language, where the sentiments are more stubborn and inalterable. Our servant, if diligent and faithful, may excite stronger sentiments of love and kindness than *Marcus Brutus*, as represented in history; but we say not upon that account, that the former character is more laudable than the latter. We know, that were we to approach equally near to that renown'd patriot, he wou'd command a much higher degree of affection and admiration. Such corrections are common with regard to all the senses; and indeed 'twere impossible we cou'd ever make use of language, or communicate our sentiments to one another, did we not correct the momentary appearances of things, and overlook our present situation.

'Tis therefore from the influence of characters and qualities, upon those who have an intercourse with any person, that we blame or praise him. We consider not whether the persons, affected by the qualities, be our acquaintance or strangers, countrymen or foreigners. Nay, we over-look our own interest in those general judgments; and blame not a man for opposing us in any of our pretensions, when his own interest is particularly concern'd. We make allowance for a certain degree of selfishness in men; because we know it to be inseparable from human nature, and inherent in our frame and constitution. By this reflection we correct those sentiments of blame, which so naturally arise upon any opposition.

But however the general principle of our blame or praise may be corrected by those other principles, 'tis certain, they are not altogether efficacious, nor do our passions often correspond entirely to the present theory. 'Tis seldom men heartily love what lies at a distance from them, and what no way redounds to their particular benefit; as 'tis no less rare to meet with persons, who can pardon another any opposition he makes to their interest, however justifiable that opposition may be by the general rules of morality. Here we are contented with saying, that reason requires such an impartial conduct, but that 'tis seldom we can bring ourselves to it, and that our passions do not readily follow the determination of our judgment. This language will be easily understood, if we consider what we formerly said concerning that *reason*, which is able to oppose our passion; and which we have found to be nothing but a general calm determination of the passions, founded on some distant view or reflection. When we form our judgments of persons, merely from the tendency of their characters to our own benefit, or to that of our friends, we find so many contradictions to our sentiments in society and conversation, and such an uncertainty from the incessant changes of our situation, that we seek some other standard of merit and demerit, which may not admit of so great variation. Being thus loosen'd from our first station, we cannot afterwards fix ourselves so commodiously by any means as by a sympathy with those, who have any commerce with the person we consider. This is far from being as lively as when our own interest is concern'd, or that of our particular friends; nor has it such an influence on our love and hatred: But being equally conformable to our calm and general principles, 'tis said to have an equal authority over our reason, and to command our judgment and opinion. We blame equally a bad action, which we read of in history, with one perform'd in our neighbourhood t'other day: The meaning of which is, that we know from reflection, that the former action wou'd excite as strong sentiments of disapprobation as the latter, were it plac'd in the same position.

I now proceed to the *second* remarkable circumstance, which I propos'd to take notice of. Where a person is possess'd of a character, that in its natural tendency is beneficial to society, we esteem him virtuous, and are delighted with the view of his character, even tho' particular accidents prevent its operation, and incapacitate him from being serviceable to his friends and country. Virtue in rags is still virtue; and the love, which it procures, attends a man into a dungeon or desart, where the virtue can no longer be exerted in action, and is lost to all the world. Now this may be esteem'd an objection to the present system. Sympathy interests us in the good of mankind; and if sympathy were the source of our esteem for virtue, that sentiment of approbation cou'd only take place, where the virtue actually attain'd its end, and was beneficial to mankind. Where it fails of its end, 'tis only an imperfect means; and therefore can never acquire any merit from that end. The goodness of an end can bestow a merit on such means alone as are compleat, and actually produce the end.

To this we may reply, that where any object, in all its parts, is fitted to attain any agreeable end, it naturally gives us pleasure, and is esteem'd beautiful, even tho' some external circumstances be wanting to render it altogether effectual. 'Tis sufficient if every thing be compleat in the object itself. A house, that is contriv'd with great judgment for all the commodities of life, pleases us upon that account; tho' perhaps we are sensible, that no-one will ever dwell in it. A fertile soil, and a happy climate, delight us by a reflection on the happiness which they wou'd afford the inhabitants, tho' at present the country be desart and uninhabited. A man, whose limbs and shape promise strength and activity, is esteem'd handsome, tho' condemn'd to perpetual imprisonment. The imagination has a set of passions belonging to it, upon which our sentiments of beauty much depend. These passions are mov'd by degrees of liveliness and strength, which are inferior to *belief*, and independent of the real existence of their objects. Where a character is, in every respect, fitted to be beneficial to society, the imagination passes easily from the cause to the effect, without considering that there are still some circumstances wanting to render the cause a compleat one. *General rules* create a species of probability, which sometimes influences the judgment, and always the imagination.

'Tis true, when the cause is compleat, and a good disposition is attended with good fortune, which renders it really beneficial to society, it gives a stronger pleasure to the spectator, and is attended with a more lively sympathy. We are more affected by it; and yet we do not say that it is more virtuous, or that we esteem it more. We know, that an alteration of fortune may render the benevolent disposition entirely impotent; and therefore we separate, as much as possible, the fortune from the disposition. The case is the same, as when we correct the different sentiments of virtue, which proceed from its different distances from ourselves. The passions do not always follow our corrections; but these corrections serve sufficiently to regulate our abstract notions, and are alone regarded, when we pronounce in general concerning the degrees of vice and virtue.

'Tis observ'd by critics, that all words or sentences, which are difficult to the pronunciation, are disagreeable to the ear. There is no difference, whether a man hear them pronounc'd, or read them silently to himself. When I run over a book with my eye, I imagine I hear it all; and also, by the force of imagination, enter into the uneasiness, which the delivery of it wou'd give the speaker. The uneasiness is not real; but as such a composition of words has a natural tendency to produce it, this is sufficient to affect the mind with a painful sentiment, and render the discourse harsh and disagreeable. 'Tis a similar case, where any real quality is, by accidental circumstances, render'd impotent, and is depriv'd of its natural influence on society.

Upon these principles we may easily remove any contradiction, which may appear to be betwixt the *extensive sympathy*, on which our sentiments of virtue depend, and that *limited generosity* which I have frequently observ'd to be natural to men, and which justice and property suppose, according to the precedent reasoning. My sympathy with another may give me the sentiment of pain and disapprobation, when any object is presented, that has a tendency to give him uneasiness; tho' I may not be willing to sacrifice any thing of my own interest, or cross any of my passions, for his satisfaction. A house may displease me by being ill-contriv'd for the convenience of the owner; and yet I may refuse to give a shilling towards the rebuilding of it. Sentiments must touch the heart, to make them controul our passions: But they need not extend beyond the imagination, to make them influence our taste. When a building seems clumsy and tottering to the eye, it is ugly and disagreeable; tho' we be fully assur'd of the solidity of the workmanship. 'Tis a kind of fear, which causes this sentiment of disapprobation; but the passion is not the same with that which we feel, when oblig'd to stand under a wall, that we really think tottering and insecure. The *seeming tendencies* of objects affect the mind: And the emotions they excite are of a like species with those, which proceed from the *real consequences* of objects, but their feeling is different. Nay, these emotions are so different in their feeling, that they may often be contrary, without destroying each other; as when the fortifications of a city belonging to an enemy are esteem'd beautiful upon account of their strength, tho' we cou'd wish that they were entirely destroy'd. The imagination adheres to the *general* views of things, and distinguishes the feelings they produce, from those which arise from our particular and momentary situation.

If we examine the panegyrics that are commonly made of great men, we shall find, that most of the qualities, which are attributed to them, may be divided into two kinds, *viz.* such as make them perform their part in society; and such as render them serviceable to themselves, and enable them to promote their own interest. Their *prudence, temperance, frugality, industry, assiduity, enterprize, dexterity*, are celebrated, as well as their *generosity* and *humanity*. If we ever give an indulgence to any quality, that disables a man from making a figure in life, 'tis to that of *indolence*, which is not suppos'd to deprive one of his parts and capacity, but only suspends their exercise; and that without any inconvenience to the person himself, since 'tis, in some measure, from his own choice. Yet indolence is always allow'd to be a fault, and a very great one, if extreme: Nor do a man's friends ever acknowledge him to be subject to it, but in order to save his character in more material articles. He cou'd make a figure, say they, if he pleas'd to give application: His understanding is sound, his conception quick, and his memory tenacious; but he hates business, and is indifferent about his fortune. And this a man sometimes may make even a subject of vanity; tho' with the air of confessing a fault: Because he may think, that his incapacity for business implies much more noble qualities; such as a philosophical spirit, a fine taste, a delicate wit, or a relish for pleasure and society. But take any other case: Suppose a quality, that without being an indication of any other good qualities, incapacitates a man *always* for business, and is destructive to his interest; such as a blundering understanding, and a wrong judgment of every thing in life; inconstancy and irresolution; or a want of address in the management of men and business: These are all allow'd to be imperfections in a character; and many men wou'd rather acknowledge the greatest crimes, than have it suspected, that they are, in any degree, subject to them.

'Tis very happy, in our philosophical researches, when we find the same phaenomenon diversified by a variety of circumstances; and by discovering what is common among them, can the better assure ourselves of the truth of any hypothesis we may make use of to explain it. Were nothing esteem'd virtue but what were beneficial to society, I am persuaded, that the foregoing explication of the moral sense ought still to be receiv'd, and that upon sufficient evidence: But this evidence must grow upon us, when we find other kinds of virtue, which will not admit of any explication except from that hypothesis. Here is a man, who is not remarkably defective in his social qualities; but what principally recommends him is his dexterity in business, by which he has extricated himself from the greatest difficulties, and conducted the most delicate affairs with a singular address and prudence. I find an esteem for him immediately to arise in me: His company is a satisfaction to me; and before I have any farther acquaintance with him, I wou'd rather do him a service than another, whose character is in every other respect equal, but is deficient in that particular. In this case, the qualities that please me are all consider'd as useful to the person, and as having a tendency to promote his interest and satisfaction. They are only regarded as means to an end, and please me in proportion to their fitness for that end. The end, therefore, must be agreeable to me. But what makes the end agreeable? The person is a stranger: I am no way interested in him, nor lie under any obligation to him: His happiness concerns not me, farther than the happiness of every human, and indeed of every sensible creature: That is, it affects me only by sympathy. From that principle, whenever I discover his happiness and good, whether in its causes or effects, I enter so deeply into it, that it gives me a sensible emotion. The appearance of qualities, that have a *tendency* to promote it, have an agreeable effect upon my imagination, and command my love and esteem.

This theory may serve to explain, why the same qualities, in all cases, produce both pride and love, humility and hatred; and the same man is always virtuous or vicious, accomplish'd or despicable to others, who is so to himself. A person, in whom we discover any passion or habit, which originally is only incommodious to himself, becomes always disagreeable to us, merely on its account; as on the other hand, one whose character is only dangerous and disagreeable to others, can never be satisfied with himself, as long as he is sensible of that disadvantage. Nor is this observable only with regard to characters and manners, but may be remark'd even in the most minute circumstances. A violent cough in another gives us uneasiness; tho' in itself it does not in the least affect us. A man will be mortified, if you tell him he has a stinking breath; tho' 'tis evidently no annoyance to himself. Our fancy easily changes its situation; and either surveying ourselves as we appear to others, or considering others as they feel themselves, we enter, by that means, into sentiments, which no way belong to us, and in which nothing but sympathy is able to interest us. And this sympathy we sometimes carry so far, as even to be displeas'd with a quality commodious to us, merely because it displeases others, and makes us disagreeable in their eyes; tho' perhaps we never can have any interest in rendering ourselves agreeable to them.

There have been many systems of morality advanc'd by philosophers in all ages; but if they are strictly examin'd, they may be reduc'd to two, which alone merit our attention. Moral good and evil are certainly distinguish'd by our *sentiments,* not by *reason*: But these sentiments may arise either from the mere species or appearance of characters and passions, or from reflections on their tendency to the happiness of mankind, and of particular persons. My opinion is, that both these causes are intermix'd in our judgments of morals; after the same manner as they are in our decisions concerning most kinds of external beauty: Tho' I am also of opinion, that reflections on the tendencies of actions have by far the greatest influence, and determine all the great lines of our duty. There are, however, instances, in cases of less moment, wherein this immediate taste or sentiment produces our approbation. Wit, and a certain easy and disengag'd behaviour, are qualities *immediately agreeable* to others, and command their love and esteem. Some of these qualities produce satisfaction in others by particular *original* principles of human nature, which cannot be accounted for: Others may be resolv'd into principles, which are more general. This will best appear upon a particular enquiry.

As some qualities acquire their merit from their being *immediately agreeable* to others, without any tendency to public interest; so some are denominated virtuous from their being *immediately agreeable* to the person himself, who possesses them. Each of the passions and operations of the mind has a particular feeling, which must be either agreeable or disagreeable. The first is virtuous, the second vicious. This particular feeling constitutes the very nature of the passion; and therefore needs not be accounted for.

But however directly the distinction of vice and virtue may seem to flow from the immediate pleasure or uneasiness, which particular qualities cause to ourselves or others; 'tis easy to observe, that it has also a considerable dependence on the principle of *sympathy* so often insisted on. We approve of a person, who is possess'd of qualities *immediately agreeable* to those, with whom he has any commerce; tho' perhaps we ourselves never reap'd any pleasure from them. We also approve of one, who is possess'd of qualities, that are *immediately agreeable* to himself; tho' they be of no service to any mortal. To account for this we must have recourse to the foregoing principles.

Thus, to take a general review of the present hypothesis: Every quality of the mind is denominated virtuous, which gives pleasure by the mere survey; as every quality, which produces pain, is call'd vicious. This pleasure and this pain may arise from four different sources. For we reap a pleasure from the view of a character, which is naturally fitted to be useful to others, or to the person himself, or which is agreeable to others, or to the person himself. One may, perhaps, be surpriz'd, that amidst all these interests and pleasures, we shou'd forget our own, which touch us so nearly on every other occasion. But we shall easily satisfy ourselves on this head, when we consider, that every particular person's pleasure and interest being different, 'tis impossible men cou'd ever agree in their sentiments and judgments, unless they chose some common point of view, from which they might survey their object, and which might cause it to appear the same to all of them. Now in judging of characters, the only interest or pleasure, which appears the same to every spectator, is that of the person himself, whose character is examin'd; or that of persons, who have a connexion with him. And tho' such interests and pleasures touch us more faintly than our own, yet being more constant and universal, they counter-ballance the latter even in practice, and are alone admitted in speculation as the standard of virtue and morality. They alone produce that particular feeling or sentiment, on which moral distinctions depend.

As to the good or ill desert of virtue or vice, 'tis an evident consequence of the sentiments of pleasure or uneasiness. These sentiments produce love or hatred; and love or hatred, by the original constitution of human passion, is attended with benevolence or anger; that is, with a desire of making happy the person we love, and miserable the person we hate. We have treated of this more fully on another occasion.

SECT. II

Of greatness of mind

It may now be proper to illustrate this general system of morals, by applying it to particular instances of virtue and vice, and shewing how their merit or demerit arises from the four sources here explain'd. We shall begin with examining the passions of *pride* and *humility*, and shall consider the vice or virtue that lies in their excesses or just proportion. An excessive pride or overweaning conceit of ourselves is always esteem'd vicious, and is universally hated; as modesty, or a just sense of our weakness, is esteem'd virtuous, and procures the good-will of every-one. Of the four sources of moral distinctions, this is to be ascrib'd to the *third*; viz. the immediate agreeableness and disagreeableness of a quality to others, without any reflections on the tendency of that quality.

In order to prove this, we must have recourse to two principles, which are very conspicuous in human nature. The *first* of these is the *sympathy*, and communication of sentiments and passions above-mention'd. So close and intimate is the correspondence of human souls, that no sooner any person approaches me, than he diffuses on me all his opinions, and draws along my judgment in a greater or lesser degree. And tho', on many occasions, my sympathy with him goes not so far as entirely to change my sentiments, and way of thinking; yet it seldom is so weak as not to disturb the easy course of my thought, and give an authority to that opinion, which is recommended to me by his assent and approbation. Nor is it any way material upon what subject he and I employ our thoughts. Whether we judge of an indifferent person, or of my own character, my sympathy gives equal force to his decision: And even his sentiments of his own merit make me consider him in the same light, in which he regards himself.

This principle of sympathy is of so powerful and insinuating a nature, that it enters into most of our sentiments and passions, and often takes place under the appearance of its contrary. For 'tis remarkable, that when a person opposes me in any thing, which I am strongly bent upon, and rouzes up my passion by contradiction, I have always a degree of sympathy with him, nor does my commotion proceed from any other origin. We may here observe an evident conflict or rencounter of opposite principles and passions. On the one side there is that passion or sentiment, which is natural to me; and 'tis observable, that the stronger this passion is, the greater is the commotion. There must also be some passion or sentiment on the other side; and this passion can proceed from nothing but sympathy. The sentiments of others can never affect us, but by becoming, in some measure, our own; in which case they operate upon us, by opposing and encreasing our passions, in the very same manner, as if they had been originally deriv'd from our own temper and disposition. While they remain conceal'd in the minds of others, they can never have an influence upon us: And even when they are known, if they went no farther than the imagination, or conception; that faculty is so accustom'd to objects of every different kind, that a mere idea, tho' contrary to our sentiments and inclinations, wou'd never alone be able to affect us.

The *second* principle I shall take notice of is that of *comparison*, or the variation of our judgments concerning objects, according to the proportion they bear to those with which we compare them. We judge more of objects by comparison, than by their intrinsic worth and value; and regard every thing as mean, when set in opposition to what is superior of the same kind. But no comparison is more obvious than that with ourselves; and hence it is that on all occasions it takes place, and mixes with most of our passions. This kind of comparison is directly contrary to sympathy in its operation, as we have observ'd in treating of *compassion* and *malice.* * *In all kinds of comparison an object makes us always receive from another, to which it is compar'd, a sensation contrary to what arises from itself in its direct and immediate survey. The direct survey of another's pleasure naturally gives us pleasure; and therefore produces pain, when compar'd with our own. His pain, consider'd in itself, is painful; but augments the idea of our own happiness, and gives us pleasure.*

Since then those principles of sympathy, and a comparison with ourselves, are directly contrary, it may be worth while to consider, what general rules can be form'd, beside the particular temper of the person, for the prevalence of the one or the other. Suppose I am now in safety at land, and wou'd willingly reap some pleasure from this consideration: I must think on the miserable condition of those who are at sea in a storm, and must endeavour to render this idea as strong and lively as possible, in order to make me more sensible of my own happiness. But whatever pains I may take, the comparison will never have an equal efficacy, as if I were really on † the shore, and saw a ship at a distance,

* Book II. Part II. Sect. VIII.

† Suave mari magno turbantibus aequora ventis
E terra magnum alterius spectare laborem;
Non quia vexari quenquam est jucunda voluptas,
Sed quibus ipse malis careas quia cernere sauv' est. *Lucret.*

[There is something pleasant in watching, from dry land, the great difficulties another man is undergoing out on the high sea, with the winds lashing the waters. This is not because one derives delight from any man's distress, but because it is pleasurable to perceive from what troubles one is oneself free.]

tost by a tempest, and in danger every moment of perishing on a rock or sand-bank. But suppose this idea to become still more lively. Suppose the ship to be driven so near me, that I can perceive distinctly the horror, painted on the countenance of the seamen and passengers, hear their lamentable cries, see the dearest friends give their last adieu, or embrace with a resolution to perish in each others arms: No man has so savage a heart as to reap any pleasure from such a spectacle, or withstand the motions of the tenderest compassion and sympathy. 'Tis evident, therefore, there is a medium in this case; and that if the idea be too feint, it has no influence by comparison; and on the other hand, if it be too strong, it operates on us entirely by sympathy, which is the contrary to comparison. Sympathy being the conversion of an idea into an impression, demands a greater force and vivacity in the idea than is requisite to comparison.

All this is easily applied to the present subject. We sink very much in our own eyes, when in the presence of a great man, or one of a superior genius; and this humility makes a considerable ingredient in that *respect*, which we pay our superiors, according to our* foregoing reasonings on that passion. Sometimes even envy and hatred arise from the comparison; but in the greatest part of men, it rests at respect and esteem. As sympathy has such a powerful influence on the human mind, it causes pride to have, in some measure, the same effect as merit; and by making us enter into those elevated sentiments, which the proud man entertains of himself, presents that comparison, which is so mortifying and disagreeable. Our judgment does not entirely accompany him in the flattering conceit, in which he pleases himself; but still is so shaken as to receive the idea it presents, and to give it an influence above the loose conceptions of the imagination. A man, who, in an idle humour, wou'd form a notion of a person of a merit very much superior to his own, wou'd not be mortified by that fiction: But when a man, whom we are really persuaded to

*Book II. Part II. Sect. X.

be of inferior merit, is presented to us; if we observe in him any extraordinary degree of pride and self-conceit; the firm persuasion he has of his own merit, takes hold of the imagination, and diminishes us in our own eyes, in the same manner, as if he were really possess'd of all the good qualities which he so liberally attributes to himself. Our idea is here precisely in that medium, which is requisite to make it operate on us by comparison. Were it accompanied with belief, and did the person appear to have the same merit, which he assumes to himself, it wou'd have a contrary effect, and wou'd operate on us by sympathy. The influence of that principle wou'd then be superior to that of comparison, contrary to what happens where the person's merit seems below his pretensions.

The necessary consequence of these principles is, that pride, or an over-weaning conceit of ourselves, must be vicious; since it causes uneasiness in all men, and presents them every moment with a disagreeable comparison. 'Tis a trite observation in philosophy, and even in common life and conversation, that 'tis our own pride, which makes us so much displeas'd with the pride of other people; and that vanity becomes insupportable to us merely because we are vain. The gay naturally associate themselves with the gay, and the amorous with the amorous: But the proud never can endure the proud, and rather seek the company of those who are of an opposite disposition. As we are, all of us, proud in some degree, pride is universally blam'd and condemn'd by all mankind; as having a natural tendency to cause uneasiness in others by means of comparison. And this effect must follow the more naturally, that those, who have an ill-grounded conceit of themselves, are for ever making those comparisons, nor have they any other method of supporting their vanity. A man of sense and merit is pleas'd with himself, independent of all foreign considerations: But a fool must always find some person, that is more foolish, in order to keep himself in good humour with his own parts and understanding.

But tho' an over-weaning conceit of our own merit be vicious and disagreeable, nothing can be more laudable, than to have a value for ourselves, where we really have qualities that are valuable. The utility and advantage of any quality to ourselves is a source of virtue, as well as its agreeableness to others; and 'tis certain, that nothing is more useful to us in the conduct of life, than a due degree of pride, which makes us sensible of our own merit, and gives us a confidence and assurance in all our projects and enterprizes. Whatever capacity any one may be endow'd with, 'tis entirely useless to him, if he be not acquainted with it, and form not designs suitable to it. 'Tis requisite on all occasions to know our own force; and were it allowable to err on either side, 'twou'd be more advantageous to over-rate our merit, than to form ideas of it, below its just standard. Fortune commonly favours the bold and enterprizing; and nothing inspires us with more boldness than a good opinion of ourselves.

Add to this, that tho' pride, or self-applause, be sometimes disagreeable to others, 'tis always agreeable to ourselves; as on the other hand, modesty, tho' it gives pleasure to every one, who observes it, produces often uneasiness in the person endow'd with it. Now it has been observ'd, that our own sensations determine the vice and virtue of any quality, as well as those sensations, which it may excite in others.

Thus self-satisfaction and vanity may not only be allowable, but requisite in a character. 'Tis, however, certain, that good-breeding and decency require that we shou'd avoid all signs and expressions, which tend directly to show that passion. We have, all of us, a wonderful partiality for ourselves, and were we always to give vent to our sentiments in this particular, we shou'd mutually cause the greatest indignation in each other, not only by the immediate presence of so disagreeable a subject of comparison, but also by the contrariety of our judgments. In like manner, therefore, as we establish the *laws of nature*, in order to secure property in society, and prevent the opposition of self-interest; we establish the *rules of good-breeding*, in order to prevent the opposition of men's pride, and render conversation agreeable and inoffensive. Nothing is more disagreeable than a man's over-weaning conceit of himself: Every one almost has a strong propensity to this vice: No one can well distinguish *in himself* betwixt the vice and virtue, or be certain, that his esteem of his own merit is well-founded: For these reasons, all direct expressions of this passion are condemn'd; nor do we make any exception to this rule in favour of men of sense and merit. They are not allow'd to do themselves justice openly, in words, no more than other people; and even if they show a reserve and secret doubt in doing themselves justice in their own thoughts, they will be more applauded. That impertinent, and almost universal propensity of men, to over-value themselves, has given us such a *prejudice* against self-applause, that we are apt to condemn it, by a *general rule*, wherever we meet with it; and 'tis with some difficulty we give a privilege to men of sense, even in their most secret thoughts. At least, it must be own'd, that some disguise in this particular is absolutely requisite; and that if we harbour pride in our breasts, we must carry a fair outside, and have the appearance of modesty and mutual deference in all our conduct and behaviour. We must, on every occasion, be ready to prefer others to ourselves; to treat them with a kind of deference, even tho' they be our equals; to seem always the lowest and least in the company, where we are not very much distinguish'd above them: And if we observe these rules in our conduct, men will have more indulgence for our secret sentiments, when we discover them in an oblique manner.

I believe no one, who has any practice of the world, and can penetrate into the inward sentiments of men, will assert, that the humility, which good-breeding and decency require of us, goes beyond the outside, or that a thorough sincerity in this particular is esteem'd a real part of our duty. On the contrary, we may observe, that a genuine and hearty pride, or self-esteem, if well conceal'd and well founded, is essential to the character of a man of honour, and that there is no quality of the mind, which is more indispensibly requisite to procure the esteem and approbation of mankind. There are certain deferences and mutual submissions, which custom requires of the different ranks of men towards each other; and whoever exceeds in this particular, if thro' interest, is accus'd of meanness; if thro' ignorance, of simplicity. 'Tis necessary, therefore, to know our rank and station in the world, whether it be fix'd by our birth, fortune, employments, talents or reputation. 'Tis necessary to feel the sentiment and passion of pride in conformity to it, and to regulate our actions accordingly. And shou'd it be said, that prudence may suffice to regulate our actions in this particular, without any real pride, I wou'd observe, that here the object of prudence is to conform our actions to the general usage and custom; and that 'tis impossible those tacit airs of superiority shou'd ever have been establish'd and authoriz'd by custom, unless men were generally proud, and unless that passion were generally approv'd, when well-grounded.

If we pass from common life and conversation to history, this reasoning acquires new force, when we observe, that all those great actions and sentiments, which have become the admiration of mankind, are founded on nothing but pride and self-esteem. *Go*, says *Alexander* the Great to his soldiers, when they refus'd to follow him to the *Indies, go tell your countrymen, that you left Alexander compleating the conquest of the world.* This passage was always particularly admir'd by the prince of *Conde*, as we learn from *St Evremond*.

> '*Alexander*,' said that prince, 'abandon'd by his soldiers, among barbarians, not yet fully subdu'd, felt in himself such a dignity of right and of empire, that he cou'd not believe it possible any one cou'd refuse to obey him. Whether in *Europe* or in *Asia*, among *Greeks* or *Persians*, all was indifferent to him: Wherever he found men, he fancied he found subjects.'

In general we may observe, that whatever we call *heroic virtue*, and admire under the character of greatness and elevation of mind, is either nothing but a steady and well-established pride and self-esteem, or partakes largely of that passion. Courage, intrepidity, ambition, love of glory, magnanimity, and all the other shining virtues of that kind, have plainly a strong mixture of self-esteem in them, and derive a great part of their merit from that origin. Accordingly we find, that many religious declaimers decry those virtues as purely pagan and natural, and represent to us the excellency of the *Christian* religion, which places humility in the rank of virtues, and corrects the judgment of the world, and even of philosophers, who so generally admire all the efforts of pride and ambition. Whether this virtue of humility has been rightly understood, I shall not pretend to determine. I am content with the concession, that the world naturally esteems a well-regulated pride, which secretly animates our conduct, without breaking out into such indecent expressions of vanity, as many offend the vanity of others.

The merit of pride or self-esteem is deriv'd from two circumstances, *viz.* its utility and its agreeableness to ourselves; by which it capacitates us for business, and, at the same time, gives us an immediate satisfaction. When it goes beyond its just bounds, it loses the first advantage, and even becomes prejudicial; which is the reason why we condemn an extravagant pride and ambition, however regulated by the decorums of good-breeding and politeness. But as such a passion is still agreeable, and conveys an elevated and sublime sensation to the person, who is actuated by it, the sympathy with that satisfaction diminishes considerably the blame, which naturally attends its dangerous influence on his conduct and behaviour. Accordingly we may observe, that an excessive courage and magnanimity, especially when it displays itself under the frowns of fortune, contributes in a great measure, to the character of a hero, and will render a person the admiration of posterity; at the same time, that it ruins his affairs, and leads him into dangers and difficulties, with which otherwise he wou'd never have been acquainted.

Heroism, or military glory, is much admir'd by the generality of mankind. They consider it as the most sublime kind of merit. Men of cool reflection are not so sanguine in their praises of it. The infinite confusions and disorder, which it has caus'd in the world, diminish much of its merit in their eyes. When they wou'd oppose the popular notions on this head, they always paint out the evils, which this suppos'd virtue has produc'd in human society; the subversion of empires, the devastation of provinces, the sack of cities. As long as these are present to us, we are more inclin'd to hate than admire the ambition of heroes. But when we fix our view on the person himself, who is the author of all this mischief, there is something so dazzling in his character, the mere contemplation of it so elevates the mind, that we cannot refuse it our admiration. The pain, which we receive from its tendency to the prejudice of society, is over-power'd by a stronger and more immediate sympathy.

Thus our explication of the merit or demerit, which attends the degrees of pride or self-esteem, may serve as a strong argument for the preceding hypothesis, by shewing the effects of those principles above explain'd in all the variations of our judgments concerning that passion. Nor will this reasoning be advantageous to us only by shewing, that the distinction of vice and virtue arises from the *four* principles of the *advantage* and of the *pleasure* of the *person himself*, and of *others*: But may also afford us a strong proof of some under-parts of that hypothesis.

No one, who duly considers of this matter, will make any scruple of allowing, that any piece of ill-breeding, or any expression of pride and haughtiness, is displeasing to us, merely because it shocks our own pride, and leads us by sympathy into a comparison, which causes the disagreeable passion of humility. Now as an insolence of this kind is blam'd even in a person who has always been civil to ourselves in particular; nay, in one, whose name is only known to us in history; it follows, that our disapprobation proceeds from a sympathy with others, and from the reflection, that such a character is highly displeasing and odious to every one, who converses or has any intercourse with the person possest of it. We sympathize with those people in their uneasiness; and as their uneasiness proceeds in part from a sympathy with the person who insults them, we may here observe a double rebound of the sympathy; which is a principle very similar to what we have observ'd *.

SECT. III

Of goodness and benevolence

HAVING thus explain'd the origin of that praise and approbation, which attends every thing we call *great* in human affections; we now proceed to give an account of their *goodness*, and shew whence its merit is deriv'd.

When experience has once given us a competent knowledge of human affairs, and has taught us the proportion they bear to human passion, we perceive, that the generosity of men is very limited, and that it seldom extends beyond their friends and family, or, at most, beyond their native country. Being thus acquainted with the nature of man, we expect not any impossibilities from him; but confine our view to that narrow circle, in which any person moves, in order to form a judgment of his moral character. When the natural tendency of his passions leads him to be serviceable and useful within his sphere, we approve of his character, and love his person, by a sympathy with the sentiments of those, who have a more particular connexion with him. We are quickly oblig'd to forget our own interest in our judgments of this kind, by reason of the perpetual contradictions, we meet with in society and conversation, from persons that are not plac'd in the same situation, and have not the same interest with ourselves. The only point of view, in which our sentiments concur with those of others, is, when we consider the tendency of any passion to the advantage or harm of those, who have any immediate connexion or

* Book II. Part II. Sect. V.

intercourse with the person possess'd of it. And tho' this advantage or harm be often very remote from ourselves, yet sometimes 'tis very near us, and interests us strongly by sympathy. This concern we readily extend to other cases, that are resembling; and when these are very remote, our sympathy is proportionably weaker, and our praise or blame fainter and more doubtful. The case is here the same as in our judgments concerning external bodies. All objects seem to diminish by their distance: But tho' the appearance of objects to our senses be the original standard, by which we judge of them, yet we do not say, that they actually diminish by the distance; but correcting the appearance by reflection, arrive at a more constant and established judgment concerning them. In like manner, tho' sympathy be much fainter than our concern for ourselves, and a sympathy with persons remote from us much fainter than that with persons near and contiguous; yet we neglect all these differences in our calm judgments concerning the characters of men. Besides, that we ourselves often change our situation in this particular, we every day meet with persons, who are in a different situation from ourselves, and who cou'd never converse with us on any reasonable terms, were we to remain constantly in that situation and point of view, which is peculiar to us. The intercourse of sentiments, therefore, in society and conversation, makes us form some general inalterable standard, by which we may approve or disapprove of characters and manners. And tho' the *heart* does not always take part with those general notions, or regulate its love and hatred by them, yet are they sufficient for discourse, and serve all our purposes in company, in the pulpit, on the theatre, and in the schools.

From these principles we may easily account for that merit, which is commonly ascrib'd to *generosity, humanity, compassion, gratitude, friendship, fidelity, zeal, disinterestedness, liberality*, and all those other qualities, which form the character of good and benevolent. A propensity to the tender passions makes a man agreeable and useful in all the parts of life; and gives a just direction to all his other qualities, which otherwise may become prejudicial to society. Courage and ambition, when not regulated by benevolence, are fit only to make a tyrant and public robber. 'Tis the same case with judgment and capacity, and all the qualities of that kind. They are indifferent in themselves to the interests of society, and have a tendency to the good or ill of mankind, according as they are directed by these other passions.

As Love is *immediately agreeable* to the person, who is actuated by it, and hatred *immediately disagreeable*; this may also be a considerable reason, why we praise all the passions that partake of the former, and blame all those that have any considerable share of the latter. 'Tis certain we are infinitely touch'd with a tender sentiment, as well as with a great one. The tears naturally start in our eyes at the conception of it; nor can we forbear giving a loose to the same tenderness towards the person who exerts it. All this seems to me a proof, that our approbation has, in those cases, an origin different from the prospect of utility and advantage, either to ourselves or others. To which we may add, that men naturally, without reflection, approve of that character, which is most like their own. The man of a mild disposition and tender affections, in forming a notion of the most perfect virtue, mixes in it more of benevolence and humanity, than the man of courage and enterprize, who naturally looks upon a certain elevation of mind as the most accomplish'd character. This must evidently proceed from an *immediate* sympathy, which men have with characters similar to their own. They enter with more warmth into such sentiments, and feel more sensibly the pleasure, which arises from them.

'Tis remarkable, that nothing touches a man of humanity more than any instance of extraordinary delicacy in love or friendship, where a person is attentive to the smallest concerns of his friend, and is willing to sacrifice to them the most considerable interest of his own. Such delicacies have little influence on society; because they make us regard the greatest trifles: But they are the more engaging, the more minute the concern is, and are a proof of the highest merit in any one, who is capable of them. The passions are so contagious, that they pass with the greatest facility from one person to another, and produce correspondent movements in all human breasts. Where friendship appears in very signal instances, my heart catches the same passion, and is warm'd by those warm sentiments, that display themselves before me. Such agreeable movements must give me an affection to every one that excites them. This is the case with every thing that is agreeable in any person. The transition from pleasure to love is easy: But the transition must here be still more easy; since the agreeable sentiment, which is excited by sympathy, is love itself; and there is nothing requir'd but to change the object.

Hence the peculiar merit of benevolence in all its shapes and appearances. Hence even its weaknesses are virtuous and amiable; and a person, whose grief upon the loss of a friend were excessive, wou'd be esteem'd upon that account. His tenderness bestows a merit, as it does a pleasure, on his melancholy.

We are not, however, to imagine, that all the angry passions are vicious, tho' they are disagreeable. There is a certain indulgence due to human nature in this respect. Anger and hatred are passions inherent in our very frame and constitutions. The want of them, on some occasions, may even be a proof of weakness and imbecillity. And where they appear only in a low degree, we not only excuse them because they are natural; but even bestow our applauses on them, because they are inferior to what appears in the greatest part of mankind.

Where these angry passions rise up to cruelty, they form the most detested of all vices. All the pity and concern which we have for the miserable sufferers by this vice, turns against the person guilty of it, and produces a stronger hatred than we are sensible of on any other occasion.

Even when the vice of inhumanity rises not to this extreme degree, our sentiments concerning it are very much influenc'd by reflections on the harm that results from it.

And we may observe in general, that if we can find any quality in a person, which renders him incommodious to those, who live and converse with him, we always allow it to be a fault or blemish, without any farther examination. On the other hand, when we enumerate the good qualities of any person, we always mention those parts of his character, which render him a safe companion, an easy friend, a gentle master, an agreeable husband, or an indulgent father. We consider him with all his relations in society; and love or hate him, according as he affects those, who have any immediate intercourse with him. And 'tis a most certain rule, that if there be no relation of life, in which I cou'd not wish to stand to a particular person, his character must so far be allow'd to be perfect. If he be as little wanting to himself as to others, his character is entirely perfect. This is the ultimate test of merit and virtue.

SECT. IV

Of natural abilities

No distinction is more usual in all systems of ethics, than that betwixt *natural abilities* and *moral virtues*; where the former are plac'd on the same footing with bodily endowments, and are suppos'd to have no merit or moral worth annex'd to them. Whoever considers the matter accurately, will find, that a dispute upon this head wou'd be merely a dispute of words, and that tho' these qualities are not altogether of the same kind, yet they agree in the most material circumstances. They are both of them equally mental qualities: And both of them equally produce pleasure; and have of course an equal tendency to procure the love and esteem of mankind. There are few, who are not as jealous of their character, with regard to sense and knowledge, as to honour and courage; and much more than with regard to temperance and sobriety. Men are even afraid of passing for good-natur'd; lest *that* shou'd be taken for want of understanding: And often boast of more debauches than they have been really engag'd in, to give themselves airs of fire and spirit. In short, the figure a man makes in the world, the reception he meets with in company, the esteem paid him by his acquaintance; all these advantages depend almost as much upon his good sense and judgment, as upon any other part of his character. Let a man have the best intentions in the world, and be the farthest from all injustice and violence, he will never be able to make himself be much regarded, without a moderate share, at least, of parts and understanding. Since then natural abilities, tho', perhaps, inferior, yet are on the same footing, both as to their causes and effects, with those qualities which we call moral virtues, why shou'd we make any distinction betwixt them?

Tho' we refuse to natural abilities the title of virtues, we must allow, that they procure the love and esteem of mankind; that they give a new lustre to the other virtues; and that a man possess'd of them is much more intitled to our good-will and services, than one entirely void of them. It may, indeed, be pretended, that the sentiment of approbation, which those qualities produce, besides its being *inferior*, is also somewhat *different* from that, which attends the other virtues. But this, in my opinion, is not a sufficient reason for excluding them from the catalogue of virtues. Each of the virtues, even benevolence, justice, gratitude, integrity, excites a different sentiment or feeling in the spectator. The characters of *Caesar* and *Cato*, as drawn by *Sallust*, are both of them virtuous, in the strictest sense of the word; but in a different way: Nor are the sentiments entirely the same, which arise from them. The one produces love; the other esteem: The one is amiable; the other awful: We cou'd wish to meet with the one character in a friend; the other character we wou'd be ambitious of in ourselves. In like manner, the approbation, which attends natural abilities, may be somewhat different to the feeling from that, which arises from the other virtues, without making them entirely of a different species. And indeed we may observe, that the natural abilities, no more than the other virtues, produce not, all of them, the same kind of approbation. Good sense and genius beget esteem: Wit and humour excite love *.

Those, who represent the distinction betwixt natural abilities and moral virtues as very material, may say, that the former are entirely involuntary, and have therefore no merit attending them, as having no dependance on liberty and free-will. But to this I answer, *first*, that many of those qualities, which all moralists, especially the antients, comprehend under the title of moral virtues, are equally involuntary and necessary, with the qualities of the judgment and imagination. Of this nature are constancy, fortitude, magnanimity; and, in short, all the qualities which form the *great* man. I might say the same, in some degree, of the others; it being almost impossible for the mind to change its character in any considerable article, or cure itself of a passionate or splenetic temper, when they are natural to it. The greater degree there is of these blameable qualities, the more vicious they become, and yet they are the less voluntary. *Secondly*, I wou'd have anyone give me a reason, why virtue and vice may not be involuntary, as well as beauty and deformity. These moral distinctions arise from the natural distinctions of pain and pleasure; and when we receive those feelings from the general consideration of any quality or character, we denominate it vicious or virtuous. Now I believe no one will assert, that a quality can never produce pleasure or pain to the person who considers it, unless it be perfectly voluntary in the person who possesses it. *Thirdly*, As to free-will, we have shewn that it has no place with regard to the actions, no more than the qualities of men. It is not a just consequence, that what is voluntary

* Love and esteem are at the bottom the same passions, and arise from like causes. The qualities, that produce both, are agreeable, and give pleasure. But where this pleasure is severe and serious; or where its object is great, and makes a strong impression; or where it produces any degree of humility and awe: In all these cases, the passion, which arises from the pleasure, is more properly denominated esteem than love. Benevolence attends both: But is connected with love in a more eminent degree.

is free. Our actions are more voluntary than our judgments; but we have not more liberty in the one than in the other.

But tho' this distinction betwixt voluntary and involuntary be not sufficient to justify the distinction betwixt natural abilities and moral virtues, yet the former distinction will afford us a plausible reason, why moralists have invented the latter. Men have observ'd, that tho' natural abilities and moral qualities be in the main on the same footing, there is, however, this difference betwixt them, that the former are almost invariable by any art or industry; while the latter, or at least, the actions, that proceed from them, may be chang'd by the motives of rewards and punishments, praise and blame. Hence legislators, and divines, and moralists, have principally applied themselves to the regulating these voluntary actions, and have endeavour'd to produce additional motives for being virtuous in that particular. They knew, that to punish a man for folly, or exhort him to be prudent and sagacious, wou'd have but little effect; tho' the same punishments and exhortations, with regard to justice and injustice, might have a considerable influence. But as men, in common life and conversation, do not carry those ends in view, but naturally praise or blame whatever pleases or displeases them, they do not seem much to regard this distinction, but consider prudence under the character of virtue as well as benevolence, and penetration as well as justice. Nay, we find, that all moralists, whose judgment is not perverted by a strict adherence to a system, enter into the same way of thinking; and that the antient moralists in particular made no scruple of placing prudence at the head of the cardinal virtues. There is a sentiment of esteem and approbation, which may be excited, in some degree, by any faculty of the mind, in its perfect state and condition; and to account for this sentiment is the business of *Philosophers*. It belongs to *Grammarians* to examine what qualities are entitled to the denomination of *virtue*; nor will they find, upon trial, that this is so easy a task, as at first sight they may be apt to imagine.

The principal reason why natural abilities are esteem'd, is because of their tendency to be useful to the person, who is possess'd of them. 'Tis impossible to execute any design with success, where it is not conducted with prudence and discretion; nor will the goodness of our intentions alone suffice to procure us a happy issue to our enterprizes. Men are superior to beasts principally by the superiority of their reason; and they are the degrees of the same faculty, which set such an infinite difference betwixt one man and another. All the advantages of art are owing to human reason; and where fortune is not very capricious, the most considerable part of these advantages must fall to the share of the prudent and sagacious.

When it is ask'd, whether a quick or a slow apprehension be most valuable? whether one, that at first view penetrates into a subject, but can perform nothing upon study; or a contrary character, which must work out every thing by dint of application? whether a clear head, or a copious invention? whether a profound genius, or a sure judgment? in short, what character, or peculiar understanding, is more excellent than another? 'Tis evident we can answer none of these questions, without considering which of those qualities capacitates a man best for the world, and carries him farthest in any of his undertakings.

There are many other qualities of the mind, whose merit is deriv'd from the same origin. *Industry, perseverance, patience, activity, vigilance, application, constancy,* with other virtues of that kind, which 'twill be easy to recollect, are esteem'd valuable upon no other account, than their advantage in the conduct of life. 'Tis the same case with *temperance, frugality, economy, resolution*: As on the other hand, *prodigality, luxury, irresolution, uncertainty,* are vicious, merely because they draw ruin upon us, and incapacitate us for business and action.

As wisdom and good-sense are valued, because they are *useful* to the person possess'd of them; so *wit* and *eloquence* are valued, because they are immediately agreeable to others. On the other hand, *good humour* is lov'd and esteem'd, because it is *immediately agreeable* to the person himself. 'Tis evident, that the conversation of a man of wit is very satisfactory; as a chearful good-humour'd companion diffuses a joy over the whole company, from a sympathy with his gaiety. These qualities, therefore, being agreeable, they naturally beget love and esteem, and answer to all the characters of virtue.

'Tis difficult to tell, on many occasions, what it is that renders one man's conversation so agreeable and entertaining, and another's so insipid and distasteful. As conversation is a transcript of the mind as well as books, the same qualities, which render the one valuable, must give us an esteem for the other. This we shall consider afterwards. In the mean time it may be affirm'd in general, that all the merit a man may derive from his conversation (which, no doubt, may be very considerable) arises from nothing but the pleasure it conveys to those who are present.

In this view, *cleanliness* is also to be regarded as a virtue; since it naturally renders us agreeable to others, and is a very considerable source of love and affection. No one will deny, that a negligence in this particular is a fault; and as faults are nothing but smaller vices, and this fault can have no other origin than the uneasy sensation, which it excites in others, we may in this instance, seemingly so trivial, clearly discover the origin of the moral distinction of vice and virtue in other instances.

Besides all those qualities, which render a person lovely or valuable, there is also a certain *je-ne-sçai-quoi* of agreeable and handsome, that concurs to the same effect. In this case, as well as in that of wit and eloquence, we must have recourse to a certain sense, which acts without reflection, and regards not the tendencies of qualities and characters. Some moralists account for all the sentiments of virtue by this sense. Their hypothesis is very plausible. Nothing but a particular enquiry can give the preference to any other hypothesis. When we find, that almost all the virtues have such particular tendencies; and also find, that these tendencies are sufficient alone to give a strong sentiment of approbation:

We cannot doubt, after this, that qualities are approv'd of, in proportion to the advantage, which results from them.

The *decorum* or *indecorum* of a quality, with regard to the age, or character, or station, contributes also to its praise or blame. This decorum depends, in a great measure, upon experience. 'Tis usual to see men lose their levity, as they advance in years. Such a degree of gravity, therefore, and such years, are connected together in our thoughts. When we observe them separated in any person's character, this imposes a kind of violence on our imagination, and is disagreeable.

That faculty of the soul, which, of all others, is of the least consequence to the character, and has the least virtue or vice in its several degrees, at the same time, that it admits of a great variety of degrees, is the *memory*. Unless it rise up to that stupendous height as to surprize us, or sink so low as, in some measure, to affect the judgment, we commonly take no notice of its variations, nor ever mention them to the praise or dispraise of any person. 'Tis so far from being a virtue to have a good memory, that men generally affect to complain of a bad one; and endeavouring to persuade the world, that what they say is entirely of their own invention, sacrifice it to the praise of genius and judgment. Yet to consider the matter abstractedly, 'twou'd be difficult to give a reason, why the faculty of recalling past ideas with truth and clearness, shou'd not have as much merit in it, as the faculty of placing our present ideas, in such an order, as to form true propositions and opinions. The reason of the difference certainly must be, that the memory is exerted without any sensation of pleasure or pain; and in all its middling degrees serves almost equally well in business and affairs. But the least variations in the judgment are sensibly felt in their consequences; while at the same time that faculty is never exerted in any eminent degree, without an extraordinary delight and satisfaction. The sympathy with this utility and pleasure bestows a merit on the understanding; and the absence of it makes us consider the memory as a faculty very indifferent to blame or praise.

Before I leave this subject of *natural abilities*, I must observe, that, perhaps, one source of the esteem and affection, which attends them, is deriv'd from the *importance* and *weight*, which they bestow on the person possess'd of them. He becomes of greater consequence in life. His resolutions and actions affect a greater number of his fellow-creatures. Both his friendship and enmity are of moment. And 'tis easy to observe, that whoever is elevated, after this manner, above the rest of mankind, must excite in us the sentiments of esteem and approbation. Whatever is important engages our attention, fixes our thought, and is contemplated with satisfaction. The histories of kingdoms are more interesting than domestic stories: The histories of great empires more than those of small cities and principalities: And the histories of wars and revolutions more than those of peace and order. We sympathize with the persons that suffer, in all the various sentiments which belong to their fortunes. The mind is occupied by the multitude of the objects, and by the strong passions, that display themselves. And this occupation or agitation of the mind is commonly agreeable and amusing. The same theory accounts for the esteem and regard we pay to men of extraordinary parts and abilities. The good and ill of multitudes are connected with their actions. Whatever they undertake is important, and challenges our attention. Nothing is to be over-look'd and despis'd, that regards them. And where any person can excite these sentiments, he soon acquires our esteem; unless other circumstances of his character render him odious and disagreeable.

SECT. V

Some farther reflections concerning the natural virtues

It has been observ'd, in treating of the passions, that pride and humility, love and hatred, are excited by any advantages or disadvantages of the *mind, body*, or *fortune*; and that these advantages or disadvantages have that effect by producing a separate impression of pain or pleasure. The pain or pleasure, which arises from the general survey or view of any action or quality of the *mind*, constitutes its vice or virtue, and gives rise to our approbation or blame, which is nothing but a fainter and more imperceptible love or hatred. We have assign'd four different sources of this pain and pleasure; and in order to justify more fully that hypothesis, it may here be proper to observe, that the advantages or disadvantages of the *body* and of *fortune*, produce a pain or pleasure from the very same principles. The tendency of any object to be *useful* to the person possess'd of it, or to others; to convey *pleasure* to him or to others; all these circumstances convey an immediate pleasure to the person, who considers the object, and command his love and approbation.

To begin with the advantages of the *body*; we may observe a phaenomenon, which might appear somewhat trivial and ludicrous, if any thing cou'd be trivial, which fortified a conclusion of such importance, or ludicrous, which was employ'd in a philosophical reasoning. 'Tis a general remark, that those we call good *women's men*, who have either signaliz'd themselves by their amorous exploits, or whose make of body promises any extraordinary vigour of that kind, are well received by the fair sex, and naturally engage the affections even of those, whose virtue prevents any design of ever giving employment to those talents. Here 'tis evident, that the ability of such a person to give enjoyment, is the real source of that love and esteem he meets with among the females; at the same time that the women, who love and esteem him, have no prospect of receiving that enjoyment themselves, and can only be affected by means of their sympathy with one, that has a commerce of love with him. This instance is singular, and merits our attention.

Another source of the pleasure we receive from considering bodily advantages, is their utility to the person himself, who is possess'd of them. 'Tis certain, that a considerable part of the beauty of men, as well as of other animals, consists in such a conformation of members, as we find by experience to be attended with strength and agility, and to capacitate the creature for any action or exercise. Broad shoulders, a lank belly, firm joints, taper legs; all these are beautiful in our species, because they are signs of force and vigour, which being advantages we naturally sympathize with, they convey to the beholder a share of that satisfaction they produce in the possessor.

So far as to the *utility*, which may attend any quality of the body. As to the immediate *pleasure*, 'tis certain, that an air of health, as well as of strength and agility, makes a considerable part of beauty; and that a sickly air in another is always disagreeable, upon account of that idea of pain and uneasiness, which it conveys to us. On the other hand, we are pleas'd with the regularity of our own features, tho' it be neither useful to ourselves nor others; and 'tis necessary at a distance, to make it convey to us any satisfaction. We commonly consider ourselves as we appear in the eyes of others, and sympathize with the advantageous sentiments they entertain with regard to us.

How far the advantages of *fortune* produce esteem and approbation from the same principles, we may satisfy ourselves by reflecting on our precedent reasoning on that subject. We have observ'd, that our approbation of those, who are possess'd of the advantages of fortune, may be ascrib'd to three different causes. *First,* To that immediate pleasure, which a rich man gives us, by the view of the beautiful cloaths, equipage, gardens, or houses, which he possesses.

Secondly, To the advantage, which we hope to reap from him by his generosity and liberality. *Thirdly*, To the pleasure and advantage, which he himself reaps from his possessions, and which produce an agreeable sympathy in us. Whether we ascribe our esteem of the rich and great to one or all of these causes, we may clearly see the traces of those principles, which give rise to the sense of vice and virtue. I believe most people, at first sight, will be inclin'd to ascribe our esteem of the rich to self-interest, and the prospect of advantage. But as 'tis certain, that our esteem or deference extends beyond any prospect of advantage to ourselves, 'tis evident, that that sentiment must proceed from a sympathy with those, who are dependent on the person we esteem and respect, and who have an immediate connexion with him. We consider him as a person capable of contributing to the happiness or enjoyment of his fellow-creatures, whose sentiments, with regard to him, we naturally embrace. And this consideration will serve to justify my hypothesis in preferring the *third* principle to the other two, and ascribing our esteem of the rich to a sympathy with the pleasure and advantage, which they themselves receive from their possessions. For as even the other two principles cannot operate to a due extent, or account for all the phaenomena, without having recourse to a sympathy of one kind or other; 'tis much more natural to chuse that sympathy, which is immediate and direct, than that which is remote and indirect. To which we may add, that where the riches or power are very great, and render the person considerable and important in the world, the esteem attending them, may, in part, be ascrib'd to another source, distinct from these three, *viz.* their interesting the mind by a prospect of the multitude, and importance of their consequences: Tho', in order to account for the operation of this principle, we must also have recourse to *sympathy*; as we have observ'd in the preceding section.

It may not be amiss, on this occasion, to remark the flexibility of our sentiments, and the several changes they so readily receive from the objects, with which they are conjoin'd.

All the sentiments of approbation, which attend any particular species of objects, have a great resemblance to each other, tho' deriv'd from different sources; and, on the other hand, those sentiments, when directed to different objects, are different to the feeling, tho' deriv'd from the same source. Thus the beauty of all visible objects causes a pleasure pretty much the same, tho' it be sometimes deriv'd from the mere *species* and appearance of the objects; sometimes from sympathy, and an idea of their utility. In like manner, whenever we survey the actions and characters of men, without any particular interest in them, the pleasure, or pain, which arises from the survey (with some minute differences) is, in the main, of the same kind, tho' perhaps there be a great diversity in the causes, from which it is deriv'd. On the other hand, a convenient house, and a virtuous character, cause not the same feeling of approbation; even tho' the source of our approbation be the same, and flow from sympathy and an idea of their utility. There is something very inexplicable in this variation of our feelings; but 'tis what we have experience of with regard to all our passions and sentiments.

SECT. VI

Conclusion of this book

THUS upon the whole I am hopeful, that nothing is wanting to an accurate proof of this system of ethics. We are certain, that sympathy is a very powerful principle in human nature. We are also certain, that it has a great influence on our sense of beauty, when we regard external objects, as well as when we judge of morals. We find, that it has force sufficient to give us the strongest sentiments of approbation, when it operates alone, without the concurrence of any other principle; as in the cases of justice, allegiance, chastity, and good-manners. We may observe, that all the circumstances requisite for its operation are found in most of the virtues; which have, for the most part, a tendency to the good of society, or to that of the person possess'd of them. If we compare all these circumstances, we shall not doubt, that sympathy is the chief source of moral distinctions; especially when we reflect, that no objection can be rais'd against this hypothesis in one case, which will not extend to all cases. Justice is certainly approv'd of for no other reason, than because it has a tendency to the public good: And the public good is indifferent to us, except so far as sympathy interests us in it. We may presume the like with regard to all the other virtues, which have a like tendency to the public good. They must derive all their merit from our sympathy with those, who reap any advantage from them: As the virtues, which have a tendency to the good of the person possess'd of them, derive their merit from our sympathy with him.

Most people will readily allow, that the useful qualities of the mind are virtuous, because of their utility. This way of thinking is so natural, and occurs on so many occasions, that few will make any scruple of admitting it. Now this being once admitted, the force of sympathy must necessarily be acknowledg'd. Virtue is consider'd as means to an end. Means to an end are only valued so far as the end is valued. But the happiness of strangers affects us by sympathy alone. To that principle, therefore, we are to ascribe the sentiment of approbation, which arises from the survey of all those virtues, that are useful to society, or to the person possess'd of them. These form the most considerable part of morality.

Were it proper in such a subject to bribe the reader's assent, or employ any thing but solid argument, we are here abundantly supplied with topics to engage the affections. All lovers of virtue (and such we all are in speculation, however we may degenerate in practice) must certainly be pleas'd to see moral distinctions deriv'd from so noble a source, which gives us a just notion both of the *generosity* and *capacity* of human nature. It requires but very little knowledge of human affairs to perceive, that a sense of morals is a principle inherent in the soul, and one of the most powerful that enters into the composition. But this sense must certainly acquire new force, when reflecting on itself, it approves of those principles, from whence it is deriv'd, and finds nothing but what is great and good in its rise and origin. Those who resolve the sense of morals into original instincts of the human mind, may defend the cause of virtue with sufficient authority; but want the advantage, which those possess, who account for that sense by an extensive sympathy with mankind. According to their system, not only virtue must be approv'd of, but also the sense of virtue: And not only that sense, but also the principles, from whence it is deriv'd. So that nothing is presented on any side, but what is laudable and good.

This observation may be extended to justice, and the other virtues of that kind. Tho' justice be artificial, the sense of its morality is natural. 'Tis the combination of men, in a system of conduct, which renders any act of justice beneficial to society. But when once it has that tendency, we *naturally* approve of it; and if we did not so, 'tis impossible any combination or convention cou'd ever produce that sentiment.

Most of the inventions of men are subject to change. They depend upon humour and caprice. They have a vogue for a time, and then sink into oblivion. It may, perhaps, be apprehended, that if justice were allow'd to be a human invention, it must be plac'd on the same footing. But the cases are widely different. The interest, on which justice is founded, is the greatest imaginable, and extends to all times and places. It cannot possibly be serv'd by any other invention. It is obvious, and discovers itself on the very first formation of society. All these causes render the rules of justice stedfast and immutable; at least, as immutable as human nature. And if they were founded on original instincts, cou'd they have any greater stability?

The same system may help us to form a just notion of the *happiness*, as well as of the *dignity* of virtue, and may interest every principle of our nature in the embracing and cherishing that noble quality. Who indeed does not feel an accession of alacrity in his pursuits of knowledge and ability of every kind, when he considers, that besides the advantage, which immediately result from these acquisitions, they also give him a new lustre in the eyes of mankind, and are universally attended with esteem and approbation? And who can think any advantages of fortune a sufficient compensation for the least breach of the *social* virtues, when he considers, that not only his character with regard to others, but also his peace and inward satisfaction entirely depend upon his strict observance of them; and that a mind will never be able to bear its own survey, that has been wanting in its part to mankind and society? But I forbear insisting on this subject. Such reflections require a work a-part, very different from the genius of the present. The anatomist ought never to emulate the painter; nor in his accurate dissections and portraitures of the smaller parts of the human body, pretend to give his figures any graceful and engaging attitude or expression. There is even something hideous, or at least minute in the views of things, which he presents; and 'tis necessary the objects shou'd be set more at a distance, and be more cover'd up from sight, to make them engaging to the eye and imagination. An anatomist, however, is admirably fitted to give advice to a painter; and 'tis even impracticable to excel in the latter art, without the assistance of the former. We must have an exact knowledge of the parts, their situation and connexion, before we can design with any elegance or correctness. And thus the most abstract speculations concerning human nature, however cold and unentertaining, become subservient to *practical morality*; and may render this latter science more correct in its precepts, and more persuasive in its exhortations.

APPENDIX

There is nothing I wou'd more willingly lay hold of, than an opportunity of confessing my errors; and shou'd esteem such a return to truth and reason to be more honourable than the most unerring judgment. A man, who is free from mistakes, can pretend to no praises, except from the justness of his understanding: But a man, who corrects his mistakes, shews at once the justness of his understanding, and the candour and ingenuity of his temper. I have not yet been so fortunate as to discover any very considerable mistakes in the reasonings deliver'd in the preceding volumes, except on one article: But I have found by experience, that some of my expressions have not been so well chosen, as to guard against all mistakes in the readers; and 'tis chiefly to remedy this defect, I have subjoin'd the following appendix.

We can never be induc'd to believe any matter of fact, except where its cause, or its effect, is present to us; but what the nature is of that belief, which arises from the relation of cause and effect, few have had the curiosity to ask themselves. In my opinion, this dilemma is inevitable. Either the belief is some new idea, such as that of *reality* or *existence*, which we join to the simple conception of an object, or it is merely a peculiar *feeling* or *sentiment*. That it is not a new idea, annex'd to the simple conception, may be evinc'd from these two arguments. *First*, We have no abstract idea of existence, distinguishable and separable from the idea of particular objects. 'Tis impossible, therefore, that this idea of existence can be annex'd to the idea of any object, or form the difference betwixt a simple conception and belief. *Secondly*, The mind has the command over all its ideas, and can separate, unite, mix, and vary them, as it pleases; so that if belief consisted merely in a new idea, annex'd to the conception, it wou'd be in a man's power to believe what he pleas'd. We may, therefore, conclude, that belief consists merely in a certain feeling or sentiment; in something, that depends not on the will, but must arise from certain determinate causes and principles, of which we are not masters. When we are convinc'd of any matter of fact, we do nothing but conceive it, along with a certain feeling, different from what attends the mere *reveries* of the imagination. And when we express our incredulity concerning any fact, we mean, that the arguments for the fact produce not that feeling. Did not the belief consist in a sentiment different from our mere conception, whatever objects were presented by the wildest imagination, wou'd be on an equal footing with the most establish'd truths founded on history and experience. There is nothing but the feeling, or sentiment, to distinguish the one from the other.

This, therefore, being regarded as an undoubted truth, *that belief is nothing but a peculiar feeling, different from the simple conception,* the next question, that naturally occurs, is, *what is the nature of this feeling, or sentiment, and whether it be analogous to any other sentiment of the human mind?* This question is important. For if it be not analogous to any other sentiment, we must despair of explaining its causes, and must consider it as an original principle of the human mind. If it be analogous, we may hope to explain its causes from analogy, and trace it up to more general principles. Now that there is a greater firmness and solidity in the conceptions, which are the objects of conviction and assurance, than in the loose and indolent reveries of a castle-builder, every one will readily own. They strike upon us with more force; they are more present to us; the mind has a firmer hold of them, and is more actuated and mov'd by them. It acquiesces in them; and, in a manner, fixes and reposes itself on them. In short, they approach nearer to the impressions, which are immediately present to us; and are therefore analogous to many other operations of the mind.

There is not, in my opinion, any possibility of evading this conclusion, but by asserting, that belief, beside the simple conception, consists in some impression or feeling, distinguishable from the conception. It does not modify the conception, and render it more present and intense: It is only annex'd to it, after the same manner that *will* and *desire* are annex'd to particular conceptions of good and pleasure. But the following considerations will, I hope, be sufficient to remove this hypothesis. *First,* It is directly contrary to experience, and our immediate consciousness. All men have ever allow'd reasoning to be merely an operation of our thoughts or ideas; and however those ideas may be varied to the feeling, there is nothing ever enters into our *conclusions* but ideas, or our fainter conceptions. For instance; I hear at present a person's voice, whom I am acquainted with; and this sound comes from the next room. This impression of my senses immediately conveys my thoughts to the person, along with all the surrounding objects. I paint them out to myself as existent at present, with the same qualities and relations, that I formerly knew them possess'd of. These ideas take faster hold of my mind, than the ideas of an inchanted castle. They are different to the feeling; but there is no distinct or separate impression attending them. 'Tis the same case when I recollect the several incidents of a journey, or the events of any history. Every particular fact is there the object of belief. Its idea is modified differently from the loose reveries of a castle-builder: But no distinct impression attends every distinct idea, or conception of matter of fact. This is the subject of plain experience. If ever this experience can be disputed on any occasion, 'tis when the mind has been agitated with doubts and difficulties; and afterwards, upon taking the object in a new point of view, or being presented with a new argument, fixes and reposes itself in one settled conclusion and belief. In this case there is a feeling distinct and separate from the conception. The passage from doubt and agitation to tranquility and repose, conveys a satisfaction and pleasure to the mind. But take any other case. Suppose I see the legs and thighs of a person in motion, while some interpos'd object conceals the rest of his body. Here 'tis certain, the imagination spreads out the whole figure. I give him a head and shoulders, and breast and neck. These members I conceive and believe him to be possess'd of. Nothing can be more evident, than that this whole operation is perform'd by the thought or imagination alone. The transition is immediate. The ideas presently strike us. Their customary connexion with the present impression, varies them and modifies them in a certain manner, but produces no act of the mind, distinct from this peculiarity of conception. Let any one examine his own mind, and he will evidently find this to be the truth.

Secondly, Whatever may be the case, with regard to this distinct impression, it must be allow'd, that the mind has a firmer hold, or more steady conception of what it takes to be matter of fact, than of fictions. Why then look any farther, or multiply suppositions without necessity?

Thirdly, We can explain the *causes* of the firm conception, but not those of any separate impression. And not only so, but the causes of the firm conception exhaust the whole subject, and nothing is left to produce any other effect. An inference concerning a matter of fact is nothing but the idea of an object, that is frequently conjoin'd, or is associated with a present impression. This is the whole of it. Every part is requisite to explain, from analogy, the more steady conception; and nothing remains capable of producing any distinct impression.

Fourthly, The *effects* of belief, in influencing the passions and imagination, can all be explain'd from the firm conception; and there is no occasion to have recourse to any other principle. These arguments, with many others, enumerated in the foregoing volumes, sufficiently prove, that belief only modifies the idea or conception; and renders it different to the feeling, without producing any distinct impression.

Thus upon a general view of the subject, there appear to be two questions of importance, which we may venture to recommend to the consideration of philosophers, *Whether there be any thing to distinguish belief from the simple conception beside the feeling of sentiment?* And, *Whether this feeling be any thing but a firmer conception, or a faster hold, that we take of the object?*

If, upon impartial enquiry, the same conclusion, that I have form'd, be assented to by philosophers, the next business is to examine the analogy, which there is betwixt belief, and other acts of the mind, and find the cause of the firmness and strength of conception: And this I do not esteem a difficult task. The transition from a present impression, always enlivens and strengthens any idea. When any object is presented, the idea of its usual attendant immediately strikes us, as something real and solid. 'Tis *felt*, rather than conceiv'd, and approaches the impression, from which it is deriv'd, in its force and influence. This I have prov'd at large. I cannot add any new arguments; tho' perhaps my reasoning on this whole question, concerning cause and effect, wou'd have been more convincing, had the following passages been inserted in the places, which I have mark'd for them. I have added a few illustrations on other points, where I thought it necessary. [...*]

I had entertain'd some hopes, that however deficient our theory of the intellectual world might be, it wou'd be free from those contradictions, and absurdities, which seem to attend every explication, that human reason can give of the material world. But upon a more strict review of the section concerning *personal identity*, I find myself involv'd in such a labyrinth, that, I must confess, I neither know how to correct my former opinions, nor how to render them consistent. If this be not a good *general* reason for scepticism, 'tis at least a sufficient one (if I were not already abundantly supplied) for me to entertain a diffidence and modesty in all my decisions. I shall propose the arguments on both sides, beginning with those that induc'd me to deny the strict and proper identity and simplicity of a self or thinking being.

When we talk of *self* or *substance*, we must have an idea annex'd to these terms, otherwise they are altogether unintelligible. Every idea is deriv'd from preceding impressions;

[*Illustrative passages have been placed where Hume wished them to go, except for the long note on personal identity printed above.]

and we have no impression of self or substance, as something simple and individual. We have, therefore, no idea of them in that sense.

Whatever is distinct, is distinguishable; and whatever is distinguishable, is separable by the thought or imagination. All perceptions are distinct. They are, therefore, distinguishable, and separable, and may be conceiv'd as separately existent, and may exist separately, without any contradiction or absurdity.

When I view this table and that chimney, nothing is present to me but particular perceptions, which are of a like nature with all the other perceptions. This is the doctrine of philosophers. But this table, which is present to me, and the chimney, may and do exist separately. This is the doctrine of the vulgar, and implies no contradiction. There is no contradiction, therefore, in extending the same doctrine to all the perceptions.

In general, the following reasoning seems satisfactory. All ideas are borrow'd from preceding perceptions. Our ideas of objects, therefore, are deriv'd from that source. Consequently no proposition can be intelligible or consistent with regard to objects, which is not so with regard to perceptions. But 'tis intelligible and consistent to say, that objects exist distinct and independent, without any common *simple* substance or subject of inhesion. This proposition, therefore, can never be absurd with regard to perceptions.

When I turn my reflection on *myself*, I never can perceive this *self* without some one or more perceptions; nor can I ever perceive any thing but the perceptions. 'Tis the composition of these, therefore, which forms the self.

We can conceive a thinking being to have either many or few perceptions. Suppose the mind to be reduc'd even below the life of an oyster. Suppose it to have only one perception, as of thirst or hunger. Consider it in that situation. Do you conceive any thing but merely that perception? Have you any notion of *self* or *substance*? If not, the addition of other perceptions can never give you that notion.

The annihilation, which some people suppose to follow

upon death, and which entirely destroys this self, is nothing but an extinction of all particular perceptions; love and hatred, pain and pleasure, thought and sensation. These therefore must be the same with self; since the one cannot survive the other.

Is *self* the same with *substance*? If it be, how can that question have place, concerning the subsistence of self, under a change of substance? If they be distinct, what is the difference betwixt them? For my part, I have a notion of neither, when conceiv'd distinct from particular perceptions.

Philosophers begin to be reconcil'd to the principle, *that we have no idea of external substance, distinct from the ideas of particular qualities.* This must pave the way for a like principle with regard to the mind, *that we have no notion of it, distinct from the particular perceptions.*

So far I seem to be attended with sufficient evidence. But having thus loosen'd all our particular perceptions, when * I proceed to explain the principle of connexion, which binds them together, and makes us attribute to them a real simplicity and identity; I am sensible, that my account is very defective, and that nothing but the seeming evidence of the precedent reasonings cou'd have induc'd me to receive it. If perceptions are distinct existences, they form a whole only by being connected together. But no connexions among distinct existences are ever discoverable by human understanding. We only *feel* a connexion or determination of the thought, to pass from one object to another. It follows, therefore, that the thought alone finds personal identity, when reflecting on the train of past perceptions, that compose a mind, the ideas of them are felt to be connected together, and naturally introduce each other. However extraordinary this conclusion may seem, it need not surprize us. Most philosophers seem inclin'd to think, that personal identity *arises* from consciousness; and consciousness is nothing but a reflected thought or perception. The present philosophy, therefore, has so far a promising aspect. But all my hopes vanish, when I come to explain the principles,

* Vol. I. page 308.

that unite our successive perceptions in our thought or consciousness. I cannot discover any theory, which gives me satisfaction on this head.

In short there are two principles, which I cannot render consistent; nor is it in my power to renounce either of them, viz. *that all our distinct perceptions are distinct existences,* and *that the mind never perceives any real connexion among distinct existences.* Did our perceptions either inhere in something simple and individual, or did the mind perceive some real connexion among them, there wou'd be no difficulty in the case. For my part, I must plead the privilege of a sceptic, and confess, that this difficulty is too hard for my understanding. I pretend not, however, to pronounce it absolutely insuperable. Others, perhaps, or myself, upon more mature reflections, may discover some hypothesis, that will reconcile those contradictions.

I shall also take this opportunity of confessing two other errors of less importance, which more mature reflection has discover'd to me in my reasoning. The first may be found in Vol. I. page 106. where I say, that the distance betwixt two bodies is known, among other things, by the angles, which the rays of light flowing from the bodies make with each other. 'Tis certain, that these angles are not known to the mind, and consequently can never discover the distance. The second error may be found in Vol. I. page 144. where I say, that two ideas of the same object can only be different by their different degrees of force and vivacity. I believe there are other differences among ideas, which cannot properly be comprehended under these terms. Had I said, that two ideas of the same object can only be different by their different *feeling*, I shou'd have been nearer the truth.